# ADVENTURES
## IN THE
# ORGASMATRON

# ADVENTURES
## IN THE
# ORGASMATRON

*How
the Sexual Revolution
Came to America*

CHRISTOPHER TURNER

*Farrar, Straus and Giroux / New York*

FARRAR, STRAUS AND GIROUX
18 West 18th Street, New York 10011

Library of Congress Cataloging-in-Publication Data
Turner, Christopher, 1972–
    Adventures in the orgasmatron : how the sexual revolution came to America / Christopher Turner.
        p.   cm.
    Includes bibliographical references and index.
    ISBN 978-0-374-10094-0 (alk. paper)
    1. Sex customs—United States—History—20th century.   2. Sex (Psychology)—History—20th century.   3. Reich, Wilhelm, 1897–1957.   I. Title.

HQ18.U5T85   2011
306.770973'0904—dc22

                                                                2010046549

Designed by Abby Kagan

www.fsgbooks.com

1   3   5   7   9   10   8   6   4   2

FOR GABY

My life is revolution—from within and from without—or it's comedy! If I could only find someone who has the correct diagnosis!

—WILHELM REICH, July 9, 1919

Perhaps the history of the errors of mankind, all things considered, is more valuable and interesting than that of their discoveries. Truth is uniform and narrow; it constantly exists, and does not seem to require so much an active energy, as a passive aptitude of soul in order to encounter it. But error is endlessly diversified; it has no reality, but is the pure and simple creation of the mind that invents it. In this field the soul has room enough to expand herself, to display all her boundless faculties, and all her beautiful and interesting extravagancies and absurdities.

—BENJAMIN FRANKLIN, *Report of Dr. Benjamin Franklin, and other commissioners, charged by the King of France, with the examination of the animal magnetism, as now practiced in Paris* (1784)

# CONTENTS

INTRODUCTION

3

EUROPE

15

AMERICA

203

NOTES

449

BIBLIOGRAPHY

493

ACKNOWLEDGMENTS

509

INDEX

513

# ADVENTURES
## IN THE
# ORGASMATRON

# INTRODUCTION

I n 1909, Sigmund Freud was invited to give a series of lectures
at Clark University in Worcester, Massachusetts. On the way
there from Vienna his cabin steward was reading *The Psychopathology of Everyday Life*, an event Freud claimed was the first indication he ever had that he was going to be famous. In the United
States, the philosopher and psychologist William James and many
other leading American intellectuals turned out to hear Freud talk,
giving psychoanalysis official recognition, as Freud saw it, for the
first time. He later wrote about what the Clark lectures meant to
him: "In Europe I felt as though I was despised; but over there I
found myself received by the foremost men as an equal. As I stepped
onto the platform at Worcester to deliver my *Five Lectures upon Psychoanalysis* it seemed like the realization of some incredible daydream: psychoanalysis was no longer a product of delusion, it had
become a valuable part of reality."[1]

Little did Freud know how his intellectual discoveries would
transform America, which he dismissed as an "anti-paradise" or a "gigantic mistake." Though he feared that Americans would enthusiastically "embrace and ruin psychoanalysis" by popularizing it and
watering it down, he already suspected that his theories would in
some way shake the country to the core. While watching the waving
crowds from the deck of his ship as it docked in New York, he turned

to his fellow analyst Carl Gustav Jung and said, "Don't they know we're bringing them the plague?"

Well before the hedonism of the 1920s, a Freud-inspired revolution in sexual morals had begun. Greenwich Village bohemians, such as the writers Max Eastman and Floyd Dell, the anarchist Emma Goldman, who had been "deeply impressed by the lucidity" of Freud's 1909 lectures, and Mabel Dodge, who ran an avant-garde salon in her apartment on Fifth Avenue, adapted psychoanalysis to create their own free-love philosophy. In the radical journal *The Masses*, Floyd Dell warned that "sexual emotions would not be repressed without morbid consequences."[2] Eastman, one of America's first analysands, wrote a book comparing Freud and Marx: "Weren't all forms of repression evil?" he asked rhetorically. Dell's left-leaning analyst, a Shakespeare scholar called Dr. Samuel A. Tannenbaum who treated many of Greenwich Village's artists, argued that it was healthier for young men to frequent prostitutes than to practice abstinence or masturbation.[3]

Together they fashioned a cult of the orgasm—Mabel Dodge even went so far as to call her dog Climax. However, as Dell later admitted, their experiment was an isolated one, like that of the Oneida Community in the nineteenth century and a handful of other "obscure but pervasive sexual cults."[4] It was only after the Second World War that the idea of sexual liberation would permeate the culture at large.

When Wilhelm Reich, the most brilliant of the second generation of psychoanalysts who had been Freud's pupils, arrived in New York in late August 1939, exactly thirty years after his mentor and only a few days before the outbreak of war, he was optimistic that his ideas about fusing sex and politics would be better received there than they had been in fascist Europe. Despite its veneer of Puritanism, America was a country already much preoccupied with sex—as Alfred Kinsey's renowned investigations, which he began that same year, were to show. Reich could be said to have instigated "the sexual revolution"; a Marxist analyst, he coined the phrase in the 1930s in order to illustrate his belief that a true political revolution would only be possible once sexual repression was overthrown, the one obstacle Reich felt had scuppered the efforts of the Bolsheviks.[5] "A sexual revolution is already in progress," he declared, "and no power on earth will stop it."

Reich was a sexual evangelist who held that the satisfactory orgasm made the difference between sickness and health. "There is only one thing wrong with neurotic patients," he concluded in *The Function of the Orgasm* (1927): "*the lack of full and repeated sexual satisfaction*" (the italics are his).[6] The orgasm was the panacea to cure all ills, he thought, including the fascism that had forced him to leave Europe. Reich sought to reconcile psychoanalysis and Marxism, thereby giving Freudianism an optimistic gloss, arguing that repression, which Freud came to believe was an inherent part of the human condition, could be shed. This would lead to what his critics dismissed as a "genital utopia" (they mocked him as "the prophet of bigger and better orgasms"). His ideas became influential in Europe, which Henry Miller, finding a new sense of purpose through sex, characterized as "the Land of Fuck." Reich was a figurehead of the vocal sex reform movement in Vienna and Berlin before the *Anschluss*, after which the Nazis, who deemed it part of a Jewish conspiracy to undermine the continent, crushed it. His books were burned in Germany along with those of the German sexologist Magnus Hirschfeld and Freud.

Soon after he arrived in the United States, Reich invented the orgone energy accumulator, a wooden cupboard about the size of a telephone booth, lined with metal and insulated with steel wool—a box in which, it might be said, his ideas came almost prepackaged. Reich considered his orgone energy accumulator an almost magical device that could improve its users' "orgastic potency" and by extension their general, and above all mental, health. He claimed that it could charge up the body with the life force that circulated in the atmosphere (a force which he christened "orgone energy")—mysterious currents that in concentrated form could not only help dissolve repressions but also treat cancer, radiation sickness, and a host of minor ailments.[7] As he saw it, the box's organic material absorbed orgone energy, and the metal lining stopped it from escaping, so the box acted as a greenhouse; and, supposedly, there was a noticeable rise in temperature in the box.

Reich persuaded Albert Einstein to investigate the machine,

whose workings seemed to contradict all known principles of physics, but after two weeks of tests Einstein refuted Reich's claims. Nevertheless, the orgone box became fashionable in America in the 1940s and 1950s, when Reich rose to fame as the leader of the new sexual movement that seemed to be sweeping the country. Orgone boxes were used by such countercultural figures as Norman Mailer, J. D. Salinger, Paul Goodman, Allen Ginsberg, Jack Kerouac, and William Burroughs—who claimed to have had a spontaneous orgasm in his. At the height of his James Bond fame, Sean Connery swore by the device, and Woody Allen parodied it in the movie *Sleeper*, giving it the immortal nickname "Orgasmatron." Bohemians celebrated the orgone box as a liberation machine, the wardrobe that would lead to utopia, while to conservatives it was Pandora's box, out of which escaped the Freudian plague—the corrupting influence of anarchism and promiscuous sex.

Because of his radical past, Reich was placed under surveillance almost as soon as he arrived in the United States (his FBI file is 789 pages long). In 1947, after *Harper's Magazine* introduced Reich to Americans as the leader of "a new cult of sex and anarchy," the Food and Drug Administration began investigating him for making fraudulent claims about the orgone accumulator, and in 1954 a court ruled that he must stop leasing and selling his machine. When he broke the injunction he was sentenced to two years in prison. The remaining accumulators, along with thousands of copies of the journals and eleven books Reich self-published in America (including copies of *The Sexual Revolution*), which were thought to constitute "false advertising" for them, were incinerated.

In the ideological confusion of the postwar period, when the world was trying to get its head around what came to be called the Holocaust and intellectuals disillusioned with communism were abandoning the security of their earlier political positions, Reich's ideas landed on fertile ground. With his tantalizing suggestion that sexual emancipation would lead to positive social change, Reich seemed to capture the mood of this convulsive moment. People sat in the orgone box hoping to dissolve the toxic dangers of conformity, which, as Reich had eloquently suggested as early as 1933, bred fascism. The literary critic Alfred Kazin wrote in his journal,

"Everybody of my generation had his orgone box . . . his search for fulfillment. There was, God knows, no break with convention, there was just a freeing of oneself from all those parental attachments and thou shalt nots."[8]

In his essay "The New Lost Generation," James Baldwin described how that generation crystallized around Reich's thinking in the late 1940s and early 1950s:

> It was a time of the most terrifying personal anarchy. If one gave a party, it was virtually certain that someone, quite possibly oneself, would have a crying jag or have to be restrained from murder or suicide. It was a time of experimentation, with sex, with marijuana, with minor infringements of the law. It seems to me that life was beginning to tell us who we were, and what life was—news no one has ever wanted to hear: and we fought back by clinging to our vision of ourselves as innocent, of love perhaps imperfect but reciprocal and enduring. And we did not know that the price of this was experience. We had been raised to believe in formulas.
>
> In retrospect, the discovery of the orgasm—or, rather, of the orgone box—seems the least mad of the formulas that came to hand. It seemed to me . . . that people turned from the idea of the world being made better through politics to the idea of the world being made better through psychic and sexual health like sinners coming down the aisle at a revival meeting. And I doubted that their conversion was any more to be trusted than that. The converts, indeed, moved in a certain euphoric aura of well-being. Which would not last . . . There are no formulas for the improvement of the private, or any other, life—certainly not the formula of more and better orgasms. (Who decides?) The people I had been raised among had orgasms all the time, and still chopped each other with razors on Saturday nights.[9]

"There was, God knows, no break with convention"; "the least mad of the formulas that came to hand"—both Kazin and Baldwin saw their bewildered peers breaking out of one ideological prison only to find themselves in another. Theirs was a generation teetering on a new kind of brink—full of optimism about the possibility of change, they were unsuspecting accomplices in the authorship of more insidious forms of control.

I first learned about Reich's orgone energy accumulator in 1993 when I visited Summerhill, the "free" school in Suffolk, England, founded in 1921 by A. S. Neill. I was an anthropology student at Cambridge University and, when I asked whether I could stay for a while as a participant-observer, I was offered a large tepee as a place to sleep. I liked the idea of living in it: a wigwam seemed a suitable home for a backyard anthropologist. However, everything at Summerhill—where lessons are voluntary and the pupils invent their own laws—is put to a vote, and the children decided they wanted to keep the tepee for themselves. So for that summer I lived in a bed-and-breakfast in Leiston. All the other guests worked for the nuclear power station Sizewell B: every piece of crockery and all the towels and cutlery were stamped with the nuclear power station's logo. The owner of the B&B had been given a free pullover after a random Geiger counter inspection had determined that his own, hung out on the clothesline, harbored dangerously elevated levels of radiation.

While I was there I read the lengthy correspondence between Neill and Reich that offered an articulate commentary on the rise of fascism and on the idea of sexual liberation as a coherent strategy to oppose totalitarianism, a philosophy that held over awkwardly and controversially into the era of the cold war. I also discovered that an orgone energy accumulator had once been used at the school, though it had recently been dismantled because the nearby nuclear power station was thought to have reversed its positive effects. Reich came to believe that atomic energy, the fear of which clouded the American psyche in the 1950s, aggravated the orgone energy that he had discovered, which explained, in his view, why not everyone who was prescribed his box could be cured.

A. S. Neill met Reich in Oslo in 1936 and soon afterward became his analysand, fitting in a dozen sessions with him on a return trip. Reich had by that time been expelled from the International Psychoanalytic Association (he had once been considered Freud's heir apparent, but his attempts to reconcile psychoanalysis and Marxism ended up alienating practitioners of both), and pioneered a new form of analysis called "vegetotherapy," a repudiation of the talking cure.[10] Reich's third wife, Ilse, described it as "doing away with the psychoanalytic taboo of never touching a patient," and replacing it with "a physical attack by the therapist."[11] Reich would relax the patient's taut muscles with deep breathing exercises and painful massage, until he or she broke down in involuntary convulsions, which Reich called the "orgasm reflex."

Though his school had already been running for fifteen years, Neill found in Reich's work its ideological justification, and he once referred to himself as Reich's "John the Baptist." His many books are littered with references to Reich's concepts of "character armor" and "self-regulation." For his part Reich saw Neill's project as a practical test of his ideas, and he sent his own son, Peter, to Summerhill for a while. He once threatened to give up his research and come and teach at the school, but Neill laughed and declined his offer, saying that Reich would frighten the children. Neill did, however, ask him to be the legal guardian of his daughter, Zoë. Reich invited Neill to start an orgonomic infant research center at his research institute in Maine and encouraged him to replace his Summerhill staff with people schooled in Reichian practice. Neill rejected both suggestions, but continued to read aloud from Reich's books at staff meetings.

Reich and Neill shared a belief in the redemptive power of unconstricted development in children. For Reich this had an urgent political significance: he thought that only when children were raised free would it be possible to lay the foundations of a utopia. Neill thought that a radical reform of the education system was an essential preliminary to the creation of a better world. Both men believed that children were inherently good: it was an authoritarian, sexually repressive upbringing that corrupted them. Summerhill was designed to offer children a sanctuary from the moral contamination of the world, where they could live out their desires without the fear of punishment and play without the pressure of indoctrination: "We set out to make a school in which we would allow children freedom to be themselves," Neill wrote. "In order to do this we had to renounce all discipline, all direction, all suggestion, all moral training, all religious instruction."[12] The school's motto continues to be "Giving children back their childhood."

By the summer of 1944, Neill had begun to practice Reich's analytic technique on his pupils at Summerhill. "I have given up teaching and am doing only veg.-ther. analysis," he wrote to Reich. "The more I see the results with adolescents the more I consider that bloody man Reich a great man . . . Marvelous how patients weep so easily when lying on their backs. Some do so in the first hour. Why?"[13] One former student remembers being instructed to lie down and "breathe deeply, as though you're having sexual intercourse," while Neill prodded her stomach (she was too young to know what sex was, so she just panted).[14] "The repressed ones have stomachs like wooden boards," Neill wrote to Reich of his pupils' resistance, "but children begin to loosen up very quickly, and at once begin to be hateful and savage."[15]

The philosopher Bertrand Russell, like Neill, preached the benefits of an unconstrained childhood and campaigned for new sexual mores. Neill said that Russell's *On Education* (1926) was the only book on the topic he'd read without uttering an expletive. Russell spent a week at Summerhill in 1927 before opening a school of his own, Beacon Hill, based on similar principles. He was soon disillusioned, however, and left the school after five years. The children in his care, Russell wrote, were "sinister," "cruel," "destructive." The effect of giving them their freedom "was to establish a reign of terror, in which the strong kept the weak trembling and miserable."[16] Russell's own children, for whom Beacon Hill was partly created (it had only twelve pupils), were, like their father, traumatized by their time at the school. "I learned to get along inside a shell," Kate Russell said, "fending off physical and emotional assaults from others and trusting nobody."[17] But for Neill, the monstrous behavior of children was a stage along the path to liberation: if they were "hateful and savage" it was only because they were sloughing off the final carapace of their repressions.

The accumulator that Reich gave Neill arrived in England on the *Queen Elizabeth* in April 1947, along with a smaller "shooter" box with a protruding funnel for directing orgone energy rays at infections and wounds. "I sit in the Accumulator every night reading," Neill wrote appreciatively, "re-reading the *Function of the O.* while I sit in the box."[18] Neill soon became convinced of the machine's effectiveness: "We used the small Accu on a girl of 15 with a boil on her leg," he said. "It cleared up in three days, and we are to have her in the big box next term." The effects apparently defied scientific explanation: "When Lucy had a new lump on her face under the operation scar, she applied the small Accu and it went in a fortnight," Neill marveled.[19] He bombarded Reich with questions: Was it safe to keep an accumulator in one's bedroom? Did you have to be naked inside it? Would it be as effective in the damp English climate? How long could his daughter safely sit in the box?

Neill's daughter, Zoë Readhead, has run Summerhill since 1985. Neill was sixty-four when his only child was born; when she was two, *Picture Post* ran a story saying that of all the children in Britain, she had the best chance of being free. "I remember the orgone accumulator vividly," she told me. "It was quite chilly in there because of the zinc."[20] As a child Readhead was prescribed half an hour a day in the device; she recalls the red plastic cushion she sat on and the funnel or "shooter" she was encouraged to position over her ear to try to cure a recurrent earache. She also remembers that as she grew up Neill lost interest in the machine (he thought he'd been mistaken in putting an extra layer of asbestos around it), and moved it to a corner of the garage.

By the time Reich died, in 1957, he and Neill were no longer communicating. In December 1954 Neill wrote, "It gave me a great shock to find you believing in visits from other planets. No, I said, it can't be true; Reich is a scientist and unless he sees a flying saucer he won't accept it as a reality. I can't understand it."[21] Reich, whose sanity had long been an open question (Sandor Rado, who analyzed Reich for a few months in 1931, said that he was "schizophrenic in the most serious way"), had started to suffer from paranoid delusions about the world being under attack by UFOs.[22] The armor-clad orgone box was always something of a protective shield, illustrative of Reich's sense of being besieged, but he now built a "cloudbuster," an orgone gun that was designed not only to influence the weather—diverting hurricanes and making it rain in the desert—but to be the first line of defense against an alien invasion. It was a kind of orgone box turned inside out, so that it could work its therapeutic magic on the cosmos.

Reich initiated the break with Neill; his young son, Peter, who was spending the summer at Summerhill, told Neill that that the American planes passing over the school had been sent to protect him, or so his father said. Neill replied that this was nonsense (there was a large U.S. air base nearby), and when Reich heard of Neill's response he wrote to his remaining supporters that Neill was no longer to be trusted. In the American edition of Neill's *Summerhill: A Radical Approach to Childhood*, published in 1960, all references to Reich were deleted because the publishers considered him too controversial. (The book sold two million copies in the United States.) But Neill never turned his back entirely on his friend's philosophy, and long after Reich's death he persuaded Zoë to go to Norway to have vegetotherapy with another of Reich's disciples, Ola Raknes.

Reich died of a heart attack in Lewisburg Federal Penitentiary in 1957, eight months after being sentenced. If Reich's claims were no more than ridiculous quackery, as the FDA doctors who refuted them suggested, and if he was just a paranoid schizophrenic, as one court psychiatrist concluded, then why did the U.S. government consider him such a danger? What was happening in America that led Reich to become an emblem of such a deep fear?

The critic Louis Menand described Arthur Koestler, with whom Reich shared a Communist cell in Berlin, as "a slightly mad dreidel that spun out of Central Europe and across the history of a bloody century."[23] Reich's story traces a similarly erratic path, and looking back at his era can help to shed new light on it. Through the history of Reich's box it's possible to unpack the story of how sex became political in the twentieth century, and how it encountered Hitler, Stalin, and McCarthy along the way. Reich created the modern cult of the orgasm and, influentially, held that ecstasy was a point of resistance, immune to political control. Of course, the birth control pill—licensed by the FDA in 1957 (the year Reich died) for treating women with menstrual disorders—ultimately provided the technological breakthrough that facilitated the sexual liberation of the following decade. But Reich, perhaps more than any other sexual philosopher, had already given the erotic enthusiasm of the 1960s an intellectual justification, and laid the theoretical foundations for that era.

His ideas rallied a new generation of dissenters, and his orgone box, however unlikely an idea it may now seem, became a symbol of the sexual revolution. In January 1964, *Time* magazine declared that "Dr. Wilhelm Reich may have been a prophet. For now it sometimes seems that all America is one big Orgone Box":

> With today's model, it is no longer necessary to sit in cramped quarters for a specific time. Improved and enlarged to encompass the continent, the big machine works on its subjects continuously, day and night. From innumerable screens and stages, posters and pages, it flashes the larger-than-life-sized images of sex. From countless racks and shelves, it pushes the books which a few years ago were considered pornography. From myriad loudspeakers, it broadcasts the words and rhythms of pop-music erotica. And constantly, over the intellectual Muzak, comes the message that sex will save you and libido make you free.[24]

*Time* called this new "sex-affirming culture" the "second sexual revolution"—the first having occurred in the 1920s, "when flaming youth buried the Victorian era and anointed itself as the Jazz Age." In contrast, the children of the 1960s had little to rebel against and found themselves, *Time* commented, "adrift in a sea of permissiveness," which they attributed to Reich's philosophy: "Gradually, the belief spread that repression, not license, was the great evil, and that sexual matters belonged in the realm of science, not morals."[25]

In 1968 student revolutionaries graffitied Reichian slogans on the walls of the Sorbonne, and in Berlin they hurled copies of Reich's book *The Mass Psychology of Fascism* at police. At the University of Frankfurt 68ers (as they were called in German) were advised, "Read Reich and act accordingly!"[26] According to the historian Dagmar Herzog, "No other intellectual so inspired the student movement in its early days, and to a degree unmatched either in the United States or other Western European nation."[27] In the 1970s, feminists such as Shulamith Firestone, Germaine Greer, and Juliet Mitchell continued to promote Reich's work with enthusiasm.[28]

However, even in his lifetime, Reich came to believe that the sexual revolution had gone awry. Indeed, his ideals seemed to run aground in the decade of free love, which saw erotic liberation co-opted and absorbed into what the historian of psychoanalysis Eli Zaretsky calls a "sexualised dreamworld of mass consumption."[29] Herbert Marcuse, another émigré who became the hero of a younger generation, provided the most rigorous critique of the darker side of liberation. After his initial enthusiasm for a world characterized by "polymorphous perversity," Marcuse became cynical about it, and he ended his career with a series of brilliant analyses of the ways in which the establishment adapted all these liberated ideas (the "intellectual Muzak" of the time) into an existing system of production and consumption. Reich had propagated an expressive vision of the self, but his sexualized politics of the body soon dissolved into mere narcissism as consumers sought to express themselves through their possessions. In the process, as Marcuse was early in detecting, sex and radical politics became unstuck.

It is a testament to the popularity Reich once had that his name is still remembered at all—so many of his colleagues have been forgotten. But he is now known more for his mad invention rather than for the sexual radicalism that box contained. Reich's eccentric device might be seen as a prism through which to look at the conflicts and controversies of that era. Why did a generation seek to shed its sexual repressions by climbing into a closet? And why were others so threatened by it? What does it tell us about the ironies of the sexual revolution that the symbol of liberation was a box?

# EUROPE

# *One*

In 1919, Wilhelm Reich, a twenty-two-year-old medical student at the University of Vienna, made a pilgrimage to Sigmund Freud's apartment building at Berggasse 19, a large eighteenth-century dwelling whose ground floor housed a butcher shop. Upstairs, the psychoanalyst's study was an Aladdin's cave of archaeological finds: glass cabinets were crammed with ancient Egyptian scarabs, antique vases, and intaglio rings; Freud's desk swarmed with antique statuettes and other mythological figurines, which led one of Freud's patients, the modernist poet H.D. (Hilda Doolittle), to portray him as an "old man of the sea" and describe these objects as treasures salvaged from the depths of the unconscious. In the center of this crowded stage was the famous analyst's couch, covered with a colorful Persian rug and padded with opulent velvet cushions.

The young man who set his eyes on all of this had just left the Austro-Hungarian army, where he had served as an infantry officer on the Italian front during the First World War. He was intellectually ardent and socially insecure, so poor that he wore his military uniform to lectures because he couldn't afford to buy civilian clothes; he was an orphan with a past full of damage, an outsider in search of some kind of home.

Yet Reich had not come to see the self-described "archaeologist of the mind" to offer up his own war-torn brain for study. He had come to request a reading list. At an anatomy class, Reich's friend Otto Fenichel, who would later become a psychoanalyst and one of his closest allies, had passed a note to all the cadaver-dissecting students urging them to sign up for an extracurricular seminar on sexology. The seminar covered topics, such as homosexuality and masturbation, that the medical school curriculum was too prudish to address. It was at the sexology seminar that Reich was first exposed to psychoanalysis; several analysts—including Wilhelm Stekel and Alfred Adler, disciples of Freud who had since parted ways with their master—came to speak to the young students.

Reich, unlike Fenichel, wasn't an immediate convert to the new science; he thought psychoanalysis made sexuality sound "bizarre and strange . . . The unconscious was full of nothing but perverse impulses."[1] But whatever lingering doubts Reich may have had were dispelled when Reich was won over by the man behind the science.

The encounter would change Reich's life. "Freud spoke to me like an ordinary human being," Reich recalled thirty-three years later. "He had bright, intelligent eyes; they did not try and penetrate the listener's eyes in a visionary pose; they simply looked into the world, straight and honest . . . His manner of speaking was quick, to the point and lively . . . Everything he did and said was shot through with tints of irony."[2]

Freud, evidently excited by Reich's curiosity, scanned his bookcases, which supplemented his cabinet of archaeological oddities with another sort of oddity: a leather-bound collection of dreams, jokes, mistakes, and perversions. As Freud handed Reich special editions of his essays—*The Unconscious, The Vicissitudes of Instincts, The Interpretation of Dreams,* and *The Psychopathology of Everyday Life*—Reich was struck by the grace with which Freud moved his hands. "I had come in a state of trepidation and left with a feeling of pleasure and friendliness," he wrote. "It was the starting point of fourteen years of intense work in and for psychoanalysis."[3]

Freud, for his part, was immediately impressed with his handsome, brilliant, and "worshipful disciple," as Reich described himself. "There are certain people who click, just click," Reich said. "I knew Freud liked me."[4] Freud began referring patients to Reich that same year. Reich was only twenty-two and had not yet started his own analysis with Isidor Sadger (that analysts must themselves be analyzed wasn't stipulated until 1926). The following October, Reich nervously presented a paper on Ibsen's *Peer Gynt* to the Vienna Psychoanalytic Society, and was formally accepted by Freud as its youngest member. He hadn't yet completed his medical degree, and wouldn't graduate as a doctor until two years later, in 1922.

Reich was to become one of the most celebrated of the second generation of analysts. The psychoanalyst Martin Grotjahn described Reich in his memoir as "the Prometheus of the younger generation," who "brought light from the analytic Gods down to us."[5] In the 1920s, Reich's second analyst, Paul Federn, called him the best diagnostician among the younger therapists—he was, in the eyes of many, Freud's natural successor. One person who knew them both would later describe Reich as having been "Freud's fair-haired boy."[6] Anna Freud reported that her father had called him "the best head" in the International Psychoanalytic Association, and he lived and had his rooms at Berggasse 7, just a block down the street from his mentor.

Freud had first called his new method of treatment "psychoanalysis" in 1896. Ten years earlier, Freud, then twenty-nine and a lecturer in neurology at the University of Vienna best known for his study of the medical effects of cocaine, traveled to Paris to study under Jean-Martin Charcot at the Salpêtrière Hospital. Freud spent four and a half months at the famous asylum, known as a "mecca for neurologists," accompanying its famous director on ward rounds of the institution's five thousand patients. The charismatic Charcot would hypnotize the people he deemed hysterics so as to break through, he said, to the "lower" or "feminine" parts of their minds (he thought hysterical patients were more susceptible to hypnosis because they suffered from hereditary degeneracy). While they were under hypnosis Charcot was able to induce and dissolve their mysterious hysterical symptoms by the powers of suggestion, a process he demonstrated in a series of legendarily theatrical lectures.

Until then hysteria had been thought of as the product of a "wandering womb," which could be repositioned by hydrotherapy or electrotherapy, or cured by the massage or surgical removal of the clitoris. Charcot, in showing that males could also suffer from hysteria, transcended these primitive techniques, but in so doing he gave scientific legitimacy, ironically, to the dubious art of mesmerism, which had been fashionable a hundred years earlier. Franz Anton Mesmer's art of "animal magnetism" was dismissed by the French Academy of Sciences in the eighteenth century as charlatanism, and ever since then it had been considered the realm of mystics and quacks. Yet Freud returned to Vienna from Paris in 1886 and, under Charcot's influence, set up a clinic as "a practicing magnétiseur." Hypnosis was so frowned upon that he found himself excluded from the university's laboratory of cerebral anatomy as a result. "I withdrew from academic life," Freud wrote in his autobiography, "and ceased to attend the learned societies."[7] He referred to the following years in the scientific wilderness as his decade of "splendid isolation."[8]

Ten years later, Freud and his coauthor, the Viennese physician Josef Breuer, published *Studies on Hysteria* (1895), the book of five case studies that could be said to have launched the "talking cure," as one of Breuer's patients (Anna O.) described the nascent art of psychoanalysis. Freud and Breuer discovered that if hysterics, once hypnotized, were encouraged to recall the traumas that had caused their symptoms, they achieved a degree of catharsis in describing them. For example, Anna O. (her real name was Bertha Pappenheim) had stopped drinking liquids, quenching her thirst only by eating fruit, but during one session under hypnosis she recalled an occasion when she had been disgusted by the sight of a dog drinking out of her glass. On coming out of her hypnotic trance, she found herself able to drink once again. Freud and Breuer positioned themselves as psychic detectives, tracking down unconscious memories from the clues—both spectacular and mysterious—that were produced by the bodies of their hysterical patients: a dead arm, an inexplicable cough, the sudden ability to speak only in a foreign tongue.

Following Breuer's example, Freud would put his own patients under hypnosis and then apply pressure to their foreheads or hold their heads in his hands, a "small technical device" that served to distract patients from their conscious defenses in the same sort of way, he wrote, as "staring into a crystal ball."[9] He would then instruct the patient to recollect, "in the form of a picture," the forgotten event.[10] He found that naming the trauma, turning the picture into words, would free up the patient's field of vision and clear the unpleasant memory. Freud would then stroke his patient over the eyes to emphasize the fact of the memory's having been wiped away. Though he gave up hypnosis in 1892, favoring instead the technique of free association, Freud's practice, with its reported miraculous cures, was at first seen as no less occult than spiritualism or mesmerism. According to the historian Peter Swales, Freud was known as *der Zauberer*, the magician, by the children of one of his patients.

Unlike Breuer, Freud always found a sexual origin to the repressed memories he unearthed. Freud thought that "symptoms constitute the sexual activity of the patient," and that these would disappear after the neurotic became conscious of the repressed sexual traumas that had caused them.[11] (He initially believed that most of his hysterical patients had been sexually abused, an idea he would renounce in 1897, when he decided that most accusations of childhood sexual abuse were sexual fantasies). Breuer disagreed with him, and the difference of opinion led them to a parting of ways. According to Freud's biographer Ernest Jones, Freud's subsequent emphasis on the unconscious, on instincts, and on sexuality, especially infantile sexuality (which Breuer had found so distasteful), breached all contemporary norms of decorum and respectability and consequently "brought the maximum of odium on Freud's name."[12] It was as though Freud had soiled the tabula rasa of the child's pure mind.

Jones met Freud in 1908 at the First International Congress of Psychoanalysis in Salzburg. (Jones had come from London). He found the fifty-one-year-old Freud's whispering voice "unmusical and rather rough," but he was very taken—as Reich would later be—with Freud's eyes, which "constantly twinkled with perception and often with humor."[13] However, when he visited Freud in Vienna after the congress, Jones admitted that he "was not highly impressed with the assembly" that had gathered around the great genius.[14] (Jones wrote in his biography that Freud was "a poor *Menschenkenner*—a poor judge of men.")[15] Jung, one of the earliest of these disciples, had warned Jones that they were "a degenerate and Bohemian crowd," a comment Jones thought vaguely anti-Semitic, but Jones himself was free with his insults, dismissing the analyst Isidor Sadger as "morose, pathetic, very like a specially uncouth bear" and Alfred Adler as "sulky and pathetically eager for recognition."[16] Jones wrote in his autobiography, *Free Associations*, that there was so much prejudice against psychoanalysis at that time that it was hard for Freud to "secure a pupil with a reputation to lose, so he had to take what he could get."[17] As it happens, Jones was as good an example of these tarnished students as any, having been recently dismissed from a London hospital after being accused of exposing himself to two young girls.

Even many years later, when Reich met Freud after the First World War, psychoanalysis was still at an uncodified, experimental stage, practiced only by a small coterie of faithful apostles—"There were only about eight men," Reich remembered—who were dismissed as sex-obsessed perverts by their enemies. By then, Freud had excommunicated three of his closest adherents as traitors to the cause: Carl Jung, Wilhelm Stekel, and Alfred Adler. Many of Freud's closest remaining adherents came from outside Vienna: Britain (Jones), Berlin (Karl Abraham, Max Eitingon, Hanns Sachs), and Budapest (Sándor Ferenczi, Sandor Rado). The small Viennese contingent to which Reich referred included Otto Rank, Eduard Hitschmann, Paul Federn, Ernst Silberer, Theodor Reik, Isidor Sadger, and Hermann Nunberg.

In 1919 Freud was appointed a full professor at the University of Vienna, the first honor granted him in Austria as the inventor of psychoanalysis. But he described this as an "empty title" because he wasn't invited to give any official lectures or to sit on the faculty board, and the post was without pay. Though Freud now had enthusiasts all over the world (after his seminal lecture series in America in 1909), he was still deemed a maverick, and was forced to operate almost totally outside the university system. Freud liked to joke that "his reputation extends far beyond the frontier of Austria. It begins at the frontier."[18] "They were laughed at," Reich remembered. "In the medical school, they were laughed at. Freud was laughed at."[19] To join *die Sache*, "the cause," as Freud referred to psychoanalysis, continued to involve renouncing a conventional career and going into a kind of exile.

Reich first arrived in Vienna at the end of August 1918. He was twenty-one and had been given a three-month leave from the military to study, even though the First World War would continue until that November. As a lieutenant in the army, he'd been entrenched on the Italian front for the past three years. Reich and the forty men under his command lived in a cramped dugout meant for half as many, about five hundred yards from the enemy front line. Knee-deep in mud, caught in the stalemate of trench warfare, blindly obeying orders from above, they sometimes went without provisions for a week or more when the Italians, who were trying to break through to capture the port of Trieste, conducted sustained bouts of heavy bombardment.

"Many cried out in a most unsoldierly manner for their mothers or just whimpered quietly to themselves," Reich wrote of life under constant fire.[20] However, most of the troops quickly became inured to the haunting screams of the dying and wounded, the dampness, shrapnel showers, cholera outbreaks, and perpetual bombardment. "Soon it became unnoticed," Reich wrote of the "habituation and dulling" effect of war. The troops, Reich wrote, protected themselves from thoughts of imminent death with gallows humor, drunkenness, and, when away from the front line, visits to brothels.

After three years of fighting, advancing and retreating only frustratingly small distances, the Austro-Hungarians, bolstered by German forces, managed to penetrate the Italian lines. They took 400,000 Italian soldiers prisoner and advanced to within a few miles of Venice. Reich found himself in the second line of attack: "The first line was a little ahead. Nobody knew quite where we were going or how. But we trotted along, past the Italian trenches. The bodies lay in rows from earlier attacks. We rested in an abandoned dugout. In front of the dugout were barbed-wire fences, hung with bodies. They made no impression."[21]

Reich's battalion was subsequently stationed in the picturesque village of Gemona del Friuli, just north of Venice, an area their forces now occupied. Reich, thoroughly disillusioned with the war and with the chances of victory for his side, allowed discipline to relax in this less hostile environment; his hungry, fatigued troops fraternized with the enemy. Reich found an Italian girlfriend, a woman whose husband had been conscripted two years earlier and hadn't been heard from since, leaving her to look after their young daughter.

When news of the revolution in Russia reached Reich and his men in 1917, it failed to excite them; they were "inwardly laid waste, no longer capable of taking anything in."[22] All they could focus on was where their next meal was coming from, and lazily performing the numerous drills and maneuvers they were assigned. One of Reich's fellow officers lamented that their "professional future was lost." He told Reich that their only option was to stay in the army after the war—they were now of little use for anything else. Reich had other aspirations. When he took leave he was, he wrote later, "looking for the way back into life."[23]

Reich arrived in Vienna penniless, despite having had a privileged upbringing as the eldest son on a two-thousand-acre family estate in Bukovina. He'd been forced to abandon the property he'd inherited after his father's death, which left him an orphan at the age of seventeen, when the Russians invaded Austria-Hungary at the outbreak of the war. To make matters worse, his father's life insurance payout was rendered worthless by the catastrophic rate of inflation. (To put this in some perspective, Freud discovered that, if he'd died at this time, his own life insurance policy of 100,000 crowns—worth $19,500 in 1919—wouldn't have left his heirs with enough money to pay a cab fare.)

Reich enrolled at the prestigious University of Vienna to study law, hoping a qualification in that subject would swiftly change his financial prospects. But he was bored by the required rote learning, and unexcited by the prospect of a life in the legal profession, and he switched to medicine before the end of the three-month cram course. In so doing, he joined a prestigious department that included Paul Schilder, Julius Wagner-Jauregg, and Sigmund Freud.

Reich's change in subjects was well timed. Only a few weeks after he began his medical studies, Austria-Hungary ceded defeat and the almost one-thousand-year-old Habsburg monarchy collapsed. (The Austrian Revolution, as the emperor's overthrow was known, was so bloodless, with only a few shots being fired, that the psycho-analyst Hanns Sachs joked about the genteel notice he imagined might have announced it: "The Revolution will take place tomorrow at two-thirty; in the case of unfavourable weather it will be held indoors."[24]) Austria, mired in war debt, was severed from its surrounding empire and, as a result, lost 80 percent of its industry and much of its trade and natural resources to its successor states. Freud's eldest son, Martin, who had read law at the University of Vienna before the war and who, like Reich, had served on the Italian front, noted in his autobiography that the end of hostilities saw thousands of lawyers suddenly unemployed. Austria-Hungary's huge bureaucracy (satirized by Kafka) crumbled and left few contracts for Austrian lawyers to draw up.

The 261,000-square-mile-dominion some called the "China of Europe," which encompassed eleven countries, fourteen different languages, and fifty-two million inhabitants, was dismantled, cut down to an eighth of its prewar size. Postwar Austria was now just a "truncated torso," as Freud called it, compared to its former self, cut off from its major sources of coal, oil, and food. Czechoslovakia, Yugoslavia, and Hungary were created out of the ruins, and Italy, Poland, and Romania laid claim to huge chunks of territory. Reich's birthplace in Galicia, the poorest and largest province of the Austro-Hungarian Empire, and his childhood home in Bukovina, also on the eastern border of the empire—places to which he'd never return—were now parts of Poland and the Ukraine, respectively. "More or less the whole world," Freud complained from his apartment in the former imperial city, "will become foreign territory."[25]

The Republic of German Austria was proclaimed on November 12, 1918, the day after the Armistice. The name of the nascent state reflected the popular desire for annexation to Germany, but the Entente powers, preparing to meet in Versailles the following year to discuss the terms of peace, forbade this strategy of reenlargement for fear of restrengthening Germany, preferring a policy of divide and rule. (The then-popular idea of *Anschluss*—merging with Germany—would, of course, be realized by Hitler under different circumstances twenty years later.) Freud never forgave President

Woodrow Wilson for carving up the map of Europe forever, guaranteeing self-determination to Austria-Hungary's "captive peoples" in his famous fourteen-point plan for peace, while reneging on his other promises. In 1930 Freud cooperated with William Bullitt—a former ambassador to Russia who had once been a patient of his and who had resigned in protest from the American delegation at Versailles—on a book-length character assassination of the ex-president; they accused Wilson of having a "Christ complex" and of suffering a complete "moral collapse" at the peace conference. (The book, which attempts to psychoanalyze someone Freud never met, is widely thought to be Freud's flimsiest work, so much so that many orthodox Freudians have tried to deny the extent of Freud's involvement with it and it is omitted from the standard edition of his writings.)

Hoping for greater concessions at Versailles, Austrian politicians declared that their bankrupt nation was *lebensunfähig,* not viable on its own, a notion that served only to cement a national lack of confidence. As Freud bluntly put it in a misanthropic letter to his colleague Sándor Ferenczi, the Habsburgs had "left behind nothing but a pile of crap."[26] The population of Vienna was half starved, Freud explained to his Welsh disciple Ernest Jones, reduced to the position of "hungry beggars."[27] Jones visited Freud in late September of that year and was struck by the sight of Vienna's skinny citizens and ragged dogs. He took a gaunt Freud out to dinner with some other analysts: "It was moving to see what an experience a proper meal seemed to mean to them," Jones wrote.[28]

"It was in the great hunger winter of 1918," Reich recalled of his arrival in the city, "an eighth of a loaf of bread for a whole week, with no meat or milk or butter."[29] The official rations were so paltry that in order to survive, people supplemented them by purchasing on the black market, where they were at the mercy of tough profiteers. Reich lived off a monotonous diet of oatmeal, watery soup, and dried fruit served in the student canteen, where he had to queue for up to two hours every day. He got a piece of jam cake every Sunday. Others weren't so lucky. In November 1918, the *International Herald Tribune* reported on the appalling conditions in Vienna from one of the city's numerous soup kitchens, each of which fed about six thousand people a day:

Each person receives half a litre of soup daily. The soup is made from rotten cabbage and flour. On Sundays a small portion of horse-flesh is dropped into the soup. I have a sample of the flour beside me. It looks like sand, but a closer inspection reveals a quantity of sawdust which it contains. All these human wrecks, with their bones protruding through their skin, exist on this soup. Hundreds die daily and are buried in paper coffins, because wood must be used for [cooking] food.[30]

Until 1920, when the Inter-Allied Commission on Relief of German Austria took over the distribution of food and prevented famine, conditions only got worse: it would be five years before *Schlagober*, fresh whipped cream, reappeared in the city's cafés. On top of the shortages of food, there was a dearth of fuel, homes, and jobs. To cause even greater devastation, that October the influenza virus reached Vienna, killing tens of thousands, mostly within three days of their being infected (the virus would ultimately kill more people worldwide than had died in the war itself). Freud lost his daughter Sophie to the flu.

Before the war, Vienna had been the most sophisticated, multi-cultural, modern, and decadent of cities—the so-called City of Dreams. The capital of glamour, hedonism, and experimentation was embodied in the ornate, highly decorative style of the Viennese Secession, in the paintings of Gustav Klimt, Egon Schiele, and Oskar Kokoschka. While the avant-garde gave expression to the city's excesses, beneath the opulence there was a sense of sturdiness and certainty. The Viennese novelist Stefan Zweig described the pre-war "golden age of security" in which he grew up as characterized by a sense of permanence, duty, stability, and optimistic belief in technology and progress. "The nineteenth century was honestly convinced," he wrote in his autobiography, *The World of Yesterday*, "that it was on the straight and unfailing path towards being the best of all worlds."[31] However, the First World War, which resulted in the deaths of 10 million people (1.2 million of them from Austria-Hungary), dispelled this delusion, leaving behind a spiritually crushed and apathetic populace.

"We of the new generation," Zweig wrote, speaking for the survivors, "who have learned not to be surprised by any outbreak of bestiality, we who each new day expect things worse than the day before, are markedly more skeptical about a possible moral improvement of our culture . . . We have had to accustom ourselves gradually to living without the ground beneath our feet, without justice, without freedom, without security."[32] Freud, who wrote about the thin layer of ice that insulated civilization from an ever-present destructive force, became the spokesman for this dejected generation. "He enlarged the sincerity of the universe," Zweig wrote in praise of his friend.[33]

The Vienna that Reich first encountered was a ghost of its sumptuous past; it was now a huge poorhouse, full of itinerant soldiers returning from the battlefields and homeless beggars who had drifted in from the provinces. With agricultural production at half its prewar levels, and with Czech, Yugoslav, and Hungarian food blockades in place, a starving rural population emigrated to the city, leading to severe overcrowding and unsanitary conditions; a third of Austria's population crowded together in the faded grandeur of the capital.

Twenty-five thousand of Reich's fellow Galician Jews were among these new arrivals to Vienna. Though he shared their provincial roots, Reich didn't identify with this group. He recalled that when he was a child, his grandfather pretended to fast at Passover—Reich was once sent to the local temple to fetch him for dinner, and indiscreetly shouted out his message—but his own family didn't even feign observance of Jewish customs. He was raised in a secular, German-speaking household, and his father, who thought assimilation was the key to social advancement, used to punish him for using Yiddish expressions (a census report from as late as 1931 recorded that 79 percent of Jewish residents in the region spoke Yiddish as their first language).[34]

According to the historian Anson Rabinbach, although the Orthodox Galician Jews formed a small fraction of the 200,000 Jews in Vienna, they were especially prominent in their long black silk caftans and broad-brimmed hats and became scapegoats for preexisting resentments: "No one had any use for this army of impoverished peddlers," Rabinbach writes, "[and] their presence in Vienna was exaggerated in the upsurge of an already established anti-semitism."[35]

It is sometimes forgotten that anti-Semitism in Austria predated fascism; indeed, Hitler, an Austrian, learned much of his hatred of the Jews from Karl Lueger, founder of the Christian Social Party, who was mayor of Vienna when Hitler lived there as a struggling artist from 1908 to 1913. As early as 1916, Vienna was so inundated with Jewish refugees that some Viennese were calling for special camps to be established in Moravia to house them.

There had been little anti-Semitism in Bukovina when Reich was growing up—more than a third of the 800,000-strong population in the province's capital, Czernowitz, where he went to school, was Jewish—but, in Vienna, Reich witnessed thugs harassing and beating up his Jewish classmates.[36] He claimed that because he himself didn't look like a stereotypical Jew, he was able to walk down the steps of the Vienna Anatomical Institute "amidst howling crowds of nationalistic students" without eliciting their racist taunts.[37]

When Martin Freud returned to Vienna in August 1919, after spending six months bulking up on spaghetti and risotto in an Italian prisoner-of-war camp on the Riviera, he was struck by the atmosphere of simmering violence, vandalism, and disorder in his home city. There were frequent street protests against the desperate food and housing shortages, demonstrations that were often accompanied by the looting of shops and cafés in the city center. He was shocked when he saw someone rip down a curtain in a train and pocket it, in full view of the other passengers and without shame, something that would have been unimaginable before the war; and the leather straps on the carriage windows had all been cut off so that people could repair their shoes. Inflation meant that the money he'd saved in his four years of military service was now no longer enough to pay a Viennese cobbler to mend his own boots, he wrote in his memoir. Money, Stefan Zweig put it, "melted like snow in one's hands."[38] "This inflation, so devastating to the foundations of middle-class life, was bad enough," Martin Freud complained, "but the sense of insecurity, caused by an absence of discipline which permitted the mob to get out of hand, was the hardest to bear."[39]

In 1919 there were uprisings in Czechoslovakia, Bulgaria, Germany, and Hungary, where Béla Kun's Communist government held power for one hundred violent days. Many in Vienna thought that the Russian Revolution would have a domino effect throughout Europe. In Vienna, Martin Freud felt that he was observing an almost carnivalesque inversion of social hierarchy: "At my return one could still hear hooligans fearlessly singing in the Vienna streets: 'Who will now sweep the streets? The noble gentlemen with the golden stars [military decorations] will now sweep the streets.' Ex-officers like myself found it wisest to wear a scarf over their golden stars or risk having them torn off, and not too gently."[40]

However, in Austria, neither the Social Democrats, who had won the majority of the vote in the first national elections in February 1919, nor the conservative Christian Social Party (and Pan-Germans) wanted a Bolshevik state. The Social Democrats planned a peaceful and democratic social revolution, and the backward-looking Christian Social Party were committed, at least initially, to the restoration of the monarchy. In an atmosphere of deprivation and near anarchy, the two main parties formed an awkward coalition in which Social Democrat politicians held almost all the key positions, putting aside their differences in order to prevent civil war or complete national collapse. With the real threat of a popular uprising, the Christian Social Party was particularly dependent on the Social Democrats to curb the threat of the sizable workers' and soldiers' councils, which wielded power over the unemployed and the demobilized military, and thereby to prevent the Communists from exploiting the dissatisfied and revolutionary mood.

In April 1919, the newly formed Austrian Communist Party organized a demonstration in front of Parliament and attempted a putsch. The Communist Party had only three thousand members at that time, and even though a few of the agitators had rifles, most were armed just with lumps of coal, and were easily crushed by the police. The majority of the workers identified more with the Social Democrats, and the Communist Party membership slumped after this unsuccessful action.

The Christian Social Party assumed a tough and popular stance against what they considered the Bolshevist menace, which they largely attributed to Jews, and they made substantial gains in the 1920 elections. When they assumed power that year, their nineteen-month coalition with the Social Democrats ended, and the Social

Democratic Party never regained power at the national level. However, the Social Democrats still had a stronghold in Vienna, where they won 54 percent of the vote in 1919 and formed the first Socialist administration to run a major capital. Red Vienna, as the city they transformed with their social projects came to be called, became an isolated laboratory for their brand of left-wing socialism, and a fertile ground for the politically engaged expansion of psychoanalysis.

In the flux of postwar Vienna, Freud, who also had little sympathy for communism, threw in his lot with the Social Democrats. The party's leader and the country's first foreign secretary was the Marxist mathematician Otto Bauer, the brother of the patient Freud wrote about as Dora, his most famous case history. Victor Adler, a physician and one of the founders of the Social Democratic Party, had lived in the apartment now inhabited by Freud, and Freud had once visited him there. Freud admitted that he had thought at one time of becoming a politician himself, claiming that his school friend Heinrich Braun, a prominent Socialist in later life, "awakened a multitude of revolutionary trends in me."[41] Freud used whatever influence he had to help Socialist politicians like Julius Tandler, Reich's anatomy teacher, who as undersecretary of state for public health in the coalition government and then as city welfare councillor for Vienna applied his much-needed surgical expertise to Austria's body politic, developing programs for child welfare, recreation, and the control of infectious diseases.

"We related to him as a teacher," Reich said of Tandler, "not as a socialist . . . Everybody was totally taken up with his own studies, and keeping alive as best he could."[42] Reich's apparent indifference to politics was perhaps understandable, considering the more immediate concerns in Vienna at the time; he was so malnourished that he collapsed from hunger during one of Tandler's lectures. It was only later that Reich would absorb the lesson from Tandler that academics, and in particular medics, could bring about real social change.

As a student, Reich shared an unheated, erratically lit room with his eighteen-year-old younger brother, Robert, of whom he was now sole guardian, and another undergraduate who sometimes received care packages from his mother, which made Reich feel jealous and home-sick. A friend of Reich's recalled seeing a note pinned to the icebox by the brothers' flatmate that read, "Willie, I left a dish of potatoes, but don't eat them all, leave some for Robert."[43] Their room was so cold that Reich had to wear gloves and his military overcoat indoors, and even then he developed frostbite on his fingers. (It wasn't just students who suffered; Freud was no better off. He had to wear an overcoat and thick gloves as he worked in his unheated study, where his ink froze, and he accepted payment in potatoes from the patients he treated.)

Reich's future sister-in-law, Ottilie Reich Heifetz, remembers Reich's mood at this time as "open, lost, hungry for affection as well as food."[44] Reich and his brother were sent the occasional precious ten dollars by an aunt who lived in the United States, and his father's brother, Uncle Arnold, who had been a lawyer, reluctantly gave them the odd meal or small handout. Reich longed to be part of a family, but his relatives treated him and his brother as an unwanted burden, and Reich broke off all contact with them after his aunt served him a cup of watered-down coffee, which he felt she would never have offered her own children. He was too proud to eat at their table as a second-class citizen and left, slamming the door behind him. At his uncle's suggestion, he sold off what few possessions remained from better days to pay his way, but even so, he spiraled into debt. When he begged his uncle for more money he was told, "All I can do for you is offer my regrets." Robert got a job working for an international transportation firm to pay the rent and, according to his future wife, helped to support his brother through university on the understanding that the favor would be returned so that later he could also attend university; however, by the time that would have been possible Robert was already too established in his new career.

Reich had been the privileged heir to his father's estate and a respected officer in the army, but at university things were different. He was seen as provincial, a "greenhorn," lacking in the confidence and sophistication of most of his peers. He spent every Saturday listening to his fellow students debate current affairs over coffee at the Café Stadttheater, near the university, but felt unable to join in. "Being clever was a special sport of the bourgeois elite," Reich wrote, "especially of the Jewish youth. Cleverness for its own sake, to be able to talk wittily, to develop ideas, and to philosophize about the thoughts of others, were some of the essential attributes of a person who thought something of himself. I admit that I could not keep up with this, even though I was not stupid."[45]

Having been "intellectually starved," as he put it, during his military service, Reich felt academically insecure—he had enlisted early, full of nationalist spirit, and had completed a rushed and leniently examined version of his *Gymnasium* diploma at officer training college. Reich sought to rectify his feelings of inadequacy by spending most of his time absorbed in his studies, reading from five to eight in the morning, huddled next to the small iron stove in the café across the road from his freezing room, before heading to lectures. He struggled with the philosophy of Kant and Schopenhauer, and consumed extracurricular sexology books by Bloch, Forel, Moll, and Freud.

He went to theatrical performances at the Kammerspiel and to free recitals at the Arnold Schoenberg Society, where he befriended the composer's brother-in-law, the violinist Rudolf Kolisch. However, Reich wasn't wealthy enough to keep up with the more active social life of his fellow students, most of whom were supported by their families. He had to spend his free time earning money by giving lessons to younger students, helping them cram for the oral examinations in physics, chemistry, and biology that he'd passed with top grades. "When I consider what I do on a given day," Reich wrote in *Passion of Youth*, describing his diary for June 24, 1919,

> I find very little which is purposeful but much that is exhausting: 6:30–9:00 tutoring; 9:00–11:00 lectures; 11:00–11:45 waiting on line at the student cafeteria; 11:45–12:15 spent in the cafeteria's noisy rush and turmoil; 2:00–3:30 tutoring (chemistry); 3:00–6:00 wanted to do dissecting but had to stand in line at university offices until 6:00; 6:00–6:45 waiting on line, dinner, and now I am so tired that I am no longer capable of serious mental work . . . I have only two hours in the evening to study, and even then, frequently either the lights or my brain fails.[46]

Grete Lehner, a fellow student who also later became a psychoanalyst, found Reich enthusiastic but domineering, unworldly, and more lacking in culture than her other student friends. Reich placed Lehner on a pedestal for a while: "How greatly she resembles my ideal woman," he wrote in his diary, describing her as "smooth, sleek, studious, a grave academician, at times naïve, and charming."[47] Their friendship became strained after she began seeing one of Reich's friends, another medical student named Eduard Bibring. On one occasion when she did not invite Reich to the theater because her future husband felt uncomfortable with him there, Reich wrote to her:

> You, Bibring, and Singer [another student] are certainly not over-burdened with riches, but you are still more or less without material worries. I live from one day to the next and have been forced to go into debt for six months, to accept charity in order to struggle through. In my opinion, this is enough to make me a sullen, irritable, and frequently unpleasant fellow. Recently, I have withdrawn somewhat in order not to disturb anyone. If this makes me appear arrogant or ill-natured, it cannot be helped, for I do not like to bother others with my complaints. I bear this misfortune as well as I am able, after a pampered childhood—without annoying others. You may have some vague idea, but by no means can one fully judge what it means to be completely alone, to have no one with whom to share one's head-splitting thoughts, to be at odds with everyone, yes, even with oneself.[48]

Reich soon fell in love with another medical student, Lia Laszky, with whom he shared a corpse in anatomy class (there were four students per body; Laszky and Reich were working on the brain together). He also shared the contents of her lunchbox; Laszky was going through so much hard-to-come-by food while remaining very thin that her mother suspected her of having a tapeworm and demanded she have a medical exam. Reich described Laszky as having a "soft face, a small nose and mouth, blonde hair" and remarked that she "could give one a very knowing look."[49] He grew so infatuated with her that he worried he'd end up in the psychiatric clinic of Julius Wagner-Jauregg, the famous doctor at the University Hospital.

Laszky told Reich's student and biographer Myron Sharaf that she found Reich both "fascinating and abhorrent" when they first met, dynamic and charismatic but bullying in his attempted seduction of her, and she resisted his advances, being "too frightened, too inhibited"—she found one of Reich's talks on psychoanalysis at the sexology seminar "disgusting." "I was a virgin," Laszky later said, "and he was a steamroller."[50] Reich chastised Laszky for "being surrounded by an iron band which prevented unwanted individuals from entering her sphere," and presented her with a book by the psychoanalyst Eduard Hitschmann, a specialist in female frigidity, in the hope of persuading her to sleep with him.[51]

"I had no idea that the wild enthusiasms which overcame me at times, the overexcitement of my senses, and a certain restlessness, were the result of a lack of sexual gratification," Reich wrote later, looking back on his student days.[52] Reich had not yet articulated his theory of the grave dangers of sexual abstinence. Although it's tempting to project his future status as a sexual revolutionary back into his past, this would be misleading—at the time, Reich felt ambivalent about his sexuality, intellectually and physically.

Reich was embarrassed by the psoriasis that had afflicted him since he was a teenager and that scarred his face and body with dry red patches, watery blisters, and acne-like sores. In 1913, on his only previous visit to Vienna, Reich had been hospitalized for nine months. He underwent X-ray treatment for the chronic psoriasis that had flared up all over his body. During the war he was sent back from the front on two occasions for treatment. The condition would plague him for the rest of his life.

Reich's skin disease, which he'd suffered from since being a teenager, may have influenced his later sexual theories. John Updike, who developed psoriasis in 1938, wrote of the humiliation he felt at being a prisoner of his "flaming scabbiness" in a chapter of his memoir, "At War with My Skin": "Of course my concern with my skin was ultimately sexual, the skin being a sexual organ, and the moment of undressing the supreme revelation and confiding."[53] In fact, Reich's whole theory of character analysis emphasizes the deceptions of the "skin ego," which covers you like an armor, or scab. To find the truth you have to delve to an authentic core hidden below the surface. Perhaps in the sexual act, when a partner proved that she had conquered her disgust at his condition, Reich felt finally at home in his awkward epidermis. Could a sexual revolution have been born from one man's uneasy relationship to his own body?

Until he met Freud, the impressionable Young Reich had subscribed to a philosophy completely antithetical to the ideas that he would later develop for himself. He fell under the influence of Otto Weininger, the author of *Sex and Character* (1903), a book that presents a number of theories that now seem bizarre and offensive, but, as Reich wrote in *Passion of Youth*, was "read by all intellectuals and raved over" at the time.[54] At the age of twenty-three, only two years after his book came out, Weininger shot himself in the house where his hero Beethoven had died, and by 1919 he had achieved a posthumous cult status. Ludwig Wittgenstein, who was training to be a primary school teacher in Vienna as he completed the work that would make him famous, *Tractacus logico-philosophicus*, enthusiastically handed out copies of *Sex and Character* to his friends. Though Reich did not know Wittgenstein, he shared his zeal; when he sat next to a rich merchant's wife at a dinner in April 1919, he offered to read several chapters of *Sex and Character* with her, and they discussed Weininger's work alongside that of Freud and Jung.[55]

Weininger promoted hard work, self-control, and sexual abstinence; he considered sexual longing to be a weakness. He railed against the permissive, anarchic atmosphere he saw everywhere in fin-de-siècle Vienna, the city the journalist Karl Kraus called a "laboratory of world destruction," and especially against what Weininger termed its "modern coitus culture."[56] Sexual excess, he complained, had become a symbol of status, so much so that women without lovers had become figures of shame. He blamed women, homosexuals, and Jews for dragging society down into a pit of sensuality. (Hitler later applauded Weininger's racial bigotry and declared that there was "just one good Jew: Otto Weininger, who killed himself on the day when he realized that the Jew lives upon the decay of peoples." Weininger had converted to Christianity in self-hatred.[57])

In 1919, the year women were first able to vote in Austria, Weininger's ideas on the "emancipation question" were being newly debated; the Christian Socials feared that the polls would be overrun with radicals, while less activist women, more likely to vote conser-

vative, would stay away (they proposed that voting should be obliga-
tory). Weininger thought that women were passive, purely sexual
beings—even if they weren't fully conscious of their sexuality—
who longed to be dominated. They were therefore not fully in possession of their reason, and not worthy of the vote. He believed that
only men were capable of rationality and genius. By transcending
sexuality and the body, exercising the sexual restraint of which
women were incapable, men were able to allow these energies to be
sublimated into the disinterested realms of art and politics. "Man
possesses the penis," Weininger explained, in an aphorism that was
to become popular, "but the vagina possesses the woman."[58] In the
years after the war, Weininger's ideas seemed more urgent to his followers, who felt that Weininger had predicted the social disintegration in which they now found themselves and had articulated the
sacrifices required for much-needed cultural regeneration.

Freud would no doubt have disapproved of Reich's interest in
Weininger's work. Freud thought Weininger's book "rotten," even
though he concurred with one of Weininger's opinions: that man
was bisexual, with conflicting male and female characteristics. When
Freud had met Weininger in 1901, he declared the "slender, grown-
up youth with grave features and a veiled, quite beautiful look in his
eyes" to be "highly gifted but sexually deranged."[59] Helene Deutsch,
who in 1918 became the first woman to join the Vienna Psychoanalytic Society (and who was in analysis with Freud in 1919), considered the misogynistic Weininger to be schizophrenic.

No doubt Reich's reading of Weininger contributed to the sexual
confusion from which he suffered at this time. Aside from his skin
complaint, Reich feared disease. In the army he had been repulsed
when he watched a company of soldiers visiting a brothel in Trieste,
queuing in alphabetical order to sleep with an Italian prostitute;
three days later, he wrote, "A whole column marched back to the front
with gonorrhea."[60] "The present erotic tension dominating me is
noteworthy," he wrote in a diary entry in 1919. "It increases from
day to day, and only disgust and fear of infection have prevented
me from releasing it before now."[61]

Reich was also "disgusted" by the promiscuity of upper-class
girls at the university who taunted him by, as he saw it, sleeping

with everyone but him. On the other hand, he was aggravated by the "sexual restraint" of the other educated girls he fraternized with. Reich acknowledged that his problem was that he tended to idealize women, preferring to worship them from afar, and that he felt disappointment after any real sexual experience. In *Passion of Youth*, Reich admitted that all of his relationships were filtered through his search for his mother, whom he pictured as both madonna and whore, for reasons that would become clearer to him when he began his own analysis. "The girls to whom I have felt attracted have always been peaceful, gentle types, and all of them with a soft expression around the mouth," he wrote, with reference to his mother, before distancing himself a degree. "However, I do have a preference for blondes, while my mother's hair was dark."[62] He also attributed to his mother his love of "breasts which are round, full, supple, do not sag, and have a rosy white hue."[63]

But Reich had not yet found requited love with such an ideal woman. Lia Laszky had started seeing the conductor Hans Swarowski, whom she eventually married, quitting medical school to go on tour with him. Hungry, parentless, penniless, and smarting from Laszky's rejection of him—and no doubt with Weininger's romantic suicide in mind—Reich wrote that he contemplated using his army revolver against himself. As a student he was frequently depressed, alienated from others, and riddled with self-doubt. "What is causing my constant inner disquiet, this lack of a desire to participate, this withdrawal into my own shell, this hatred for my environment?" Reich asked himself in one particularly melancholic diary entry. "Yes, I hate everything and everyone, I shake my fists (albeit in my pockets, out of cowardice!) at everything that goes against my will."[64]

He sought a kind of resolution to these feelings, which pitted him against the world, in psychoanalysis.

On September 15, 1919, Freud referred to Reich his first patient, a waiter suffering from impotence and a compulsion to speed-walk. Compared to the little extra money he made tutoring first-year medical students, psychoanalysis promised a good income. "I am alive," Reich exclaimed in his diary. "[I] have two paying patients sent to me by Freud himself."[65] At that time Freud didn't believe psychoanalysis to be interminable but, in the cases entrusted to Reich, hoped for speedy cures. Reich treasured the small calling cards on which Freud wrote referrals, for example: "For psychoanalysis, impotence, three months."[66] (In 1910 Freud claimed to have cured Gustav Mahler of impotence in just four hours.) Freud's estimate proved optimistic: Reich would eventually treat the waiter for three years.

Though it was not yet mandatory for an analyst to have been analyzed before he could treat others, Freud did recommend that students of psychoanalysis undergo therapy ("The only way to learn analysis is to be analyzed," he constantly reiterated). So Reich began his own analysis in parallel to his work with his first patient. For this purpose Reich chose Isidor Sadger, whose course on psychoanalysis he had attended at the university. Sadger, who like Reich was born in Galicia, was twenty years older than his patient. In 1898, when he became one of the first practitioners of psychoanalysis (he was never analyzed himself), Sadger sent Freud one of his essays. Freud couldn't stand his hyperbolic prose—he called Sadger's style "insufferable"—but accepted Sadger for membership of the Vienna Psychoanalytic Society in 1906.[67]

The psychoanalyst Helene Deutsch considered Sadger to have an almost pornographic interest in sex. Ernest Jones, in his autobiography, illustrated Sadger's blunt manner and lack of social grace by describing how Sadger introduced himself to a distinguished literary lady, whom he sat next to at dinner during a psychoanalytic congress, with the coarse line "Have you ever concerned yourself with masturbation?"[68] His nails, Deutsch remembered, were as filthy as his mind, and the couch on which Reich stretched out in Sadger's office was notoriously dirty: "He would not even keep his analytic couch clean for a patient's head and feet," she remarked.[69]

Staring at the ceiling from this unsanitary bed, Reich confided in someone for the first time the guilty secrets and horrible tragedies that had scarred his childhood.

Reich was born on March 24, 1897, in the small village of Dobrzanica, an outpost of the Austro-Hungarian Empire in what is now

Ukraine. The nearby town of Drohobycz had about ten thousand inhabitants but was expanding rapidly as speculators were drawn to the area's rich oil fields. Oil was in high demand for city lighting, and the crude oil mined from Drohobycz illuminated Vienna and Prague. As early as 1873 there were twelve thousand derricks holding the machinery that extracted the so-called black gold; the area was nicknamed "Galician California."[70]

The writer Bruno Schulz, born in Drohobycz five years before Reich, would capture the resulting clash of cultures in his novel *The Street of Crocodiles* (1934). The oil works on the outskirts of the town polluted the Tysmienica, the river that ran through it, and seemed to infect the place with greed and corruption. Shoddy new houses with garish façades sprang up in the gray suburbs to house the oilmen. Existing alongside it, though seemingly doomed to obsolescence by the brash modernity that choked it, was the town's crumbling core with its wild gardens and musty shops. In his novel Schulz describes with great accuracy the exotic treasures these contained: Bengal lights, magic boxes, mandrakes, automatons, microscopes, homunculi in jars, salamanders, and rare folios of engravings. It was at this juncture between the old and the new that Reich was born.

Soon after his son's birth, Leon Reich moved the family to Jujinetz, south of Drohobycz in the province of Bukovina, where he leased a cattle farm that supplied beef to the Austrian army. He ran it like a feudal fiefdom, and was felt by his son to be a large, sadistic, bruising presence. "I cannot remember my father ever having cuddled or treated me tenderly at that time," Reich wrote in *Passion of Youth*, "nor can I recollect feeling any attachment to him."[71] He did recall being beaten by him, and also witnessed his father hit his workers. Reich remembered how his father used oppressive rage when he home-schooled him and his younger brother.

In one of Reich's photographs of his father, Leon Reich is shown to be a burly man with a handlebar mustache, his fat face held up by his stiffly starched collar. Reich scrawled over the image, "His ideal was the German Kaiser." In contrast, Reich described his mother, Cäcilie Reich (née Roninger), as "slender, her face round, with a beautiful, gentle profile and delicate features. She had thick, jet-black hair, which fell in natural waves all the way to her knees when she let it down. Her eyes were also black, her nose small and straight, her complexion as white as snow."[72] Though she may well have been attractive for the era, the surviving photographs of a plump hausfrau don't correspond with his memories, although it is clear that Reich inherited her black hair and eyes. According to Ilse Ollendorff, Reich's third wife, who felt she failed to live up to Reich's idealized memory of his mother (and her cooking), Cäcilie was "much subdued by her husband" and "rather unintellectual"—she was nicknamed *das Schaf*, the sheep, which, as Ollendorff explained in her biography of her husband, "very definitely has the connotation of the 'dumb one.'"[73]

Reich lived an isolated life, cocooned from the farmworkers' children and prevented from playing with the Yiddish-speaking children in the nearby village. Reich wrote of having looked longingly over the fence at the other children's games. Robert, his younger brother, was his only playmate. Despite his sense of isolation, Reich retained a rose-tinted vision of his lonely semifeudal childhood in the Bukovinian countryside. He collected butterflies in the fields of his father's estate, rode, hunted, swam, fished, and would remember this privileged, austere, rustic experience as the happiest time of his life.

Reich's parents were well-off; they had a housemaid, a nurse, and a cook. Each was to play a role in Reich's precocious sexual awakening, the story of which the supposedly sex-obsessed Sadger no doubt drew out in his analysis. Sadger encouraged him to publish an account of his childhood. Reich's diaries of the time of his analysis—from February 25, 1919, to October 5, 1922—interspersed with his memories of his upbringing, would be released only in 1988 as *Passion of Youth*.

Reich wrote that he was four and a half when he eavesdropped on the housemaid having sex with the coachman; at five he masturbated his younger brother's nurse; at eleven and a half he lost his virginity to Sosha, the cook. His memoir describes these scenes with the detailed relish of a sexologist ("Diaries," he wrote, "are the receptacles of filth!!")—how he stumbled across his father's pornography collection, discovered and devoured his parents' sex guide, *The Marriage Counselor*, and repeatedly pleasured the family horse with a riding crop.[74]

When Reich was ten his father arranged for him to have a tutor. Reich's mother, then thirty-three, began an affair with this teacher, Dr. Sachter, a much younger man, when her husband was away. Reich witnessed snatched moments of indiscretion night after night, which both horrified and aroused him. In Reich's description of the primal scene, his mother had to tiptoe through his room to get to that of her young lover. "I heard them kissing, whispering," Reich wrote, "and the horrible creaking of the bed in which my mother lay . . . And so it went, night after night. I followed her to his door and waited there until morning. Gradually I became accustomed to it! My horror gave way to erotic feelings. Once I even considered breaking in on them, and demanding that she have intercourse with me too (shame!), threatening that otherwise I would tell Father."[75]

Leon Reich was a jealous man who already suspected his wife of having an affair with his own brother. Leon and Arnold Reich looked almost identical, their only distinguishing feature seeming to have been their mustaches—Leon's twirled up, Arnold's drooped down. Leon became convinced that she was consorting with another of his sons' tutors when he startled them alone together. "What were you doing with him alone in the hall, you whore?" he screamed, as Reich recalled the scene. "Tell me! Why did he jump back a few steps when I came in!? Why did he jump back, I ask you?"[76] He dragged her upstairs, where his children could hear him continuing to shout in a crazed voice, "You tell me everything or I'll murder you—every detail of the love affairs you've had up to now."[77]

Leon Reich soon reappeared, with beads of sweat on his forehead, and threatened to beat confirmation of his suspicions out of the trembling twelve-year-old Reich, who soon confessed that he'd witnessed the earlier affair. His father then took him off to confront his mother.

Cäcilie Reich had locked herself in her bedroom to escape her husband's fury; a "deep groan" was heard through the door, and she was discovered in the dark, writhing and foaming at the mouth, having downed a bottle of household cleaner. Her husband force-fed her an emetic and saved her, only to subject her, in Reich's account, to almost a year of taunts and severe beatings. Leon Reich accused her of having slept with almost every man they knew; he even be-

gan to doubt that the blond Robert was really his son (later in life
Reich often fantasized that he, too, was illegitimate, the result of his
mother's affair with a Ukrainian peasant).

Cäcilie sought refuge in a hotel for several days to escape the
barrage of abuse. Soon afterward she tried, once more, to kill herself
by drinking poison, but it did nothing more than burn her mouth
and strip her stomach lining raw, forcing her to recover in bed for
several weeks. "Driven to death like a hunted animal," as Reich put
it, she tried a third time and hemorrhaged violently.[78] She died two
days later with her family by her side. Reich wrote that he'd never
seen her look so beautiful as in the moments before she passed
away. He was thirteen years old.

In the first psychoanalytic article Reich published, "A Case of Pubertal Breaching of the Incest Taboo" (1920), he described a depressed patient, "a thoroughly intelligent, capable man in his
twenties," who was a student, like him.[79] The patient was afflicted
with a crippling inferiority complex and felt "all choked up" in company, worried he'd say something stupid, and he therefore stayed
apart from his peers. His brooding melancholy made him blow even
the smallest trouble out of proportion. Over a month of daily therapy,
the patient told Reich of his close relationship with his mother,
whom he'd tried to defend against his father's violent and jealous
rages when he was a young boy. It seemed, Reich wrote, that they
were always circling some indescribable memory in these sessions.
However, to the frustration of the inexperienced analyst, the student
mysteriously broke off his therapy before they ever reached it.

Two weeks later the former patient sent Reich a long letter explaining the trauma that had been too painful for him to discuss.
After a lengthy passage in which he lavishly praised his mother's
beauty, as if to excuse her subsequent actions, the young student
wrote of the adulterous affair he'd witnessed at the age of twelve
between his mother and his tutor:

> I am not quite sure just how the affair began because I didn't notice
> anything. I first became conscious of the situation and began to

keep track of it one afternoon when Father was asleep and I saw my mother going into the tutor's room. The feelings I had at the time were partly erotic curiosity and partly fear (fear that Father might wake up—I thought no further) . . .

Shortly after Christmas, Father went away for three weeks. During that time I had the most horrible and repulsive experiences imaginable, which buried themselves deep in my thought and emotions.

The very first night (I hadn't shut my eyes from excitement) I heard Mother get up and—even now disgust seems to be strangling me—tiptoe through our bedroom in her nightgown. I heard his door open, and close partially. Then all was quiet. I jumped out of bed and crept after her, freezing, with my teeth chattering from cold and fear and horror. Slowly I made my way to the door of his room. It was ajar. I stood there and listened. Oh, the frightful memories that drag each recollection of my mother down into the dust, that soil my image of her with muck and filth! Must I go into details?

. . . I heard them kissing, whispering, and the horrible creaking of the bed on which my mother lay.[80]

Reich bluntly paraphrases the patient's account of what happened next: the man's father discovered the affair and, in response, his mother killed herself by taking poison.

The supposed patient was, of course, Reich himself. The patient's letter and the related passages in *Passion of Youth* are almost identical. His mother's death was something Reich almost never spoke about, and he would confide the story of how she died only to those who knew him best; interestingly, in the disguised case history, Reich omitted to mention the patient's role in how his father found out about his wife's affair.

Instead of publishing a book-length account of his childhood as Sadger had proposed, Reich evidently preferred to publish a version of this central event in an eight-page paper consisting of veiled autobiography. Reich broke off his analysis with Sadger before it was finished, which is perhaps reflected in the convoluted, epistolary form of his interrupted fictional analysis (one is reminded of Goethe's *The*

*Sorrows of Young Werther*). The process of fictionalizing one's self-analysis was not uncommon—Freud's daughter, Anna, in the paper that initiated her psychoanalytic career ("Beating Fantasies and Daydreams"), also wrote of herself in disguised form when she documented her masochistic fantasies of being beaten by her father.

Reich felt betrayed by his mother, and was racked with guilt over his betrayal of her; he thought that if he'd confronted his mother earlier, instead of being an excited voyeur, he might have been able to put an early stop to his mother's affair and thereby spared her his father's wrath. Even into his thirties he would wake abruptly from the recurrent nightmare that he'd killed her. "That Reich was unable to resolve this question may be one of the reasons that he was never able to successfully finish his own analysis," Ilse Ollendorff concluded in her biography of Reich. This inability colored the rest of his life. Ollendorff suspected that his "subsequent guilt over it may well have added to his personality that obsessive note of absolute, relentless dedication which so frequently is a characteristic of the intellectual pioneer."[81]

Reich certainly seems to have sought to compensate for his mother's death with his work. When he was almost fifty and had devoted over half his life to battling sexual repression, Reich wrote of a photograph of his mother that he kept on display in his study, "I have set up an image of that noble woman so that I can look at it over and over again. What a noble creature, this woman—my mother! May my life's work make good for my misdeed. In view of my father's brutality, she was perfectly right!"[82]

In an unpublished autobiographical sketch also written at that time, in the third person, in Reich's awkward, unedited English, he made a rare comment about the radical effect her loss had on him. It had robbed him of any possibility of having a normal life:

> WR was forever ripped from the ways of a sitting life. He was put upon the road of continuous motion and he has kept moving ever since . . . WR's life since 1910 had never been a smooth ride in rolling hill countryside with flowers at the wayside and birds singing in the air. He had known and lived that, too, of course. But his life was

rather to be compared to the stormy flight of a jet through hurricanes and blizzards, through the steepness of thousands of feet up and down the atmosphere, through mild sunshine and springy hopefulness as well as through peril and breathlessness.[83]

In *Passion of Youth*, Reich described how five days after his mother died he spent the evening with his father and younger brother in a nightclub, "crying over our champagne."[84] Leon Reich presumably took his sons along to watch him drown his own sense of guilt. According to Reich, his relationship with his father improved after they were stripped of the object of their Oedipal rivalry. That is not to say their relationship was unambivalent. Reich blamed his father for keeping him isolated from other children until after his mother's death, when he continued his education at the local *Gymnasium* (secondary school); he felt this had made him socially awkward and "serious and moody." "My father barred my way," Reich wrote of his upbringing. "He infected me with his ambition and caused my problems . . . And yet he was an intelligent man whom I not only hated but loved."[85]

Two years after his mother died, the fifteen-year-old Reich sought solace in the local brothel, drunk and "yearning for maternal love" (hadn't his father repeatedly called his mother a whore?). "Was it the atmosphere, the clothing, the red light, the provocative nakedness, the smell of whores—I don't know!" he wrote of his inaugural visit to a brothel. "I was pure sensual lust; I had ceased to be—I was all penis! I bit, scratched, thrust, and the girl had quite a time with me! I thought I would have to crawl inside her. In short, I had lost myself!"[86]

Reich, marveling at the "staggering intensity" of the experience, which was allegedly exacerbated by the prostitute's "hysterical writhing," begged her to be his exclusive mistress, but when he returned the following evening she was entertaining another client, and Reich, like his jealous father, was furious and crushed.[87] He didn't visit a brothel for three years, when, he says, he became a habitué, despite his announced "ever-increasing disgust for whores."[88] He tried to "save" another prostitute, paying her to tell him the unhappy story of her life, and when she also rejected him, he recalled feeling suicidally depressed. Reich sublimated his sexual energies by writing a play, *The Reunion*, about a noble prostitute and a dastardly hero (himself) who had seduced and then deserted her.

Instead, Reich "succumbed to excessive masturbation," as he termed it, despite a cousin's having warned him that the practice would make him impotent. He often fantasized about his mother, and in *Passion of Youth* he attributed his frequent depressions to his guilt over this incestuous compulsion. Reich summed up his lonely school years at the *Gymnasium* in Czernowitz: "I read a lot, devoured both belles lettres and scientific writings, improvised on the piano for hours, and gave lessons to add to my pocket money. I worked, played, brooded, dreamed, and masturbated!"[89]

Reich's teenage years were marked by a good deal of sexual confusion, which he carried with him to university. He fell in love with a cousin and gave her all his late mother's jewelry, but was too shy to kiss her. Once, when he leaned in to embrace a friend's sister, Reich blacked out. "My field of vision grew dark," he recalled, explaining why he fled the scene "as if the devil himself were after me": "I saw red and green lights, balls of light, glowing rays, and between them something white."[90]

Four years after his mother's death, Reich's father lost a lot of money in a series of "unfortunate investments." He took out a life insurance policy and then stood in water up to his waist in a freezing pond, supposedly fishing, but, Reich thought, really in order to catch pneumonia, since a more obvious form of self-harm would invalidate the policy. If this is what he intended, he may well have been successful. His lungs became seriously infected soon afterward.

Reich borrowed money from his uncle to take his father for treatment, and they traveled three hours south to a health resort in the Tyrol. Reich left his father, who had lost a quarter of his weight, wrapped in a blanket on one of the sanatorium's balconies, where he was supposed to recover from his tubercular condition by soaking in the sun and breathing the healing mountain air. "In surroundings like this, one simply has to recover, and I am already feeling so well!" his father said optimistically, before suffering a convulsive coughing fit that wasn't at all reassuring to his son.[91] By the time Reich arrived home to take over the running of the family farm, a telegram was waiting for him with the news that his father had died from his illness. Reich always suspected that he had committed suicide. At seventeen, Reich was an orphan, responsible for a large estate, and his brother's principal guardian.

On June 28 of that year, Archduke Franz Ferdinand, the heir to the Austro-Hungarian Empire, was assassinated in Sarajevo by a member of the Black Hand, a secret Serb nationalist group. A month later, after various aggressive ultimatums were rejected, Austria-Hungary declared war on Serbia. This provoked Russia to mobilize its own army in the Balkan state's defense. Germany, coming to the aid of her ally Austria-Hungary, then declared war on Russia. The Austro-Hungarian soldiers, confident of an easy victory, were garlanded with flowers as they marched off toward the front, singing, "We shall conquer the Russians and beat the Serbs and show that we are Austrians."[92]

The Russians invaded the Austro-Hungarian Empire from the east in large numbers on August 18. Soon tales of ferocious Cossack forces undermined the confident Austrian patriotism. Many wealthy landowners vacated their country houses, abandoned their possessions, and retreated to the safety of Vienna. In the two days before the war started, thousands of Jews fled Galicia and Bukovina; eventually about 400,000 refugees would flee the two provinces. Jews were the victims of frequent pogroms in Czarist Russia, where they didn't enjoy the full civil rights granted them in Austria, and the refugees feared the Russian army's well-known anti-Semitism. Russian troops did indeed harass and rob the Jews who remained. Bruno Schulz's father's textile shop in Drohobycz was burned down by the Russians during the early days of the war.[93]

Reich dispatched his fifteen-year-old brother to live with their maternal grandmother, while he stayed on with an elderly housekeeper to protect the farm. He set up some barrels of strong schnapps at the side of a nearby road to appease the thirsty Russian infantryman who marched past, not because he sided with the Russian liberators—which was how they presented themselves—but because he had been advised that this would discourage plundering.

It had precisely the opposite effect. A division of troops, who interpreted the gesture as an invitation, took up residence in Reich's house for the night, helping themselves to his supplies. Though Reich seems to have witnessed only the occasional skirmish at this time, the eastern front was a bloody battlefield. In mid-September the Austrians abandoned Galicia, leaving behind 130,000 dead.

In the winter of 1915, German troops bolstered the Austrians in a new offensive and the Russians retreated. Reich was dragged from his bed by two soldiers early one morning and taken hostage along with some other local citizens. Reich liked to play down his Jewishness, and he does not mention the logic to this roundup—he thought he was taken along because of his "supposed 'importance.'"[94] These were almost certainly delusions of grandeur. In fact, Russian military policy was to deport Jews en masse to Russia; in the first year of the war, 35,000 Jews were sent to internment camps in Siberia, which were prototypes for the later Soviet gulags.[95]

As he was being escorted from his property, Reich met one of his farm stewards and instructed him in a whisper to collect as much money as he could to bribe his captors; Reich had little cash of his own and was dependent on his friends for help. A farmhand was recruited to drive Reich's horse-drawn sleigh in the direction of the Russian border, where Reich was being deported. Reich sat in the backseat wrapped in layers of fur, protection against the minus-40-degree cold. He had been traveling for a tense hour when the steward caught up with them and bribed the Russian sergeant major with a packet of banknotes. Reich does not record who his generous benefactors might have been. He had ensured his was the last sleigh in the convoy, and with a wink to the sergeant riding on horseback behind, he was allowed to drop back and return home. He later heard that one of his neighbors had died in the Russian camps.

Austrian forces temporarily moved back into the district but almost none of the displaced populace returned with them. When the Russians regrouped and attacked once again, Reich decided to join the second Austrian retreat in a convoy of thousands of other refugees. He arranged for the farm horses and remaining livestock to be driven south, where they were sold to the Austrian army. He followed in a farm cart laden with sacks of feed. As he left, Reich looked up to see that the hill above his house was swarming with Cossack riders. They were chasing down a patrol of Austrian cavalry, firing on them at full gallop.

He decided to enlist in the army, even though it was a year and a half before he was legally bound to do so and he had not yet graduated from the *Gymnasium*. He was sent to officers' school in Hungary for training. Reich would never see his homeland again: "Of a well-to-do past," Reich wrote, "nothing was left."[96]

The Vienna Psychoanalytic Society met every Wednesday evening in Freud's study, where a member would give a talk on an aspect of psychoanalysis and it would be dissected over black coffee and cigars (the theme of the first talk was the psychological implications of smoking). Lots would be drawn from one of Freud's Greek urns to decide the order of discussants. In the autumn of 1919, after Reich nervously presented his paper "Libidinal Conflicts and Delusions in Ibsen's *Peer Gynt*," he was accepted into Freud's inner circle. Reich was the youngest member by about twenty years. At one such gathering Freud reminded Reich of his junior status when he said, "You are the youngest here. Would you close the door?"[97]

It was perhaps Sadger who proposed Reich for membership in the society. Sadger was an expert on Ibsen, about whom he'd written extensively, and his influence may also have explained Reich's choice of subject for his inaugural paper. Otto Weininger was perhaps a greater impetus. He had devoted an essay to *Peer Gynt*, published the same year as *Sex and Character*; Reich thought it "beautiful and often profound."[98] Weininger had been so enamored with Ibsen's play, which had premiered in German translation in Vienna in 1902, that he learned Norwegian in order to read it in the original and traveled to Oslo to see a performance.

Peer Gynt is a dreamer, a libidinous prankster, an unscrupulous egotist and lying braggart, who gets swept up in all sorts of exotic adventures. He habitually retreats from the harsh realities of his life to a fairy-tale world of his own invention. According to Weininger, the lesson of Ibsen's play was that we are all condemned to self-deception: "In this life people can never live in complete truth, something always separates them from it . . . [be it] lies, errors, cowardice, obstinacy."[99]

Reich used psychoanalytic language to elaborate on Weininger's idea of our being always irrevocably split from our unconscious—it was impossible, Weininger believed, to be entirely self-aware. Peer Gynt blurs this line in his bouts of madness, which Reich termed "narcissistic psychosis," because his insanity was accompanied by delusions of grandeur. Only in an Egyptian asylum, where the inmates hail him as an emperor, does Peer Gynt achieve the recognition and heroic destiny he craves. In commentating on this journey, Reich—who, it must be remembered, was himself auditioning for a part as a psychoanalyst—made sure to name-check as many analysts as possible, and to make numerous laudatory remarks about Freud's work.

Reich suspected Weininger of unconsciously identifying with Peer Gynt, and in his own diary he himself did so quite consciously. Reich had first seen the play performed in 1919 at the German People's Theater (Deutsches Volkstheater) in Vienna; he read it again and again, and struggled with the issues of identity that it explored. When retracing Reich's account of his life, and questioning the reliability of his own narration, one might wonder what it means that he identified so closely with Peer Gynt, a famous literary fantasist he described in his paper as an "inveterate liar."[100]

Reich interpreted his own interest in Ibsen's archetypal outsider as a reflection of the leap into the dark that he made when he chose to pursue a career in the stigmatized profession of psychoanalysis. "He who departs from the normal course easily becomes a Peer Gynt, a visionary, a mental patient," Reich declared in a 1940 edition of *The Function of the Orgasm*:

> It seems to me that Peer Gynt wanted to reveal a deep secret, without quite being able to do so. It is the story of a young man who, though insufficiently equipped, tears himself loose from the closed ranks of the human rabble. He is not understood. People laugh at him when he is harmless; they try to destroy him when he is strong. If he fails to comprehend the infinity into which his thoughts and

actions reach, he is doomed to wreak his own ruin. Everything was seething and whirling in me when I read and understood Peer Gynt and when I met and comprehended Freud. I was ostensibly like Peer Gynt. I felt his fate to be the most likely outcome if one ventured to tear oneself from the closed ranks of acknowledged science and traditional thinking.[101]

When Reich's university friend Otto Fenichel visited Berlin for a few months in the fall of 1919 (he would move there full-time in 1922), Reich temporarily assumed leadership of the student sexology seminar, which had about thirty participants; it was a task he took very seriously. Fenichel was one of Reich's most radical and articulate friends, and Reich was a little intimidated by him.

Fenichel had been born in Vienna, in the same year as Reich, and during his teenage years he had been an integral part of a Jewish faction of the Wandervögel (literally, "birds of passage") youth movement. The right wing of this movement, which would become the Hitler Youth, was full of nationalists and anti-Semites. The left wing was composed of Socialists, pacifists, and sexual libertarians who rebelled against authority, escaping their parents' bourgeois lifestyles by escaping to the freedom of the mountains on hikes. The psychoanalyst Bruno Bettelheim recalled hearing of Freud for the first time on one of these weekend outings to the Vienna Woods: "A young man, Otto Fenichel, dressed in [military] uniform, joined me and the person I considered my girlfriend. They started to talk about dreams and dream interpretation and the sexual meaning of dreams and all that . . . My girlfriend became fascinated . . . but I didn't want [her] to become attracted to this man. As the day went on I became more and more furious."[102]

Bettelheim made sure to immerse himself in psychoanalysis so that he could compete with Fenichel, and when he returned to Vienna he immediately bought as many books by Freud as he could afford. It was as if they were seduction manuals.

Fenichel conducted and published a study on the "sexual enlightenment" of the youth movement's more adventurous members as early as 1916; the paper almost got him expelled from his

*Gymnasium*. But Reich, having been isolated in the provinces and having enlisted so early in the military, had missed all of this bohemianism, which centered on Vienna. He would no doubt have enjoyed the sense of camaraderie the movement offered. Only in 1920, when Lia Laszky, who was also an active member, gave Reich a copy of the romantic anarchist Gustav Landauer's *Aufruf* (The Call), which introduced him to Landauer's anarchist ideal of a spontaneous community, was Reich primed in the central principles that inspired the young utopians.

Fenichel was also the author of "Esoterik" (1919), a radical paper written for a Jewish youth journal, *Jerubbaal*, in which Fenichel linked a militant advocacy of free love to an idea of social emancipation and documented the inroads made by the youth movement against sexual repression. When he first read Fenichel's essay alongside Landauer's book in 1920, Reich was resistant to its themes, and—perhaps like Bettelheim a little jealous of his friend's intellectual confidence—he did not engage with his arguments, even though he'd later adopt them as his own.[103] "Otto is blind and inconsiderate in his attitude toward young people," Reich grumbled, "who he thinks are all just like himself!"[104]

Nevertheless, under the tutelage of Fenichel, who held frequent symposia attended by members of the youth movement and other young radicals, Reich found that, by the summer of 1920, he "was moving more and more toward the left."[105] When he returned to Vienna from his travels in time for Easter 1920, Fenichel delivered a lecture titled "On Founding a Commune in Berlin," a proposal that appealed to Reich. At another Sunday evening meeting, Fenichel spoke for two and a half hours in answer to the question "How can we improve the situation?"—a reference to the desperate social conditions in Vienna. He captivated his audience with his sense of spontaneous outrage, and Reich wrote that he was "overwrought" and intimidated by the company. He stayed on the fringe of the discussion and admitted to having been unable to contribute anything more than "timid comments and incomplete sentences."[106] Among those present were Willy Schlamm, who would go on to publish the Communist newspaper *Die Rote Fahne* (The Red Flag); Deso Julius, a Communist who had escaped to Vienna in 1919 after the Hungarian Soviet Republic was quashed by Romanian forces; and a nineteen-year-old teacher trainee at an experimental kindergarten for Jewish orphans. Her name was Lore Kahn and soon afterward she would begin therapy with Reich. The consequences were to be disastrous.

Freud's colleague and mentor, Josef Breuer, was psychoanalysis's first victim of what Freud called "transference." Breuer's patient, the famous Anna O., flung her arms around his neck and, to his embarrassment, declared that she was about to give birth to his child, though the pregnancy, and the act that would have led to it, were fantasies. Shaken by this experience, Breuer left for Venice the next day to enjoy a second honeymoon with his wife. Freud himself gave up using hypnosis as an analytical tool after another patient threw herself at him when she emerged from a deep trance. Fortunately, Freud wrote, they were interrupted by his maid. He was too modest about his own appeal to think her attraction for him was anything other than a trick of the psyche: he thought his patients were just acting out their Oedipal desire to be seduced by their fathers. In 1915 he imposed what was known as the "rule of abstinence" on the analytic process, requiring the analyst to deny the patient's craving for love.

Nevertheless, as Freud wrote to Jung of the erotic attraction between analyst and analysand, "in view of the kind of matter we work with, it will never be possible to avoid little laboratory explosions."[107] Affairs with patients, later considered strict boundary violations, were not at all uncommon in the early days of psychoanalysis, though they were fraught with problems; Ernest Jones, Sándor Ferenczi, Carl Jung, and Wilhelm Stekel all had affairs with patients. "One should not sleep with one's patients; it is too complicated and dangerous," Reich reminded himself, heeding Freud's warnings about the pitfalls inherent in psychoanalysis.[108]

But by the time Reich's affair with Lore Kahn began, she no longer was a patient: she was, as Reich put it, "at last 'herself.'" Kahn embarked on therapy after her heart had been broken by Karl Frank, a charismatic and radical member of the youth movement. As a result of their separation, Kahn completely lost her self-confidence. As she recovered from her dependence on her revolutionary ex-boyfriend, she transferred her affections to her new analyst, who found her to be "lively, clever, and somewhat 'messed up.'"[109] One day, Reich reported, Kahn declared that she was terminating her analysis because she thought she was cured and she now wanted him.

After Kahn's analysis was curtailed, she and Reich met again at one of Fenichel's sexology seminars, where Kahn gave a lecture on kindergartens, a movement that was intimately connected to the rise of radical feminism in Austria ("Women and children . . . are the most oppressed and neglected of all," wrote Friedrich Froebel, who founded the first kindergarten in 1848).[110] After her talk, and emboldened by her newly restored confidence, Kahn took the opportunity to invite Reich to go hiking with her in the Vienna Woods, where Reich and Kahn embarked on an affair. "Lore had loosened her hair," Reich wrote. "She knew what she wanted and did not hide it. After all, she was no longer a patient. And it was nobody's business. I loved her, and she grew very happy."[111]

Kahn's parents immediately pressured the couple to marry, which Reich wouldn't consent to do because he felt he was too young and also was still in love, albeit unrequitedly, with Lia Laszky. Once again, citing Otto Weininger, Reich characterized Kahn as the noble "mistress-mother" and Laszky, who had spurned him for Swarowski, as the whore. Reich and Kahn used to sleep together on their hiking outings, but back in Vienna Reich's landlady wouldn't permit female guests, and Kahn's parents expressly forbade any premarital affair. Kahn left home and took a room at a friend's so that they could continue to see each other without parental interference. "It was unheated and bitter cold," Reich reported in *Passion of Youth*. "Lore became ill, ran a high fever, with dangerous articular rheumatism, and eight days later died of sepsis, in the bloom of her young life."[112]

Kahn's mother, who found some bloody undergarments in a closet, accused Reich of having arranged an illegal abortion for her daughter and suggested that it was this that killed her—she called

Reich a murderer, implying that he'd botched the operation himself. Reich showed Mrs. Kahn her daughter's final diary entry, dated October 27, 1920, hoping to prove his innocence:

> I am happy, boundlessly happy. I would never have thought that I could be—but I am. The fullest, deepest fulfillment. To have a father and be a mother, both in the same person. Marriage! Monogamy! At last! Never was there coitus with such sensual pleasure, such gratification, and such a sense of oneness and interpenetration as now. Never such parallel attraction of the mind and body. And it is beautiful. And I have direction, clear, firm, and sure—I love myself this way. I am content as nature intended! Only one thing: a child![113]

This excited entry, though it shows Kahn was happy in her last days, is inconclusive on the matter of an abortion—it suggests that Lore Kahn either was pregnant or wanted to be. She could have died of a miscarriage or an infection that was the result of an abortion (the "sepsis" Reich describes).[114] Perhaps Reich thought that if he demonstrated that Kahn desperately wanted a child, it would make the idea of her agreeing to terminate her pregnancy seem far-fetched. Mrs. Kahn remained unpersuaded, and Reich issued further overly defensive denials, claiming that Kahn's mother was sexually attracted to him and that she now wanted some of her daughter's happiness for herself. "This is the hysterical comedy of a woman in menopause," he wrote in his diary, exploiting all the slippery logic of his newly acquired psychoanalytic reasoning, "who has identified with her daughter and is lustfully wallowing in the idea of an 'operation' despite its obvious absurdity. This wallowing is the hysterical symptom of a desire for an operation she really wanted—from me!"[115]

Reich later became a committed advocate for legalizing abortion, a right that was first granted in Russia the year of Kahn's death; his first wife, whom he began seeing soon after Lore died, had several abortions.[116] In 1962, Reich's second, common-law wife, Elsa Lindenberg, who also aborted one of Reich's children at his insistence, told Reich's student and biographer Myron Sharaf that Kahn had died from an illegal abortion, which suggests that this is how Reich recounted the story to her after they met in the early 1930s.

But at the time Reich fiercely denied this version of events. He diagnosed Frau Kahn as paranoid and arranged for her to see Professor Paul Schilder, his teacher and one of the few psychiatrists at the University of Vienna who took Freud seriously. Kahn's grieving mother never consulted him; she gassed herself to death. Reich felt that he'd destroyed first his own family and then another: "Didn't my mother also die—better said, also commit suicide—because I had told all?"[117] However, one might venture to suspect that in this case he had told less than everything.

In January 1921, barely two months after Lore Kahn's death, Reich began the analysis of one of her friends, the attractive and flamboyant Annie Pink, the daughter of a Viennese cocoa trader. Fenichel had been close to her brother Fritz, who had died in the war, and on his recommendation the eighteen-year-old Pink went to Reich for treatment. Pink's mother, who had been a teacher, had died in the influenza epidemic of 1919, and Pink joined the Wandervögel to escape Malva, the much-hated stepmother who replaced her. However, she didn't indulge in the promiscuity for which the left-wing part of the youth movement was known. In fact, when she came to see Reich, Pink had never had a boyfriend. She was his fourth female patient.

Reich, who described Pink as "extremely neurotic," diagnosed a father and brother fixation. He soon realized that he was analyzing her "with intentions of later winning her for myself—as was the case with Lore": "She flees from men; I am supposed to enable her to release her drives and at the same time to become their first object. How do I feel about that? What must I do? Terminate the analysis? No, because afterwards there would be no contact! But she—what if she remains fixated on me, as Lore did? Resolve the transference thoroughly! Yes, but is transference not love, or, better said, isn't all love a transference?"[118]

For Reich, who had had such bad luck with women in the student dance halls, psychoanalysis provided a free pass to—and increasingly a rationale for—promiscuity. The sort of young, well-educated, and neurotic women who had previously ignored him were now patients in thrall to him. But it was a forbidden attraction. "A young man in his twenties," Reich noted, crippled by temptation, "should not treat female patients."[119]

Reich started to fantasize during sessions about marrying Pink, admiring her "lithe body" as she lay on his couch. He noted how Pink's urbane personality complemented his rustic one, and he wondered what beautiful and intelligent children they'd have. "It is awful when a young, pretty, intelligent eighteen-year-old girl tells a twenty-four-year-old analyst that she has long been entertaining the forbidden idea that she might possibly embark on an intimate friendship with him—yes, that she actually wishes it, says it would be beautiful—and the analyst has to resolve it all by pointing at her father."[120]

Annie Pink called an end to their analysis after six and a half months, perhaps after Reich confessed his feelings to her (in his diary Reich wrote of drafting such a letter). She went instead to see an older analyst, the sour Hermann Nunberg. Reich was free to take her on a day trip into the Vienna Woods, where Lore Kahn had once taken him. In a hotel called the Sophienalpe, the couple undressed and Reich embraced his former patient. Annie had never kissed a man before.

"Is an analyst permitted to enter into a relationship with a female patient after a successful analysis?" Reich wrote, justifying the transgression to himself. "Why not, if I desire it!"[121] According to Pink's best friend, the child analyst Edith Buxbaum, Pink was "spellbound" by Reich, still in the grip of a powerful transference: "It would turn any patient's head," she added knowingly, "to have her analyst fall in love with her."[122] "I corresponded somewhat to her hero fantasy," Reich wrote of their mutual attraction, "and she looked a little like my mother."[123]

At the sexology seminar, not long after they began seeing each other, Reich delivered a thirteen-page paper on the orgasm: "Coitus and the Sexes." It was his first reference to the topic that would intellectually captivate him for the rest of his life, though he did not yet connect the libido or orgasm to politics. Reich sought to answer the question posed by a contemporary sexologist: Why were the male and female climax so infrequently simultaneous? This wouldn't be the case if castration fears were eliminated and tender and sensual impulses were allowed to coincide, Reich boasted, hinting at a new sexual assurance with Annie Pink.

Reich, Pink, Fenichel, and Berta Bornstein, Fenichel's girlfriend at the time, went on a cycling holiday together to the Wachau, a beautiful stretch of the Danube River Valley. Back in Vienna, because of his suspicious landlady, Reich would have to creep into the Pinks' apartment at night to continue their affair. After several weeks of secret liaisons, Pink's stepmother discovered them in bed together. At first Pink had no intention of getting married, despite Reich's fantasies that they would, which made her, according to Reich, a "modern sexual rebel" in her father's eyes.[124] But Alfred Pink tracked Reich down and confronted him, demanding that Reich make an honest woman of his daughter. What Reich refers to in his memoir as "My Early Forced Marriage" took place on March 17, 1922, without fanfare. There were only two witnesses: Edith Buxbaum and Otto Fenichel. Annie Pink was nineteen, and Reich was twenty-four.

Reich and Annie moved into a small apartment together, and Reich graduated from the University of Vienna that summer (war veterans at the university were compensated for their service by being able to complete a six-year course in four). Pink, with his encouragement, was just beginning her own medical training there. Reich had already been a practicing psychoanalyst for three years, and was so in demand that he had to rush from an analytic session to collect his diploma. All the other male students were in morning coats for the occasion; he was underdressed in a light summer suit. Reich didn't like ceremonies, and he didn't mind that no one was there to congratulate him. "Only my mother's good wishes," he wrote, "would have made me happy."[125]

Sadger would come to bitterly dislike Reich, apparently jealous of Reich's growing relationship with Freud, who was increasingly impressed by his youngest disciple. Sadger evidently disapproved of Reich's sleeping with a former patient. Reich would later retaliate by accusing Sadger of masturbating his own analysands during sessions. Reich had persuaded him to treat Lia Laszky for free. When Laszky told Sadger that the only contraception she used with Swarowski was withdrawal, Sadger took the opportunity, Reich contended, to fit her with a diaphragm right there on the analytic couch. "He behaved like a sick man," Laszky remembered of Sadger. "When I told him I practiced coitus interruptus, he said it produced 'actual neurosis' and he refused to treat me unless I gave it up. He said he would teach me how to use a diaphragm."[126] Laszky added, confirming Sadger's attitude to Reich: "Sadger was terribly jealous of Reich, who by now had left him and become the pet of Freud. I found that if I didn't want to talk during a session, all I had to do was mention Reich's name and he would rant and rave and that would be the end of my hour."[127]

Reich broke off his analysis as a result of these differences. The psychoanalyst Lou Andreas-Salomé, who had been the muse of both Nietzsche and Rilke, once wrote that Freud had remarked that Sadger "presumably enjoys his analysands more than he helps them or learns anything from them."[128] Whether Reich's analysis served to enlighten him or to titillate Sadger is an open question. Reich no doubt gauged the low esteem in which Sadger was held in psychoanalytic circles, and sought a more politically advantageous mentor. He continued treatment with Paul Federn, the talented, depressive, and disorganized vice president of the Vienna Psychoanalytic Society, who not only analyzed Reich for free but also would often feed his impoverished patient.

Federn had been an analyst since 1903 (he was the fifth member of Freud's Wednesday Society), and was an active Socialist, committed to reform. Despite their later differences, he more than anyone else opened up Reich to the possibilities psychoanalysis had for improving the world. Federn's father had been a distinguished physician, and his mother had founded the Settlement House, dedicated to advancing social welfare in slum areas in Vienna, initiating public education and health programs. Paul Federn sat on the board of the institution, which his sister now ran. Federn was one of only two psychoanalysts elected to parliamentary office. (The other was Josef K. Friedjung. Federn became a district councilman in Vienna, responsible for conducting a survey of housing conditions for janitors and clearing the army prison of lice.)

According to Federn's son, Ernst, who followed his father into the psychoanalytic profession, Federn was such a "friend of the 'common man'" that he was nicknamed "Haroun al Raschid," after the legendary caliph in *A Thousand and One Nights* who benevolently transformed living conditions for the poor in Baghdad.[129] Ernst Federn, who thought his father had been sidelined in Jones's biography of Freud and was keen to rehabilitate him, summed up his life's work: "A pioneer in the field of mental health and the application of psychoanalysis to social problems, he strove to transform psychoanalysis into an instrument for social and political change, thus remaining faithful to his socialist convictions."[130]

Federn was Freud's most senior disciple in Vienna (he was also known as "Paul the Apostle"), and he assumed the post of acting chairman and director of the Vienna Psychoanalytic Society when Freud became ill in 1922. However, Freud once told Jung that he thought Sadger the better analyst. Federn's therapeutic skill was also questioned by Helene Deutsch in her memoir, where she drew attention to the high suicide rate among his patients. In the summer of 1922 her husband, Felix Deutsch, who was also Freud's personal physician, had been called when one of Federn's patients committed suicide by poisoning herself. The patient was Freud's niece, Cäcilie Graf. Reich was in analysis with Federn at precisely this time. Like his fictional patient, and as he had with Sadger, Reich broke off the analysis he had begun with Federn before he got to the core of his troubles. There were, Ilse Ollendorff put it in her biography, "certain problems that he was never able to face."[131]

# *Two*

By 1922 the Austrian economy, which had been in free fall since 1919, teetered on the brink of collapse. The country was still devastated by its wartime expenditures, and the rate of inflation was out of control. Immediately after the war there had been twelve billion Austrian crowns in circulation; by the end of 1922 this figure had reached four trillion.[1] While the country's industry lay idle, lacking the coal and oil needed to power factories, the government's printing presses ran at full speed, working day and night to produce new banknotes. Knapsacks replaced wallets as people carried around bundles of virtually worthless paper. In 1922 a 500,000-crown note was issued, a denomination no one would have believed possible a year earlier. Despite its incessant printing, the central bank couldn't keep up with the hyperinflation, and provincial towns had to produce their own emergency money.

Visitors flocked to Austria to exploit the favorable rate of exchange. Stefan Zweig wrote of Austria's "calamitous 'tourist season,'" during which the nation was plundered by greedy foreigners: "Whatever was not nailed down, disappeared."[2] Even England's unemployed turned up to take advantage, finding that they could live in luxury hotels in Austria on the government benefits with which they could hardly survive in slums back home. None of the indigenous population wanted Austrian crowns, which most merchants no longer accepted, and there was a scramble to swap them for secure foreign currency, or any goods available. Freud hired a language tutor to brush up on his shaky English so that he could take Americans into analysis, who paid him in U.S. dollars.

In October 1922 the Christian Social chancellor, Ignaz Seipel, secured a large loan of 26 million pounds sterling from the League of Nations to stabilize the depleted economy. The budget was balanced the following year under draconian foreign supervision by the league's permanent members, who insisted that Austria unburden itself of a bloated bureaucracy. That year Vienna, which unlike the rest of the country had a clear Social Democratic majority, was declared a separate province from the otherwise predominantly rural province of Lower Austria. This gave the Social Democrats the power to raise their own taxes and implement an ambitious reform program without the need for their radical policies to be ratified by an unsympathetic assembly in Lower Austria. Excluded from national power, and exploiting the new period of prosperity, the Social Democrats concentrated on turning Vienna into a Socialist mecca, a model Western alternative to the Bolshevik experiment.

In 1923 the new city-state instituted a housing construction tax (the burden of which was on businesses and the diminishing middle class); 2,256 new residential units were built by the end of the year to redress the desperate housing shortage and to help clear the slums. Over the next decade, four hundred large communal housing blocks were built, planned around spacious courtyards, some of which spanned several city blocks. These increased the housing stock by 11 percent and housed 200,000 people, who were charged only token rents. The new "people's apartment palaces," as they were referred to, contained libraries, community centers, clinics, laundries, gyms, swimming pools, cinemas, and cooperative stores. The pride of these super-blocks, called the Karl-Marx-Hof, was built by a student of the architect Otto Wagner. Another was named after Freud.

These bastions were described by their Christian Social critics as "red fortresses," suspected of being strategically sited and designed to be easily defendable in case of civil war. Vienna was hemmed in by the surrounding provinces from which it was now separated politically, and planners were therefore unable to enlarge the capital with garden city satellites. The historian Helmut Gruber describes the new housing blocks as reflecting the status of Vienna itself, a Social Democratic island in a national sea of Christian Socials: "Enclosed, isolated and defensive," he writes, "they were enclaves within an enclave."[3]

However, the Social Democratic politicians hoped that their form of "anticipatory socialism" would be infectious and serve as a springboard back to government. In 1923 their share of the national vote stood at 39 percent, but in Vienna they could count on a two-thirds majority in municipal elections. In Vienna, after the disillusionment of the immediate postwar years, the Social Democrats had managed to restore confidence in the revolutionary idea that modernism—reflected in the functional, streamlined forms of the architecture they sponsored—could reshape people's lives for the better. The Social Democratic politician Otto Bauer claimed proudly that his party was "creating a revolution of souls."[4]

As the Christian Socials grumbled about "tax sadism," Vienna, like Weimar Berlin, became a model of social welfare, with not only excellent public housing but also enviable public health services. As city welfare councillor for Vienna, Julius Tandler, Reich's former anatomy teacher, was responsible for the health and well-being of every citizen. The Social Democrats extended to everyone "cradle-to-grave" care. Tandler was also in charge of early childhood education and initiated kindergartens and child welfare centers, and arranged for the building of numerous swimming pools and gyms. Under his tenure mortality rates dropped to 25 percent of prewar levels and, thanks to a government-sponsored proliferation of maternity clinics, the rate of child mortality halved.

Though it was not state-funded, the free psychoanalytic clinic, the Ambulatorium, that opened at Pelikangasse 18 in May 1922, offering free therapy for all, regardless of their capacity to pay, should be seen in the context of Tandler's and the Social Democrats' politics of benevolent paternalism. In September 1918, Sigmund Freud had given a speech at the Fifth International Congress of Psychoanalysis in Budapest. It was two months before the Armistice (Reich had just reached Vienna on leave), and almost all the forty-two analysts who attended appeared in military uniform, having been conscripted as army doctors to treat war neuroses, their success at which had won psychoanalysis begrudging respect from conventional psychiatry. But Freud looked to the future rather than dwelling on civilization's obvious discontents, promising his audience, "The conscience of society will awake and remind it that the poorest man should have just as much right to assistance for his mind as he now has to life-saving help offered by surgery."[5] To this end, and sounding more like a health reformer than a psychoanalyst, Freud urged his followers to create "institutions or out-patient clinics . . . where treatment shall be free." Keen to contribute to a better postwar world, Freud hoped that one day these charitable clinics would be state-funded. "The neuroses," he insisted, "threaten public health no less than tuberculosis."[6]

The psychoanalyst Max Eitingon, who came from a wealthy family of Galician fur traders and had funded the first of these clinics, established in Berlin in 1920, later wrote that Freud had spoken "half as prophecy and half as challenge."[7] Eitingon had directed the psychiatric divisions of several Hungarian military hospitals during the war. He set up the Berlin Poliklinik with Ernst Simmel, who had been director of a Prussian hospital for shell-shocked soldiers. The Poliklinik, which reflected a postwar spirit of practicality, might be seen as the psychoanalysts' attempt to adapt the intensive treatment of war neuroses to shattered civilian life.

The Berlin Poliklinik was a chic but modest outpost for this military-style campaign against nervous disease; it occupied the fourth floor of an unassuming block and it had only five rooms. Freud's son Ernst, an architect who had trained with Adolf Loos, designed the Spartan, minimalist interior. There was a large lecture hall–cum–waiting room with dark wooden floors, a blackboard, and forty chairs; four consulting rooms led off it through soundproofed double doors, and were tastefully furnished with heavy drapes, portraits of Freud, and simple cane couches. One patient was struck by the apparent lack of medical paraphernalia and walked out disappointed, muttering, "No ultraviolet lamps?"

We don't tend to think of Freud as a militant social worker, and imagine he was more likely to be found excavating the minds of the idle and twitchy rich. The psychoanalyst Karl Abraham, who was to become director of the Berlin Poliklinik, complained of just such a clientele in a letter to Freud written before the outbreak of World War One: "My experience is that at the moment there is only one kind of patient who seeks treatment—unmarried men with inherited money."[8] But Abraham's six Poliklinik staff were soon swamped with patients from all social backgrounds: they performed twenty analytic sessions on opening day. Though it was supposedly free, most patients did in fact make a modest contribution, evaluated on a sliding scale according to their means. Factory workers, office clerks, academics, artisans, domestic servants, a bandleader, an architect, and a general's daughter were expected to pay, Eitingon explained, only "as much or as little as they can or think they can for treatment." Freud praised Eitingon for initiating the drive to make psychoanalysis accessible to "the great multitude who are too poor themselves to repay an analyst for his laborious work."[9]

The Berlin Poliklinik was always intended to be a flagship institution, and following its rapid success—350 people applied for treatment in its first year—a second free clinic was founded two years later in Freud's native city (between the wars at least a dozen more were opened in seven countries and ten cities, from Paris to Moscow). According to Ernest Jones, who set up a clinic in West London in 1926, Freud was initially "lukewarm" about the idea of having a free clinic in Vienna, because he felt that only he could head it. However, the Berlin Poliklinik seemed to have turned its city into the new capital of psychoanalysis—Fenichel emigrated there in 1922, attracted by its vibrant reputation—and the Viennese analysts didn't want to be upstaged. Paul Federn (then Reich's analyst), Helene and Felix Deutsch, and Eduard Hitschmann pressed the idea upon Freud.

In May 1922 Hitschmann, a specialist in female frigidity (Reich had given Hitschmann's book on the subject to Lia Laszky), was appointed the first director of Vienna's Ambulatorium. Helene Deutsch later described Hitschmann, a resolute Social Democrat who had been practicing analysis since 1905, as "a cultured, witty man . . . 200 percent 'normal.'"[10] Reich became Hitschmann's first clinical assistant and would remain at the Ambulatorium for the rest of the decade. In 1924, he became the clinic's deputy medical director with the job of interviewing and examining all prospective patients, sending off the ones he suspected of having a physical rather than a psychosomatic illness for X-rays and blood tests, and assigning the rest to an analyst. Each member of the Vienna Psychoanalytic Society promised to treat at least one patient for free to support the clinic, which represented a fifth of their practice. If they couldn't spare the time, Reich would collect the equivalent in monthly dues.

The Ambulatorium had been two years in the planning not only because of Freud's initial intransigence but because the psychiatrist Julius Wagner-Jauregg, a member of the conservative Christian Social Party and the head of the Society of Physicians, had blocked the proposals to launch a free clinic connected to the *Garrisons-Spital* (military hospital). Wagner-Jauregg, the director of the University Clinic for Psychiatry and Nervous Diseases, was then Vienna's most celebrated doctor and one of Freud's most notorious and sarcastic critics—"His whole personality," his onetime assistant Helene Deutsch wrote in describing his resistance to psychoanalysis, "was too deeply committed to the rational, conscious aspects of life."[11] With the support of other psychiatrists who were not well-disposed toward psychoanalysis, Wagner-Jauregg, who took an entire year to examine Hitschmann's proposal for the free clinic before he rejected it, argued that the clinic was an unnecessary supplement to existing ones like his own and constituted a breach of trade.

Reich would no doubt have been aware of Wagner-Jauregg's efforts to block the Ambulatorium when he began a two-year stint of postgraduate work in neuropsychiatry with Wagner-Jauregg and Paul Schilder, the doctor to whom Reich had referred Lore Kahn's mother. When Reich studied under him, Wagner-Jauregg was experimenting with electrotherapy and insulin shock treatments, and with inducing malaria to cure the dementia associated with the final stages of syphilis. It was found that the resulting fever could kill all pathogenic bacteria; the innovation would win him the Nobel Prize in 1927.

Wagner-Jauregg had been a friend of Freud's when they were students. He once carried him to bed after Freud blacked out from drink, and he was one of the few to use the familiar *du* to address him. However, the pair fell out in 1920 when Freud testified against Wagner-Jauregg before a parliamentary commission. Wagner-Jauregg had been accused of excessive use of force in treating the military "malingerers," as he called those he felt were feigning illness as a form of desertion. At the beginning of the war he had treated war neurotics with isolation and a milk diet, but he soon found that a strong dose of electric shock therapy was the best method of getting "simulators" to return to active duty, a feat he claimed to have achieved after as little as one session of torture. Freud accused him of having used psychiatry like a machine gun to force sick soldiers back to the front. In his autobiography, Wagner-Jauregg wrote that he considered Freud's public statement a "personal attack."[12]

Reich received his first exposure to schizophrenic patients when he worked as an intern for a year on the "chronic ward" at the Steinhof State Lunatic Asylum in Vienna. There Wagner-Jauregg used bromides and barbiturates to sedate patients, which, Reich noticed critically, had no effect on their underlying psychotic symptoms. He wrote sympathetically of the inmates, "Each and every one of them experienced the inner collapse of his world and, in order to keep afloat, had constructed a new delusional world in which he could exist."[13] His own analyst, Paul Federn, claimed some success in penetrating and curing schizophrenic fantasies using psychoanalysis. Reich liked Wagner-Jauregg's "rough peasant candour" and admired his impressive diagnostic skill, but working with him created split loyalties.[14] Reich had already decided to give over his career to psychoanalysis, but to avoid being a target of his professor's derisive wit, at Wagner-Jauregg's clinic he made sure to exclude all mention of sexual symbolism from his patients' case histories.

The Ambulatorium, which eventually opened at the General Hospital (where Felix Deutsch was a physician) just after Freud turned sixty-six, couldn't have been more different from its sleek, modernist cousin in Berlin. Its shabby clapboard building was a carbuncle on the Beaux Arts architecture that surrounded it. The building was shared with the Society of Heart Specialists, whose physicians vacated it in the afternoons. The psychoanalysts used the emergency entrance for heart-attack victims as a meeting room, and the unit's four ambulance garages made makeshift consulting rooms. A metal examination table with an uncomfortable spring-board mattress doubled as a couch (patients had to use a stepladder to get onto it), and the analyst perched on a hard wooden stool. "After five sessions we felt the effects of so long a contact with the hard surface," recalled the psychoanalyst Richard Sterba.[15] He had occupied both the stool and the table, having been analyzed at the Ambulatorium for free by Hitschmann and later, with Reich's help, having gotten his first job at the clinic.

There was nothing elitist about psychoanalysis as Reich practiced it at the Ambulatorium. According to a report published by Hitschmann in 1932, 22 percent of the clinic's patients were either housewives or unemployed, and another 20 percent were laborers. In its first decade, 1,445 men and 800 women were treated in the Ambulatorium's improvised space, more than the 1,955 people treated at the Berlin Poliklinik. "The consultation hours were jammed," Reich recalled, "There were industrial workers, office clerks, students, and farmers from the country. The influx was so great that we were at a loss to deal with it."[16]

These figures are especially impressive, considering the skeleton staff with which the institution operated, and show how accepted psychoanalysis was increasingly becoming among the general public. But they also show how far psychoanalysis was from providing what Eitingon ambitiously called "therapy for the masses."[17] Eitingon himself regretted that the clinics couldn't reach more "authentic proletarian elements." Yet it was specifically the ambition of the second-generation analysts to do this—to universalize psychoanalysis with the aim of treating the social causes of neurosis rather than merely patching up the mental health of individual sufferers—that led to ruptures that almost destroyed the profession.

Freud, in launching the radical social project that was the free clinics, inspired the "revolutionism" of the second generation of analysts, as one of their members, Helene Deutsch, termed it (echoing Otto Bauer's idea of a "revolution of souls"). They were, she said, "drawn to everything that is newly formed, newly won, newly achieved."[18] These now legendary figures, who staffed the free clinics in Berlin and Vienna and came to believe that psychoanalysis could play a utopian role in liberating man from social and sexual repression, included Deutsch herself (who had been a lover of the socialist leader Herman Lieberman), Wilhelm and Annie Reich, Otto Fenichel, Edith Jacobson, Karen Horney, and Erich Fromm.

The year Reich joined the Ambulatorium staff, Fenichel instituted what became known as the children's seminar for young psychoanalysts in Berlin, so called not because it was devoted to child analysis but because Fenichel liked to think of the rebellious analysts as "naughty children."[19] In Vienna there was a similar generational gap, and a corresponding rebellion of values. It is notable that in a photograph of the Ambulatorium's volunteers taken in the mid-1920s, there were only two gray-haired members: Ludwig Jekels and Hitschmann, who were both about thirty years older than Reich. For the young recruits, even more than for their superiors, psychoanalysis was, as the historian Elizabeth Danto puts it, "a challenge to conventional political codes, a social mission more than a medical discipline."[20]

Swamped with patients at the Ambulatorium, Reich felt he was "'swimming' in matters of technique," at sea in trying to apply psychoanalytic theory to an inundated practice.[21] He knew that he was supposed to break down the barrier of unconscious resistance with which the patient repressed any childhood sexual conflict so that the emotion-laden memory could break through and evaporate into consciousness, and he knew how to work with the transference so that it became a curative force in therapy. But what was one to do with uncooperative or catatonic analysands who refused to play the game of free association or did not want to have dreams? How to communicate with patients to whom the language of psychoanalysis was entirely foreign? When Reich told his uneducated patients, as he was supposed to, that they had a resistance or that they were defending themselves against their unconscious, they just responded with vacant stares.

There was no training institute or organized curriculum where Reich could discuss these practical problems. When he expressed his concerns to more experienced analysts, he said, "the older colleagues never tired of repeating, 'Just keep on analyzing!' . . . 'you'll get there.'" Where one was supposed to "get," Reich added, no one seemed to know.[22] Reich would take particularly puzzling cases to Freud, to whom he seems to have had privileged access. One of the cases about which he sought advice was that of his first analysand, the impotent waiter Freud had referred to Reich who was still not cured three years later.

Reich had managed to trace the origin of the man's problem to his having witnessed, at the age of two, the bloody scene of his mother's giving birth to a second child. This had left his patient, Reich noted, with severe castration anxiety, "a feeling of 'emptiness' in his own genitals."[23] However, though he had theoretically solved the case by unearthing the unconscious root of his problem, an epiphany to which the patient displayed no obvious signs of resistance, the waiter remained uncured.[24] Freud warned against too much "therapeutic ambitiousness" and advised Reich to be patient and not force things; he also suggested, "Just go ahead. Interpret."[25] However, Reich declared a stalemate and dismissed the patient a few months later. His first case was a defeat that would plague him.

Freud told his disciples only what not to do in therapy, preferring to leave what one should do, as he told Ferenczi, to "tact." Freud later admitted that his more "docile" followers did not perceive the elasticity of his rules and obeyed them as if they were rigid taboos. According to Reich, Freud deemed only a handful of analysts to have truly mastered his technique. At the Seventh International Psychoanalytic Congress, in Berlin in 1922, where Freud gave a lecture that was the germ of the following year's paper "The Ego and the Id," he looked out at all the people in attendance and whispered conspiratorially to Reich, "See that crowd? How many do you think can analyse, can really analyse?"[26] Freud held up only five fingers, even though there were 112 analysts present.

Many psychoanalysts thought of themselves as passive screens for their patients' unconscious projections and hardly intervened in their free associations. If their analysands were silent, they advocated matching these silences; they joked among themselves that they had to smoke a lot to keep awake during such unproductive sessions. (One analyst who had awoken to find an empty couch justified his having dozed off by claiming that his unconscious was able to dutifully watch over his patient even as he slept.) Reich experimented with this passive technique, but it did not suit his energetic character—he had been attracted to analysis by Freud, who was, as Reich saw it, a dynamic conquistador of the psyche. When Reich put up a blank façade, as some advised, he found that his patients "only developed a profound helplessness, a bad conscience, and thus became stubborn."[27]

Soon after he joined the staff at the Ambulatorium, Reich suggested to Freud the establishment of a technical seminar to explore alternative techniques. When the idea received Freud's blessing, the first-ever teaching program for psychoanalysts was launched. The technical seminar, initially led by Reich's superiors, Eduard Hitschmann and Hermann Nunberg (Reich took over in 1924), was aimed at less experienced analysts, but senior analysts regularly joined the debate. It took place in the Society of Heart Specialists' windowless basement; the "long room with a long table and big heavy chairs," according to Helen Ross, a trainee who had made the pilgrimage to Vienna from Chicago, was made even more claustrophobic by the fact that it was clouded in cigar smoke.[28] The seminar propelled Reich to the center of the theoretical debates then taking place within the profession. In this concentrated, heavy atmosphere, the analysts presented the stories of their therapeutic struggles (Reich offered his foundering case of the impotent waiter) and thrashed out possible solutions in the hope of forging a new, clinically grounded psychoanalytic technique.

When Freud had introduced the idea of free clinics, in Budapest in 1918, he had also spoken optimistically about "a new field of analytic technique" that was "still in the course of being evolved."[29] In the early 1920s there were two main areas of innovation to which Freud might have been referring: Ernest Jones and Karl Abraham were pioneering "character theory," and Otto Rank and the Hungarian analyst Sándor Ferenczi (who made sure to attend the technical seminar when he was in Vienna) were pursuing what they called "active therapy." Reich would ultimately try to fuse these two strands, but the former played a greater role in the birth of his theory of the function of the orgasm.

Freud supposed that a child went through a series of developmental stages during which the infantile libido was concentrated on the mouth (the oral stage), then the anus (the anal stage), and the genitals (the phallic stage)—these phases were normally surmounted in weaning, toilet training, and the developing of the Oedipus complex; only after making these rites of passage could a person accede, finally, to full, adult genitality (the genital stage). Freud thought that neurotics had stalled at one of these earlier stages, where their libidos were prematurely dammed up and spilled over not only into symptoms and perversions but also into negative character traits. In his 1908 essay on the anal character, for example, Freud observed that many of his patients who were unconsciously fixated on the anal stage displayed traits such as orderliness, parsimoniousness, and obstinacy.

Ernest Jones and Karl Abraham built on Freud's observations to elaborate on a further series of personality traits for the oral, anal, phallic, and genital types. It was hoped that the analyst, armed with a list of character types, would immediately be able to recognize and understand defective developments, and therefore correct them more quickly.[30] Reich's first book, *The Impulsive Character: A Psychoanalytic Study of Ego Pathology* (1925), based on his treatment of patients at the Ambulatorium with especially troubled backgrounds, represented his attempt to contribute to this trend toward characterology; in the book he argued for a "single, systematic theory of character . . . a psychic embryology."[31]

Because Freud saw psychosexual development as a linear progression culminating in full genitality, it was inevitable that the genital character was destined to display virtues lacking in the other stages. As the historian of psychoanalysis Nathan G. Hale has observed, the genital character was held up by many analysts as the "norm of human attainment." The individual who had conquered all other stages to achieve the primacy of the genital phase was able to blend the most useful features of these earlier stages in a harmony of traits; from the oral stage, Abraham wrote of this ideal type, the genital character had retained "forward-pushing energy; from the anal stage, endurance and perseverance; from sadistic sources [which Freud traced to both the oral and anal phases] the necessary power to carry on the struggle for existence."[32]

Reich, like most analysts, came to assert that establishing genital primacy was the only goal of therapy, but he equated this achievement with orgasm (of which his ex-patient, the impotent waiter, remained deprived). He asserted that genital disturbance was the most important symptom of neurosis. "It is quite striking," Reich wrote in his essay "On Genitality" (1924), that "amongst the twenty-eight male and fourteen female neurotics I have treated, there was not one who did not manifest symptoms of impotence, frigidity, or sexual abstinence. A survey of several other analysts revealed similar findings."[33] Reich thought a wave of genital excitement in orgasm would rupture the stagnant dams of repression he saw in these patients and shortcut the long, slow process of analysis by leading them more quickly to full genitality.

Reich would encourage, indeed teach, his patients to have regular orgasms. When he instructed one of his patients, an elderly woman suffering from a nervous tic that interfered with her breathing, how to masturbate, Reich wrote that her symptom suddenly subsided. He worked with another young man to dissolve the guilt he felt over masturbation, the cause, Reich thought, of his patient's headaches, nausea, back pains, and absentmindedness. These symptoms apparently cleared up when he discovered complete gratification in the act. ("Guidance of masturbational practices during treatment," Reich concluded in a 1922 study of several of the eccentric sexual habits of the Ambulatorium's patients, is "an essential and active therapeutic tool in the hands of the analyst.")[34]

Reich persuaded one woman who was in a sexless marriage to have an affair with a young suitor; he seemed to encourage, or at least condone, others' sleeping with prostitutes. Reich came increasingly to believe that enabling the patient to achieve orgasm was the measure of successful therapy. The process of analysis had troubled Reich because it had no clearly defined goal, and now he felt he'd found the means to the end of resolving neurosis in the orgasm.

Though there was considerable resistance to this theory from other analysts, Reich's ideas would later position him at the forefront of the group of younger psychoanalysts. As the second generation of therapists sought to redefine the relationship between the erotic demands of an increasingly liberated youth and the repressive moral pressures that constrained them, Reich's theory of the orgasm became the defining metaphor for their sexual revolt.

Inducing orgasm to treat hysteria was an ancient cure that went back to the classical Greeks, who thought that an orgasm might reposition the wandering womb from which hysteria took its name. As the historian Rachel Maines has shown in *The Technology of Orgasm*, "massage to orgasm of female patients was a staple of medical practice among some (but certainly not all) Western physicians from the time of Hippocrates until the 1920s."[35] The treatment, aimed at relieving congestion of the womb, was not without its moral risks; one turn-of-the-century doctor claimed that the task "should be entrusted to those who have 'clean hands and a pure heart.'"[36]

In 1878 an electro-mechanical vibrator was used at Paris's Salpêtrière Hospital to treat female hysterics, which introduced a further degree of clinical distance. That year a male doctor at the institution, Desiré Magloire Bourneville, published a three-volume photographic atlas depicting patients suffering from hysteria and epilepsy that contained photos of women in the throes of mechanically stimulated orgasms. One eighteen-year-old patient referred to as "Th." in Bourneville's notes is reported to have cried "Oue! Oue!" as she approached climax, before throwing back her head and rocking her torso violently: "Then her body curves into an arc and holds this position for several seconds," Bourneville wrote. "One then observes some slight movements of the pelvis . . . she raises herself, lies flat again, utters cries of pleasure, laughs, makes several lubricious movements and sinks down on to the vulva and right hip."[37] During her ecstasy Bourneville made detailed physiological notes from his vantage point as the machine's operator: "La vulve est humide . . . La secretion vaginale est très abondante."[38] From the 1880s, the vibrator became a widely used tool, an essential piece of equipment in many doctors' offices and sanatoriums, which gave speed and efficiency to a previously manual process. By the 1920s the device began to appear in the first pornographic films, which discredited it somewhat as a purely medical tool.

Freud would have been aware of Bourneville's innovations when he interned at the Salpêtrière in 1885, as well as the other vibrating helmets and shaking chairs Charcot used to calm his hysterical patients. At one evening reception he attended at the hospital, Freud heard Charcot excitedly telling a colleague that hysteria always had a genital origin ("C'est toujours la chose génitale, toujours! Toujours! Toujours!"), explaining that all neuroses could be traced back to the "marriage bed" (as in the particular case under discussion, which involved an impotent husband).[39] Freud wrote that he was "almost paralyzed with astonishment" at the time, the idea was so shocking, and he soon repressed Charcot's never-published observation.[40]

When Freud returned to Vienna and established his private practice, he was reminded of Charcot's controversial remark when his colleague Rudolf Chrobak referred a hysterical patient to him who was still a virgin despite having been married for eighteen years. Chrobak commented sarcastically, "We know only too well what the only prescription is for such cases, but we can't prescribe it. It is: 'Penis normalis. Dosim repetatur!'"[41] At his clinic Freud employed hydrotherapy, electrotherapy, massage, and the Weir-Mitchell rest cure before abandoning these methods in favor of hypnosis. Rachel Maines wonders whether Freud, who claimed a certain expertise when he distinguished the vaginal from the clitoral orgasm (he considered the latter immature and inferior, to the annoyance of many 1960s feminists), ever operated as a "gynaecological masseur." In *Studies on Hysteria* Freud wrote of the case of "Elisabeth von R.," who had an orgasm when he "pressed or pinched" her legs, supposedly to test her response to pain.[42]

In a letter dated 1893 to his friend and mentor Wilhelm Fliess, Freud noted that nervous illness was frequently a consequence of an abnormal sex life and speculated about a possible cure for neuroses along free-love lines: "The only alternative would be free sexual intercourse between young men and women. Otherwise the alternatives are masturbation, neurasthenia . . . In the absence of such a solution society seems doomed to fall victim to incurable neuroses."[43] In his first decade of practicing psychoanalysis, Freud continued to maintain that neuroses were caused by enforced abstinence and coitus interruptus (a belief his diaphragm-fitting colleague, Isidor Sadger, evidently still held in the early twenties), which forced the libido to find alternative outlets in hysterical and neurotic behavior. In 1905, even after his relationship with Fliess had disintegrated, Freud continued to maintain that "in a normal vita sexualis no neurosis is possible."[44]

Some of Freud's colleagues, one of them the Austrian doctor Otto Gross, took these ideas to extremes, encouraging people to throw off what he considered to be the out-of-date moral prejudices that caused sickness: "Repress nothing!"[45] Freud held Gross in high esteem, and thought he had the most original mind among his followers (according to Ernest Jones, who befriended Gross and considered their conversations to have constituted his first analysis, Gross was "the nearest approach to a romantic genius I ever met"), though Gross's morphine and cocaine addiction made him a paranoid and a particularly wild analyst.[46] In September 1907, Jung wrote to Freud of Gross's radical ideas: "Dr. Gross tells me that he puts a quick stop to the transference by turning people into sexual immoralists. He says the transference to the analyst and its persistent fixation are mere monogamy symbols and as such symptomatic of repression. The truly healthy state for the neurotic is sexual immorality."[47] (Jung would treat Gross in Switzerland the following year for his drug addiction.)

In his paper "'Civilized Sexual Morality and Modern Nervousness,'" published in 1908, Freud criticized the puritanical sexual mores that so often lead to neurosis and sadism, such as enforced monogamy and abstinence. Freud implied that a lack of sex was as degenerative to the species as inbreeding, and that further repressions of the sexual instincts might endanger the very existence of the human race. "I have not gained the impression," Freud wrote, "that sexual abstinence helps to shape energetic, self-reliant men of action, nor original thinkers, bold pioneers and reformers; far more often it produces 'good' weaklings who later become lost in the crowd."[48] Freud posed the question: Is civilized sexual morality worth the sacrifice it imposes upon us? It was this fundamental question that Reich took up.

Reich thought he noticed the same sex-deprived weakness in his patients and, like Gross, celebrated sexual immorality as a cure. Reich followed Freud in believing that a core of dammed-up sexual energy acted as a reservoir for neuroses to sprout up. Adopting Freud's hydraulic notion of the libido, he came to believe that a healthy sex life, full of orgasms—at least one a day if possible— would deprive these symptoms of the sustenance that they needed to grow by maintaining a healthy flow of sexual energy. (The writer Arthur Schnitzler, a caddish bachelor, former doctor, and a friend of Freud's, kept a diary in which he recorded his orgasms, sometimes as many as eight a night, and drew up monthly totals subdivided by each mistress; he omitted tallying theirs.)

However, by the time Reich first visited him at Berggasse 19, Freud was moving away from such a sexually radical solution to mental health problems. In 1920, the year after Reich met him, Freud published *Beyond the Pleasure Principle*, which set Thanatos against Eros, the death drive against the sex drive, and marked a decisive shift away from his early thinking about repression. In that essay he argued that the drive for gratification, love, and life is always over-shadowed by a self-destructive urge toward aggression and death.

Freud's theory of anxiety evolved in parallel with this shift in his thinking. In his *Introductory Lectures on Psychoanalysis* (1917), Freud regarded anxiety, like hysteria, as an outgrowth of sexual repression, caused by unsatisfied libido, which—like wine turning to vinegar— seeks discharge in palpitations and breathlessness, dizziness and nausea. However, Freud now asserted that anxiety was a cause rather than an effect of repression: "It was not the repression that created the anxiety," Freud wrote in *Inhibitions, Symptoms and Anxiety* (1926). "The anxiety was there earlier; it was the anxiety that made the repression."[49] Freud now suggested that repression wasn't something that could be thrown off, as Reich would maintain, but was an intrinsic part of the human condition. To Freud, misery came from within; to Reich, it was imposed from without.


Reich claimed to have kept his discovery of the therapeutic powers of the orgasm to himself at first, because he thought that the world of psychoanalysis wasn't yet ready for his theory: "The actual goal of therapy," he recalled, "that of making the patient capable of or-gasm, was not mentioned in the first years of the seminar. I avoided the subject instinctively."[50] In fact, Reich did air his theory quite early, at a meeting of the Vienna Psychoanalytic Society in November 1923, where it met with a frosty reception:

> During my presentation, I became aware of a growing chilliness in the mood of the meeting. I was a good speaker and had always been listened to attentively. When I finished, an icy stillness hung over the room. Following a break, the discussion began. My contention that the genital disturbance was an important, perhaps the most important symptom of the neurosis was said to be erroneous . . . Two analysts literally asserted that they knew any number of female patients who had a "completely healthy sex life." They appeared to me to be more excited than was in keeping with their usual scientific reserve.[51]

The only member of the older generation to support him on that occasion (and only privately) was his boss at the Ambulatorium, Eduard Hitschmann, who told him afterward, "You hit the nail on the head!"[52] Reich had evolved his ideas under Hitschmann's supervision. Hitschmann, the expert in curing frigidity and impotence, was famous for treating sexual disturbances with a calm practicality; when the analyst Fritz Perls, who later went back into analysis with Reich to be treated for impotence, lay on Hitschmann's couch and told him of the anxieties he had about his manhood, Hitschmann said, "Well, take out your penis. Let's have a look at the thing."[53] According to the *Minutes of the Vienna Psychoanalytic Society*, Hitschmann "always advocated searching for 'organic factors' as a background of the neurosis," which is just what Reich thought he'd discovered in the orgasm.[54]

Encouraged by Hitschmann, and desperate to prove the universality of his theory, Reich began to collect case histories that same month, grilling patients at the Ambulatorium about the minutiae of their sex lives. In 1924 he was promoted to assistant director, and could incorporate in his study information from the weekly written summaries his colleagues were required to submit to him (patients were assigned case numbers to protect their privacy); statistics were collected on 410 individuals, 72 of them Reich's own patients.

At the congress in Salzburg later that year, Reich, armed with this data, insisted that there was now no doubt that "the severity of neurotic disturbance is directly proportionate to the psychogenital disturbance."[55] Reich maintained that the majority of the people who came to the Ambulatorium had some form of genital problem. The incidence of impotence at the clinic, where it was reported to be the most common condition, might have been so high, the historian Elizabeth Danto has suggested, because impotence was one of the most prevalent effects of shell shock. But it might equally be understood in terms of Reich's own diagnostic agenda: according to Hitschmann's report on the clinic, cases of impotence slumped in 1930, when Reich left for Berlin. Furthermore, Reich claimed that the problem afflicted not just patients. He estimated that 80 to 90 percent of all women and about 70 to 80 percent of all men were sexually sick, victims of libidinal stasis.[56] He warned that, as well as neurosis, such genital stagnation could bring about "heart ailments . . . excessive perspiration, hot flashes and chills, trembling, dizziness, diarrhea, and, occasionally, increased salivation."[57]

In reply to the critics, who claimed to have plenty of neurotic but sexually active patients in treatment, Reich made a distinction between sexual activity and sexual satisfaction; the neurotic patients who seemed to be exceptions to his rule weren't enjoying "total orgasms," he said. These, Reich argued, went beyond mere ejaculation, which even a neurotic might occasionally manage; they completely absorbed the participants in tender and all-consuming pleasure. In *Thalassa*, the influential theory of genitality that Ferenczi published in 1924, Ferenczi wrote that there was a satisfying "genitofugal" backflow of libido on orgasm, from the genitals to the rest of the body, which gave "that ineffable feeling of bliss."[58] In idealizing non-neurotic sex, Reich similarly united tenderness and sensuousness in an almost sacred act, as he emphasized when summarizing his theory: "It is not just to fuck, you understand, not the embrace in itself, not the intercourse. It is the real emotional experience of the loss of your ego, of your whole spiritual self."[59]

Each sexually ill or disturbed patient Reich saw failed to live up to this increasingly refined standard of "orgastic potency." In his paper "The Therapeutic Significance of Genital Libido" (1924), Reich laid down eight rules for the "total orgasm":

The forepleasure acts may not be disproportionately prolonged; libido released in extensive forepleasure weakens the orgasm.

Tiredness, limpness, and a strong desire to sleep following intercourse are essential.

Orgastically potent women often feel a need to cry out during the climax.

In the orgastically potent, a slight clouding of consciousness regularly occurs in intercourse if it is not engaged in too frequently. [He doesn't qualify what an overdose might be.]

Disgust, aversion, or decrease of tender impulses toward the partner following intercourse imply an absence of orgastic potency and indicate that effective counterimpulses and inhibiting ideas were present during coition. Whoever coined the expression "Post coitum omnia animalia tristia sunt" [After intercourse, all animals are sad] must have been orgastically impotent.

Male lack of consideration for the woman's satisfaction indicates a lack of tender attachment. ["Don Juan types are attempting to compensate for an inordinate fear of impotence," he wrote elsewhere.]

The fear of some women during coition that the male member will become limp too early and that they will not be able to "finish" also makes the presence of orgastic potency questionable, or at least indicates severe instability. Usually active castration desire is at the root of this fear, and the penis becoming flaccid after ejaculation is interpreted as castration. This reaction may also be caused by the fear of losing the penis, which the woman fantasizes as her own.

It is also important to discover the coital position assumed, especially that of the woman. Incapability of rhythmic responsive movements inhibits the orgasm; likewise, maximal stretching of lower pelvic muscles in women from wide spreading of the legs is indispensable for intense orgastic sensations.[60]

Reich, as already mentioned, would give his neurotic patients advice on technique so that they could achieve the ideal orgasm, as if he were a sex educator rather than a psychoanalyst. He would even visit his patients' homes, asking to see the person's spouse to enlighten him or her as to the partner's needs. "No analysis may be considered complete," Reich wrote, "as long as genital orgastic potency is not guaranteed."[61]

Reich asked several of his patients to draw graphs, illustrating their different experiences of orgasm before and after he cured them, intended to illustrate the seismic difference in levels of satisfaction. Theodoor H. Van de Velde's popular 1926 sex guide, *Ideal Marriage: Its Physiology and Technique* (there were forty-two German reprintings by 1933), contained similar graphs depicting the comparative trajectories of women's and men's sexual excitement as they approached mutual orgasm. Some of these coital timelines were included in Reich's *The Function of the Orgasm* (1927), the first full-length book on the topic. (Despite his busy schedule, Reich was very disciplined about his writing, to which he devoted a few hours every day except Sunday.) For Reich, as these diagrams show, a potent orgasm built up slowly through friction in foreplay into a tsunami-like wave, to peak in a huge crest that dropped off with a shudder and an explosion.

Until he conducted his survey, Reich's theory lacked any empirical foundation and he was accused of operating solely on autobiographical evidence. Indeed, Reich told Richard Sterba that if he didn't have an orgasm for two days, "he felt physically unwell and 'saw black before his eyes' as before an approaching spell of fainting. These symptoms disappeared immediately with an orgasmic experience."[62] Sterba described Reich as a "genital narcissist." Indeed, when Reich writes of the "genital character" he might be describing the way he'd like to be perceived: "[He] can be very gay but also intensely angry. He reacts to an object-loss with depression but does not get lost in it; he is capable of intense love but also of intense hatred; he can be . . . childlike but he will never appear infantile; his seriousness is natural and not stiff in a compensatory way because he has no tendency to show himself grown-up at all costs."[63] Reich believed that other analysts were resistant to his theory because of unconscious sexual jealousy; they weren't as "potent" as he.

In his diary Reich provides two early glimpses of his own orgastic potency: his momentous night with a prostitute as a fifteen-year-old boy ("I was all penis!"), and an apparently earth-shattering experience he had at nineteen with the young Italian woman he lived with in Gemona del Friuli, the village to the north of Venice where he stayed as a reservist during the last stages of the war. In an unpublished memoir of his sex life, a copy of which is in the National Library of Medicine in Washington, again written in the third person, Reich described how, while sleeping with this woman, "he and she felt completely One, not only in the genital but all over; there was not the least experiential distinction between the two organisms; they were ONE organism, as if united or melted into each other . . . When the orgasm finally mounted and overtook them, they burst into sweet crying, both of them, in a calm, but intense manner, and they sank deeper and deeper into each other."[64]

On April 27, 1924, Annie Reich gave birth to the couple's first child, a daughter they named Eva. They moved into a large double apartment in an opulent stucco building on Lindenstrasse, which looked out onto a women's prison. It was sumptuously furnished, thanks to the wealth of the bourgeois family Reich had married into. They employed a nursemaid, who enforced a strict feeding schedule, and kept careful Freudian records of Eva's development through the early oral and anal stages of her life.

Reich was enjoying what he would later call his "dancing and discussing Goethe stage"—he and Annie had active professional and social lives.[65] They went to the Austrian Alps for frequent winter skiing trips, a sport at which Reich excelled, and visited the Austrian lakes with their friends in the summer; they went to parties in Vienna, and on picnics and hikes. When Reich joined the psychoanalysts, they were an isolated group of dissenters; but now Freud was fast gaining acceptance, and Reich and his friends—almost all analysts—were enjoying their new status as a more reputable part of the avant-garde. That year, to celebrate Freud's sixty-eighth birthday, Vienna's City Council gave Freud the *Bürgerrecht*, an honor akin to the freedom of the city.

Reich was now at the forefront of the psychoanalytic movement, the acknowledged leader of its second generation, just as Freud was withdrawing from that scene. In October 1923, Freud's upper palate was excised because of the cancer that riddled his jaw, an affliction for which he underwent thirty more operations in his final sixteen years. After his malignant tumor was cut out, Freud had to wear a prosthesis, known as "the monster" by his family, to shut off his mouth from his nasal cavity so that he was able to eat and talk. Freud stubbornly continued to smoke; to get a cigar between his teeth, he now had to hold open his jaw with the help of a clothes peg. "The monster" had to be adjusted every few days, to stop it from grating against his cancer-raw inner cheek, and a related infection would soon make him deaf in one ear—his right, luckily, which made it unnecessary for him to turn around the analytic couch at whose head he sat.

The analysts Karl Abraham and Felix Deutsch both visited Freud in a villa he'd rented in Semmering, a village in the Austrian Alps, as he recuperated from this first of many operations. "We spoke a lot about Professor [Freud]," Deutsch wrote afterward, "how he withdraws more and more from people, which A[braham] had occasion to experience for himself when he was staying at Semmering. Up in his workroom Professor [Freud] has a telescope with which he studies the moon and the stars, and by day he studies the hills and the mountains of the region. He withdraws more and more from the world."[66]

Paul Federn, Reich's former analyst, the vice president of the Vienna Psychoanalytic Society, had increased power as acting chairman in Freud's absence. Like Sadger, he had lost all enthusiasm for his protégé Reich in the course of analyzing him. Federn had decided that Reich was "aggressive, paranoid and ambitious," all traits he found distasteful.[67] One of Reich's biographers, Myron Sharaf, suggests that Federn especially disapproved of the frequent extramarital affairs Reich spoke about in his analysis. Futhermore, Federn—whom Reich later described mockingly as "a prophet, with a beard"—did not share Reich's celebration of the orgasm. In 1927, the year *The Function of the Orgasm* appeared, Federn published a book (with Heinrich Meng) in which it was claimed that "abstinence is not injurious to health"; cold baths, holding one's breath, and swimming were prescribed to temper the sex drive.[68]

Federn would start "digging" against him, as Reich put it, by trying to convince Freud that Reich's behavior was belligerent to the point of being pathological, and he encouraged Freud to take action in response to the increasing complaints from colleagues about Reich's orgasm fanaticism. "His collaboration was for a time welcoming and stimulating," Helene Deutsch recalled of the shifting mood concerning Reich. "He worked at the Ambulatorium and his clinical reports were usually very informative for his younger colleagues. After a time he himself devalued the quality of his work by trying to make certain ideas, correct in themselves, but obvious and not entirely original, into the central concept of psychoanalysis. His aggressive way of advancing these ideas was typical of him . . . His presumptuous and aggressive, I might even say paranoid, personality was hard to bear."[69]

Federn was in charge of who was invited to attend the monthly meetings held in Freud's drawing room at Berggasse 19, which took place on the second Friday of every month. Freud, working on his autobiography, was seriously ill and preoccupied with the specter of death; he attended only one further general meeting and never went to another psychoanalytic congress, so these private meetings were the only chance many of his devotees had of seeing him. Freud had decided that only twelve disciples could come at one time—there were six places for the permanent members of the society's executive committee and six to be rotated among the remaining members.

In 1924 Reich put himself forward for the role of second secretary of the Vienna Psychoanalytic Society, a junior position that would have guaranteed him one of the much-desired regular spots at these monthly meetings. He was elected, but without Reich's knowledge, Federn persuaded Freud to overrule the ballot in favor of Robert Jokl, Reich's older colleague at the Ambulatorium. Freud regretted his unethical decision when he read and was impressed by the proofs of Reich's *The Impulsive Character*, which was published the following year and in which Reich made no explicit reference to his theory of the orgasm. In treating the "drifters, liars, and contentious complainers," who like psychotic patients seemed to have no control over their impulses, Reich had bravely put himself on the front line of the profession.[70] Reich was attracted to these characters because they didn't exhibit the sexual repression that he thought so pernicious—seemingly free of a superego, impulsive characters acted on every whim thrown up by their unconscious. They were the clinical equivalent of Peer Gynt.

Reich found that all the patients he deemed impulsive characters had been sexually active from a very young age, but that their youthful curiosity about sex had been suddenly repressed by a guilt-inducing trauma. Reich's American disciple Elsworth Baker would later refer to Reich himself as an "impulsive character" and, knowing the circumstances of his mother's death, would presume Reich identified with the troubled childhoods of these difficult patients.

One of the patients Reich wrote about in his book was a twenty-six-year-old masochist and nymphomaniac who could feel pleasure only when she masturbated with a knife, deliberately cutting herself in the process until she caused a prolapse of her uterus. This woman's mother had thrown a knife at her when she had caught her masturbating as a young girl, which, he thought, explained her method of self-mutilation. The nymphomaniac's bullying older brother, with whom she'd had sex when she was ten, was now in prison serving a sentence for rape. She had married but was having an affair with a sadist who whipped her, and when Reich forbade her from continuing that relationship—threatening to end the analysis if she didn't—she brought a whip to her sessions and began to strip, demanding that her analyst lash her instead. Reich had to physically stop her from undressing. She then took to following him as he walked the streets of Vienna. She came to his door at ten o'clock one night, wanting him to have sex with her or whip her. She said that she desired a child by him and, Reich discovered, she attempted to poison her husband and older sister with rat poison to clear the way—only Reich could satisfy her, she said. When he told her that would be impossible, she went to a shop and bought a revolver with the intention of murdering him.

Reich managed to break through his patient's initial mistrust and ambivalence toward him (she wanted both to have sex with him and to kill him), and her refusal to recognize that she might be ill, to cultivate a positive transference. The patient would frequently declare that she didn't want to end their sessions, manipulating Reich into a position where he had to be strict and threaten to have her removed by force; she'd leave screaming, her masochism satisfied, crying that nobody loved her. Over fourteen months of treatment, Reich succeeded in assuaging her anxieties and in stopping her practice of self-harm, and she was able to start a job.

Freud, who limited his practice to neurotics, was impressed with Reich's handling of such dangerous cases, which extended psychoanalysis into the treatment of the early stages of schizophrenia. On December 14, 1924, Freud backed down on his decision to oust Reich from his rightful post, writing to Federn that Reich should be judged by his work, not his character:

> Shortly after you left I read a manuscript by Dr. Reich which he sent me this morning. I found it so full of valuable content that I very much regretted that we had renounced the recognition of his endeavors. In this mood it occurred to me that for us to propose Dr. Jokl as second secretary is improper because we had no right to change arbitrarily a decision made by the Committee. In the light of this fact, what you told me about private animosities against Dr. Reich is not significant.[71]

When Federn protested, saying that he'd already told Jokl of his appointment, Freud refused to save him the embarrassment of having to put the situation right. Reich never was given the appointment, though at this stage Reich did not seem to be aware of the snub. It is not clear how Federn managed to finally persuade Freud to oust Reich; Reich later came to believe that Federn told Freud that Reich slept with his patients.

At the end of 1924, Reich's brother, Robert, contracted tuberculosis, the disease that had killed his father, and he returned to Vienna from Romania, where he was in charge of arranging shipping on the Danube for his transportation company. He had married Ottilie Heifetz three years earlier and now had a young daughter of his own, Sigrid. Reich met his brother at the station and used his medical connections to ensure that Robert saw the best doctors in the city. Robert was advised to go to a sanatorium in Italy to recover; Reich sent morphine and other expensive medicine and, in anticipation of his later theories, advice on breathing techniques to help his brother aerate his consumption-spotted lungs. But, to Robert's disappointment, Reich never visited him there—he claimed he was too busy, no doubt embroiled in the battles within the Vienna Psychoanalytic Society.

Robert died in April 1926, and his widow and daughter lived with the Reichs for a year in Vienna, where Reich helped Ottilie start a new career as a nursery teacher. In a curious twist, Ottilie married Annie Pink's father after his wife died, thereby becoming Reich's new mother-in-law.

In January 1925, the Training Institute, a teaching arm of the Vienna Psychoanalytic Society, was set up in order to instruct psychoanalysts-to-be. Freud wanted this entity to be able to accept lay practitioners, which the Ambulatorium wasn't able to do, as it had received a license on condition that only M.D.'s would practice there.

Located about half an hour's walk from the Ambulatorium, in the Wollzeile, the Training Institute of the Vienna Psychoanalytic Society was run by Helene Deutsch, who was thirteen years Reich's senior. She had been the only female psychiatrist at Julius Wagner-Jauregg's clinic during the war (she lost her job when Paul Schilder returned from the battlefield), and had just spent a year at the training institute in Berlin, where she studied under its director, Karl Abraham.

Deutsch told her biographer, Paul Roazen, that the Training Institute was designed in part to alienate Reich, and that measures were taken to submit Reich's "obstinate insistence upon his ideas ["the false propaganda of the 'orgiastic' ideology"] . . . to an objective control."[72] Despite having been denied a place on the executive committee, Reich had assumed the position of leader of the technical seminar, and he was also promoted to deputy medical director of the Ambulatorium, roles he occupied until he joined Fenichel in Berlin in 1930, despite Federn's continued attempts to persuade Freud to replace him. Federn and Freud worried that

Reich would use the technical seminar to indoctrinate trainees with his orgasm theory, and the Training Institute was a way to disperse his power. Its four-term curriculum subsumed many of the technical seminar's educational tasks, and even though he was granted a seat on the institute's training committee, Reich's monopoly on teaching effectively ended.

Though at that time many analysts in Vienna didn't share Reich's views on sex—or considered them "obvious," as Deutsch did—he was thought to be a brilliant analyst of certain types of patient. Even Federn claimed that Reich was the best diagnostician among the younger generation, and his technical seminar at the Ambulatorium was so instructive that many of the older members of the society attended it regularly. Reich conducted the seminar "with informality and spontaneity," recalled his American pupil Walter Briehl.[73] Reich made sure that each session was devoted to discussing a therapeutic failure (Reich, it must be remembered, never completed his own analysis), and the discussions of these cases sometimes went on until one in the morning. "Reich had an unusual gift of empathy with his patients," Richard Sterba wrote of Reich's precise and clear diagnoses. "He was an impressive personality full of youthful intensity. His manner of speaking was forceful; he expressed himself well and decisively. He had an unusual flair for psychic dynamics. His clinical astuteness and technical skill made him an excellent teacher."[74] Anna Freud attended Reich's technical seminar and once sent Reich an admiring postcard saying that he was a *spiritus rector*, an "inspiring teacher."[75]

The year that Reich took over the technical seminar, Freud's disciples Sándor Ferenczi and Otto Rank, both of whom Freud considered potential heirs after Jung had fallen out of favor, published *The Development of Psychoanalysis* (1924). They criticized "classical technique" for its arid devotion to theory rather than therapy, and proposed a new method to speed up and refine the talking cure and to break through the most stagnant cases; they pointed out that in the early days of analysis it was not unusual for cures to be achieved in a matter of days or weeks. Ferenczi and Rank suggested an "active technique of interference," in which the psychoanalyst would set a definite time limit to therapy and act less as an emotionally detached surgeon of the psyche, listening from his unseen position behind the couch and offering cool interpretations, and more as an assertive guide who would goad and challenge the patient. Ferenczi termed this "obstetrical thought assistance." They disregarded childhood memories, believing that it was more economical and just as therapeutically valuable for patients to act out and relive their traumas in the interaction of the transference situation. "We see the process of sublimation, which in ordinary life requires years of education, take place before our eyes," Rank wrote with new therapeutic optimism.[76]

Though Freud described Ferenczi and Rank's efforts as a "fresh daredevil initiative," he was suspicious of the quick cures they promised.[77] Freud had had his beard shaved off before his cancer operation, and it had taken six weeks to grow back. Three months later the scar had yet to heal. Wouldn't it take a bit longer than a scar takes to heal, he asked cynically of Ferenczi and Rank's work, to penetrate to the deepest levels of the unconscious? Their practice sparked a controversy between progressive and more traditional analysts; the British analyst Edward Glover, a proponent of passive therapy who believed that shaking hands with patients might provoke needless emotional contagion, was the most vocal defender of orthodoxy. It is important to stress, however, that Ferenczi and Rank were not doubters but zealous reformers in psychoanalysis's name— as was Reich. They found fault with classical analysis only because they had higher hopes for analysis itself.

Freud expressed concern that active therapy might be "a risky temptation for ambitious beginners."[78] Reich, disappointed with the "[Egyptian] mummy-like" attitude required of him in passive analysis, was one of the "ambitious beginners" drawn to Ferenczi and Rank's cutting-edge and more dynamic technique. He sought to fuse their innovations with Abraham and Jones's parallel developments in characterology and with his own theory of the orgasm, a synthesis that culminated in his book *Character Analysis* (1933). Reich later claimed that in 1930, the year he left for Berlin, Freud had credited him with being "the founder of the modern technique in analysis."[79] Reich is indeed almost universally acknowledged as the founder of a new method of analyzing a patient's defenses, a technique that evolved into what became known as ego psychology. This was the dominant therapeutic practice in the 1950s, especially in the United States, where *Character Analysis* became a standard training manual for many years—though it was employed in the States to very different ends from those for which Reich first imagined it.

Reich shifted the focus from what the patient told him in analysis to how it was said. He would be deliberately provocative and confrontational with his patients. Instead of dissolving the traumatic nature of childhood events by going over them in words again and again, as an orthodox analyst would do, Reich would seize upon physical evidence of a resistance and goad the patient with his observation of his or her resistances (Ferenczi had referred to his own brand of dynamic psychoanalysis as "irritation therapy"). "We confront . . . the patient with it repeatedly," Reich stated, explaining how he sought to puncture the defensive shield of the patient's ego—or, as he termed it, "character armor"—"until he begins to look at it objectively and to experience it like a painful symptom; thus, the character trait begins to be experienced as a foreign body which the patient wants to get rid of."[80]

Reich thought that patients were always producing material that could be interpreted; even their silences revealed a mutating façade of resistance, Reich believed, and he was very attentive to these awkward phenomena. Reich used to act out for his students the various nonverbal clues, facial expressions, and bodily postures with which neurotic patients revealed this emotional barrier: "the manner in which the patient talks, in which he greets the analyst or looks at him, the way he lies on the couch, the inflection of his voice, the degree of conventional politeness."[81] In so doing, he transferred Freud's cerebral notion of resistances to the body.

One of Reich's patients, Ola Raknes, praised Reich's undisputable therapeutic gift:

> As a therapist he was naturally and absolutely concentrated on the patient. His acuity to detect the slightest movement, the lightest inflection of the voice, a passing shadow of a change in the expression, was without a parallel, at least in my experience. And with that came a high degree of patience, or should I call it tenacity, in

bringing home to the patient what he had discovered, and to make the patient experience and express what has not been discovered. Day after day, week after week, he would call the patient's attention to an attitude, a tension or a facial expression, until the patient could sense it and feel what it implied.[82]

The American psychiatrist O. Spurgeon English visited Reich's fourth-floor apartment near the General Hospital teaching hospital seven days a week for therapy:

> It was at this time that I recall Dr. Reich utilizing his interest in other than verbal presentations of the personality. For instance, he would frequently call attention to the monotony of my tone of voice as I free associated. He would also call attention to my position on the couch, and I remember particularly that he confronted me with the fact that when I entered and left the office, I made no move to shake hands with him as was the custom in both Austria and Germany.[83]

English found Reich "taciturn" and "cold and unfriendly," and he was encouraged by Reich to voice these criticisms; in their sessions English complained of Reich's chain-smoking and his habit of interrupting the analysis to take frequent phone calls, and his suspicion that Reich insisted on such an intensive schedule of treatment only because he wanted to relieve him all the more speedily of his dollars. Despite their frequent arguments, in the end English was enthusiastic about his therapy, concluding that Reich was "serious . . . although not without humor."[84] English wrote in an essay on Reich (one can almost hear English's monotonous tone): "I have always felt a great gratitude that somehow or other I landed in the hands of an analyst who was a no-nonsense, hard-working, meticulous analyst who had a keen ear for the various forms of resistance and a good ability to tolerate the aggression which almost inevitably follows necessary confrontation in subtly concealed or subtly manifested resistance."[85]

Reich believed that unless patients were provoked into expressing their pent-up hatred of him, he wouldn't be able to clear up their resistances; no genuine positive transference would be achieved and the analysis would invariably falter. A humanitarian optimism underlay Reich's new therapeutic scheme that wasn't immediately apparent in his aggressive practice. In Reich's onion-like model of the psyche, man is inherently good, with a loving and decent core of "natural sociality and sexuality, spontaneous enjoyment of work, capacity for love" (the id). However, this is sheathed in a layer of spite and hatred, the residue of all our frustrations and disappointments (the realm of the Freudian unconscious). We protect and distract ourselves from these horrors with a third and final layer of "character armor," he believed, an "artificial mask of self-control, of compulsive, insincere politeness and of artificial sociality" (the ego—the buffer between the id and the outer world, or superego). Freud thought that the ego was the locus not only of resistance but also of reason and of the necessary control of the instincts; Reich, in contrast, thought the instincts were good, if only we could bypass the ego's resistances. In therapy, he wanted to smash through to the garden of Eden that he thought we all harbored deep within us.

Using a metaphor from his farm days, Reich explained:

> Human beings live emotionally on the surface, with their surface appearance . . . In order to get to the core where the natural, the normal, the healthy is, you have to go through the middle layer. And in the middle layer there is terror. There is severe terror. Not only that, there is murder there. All that Freud tried to subsume under the death instinct is in that middle layer. He thought it was biological. It wasn't. It is an artifact of culture . . . A bull is mad and destructive when it is frustrated. Humanity is that way, too. That means that before you can get to the real thing—to love, to life, to rationality—you must pass through hell.[86]

According to the psychoanalyst Martin Grotjahn, who knew Reich in the 1920s, Reich was known by his colleagues as "the character smasher." Of his analytic technique Reich wrote, "I was open, then I met this wall—and I wanted to smash it." Reich hoped to free the reservoir of libido that the ego had frozen over, so that the patient could achieve the curative warmth of total orgasm. To that end, Reich asserted, the therapist had to be "sexually affirmative," open to "repressed polygamous tendencies and certain kinds of love play."[87]

Naturally, the patient didn't like being perpetually reminded of his weaknesses, and frequently acted aggressive in the face of Reich's sometimes abusive and excessively authoritarian method. Richard Sterba remembered that "Reich became more and more sadistic in 'hammering' at the patient's resistive armor."[88] He suggested that his therapeutic emphasis reflected not simply the theoretical development of a technique but Reich's "own suspicious character and the belligerent attitude that stems from it."[89]

The year before it was published, Reich presented to Freud the manuscript of his major work, *The Function of the Orgasm*, for his seventieth birthday (May 6, 1926), inscribing it to "my teacher, Professor Sigmund Freud, with deep veneration."[90] Freud's sarcastic response to Reich's 206-page tome was "That thick?"—as if to suggest that the function of the orgasm was rather self-evident. Freud evidently didn't share Reich's belief in the potent orgasm as the summation of human health. Two months later he wrote Reich a tardy but polite note: "I find the book valuable, rich in observation and thought. As you know, I am in no way opposed to your attempt to solve the problem of neurasthenia by explaining it on the basis of genital primacy."[91]

Freud adopted a more acerbic tone when he wrote to the psychoanalyst Lou Andreas-Salomé in Berlin: "We have here a Dr. Reich, a worthy but impetuous young man, passionately devoted to his hobbyhorse, who now salutes in the genital orgasm the antidote to every neurosis. Perhaps he might learn from your analysis of K. to feel some respect for the complicated nature of the psyche."[92] K. was one of Lou Andreas-Salomé's hysterical patients who seemed to refute Reich's claims; K.'s sex life revealed, according to Andreas-Salomé, a "capacity for enjoyment, a spontaneous and an inner physical surrender such as in this combination of happiness and seriousness is not often to be met with."[93]

In the summer of 1926, Reich again put himself forward as a candidate for second secretary of the Vienna Psychoanalytic Society. This time Federn abolished the position without explanation. Reich wrote Federn a letter, which he never sent, to complain about what he felt was a definite slight. He only sought the appointment, he wrote, because he wanted to see and hear Freud more frequently: "infantile, perhaps, but neither ambitious nor criminal," he argued. "My organizational work in the Society, combined with my scientific activity, gave me the sense of justified expectation."[94] He admitted to having been "stung by an irrelevant scientific opposition" to his ideas, and to having perhaps been overdefensive in the face of criticism: "I never intended any personal offense," Reich wrote in protest, "but always objectively said what I was convinced I was justified in saying—without false consideration, however, for age or position of the criticised party."[95]

In a letter that he subsequently wrote to Freud, Reich complained of Federn's "hateful, high-handed tone" and "supercilious condescension."[96] Reich didn't send this letter either, though he evidently hoped for some sympathy; in an indiscreet moment at the Ambulatorium, Hitschmann had told Reich, to the latter's satisfaction, that Freud had commented that Federn had "patricidal eyes."[97] Reich chose to complain about his treatment at the hands of Federn in person instead. After Reich visited him for this purpose, Freud wrote Reich a letter, dated July 27, 1926, assuring him that any personal differences between him and Federn would not influence his own high regard for Reich's competence, a view that he said was shared by many others.[98]

Though Freud had defended Reich against Federn two years earlier, by this time he had transferred his paternal attention to two fresh protégés, Franz Alexander and Heinrich Meng. The latter was editing a popular manual of psychoanalysis with Federn. Freud humiliated Reich by cutting him down in public at one of his monthly meetings, revealing his new impatience with the cantankerous twenty-nine-year-old. After Reich gave a talk in December 1926 in which he argued that every analysis should begin with a discussion of the patient's negative transference, Freud, who had decided that his "classical technique" was superior to the proposed innovations of Ferenczi, Rank, and Reich, interrupted, "Why would you not interpret the material in the order in which it appears? Of course one has to analyze and interpret incest dreams as soon as they appear."[99] His "biting severity," as Reich called Freud's response, sent out a clear signal to all that Reich had fallen out of favor.

"I was regarded very highly from 1920 up to about 1925 or 1926," Reich recalled in 1951 when speaking to Kurt Eissler, the founder and keeper of the Sigmund Freud Archives, who was compiling an oral history of Freud and his circle. "And then I felt that animosity. I had touched on something painful—genitality. They didn't like it."[100] Until then Reich had thought of himself "as a sincere and unhesitating champion of psychoanalysis," completely dedicated to what Freud called "the cause."[101] Now he was increasingly aware that he had largely alienated his psychoanalytic colleagues with his dogged insistence that everyone lay their patients bare to the pleasures of "ultimate involuntary surrender."

Reich confessed to finding the hierarchical attitude of the Vienna Psychoanalytic Society stifling: no one showed much interest in the Ambulatorium anymore, and the conservative analysts were resistant to his, or indeed anyone's, efforts to revive psychoanalytic technique. He was the only one who was not afraid to report on or publish therapeutic failures, or to argue that patients should be discharged if the analyst thought he or she couldn't help them. The society, Reich complained, was characterized by "intramural envy" and a "paralyzing skepticism." As a result he was becoming increasingly antagonistic. At their meetings he acted, as he himself later admitted, "like a shark in a pond of carps."[102]

Reich felt he had outgrown the possibilities offered by the Ambulatorium, which only had the capacity to treat about two hundred fifty patients a year, and now wanted to spread his message out into the city that he saw as a macrocosm of the clinic. "Neurosis is a mass sickness," Reich believed, "an infection similar to an epidemic."[103] He wanted to change the societal norms responsible for the unnecessary sexual repressions that he felt were causing such mass illness. If Freud cast himself as Moses, Reich saw himself as returning to the unfulfilled potential of Freud's early work on the libido, completing Freud's journey to discover the promised land. As Reich later put it, Freud was "a peculiar mixture of a very progressive free thinker and a gentleman professor of 1860," and he was too polite to imagine a world free of sexual alienation, a world that the free-thinker in Freud would have wanted, Reich was convinced, and that he now had in his sights.[104]

Searching for a fresh allegiance to compensate for the rejection he had experienced at the hands of Freud's immediate circle, Reich was driven to politics, where he found a new group of admirers. In his own account of his political awakening, the moment when he realized that a revolution in sexual attitudes could bring about a true political revolution was a dramatic epiphany.

On January 30, 1927, in the small Austrian town of Schattendorf, near the Hungarian border, members of the Heimwehr (home guard), a right-wing paramilitary group associated with the Christian Social Party, randomly shot into a Social Democratic Party rally. A war veteran and an eight-year-old boy were killed, and another six-year-old child was critically wounded. Six months later in Vienna, the three accused gunmen were acquitted of "all wrongdoing" by a right-wing judge.

Ignaz Seipel, the Christian Social chancellor, supported this controversial decision. However, the next day an editorial in the Social Democrat newspaper, the *Arbeiter-Zeitung* (Workers' Newspaper), declared the acquittal "an outrage such as has seldom if ever been experienced in the annals of justice." In Vienna, a huge number of workers went on strike and assembled to stage a spontaneous protest rally on the Ringstrasse, the main artery around the inner city. They marched together to the square in front of the Palace of Justice. The Christian Social–dominated police force was unprepared for the angry mob. The spontaneous demonstration turned into a riot as the crowd threw stones at the law courts before storming the building, overpowering the police cordon, and breaking down the large iron doors. The unarmed police officers had their uniforms stripped from them and paraded on flagpoles like trophies. Four officers were killed, court records and books were thrown out of the windows like confetti, and the building was set ablaze.

When a patient arrived at Reich's apartment for therapy and informed him that several protesters had already been killed by the police, Reich canceled their session and went to join the demonstrators, who were massing in the Schottenring, not far from his home. He joined the ranks of unarmed workers marching in silence toward the university. When Reich saw that the Palace of Justice was ablaze, he ran home to collect his wife. He and Annie stood by the Arcaden Café with about four hundred others, watching the fire, sharing in the sense of collective retribution. Reich heard someone shout, "That shack had it coming."[105] The offices of the conservative *Reichspost*, which had declared the court ruling "a just judgment," were also burned down that day.

The demonstrators refused to let fire engines through to put out the fire, and Johann Schober, the Christian Social police chief responsible for crushing the 1919 Communist uprising, issued rifles to his forces so that they could clear a path. Members of the fifty-thousand-strong Republikanischer Schutzbund (Republican Defense League), the Social Democratic militia formed in 1923 for precisely the purpose of defending the workers in such a situation, had been ordered by Otto Bauer to return to barracks: the Social Democrats wanted to avoid a full-scale confrontation, and had sent the militia home under threat of expulsion or disciplinary action. Reich recalled that two hundred yards from where he was standing a phalanx of policemen started to advance, inching forward slowly with their gun barrels lowered. When they were fifty yards away their captain ordered them to shoot at the crowd. A few disobeyed and fired over the onlookers' heads, but dozens in the crowd fell dead or wounded.

Without the Schutzbund to defend them, the crowd was completely helpless. Reich dragged Annie behind a tree, where they hid to avoid the bullets; others fled down alleys. Ernest Fisher, a journalist for the *Arbeiter-Zeitung* whose editorial had helped spark the events, wrote that he'd seen one worker tear open his shirt and shout at the police, "Shoot, if you have the guts." He was shot in the chest. Others screamed, "Worker killers! You are workers yourselves!" and begged them to stop. The killing went on for three hours.[106]

Eighty-nine people were killed, and about a thousand wounded.

The historian David S. Luft has called the violence "the most revolutionary day in Austrian history," and refers to the "generation of 1927 . . . a generation whose adult political consciousness was defined in terms of the events of 15th July 1927."[107] Reich was very much part of that generation. In his book *People in Trouble* (written in 1937 but not published until 1953) he wrote of the events he witnessed as the defining moment in his political awakening; he called the brutal police oppression a "practical course on Marxian sociology." He was deeply disturbed by the violence, and described the police as mindless automatons, part of "a senseless machine," just as he himself had been in the war, firing "blindly on command, without thinking."[108]

That evening, Reich and Annie walked through the deserted streets to the house of a friend whose father and brother were important figures in the Social Democratic Party, hoping to discuss what might be done in the wake of the violence. When they arrived the family was expecting dinner guests, and the table was laid. One is reminded, reading Reich's description, of the scene from the film *Dr. Zhivago* in which a group of aristocrats sits down for a feast, oblivious to the revolution beyond the windows that will make it their last. Reich was underdressed, without a jacket or tie, and shaken to the core by what he'd seen:

> The gory events appeared not to have penetrated this room. In my agitated state of mind, I suddenly felt out of place and ludicrous in this cool, reserved atmosphere. I wanted to leave but was asked to stay. Then the guests arrived. A very intelligent conversation about the events of the day began in truly cultured Viennese fashion. It was obvious that no one knew what had really happened. They spoke of the bloodshed as they might ordinarily have spoken of Goethe. We said goodbye and took our leave. We had both remained polite. I would have liked, at the very least, to have overthrown their table, but I was sufficiently well-bred to discipline myself.[109]

Like many others, Reich was disappointed by the Social Democrats' reaction to the day's violence, especially the fact that they failed to take a decisive stand, despite their constant rhetoric of revolution, and protect the workers by mobilizing the Schutzbund when civil war looked imminent. By returning his troops to barracks, Otto Bauer had exhibited, Reich thought, a "dangerously irresolute politics" and thereby failed to prevent the massacre.[110]

In the April elections earlier that year the Social Democrats had received their largest electoral vote to date. Otto Bauer was confident that the Social Democrats could further increase their vote nationally from 42 percent (up from 39 percent in 1923) to a controlling 51 percent in the future, and he didn't want to jeopardize this ascent by risking civil war. Chancellor Ignaz Seipel's conservative coalition government, made up of Christian Socials and Pan-Germans, lost 10 percent of their lead and no longer had an absolute majority; they had to form a coalition with the Agrarian League to remain in power. However, the events of July 15 ended Bauer's illusory optimism, revealing the impotence of the Social Democrats on the national stage. Even in the capital they supposedly controlled (in Vienna they had won 60 percent of the vote), the government was prepared to use violence to suppress what it saw as an irksome "red tide."

On the evening of July 15, Reich joined the Internationale Arbeiter-Hilfe (Workers International Relief), a medical corps affiliated with the Austrian Communist Party, hoping to help the wounded. The Austrian Communist Party had dwindled to two thousand members by the mid-1920s, but it was reorganized soon after the July revolt, and by the following year, when Reich joined the party proper, he had five thousand comrades, the majority of whom were unemployed. At the time of the July revolt, however, the Communist opposition was so disorganized that its members only managed to distribute their insurgent literature the following day.

By then the rioting had spread to the northern suburbs of the city, and elsewhere people stayed indoors in self-imposed curfew, watching from their windows as the police patrolled the city streets in heavily armored riot trucks. A twenty-four-hour general strike was broken up by the right-wing Heimwehr, destroying what the government feared was a looming revolution. Order was swiftly restored, followed by a reactionary crackdown that, Reich wrote in hindsight, led directly to Hitler's rise to power. The resulting crisis of confidence in the Social Democratic leadership would ultimately

lead to the collapse of the party and the triumph of fascism. Heimito von Doderer, who witnessed the events and later centered his
novel, *The Demons* (1956), on them, wrote that the violence "turned
the Austrian middle-class towards fascism" and signaled the end of
freedom in Austria.[111] Doderer would have known: he was a member of the Austrian Nazi Party from 1933 to 1938.

Reich met Freud at the end of the month in the villa Freud
liked to rent on the Semmering Pass. Freud was troubled with
stomach problems in addition to the painful complications of his
cancer. He complained to Jones of being "eternally ill and plagued
with discomfort."[112] Reich talked to Freud about the recent political events and concluded that Freud had completely failed to understand the true significance of the uprising, like the dinner guests
who'd so upset him on that day. Martin Freud revealed the family's
collective stance when he wrote of the "civil war" in his memoir:
"When the Socialists, inspired by Communist influence, were at
the throats of the Conservatives, who at this time appeared to have
a strong leaning towards the new Nazi theories, the Freuds remained neutral. Unable to decide which was the lesser evil, we kept
out of the struggle and were not hurt."[113]

Freud thought of July 15 in terms of a natural disaster rather
than a political turning point; he viewed it, Reich found, "as a catastrophe similar to a tidal wave."[114] Freud had little confidence in the
readiness of the masses for freedom. For him, the crowd was a "primal horde," a surging unconscious throng that was searching, herd-
like, for an authority figure to guide it. On the street Reich felt he
had witnessed something different: a crowd nobly seeking justice
and viciously suppressed.

Later that year, in response to the riots, Freud wrote *The Future of
an Illusion*, in which he stated that the masses were "lazy and unin-
telligent: they have no love for instinctual renunciation."[115] Freud
believed that as a result the masses had to be educated and coerced
by an elite into accepting repression as a requirement of civilization
(the crowd psychologist Gustav Le Bon, whom Freud cites in his
essay, wrote of the masses as "extraordinarily credulous and open to
influence").[116] This belief was exported to the United States by
Freud's nephew, Edward Bernays, who sought to use Freud's in-

sights to manipulate public opinion. In 1928, Bernays wrote his book *Propaganda*, which explored the ways in which a small band of "invisible wire pullers" might "regiment the public mind."[117] In a letter to his nephew, Freud praised *Propaganda* as "clear, clever, and comprehensive . . . I read it with pleasure [and] . . . wish you all possible success."[118] To its author's horror, Joseph Goebbels was an enthusiast of the book; Bernays wrote that he later used its ideas as "the basis for his destructive campaign against the Jews."[119]

The future Nobel literature laureate Elias Canetti, then a chemistry student at the University of Vienna, was, like Reich, a member of the "generation of 1927"; it was "the most important day of my life," he wrote in his autobiography, *The Conscience of Words* (1979), of the events he witnessed that day in Vienna: "Since then I have known exactly what the storming of the Bastille was like. I had become part of the crowd, I fully dissolved in it, I did not feel the slightest resistance to what the crowd was doing."[120] Angered by the contempt for any feeling of justice in the court ruling on the Schattendorf killers, he had bicycled to the Palace of Justice to join the demonstration. "The agitation," he wrote, explaining how the riots influenced his classic study *Crowds and Power* (1960), "is still in my bones. It was the closest thing to a revolution that I have physically experienced."[121]

Canetti read Freud's *Group Psychology* (1921) when he returned home from the riot and was repulsed by it. Freud and other writers such as Le Bon, he wrote thirty-three years later, "had closed themselves off against masses, crowds; they found them alien or seemed to fear them; and when they set about investigating them, they gestured: Keep ten feet away from me! A crowd seemed something leprous to them, it was like a disease . . . It was crucial for them, when confronted with a crowd, to keep their heads, not to be seduced by the crowd, not melt into it."[122] Unlike Freud, Canetti said, he "knew the crowd from the inside . . . I saw crowds around me, [and] I also saw crowds within me."[123]

Reich also felt the crowd's contagious energy within him. "When a crowd runs," he wrote after July 15, "one feels an irresistible urge to run with it."[124] Seeking an explanation for what had happened on that day, and disappointed with Freud, Reich turned to Karl Marx.

Hadn't Vienna been on the brink of the kind of revolution that Marx eagerly anticipated? After his meeting with Freud on the Semmering, Reich and his family went on holiday to Lans, a scenic alpine village near Innsbruck. There Reich read *Das Kapital* for the first time, somewhat late, given Marx's popularity among Social Democrats. He realized that what Marx had done for economics was as radical as what Freud had done for psychiatry, and he imagined a fusion of their respective insights. Marx led him to Engels's *Origins of the Family, Private Property and the State*, and to other critics of patriarchy such as Johann Jakob Bachofen. The very status of the father, a vacant role in Reich's life that Freud had filled, was now thrown into doubt. Reich would emerge from his summerlong studies a different person, thoroughly radicalized.

When he visited him on the Semmering, Reich asked Freud to analyze him, and when Freud refused, Reich took it as a great insult, even though Freud was now so weak that he had only three patients. Annie Reich held that it was the refusal of Freud to take Reich for personal analysis that led to Reich's break not only with Freud but also with reality. At the time, Annie Reich was being analyzed by Anna Freud; from what Reich's wife said in these sessions, Anna Freud wrote to Jones (in a breach of doctor-patient confidentiality) that she deduced that Reich, though charismatic and impressive, was unstable and that things "could end up badly for him."[125]

In the early 1920s, a quarter of the fatalities in Vienna were attributed to tuberculosis. TB was so rife there that it was popularly known in Europe as the "Viennese disease." Mainly affecting working-class neighborhoods, it was one of the catalysts for the Social Democrats' policy of housing reform.

For those who were better-off, there was at least the hope of a cure in a number of alpine sanatoriums that had sprung up in Switzerland in areas where the well-to-do went for winter sports. In the 1860s, Dr. Alexander Spengler, who had fled Germany after the collapse of the 1848 revolution, discovered that TB was almost nonexistent in Davos, which he attributed to the purity of the mountain air at 5,250 feet above sea level. The intensity of the sunshine, with its abundance of ultraviolet rays, was also thought to be an important factor. Another doctor supposed that in Davos, closer to the sun, there was three times as much radioactive emanation as in the lowlands, which he believed accumulated on the surface of the body to beneficial effect. (In 1907 the bioclimatologist Carl Dorno founded the World Radiation Center there to study these biological effects. The center is still based in the town and measures global warming.)

Until the discovery in 1946 of antibiotics, which virtually eliminated tuberculosis in Europe and led to the closure of many of Davos's hotels, the resort represented many patients' last hope. In 1906 it was reported that an amazing 48 percent of TB sufferers were fit for work after one to seven years of treatment in Davos. The rest, who arrived in the latter stages of the disease vainly hoping for a miracle cure, were buried in the town's wooded graveyard.

TB had killed Reich's father and brother. At the end of 1927 he found himself afflicted, and spent the winter in Davos. Yet Reich thought all illness was psychosomatic and blamed the depression and illness from which he suffered at the time on Freud's reaction to him and to his work. Reich, overextended at the psychoanalytic clinic and with many railing against his theory of the orgasm, felt burned-out. The doctor had become the patient.

There is a photograph of Reich at thirty, standing in the snow outside an alpine sanatorium in ski clothes, brooding, with his hands in his pockets. Under another image of himself taken at this time, showing the same wounded expression, Reich wrote, "Conflict with Freud." Reich's third wife, Ilse Ollendorff, later wrote in her biography of Reich: "Freud had become . . . a father substitute for Reich. The rejection, as Reich felt it, was intolerable. Reich reacted to this rejection with deep depression."[126]

Reich no doubt stayed in one of the thirty large private sanatoriums, which had up to seven hundred beds (there were also a few people's sanatoriums for the less well-to-do). The rooms in these facilities had linoleum floors and walls covered in washable paper, so that they could be easily disinfected between occupants. Patients were encouraged to sleep with the window open, despite the cold, so that they could breathe in the curative air even at night.

For breakfast patients were fed a diet of large portions of milk, supplemented with liberal doses of beer or Grüner Veltliner wine, which were thought to fortify and settle the stomach. After breakfast patients were subjected to freezing forty-five-second showers in water of a perishing 40 degrees. Administered by a physician, they were followed by a cold rubdown. For most of the day patients stretched out on fur-covered chaise longues on the south-facing balconies outside their rooms, soaking up the healing power of the sun and the fresh mountain air. They were also led on long alpine hikes.

According to an antique guide, a typical day for a "well-acclimatized, slightly ill patient" at a standard facility in Davos (in this case Dr. Turban's Sanatorium) was as follows:

| | |
|---|---|
| 7 o'clock | Get up |
| 7.30    " | First breakfast |
| 8      " | Douche |
| 8.15–9.45 o'clock | Uphill walk, with rest at intervals |
| 9.45–10.30    " | Rest cure |
| 10.30–11    " | Second breakfast |
| 11–12    " | Level walk, with rest at intervals |
| 12–1    " | Rest cure |
| 1–2    " | Lunch |
| 2–2.30    " | Standing or sitting in open air |
| 2.30–4    " | Rest cure |
| 4–4.30    " | Afternoon refreshment |
| 4.30–6    " | Level walk, with rest at intervals |
| 6–7    " | Rest cure |
| 7–7.45    " | Dinner |
| 8–9.30    " | Rest, milk at 9 |
| 10    " | Bed.[127] |

As a result of this regimen, which required patients to spend ten and a quarter hours a day in the open air, Davos was full of sunburned faces.

Between hikes, while confined to his balcony for silent rest cures, Reich spent his convalescence reading Marx, Engels, and Lenin and correcting the galleys of *The Function of the Orgasm*, the summation of all his theories about sex to date. As the coughing of the other sick and emaciated patients echoed around him, Reich added a new chapter to the book, "The Social Significance of Genital Strivings," which represented his first attempt to apply his insights to social problems, thereby fusing his interest in both Marx and Freud.

If Reich thought that all neuroses were caused by sexual repression, he extended this idea when he thought of possible solutions to mass neuroses. It was sexual frustration, he now argued, that led to social disorder and that held people back from embracing revolutionary change. If people were sexually satisfied, liberated, and willingly polygamous, he suggested, there would be no war, sadism, or drive to destructiveness, but a kind of genital utopia instead. His optimistic theory about the repressive but surmountable obstacles to orgastic bliss was developed in a mood of melancholy and injured pride. When *The Function of the Orgasm* was published the following year the ideas contained within it were so disputed by his colleagues that Reich wrote a disclaimer admitting that his views were "not as yet accepted by psychoanalysis."[128]

Reich may have found further confirmation of his sexual theories in the seclusion of his alpine retreat: Three years before Reich's stay, Thomas Mann had published *The Magic Mountain* (*Der Zauberberg*), a novel set in a sanatorium above Davos like the one Reich was now in, that emphasized the theme of sexual repression. (The book was banned by some Davos doctors, who forbade patients to read it because of its negative portrait of the town.)[129] In 1912, Mann's wife had been confined for six months to Dr. Friedrich Jessen's Waldsanatorium, and, like his protagonist Hans Castorp, Mann was also diagnosed with a spot on his lung when he visited her there. Castorp stays for several years in Davos, but Mann left after only a few weeks to seek a second opinion and was given the all-clear by a doctor in Munich.

In Mann's novel, lust is heightened in the rarefied, lethargic atmosphere of the health spa, where patients, away from their families for long stints, enjoy a diet of breakfast beer and a regimen of boring rest cures. "The demands of love could not be fettered, or coerced," warns Mann's fictional clinician, Dr. Krokowski, of the dangers of sexual repression. "Suppressed love was not dead, it continued to live on in the dark, secret depths, straining for fulfillment—

and broke the bands of chastity and reappeared, though in transmuted, unrecognizable form . . . in the form of illness!"[130]

It is often supposed that the character of Dr. Krokowski is based on Georg Groddeck, a physician and novelist who had just published *The Book of the It* (1923), from which Freud took the term "id" and Reich took the idea that all illnesses were psychosomatic. Is it possible that Mann might have also known about Reich's theories? Dr. Krokowski recommends uninhibited love as a cure for consumption, just as Reich did for neuroses, and he therefore takes a permissive view of his patients' frequent sexual liaisons. A copy of a fictitious sex manual, *The Art of Seduction*, an "exposition of a philosophy of physical love and debauchery," does the rounds of Dr. Krokowski's sickrooms.[131]

In an article about his novel published in *The Atlantic Monthly* in 1953, Mann described life at Davos:

> It is a sort of substitute existence, and it can, in a relatively short time, wholly wean a young person from actual and active life . . . The cure is always a matter of several months, often of several years. But after the first six months the young person has not a single idea left save flirtation and the thermometer under his tongue. After the second six months in many cases he has even lost the capacity of any other ideas. He will become completely incapable of life in the flatland.[132]

When Albert Einstein visited Davos from Berlin in March 1928 (by which time Reich had left the health resort) to initiate university courses there so as to give these bored patients something to do, he invoked Mann's book. The theorist of relativity, who had won his Nobel Prize for Physics seven years earlier, spoke about how Davos's young patients were understimulated, describing them as "hot-house plants," prone to melancholy: "Thus withdrawn for long periods from the will-hardening discipline of normal work and a prey to morbid reflection on his physical condition, [the patient] easily loses the power of mental effort and the sense of being able to hold his own in the struggle for existence."[133]

With the luxury (or misfortune) of so much time to think, Reich had a sort of existential crisis in the mountains. The rest cure acted like a crucible. He felt, he wrote, that everything he had believed in and worked for had been put into question by the recent events in politically divided Austria. "[My] first encounter with human irrationality," Reich wrote of the July 15 riots, "was an immense shock. I can't imagine how I bore it without going mad. Consider that when I underwent this experience I was comfortably adjusted to conventional modes of thinking."[134]

It was as though he'd landed in a meat grinder, his brain ground to pulp—nothing made sense anymore:

It may be best described as follows: As if struck by a blow, one suddenly recognizes the scientific futility, the biological senselessness, and the social noxiousness of views and institutions, which until that moment had seemed altogether natural and self-evident. It is a kind of eschatological experience so frequently encountered in a pathological form in schizophrenics. I might even voice the belief that the schizophrenic form of psychic illness is regularly accompanied by illuminating insight into the irrationalism of social and political mores.[135]

Annie Reich felt that a "deterioration process" set in during Reich's recuperation in Davos, one that marked the beginning of an incipient psychosis.[136] She reported that Reich returned from Davos a different person: angry, paranoid, and suspicious of her. Against Anna Freud's advice, a second child (named Lore, after the ill-fated Lore Kahn) was conceived soon after his homecoming in a desperate attempt to consolidate the marriage.

But Reich, like Peer Gynt, thought that the world was mad, not him—he felt he was a lucid and sane observer of its delusions. Reich's mind raced with new questions: Why were the young forbidden from satisfying their libidinous drives? Why were so many people psychically sick? Why was there such a barrier to natural sexuality? Where did sexual repressions come from? In 1928, the year Lore Reich was born, Reich joined the Communist Party of Austria. Now marginalized by psychoanalysts in Vienna and increasingly disillusioned with psychoanalysis itself, he referred to the party as a "second home."[137]

*Three*

In October 1928, the Heimwehr, the Christian Social Militia, chose to conduct a mass rally in Wiener Neustadt, an industrial town south of Vienna. The town was a bastion of socialism, so to bring twenty thousand fascists there was a deliberate provocation. It was the Heimwehr's first show of strength since the July 15 riots in Vienna; the implication was that their next move would be on the capital itself. In response, the Social Democrats declared that they would plan a rally there for the same day, to be attended by 15,000 Schutzbund troops and thousands of party members. The Social Democratic leader Otto Bauer thought that the government, when faced with the prospect of what seemed an inevitable clash, would be provoked into banning both marches, and he called for internal disarmament.

Reich set off with two hundred other unarmed Communist Pary members for Wiener Neustadt. They hoped to "spearhead" the Social Democratic Schutzbund into violence against the Heimwehr and thereby incite civil war, which they believed would precipitate a revolution. In his role as a physician in the Communist Party of Austria, Reich was in charge of first-aid supplies: "I packed my rucksack, [and] said goodbye to my wife and children," Reich wrote, adding melodramatically, "It was questionable whether I would ever return."[1] The agitators seemed hopelessly outnumbered. Disguised in tourist attire so as not to attract the attention of the secret police, they met at the train station in Vienna, where they bought third-class tickets to Pottendorf, a small village within walking distance of Wiener Neustadt. Those who couldn't afford the fare had set off the day before on foot to walk the twenty-five miles.

When they arrived in Pottendorf, the Social Democratic mayor of the town offered them a large dance hall in which to stay the night. His apparent generosity was a trap. At 7:00 a.m. they woke to find themselves surrounded by armed police, and they were marched to the train station at bayonet point, proudly singing the "Internationale" as they went, and were packed off back to Vienna. When they got close to the city one of their members pulled the emergency cord and Reich and his comrades jumped from the train and marched the final few miles on foot. In Baden, which also neighbored Wiener Neustadt, the secretary of the German Communist Party was arrested along with ten members of the executive committee, accused of hindering the arrival of the Heimwehr with sabotage and of trying to incite railway strikes.

In Wiener Neustadt the majority of the population had fled in anticipation of violence, closing and shuttering stores, removing electric signs, and barricading buildings. The Red Cross had set up field tents to treat the wounded. However, the government arranged for a third of the army to be deployed there, and under the watchful eyes of military machine gunners, four batteries of light artillery, and cavalry squadrons, both rallies took place without incident, and without Reich. The Heimwehr troops, dressed in olive green knickerbockers and green bonnets that were decorated with a Tyrolese feather, paraded the black, white, and red colors of pre-1918 Imperial Germany. The organization's shock troops, the *Frontkämpfer*, wore military helmets and marched with drill-like precision. Two hundred yards away, behind a police cordon, members of the Schutzbund, wearing gray-green windbreakers and peaked caps with a red flower in the band, carried the scarlet banners of socialism. A reporter for *The New York Times* estimated the cost of policing the operation—which involved ten thousand troops and three thousand policemen—at $1 million.

The few Communists who did make it through attempted to distribute leaflets among the Schutzbund and "received a terrible thrashing," according to Reich, for their revolutionary efforts.[2] Sixty

Communists, led by Victor Stern, the Moravian member of the Czech parliament, were arrested in the town. Even if they had managed to goad the Social Democrats into violent action, it is questionable whether Reich and his comrades would have succeeded in catalyzing revolution; the better-equipped Heimwehr hoped to provoke just such a clash, which they thought would cause a government backlash and a right-wing coup d'état. A document that was stolen from the Heimwehr headquarters in Graz and leaked to the press revealed that Ignaz Seipel had advised Austrian industrialists to fund the Heimwehr, which also received money from Italian fascists, and that he had ordered the police to arm and protect the militia. The police frequently raided Schutzbund armories and confiscated weapons, which were given to the Heimwehr.

Reich and his revolutionary friends, he later explained, were full of belief in the "inevitable collapse of capitalism" and "the immutable course of history."[3] Whenever demonstrations were announced in the Communist newspaper, *The Red Flag*, Reich would join them, marching with the unemployed, of which there were now one hundred thousand in Vienna, shouting "Down with capitalism" and "Freedom and bread." On such occasions, Reich admitted to feeling guilty about his six-room apartment and the two servants he employed; he contributed a large portion of his earnings to the party in an attempt to assuage this guilt. Among the raggedly dressed masses, Reich would try to blend in by wearing a leather jacket rather than his usual, more bourgeois overcoat.

Reich glamorized the hungry and sex-starved working class. "Thievery, drunkenness, beatings and sexual brutality all occurred frequently," he admitted of his proletarian friends, "but in relation to the misery in which [the workers] lived, they were more decent, moral, ready to help, honest and aware than the vain, fat-stomached, high-nosed and no-good spenders and phrase-makers who could generate no trace of humanity and who were sexually far sicker, only in a less honest way."[4] Reich spoke about society's sexual problems at party meetings, and promised that if the cornerstone of sexual repression was removed, the whole edifice of class submission would crumble.

After the failed action in Wiener Neustadt, Reich tried to convert a revolutionary faction within the Social Democratic Party to communism. Reich had met some members of the Social Democratic Party's Youth Guard who had formed a secret machine-gun division and planned to take over the inner city. This was a sign of the increasing political desperation among Social Democrats: Ignaz Seipel had initiated emergency legislation that was deliberately intended to undermine Red Vienna's considerable social achievements, and the Social Democrats' neutered response was frustrating to its supporters. Reich used his own money to establish what he called the Committee of Revolutionary Social Democrats; he rented a meeting hall and gave a keynote speech in which he criticized the Social Democratic leadership and tried to recruit the two thousand Social Democrats in attendance, mostly members of the Schutzbund, to his own party: "There was much shouting; the atmosphere was explosive," he recalled.[5]

As at Wiener Neustadt, no alliance was forged, and the Social Democrats, who felt Reich was trying to sow dissent in their ranks, stormed out of the meeting en masse. "By openly confronting the leadership with almost no support in the party except among certain discontented elements among the youth and the Schutzbund," wrote the historian Anson Rabinbach of this riotous meeting, "Reich clearly put himself in a position that courted expulsion."[6] Reich was indeed expelled from the Social Democratic Party, of which he was still also a member, a month later. The witnesses against him were two committee members who claimed they did not know that the meeting was to be attended by Communists. One of them, successfully arguing against his own expulsion, said that he'd met Reich after a long stint of being unemployed and was therefore especially vulnerable to Reich's "seductive influences."[7]

In *The Question of Lay Analysis* (1926), Freud seemed to expand on his inspirational idea of free clinics when he imagined that social workers might "mobilize a corps to give battle to the neuroses springing from our civilization."[8] He thought that funding such a "new Salvation Army" was a worthy philanthropic project and he urged that "some American millionaire apply part of his fortune" to it. On his return from the sanatorium to which he had been confined in Davos, Reich poured his energy into mobilizing just such a force.

"Go ahead, just go ahead," Reich remembered Freud saying enthusiastically when he visited him in his country retreat and asked his permission to open free psychoanalytic clinics, modeled on the Ambulatorium, on a mass scale in poorer areas of the city and suburbs. (Wilhelm Stekel and Alfred Adler had already set up their own chain of clinics, which competed with the Ambulatorium for sexually disturbed patients, and Reich's old teacher Julius Tandler had also instituted a network of marriage guidance centers in Vienna.)[9] "Freud agreed wholeheartedly," Reich said. "He knew as little as I where it would lead."[10]

Reich believed that sexual repression, as encouraged by the institution of the family, was not an intrinsic part of the civilizing process, as Freud maintained, but that it functioned to support the existing class structure. In *The Communist Manifesto* Marx had argued that one of the main tasks of the social revolution was to abolish the nuclear family. At his meeting with Freud, Reich asserted the importance he attributed to "treating the family problem vigorously." Reich, once again a father, declared the family to be "a factory for authoritarian ideologies" that suppressed the natural sexuality of children. He spoke of it as a disease—"familitis"—and proposed that children be brought up in collectives instead. Freud warned, "You'll be poking into a hornet's nest."[11]

Reich founded and appointed himself "scientific director" of the Socialist Society for Sex Counseling and Sex Research; among its members were Anny Angel, Edmund Bergler, Richard Sterba, and Annie Reich. In January 1929, to launch his enterprise, Reich placed an ad in the Social Democratic newspaper, *Die Arbeiter-Zeitung* (The Workers' Newspaper), offering "Free counseling on sexual problems, the rearing of children, and general mental hygiene to those seeking advice."[12] Over the next three years Reich's organization—whose motto was "Free Sexuality Within an Egalitarian Society"—established six free clinics in Vienna, which were open one or two days a week. "The new centers immediately became so overcrowded," Reich wrote, "that any doubt as to the significance of my work was promptly removed."[13]

Lacking a rich American patron, Reich funded the organization from his own pocket with the money he earned analyzing Americans. Sándor Ferenczi, who thought Reich "original" and "gifted" and went to the States on frequent lecture tours, had referred several lucrative American trainees to him: Walter Briehl, M. Ralph Kaufman, John Murray, and O. Spurgeon English all came to Reich for analysis, each paying five to fifteen dollars or even more an hour, compared to the one-dollar fee Austrians were charged, if they were charged at all (English was warned that he would be contaminated by Reich's radical politics, and that this would make him unemployable back home, but Helene Deutsch reassured him—somewhat misleadingly—that politics was an extracurricular activity for Reich).

Reich also operated a van that doubled as a mobile clinic on the weekends, taking his message of liberation to the people, distributing sex education pamphlets and contraceptives door-to-door, and inviting his audience to throw off their repressions as he lectured to them on "the sexual misery of the masses under capitalism" in squares and parks. Reich spoke from his soapbox about the dangers of abstinence, the importance of premarital sex, and the corrupting influence of the family, arguing for a "politics of everyday life." With his emphatic gesticulations, darting black eyes, and scarlet face (a result of his psoriasis), Reich made an impassioned speaker.

It was perhaps the most radical, politically engaged psychoanalytic enterprise to date. Reich abandoned his doctor's office to get to the "sickbed of society, on the streets, in the slums, among the unemployed and poverty-stricken." It was new, Reich said, "to attack the neuroses by prevention rather than treatment," trying to stop the causes of illness rather than just treating the sick.[14] His talks, which combined sex education with political indoctrination along with the other services offered by his mobile clinic, presented a deliberate provocation to the Catholic Church, which was politically powerful in Austria. As a result he and his band were often moved on by the police.

Reich wasn't alone in thinking that if people jettisoned their sexual repressions, all other authoritarian repressions would evaporate with them—he had the support of many of the younger analysts at the Ambulatorium. Reich's old friend Lia Laszky became his closest collaborator. After suffering through unrequited love for her as a student, Reich had begun a not particularly secret affair with Laszky, who had separated from Swarowski and now worked at the local Montessori school, where she was Eva Reich's teacher. Her job in the mobile clinic was to enlighten the children about sexual matters, and she would sing songs with lyrics by Reich that were designed to do this to the tunes of popular songs such as Marlene Dietrich's hit from Josef von Sternberg's *The Blue Angel* (1930), "Falling in Love Again."

The team's gynecologist would offer health advice, fitting contraceptive devices in the privacy of the van and arranging illegal but medically safe abortions, euphemistically known as "therapeutic" abortions. Like many of his colleagues, Reich believed in eugenics, or "sexual improvement." Eugenics was "aimed at raising the health and morale of the people," wrote the psychologist and sex reformer Charlotte Wolff, after the Nazis had given eugenics a bad name. "None of the scientists and physicians who practiced it in this way would have foreseen that one day it would be used as a poison, ruining a whole nation."[15] Most of the women operated on were, Reich wrote dispassionately, justifying his transgression of what he considered an outdated law (abortion was legal in the Soviet Union), "frigid, careworn, covertly sadistic or overtly masochistic . . . latent schizophrenics, or morbid depressives . . . Such women should not be allowed to bear children!"[16]

When she was interviewed in the early 1970s by the British writer and theater critic Kenneth Tynan, the picture Laszky painted of the success of their agitprop enterprise greatly differed from Reich's:

> We would stop in a workers' district, hand out pamphlets and make speeches explaining birth control, which was a forbidden subject in a Catholic country. But we attracted no publicity, except in the most conservative papers, which just made fun of our efforts. Willi spent almost everything he earned on these pamphlets and public meetings. He would go down to the basement of a coffee-house and talk to maybe a hundred people about reconciling Freud and Marx. And then *Pravda* would say: "Mass Assembly of Viennese People to hear Dr. Wilhelm Reich."[17]

Despite these disappointing audiences, which were exaggerated by the Soviet propaganda machine, "Reich loved it," remembered Laszky. "It was meat and potatoes to him."[18]

In 1929, Stalin launched his megalomaniacal five-year plan, which imposed a program of rapid industrialization and the compulsory collectivization of farms (the party projected a fanciful 330 percent rise in industrial production as a result of this technological push, as well as a 50 percent increase in agricultural production). Numerous posters trumpeted the success of these schemes. The reality was, of course, that when farmers burned grain and slaughtered livestock to protest the requisitioning of their land, rationing had to be introduced in the capital and over a million peasant dissenters were arrested and deported to forced-labor camps.

That August, Wilhelm and Annie Reich made a pilgrimage to Moscow. Already—two months before the Wall Street crash—there was mass unemployment in Europe (between 1928 and 1932, after five years of relative prosperity, unemployment doubled in Austria). The Soviet Union the Reichs visited was a utopian place of their imagination, seemingly immune to these difficulties. The first thing Reich did when he crossed the border into the Soviet Union, beginning a two-month visit, was to embrace the Red Army guard, who, Reich thought, was standing there to welcome him: "He only looked at me in bewilderment and without understanding," Reich wrote later of the warmth that was unreciprocated by his comrade. "It was this way with me for a long time in my life. Something was very earnestly propagandized and I would take it seriously. Then, time and again, I discovered that I had taken it more seriously than the propagandizer."[19]

The Reichs were hoping to see for themselves the changes wrought by the country's liberalized sex laws, which they saw as a useful model in their campaign for similar changes in Austria (Reich's mobile clinic was based on Soviet mobile birth-control units). After the October Revolution of 1917, Alexandra Kollontai, a staunch feminist who was the first people's commissar for social welfare, had ushered in emancipatory decrees that secularized marriage, facilitated divorce and abortion, and decriminalized homosexuality—these progressive policies presented a beacon of hope to sex reformers like

Reich, who battled in their own countries against sexual oppression and the nuclear family that many of them believed perpetuated it. An advocate of "free love" and the social emancipation of women, Kollontai was famous for arguing that sex in a postrevolutionary society should be as accessible and easily satisfied as quenching one's thirst by drinking a glass of water. She spawned an era of free-love leagues and nude marches in the Soviet Union; there was even a campaign calling for special booths to be built next to public toilets for the sexual convenience of the masses.[20] Kollontai occupied an important government position and was a close friend of Lenin's, so her arguments couldn't be dismissed as belonging to the lunatic fringe. However, Reich naïvely accepted Kollontai's free-love version of communism as orthodoxy.

In 1921, Lenin had noted to the German Communist leader Clara Zetkin, "Communism will not bring asceticism, but joy of life, power of life, and a satisfied love life will help to do that."[21] However, Lenin was not willing to make free sexuality a cornerstone of a new society, as Kollontai believed it should be. After Lenin's death in 1924, Zetkin's full exchange with him was published, which revealed his more sexually conservative position. Lenin warned against the potential corruption of youth by faddish Freudians seeking a rationale for their own "overheated sexuality":

> Although I am nothing but a gloomy ascetic, the so-called "new sexual life" of the youth—and sometimes of the old—often seems to me to be purely bourgeois, an extension of bourgeois brothels. That has nothing whatever in common with freedom of love as we communists understand it. You must be aware of the famous theory that in communist society the satisfaction of sexual desires, of love, will be as simple and unimportant as drinking a glass of water. This glass of water theory has made our young people mad, quite mad. It has proved fatal to many young boys and girls . . . Of course, thirst must be satisfied. But will the normal person in normal circumstances lie down in the gutter and drink out of a puddle, or out of a glass with a rim greasy from many lips? . . . The revolution demands concentration, increase of forces . . . Dissoluteness in sexual life is bourgeois, [it] is a phenomenon of decay.[22]

By 1921, when he wrote these words, Lenin (a man rumored to be impotent, with little interest in sex) had fallen out with Kollontai, angry at the role she played in founding the Workers' Opposition, an organization that was scathing of repressive government bureaucracy. The Workers' Opposition was banned at the Party Congress in 1922 and Kollontai was discharged from the party administration and reassigned to the diplomatic service. When Reich visited the Soviet Union, Stalin had effectively exiled her to Norway, where she served as the world's first woman ambassador. In 1929, Stalin abolished the Women's Department Kollontai had once headed; eventually Kollontai's sex reforms were all reversed—abortion was outlawed again, divorce made more difficult, pornography banned, homosexuality recriminalized, and sex education abolished.

Though these warning signs were already there, Reich continued to see the country through rose-tinted spectacles (in her biography of the German sexologist Magnus Hirschfeld, who was an admirer of Kollontai and visited the Soviet Union on a study tour in 1926, Charlotte Wolff wrote that Hirschfeld was, similarly, "mentally blindfolded or afraid of facing the truth").[23] Reich and Annie visited several progressive Soviet institutions that were intended to showcase how the family had been broken down and superseded by more collectivized ways of living. Reich was especially interested in the many communes that had been formed—in one, he noted approvingly, the communards even shared underpants. The Bolshevo Commune, a model prison for youth offenders that had been started in 1924 by inmates of the Butyrka prison on the outskirts Moscow, was a typical stop on the propaganda tour. The running of the commune and attached shoe factory—which was turning out four hundred pairs of shoes and a thousand ice skates a day when Reich visited—was solely administered by the thousand adolescents who formed it.

Reich also visited several Soviet kindergartens and made a point of visiting Vera Schmidt, the founder of the famous psychoanalytic orphanage-laboratory, a school intended to foster intensive group rather than parental ties. The only place that conformed to Reich's sex-positive pedagogical line, Schmidt's Experimental Home for Children had opened in 1921, on the second floor of the Psychoanalytic Institute, in an art nouveau building that had been a banker's mansion before the revolution. It had thirty children; alumni included Schmidt's son, Alik, and, before his father denounced psychoanalysis, Stalin's son, Vasily. In her book *Psychoanalytic Education in Soviet Russia* (1924), Schmidt explained that most of the children were the offspring of party officials, "who spend most of their time doing important party work, and are therefore unable to raise children." The new citizens in her care were to be raised completely free of all traditional repressions.

There were no punishments at Schmidt's school; teachers were forbidden from praising or condemning children because moral judgments were thought to be unnecessarily guilt inducing and to result in neurosis later in life. The teachers were also banned from displaying affection for the children, as kissing and hugging were thought to gratify the adult's rather than the child's needs. Potty training wasn't attempted until the children were almost three. A girl who smeared herself with feces was simply washed and changed rather than punished, and was gently encouraged to play with paints instead.

The school collected Freudian data on the uncontrolled sexual development of children, and Schmidt kept a meticulous day-to-day diary about her own son. Controversially, teachers were trained to tolerate rather than suppress childhood masturbation and to allow the children to pursue their sexual curiosity with each other. Rumors abounded that Schmidt's charges were subjected to perverse experiments aimed at stimulating their sexuality prematurely, and the institution was investigated by the authorities as a result.[24] Though the rumors were not confirmed, state funding was withdrawn after the school had been open only eight months and it survived on donations until it closed three years later.

Reich presented an enthusiastic account of his trip to the Soviet Union in a meeting at Freud's home that December, arguing that Schmidt's school promised a way of abolishing neuroses in future generations. However, his fellow analysts took a half skeptical, half hostile view of her pedagogical experiments. Freud, aware of the turning tide against psychoanalysis in the Soviet Union—in 1927 Stalin had forbidden future translations of Freud's work; a decade later he would ban psychoanalysis altogether—ridiculed Reich's faith in the idea that Soviet reforms of marriage and the family could render extinct the Oedipus complex and therefore all mental illnesses. He compared this notion "to treating a person's intestinal disorders by having him stop eating and at the same time putting a stopper into his anus."[25] Freud suggested sarcastically that time was the only test of a child's neurosis and that they should continue Reich's discussion of Schmidt's orphanage in thirty years' time. Freud was already seventy-three, and he died ten years later.

Furthermore, Freud said that "total orgasms" were not the answer to neuroses, which had no single cause. When Reich continued to argue his position, maintaining that analysis "must shift from therapy to prophylaxis—prevention,"[26] Freud lost his temper, which he rarely did: "He who wants to have the floor again and again shows that he wants to be right at any price. I will not let you talk any more." Richard Sterba, who attended Reich's presentation, wrote that it was the only time he saw Freud adopt an "authoritarian attitude."[27]

By 1930 the psychoanalytic profession was completely polarized. That year Freud published *Civilization and Its Discontents*, in which he maintained that civilization demanded the sacrifice of our freedom. "The intention that men should be 'happy' is not in the plan of creation," Freud put it with what he called his "cheerful pessimism."[28] But the younger, more radical analysts believed that these repressions of our natural instincts might be jettisoned. Reich, who was becoming the leader of the dissident group, thought that Freud's essay was a direct response to his own ideas, specifically his lecture "The Prophylaxis of the Neuroses," a summary of *The Function of the Orgasm* that he'd delivered on his return from the Soviet Union. "I was the one," he immodestly told Kurt Eissler in the 1950s, "who was 'unbehaglich in der Kultur' ["discontented" by civilization]."[29]

In fact, Freud had been working on the book well before Reich gave his talk, but it is not unlikely that Reich's subversive ideas about orgasms, formulated three years earlier, had an effect on Freud's final thesis. In *Civilization and Its Discontents*, Freud argued that there is always a fundamental conflict between our primal instincts and the restraints of civilization, which make us sacrifice the former. The orgasm might offer us a glimpse of former freedoms, Freud wrote, as if addressing Reich directly, and it is tempting to let the "overwhelming sensation of pleasure" we experience in sexual love serve as a paradigm in our search for happiness, but this quest is fundamentally flawed: "We are never so defenseless against suffering as when we love," Freud warned.[30]

"It is a bad misunderstanding," Freud stated, "explained only by ignorance, if people say that psychoanalysis expects the cure of neurotic illness from the 'free living out' of sexuality. On the contrary, the making conscious of the repressed sexual desires makes possible their control."[31]

Freud told Reich that it was not the task of psychoanalysis to change the world; its true role, he implied, was to adjust people to it. This strategy of adjustment to the status quo would come to define psychoanalysis, but at the time many of the second generation of analysts believed sexual liberation would bring about cataclysmic changes in society, and they practiced what they preached. In the summer of 1930, the two embattled poles of psychoanalysis coincidentally set up camp at opposite ends of the Grundlsee, a lake southeast of Salzburg.

Peter Heller was analyzed by Anna Freud as a child and painted a picture of that summer in his memoir. His mother, who was having an affair with Reich's friend the dashing Communist Karl Frank, was friendly with many of the left-wing analysts. The lake attracted an avant-garde group of writers, actors, painters, and, Heller writes, "psychoanalysts of the left-wing liberal-to-radical observance . . . The grown-ups indulged in a voyeuristic exhibitionistic fashion of semi-public love affairs, dramatized promiscuity, risqué parties and play-acting, and bathing in the nude."[32] Heller described how they "dramatized their sexuality, and let themselves go, in order to parade their opposition to convention."[33] They "experimented with themselves and their modernity to the point of self-destruction."[34]

While this festival of bohemian promiscuity was occurring at one end of the lake, the more prudish Freud and his daughter Anna were holidaying at the other; it was, as Heller puts it, "the orthodox and proper psychoanalytic establishment, guardian of convention and morality . . . vis-à-vis the clique of progressive socio-utopians and sexually superfree protagonists of the psychoanalytic left."[35]

Heller's mother had her son analyzed by the old guard while

sleeping with the new, so Anna Freud had a young spy in the opposing camp. She quoted Heller's childhood description of his holiday in her case notes: "The married people there do not act in love with one another but are friendly with other men and women 'they do not really care for.'"[36] (Karl Frank, with whom Heller's mother was sleeping, not only had a brief love affair with Lore Kahn before Reich's analysis of her but, according to Reich, also had sex with Annie Reich at Grundlsee in 1929.) In a boat in the middle of the Grundlsee was Fenichel's ex-girlfriend Berta Bornstein, who along with her sister Steff played an active role in Fenichel's radical "children's seminar"; Heller reports that the children, glued to their binoculars, "observed Berta Bornstein when she disappeared in the bottom of the rowboat with the art historian Dr. Ernst, in the course of their short-lived grand passion."[37]

That summer Reich went to see Freud in his lakeside villa. Reich had just published the first part of *The Sexual Revolution* ("Sexual Maturity, Abstinence, Marital Morality"), and their conversation, once again about the need to remove children from the family setting if the Oedipus complex and correlating neuroses were to be avoided, marked a final break. "I stressed that a distinction must be made between a family based on love, and a coercive family," Reich recalled. "I said that everything possible had to be done to prevent neuroses. And he replied: 'Your viewpoint is no longer compatible with the middle path of psychoanalysis.'"[38]

"It was not the character-analytic technique, it was the sexual revolution that bothered him," Reich said later. "He was angry . . . Instead of developing into one of his best supporters, one of his students, one who would carry his ideas forward, here I was, going 'off the beam' . . . But I didn't. I didn't go off the beam."[39] Reich, not recognizing his own father complex with all of its attendant ambivalence, thought he was developing rather than diverging from Freud's theories. In using the phrase "off the beam" it seems that Freud was referring to Reich's mental as well as theoretical departure. Sometime in the middle of their inflammatory argument, Freud advised Reich to go to Berlin to see Sandor Rado or Siegfried Bernfeld for a third analysis, and Reich, ever attentive to his mentor's recommendations, chose to obey him.

As he left, Reich looked back and saw Freud anxiously pacing the floor of his room. He reminded Reich of "a beautiful and restless animal, caught and confined in a cage."[40] It was to be the last time he saw him.

Berlin had a decadelong reputation as "Babylon on the Spree." The golden twenties in the capital were, in contrast to the quiet elegance of Vienna, an era of erotic revues, cocaine, prostitution, avant-garde art, and sexual experimentation; an estimated 120,000 female and 35,000 male prostitutes catered to every sexual proclivity. One 1927 guidebook, aimed at the numerous sex tourists who flocked to the city, waxed enthusiastic about the "light-filled, sparkling, champagne-bubbling, jazz-droning, noisy, too noisy, always overflowing Berlin night."[41] Psychoanalysis became part of this sexual language; Grete Ujhely, the author of *A Call for Sexual Tolerance* (1930), complained of the new rhetoric of persuasion: "The result [of refusing a request for sex] is a popular lecture for the next half hour from the angle of psychoanalysis, with primary emphasis on that nice handy word inhibitionism."[42]

Christopher Isherwood moved to Berlin in 1929 at the age of twenty-four, attracted by its reputation as the world capital of sexual liberation—his school friend W. H. Auden had written him a letter from Germany telling him that "Berlin is a Bugger's daydream" with 170 police-controlled male brothels. Isherwood's famous novel, *Goodbye to Berlin*, was written in 1939; it was only with hindsight that he saw the promiscuous city of his early sexual adventures against the "miseries of political violence and near-starvation" suffered by its indigenous population: "The 'wickedness' of Berlin's nightlife was of a most pitiful kind," Isherwood remembered. "The kisses and embraces, as always, had price-tags attached to them, but here the prices were drastically reduced in the cut-throat competition of an overcrowded market."[43]

Isherwood wrote that Berlin, hit particularly hard by the worldwide depression, was almost in a state of civil war when he arrived there: "Here was the seething brew of history in the making—a brew which would test the truth of all the political theories, just as actual cooking tests the cookery books. The Berlin brew seethed with unemployment, malnutrition, stock market panic, hatred of the Versailles Treaty and other potent ingredients."[44] Auden wrote of his time in Berlin, "One suddenly realized that the whole foundations of life were shaking."[45]

Reich didn't spend his Berlin years exclusively in the pursuit of private pleasures, as Isherwood and Auden did, but in trying to impose his recipe for utopia on the volatile city. He was attracted to Berlin because it was the home of what he referred to as the "great freedom movement," with which he wanted to join forces. Reich was well aware of Germany's leading role in the sex reform movement: "Berlin now offered me splendid opportunities," he wrote.[46]

Reich joined the Communist Party of Germany as soon as he arrived, and his Berlin was one of factories, strikes, unemployment, demonstrations, and rallies rather than nightclubs. Sandor Rado recalled that Reich was "heavily involved in communist propaganda" when he arrived in Germany, an "admirer of Lenin and Stalin." Reich, he said, was "both leftist and outspoken."[47]

In the September 1930 elections in Germany the Communist Party garnered 4.6 million votes, making it the largest Communist Party outside the Soviet Union. In the capital itself the Communists overtook the Social Democrats and were now the leading party. Yet nationally, the Nazis surged past them with 6.5 million votes, dramatically increasing their number of seats in the Reichstag from 12 to 107. The Russian Communist leader Karl Radek wrote that the Nazi Party burst onto the political scene "just as an island suddenly emerges in the middle of the sea owing to volcanic forces."[48] The slight, clubfooted Joseph Goebbels had been the *Gauleiter* (Nazi district leader) of Berlin since 1926; his violent campaigning had seen the Nazi vote increase fourfold, even in this bastion of free-thinking and liberalism. The Nazis celebrated their electoral success by wreaking havoc in the capital. They smashed the windows of the Jewish-owned department stores in the Leipziger Strasse before assembling in Potsdamer Platz to chant "Germany awake!" "Death to Judah," and "Heil Hitler."[49]

In July 1931 there was a devastating financial crash in Germany, which saw unemployment double, to six million, by the following

January. In the volatile months that followed, the Communist Red Front and the Nazi Brownshirts clashed frequently in Berlin, an escalation of violence that led to near anarchy. The expressionist painter George Grosz wrote to a friend that the Nazis were perpetrating a political murder "almost every third day."[50] That September the head of the Berlin storm troopers, the ominously named Wolf Heinrich von Helldorf, was driven up and down a busy boulevard in broad daylight as he stood in his convertible and pointed imperiously at anyone who looked Jewish. These people were immediately set upon by storm troopers dressed in civilian clothes and mixed in with the crowds. This "mini-pogrom," as one historian has called it, went on for two hours before the police intervened to stop it.[51]

The Communist demonstrations Reich attended in Berlin were much more impressive and better organized than those in Vienna. "One marched in military formation and sang revolutionary songs lustily," Reich recalled.[52] Reich volunteered as a marshal at the May Day parade, in which nearly one hundred thousand Communists participated. He gave an average of two lectures a week to youth groups on subjects such as "The Fiasco of Bourgeois Morality," distributed leaflets in unemployment offices, daubed revolutionary and anti-Nazi slogans on walls in red paint, and on Sundays recruited door-to-door in the working-class sections of the city. "Social Democrats furiously slammed the door at the sight of a Communist brochure," Reich recalled, "and the indifferent brusquely declined."[53] He even traveled to rural districts to speak to farmers about the Soviet collectivization of farms.

Among his comrades was the writer Arthur Koestler, who moved from Paris to Berlin in September 1931 to become the science editor of the liberal Berlin newspaper *Vossische Zeitung* and now found himself in the Communist cell of thirty writers and intellectuals associated with the "Red Housing Block" on Wilmersdorfer Strasse. "We sold the World Revolution like vacuum cleaners," Koestler wrote in *The God That Failed* (1949) of their dogged, unglamorous brand of activism:

Among other members of our cell, I remember Dr. Wilhelm Reich. He . . . had just published a book called *The Function of the Orgasm,* in which he had expounded the theory that the sexual frustration of the proletariat caused a thwarting of its political consciousness; only through a full, uninhibited release of the sexual urge could the working-class realize its revolutionary potentialities and historic mission; the whole thing was less cockeyed than it sounds.[54]

Reich found an audience in Berlin that was much more receptive to his utopian project (Koestler was, by his own admission, "fanatically promiscuous"); the psychoanalysts he met there were "far more progressive in social matters than the Viennese," he wrote. "The young psychoanalysts could breathe more freely and my orgasm theory was much better received."[55] In an oral history at Columbia University, recorded in 1971, Edith Jacobson, a young dissident analyst, convincingly explained why "renegades" such as Reich flourished in the less conservative environment of Berlin, far removed from Freud and Vienna: "Some of these people felt, 'Now I am in a new country. Now I can be myself completely.' And they wanted to resolve their ties to Freud. It had something to do with acting out unresolved transference problems and underlying ambivalences that may not have been so fully analyzed."[56]

According to Reich's future disciple Ola Raknes (who would be bowled over by his "vitality, his vivacity and his charm"), Reich was already much talked about in Berlin, with "a reputation of an outstanding clinician and teacher and of a remarkable, though somewhat wild theorist."[57] In 1924 Otto Fenichel, now teaching at the Berlin Psychoanalytic Institute, had started the "children's seminar," which met to debate radical ideas, and on his arrival in the city Reich immediately fitted into this circle of younger dissident left-wing analysts (Erich Fromm, Karen Horney, Edith Jacobson). In fact, Reich hijacked Fenichel's Marxist group. It was now Reich's ideas that a splinter group met to discuss ("The opposition," Reich said proudly, "had sprung up around my scientific research"). They often met in Reich's house on Schwäbische Strasse to plot their coup against conventional analysis. Following the slogan "[For] Freud against Freud," Reich wanted the group to reassert the early radical work of psychoanalysis, to show "where Freud the scientist came into conflict with Freud the bourgeois philosopher."[58] "We specifically dealt with therapeutic 'character' problems," Edith Jacobson remembered of the group, "discussed Reich's ideas, and also socio-psychological questions . . . This was a very lively, smart, special group."[59]

In 1930 the German psychoanalyst Fritz Perls, whose genitalia Hitschmann had examined when he was his analyst, was thinking of going back into therapy. When he asked Karen Horney to refer him to a doctor, she said, "The only analyst who I think would get through to you would be Wilhelm Reich."[60] Perls had been in therapy for eighteen months with the conservative analyst Eugen Harnick, who had terminated the therapy in August 1929 when Perls got married against his advice (according to Freud, patients were to be discouraged from making any life-changing decisions while undergoing therapy). Harnick, who believed in classic "passive analysis," refused to shake Perls's hand when he arrived or left his office and, according to Perls, limited his own verbal contribution to a frustrating one sentence a week; he was so mute that he would signal the end of the allotted hour merely by scratching the floor with his foot.

"Well, the next year was a completely different story," Perls wrote of character analysis with Reich, who was two years younger than him. "Reich was vital, alive, rebellious. He was eager to discuss any situation, especially political and sexual ones, yet of course he still analyzed and played the usual genetic tracing games. But with him the importance of facts begins to fade. The interest in attitudes moved more to the foreground."[61] Perls once said that Reich, whom he saw for three years, was the first man he had been able to trust. From Reich he also learned "brazenness," he wrote.

Perls's experience goes some way toward showing how Reich became influential among a second generation of analysts, and how, in his zeal, Reich fused what he saw on the street with what he did in the consulting room. In his book *Ego, Hunger and Aggression* (1942), Perls singled out for particular praise Reich's healthy attitude to sexuality: "One of the best points which W. Reich made is his demand that the regulation of our sex life by morality should be replaced by the rhythm of self-regulation."[62] In other words, the orgasm was a homeostatic valve through which steam had to be regularly let off. Perls also considered Reich's technique of concentrating on the patient's character armor a great therapeutic innovation, but (without saying in the book that he himself had been a patient) he disapproved of the "mocking and even bullying" Reich used to break down resistances. He criticized Reich for "making the patient swallow ideas which he cannot digest."[63]

In his later autobiography, *In and Out the Garbage Pail* (1969), Perls gave an example of this kind of unpalatable assertion. Reich apparently confronted Perls with the unsubstantiated suggestion that his uncle, a celebrated attorney and philanderer named Herman Staub, was in fact his real father. Staub's name came up when Perls recounted to his analyst the story of the passionate affair he had with his cousin Lucy, also a niece of Staub's who was a victim of Berlin's fast-paced nightlife; she introduced Perls to orgies and bisexuality, and later became a morphine addict and killed herself. If Perls felt guilty about these taboo adventures, which was indeed one of the things that led him to seek analysis, they were given a certain license when Lucy told Perls that Staub had slept with her when she was thirteen. Perls was shocked when Reich subsequently told him the far-fetched secret of his paternity and he noted in his autobiography that Reich "never revealed to me how he came to that conclusion."[64] Whether Reich's hypothesis was designed to provoke Perls in some way is unclear. Perls never really accepted the idea, though he confessed it flattered him. His own much hated and mostly absent father, a traveling wine salesman, was to him rather unimpressive.

Perls absorbed Reich's theory of the orgasm in the course of his therapy. "Believing, as I previously did, in the libido-theory (especially in Reich's ideal of the genital character), I made a kind of phallic religion out of it, rationalized and justified by what seemed a sound scientific foundation."[65] Under Reich's influence, Perls, like many other young analysts and analytic trainees in Berlin, merged orgasms with politics; he was an enthusiastic member of the Anti-Nazi League and a teacher at the Marxist Workers' University, where Reich gave lectures on sexology and on Marxism and psychology, and expounded revolutionary ideas in the smoke of Berlin's legendary Romanisches Café. Therapy, this generation felt, was also an ideology, and one had to accept the latter if the former was to succeed. Perls wrote of this optimistic spirit, "We fools believed we could build a new world without wars."[66]

When Reich moved to Germany he estimated that the country had about eighty organizations devoted to sex reform, with about 350,000 members between them and a well-established network of marriage guidance and birth control clinics. These politically diverse organizations were mainly devoted to the campaign to repeal the laws against homosexuality and abortion, and formed the backbone of the "freedom movement" that so attracted Reich to Berlin.

The world headquarters of the sex reform movement was Magnus Hirschfeld's Institute for Sexual Science in the chic Tiergarten district (next door to the house where Christopher Isherwood lived). Hirschfeld had started the Berlin Psychoanalytic Society in 1908 with Karl Abraham, but withdrew in 1911 to focus on his sex research. Hirschfeld, who was homosexual, campaigned for all consensual sex among adults to be considered outside the purview of law. Freud found the portly, walrus-mustached, and bespectacled Hirschfeld "flabby and unappetizing" but admired his idealism.[67]

Hirschfeld's institute occupied the mansion of the former French ambassador, and it was decorated in the Biedermeier style, more like a wealthy private residence than a scientific institute, with Persian carpets, a grand piano, and glass cabinets full of porcelain. Free sexual advice was offered in a number of consulting rooms, and leading sexologists gave public talks in a large lecture hall (each week the popular Communist doctor Max Hodann, the head of the German-Soviet Friendship Society, answered anonymous questions on sex that were left in a drop box inside the institute). There were medical clinics for the treatment of venereal diseases and other sexual illnesses, research laboratories where Hirschfeld formulated dubious aphrodisiacs and anti-impotence medicines, a library with the largest collection of literature on sex in the world, and—an unlikely tourist attraction—a museum of sexual pathology that held up a mirror to the risqué desires of Berlin's inhabitants. It was stuffed, Christopher Isherwood noted when he visited, with sado-masochistic and fetishistic props: whips and chains, complicated masturbation devices, flashers' attire, and oversized lacy underwear that had been worn by macho Prussian officers under their uniforms.

Before he arrived in Berlin, Reich had established links with Hirschfeld and his institute, which maintained close connections with the psychoanalytic circle. In 1930 Reich gave the first talk at the congress of the World League for Sexual Reform, an organization founded by Hirschfeld, and he published his first articles on sexology in the institute's journal, *Jahrbuch für sexualle Zwischenstufen*. However, Reich and Hirschfeld never worked together in Berlin. Immediately after the congress and before Reich arrived in Berlin, Hirschfeld went on a lecture tour of the United States and never returned to Germany. As a homosexual, a Jew, and a leftist, he represented everything Hitler abhorred; as early as the 1920s he had been attacked by Nazi thugs for his permissive views, on one occasion suffering a fractured skull, and he now thought the city too dangerous.

Reich, seeking to fill Hirschfeld's shoes, drafted a series of proposals in January 1931 for what he called the German Association for Proletarian Sexual Politics (*Sexualpolitik* was shortened to Sex-Pol), an organization whose aim was to unify the diverse groups committed to sex and welfare reform, and to unite the ideas of Freud and Marx. Reich wanted to give his theory of the orgasm a national platform and get the whole sex reform movement behind his plan to rid the country of sexual repression and neurosis. The Sex-Pol manifesto was based on Reich's own lecture at the World League for Sex Reform the year before. Reich called for:

The free distribution of contraceptives to those who could not obtain them through normal channels; massive propaganda for birth control.

Abolition of laws against abortion; provision of free abortions at public clinics; financial and medical safeguards for pregnant [women] and nursing mothers.

Abolition of any legal distinctions between the married and the unmarried; freedom of divorce; elimination of prostitution through economic and sex economic changes to eradicate its causes.

Elimination of venereal diseases through comprehensive sex education.

Avoidance of neuroses and sexual problems through life-
affirmative education; study of principles of sexual pedagogy;
establishment of therapeutic clinics.
Training of doctors, teachers, social workers . . . in all relevant
matters of sexual hygiene.
Treatment rather than punishment for sexual offenses; protection
of children and adolescents against adult seduction.[68]

Reich wrote that he presented his scheme to the cultural adviser
of the Communist Party Central Committee, who approved it, but
the World League of Sexual Reform refused to ratify it. Even though
many members were also Communist Party members or Communist sympathizers, they didn't want their organization, which had
built up a broad coalition from across the political spectrum, to be
totally co-opted by the Communists.

The first meeting of Sex-Pol took place in Düsseldorf in the fall
of 1931, and was attended by representatives of eight sex reform
groups whose organizations together had twenty thousand members.
Reich gave the keynote speech. In only a few months Sex-Pol doubled in size, Reich wrote proudly in *People in Trouble*, with counseling
centers established in Leipzig, Dresden, and Stettin, to which Reich
traveled to promote his politically explosive fusion of Freud and
Marx and further expound his message about orgasms. He argued
provocatively that the bonds of the family and marriage were bourgeois shackles and that, as in the Trobriand Islands (a society studied
by the Polish anthropologist Bronislaw Malinowski), adolescents
should be encouraged to have free sex. Never before had he enjoyed
such large audiences, and—rivaling Hirschfeld—he enjoyed a new
fame as the leading advocate of sexual liberation in Germany. For his
exhaustive propagandistic efforts, Reich wrote in his account of
Sex-Pol, "I enjoyed great recognition from the party leadership.[69]

Reich so hoped to change society by freeing the working class of
its sexual hang-ups that he told Kurt Eissler in 1951 that these public demonstrations were among the most profound experiences he
ever had as a doctor. "I shall never forget the warm, flushed faces,
the glowing eyes, the tension, the contact. There's no doubt about
it, Dr. Eissler, this issue will win out everywhere. It will kill any dic-

tator. There's no doubt about the social force in it. It is the force of the future. It is the sexual revolution."[70]

In *Reforming Sex: The German Movement for Birth Control and Abortion Reform, 1920–1950*, Atina Grossmann has criticized Reich for exaggerating his role in the German sex reform movement. In her corrective account, the Unity Committee for Proletarian Sex Reform and not Sex Pol represented the Communist Party's effort to unify and politicize sex reform organizations in Germany. The Unity Committee published a manifesto in June 1931, *Forbidden Love*, which featured a blond woman looking up admiringly at a muscled male worker. It claimed that "sexual desire" was "one of the few pleasures left to those oppressed people," and called for free treatment for the sexual disturbances that were caused by capitalism and the bourgeois family. Grossmann writes that it was this manifesto, rather than Reich's, that was adopted at Düsseldorf. She maintains that there was "no organization known as Sexpol. [The Unity Committee] functioned as the organizational embodiment of Sexpol ideas, and those were not the exclusive property of Wilhelm Reich."[71]

The Unity Committee launched a journal in January 1932, *Die Warte* (The Lookout), described as "the Voice of Struggle in the Fight for Proletarian Sexual Reform and the Protection of Mothers." It praised the Soviet Union as "the healthiest country in the world" and predicted a sexually repressive Nazi future in which anybody who wanted to get married, or even to have sex, would have to get a permit from a counseling center to see if they fulfilled the racial requirements. Grossmann points out that Reich doesn't mention *Die Warte* in his "copious and often self-serving" account of the sex reform movement, nor does the journal mention him, which she takes as proof of his marginal status.[72] In fact, Reich published several articles in the journal under the pseudonym Ernst Roner (Roninger was his mother's maiden name), and many of the other articles on the sexual misery of youth forced "to satisfy their sexual needs in halls and basements" specifically reflect Reich's own peculiar bugbears.[73]

However, Grossmann shows convincingly that Reich's sex-political work mainly took place within the framework of the Unity Committee, rather than through his own independent pioneering efforts. It was only later that he positioned himself as the leader of the "great freedom movement" that he had come to join. In 1931 Reich opened a clinic in Berlin on behalf of the Unity League, which gave out sex advice and "mountains" of free contraception and lubricants, and put on lectures with titles like "Sexual Oppression in the Capitalist Economic System" and "The Woman in the Soviet Union." Reich's clinic also reflected his own particular interests. Reich used the language of psychoanalysis to argue that better orgasms would mean better comrades, and to this end he placed special emphasis on encouraging premarital sex. Reich warned teenagers that if they hadn't lost their virginity by twenty, it would lead to problems later on, and introduced the popular slogan "A room of his own for every adolescent."

When Sandor Rado took Reich on as a patient in Berlin, he worked to dissolve what he diagnosed as a "mild paranoid tendency."[74] However, Rado let Reich down by leaving for America after Reich had been in analysis for only four months. Rado decided to stay there when he was offered the chance to direct training at the New York Psychoanalytic Institute.

Annie Reich thought that Rado should never have begun the analysis if he was planning to break it off for his transatlantic trip. She was concerned because their marriage finally seemed to be falling apart. In early 1930, Reich pursued his affair with Lia Laszky quite openly and he left for Berlin alone at the end of that year. Around this time Reich wrote an essay entitled "Compulsory Marriage and Enduring Sexual Relationship" in which he argued that sooner or later sexual attraction between a couple dried up and they were invariably drawn to others. "The healthier the individual," Reich wrote, perhaps with himself in mind, "the more conscious he is of his desires."[75] Was it modern to be married? he asked. If one takes his writing to be autobiographical, one gets a sense that Reich was frustrated that Annie tolerated his adultery. "It only seems to be a paradox," Reich continued in his essay, "that the unconscious hatred [toward the partner to which you are no longer as sexually attracted as you once were] can become all the more intense the kinder and more tolerant the partner is."[76] One compensated for this, Reich observed of disintegrating relationships, with guilty tenderness, a "sticky attachment" that only prolonged the relationship in "mutual torment."[77]

In 1931, against the advice of both Rado and her own analyst, Anna Freud, Annie followed Reich to Berlin with Eva and Lore, hoping to give their marriage a final chance.

Lore Reich now lives in a large apartment in Pittsburgh, right at the heart of the university campus, where her husband, who died a month before our October 2004 meeting, used to teach economic history. She greeted me at the door, with her shock of white hair and her warm, generous face. She was a psychoanalyst, like both her parents, and had retired four years earlier when, she said, her mind began to wander during sessions. Her apartment was decorated with paintings by her mother, scratchy and colorful Austrian scenes, like illustrations from a children's book whose text has been lost: hikers in the Alps, a schoolyard fight, an orchestra in full swing. The furniture consisted of several comfortable analysts' chairs; there was a brown leather Eames chair and a stylish, felt-covered Danish armchair that, Lore told me, was the one she had used when she practiced psychoanalysis.

I ask Lore why she thought her mother returned to Reich, and why her analyst at the time advised against it. "Anna Freud was adamant that my mother should leave my father and she was very angry when my mother went back to him," Lore Reich said. "She was into good behavior—Anna Freud and Willie [as she calls her father] also deviated there, because she thought that you should have ego strength and the instincts were really bad, and you were supposed to control them. She was the 'iron maiden,' a virgin, all about self-control, and against the id. Whereas for him the instincts were good, and he was trying to release them."[78]

Lore Reich believes that Anna Freud not only had a conflict of ideology with her father but also was disgusted by what she learned about Reich's behavior during her analysis of Annie. "My father was having an affair with Lia Laszky at the time, we have photographs, well, never mind . . . He had lots of affairs, and he felt that if you didn't go along with that you were just clingy and neurotic. This was totally different if women cheated on him. But anyway, he was having these yelling matches and things, and he was being crazy in many ways and she was in analysis, so she was telling all this to Anna Freud, and I'm sure she told Freud.

"My mother was a very modern woman," Lore continued. "She became a psychoanalyst. She was highly intellectual, very cultured, and she became very successful in her field. Her problem was that she should have left him when he went to Berlin, but she didn't, she went back to him. She writes about it . . . she writes these articles that are really about herself, you know how analysts do—about 'Extreme Submissiveness in Women,' and I'm sure that's about her questioning why she stayed with this guy, or got together with him."

As Annie Reich explained it in the paper Lore Reich refers to, submissive women are almost always married to narcissistic men, who maltreat or cheat on them. These women tolerate this because they have renounced their own narcissism, projecting it onto their "brilliant" lovers:

> Intercourse is an experience of extraordinary intensity in these cases of extreme submissiveness in women. It is worthy of note that the self-esteem of the submissive woman falls to a strikingly low level when she is away from her lover. The man, on the other hand, is overrated; he is considered to be very important, a genius. He is the only man worthy of love . . . she develops a sort of megalomania in regard to him. In the magic of unio mystica she finally regains, through identification, the narcissism which she had renounced.[79]

Reich's condition for the reconciliation with Annie was that their children should be educated in a Communist school in Berlin. Eva was suffering from night terrors and temper tantrums, and Reich thought that a Communist education would resolve the Oedipus complex that he thought was developing in her. Both girls were sent to an institution similar to Vera Schmidt's psychoanalytic orphanage in the Soviet Union that Reich so admired. At the Berlin school, no toilet training was enforced and a positive sex education was given; if children masturbated, Reich wrote of the school's educational philosophy, they were allowed to "satisfy themselves without embarrassment . . . without any secrecy, under the eyes of the teachers."[80]

"It was terrible!" Lore Reich said. "I was three, my sister was seven. There was no food. Eva said she slept on straw—we actually had mattresses, but it was very primitive. I don't know that we had toilets, maybe outhouses. The counselors weren't really interested in children, but were idealistic Communists. Eva said she went around with other people and they made all these little shit piles. It wasn't pretty, very regressed, unfortunate. I was only there for about six months. I got sick, my mother took me out. But it was one of the conditions of them getting back together . . . We suffered for his convictions. I came home and I was singing 'Tannenbaum,' you know the Christmas song, and he got into an absolute rage that I wasn't singing the 'Internationale.'"

Reich's theory was that people shouldn't live with their families—"the kibbutz idea," Lore Reich described it, "except it was more like the Russian crèches, whereby you would separate the child from the family and the Oedipus complex. The child wouldn't have the Oedipus complex because it would be brought up in a group home where they would learn Socialist, sharing ideals, instead of bourgeois ideas, and they would have sex all over the place. He didn't know that when you raise people on a kibbutz they don't have sex with each other; they all become like brothers and sisters because of the incest taboo."

According to Reich's sister-in-law, Ottilie Heifetz, Eva told her father on a visit home from the collective, "You are the Communist. You go live at the center. I'm staying here."[81]

At least one person at that time had identified a place where the Oedipus complex was absent. Bronislaw Malinowski, the anthropologist whose accounts of the sexually permissive, politically peaceful Trobriand Islanders in the archipelago of coral atolls off New Guinea were deeply influential among advocates of sexual liberation, wrote of the islanders' "happy, free, arcadian existence, devoted to amusement and the pursuit of pleasure."[82] Malinowski believed that the islanders' matrilineal kinship patterns and their open encouragement of adolescent sexuality left them free of neurosis, sadism, and sexual perversion. (Both Ernest Jones and the psychoanalyst-anthropologist Geza Roheim openly disputed this, defending Freud's notion that sexual repression was an intrinsic component of civilization.)

Reich felt that Malinowski had shown the possibility of primitive communism, of utopia on earth. His ideas about education were heavily influenced by Malinowski's writings, specifically, *The Sexual Lives of Savages in Northwestern Melanesia* and *Sex and Repression in Savage Society*, which Reich read in 1930. He became a close friend of Malinowski's; Malinowski would be instrumental in helping Reich emigrate to the United States in the late 1930s, where an ornately carved cane from the Trobriand Islands, given to Reich by the ethnographer, had pride of place in his study.

In *The Invasion of Compulsory Sex-Morality* (1931), Reich's account of the origins of sexual repression, Reich looked to Malinowski's account of the Trobriand Islanders for confirmation of his sexual theories. He thought it demonstrated "irrefutably that common property, matriarchy, a lack of rigid family organization, sexual freedom for children and adolescents, openness and generosity in character structure, are just as interrelated as private property, patriarchy, asceticism in children and adolescents, enslavement of women, rigidity in family and marriage, character armoring, sexual perversion, and mental illness, all of which are the ever-present symptoms of sexual suppression."[83]

However, Reich's vision of a sexually permissive future, where primitive sexuality was unleashed, didn't appeal to either orthodox Marxists or Freudians. The German Communist Party was alarmed by the youth cult that was growing around Reich as a consequence of his popular appeal to sexual freedom, especially for adolescents. One Communist sports organization complained that students influenced by Reich had demanded that they be provided with rooms where they could pursue their sexual relationships. When the Communist Party, which feared alienating Catholic voters, wavered on whether or not to clear for publication Reich's book endorsing adolescent sexuality, *The Sexual Struggle of Youth*, Reich simply founded and financed a press devoted to sex education literature and published the book himself. The book took him several weeks to write and was intended to counter the Nazis' nationalistic appeals to youth; ten thousand copies were printed, almost half of which sold within six weeks of publication. The press was run by Arnold Deutsch, a Communist and former student of Reich's; it also published Annie Reich's *When Your Child Asks Questions*, which taught mothers how to give sex education, and her "birds and the bees" children's book, *The Chalk Triangle: Group for the Study of Adult Secrets*, which Reich claimed had a revolutionary and liberating impact on his own daughters' school.

The party's hierarchy didn't like being sidestepped in this way and subsequently branded Reich a counterrevolutionary, accusing him of making brothels of their youth associations and turning the class struggle into the battle between adolescents and adults. As one critic asked at the time, was Reich politicizing sexuality or sexualizing politics? Martha Ruben-Wolf, a Marxist physician and leading luminary in the sex reform movement, argued that there were no orgasm disturbances among the proletariat because neurosis was a bourgeois disease. The party had dwindling sympathies for Reich's psychoanalytic arguments. Reich's old friend Grete Bibring recalled in an interview that Communists had to leave the party when they entered analysis: "It sounds like an operetta but it's true, the Communists were relieved from the party when they were in analysis, so . . . that they could have an analysis without betraying the party."[84]

In December 1932, Sex-Pol's publications, which Moscow declared "ideologically incorrect," were banned from party bookstores.

At the same time that the Communist Party was beginning to disown Reich, preferring Lenin's revolutionary regimen of sport and sublimation for their young members, similar machinations against him began in the psychoanalytic inner circle precisely because he was a Communist, though the analysts were a lot less direct in their approach. Freud told his American patient Joseph Wortis that he disapproved of Reich's activism. "An analyst by the name of Wilhelm Reich went to Russia and lectured there, and talked so much about promiscuity that they [the Russians] finally asked him to leave," Wortis recalls Freud saying. "Reich, a talented psychoanalyst, will probably have to leave the [psychoanalytic] movement because he has turned Communist and altered his views. He believes, e.g., that the aggressive instinct and sex problems are products of the class struggle instead of inborn biological drives."[85]

When Reich submitted an article on masochism to the *International Journal of Psychoanalysis* in 1932 in which he claimed that sadism and masochism, which Freud explained as the work of the death instinct, were not biologically innate in man but products of capitalism, Freud insisted that it should be accompanied by a disclaimer: "Bolshevism places restrictions on the freedom of scientific research similar to those of the Church."[86] Reich's article was eventually published without Freud's disclaimer after Fenichel and the Marxist analyst Siegfried Bernfeld negotiated with Freud on Reich's behalf. Bernfeld said that such a note would be read as a declaration of war on Soviet Russia, and agreed instead to write a thirty-page rebuttal. Fenichel was removed from the editorship of the journal as punishment for defending Reich.

Freud thought that Reich had so departed from orthodoxy that he needed to cut him off as he had done earlier dissenters and revisionists, such as Jung, Adler, Stekel, and Rank. "First one then another turns out to be unusable or unguidable," Freud wrote to Max Eitingon of the Bolshevik propagandists Fenichel and Reich. "Everything shows that under the corrosive influence of these times characters rapidly decompose."[87]

Freud responded to the increasing radicalism of the latest heretic with a blunt New Year's resolution for 1932. He made a note of it in his diary: "Step against Reich."[88] That year Eitingon, then president of the German Psychoanalytic Institute, was pressed into action as Freud's henchman and forbade Reich from inviting training analysts to his seminar at the Berlin Psychoanalytic Institute, effectively depriving him of students. By the end of the year, and without his knowledge, Reich's name was deleted from the German Psychoanalytic Society's membership roll. The International Psychoanalytic Association's press also reneged on its plan to publish *Character Analysis*, which was already in galleys. Freud feared Reich because he was so articulate, single-minded, and persuasive. At that stage Freud thought that communism rather than Nazism was the main danger, as it threatened to topple everything with world revolution, and he didn't want people to oppose psychoanalysis because it was identified with such a left-wing worldview.

In Germany, Hitler was appointed chancellor of a coalition government in January 1933, in a ceremony that was celebrated with the soon-to-be-familiar sight of a Nazi torchlight procession through the Brandenburg Gate. The Nazis still didn't have a clear parliamentary majority, however, and President Hindenburg optimistically believed Hitler could be contained (Hindenburg had a low opinion of Hitler's political talents, famously saying he believed him unqualified for any office but postmaster general). On February 27, 1933, the Reichstag was set ablaze; the arsonist was supposedly a mentally disturbed Dutchman called Marinus van der Lubbe, who was found wandering naked through the flames. (Hitler's second-in-command, Hermann Göring, later claimed responsibility for having started the fire.) Hitler declared that the arson was part of a Communist conspiracy and played up fears of civil war. Hindenburg declared a state of national emergency and Hitler, taking advantage of the power that he was granted as a consequence, ordered storm troopers to round up thousands of Communist officials and intellectuals in the interests of so-called national security. The Reichstag fire ended the Weimer democracy and launched Hitler's dictatorship.

As a psychoanalyst, a Communist, and a Jew, Reich was thrice-marked in Nazi eyes. Reich told his American patient O. Spurgeon English that he was aware that he was under surveillance by the Gestapo. "He did not say this with bitterness or with any sense of persecution," English later wrote in an article about his analyst, "but just with a rather wry observational affect concerning his own plight."[89] During the Nazi regime of terror, political enemies were routinely taken from their beds in the middle of the night and detained. Two of Reich's friends were murdered in the storm troopers' barracks on Papestrasse, which served as a makeshift prison and torture chamber during the political violence. Reich escaped arrest by staying in hotels under false names after his apartment was ransacked by storm troopers, who stole a watch, a copy of the Kama Sutra, and a book of erotic Japanese woodcuts. One of Reich's Sex-Pol clinics was also raided, and a list of members' names confiscated.

In March 1933, Heinrich Himmler opened the first concentration camp, at Dachau, where 27,000 Social Democrats and Communists were imprisoned by the end of the year. Reich finally fled Berlin that same month, after his book *The Sexual Struggle of Youth* was attacked in the *Völkischer Beobachter*, a Nazi newspaper. Lore and Eva had already been sent back to Vienna to live with their grandparents. Reich and Annie traveled south by night train to join them and crossed the border into Austria at a small Bavarian town. They were disguised as tourists setting off on a skiing holiday.

When I asked Lore Reich whether her mother had ever recounted the story of her separation from Reich, she told me the transference "wore off on top of a mountain." "Hitler came to power and Reich was on a list to be arrested because he was a very active, noisy political person. So [to escape] they walked out with knapsacks over the mountains and when they got to the top of the mountain she realized he was falling apart, he was just a bubble of anxiety. She lost that transference, all the admiration and submissiveness, and the belief that he was a great man—she said: Who is this jerk who's so scared?" Lore laughed. "And she left him."

Against all advice, and obviously disoriented, Reich returned to Berlin without his wife, almost as if to face these fears directly. He checked into a "hotel for transients" under his own name. "My friends thought I was insane," Reich noted in *People in Trouble*.[90] Reich snuck back into his apartment, packed a suitcase with clothes, and set off again for Vienna, leaving his furniture, library, and car behind. He had only a few German reichsmarks to his name.

In April 1933 the so-called Law to Restore the Professional Civil Service was passed, after which over 16 percent of Germany's university staff were dismissed, three-quarters of them because they were Jewish and the rest because they were deemed subversive. Magnus Hirschfeld's Institute for Sexual Science was vandalized by storm troopers on May 6; they poured ink all over the archival files, smashed the exhibition cases, and played soccer with the erotic artifacts inside. A plaster bust of Hirschfeld, who had returned from his tour of America and was now in exile in Paris, was paraded on a wooden stake to the Opernplatz, where Brownshirts tossed it on an enormous pyre of "un-Germanic" books. As a brass band played, 100,000 volumes burned, including works by Thomas Mann, Sigmund Freud, and Wilhelm Reich.

When he arrived in Vienna, Reich, knapsack in hand, went to see his in-laws, where Annie and the children were staying. They refused to take him in. It was the first time he'd been back to the city in three years, and his short stay there would be his last.

During his two months in Vienna, Reich gave a lecture on fas-

cism to some students in which he called for the ceaseless politicization of sexual life in response to the rising danger of Nazism.
Freud banned him from giving any more lectures, worried that such
a provocation endangered the psychoanalytic movement, already
under attack from the Nazis, by identifying it with communism.
Anna Freud wrote to Ernest Jones in 1933:

> Here we are all prepared to take risks for psychoanalysis, but not
> at all for Reich's ideas, with which nobody is in agreement. The
> pronouncement of my father on this matter is: If psychoanalysis is
> to be prohibited, it should come to be prohibited for that which it
> is and not for the mixture of politics and psychoanalysis which
> Reich represents. My father can't wait to get rid of him inasmuch
> as he attaches himself to psychoanalysis. That which my father
> finds offensive in Reich is the fact that he has forced psychoanaly-
> sis to become political. Psychoanalysis has no part in politics.[91]

Freud tried to protect psychoanalysis by asserting its status as a
pure science and retreating entirely from political commentary. He
refused to contemplate the dangers of German fascism. Ferenczi
urged him and his family to leave Vienna as early as May 1933, but
it was five years before he would actually do so, believing that what
had happened in Berlin wouldn't spread to Austria, even though
many others disagreed with his assessment early on. The Christian
Social chancellor of Austria, Engelbert Dollfuss, had suspended
Parliament and ruled by emergency decree since March 4. The following February, in response to a general strike in Vienna, Dollfuss
banned the Social Democratic Party, declared martial law, and had
the entire inner city surrounded with barbed wire. He was determined to destroy the Social Democrats once and for all. After four
days of bloody fighting, during which Heimwehr troops shelled the
Karl-Marx-Hof, pounding the Schutzbunders out of their "forts,"
Red Vienna finally crumbled.

The German Psychoanalytic Society was purged of the Jews
who formed 80 percent of its membership, most of whom fled the
country. As president of the International Psychoanalytic Association, Jones had set up an immigration office in London to finance

and coordinate the psychoanalytic diaspora: "The situation of the German analysts is pretty terrible," Jones wrote to Abraham Brill, the founder of the New York Psychoanalytic Society, at the end of May 1933. "I understand that no Jew is allowed to hold any official position in the society there . . . Freud himself is behaving splendidly in the situation and still hopes that Austria may not succumb to the Nazi menace though I think that is doubtful."[92]

Max Eitingon escaped to Palestine, and the Berlin Poliklinik and German Psychoanalytic Society were taken over by two non-Jewish analysts, Felix Boehm and Carl Müller-Braunschweig, who proved to be effective Nazi collaborators. They signed their letters "Heil Hitler!" and replaced the photographs of Freud that decorated the Poliklinik—in some rooms there were as many as four—with portraits of the Führer. According to Boehm's account of his job interview, when Freud appointed him to take over from Eitingon, his only demand was "Free me of Reich." Jones, who had heard that Reich was "a very clever analyst," though "somewhat wild and unreliable in his theoretical judgments," at first defended Reich's right to be politically active.[93] After some cajoling by Anna Freud, Jones changed his mind and declared that Reich should choose between psychoanalysis and politics. Together, Jones and Anna Freud plotted how best to silence him.

Ernest Jones hoped that Boehm and Müller-Braunschweig would be able to appease the Nazis and that psychoanalysis would be "saved," as he put it, until it could flourish again in a less hostile era. "I prefer psychoanalysis to be practiced by Gentiles in Germany than not at all," he wrote in a letter to Anna Freud.[94] This was hopelessly naïve, as Reich and others argued. In 1936, the German Psychoanalytic Society became part of the sinister German Institute for Psychological Research and Psychotherapy, headed by Hermann Göring's cousin, a committed Nazi who advised members to read Hitler's *Mein Kampf* with "scientific zeal." The Poliklinik was personally endorsed by Hitler, who used it as a holding pen for the camps—like a "virtual psychiatric guillotine," as Elizabeth Danto describes it—in his battle against degeneracy.

Ninety percent of the analysts practicing in Germany and Austria had already fled by March 1938, when the Nazis marched into

Vienna. They draped a swastika over Freud's apartment building, and Anna Freud was taken off for interrogation by the Gestapo. Freud wrote "Finis Austriae" in his diary.[95] He was eighty-one and weak from the final stages of cancer. Storm troopers were in the process of looting his apartment when Ernest Jones came to the rescue, yet it took Jones five days to persuade Freud and his entourage to leave. (Those who were left behind ended up in the camps; four of Freud's five sisters died in Auschwitz.)

Fritz Perls fled Berlin not long after Reich, making it to Holland in the spring of 1933 with just one hundred marks hidden in a cigarette lighter. His wife, the analyst Laura Perls, remembered, "Our last few nights in Berlin we slept in a different place every night. People were getting pulled out of their beds between 3 and 4 in the morning—not only Jews but also people who were active in any leftist or communist movement."[96] Perls went to London to see Ernest Jones, who assigned him to South Africa. Perls started a psychoanalytic society in Johannesburg with Wulf Sachs, another enthusiastic follower of Reich. Perls's elder sister Grete did not escape and died in a concentration camp, as did Laura Perls's sister and her family.

Edith Jacobson was one of the few analysts to remain in Berlin, ostensibly to look after her elderly mother. In October 1935 she was caught dumping a trunk of anti-Nazi literature in a public park and was arrested for her part in the New Beginning movement, an underground group headed by Reich's erstwhile romantic rival, Karl Frank. She was interrogated by the Gestapo about her patients' sexual and political lives; despite her silence, one of these patients was later murdered by the Nazis. Jacobson spent two years in prison in Leipzig for her anti-Nazi activities (she wrote a psychoanalytic paper describing her experiences, "Observations on the Psychological Effect of Imprisonment on Female Political Prisoners") before she was temporarily released for hospital treatment in 1937 and, with the help of Otto Fenichel and Annie Reich's new partner, Arnold Rubenstein, fled to Prague and then to America.

As for Reich, he felt unwelcome in Vienna and fled to Denmark in 1934, traveling by ship via Poland. There, psychoanalysis's putative prince became haunted by his father figure and, as his friends described it, gradually went mad.

# *Four*

Denmark accepted few German refugees after the Nazis came to power. Despite its sharing a border with Germany, only 1,680 German Jews and 142 Communists were accepted into the country, most of those in the first two years of the Nazi seizure of power. The Social Democrats in Denmark, a country hit hard by the Depression, were instituting the social reforms that would establish its enviable welfare state and they didn't want the added burden of supporting large numbers of foreigners. The few refugees that the Danish authorities did welcome were given only temporary six-month visas, which did not permit them to work, and many were destitute, reduced to the status of vagabonds, dependent on the Danish-Jewish relief committee's handouts and on soup kitchens. Reich recalled the "increasing numbers of desperate shabby individuals" who were starving in the streets.[1]

In contrast to this, a number of German intellectuals in exile there—journalists, authors, academics, actors—were supported by private patrons. Bertolt Brecht also arrived in 1933, and a steady stream of distinguished physicists assembled at the Niels Bohr Institute at the University of Copenhagen. Reich had been invited to lecture at the Rockefeller Institute in Copenhagen three months earlier, and already had a network of admirers. He took up residence in the Weber Hotel on the Vesterbrogade, one of the main thoroughfares in the center of Copenhagen, and his hotel was soon swamped with so many visitors hoping for treatment and training that the hotel manager demanded that he leave. Reich moved to an apartment lent to him by the author and sex reformer Jo Jacobsen.

Psychoanalysis was still novel and exciting in Denmark. The first book on Freud had been published in Danish as recently as 1929 (in his history of the psychoanalytic movement, Freud complained that the Scandinavian countries had been the "least receptive" to his ideas), and the only analyst working there was Jenö Harnick, who had arrived from Germany in 1932.[2] Harnick's family had stayed behind in Nazi Germany, and the anxiety that the separation caused him resulted in a nervous breakdown shortly before Reich's arrival. According to the psychoanalyst and biographer Erik Erikson, who also emigrated to Denmark after the Nazis seized power, Jenö Harnick was scheduled to speak at a public meeting, but could only manage gibberish. He had to be led away from the podium and taken into psychiatric care. It is unclear what became of Harnick; Fritz Perls, who had been analyzed by Harnick before Reich treated him, heard that he had died in a mental institution outside Copenhagen.

Just as Fritz Perls had experienced an explosive change when he switched from Harnick's passive method of therapy to Reich's more impassioned technique, psychoanalysis itself was transformed in Denmark when Reich arrived on the scene. Before his breakdown, Harnick had told the journalist Ellen Siersted, who would become one of Reich's most loyal Scandinavian followers, "If Wilhelm Reich comes, you go to him. He is very skilled but watch out—he works with dynamite in your private little 'kitchen.'"[3] Reich's reputation as an analyst preceded him, but he also came with a public health warning.

Despite being petitioned by several Danish students to do so, Freud refused to sanction Reich as Harnick's replacement as a practitioner of psychoanalysis because of his "Communist creed"; he was hesitant to unleash Reich's radical version of psychoanalysis into virgin territory.[4] Reich arrived in an unofficial capacity. According to a historian of Danish psychoanalysis, he was received by Copenhagen's avant-garde "as a prophet who could renew society, and especially sexual life."[5]

From Copenhagen's relative oasis of tolerance, Reich looked back critically at his former home and began writing his classic study of dictatorship, *The Mass Psychology of Fascism*. Full of urgency, he immersed himself in the study of Hitler's *Mein Kampf* and Nazi propaganda in an attempt to explain why, when the conditions seemed so ripe for revolution, the German masses had turned to Nazism rather than communism. Reich applied all his thinking on sex and politics to the crisis at hand. Why did people so enthusiastically support Hitler, against all their best interests and at the cost of the liberty promised by the sexual revolution of which Reich dreamed?

Reich rejected the idea that the rise of fascism could be explained by Hitler's personal charisma—that the nation was gripped by "Hitler psychosis."[6] What made people open to fascist ideas, Reich argued, was the "psychic structure" that they had internalized from childhood. According to Reich, who continued to extend his orgasm theory into politics, the systematic repression of the child's natural desires by the patriarchal family created citizens who were used to being told what to do, and who were therefore prone to submissiveness, blind obedience, and irrationality. Hitler idealized the family, Reich thought, because it taught the child to police his or her unruly instincts, and represented "the authoritarian state in miniature."[7]

Hitler boosted the nation's self-esteem by making the Communists and the Jews scapegoats for all German ills; he equated the two, identifying Bolshevik Russia with the "Jewish world conspiracy" and with the dangers of sexual promiscuity. Reich asserted that Hitler was deliberately exploiting people's sexual anxiety in his propaganda, and that he, Reich, as a psychoanalyst, could see through such maneuvers. Reich thought that Hitler's emphasis on guarding the racial "purity of blood" appealed to his supporters' unconscious and hypochondriacal fear of syphilis (it was rumored in medical circles at the time that Hitler was syphilitic), while his emphasis on the Jews animated an unconscious fear of castration because of the Jews' religious practice of circumcision.[8]

At the same time that he exploited these sexual anxieties, Reich wrote, Hitler offered his subjects substitute gratifications for their repressed sexual enthusiasm in the frenzy of Nazi spectacle—in flashy uniforms, torchlight parades, and jingoistic oratory—all of which had an erotic charge that bound its subjects to the Führer and, by extension, to the nation itself. (In his 1995 biography of Hitler, Joachim Fest writes of the "copulatory character" of Hitler's public appearances. "He played the crowd like a gigantic organ," recalled one of its members, "pulling out all the stops, permitting the listeners to rave and roar, laugh and cry. But inevitably the stream flowed back, until a fiery alternating current welded speaker and listeners into one.")[9] Reich, ever single-minded, devoted a chapter to the symbolism of the ubiquitous swastika, which he thought subliminally represented two interlocked figures engaged in the sexual act.

Hitler's genius, Reich believed, was that he wasn't just a reactionary, as his Communist critics maintained. With his promise to impose a wholesale upheaval of the social system from above, Hitler satisfied both the masses' rebellious call for change and their indoctrinated craving for authority. More people followed Hitler rather than the Communist Party, Reich wrote, because they feared the freedoms promised by a genuine (Communist) revolution in which they—not an absolute ruler—would have to take complete responsibility for their own fates. Reich thought that only the "genitally satisfied" were able to make this existential leap into the dark.

Reich was damning of the German Communist Party's blinkered emphasis on economics, which he thought failed to explain fascism. He criticized the party for ignoring the sexual question; his focus on it had caused him to be increasingly marginalized in Berlin. Reich maintained his faith in the proletariat's "open and untrammeled" attitude toward sexuality, which he thought was an untapped resource of revolutionary energy. The book is a manifesto for his questioned sex-pol views: if things had been done his way, if the Communists had worked to eliminate sexual repression, Reich implied, the masses would not have swept Hitler to power.

The picture Reich painted of the Nazis as sexual puritans became the dominant view for decades. However, revisionist historians such as Dagmar Herzog have shown that as soon as the Nazis had crushed the "Jewish" sex reform movement, they appropriated many of their arguments. This fascist embrace of sexual freedom was controversial among some Nazis. One fascist critic of sexual libertarianism wrote in 1933 that "a large proportion of our Volk, comrades male and female, insists nowadays on the standpoint of complete 'free love,' love without any inhibition, that is, love that is not love, but rather a purely animalistic activation of the sex drive."[10] In 1938 a Nazi physican named Ferdinand Hoffmann complained that 72 million condoms were used a year in Germany and that only 5 percent of brides were still virgins: "There are not two sides to the Jewish question," he warned, "and it is not admissible to damn the Jew in his political, economic, and human manifestations while secretly, for personal convenience, [maintaining] the customs he has suggested in the realm of love- and sex-life."[11]

Some Nazis even seemed to share distorted versions of Reich's sexual beliefs. In his party-endorsed advice manual *Sex—Love—Marriage* (1940), the Nazi psychologist Dr. Johannes Schultz described sex as a "sacred" act and endorsed child and adolescent masturbation and extramarital sex, calling for all young women to throw off the shackles of repression to enjoy the "vibrant humanness" to which they were entitled.[12] Like Reich, Schultz differentiated between the hasty, superficial orgasm and the orgasm that led to a "very intensive resolution . . . extraordinary profound destabilizations and shakings of the entire organism."[13]

Schultz had a totalitarian solution for those who fell short of what Reich would have called an "orgastically potent" ideal: he called for the extermination of handicapped people and homosexuals, whom he deemed "hereditarily ill." Under the direction of Matthias Göring at the German Medical Society for Psychotherapy—which had absorbed the German and Austrian Psychoanalytic associations—Schultz forced homosexuals to have sex with prostitutes under his clinical gaze. Only those who achieved a satisfactory orgasm were saved a train ride to the camps.

Many on the left saw the Nazis' sexual libertarianism as proof that Reich's ideas were misguided. Reich's former colleague, the psychoanalyst Erich Fromm, who incorporated many of Reich's ideas into his best-selling *Escape from Freedom* (1941), questioned the link between sexual repression and authoritarian tendencies, arguing that the Nazis proved instead that sexual freedom did not necessarily lead to political freedom. Contrary to Reich, the philosopher Herbert Marcuse also observed how the Nazi Party actually encouraged sexual pleasure within the confines of a racial elite, thereby "nationalizing" the realm of even the most private act in the service of the state.[14]

*The Mass Psychology of Fascism* appeared in September 1933, privately published in Copenhagen by Reich's press, Verlag für Sexualpolitik (which also published *Character Analysis* the same year). A second printing was done in April of the following year. The first people to object to Reich's critique of fascism were, perversely or not, the people he considered his comrades. The opening sentence of Reich's book declared, "The German working class has suffered severe defeat," which conflicted with the Comintern's stubbornly optimistic assessment that revolution, despite a temporary setback, was still imminent in Germany.[15] Even though the once powerful German Communist Party had been outlawed in Berlin after the Reichstag fire, some of the Communist émigrés Reich encountered in Denmark naïvely thought that Hitler would last only six months and that they'd soon be back in Germany.

*The Mass Psychology of Fascism* was massacred in the Danish Communist newspaper, the *Arbeiterblad* (Workers' Newspaper), which declared it "counterrevolutionary." The same arguments that were made in Germany when Reich published *The Sexual Struggle of Youth*—that Reich was a petty bourgeois and a corruptor of Communist youth and that sexual neurosis was a bourgeois disease—were again voiced against him. The Communist Party, it seemed, had lost patience with Reich's brand of sexual politics.

Unlike the German Communist Party, which had been a leading force and was now crushed, its Danish counterpart had only won its first two parliamentary seats in 1932 (representing about 1 percent of the vote), despite 40 percent of industrial workers being unemployed. The Social Democrats, about whom even the staunch Communist Bertolt Brecht had good things to say, remained the unchallenged champions of the working class. Nevertheless, the small party bureaucracy in Denmark had the power to expel Reich from the Comintern. After Reich's committed service to the party, it was, improbably enough, this small group of Danes who finally orchestrated his exit.

Reich's relations with the Danish branch of the party were already strained because an article he had written in 1927 had been translated and published in a Danish Communist journal, *Plan*, just before he arrived in Copenhagen. The article, entitled "Where Will the Trend Toward Nudity in Education Lead?"—which argued the benefits of a sexually permissive upbringing—had landed *Plan*'s editor in jail for forty days on pornography charges. Reich published a letter in which he claimed there was no question of pornography, but he accused the editor of choosing a poor and offensive translation of the word "penis" (*wipfi* is a diminutive for "penis"), and the Danish party hierarchy interpreted his excuses as a cowardly betrayal.

The *Arbeiterblad* announced his exclusion in a formal statement from the party secretariat, published on November 21, 1933:

### COMMUNIST PARTY
### SECRETARIAT OF THE CENTRAL COMMITTEE

Exclusion from the Communist Party of Denmark
In agreement with the Central Committee of the Communist Party of Germany, we announce that Dr. Wilhelm Reich has been excluded from the Danish Communist Party. The reasons for this include: his un-Communist and anti-party behavior in a succession of cases; his publication of a counterrevolutionary book; his establishment of a publishing house without party sanction, and additionally, his statement, published by the Danish government press, wherein he renounces his own article published in *Plan*, thus facilitating official and police action against the editor of said *Plan*.[16]

Reich would later maintain that he couldn't really be expelled from the Danish party, since he'd never joined it, nor from the German party, since it had ceased to exist. Nevertheless, he was officially exiled from the political organization that he had always considered a "second home," the membership of which had strained his relationship with Freud and psychoanalysis to the breaking point. Reich still considered himself a Communist: "Against my better judgment," he wrote four years later, "I . . . clung fast to the organization to which I'd belonged and for which I had fought."[17]

Two years after it was disowned by the Communists, *The Mass*

*Psychology of Fascism* was banned and then burned by the Nazis, along with Reich's other works. This particular book, however, developed a secret afterlife. Contraband copies were smuggled into Germany by the antifascist underground, disguised to look like prayer books. It was to become Reich's most influential political work and the book on which his later intellectual reputation would principally be based, it became required reading for postwar intellectuals trying to understand the Holocaust and by the 1960s it would become a seminal text for anti-authoritarian groups in both Europe and the United States.

As it happened, Reich's expulsion from the Communist Party was only one of many problems he encountered in Denmark; his problems began almost as soon as his ship docked there. One of Reich's first patients was a teenage girl who was referred to him and whom he agreed to see for a trial period of therapy in order to make a diagnosis (his verdict: "hysteric character with a strong schizophrenic element"). Six weeks into treatment, she tried—not for the first time—to kill herself.

The psychiatrists at the hospital where she was admitted declared that her suicide attempt was "the result of treatment" under Reich, whom she'd been seeing three times a week; and since Reich was practicing medicine without a permit, in violation of the terms of his visa, they turned the case over to the police, who referred it to the Ministry of Justice.[18]

A Danish newspaper took up the story, connecting Reich to the earlier *Plan* pornography affair, and called for his six-month visa not to be extended so as "to prevent one of these German so-called sexologists from fooling around with our young men and women and converting them to this perverse pseudo-science."[19] In a country still unfamiliar with Freud, let alone the offshoots of his thought, Reich was reviled by conservatives "as a charlatan; a demagogue who had seduced the young to live in sin."[20] To them, Ellen Siersted wrote, "it seemed as if the devil had come into a gathering of angels."[21]

One of Reich's Danish followers, J. H. Leunbach, had run for office twice on the Communist ticket, and Reich tried without success to get him elected to the Danish parliament on his sex-political platform. Leunbach was one of the people who had encouraged Reich to move to Denmark. He'd met Reich in his role as the cofounder (with Magnus Hirschfeld) of the World League for Sexual Reform. The son of a priest, six years earlier Leunbach had founded a controversial free birth control clinic in Copenhagen, where he fitted diaphragms and performed illegal abortions by prescribing a uterine paste of his own invention that caused instant miscarriage. (The use of "Leunbach's paste" became a common but dangerous abortion practice. A German medical journal reported in 1932 that there had been twenty-five deaths through use of this method, and it was banned in America by the Food and Drug Administration in the early 1940s).[22]

The clinic had brought Leunbach into frequent conflict not only with his medical colleagues, who considered him a crank, but also with the law. (In 1936 Leunbach and another Reichian, Dr. Tage Philipson, were imprisoned for three months for performing illegal abortions at Leunbach's clinic and were suspended from practicing medicine for five and three years, respectively.) Having been refused a permit for his proposed Sex-Pol office, Reich encouraged his followers to volunteer in Leunbach's clinic, where eugenics was associated with abortion, free love, and communism. Reich's shared ideals and close association with Leunbach brought him under suspicion for being a similarly dangerous agitator for sex reform.[23]

In the fall of 1933, the newly formed Danish-Norwegian Psycho-analytical Society called a meeting at Borops High School near the Christiansborg Palace, which housed the Danish parliament. The aim was to campaign for Reich's visa to be renewed by the Ministry of Justice, which was investigating his case. Reich's reputation was such that seven hundred people showed up to the meeting; the auditorium overflowed, and people had to peer in through windows and crowd around the doorways to get a glimpse of the polarizing psychoanalyst. "I have had to promise not to talk politics," Reich told his audience, "but it is difficult because science isn't floating freely in the room but is standing with both of its legs in society. It is a fact that books are burned and scientists have been fired—this is big politics."[24]

"Reich didn't speak to the young to seduce them," wrote Siersted, "but to shed some light on their problems and to explain to them about society's attitude to these problems . . . He stood on the main floor of the hall, closely facing his listeners, and he spoke with them warmly and seriously about what was on his mind . . . Reich was not a tall man but he was agile and thin, with dark hair and strands of gray over his large, dark eyes. He seemed to be an extremely alive human being."[25]

A Danish reporter, evincing more than a hint of anti-Semitism, described Reich as looking like an undignified tailor's assistant. When he spoke, delivering his message about sexual liberation, Reich's evident charisma was frightening. The journalist referred to Reich as a "magician" and, as if he had made a pact with the devil, portrayed him as a "Mephistopheles with a warm heart and a streak of melancholy":

> He is a phenomenon, The moment he starts to speak, not at the lectern, but walking around it on cat's paws, he is simply enchanting. In the Middle Ages, this man would have been sent into exile. He is not only eloquent, he also keeps his listeners nailed to their seats, spellbound by his startling personality, reflected in his small, dark eyes. In a way, it must be said that he is a "dangerous" man, who with both hands plucks the fruits from the "tree of knowledge."[26]

Playing up his martyrdom, Reich concluded his talk by saying that if deported he would hire a boat and continue to teach his brand of psychoanalysis in neutral waters beyond Denmark's three-mile nautical limit (as if he were Jesus on the Sea of Galilee, preaching to the crowds onshore). Reich was so persuasive—or, as the journalist portrayed him, such a dangerous Svengali—that only two people voted against his being granted the right to stay.

Reich's supporters approached Freud yet again, requesting that he write an appeal objecting to Reich's expulsion, but Freud refused, saying that although he acknowledged Reich's stature as an analyst, Reich's politics tainted his scientific work. Ernest Jones, then president of the International Psychoanalytic Association (IPA), wrote a private letter to the Danish government distancing psychoanalysis from Reich's activities there. When Reich's visa expired it was not renewed.

Unaware of Jones's intervention, Reich traveled to London that winter, hoping he might emigrate to Britain, and met with Jones to discuss this possibility (Reich also met Bronislaw Malinowski for the first time during that trip). Jones carefully vetted every analyst who wanted to settle in England and allowed in only the ones he felt most suitable, since he felt the country was almost saturated with therapists. Jones wrote to Anna Freud that he found Reich's Communist writings "obscure and tedious" but that during the "hectic hour" he'd spent interviewing him, Reich had made a "more favorable impression" than Jones had been led to expect from Anna Freud's recent account of Reich. However, Jones felt that "this impression would not go on indefinitely improving at still closer quarters."[27] Reich's recollection of the encounter was that "Jones was cordial as usual, but always the gentleman—in other words, no involvement at any cost."[28]

Jones spent a further four hours questioning Reich with a panel of five other British analysts, including Melanie Klein, Joan Riviere, and James Strachey; Reich concluded that they were an "odd" bunch. Even though Reich had been banned from the Communist Party, his support of Marxist principles still placed his loyal Freudianism in jeopardy. "Our judgment about the problems was pretty unanimous," Jones reported to Anna Freud of this second meeting.

> Reich's communism is not so much economic; it is essentially the belief that communism would give more chance of Sexualreform, which is the central idea of his life. He has taken some of your father's early teachings very literally and pursued them with a certain consistency . . . It all sounds very plausible but the trouble with Reich altogether is that, with all his cleverness, he is really rather naïve and simpleminded. At the same time he appears to be thoroughly honest and very much in earnest.[29]

Under the influence of Anna Freud and her father, Ernest Jones and his colleagues declared Reich to be "insufficiently analyzed," implying that, among other things, he had a neurotic and unresolved hostility to Freud, and they accused him of misrepresenting psychoanalysis with his version of it. They advised him to try to emigrate to Russia or America instead, as if these places were politically equal. Jones further undermined Reich by saying that the IPA would not recognize anyone trained by him, which they hoped would divest him of his Danish students. Reich warned them that this action would cause a split in the IPA and that he would head a rival and substantial "opposition movement" of Marxist-oriented analysts that would include, he said to Jones's evident surprise, Fenichel.

"I have quite a long Reich experience behind me and I could get along with him longer than the others," Anna Freud wrote to Jones in January 1934, approving of Jones's actions,

> because I tried to treat him well instead of offending him. It helps a little way and would help more if he were a sane person which he is not . . . There is a wall somewhere where he stops to understand the other person's point of view and flies off into a world of his own . . . I always thought that he is honest as far as he himself knows, which most of the others do not believe of him. But, of course, he is not consistent of logic in his actions. Which one could expect if he were honest and sane. I think he had quite a deep understanding of psycho-analysis and is taking it in places now where it does not go together with his much less complicated beliefs. He is an unhappy person . . . and I am afraid this will end in sickness. But since he is in our world still, I am sure the way you dealt with him [in London] is the best possible way.[30]

And there it was: Reich's sanity itself was officially the subject of the Freud family's judgment. Anna Freud's prophecy that "this will end in sickness" might be seen as self-fulfilling: the verdict in this case was not so much a diagnosis as an executive decision made in order to protect psychoanalysis from what its guardians considered to be perversions of its natural course—and yet this view of Reich would crystallize among his peers into an established truth.

Reich returned to the Continent; he risked traveling through Germany on his way back to Denmark, and had a three-hour stopover in Berlin: "The scene on the streets was distressing," he wrote. "There were soldiers everywhere; people looked depressed; their movements were lethargic; there was nervous loitering."[31] Reich recognized a former comrade but avoided greeting him because he knew that many Communists had converted to Nazism; he'd heard

that since he'd left, whole divisions of the outlawed Communist Ar-
beiterwehr (Workers' Defense) had joined the Nazi storm troopers.

In the restaurant at the train station Reich was reunited with one
of his lovers, the avant-garde dancer and choreographer Elsa Lindenberg. Lindenberg was blond, Aryan, and nine years younger
than Reich, who had first met her at a May Day parade in 1932—he
called her his "Somali girl" and said that she turned heads wherever
she went. "I got to know Willie Reich when I used to walk around
Berlin at night with a pot of glue and anti-Hitler posters," Elsa Lindenberg recounted in an interview for German television in the late
1980s. "Willie told me he'd been excommunicated from the party,"
Elsa recalled. When asked what he would do next, he replied por-
tentously, "I will continue!"[32]

For Lindenberg, the Dionysian aesthetic of modern dance was
intimately linked to sexual freedom. In 1919, the year Reich met
Freud, Lindenberg won a scholarship to attend the "gifted class" of
the Helene Lange school in Berlin.[33] She went on to complete her
diploma at the Laban School, run by Herta Feist, a *Frei Körper Kultur*
("free body culture," the German nudist movement) enthusiast, famous for her choreography of naked performances and her belief in
the therapeutic powers of nude dance. From 1927 to 1933, Lindenberg danced at the Municipal Opera House in Berlin, where one of
the founders of modern dance, Rudolf von Laban, was director of
ballet.

In *Empire of Ecstasy: Nudity and Movement in German Body Culture,
1910–1935*, the historian of dance Karl Toepfer writes of the radical, frenzied, "expressive" style Laban practiced: "German dance
equated the liberated body not with an enhanced power to signify a
wide range of emotions but with the power to signify and/or experience a single, great, supreme emotion: ecstasy."[34] Ecstasy—as depicted, for instance, in the 1933 movie of that title, which shows a
close-up of Hedy Lamarr in the throes of the first (simulated) female
orgasm ever filmed—was thought by many body culture enthusiasts
to return the alienated, mechanized modern subject back into harmony with the body, nature, and the unconscious rhythm of life.

Though Annie Reich tolerated Reich's affairs, the seriousness of
his relationship to Lindenberg had been an important factor in the

breakup of their marriage. Annie Reich wrote to Lindenberg, "Your happiness will be built on my tears."[35] Eva Reich, who was impressed with Lindenberg from the moment she saw her in the Berlin Opera's production of *Petroushka*, has said that Lindenberg was certainly the love of Reich's life—she had memories "of Reich being tender to Elsa in a way [she] rarely remembered his being with her mother."[36]

A well-known Communist, Lindenberg, accused of "activity harmful to the state," had been fired from the Municipal Opera along with its Jewish dancers after the Nazis seized power in 1933.[37] A warrant had been issued for her arrest and her apartment had been searched, as Reich's had been a year earlier, and she also had to flee the city.

Unable to settle in Denmark because Reich's visa had expired, Reich and Lindenberg moved to Malmö on the southernmost tip of Sweden. Reich described it as "one of those little towns in which boredom breeds fascism . . . At least," he added, "it was better than a concentration camp."[38] His loyal Danish students would make the three-hour trip by sea from Copenhagen to visit him; trainees and analysands used to wave at each other as their ferries passed in the Øresund. Lindenberg, who was able to work in Copenhagen during the week, where she became one of the earliest exponents of modern German dance in Scandinavia, would accompany them back and forth, leaving Reich for four days at a time in what he complained was "dull asylum."[39]

Reich continued to be hounded by the authorities in Malmö; as unfamiliar with the techniques of psychoanalysis as their Danish counterparts, they suspected from the hourly visits to his hotel room that he was running some kind of brothel. Since Reich and Lindenberg were unmarried, he was suspected of being her pimp. Reich's rooms were kept under surveillance by the police from an office on the opposite side of the street; his pupils were sometimes arrested by the detective stationed at his door and taken to the chief of police for interrogation; and in April 1934 Reich's apartment was raided and searched when he was in the middle of a psychoanalytic session with Tage Philipson (the man later imprisoned with Leunbach in Denmark).

When the Swedish government also refused to extend Reich's

visa, Malinowski wrote a letter of appeal. Reich's supporters once again petitioned Freud. Freud wrote back a single exasperated line: "I am unable to voice support of your protest in the matter of Dr. Wilhelm Reich."[40]

In 1931, the more radical analysts in Berlin, all declared Marxists, formed a clandestine circle that splintered off from the "children's seminar." This rebel group arranged an emergency summit in Norway scheduled for April 1934 so that they could discuss the position they would adopt at the upcoming psychoanalytic congress in Lucerne, Switzerland. The dissidents all believed that the political defeatism of Freud and the more orthodox analysts was allowing their science to become totally compromised and crushed by the Nazis. By the time of the Lucerne congress four months later, twenty-four of the thirty-six members of the German Psychoanalytic Society had been forced to flee their country. The "radical scientific wing" knew, Reich wrote, that "psychoanalysis, as a movement, was not withstanding the test of time."[41]

The opposition caucus took place in Oslo, where Fenichel had lived and practiced since leaving Berlin the year before. Reich and Fenichel fought over tactics and the leadership of the group. The two friends were very different: Reich was romantic, explosive, uncompromising, innovative, aggressive; Fenichel, though no less politically engaged, was discreet, dispassionate, savvy, and careful. Reich scattered ideas like sparks, many of them erratic, whereas Fenichel, a compulsive list maker, had a consolidating, organizational, encyclopedic mind. Reich tried to co-opt the group as a revolutionary alternative to the International Psychoanalytic Association and wanted to form an activist psychoanalytic splinter group based around his own scientific program. He proposed a series of conditions that all opposition analysts should fulfill, such as having an "orderly sex-economy"—meaning that they should be orgastically potent, presumably something that only he could judge.[42] The less confrontational Fenichel preferred to maintain a secret, sort of double-agent role within the organization, aiming to manipulate from the inside.

After the meeting Fenichel began circulating *Rundbriefe*—newsletters—to each member, as Freud had done to the "paladins" who formed his inner circle. Fenichel typed the *Rundbriefe* on onionskin paper and sent carbon copies to the half-dozen or so Marx-ist analysts: Annie and Wilhelm Reich, Edith Jacobson, Erich Fromm, George Gerö, Nic Waal, Edith Gyömröi, and Henry Lowenfeld. "We are all convinced," Fenichel wrote in his inaugural missive, "that we recognize the germ of the dialectical-materialist psychology of the future, and therefore we desperately need to protect and ex-tend this knowledge."[43]

In his *Rundbriefe* Fenichel compiled news and gossip from his many psychoanalyst correspondents and added his voluminous edi-torial and theoretical comments. He typed a total of 119 letters, one every three to six weeks, each one between ten and eighty pages long, single-spaced—three thousand pages in all—and kept up the secret correspondence over eleven and a half years, until July 14, 1945, the year before his death. Though Reich was by now the more charismatic of the two, these letters made Fenichel the de facto leader of the group; he provided the ink that linked them.

Few copies of the *Rundbriefe* still exist, because Fenichel asked the recipients to destroy them: "One should not forget how un-pleasant it would be if these *Rundbriefe* fell into the wrong hands!" Fenichel wrote. "For that reason I have asked that they be burnt after reading. Whoever does not want to do that, has to at least han-dle them so carefully that no one uninvited can see them."[44] When Reich asked Fenichel if he could publish one of his own letters to the group in his newly founded *Journal of Political Psychology and Sex Economy* (the first issue was almost entirely written by Reich), he was told that it would compromise the secret nature of the opposi-tion. Reich would have preferred the battle to have been fought in the open. "When one sees all this narrow-mindedness around him," he responded to Fenichel, "one has a desire to let loose."[45]

"These letters were very hush-hush," Lore Reich told me. An-nie Reich, who died in 1971, did not burn hers, and Lore Reich now possesses an almost complete set. "Many years later as she lay dy-ing, a fellow recipient went into her closet and stole them because he was mentioned in them and didn't want his identity revealed . . . The thief, however, had a guilty conscience and confessed this to me and brought me the *Rundbriefe* in a shopping bag." Who was the thief? "Lowenfeld. Henry Lowenfeld. He was in Berlin . . . then he was in Prague and then he came to New York." He had stolen them because "they were all scared that their names would be known and they'd be kicked out of America for lying to the immigration people because they were all Communists. They were also worried about the psychoanalytic establishment knowing that they were part of this secret organization."

In 1997, at the centenary celebration of her father's birth, Lore Reich gave a lecture at the Goethe Institute in Boston, Massachusetts. "Reich was not a saint," she said to the assembled crowd of family and admirers. "He was a very difficult man, but I am not going to stress that on the occasion of this birthday celebration."[46] What followed was an passionate defense of her father and a damning criticism of Freud and the psychoanalytic establishment of the time, who, as she showed with new evidence gleaned from the *Rundbriefe*, cynically colluded against Reich.

The official story of Reich's break with analysis is that he voluntarily left the group in 1934 because of irreconcilable differences with Freud. "Reich's politics led to both personal and scientific estrangement," Jones wrote in the third volume of his biography of Freud, published the year of Reich's death, and so "Reich resigned from the International Psychoanalytic Association."[47] Nothing could have been further from the truth—as, Lore shows, Jones well knew. Lore Reich also attacked her mother's analyst, Anna Freud, whom she describes as a "conniving megalomaniac" and believes to be personally responsible for the disintegration of her family.

After her parents separated for good, Lore Reich and her sister left the Communist collective in Berlin and attended a Freudian school in Vienna, where they lived with Annie Reich's parents. "Anna Freud ran this collective for children," Lore Reich told me. "Rich Americans and people who wanted their children to be analyzed needed to have a place to stay, so she organized group homes for those kinds of children . . . all in analysis. At most there were ten kids. Physically we were very well taken care of. I mean, I didn't like the food, but it was nothing like the Communists'."

While Annie Reich continued her analysis with Anna Freud, the Reich children were analyzed by Berta Bornstein, Anna Freud's student and Otto Fenichel's onetime lover—she of the erotic boat ride at Grundlsee. Peter Heller, another of Anna Freud's child analysands at the collective, recalled that Bornstein "was a somewhat shapeless person with a noble Jewish profile" who used analysis like a blunt sword: "The professional cheeriness and a soft and gentle Polish accent with which she pronounced her psychoanalytic comments on everything and everyone somehow reinforced the certainty of her severe judgments."[48]

The collective had come about when Dorothy Burlingham, daughter of the jeweler Charles Tiffany and heir to his fortune, came to Vienna in 1925 to have her four children analyzed by Anna Freud. Burlingham moved into an apartment above Anna and Sigmund Freud's. She had a direct phone line to Anna Freud's bedroom so that she could discuss her children's progress, and was analyzed by Sigmund Freud (she eventually also became a psychoanalyst herself). Her close collaboration and friendship with Anna Freud was cemented when they bought a country cottage at Hochrotherd in the country together. It has long been suspected that they were also lovers (Richard Sterba visited their country cottage and reported that they shared a bed). Anna Freud's unfulfilled maternal instincts drove her not only to be analyst to Burlingham's children but a surrogate parent: "I think sometimes that I want not only to make them healthy but also at the same time to have them ... for myself," Anna Freud wrote to her father.[49]

There was a catch, however: Dorothy Burlingham was married. Robert Burlingham was a surgeon who suffered from manic depression, for which he had been hospitalized several times. He was devastated at being separated from his family and visited Vienna repeatedly in order to try to win them back. Both Freuds conspired to keep him away from his children and advised Dorothy to cease all contact with him. Anna wrote to Robert Burlingham that his visits from America were upsetting his children, and she tried to convince the children that seeing him was bad for them. When Robert Burlingham visited Sigmund Freud to appeal for his family's return, Freud told him that he was helping Dorothy overcome her sexual needs for her husband.

Lore Reich believes that Anna Freud and Berta Bornstein colluded similarly against her own father. "Anna Freud was supposedly saving the Burlingham children from this crazy father," she said, "when actually she was trying to keep the mother for her own lesbian—I think it was a sexual relationship, but this is not proven—needs. She wanted the mother and she wanted the children. She wanted to protect them, and I think that technique influenced Berta Bornstein. Bornstein had Eva in analysis for years, and the analysis consisted, very much, as I think Anna Freud's analysis of the Burlingham children did, of convincing Eva that her father was crazy. That's what the analysis was about. Hammer, hammer, hammer, hammer. I remember when my sister was around twenty, we—my mother, Berta Bornstein, my sister, and I—were climbing a mountain. Berta Bornstein was carrying on, 'Now you see that he's crazy. Can't you see?' My sister finally spat at her, she was so angry."[50]

Annie Reich, in the throes of her own analysis with Anna Freud, went along with this. "My mother was also determined that we should know he was crazy and have nothing to do with him. She was very concerned, and maybe correctly, that he would take us over and twist our heads." Eva Reich felt she was being "brainwashed," as she later put it to Myron Sharaf, into believing her father was "seductive and sick."[51]

Lore Reich later discovered that Bornstein had written a letter to Reich demanding that he cease all contact with them. "In this letter she told him to stay away from his children, and not to write or phone, because it was interfering with Eva's analysis . . . This is exactly what they did with the Burlingham guy, told him that he was interfering with the children's analysis. And Reich was manic-depressive, not diagnosed, but Richard Burlingham was diagnosed manic-depressive [Burlingham killed himself in 1938]. I guess I didn't see my father from 1936 to '39, I didn't see him at all, and he wasn't writing or anything. My father was an analyst, and he believed in analysis, and he thought my sister needed it, so he was being naïve and stupid, being pushed around by these manipulative women." She herself had absolutely no idea at the time why her father had disappeared from their lives. She has written, "This had a very deleterious effect on me."

In 1936, Anna Freud published what was to become her most famous work, *The Ego and the Mechanisms of Defense*, a book that, according to Richard Sterba, was highly influenced by *Character Analysis*. Nevertheless, it included several veiled gibes at Reich, whom she mocked for assuming that the drives were intrinsically good, and that sadism and destructiveness were the result of sexual frustration. Reich wanted to change the world. Anna Freud's version of analysis aimed to adapt the patient to reality, by which she meant the status quo, as the status of reality was never in question.

Anna Freud's orthodox, authoritarian version of analysis "had an infantilizing and often debilitating influence," Peter Heller concluded, "instead of promoting the liberation of man which seemed to be inherent in the potential of psychoanalysis" (Heller cites Reich as an example of this other, more permissive form of analysis).[52] Heller married one of the Burlingham children and his sister-in-law, Mabbie Burlingham, was one of the victims of Anna Freudianism, as he perceived it. In the summer of 1974 she made the pilgrimage to the Freud house in London (where the Freuds emigrated in 1938), "to the center of the cult at Maresfield Gardens, to take her life . . . with pills collected for this purpose over a long period of time."[53]

"In her quiet fashion," wrote Heller, "and accompanied by the clicking of knitting needles, Anna Freud spun, in all innocence, the spider web of the older generation in which later so many of us, beneficiaries and victims, got caught." It was a web in which the Reich children, in Lore Reich's view, were also trapped.[54]

Eva and Lore Reich visited their father in Denmark for the first time since their parents' separation in the summer of 1934. Reich had returned to the country illegally under the pseudonym Peter Stein, and Ellen Siersted had rented him a waterfront house next to her own in the fishing village of Sletten, on the coast just north of Copenhagen. Reich was accompanied by Elsa Lindenberg, whose mother and younger sister were also staying there, and Fenichel visited from Norway. "It was light, fun, jolly," Eva remembered many years later. "There were trips, eating out, people dancing, people coming and going . . . It was alive."[55]

In August 1934, Reich, Lindenberg, and his two daughters traveled to the International Psychoanalytic Congress in Lucerne, taking a boat to Belgium so as to circumvent Germany. At Lucerne the girls were reunited with their mother, who was also attending the congress. Eduard Bibring, Reich's friend from the University of Vienna, who had married Grete Lehner and also become an analyst, took a series of informal photographs of the assembled psychoanalysts chatting between sessions.[56] The photographs offer an intriguing glimpse into the private dynamics of the group. Reich, looking lean in a sharply creased flannel suit, his hair swept back, seems by far the most compelling member. In every photo he is shown locked in conversation; in one picture he's talking to Grete Lehner with an expression of excited engagement—one hand in his pocket, the other cradling a cigarette. Lehner, who had taken over the position of associate director of the Ambulatorium when Reich left for Berlin, looks back at him goggle-eyed as Rudolph Loewenstein and Erwin Stengel listen in. Reich had good reason to be agitated: it was at Lucerne that his brewing conflict with orthodox analysis came to a dramatic head.

"We see once more that Politics and Science do not mix any better than oil and water," Jones said in his August 26 opening address, and it was obvious to everyone that he was referring to Reich. "It follows that whoever yields to such impulses becomes by so much the less a psychoanalyst. And to attempt to propagate his particular social ideas in the name of psychoanalysis is to pervert its true nature, a misuse of psychoanalysis which I wish firmly to renounce and repudiate."[57]

On August 1, Reich had received a letter from Carl Müller-Braunschweig, the secretary of the Berlin Psychoanalytic Society, warning him that because of the political situation his name would be excluded from the list of German members (Müller-Braunschweig had actually taken this precaution a year earlier) but that this was just a formality—he could register as a member of one of the Scandinavian groups that were lobbying for membership of the IPA at the congress. However, Jones forbade the Scandinavian contingent from granting Reich membership as a condition of joining; Freud didn't want to expel the troublemaker only to have him rejoin through the back door.

Reich was summoned for a hearing before the executive committee of the IPA, a meeting that Fenichel was invited to witness. Anna Freud, the vice president and her ill father's gatekeeper, accused Reich of trying to fuse politics with psychoanalysis and of subordinating Freud's ideas to his own revolutionary "Bolshevik" message; the senior psychoanalysts objected to his communism, just as the Communists did to his psychoanalysis. Reich was to be expelled, she told him, for founding a journal and a movement to assert these radical ideas. Jones—who now labeled Reich the troublemaking "madman" of the profession—wanted him to resign from the IPA of his own free will, or take a period of sick leave.

Reich refused to accept his exclusion and told the committee that he viewed himself "as the legitimate representative of natural-scientific psychoanalytic thought."[58] He accused them of political backsliding and of accommodating fascism (he always maintained that it was his publication of *The Mass Psychology of Fascism*, which Reich was forbidden from promoting at the conference, that had resulted in his expulsion). Since it was obvious that the IPA had already secretly and undemocratically excluded him, Reich finally capitulated and said that he'd continue alone with the libido theory under the banner of the science of "sex-economy."

Fenichel, who had lost his editorship of the IPA's flagship journal when he supported Reich against Freud over Reich's essay on masochism two years earlier, did not come to Reich's defense on this occasion, choosing to remain silent. Reich accused him of putting his personal ambition ahead of his political beliefs; he would never forgive what he regarded as a great betrayal. The executive committee had successfully exploited Fenichel's split loyalties in order to isolate Reich (Fenichel was not only the joint head of the self-styled psychoanalytic opposition but the new secretary of the Norwegian-Danish would-be affiliate to the IPA). Fenichel replied in his next *Rundbrief* that revolutions began from within: "The most important thing that I can do now for the psychoanalytic movement is not to get myself thrown out."[59]

Anna Freud was right in thinking, as she predicted in a letter to Jones written on New Year's Day, 1934, that splitting Reich off from his colleagues would render the group harmless, separating, as she said, the match from the gunpowder.[60] The left-wing analysts conspicuously failed to emerge from the shadows of the *Rundbriefe* at the congress to rally around Reich and the Marxist line. None of the rebel group referenced Reich's work in the papers they delivered at the congress, even though Reich thought acknowledgment was due. Ellen Siersted witnessed Reich's student, the Hungarian analyst George Gerö—who had followed Reich to Denmark and whom Siersted had married so that he could stay in the country—burst into tears when Sandor Rado and Annie Reich told him that he had to choose between Reich and the IPA (Gerö initially chose the former, but a few years later he changed his mind, claiming that Reich had gone off "on a tangent").[61]

At the congress, Reich wrote, he felt "completely alone." Lore Reich remembered that her father "went ballistic," though she had no idea at the time why this was. "It just seemed he suddenly blew his stack," she recalled. "He was totally enraged and fought with my mother. I am sure he fought with all kinds of other people [at the conference Reich asked the analyst Heinz Hartmann if he thought he should punch Jones]. He was really very upset . . . Then analysts started stressing that Reich was 'crazy,' and that was the real reason he was kicked out."

If some of his peers thought that he was crazy before, Reich's behavior at Lucerne cemented his reputation as a wild man. He camped in a tent outside the conference center and was said to carry a large knife in his belt, which reminded one analyst of an Arab sheik, and to have cavorted with Elsa Lindenberg in front of the other analysts, who took the opportunity to falsely insinuate that she was a prostitute (Reich divorced Annie later that year). Paul Federn, who had lobbied to exclude Reich from the executive committee since the late twenties, now went so far as to label him a psychopath who slept with all his female patients. "Either Reich goes or I go," he said.[62] Rado, who in 1930 had described Reich as suffering from a "mild paranoid tendency," now claimed to have observed signs of an "insidious psychotic process" at that time, and Federn also later maintained he had detected "incipient schizophrenia" during his analysis of Reich.[63]

In a book written in the 1960s, Rado declared that he'd summoned Annie Reich to Berlin from Vienna in the spring of 1931 and broken the news about her husband's mental state: "I have very bad news. This man is schizophrenic," he claimed to have said. "And not a schizophrenic in the coffeehouse sense. He is schizophrenic in the most serious way."[64] Annie Reich was "knocked out" by this news, Rado recalled:

> Nobody had ever suspected any such thing, and he [Reich] was at the height of his medical reputation. People were already uneasy about his involvement in political matters, but his scientific contributions and his clinical gifts were widely acknowledged . . . Annie Reich was unprepared for a statement like mine. She said, "Thank you very much for telling me this." She went home to Vienna and instituted divorce proceedings and, in no time, was divorced from him. That was the only decision she could make. As much as it was possible, I gave her a few examples of my diagnosis. I said to her, "I would not make a statement like this without weighty reasons and here they are."[65]

In this account of the meeting, however, Rado omitted the supporting evidence for his diagnosis. Despite his claims to have "saved" Reich's family, whatever he did tell Annie Reich cannot have been as persuasive as Rado implied—Annie stayed in Berlin with her husband until Hitler's rise to power in 1933. Reich later claimed that Rado's attacks were motivated by jealousy, because of Rado's wife's obvious but unconsummated attraction to Reich.

Though now barred from administrative meetings and closed sessions at Lucerne, Reich was allowed to deliver his conference paper, "Psychic Contact and Vegetative Streamings." "Having been a member of the International Psychoanalytic Association for fourteen years, I am speaking to you for the first time as a guest of the congress," Reich began.[66]

Reich described his recent chance discovery of a "biopsychic energy." One of his Danish patients had exhibited an extremely stiff neck, which Reich interpreted as the bodily symptom of a severe repression: "After an energetic attack upon his resistance he suddenly gave in, but in a rather alarming manner. For three days, he presented severe manifestations of vegetative shock. The color of his face kept changing rapidly from white to yellow or blue; the skin was mottled and of various tints; he had severe pains in the head and occiput; the heartbeat was rapid, he had diarrhea, felt worn out and seemed to have lost hold."[67]

In managing to uncork the man, as it were, during analysis, Reich thought he had unleashed what he called the "vegetative currents" of sexual energy that the muscular block had frozen over. Reich thought that the patient, whose "armor" had been dissolved, could be trained to control the torrent of orgastic streamings he'd rediscovered within himself, to channel and release them in the sexual act rather than allow them to stagnate in neurotic symptoms; the genital character, Reich asserted, "did not suffer from any stasis of anxiety."[68]

The audience at the congress listened to Reich respectfully, though, to the ears of those who had not been following his recent work, all Reich's talk of "vegetative currents" must have sounded eccentric at best. They followed his lecture with what Reich interpreted as enthusiastic applause. It was a kind of farewell. "Attention was paid to me as never before," he wrote in his diary. "I had the feeling that the [IPA] had excluded the theory of sexuality which formed its very core . . . and now spoke as a guest in the homeland."[69] Reich found out later, as he noted in his diary, that "at least half of the audience had not understood me in the least."[70] No one dared add further insult to injury by publicly disagreeing with him. "Everyone had a bad conscience," Reich wrote in an account of his expulsion he filed in the Sigmund Freud Archives. "It was hateful and indecent."[71]

"I'm sure my father was a manic-depressive. Is there any doubt?" Lore Reich said. "For a while I thought he had syphilis. His ideas got more and more grandiose, his theories got bigger and bigger, and this is what they describe happening in syphilis. But Ilse Ollendorff [Reich's third wife] claims that they had a blood test when they got married and that he didn't have syphilis. Actually, schizophrenics and manic-depressives are very hard to tell apart when they get very psychotic. But I think he had these energetic happy periods, and then he got depressions. And rages. The man had horrible rages." Lore Reich compared Reich to his nemesis Hitler: "He would build up the way Hitler did. We'd listen to Hitler building up into his rages. It would start as a low rumble and it would get louder and louder and louder."

Reich wasn't the first to react badly to his rejection by Freud. Jung suffered a nervous breakdown following his excommunication, and Herbert Silberer and Victor Tausk killed themselves. The question is, was Reich's precarious sanity the cause or the result of his expulsion? "They accused him of being crazy before he was so crazy," Lore Reich asserts. "And they did it to so many people—they did it with Rado, they did it with Ferenczi, they did it with Abraham. They're dealing with crazy people all the time and the worst thing you could say about another analyst was that they're crazy. If they had handled him better . . . I don't think he would have been so angry and paranoid, so it was a kind of interaction. I don't think he was that crazy then—he became much more difficult later. He ended up really, well, psychotic, at the end. But he had some good ideas, and I think they were nuts not to listen to them."

Edith Jacobson, a member of the *Rundbriefe* group, believed that the psychoanalysts evicted him because he was a Communist and not because he was mentally unstable: it was only at Lucerne, she argued, and perhaps in part because of his expulsion, that "his paranoid ideas began to flare up."[72] Before the congress Jacobson had plenty of time to make a diagnosis; she traveled from Germany to Norway for the summit of opposition analysts, meeting up with Reich in Malmö en route, and they drove the two-and-a-half-day journey through the Nordic countryside together to Oslo. She didn't think he was crazy then.

"I liked Willie Reich quite a lot," she recounted later. "Although he began to develop the first signs of illness, we didn't recognize it. We denied it obstinately until it became so apparent that it couldn't be denied anymore, you know. He became so sick . . . Paranoid people are just always troublemakers. But he was not really paranoid at that time. He had friends. You know, we spent very many weekends with each other. We went to the seashore with each other. We had a good time with each other, and he was a very close friend of Fenichel . . . Fenichel didn't want to accept the fact that he . . . was a crazy man. It took a long time for the friends to really accept it and for his wife. She didn't want to accept it either."[73]

One of Reich's friends, the psychoanalyst and fellow Communist Edith Gyömröi, remembers a walk she took along one of Denmark's beaches accompanied by Reich and Fenichel:

> We met Reich and went to the beach, talking endlessly as we walked. Reich, who meant very much to me at the time, told us about the outline of the book he was then working on. It was the beginning of his orgone theory. Fenichel and I did not dare look at each other, and had cold shivers.
>
> Then Reich suddenly stopped, and said, "Children, if I were not so sure of what I am working on, it would appear to me as a schizophrenic fantasy." We didn't say anything. Not even on our journey back. It was for us a great loss and a great sorrow.[74]

## *Five*

In October 1934, Reich left for Norway with his "companion-wife," as he referred to Elsa Lindenberg. He had been invited to give a series of lectures on character analysis by Harald Schjelderup, a professor of psychology at the University of Oslo who had been in training with Reich in Denmark. The couple checked into "another of those horrible small hotels," in Reich's description, "which seem especially equipped to crush even the strongest spirit."[1]

He was now an exile of every possible kind—political, intellectual, and personal. He had been thrown out of Germany, Denmark, and Sweden; rejected by both the Communist Party and the International Psychoanalytic Association; and he was divorced and estranged from his family. Bertolt Brecht, who would become a friend of Reich's in Oslo, once suggested that the refugee's most laborious job was "continued hoping."[2] Reich certainly refused to be discouraged—he seemed to have an endless capacity for reinvention. He referred to himself as the eternal *Stehaufmännchen*, a toy man who always stands up and rights himself.[3]

While there Reich founded the Institute of Sex-Economic Bioresearch, another grandly named organization designed to promote his version of the libido theory. Reich threw himself with manic energy into a series of scientific experiments that he hoped would vindicate the ideas that had seen him excommunicated from Freud's circle. At Lucerne Reich had spoken of his Danish patient who had turned a range of chameleon hues when Reich broke thorough his repression, which suggested to Reich that there were currents of energy coursing around the body that were blocked in neurosis. He sought to measure these as if they were electrical, an objective that Gyömröi and Fenichel thought sounded crazy. Reich considered repression to be the "frozen state"; in contrast to everything he saw around him, he felt truly alive, burning with energy, ideas, and ambition, and this in itself led him to believe that he must be right. What others saw as a symptom of his veering off the tracks, Reich claimed as proof that he was about to make history.

There was, he believed, an uncorrupted Freudian logic to his investigations of sexual electricity. Reich had long been inspired by a theory Freud had held in the 1890s that the libido was electrical in nature or made up of some "chemical substance" (Ernest Jones would later note in his biography that Freud had dreamed of "transforming psychology into a biological or physiological discipline").[4] This idea came to be used as a metaphor in Freud's work but Reich took it literally, believing that something akin to electricity was expended in the sexual act. When he broke down his patients' repressions in therapy they apparently felt a "streaming of current, an itching, a surging, a feeling of soothing warmth or of 'sweetness' flowing around their body and in their genitals."[5] Reich hoped to quantify these pleasurable sensations in millivolts. He thought that during the friction of intercourse a charge built up in both parties— "The orgasm can be nothing other than an electrical discharge," he stated.[6]

Reich spent the equivalent of what he would have earned from three dozen analytic sessions on an oscillograph, a device designed to measure and record electrical charge, and began to try to quantify the libido, rigging up the nipples and genitalia of various volunteers with silver electrodes. "It is the beginning!" Reich wrote to Ellen Siersted in January 1935 with the news of his new purchase, "and within three years we will be able to state that Freud, long ago, had found how to measure the electrical power of sexuality!"[7]

The laboratory in which Reich's risqué experiments took place was makeshift: "I placed [the oscillograph] in the center of my small, fifteen-foot-square study amid a pile of books and manuscripts," Reich remembered.[8] His test subjects were joined to the machine by wires that ran to his bedroom. Reich would instruct them to masturbate, to suck each other's nipples, to scratch, kiss, tickle, pinch, and caress one another. They did almost everything but have sex, and they would have done that too had it not been for the difficult problem of where to attach the electrodes.

He published examples of the resulting oscillograph tracings in *The Bioelectric Investigation of Sexuality and Anxiety* (1937), distributed by his own German-language press, Sexpol Verlag (all his books after *The Impulsive Character* were self-published). He observed that fright—stimulated by screaming, bursting a balloon, or smashing a gong—produced a sudden negative charge. And he reported that by tickling a subject's sexual organs with a feather or cotton bud he could produce a gentle, wavelike oscillation on the machine, more so than when he applied the feather to other parts of the body. On one occasion, Reich reported, when his subject was at the height of orgasm, the oscillograph reading shot up from 40 millivolts to 120 millivolts before dropping back to zero. As a result of these jagged tracings, Reich began to think of the libido as a kind of tentacle into the world, expanding with pleasure and shriveling up in fear or anxiety. "Freud's concept of the libido as a measure of psychic energy is no longer merely a simile," he claimed.[9]

Several of his students and Norwegian friends served as test subjects for these bioelectric experiments: Reich was nothing if not persuasive. Willy Brandt, who later became German chancellor but was then living in Norway to escape Nazi persecution, was one of Reich's unlikely guinea pigs. Others included the catatonic inmates of the Dikemark Sykehus, a psychiatric hospital just outside Oslo; rumors spread that Reich was arranging couplings there between mental patients. The twenty-one-year-old Brandt was then the boyfriend of Reich's secretary, Gertrud Gaasland. (She married him so that he could stay in Norway, where he founded the International Bureau of Revolutionary Youth Organizations and wrote newspaper articles condemning the Nazis.) Gaasland introduced him to Reich's seminars, where he became convinced by Reich's account of the sexual origins of fascism. Lindenberg described Brandt as "very calm, with a clear, sharp mind. There was an inner restlessness there due to his political involvement but he kept it under control." She contrasted Brandt with Reich: "Wilhelm Reich was also feeling this inner restlessness but he made no attempt to control it. Yet, despite his restlessness, he looked rather calm."[10]

Reich, who had no previous experience of laboratory work, wrote to his estranged wife that in this regard he felt like an "untrained tourist . . . standing at the foot of Mount Everest."[11] He hired a physiologist from Berlin, Dr. H. Löwenbach, to help him with his experiments. Löwenbach expressed serious doubts about Reich's interpretations of the data they collected, but Reich chose to ignore his professional advice. "Löwenbach is a typical fart," he wrote in his diary, "one of those scientists who for decades examine the finest little fibrils on a leaf when they are supposed to find out what a tree looks like and how it thrives and grows. Along comes someone who describes the tree as a whole, and then they become exact— and belittle him."[12]

Another of Reich's helpers, Wilhelm Hoffmann, who had trained in physiology at the Kaiser Wilhelm Institute in Berlin, also became suspicious of Reich's thesis. He found that the catatonic patients he tested for Reich at the Dikemark Sykehus displayed similar readings to those of healthy patients (Reich expected them to be lower), and he found that the skin potential recorded on these patients' erogenous and nonerogenous zones was identical (Reich expected the erogenous zones to be more sensitive). Reich also rejected Hoffmann's criticisms, claiming that Löwenbach had poisoned Hoffmann "with lies."[13]

For Reich the oscillograph was a sort of lie detector test for orgastic potency. He claimed that his machine could distinguish between an orgasm and a "total orgasm," only the latter being properly accompanied by liberated energies, as recorded by the oscillograph, no matter what the subject said he or she felt. Scientific as these tracings may have appeared to be, the theory of total orgasm left a great deal to Reich's own subjective impressions; if the test results were negative, Reich would excuse them by saying that the subject was too repressed. He wrote to his ex-wife that he imagined laying wires all the way to Prague to connect her up to his oscillograph so that he could detect her "slightest flicker of pleasure and non-pleasure" and thereby be able to gauge her feelings toward him.[14] (She'd emigrated to Czechoslovakia with her children to escape the civil war that had erupted in Vienna in 1934.)

Liberated from psychoanalysis's strict code of professional conduct, Reich entirely repudiated the talking cure. He had verbally hammered away at the personality traits revealed to him in his patients' posture, expression, and tone of voice; influenced by Lindenberg's type of experimental dance, he began to attack the patients' taut "muscular armor" directly with deep breathing exercises and vigorous kneading of the patients' bodies.[15]

These therapeutic innovations developed in tandem with Reich's new electrical model of sexual functioning: "the cornerstones of life, namely currents and electrical charges, are disrupted in modern people, and this makes them neurotic," he explained to Lore.[16] A neurotic couldn't be electrically lit up by an orgasm, he argued, because his or her libidinous circuit boards were muddled. Believing that he'd found the physiological basis of psychological disorders, Reich hoped to rewire his patients at the cellular level. In a way it was his version of electric shock therapy, then the most popular psychiatric tool.

Freud, when he began treating hysterics, used to touch his patients, pressing their foreheads or stroking them over the eyes. Freud gave up these tactile tricks because he thought them seductive. They were also reminiscent of the theatrical flourishes used by the fashionable eighteenth-century healer Franz Anton Mesmer, who was considered by scientists to be a charlatan. (In *Mental Healers*, published in 1931, Stefan Zweig drew out the connections between Freud and Mesmer, showing how psychoanalysis was rooted in Mesmer's experiments.) Mesmer believed that the human nervous system was made up of a subtle, invisible fluid analogous to electricity but operating according to "hitherto unknown" laws, and that sickness was caused by the obstruction of the free flow of a "radiant fluid" in the body.[17] Mesmer thought this fluid was subject to the ebb and flow of planetary influence, much like ocean tides, and claimed he could restore a natural equilibrium in his patients with the powers of his own "animal magnetism." To transfer this healing current he would sit with a patient's legs squeezed between his knees, press her thumbs in his hands, stare intensely into her eyes, and stroke her limbs to manipulate what he called her "internal ether."

Reich, similarly, would attempt to redirect patients' "vegetative currents," encouraging his patients to hyperventilate by repeating the mantra "Breathe! Out—down—through." "Out" referred to the lungs, "down" to the stomach, and "through" to the genitals. Reich claimed that when patients breathed properly he could more easily locate dead or "frozen" spots in their bodies that were impervious to pleasure, and he would try to dissolve these blocks through therapy. Reich would forcefully massage a patient's forehead, slowly progressing down the body to the pelvis, loosening and unknotting his patient's repressions as he went (a stiff jaw, a tense chest, and finally a dead pelvis), until he or she broke down in uncontrollable convulsions.

To illustrate a muscular block to the free flow of energy that coursed around the healthy body, Reich drew a sketch of a worm that had been lassoed with a string around one of its segments; this prevented its natural, free serpentine movement and forced it to thrash about aimlessly (his descriptions of his new therapy were illustrated by numerous such cartoons). It was precisely these sorts of neurotic bodily chinks that he hoped to iron out so that the waves of "vegetative currents" of sexual energy could flow freely. For Reich, as for Mesmer, a healthy human was essentially an electrical machine in harmony with the energies of the cosmos.

On the whole, he reported, the patients were frightened at first by the released energy: "The loosening of the rigid muscular attitudes produced peculiar body sensations in the patients," Reich noticed of his new and rigorous technique, "involuntary trembling and twitching of the muscles, sensations of cold and hot, itching, the feeling of pins and needles, prickling sensations, the feeling of having the jitters, and somatic perceptions of anxiety, [and] anger."[18] The ultimate aim of therapy was to teach the patient to control these forces, so that they could rush through the open sluice gates of the body in an avalanche of pleasure and be channeled out through the genitals in what Reich called the "orgasm reflex."

"This was experienced all over and especially in the genitals as a nice and living current," wrote Ellen Siersted, who made the long journey from Copenhagen every month to continue her therapy in Oslo, "which was not always of a sexual nature but a sensation of life and carnality." That being said, Siersted added, "The real goal in all of Reich's treatments was that the patient should reach a full orgasm."[19]

Reich was sure that his new method was "bound to become a fad," as character analysis had, and he sought to establish training requirements to safeguard it from distortions, imagining it as a new school of therapy. He originally planned to call his technique "orgasmotherapy," but fearing this would be misleading he called it "character-analytic vegetotherapy" instead. Whereas in Reich's laboratory experiments subjects were encouraged to masturbate, his therapy was entirely different. He did aim to improve orgastic potency, but this was done through massage of other parts of the body, in the hope that such treatment would free muscular blocks. The distinction was important to Reichians—though of course to their critics the line seemed extremely fine—because actual "masturbation therapy" was at the time a competing school of thought.

One of the first practitioners of psychoanalysis in Norway, Johannes Irgens Strømme, had been a staunch advocate of masturbation therapy. In 1932, Strømme had appeared in court after the husband of one of his patients accused him of charging an "immoral treatment fee," and it was alleged that Strømme's seductive form of therapy had wrecked their marriage.[20] The controversy surrounding Strømme's practice had contributed to the bad name and slow acceptance of psychoanalysis in Norway.

The Scottish educator A. S. Neill, the founder of the progressive school Summerhill, was one of vegetotherapy's first willing victims (it was an arduous practice). His account of therapy with Reich paints a colorful picture of the new technique. Neill met Reich in Norway in 1936, when he was invited to lecture at Oslo University.

After Neill's talk the chair told him, "You had a distinguished man in your audience tonight—Wilhelm Reich."[21] Coincidentally, Neill had been reading *The Mass Psychology of Fascism* on the boat over; he thought Reich's work "moral dynamite" and invited him to dinner. The pair drank and talked into the night: "Reich," Neill recalled declaring to the man fifteen years his junior, "you are the man for whom I have been searching for years, the man to link the soma with the psyche. Can I come and study under you?"[22] Neill returned to Oslo the following year and managed to fit in a dozen analytic sessions with Reich during his two-week stay.

For the next two years Neill spent every school holiday on Reich's couch in Norway. Reich would get his patients to undress to their underwear. They lay on their backs on his couch breathing deeply and with their legs in the air, a position he thought heightened the flow of emotion, as he poked and manipulated their bodies. Reich's brand of active therapy "meant lying naked on a sofa while he attacked my stiff muscles," Neill later wrote in an appreciative tribute to his analyst. "It was a hard therapy and often a painful one."[23]

Neill had found his previous analysis, with the dissident Viennese psychoanalyst Wilhelm Stekel, to be "all head-talk and symbolism." (Furthermore, Stekel had appealed to his "Scottish thrift" because he claimed that therapy should never take longer than three months.) Though he admired Stekel as a brilliant interpreter of his dreams, Neill complained that "his words touched my head but never my emotions."[24] Reich, in contrast, "refused to touch dreams," preferring to concentrate on releasing Neill's stiff belly. "There is no neurotic individual who does not show tension in the abdomen," Reich stated as he prodded Neill's stomach. Neill wrote that Reich "tore me to pieces on his sofa," inducing "terrible weepings and anger."[25] Reich had, as another patient described it, "the claws of a hawk," and referred to sobbing as the "great softener."[26]

Like many analysts, Stekel believed that patients should be kept in an enforced state of abstinence during treatment, but by the time he met Reich, Neill had come to suspect that abstinence was perhaps the cause of his problems. He felt trapped in a sexless marriage and had begun a guilty affair with the married mother of a pupil—the pseudonymous Helga of his autobiography. Reich's theories about repression and the total orgasm seemed to Neill to explain his own fidgety nervousness. "In 6 weeks of therapy," Neill wrote in praise of Reich's new technique, "[I got] more emotional reaction and relief than in 7 years of talky analysis."[27] Stekel, who had been exiled from Freud's circle in 1912, generously reaffirmed Neill's enthusiasm by telling him that Reich was "the most brilliant analyst that Freud has produced."[28]

Reich still used the character-analytic technique of deliberately provoking his patients; he accused Neill of harboring a lot of repressed hatred toward him, and suggested that Neill hit him. Neill replied that he found it difficult to hate. "Finally I got furious. I sat up and looked him in the eye. 'Reich,' I said, 'I have just discovered something. I have discovered that I don't believe a bloody word you say. I don't believe in your muscle theory one bit. You are a sham.' I lay down on the sofa again and Reich touched the back of my neck. 'Good Lord,' I said, 'the pain's gone.'"[29]

Reich's friendship with Fenichel, called into question at Lucerne, was further strained when Fenichel lobbied against Reich's being admitted to the Danish-Norwegian Psychoanalytic Society. At Lucerne, Reich's patients Harald Schjelderup, Ola Raknes, and Nic Waal had refused to accept Reich's exclusion as a condition of their society's membership in the International Psychoanalytic Association, as Ernest Jones had dictated. Schjelderup, who served as the Norwegian group's president, now tried to persuade Reich to join it.

But Fenichel, the secretary of the society, feared the sacrifice of their precious international affiliation and was against the idea of Reich's inclusion. In *People in Trouble* Reich complained that Fenichel "circulated from member to member and agitated against my acceptance."[30] According to Reich, Fenichel expressed his negative view of Reich's sanity. "To one of the members he said I had only come to Norway to steal all his patients," Reich wrote bitterly of what he considered to be Fenichel's secret campaign against him. "To another he said that I had gone mad."[31] His closest friendship and collaboration of the past fifteen years was coming to an end.

Reich wrote to Annie Reich that he would have preferred "to have an openly declared enemy than an unconsciously hostile friend."[32]

While Fenichel increasingly distanced himself from Reich's theory of the orgasm, Reich demanded that everyone subordinate himself unconditionally to his sex-political program. He and Fenichel competed for supporters, and the dissident psychoanalysts were thus split into two factions that scarcely communicated with each other—which was exactly how Ernest Jones and Anna Freud had hoped to neuter the radical wing. Reich sent a long and scathing letter to "the psychoanalysts in Denmark, Norway, and Germany who are in conflict with Freud" (the group that had failed to materialize at Lucerne). The letter accused Fenichel of spinelessness and of stealing and distorting Reich's ideas.[33] He was painted, Fenichel wrote, as a "vacillating opportunist."[34]

In response, Fenichel took Reich off the *Rundbriefe* mailing list, thereby effectively excommunicating him from the very psychoanalytic opposition of which he'd been a leading member. Fenichel began to try to distance this group from Reich's ideas and influence by including in his letters a four-page list of quotations from Reich's publications that were designed to make Reich appear ridiculous.[35] Fenichel also defended his right to purge from the *Rundbriefe* "without warning . . . comrades who still have a relationship of trust with Reich."[36] In response, Reich issued the following decree to his supporters: "It was . . . decided yesterday [that is, by Reich] that no person may work with us who is in contact with Fenichel."[37]

A year after Reich arrived in Norway, Fenichel left in order to escape their escalating dispute. "Reich had become impossible," Fenichel explained of Reich's increasing paranoia. "Anyone who does not completely agree is an enemy."[38] He and his wife, the dancer Clare Nathanssohn, joined Annie Reich in Czechoslovakia. Reich claimed that Fenichel had really left Oslo because he could no longer make a living there after all his Norwegian patients had deserted him. Several of them—including Ola Raknes and Nic Waal—had defected to Reich, who was running popular lectures on his new and dynamic technique, and he thought that Fenichel's reaction to him was based on jealousy (one of the papers Fenichel wrote at the time was entitled "Contribution to the Psychology of Jealousy").

Waal, who later became a child psychiatrist, wrote of her analysis with Fenichel: "He stood at a four meter distance, did not take my hand, and his comments were 'yes' and 'no' . . . His voice was not kind, soft and accepting. When I said positive things about Reich, Fenichel's movements became nervous, his voice shrill, even if he only said 'yes' or 'no.' So I got scared."[39] Waal broke off her treatment with Fenichel after a year and told him that she planned to continue therapy with Reich, who was already analyzing her husband with his new technique. "[Fenichel] was furious," Waal recalled, "and indicated that Reich had seduced me in order to kill Fenichel and destroy his treatment of me."[40] When Ola Raknes also threatened to switch analysts, Fenichel told him that Reich was psychotic.

Reich and Fenichel's mutual friend Henry Lowenfeld recalled that "Reich became [mentally] ill . . . obsessed with certain ideas, the way people with paranoia can have a tremendous effect because no one can be so convincing . . . Reich was always obsessed with something. And the next year it was something else . . . Reich got a lot of young people on his side and Fenichel couldn't stand it."[41] Lowenfeld (the man who stole Annie Reich's *Rundbriefe*) had lived in Prague since 1933 and met Fenichel there. In an oral history taken in the 1990s, Lowenfeld compared Reich to the Pied Piper, who enchanted an ever-expanding crowd of children with his music and led them astray: "Reich had this ability. And they all went to him . . . One's mind [had to be] very straight, not to be overwhelmed by him."[42]

Reich's supporters found a building for his Institute of Sex-Economic Bioresearch; it served as a lab, seminar room, and publishing house, and was staffed by physicians, psychologists, kindergarten teachers, and artists, all of them left-wing. The hard-core group of about twenty followers that gathered around Reich were all in analysis, or had been in analysis, with him; these included the distinguished novelist Sigurd Hoel (then married to Nic Waal) and Norway's poet laureate, Arnulf Øverland. Hoel had therapy with Reich four times a week for two and a half years and saw him socially almost every day. He wrote that he had been "once or twice on the verge of death" in vegetotherapy because of the strong "organic reactions" it provoked, but praised Reich's new technique for "lifting his depression and replacing it with an almost mystical sense of bliss."[43] Reich's disciples were so enthralled by him that he was accused of having a hypnotic power over them.

According to one of them, the psychotherapist Marie Naevestad, "The circle around [Reich] was deeply influenced by his vital and suggestive personality but also by the fact that he demanded absolute loyalty to himself and his teachings thereby creating an obstacle for all fruitful criticism."[44] Reich's detractors nicknamed his militant supporters the Reichswehr, also the name of the German army. In a moment of anger, Lindenberg dismissed Reich's unquestioning devotees, bound to Reich by the power of psychoanalytic transference, as a bunch of needy bourgeois neurotics.

Reich always maintained that it was Fenichel and Annie Reich who spread the rumors that he'd gone mad (he didn't know that his own analysts had publicly raised questions about his sanity a year earlier).[45] Reich was said to have had a nervous breakdown in Norway and to have been institutionalized for a time. Reich denied this and made the unfounded counterclaim that it was actually Fenichel who had spent three weeks in an asylum when he broke down after the Lucerne congress, and that he sought to divert attention from this fact by claiming that it was Reich. As for his own sanity, Reich wrote in 1937 that the idea of mental illness did not alarm him; he simply assumed that he would be publicly celebrated enough to be vindicated and thus stave it off: "I was well aware of my own personal equation which threatened from within," he wrote. "I was aware that if I did not achieve an adequate degree of success I might become the victim of an old insecurity acquired in childhood, namely . . . sexual guilt."[46]

After hearing Fenichel's reports about her ex-husband's mental well-being, Annie Reich refused to let Eva and Lore visit him in Oslo. As a result, Reich, who had not seen his children for two years, arrived unannounced at Grundlsee in August of 1936, interrupting a family holiday. Reich and Annie argued bitterly over custody, mediated by the children's analyst Berta Bornstein—who had been trying to convince them their father was insane—and Annie's new lover, the Russian historian and former Soviet spy Arnold Rubenstein.

In Lore Reich's view, Rubenstein was just as complicated a figure as her father. His FBI file, compiled in the 1960s after Rubenstein's death, notes that he had been the secret head of the West European bureau of the Communist International from 1919 to 1925. "Comrade Tomas," as Rubenstein was code-named (his real name was, coincidentally, James Reich), operated out of a secondhand bookstore in Berlin and was in charge of distributing funds from Moscow to the German Communist Party and its related fronts, funding revolutionary uprisings, publishing Communist propaganda, and assisting other Comintern agents. The FBI's informant, Boris Nikolayevsky, who met Rubenstein in Prague and emigrated to America on the eve of the Second World War, reported that Rubenstein was sent to Berlin in 1919 with a million rubles in German and Swedish currency and a leather suitcase stuffed with jewels and precious stones that the secret police had confiscated from the Russian bourgeoisie after the revolution.[47]

The mismanagement and alleged embezzlement of these funds was Rubenstein's downfall. Rubenstein tendered his resignation after the 1923 bank crisis in Germany, when he only managed to save twenty-five million marks by changing them into stable dollars, but lost most of the rest in the devaluation that followed. His resignation was rejected at the time, but subsequent accounting showed his control of the party finances to have been chaotic at best; nine million marks had apparently been stuffed into a piece of furniture and forgotten.

Rubenstein—whom Lenin had handpicked to go to Germany—lived in fear of Stalin's retribution. According to Lore Reich, even after they emigrated to New York in 1938, he had a paranoid fear that Stalin's henchmen would catch up with him. On one occasion he noticed that she'd disturbed the dust he'd sprinkled on his desk as a security measure. Annie Reich had met Rubenstein in the early 1930s through her erstwhile lover Karl Frank, who had been employed by Rubenstein a decade earlier. They moved to Prague together in 1934. Lore Reich remembers that her father called Rubenstein "the rattlesnake"; Rubenstein called Reich "the skunk."

At Grundlsee, Reich fought a losing battle for the affection of his children, whom he now thought to be tainted by Anna Freud's normalizing version of psychoanalysis. "Eva has become superficial, quiet, adjusted," he wrote in his diary. "Lore neurotically superficial."[48] Reich encouraged Eva, now twelve, to come and live with him in Oslo and assist him in his research. To try to cure her demure demeanor he lent her a copy of Malinowski's *The Sexual Lives of the Savages* and encouraged her to find an outlet for her nascent sexuality. On finding this out, Annie Reich refused to let Reich be alone with his children, believing him to be a potential danger to them. After Reich had been in Grundlsee for a week, Eva—the child most fought over—demanded that he leave. On his return to Oslo, he prepared an eighty-page document entitled "How I Lost Eva," which recorded every letter, phone call, and instance in which Annie and her friends had worked to drive them apart.

Reich made the 1,850-mile trip back to Norway with, he noted in his journal, "a thousand worries."[49] Even though he had been excommunicated from the IPA in 1934, Reich couldn't help making a detour on his long journey home: the International Psychoanalytic Congress was being held at the Bohemian spa town of Marienbad in July that year, and Reich had no intention of sparing his former colleagues any embarrassment. Member or not, he continued to see himself as the uncompromising guardian of pure psychoanalysis, and he was determined to be there.

It was the year of Freud's eightieth birthday, and celebrations were planned, but the patriarch of psychoanalysis was too ill to attend. Reich had sent Freud a letter of congratulation ("My dear Professor," he began), and enclosed an expanded version of the paper he'd read at the Lucerne congress two years earlier, in 1934. Reich's hope was that Freud would see the paper as confirmation that Reich had been right all along in his clinical suppositions. He asked Freud not to view his recent work as the result of a "personal and irrational reaction" to the "grave injustice" he had suffered at the hands of the IPA but to appreciate instead that the future of psychoanalysis lay in Reich's hands.[50] Freud did not respond.

At Marienbad Reich encountered his former analysand Fritz Perls, who had flown all the way from South Africa. In the three years since Ernest Jones had sent Fritz and Laura Perls to Johannesburg to escape the Nazis, they had both established successful psychoanalytic practices. They were, in effect, Reichian missionaries: they translated Reich's books for a South African readership and incorporated many of his techniques into their work with patients, particularly his emphasis on breathing. But of course the Reich they took with them was the Reich that had existed when they left, and the fact that they knew so little about what had happened since was a testament to how dramatically things had changed in the intervening years. Just as Reich had no sense of the extent to which the Perlses had expanded the reach of his work in South Africa, they had no idea that Reich was now persona non grata in the psychoanalytic establishment. At Marienbad Perls enthusiastically delivered a paper on "oral resistances" that was his expansion of an essentially Reichian argument; he was surprised when it was not well received. "Most people didn't understand it," Laura Perls later wrote. "It was more Reichian, and Reich was already suspect."[51]

Fritz Perls was disappointed not to be greeted warmly by his mentor, but Reich was in his own world. Perls wrote that Reich "sat apart from us and hardly recognized me. He sat there for long intervals, staring and brooding."[52]


In August 1936, Leon Trotsky found the home outside Oslo where he and his wife were staying invaded by fascist thugs. He had arrived there from France in June 1935, having been offered asylum by the Labor government, but a year later he realized with terrible clarity that Norway was no longer a safe political haven. Members of Vidkun Quisling's fascist party, Nasjonal Samling (National Union), disguised themselves as policemen and broke into Trotsky's living quarters. The daughter of Trotsky's host saw them off, but not before they had stolen some of Trotsky's papers—an article on France that had been published in the American periodical *The Nation*, and a letter to a French Trotskyite. The fascists used these documents to claim that Trotsky was violating the terms of his asylum by involving himself in Norwegian politics. Though the charges were initially dismissed, Trotsky soon found himself "in the very centre of Norwegian politics."[53]

On August 25, the day after the notorious Moscow trials, in which Trotsky and other leaders of the October Revolution were accused of plotting with the Nazis to assassinate Stalin, the Soviet Union put pressure on the Norwegian government to deport Trotsky, threatening a commercial boycott if it didn't. The Labor government was already facing a violent campaign in the right-wing press, thanks to having given sanctuary to Trotsky, and now, panicking in the run-up to parliamentary elections, the government changed tack. They used the stolen documents to justify placing Trotsky under house arrest, thereby appeasing both the fascists and the Stalinists at once. This was an act, Trotsky charged, of "miserable cynicism."[54]

Trotsky later claimed that he had always been suspicious of the politicians who welcomed him; from his first dealings with them, "I got a strong whiff of the stale odor of the musty conservatism denounced with such vigor in Ibsen's plays . . . Ibsen's hatred of Protestant bigotry, provincial sottishness, and stiff-laced hypocrisy became more comprehensible to me after my acquaintance with the first Socialist government in the poet's native land."[55]

When the minister of justice, Trygve Lie (who would go on to serve as the first secretary-general of the United Nations, from 1946 to 1952), visited him to discuss his case, Trotsky warned him that his cowardly collaboration with Quisling was paving the road for fascism: "This is your first act of surrender to Nazism in your own country. You will pay for this. You think yourselves secure and free to deal with a political exile as you please. But the day is near—remember this!—the day is near when the Nazis will drive you from your country."[56] Lie and his colleagues would soon be "émigrés in a few years like . . . the German Social Democrats."[57] In December 1936, ignoring these warnings, Lie deported Trotsky to Mexico. The Soviet ambassador sent Lie flowers in thanks.

It's unclear whether Reich and Trotsky ever met in Norway. Myron Sharaf, Reich's disciple and biographer, claims in a footnote that they did, and this has subsequently become an accepted part of Reich's biography, but there is no evidence to confirm such an encounter. If Reich made the hour's drive to meet Trotsky, he certainly never kept a record of it, and it seems extremely unlikely, considering Reich's immodest personality, that he would have been able to keep any important brush with history a secret his whole life. There was a time when to admit to such an association might have been dangerous, but as Isaac Deutscher notes in his biography of Trotsky, even when Trotsky was at his most politically toxic, "nothing bestowed greater distinction on a person in Oslo's leftish circles than the ability to boast of having been received by the great exile."[58]

But Reich and Trotsky certainly corresponded. In October 1933, before Reich's exclusion from the Comintern by the Danish Communist Party, Reich wrote to Trotsky in an attempt to interest him in his sex-political ideas. The following year in Paris, Reich met with some of Trotsky's representatives, who he claimed had all not only read but were in theoretical agreement with *The Mass Psychology of Fascism*; nevertheless, Reich failed to convince them to incorporate a platform of sexual liberation into their program.

This Paris meeting was probably arranged by Otto Knobel, who had emigrated to Paris from Germany in 1933 and joined the Trotskyites before leaving for Denmark, where Reich employed him in his publishing house (Knobel may have supplied the Parisian Troskyites with copies of *The Mass Psychology of Fascism*). In 1936, after returning to Russia, Knobel was arrested as a Trotsky supporter and sent to a labor camp for five years. The Comintern document that fingered him, a 1936 memorandum titled "Trotskyists and Other Hostile Elements in the Émigré Community of the German CP," accused Knobel of helping Reich compose and mail his letters to Trotsky and asserted that Reich "had been expelled from the CPG [German Communist Party] for Trotskyism."[59] It is probable that Soviet agents intercepted Reich's letter to Trotsky, and it's possible that, unbeknownst to Reich, this contributed to his expulsion from the Danish Communist Party the following month.

Reich wrote a second letter to Trotsky a few months after Trotsky arrived in Norway, again hoping for a collaboration. Though Trotsky remained sympathetic to psychoanalysis (he had once hoped analysis could save his daughter Zina, who underwent several months of treatment before committing suicide in 1933), he wrote back to say that he had insufficient knowledge of psychology to be able to join forces with Reich. Having been rejected, Reich dismissed Trotsky's party as "stillborn and senseless," but the revolutionary leader's personal influence extended well beyond such fits of pique.[60]

Around the time the fascists invaded his house, Trotsky put the finishing touches on a manuscript that was to have an immeasurable effect on Reich's politics. In *The Revolution Betrayed* (1937), Trotsky analyzed the ways in which the Communist revolution had gone awry since Lenin's death. He considered it to have been hijacked by bureaucrats, and predicted the collapse of the Soviet Union as a result; he called for another, purifying uprising. Trotsky criticized the new "cult of the family" that was encouraged in Russia, which he thought a cynical ploy to try to discipline youths "by means of 40 million points of support for authority and power."[61] This was exactly the strategy that Reich had accused Hitler of employing in *The Mass Psychology of Fascism*. Trotsky also documented Stalin's "sexual Thermidor," which rolled back the marriage- and sex-related reforms that were instituted after the October Revolution; now abortion was banned, sodomy was recriminalized, and the divorce laws were tightened. Reich was disgusted by news of this bolstering of sexual repression, which shattered his rosy illusions of Russian communism for good. After reading Trotsky's polemic, he referred to Stalin as "the new Hitler" and to Stalinists as "red fascists."

In December 1941, the year after Trotsky's death, some of Reich's books were confiscated by FBI agents, including a copy of *The Revolution Betrayed*. This was taken as evidence of Reich's communism—certainly, to FBI agents one form of Communist was as bad as another. Ironically, though, it was that book that marked Reich's final break with the party. The year *The Revolution Betrayed* was published, Reich wrote a new preface to *The Sexual Struggle of Youth* in which he asked the reader to substitute "revolutionary" every time he or she came across the word "Communist" because of "the catastrophic political behavior of the Comintern in the past ten years." Reich proposed instead a new, non-bureaucratic political structure he called "work-democracy," which would be self-organizing—and represented to many enthusiasts a kind of anarchism.

A year after Trotsky was packed off to Mexico (where he would be assassinated by one of Stalin's henchmen) Reich, too, faced expulsion from Norway. The "stale odor" of which Trotsky had complained intensified, and Reich now found himself its victim. Fascism was taking over in Norway; Russia was no longer the utopia Reich hoped it would be. The walls were closing in.

Reich immersed himself more deeply in scientific experiments that seemed to reflect his narrowing horizons and precarious state of mind. Once again his research was aimed at vindicating his version of the libido theory, for which he craved recognition. He hoped to use a newly acquired microscope to observe at the most primitive biological level the "vegetative currents" he'd seen in therapy and the expansion and contraction he'd recorded in his bioelectric experiments.

"My knowledge of protozoology was limited," Reich admitted, having last studied biology two decades earlier, though he evidently didn't see any urgent need to fill this gap. "For the time being, I deliberately refrained from reviewing the biological literature so that I could be unbiased in my observations."[62] Reich thought he could rely on his "naïve and playful" childlike curiosity. "I am not a megalomaniac," he explained to Annie Reich, who thought he was just that. "I just have agonizingly good intuition; I sense most things before I actually comprehend them. And the most important 'intuitions' usually turn out to be correct."[63]

In *People in Trouble*, Reich described the manic nature of his research, how he "threw meat, potatoes, vegetables of all kinds, milk and eggs into a pot which I filled with water; I cooked the mixture for half an hour, took a sample and hurried with it to the microscope."[64] As Reich stared through his microscope for six hours at a time, he was hypnotized by the kaleidoscopic patterns into which he gazed. At the edges of the bouillon he saw minuscule blue vesicles breaking off, slowly clustering together and pulsating. They looked to Reich like pseudo-amoebas and he came to believe that he had discovered a hitherto unnoticed life force that existed in nature and possessed its own generative power. He was, he believed, observing nothing less than the first steps in the origins of life.

Reich realized that people would think him "crazy" if they saw him looking for the origins of life in such a hastily reconstructed version of the primordial soup. "What I saw seemed as insane as the entire venture," he admitted of the blue vesicles he named "bions," after the Greek word for life.[65] Of course, many of those around him did think him mad; the idea of spontaneous generation, which can be traced back to Aristotle, was popular before the Enlightenment, when it was thought that living organisms—including beetles, eels, maggots, and mice—could be born from putrefying matter, moist soil, or slime, animated by some vital force. However, the idea had been wholly ridiculed ever since Louis Pasteur's germ theory proved that bacteria actually came from outside the putrefying matter, carried by flies and other bugs or via airborne spores.

In 1927 the Soviet biochemist Aleksandr Oparin had published *The Origin of Life*, which reopened the discussion around spontaneous generation. Oparin discussed the conditions under which life could have been first formed on earth and concluded that spontaneous generation was only possible in an earlier epoch and under very different atmospheric conditions. In *Dialectics of Nature* (1883), one of Reich's heroes, Friedrich Engels, had warned, "It would be foolish to try and force nature to accomplish in twenty-four hours, with the aid of a bit of stinky water, that which took her many thousands of years to do."[66]

Reich believed he had done just this in his experiments. Yet the swarming soup seemed to some of his peers to be nothing so much as a metaphor for what was happening to Reich's mind: the world dissolved into an electrified substance, a seething broth, teeming with perpetual motion. But for Reich, the vitality he observed under the microscope appeared to confirm what happened in the course of vegetotherapy, where dead and blocked muscles were re-animated in treatment, and fixed borders dissolved in the ecstasy and anarchy of movement. He could see logic in the chaos: "If I feel unhappy, I let my mind wander," he wrote in 1949 in reference to his discovery of the bions by throwing food in water, "and things begin to take shape and to develop logic and beauty in their order."[67] Reich wrote excitedly in his journal, "Science! I'm going to plant a bomb under its ass!! . . . In fifty to one hundred years they'll idolize me."[68]

Reich's uncritical followers were swept along by his euphoria. One of his assistants didn't see any movement in the soup when she first looked through the microscope, but, Reich reported, after he encouraged her to stare through the microscope for a further ten minutes, the bions miraculously swam into focus. But despite Reich's supporters' willingness to see what he saw, they were ill equipped to verify his supposed discoveries. Reich's most preeminent collaborator on the bion experiments was Roger du Teil from the Centre Universitaire Méditerranéen in Nice, who was a poet and professor of philosophy, not a scientist (du Teil was suspended from his university post in June 1938 because of his controversial extracurricular work for Reich).

Nic Waal realized that to outsiders Reich's theoretical leap from therapy to theories about the origins of life must have looked like "a development from sanity to insanity."[69] (When A. S. Neill showed Reich's report on his experiments to the editor of *The Lancet*, the London-based medical journal, he was told that Reich's study was "worthless" and "that R[eich] should stick to his own subject, analysis."[70]) But, Waal asserted, "to those who went through those years in close contact with Reich, it had nothing to do with insanity. It was a logical development of his thinking and findings." Ellen Siersted, too, visited Reich's lab on one of her trips to Norway and was similarly persuaded: "He showed us in the microscope proof of the life he had found. I didn't fully understand his biological discoveries but his enthusiasm was contagious and when I, both during my treatment and with some of my patients whom I commenced to treat, got verification of his teaching about the muscular armor and the vegetative currents, I felt intuitively that Reich was on the right track in his biological work."[71]

Reich showed his bions to Albert Fischer, head of the Biological Institute in Copenhagen, which was funded by the Rockefeller and Carlsberg foundations; he thought Fischer would be dazzled by his discovery. After their meeting, Fischer told Leunbach, the controversial abortionist, that all Reich was observing was Brownian motion and that Reich, in pursuing "old fairy tales" dating back to the days before Pasteur, was "a fantasist."[72] Reich had hoped that Fischer would recommend him for a grant; he later applied for one to the Rockefeller Foundation in Paris and was rejected.

At the University of Oslo, Lejv Kreyberg, professor of pathological anatomy, and Thorstein Tjøtta, professor of bacteriology, also rejected Reich's claims. Like Fischer, they dismissed his findings as simple bacteria resulting from air infection or movement caused by Brownian motion. Kreyberg would later say that Reich knew less about anatomy and bacteriology than a first-year medical student. When Reich ignored these criticisms and published *The Bion Experiments* (1938), in which he claimed to have discovered the secret to the "origin of life," it brought on an avalanche of attacks.

Though it had a population of only three million, Norway had an extremely active press; the ruling Labor Party alone published thirty-five daily newspapers and a dozen weeklies. Between September 1937 and the autumn of 1938, over a hundred articles denouncing Reich were published in the country's print media. Reich would later refer to this period, which saw him driven out of Europe, as the "Norwegian campaign."

The campaign began when the scientists from whom Reich had sought confirmation of his bion experiments published a damning report denouncing his claims to have discovered the origins of life. In the conservative *Aftenposten* (Evening Post), Ljev Kreyberg, whom Reich later accused of being a fascist, argued that Reich's visa, which was due to expire in February 1938, should not be renewed:

> If it is a question of handing Dr. Reich over to the Gestapo, then I will fight that, but if one could get rid of him in a decent manner, that would be best. More than one million miserable refugees are knocking at our door and there is reason for us to show mercy. It seems sad to me, however, that a man of Dr. Reich's nature is admitted. Dr. Reich's visa is a blow to those of us who would like to have a more open door policy to refugees. It is people like him who have partly created the refugee problem . . . by their irresponsibility.[73]

Sigurd Hoel responded in Reich's defense: "When did it become a crime to perform some biological experiments, even if they should prove to be amateurish? When did it become a reason for deportation that one looked in a microscope when one was not a trained biologist?"[74] What is more, Reich published in German, which only a select group in Norway could read anyway.

Certainly there seemed to be little danger in Reich's experiments, even if he was wrong. Hoel was no doubt correct in maintaining, as Reich himself did, that in the subsequent avalanche of criticism he was really being persecuted for his sexual beliefs, which they feared would corrupt Norwegian youths. One newspaper claimed, "Reich is the slimiest kind of pornographer"; another article claimed that he was "destructive for the spirit and morals of society."[75] "The furious struggle against me was very painful indeed," Reich wrote. "All manner of insult, suspicion and calumny was employed."[76]

Reich was depicted as a bogus alchemist and fraudulent guru. One newspaper cartoon pictured him in a lab coat, his pockets stuffed with cash, stirring a bowl of his bouillon, surrounded by disciples who appeared on their knees as if in prayer before him. "High priest Wilhelm Reich reveals the mysteries of life to his followers," read the caption. The supposedly illicit nature of the suggested cult was emphasized by an enormous padlock on the door and by a supporter pulling down a blind over the window.

There was, Reich wrote in 1943,

> an almost daily dispute in the newspapers as to whether I was a charlatan or a genius, a Jew, a psychopath or a sexual monomaniac. They asked the police authorities to throw me out of the country; they tried to bring a charge against me concerning the seduction of minors, because I had affirmed infantile masturbation. Such indecent behavior on the part of the academic world simply cannot go unmentioned; it almost cost me my existence, in addition to the loss of many thousands of dollars and several good co-workers who became frightened.[77]

In many ways, it was a dress rehearsal for what would happen to Reich in America.

According to Randolf Alnaes, historian of psychoanalysis in Norway, Reich's opponents were for the most part the same people who had opposed Strømme and his controversial masturbation therapy five years earlier. For example, the orthodox Freudian Ingjald Nissen wrote an article in the Labor Party newspaper *Arbeiderbladet* lamenting that "psychoanalysis in this country has become sort of a weedy garden, where all kinds of parasites and climbers strike root and almost choke what is of value." He complained of the quackery of "psychoanalytic sectarians" such as Reich, who "do not call themselves psychoanalysts any longer" and practice "some sort of quasi-medicinal relaxation analysis" that "only leads to sexual relations."[78] (Reich began an affair with a patient at this time, a beautiful actress, which his supporters thought suicidal; she threatened to go to the police when it ended and Sigurd Hoel had to beg her not to.) In 1938 an act was passed with the express aim of controlling Reich's and Strømme's therapeutic factions that required all psychoanalysts to apply to the Ministry of Social Affairs for the authorization to practice. It was clear that Reich would never be granted such a permit.

The more Reich was attacked by the press—the attacks seemed to come from every political angle—the more domineering he became. He demanded, Nic Waal recalled, absolute loyalty from his supporters, who not only paid for his research but manned his laboratory. He excluded those who didn't agree with him or expressed any degree of skepticism about his discoveries. "He was a tyrant . . . He wanted your whole life," Sigurd Hoel wrote in a memoir.[79] Many of Reich's followers left because of Reich's overbearing demands on them and his frequent mood swings. "He began to take out his anger on his patients," wrote Hoel. "I saw him crush several people. That was unforgiveable because he was the strongest one in the group. Unforgivable!"[80] Reich displaced his rage onto those closest to him, whom he described as moths to the flame. "He was enormously stimulating and loveable," Nic Waal remembered, "and sometimes terribly and hopelessly disgusting."[81]

Reich had a romantic and inflated view of his predicament and didn't deign to respond to any of the criticisms launched against him. He identified himself with Galileo, the persecuted seventeenth-century scientist tried by the Inquisition (Brecht, still in Denmark, was completing his play *Life of Galileo*). When Reich read a book about Galileo he remarked, "I have just experienced Galileo's death—almost physically."[82] Reich retreated to his small modernist house in what one of his supporters described as "clamorous silence." He was absolutely sure that his version of science would prevail, that it was Nobel Prize worthy, and that he was, like Galileo, a martyr to truth and knowledge.

Reich had a dream at this time, recorded in his diary, that he was an express train thundering over wide plains; passengers got on and off, some for long trips and some for short stops. The train "rushed headlong into the unknown through the world, with no certain destination."[83] Reich doesn't put forward an interpretation of his dream in his diary, but little is needed to see in it a perfect symbol for continual dislocation, transitory disciples, and his racing thoughts.

"Today I discovered the first indication of death on my right cheek," Reich noted in his diary on November 23, 1938, "a cancerously hypertrophied piece of epithelial tissue. Added calcium chloride to a piece of it. Within five minutes blisters and ca. [cancer] cells developed . . . With death in my body I shall fight death as best I can."[84]

Two years earlier, after a period of relative depression, Reich had seen a film about cancer and was inspired to a new spurt of energy; he came to believe that his bions might be able to combat cancer's swarming cells—life versus death. For Reich, cancer was the result of sexual stasis and political repression (Max Eastman had introduced psychoanalysis to the American public in 1915 as a kind of surgery that could remove "mental cancer," leaving the patient "sound and free and energetic"). Reich observed that "the majority of women contract cancer specifically in the sexual organs, such as the genitals and breasts."[85] This, he was convinced, was more than a coincidence, and since for him sex and politics were always intertwined, he believed fascism to be a root cause, too. ("Fascism," he wrote of the looming situation in Europe, "is sitting here on the far edge of Europe under the nose of a socialist government like a cat waiting for victims.")[86] Seeing an opportunity to extend his biological discoveries outside the treatment room, he wrote excitedly that the disease was, as he put it, now "the main issue—in every respect, even political."[87]

The day after Kristallnacht—November 9, 1938—Reich wrote, "The most beautiful and effective revenge for Hitler's atrocities will be my victory over cancer."[88] He had the fantasy, he later reported to a friend, that he would ride back into Berlin "as a triumphant knight mounted on a white horse, while the band played Ravel's Bolero."[89] Now he thought he was afflicted by the disease on which he was waging war.

The Nazis themselves were waging a military-style offensive against the disease, which killed one in eight Germans (the statistic was used for the title of a Nazi propaganda film, *Jeder Achte*, which encouraged people to go for regular cancer screenings).[90] Cancer was one of Hitler's personal obsessions; in *Mein Kampf* Hitler claimed that his mother's death from breast cancer in 1907 was the only occasion in his life when he'd cried (in *The Mass Psychology of Fascism* Reich connected Hitler's early loss with his excessive idealizations of motherhood).

Certainly the Nazis' public health campaign was admirable, yet cancer became, in Hitler's view, a symptom of everything that was wrong with modernity; by extension of his racist logic, Jews were converted into the embodiment of the disease, castigated as alien and cancerous tumors in the otherwise healthy Aryan body politic. In 1936 one SS radiologist gave lectures that included a slide depicting radium rays as Nazi storm troopers attacking hook-nosed cancer cells.

In *The Mass Psychology of Fascism*, Reich had brilliantly diagnosed the way the Nazis exploited the irrational fear of syphilis for anti-Semitic and politically opportunistic purposes. Five years later, however, Reich was not able to see that the Nazis were exploiting cancer for the same purpose, or that he shared their rhetoric. Reich believed Nazism was spreading cancer, just as the Nazis believed the Jews were—they accused each other of the same thing. In *Illness as Metaphor*, Susan Sontag made the point that "although he perceived sexual and political phobias being projected onto a disease in the grisly harping on syphilis in *Mein Kampf*, it never occurs to Reich how much was being projected in his own persistent use of cancer as a metaphor for the ills of the modern era." Cancer was, Sontag wrote, a particularly flexible metaphor with which to charge that society was in danger, one that Hitler and Reich shared: it was "a good metaphor for paranoids, for those who need to turn campaigns into crusades."[91]

The fight against cancer not only offered Reich—theoretically—a weapon against fascism, it was also aligned with his own individual psychology. While in Norway, Reich considered going into therapy with his pupil, Ola Raknes, thinking Raknes might cure him of his excessive dependency on Freud. It is tempting to interpret his search for a cancer cure as yet another way of trying to get closer to his mentor; it is notable that he thought the disease had struck him in the same place it had Freud, on the right jaw. Reich once remarked that his interest in finding a solution to the cancer problem stemmed from seeing Freud afflicted with the illness, with which he was diagnosed in 1923.

Reich thought that Freud had developed cancer as a direct result of his sexual stasis, rather than his habit of smoking a box of cigars a day: "[Freud] lived a very calm, quiet, decent family life, but there is little doubt that he was very much dissatisfied genitally," Reich told Kurt Eissler in 1952. "Both his resignation and his cancer were evidence of that. Freud had to give up, as a person. He had to give up his personal pleasures, his personal delights, in his middle years . . . If my view of cancer is correct, you just give up, you resign—and then, you shrink." Freud was "very beautiful . . . when he spoke," Reich said. "Then it hit him just here, in the mouth. And that is where my interest in cancer began."[92]

Freud himself implied a link between an improvement in his cancerous jaw and his renewed sexual health. Freud told the sexologist Harry Benjamin that he had undergone a "Steinach operation" the year he found out he had cancer, a then-popular vasectomy procedure that was thought to increase one's sex drive and make one look and feel years younger by stimulating the production of hormone-producing Leydig cells (W. B. Yeats described the result of his operation as "a strange second puberty"). Freud thought his vasectomy had increased his vitality and helped his cancer of the jaw.

With Europe on the brink of war and his mentor dying in London, forbidden from teaching or practicing in Norway, and afraid to go out in public, Reich isolated himself in his laboratory. It was there in January 1939 that he made a discovery he believed to be as dramatic as that of radium. One of his assistants heated a culture containing ocean sand by mistake; Reich thought that the resulting "sand packet bions"—or "SAPA-bions," as he called them—glowed much more strongly than the blue forms he'd observed in his original bouillon. When he looked at these new cultures through his microscope "daily for several hours" he got severe conjunctivitis, which suggested to him that they were emitting radiation. When he held the slide to his wrist, he observed that the SAPA-bions caused a reddening irritation of the skin even through the quartz glass, which seemed to confirm this power. This also happened to his more suggestible friends, the loyal supporters who had not yet deserted him. Reich said of this skin test, "Those among them who were vegetatively strongly mobile regularly gave a strong positive result; those with less emotional mobility reacted only slightly or not at all."[93]

In 1901 Pierre and Marie Curie had observed the same burning phenomenon when exposed to radioactive materials. (Reich no doubt empathized with the dedicated, humble, underfunded, and institutionally unrecognized work that lead to their Nobel Prize–winning discovery: Eve Curie's biography of her mother, which created this romantic portrait, was published in 1937.) Reich therefore concluded that the SAPA-bions were emitting a radiumlike energy, and supposed that they could have a similarly powerful curative and paralyzing effect on cancer cells. In his journal he wrote the grandiose claim that he'd succeeded in freeing the solar energy that the sand had absorbed. He called this radiation "orgone": it was a sexual energy, named in acknowledgment of the role the orgasm played in its discovery. "I yearn for a beautiful woman with no sexual anxieties who will just take me!" Reich wrote soon after his forty-second birthday. "Have inhaled too much orgone radiation."[94]

Reich began injecting himself with cultures of SAPA-bions as a remedy for the growth on his cheek that he thought might be cancerous. He also held a test tube of the bions against his skin for several minutes at a time to clean up patches of psoriasis. Reich would then anxiously examine his "scales," as he referred to his flaky skin, under a microscope, looking for evidence of deadly cancer cells. The growth miraculously seemed to disappear. An "erosion on the left side of his tongue" apparently also cleared up in the same way. Reich was so sure his treatment worked that he persuaded three of his female followers to experiment with inserting test tubes filled with the SAPA-bions into their vaginas as a security against cervical cancer.

A radium physicist at the Cancer Hospital in Oslo was persuaded to test a culture with an electroscope. He got no reaction and concluded that the SAPA-bions weren't at all radioactive. A scientist at Niels Bohr's Institute of Theoretical Physics in Copenhagen declared Reich's claims to be "fantastic"; in January 1939 Bohr was in Washington, where he reported on a successful uranium fission experiment in Germany and raised the possibility of an atomic bomb. Reich, not keen to invite more criticism and questions about his sanity, dismissed the idea of further consultations with experts: "I preferred not to expose my new discovery to a kind of investigation which was biased by disbelief on principle."[95]

"The final solution to the cancer problem" would be—if he could work out a way to fashion it—a thing he now termed an "orgone accumulator," Reich wrote in his diary.[96] He retreated to his basement, where he made a copper Faraday cage filled with SAPA-bion cultures. He thought the metal structure would amplify their power. He sat inside it.

Reich reported that he felt a "curious heaviness" when he spent even as little as ten minutes in the cage. When his eyes slowly adapted to the dark, the room appeared gray-blue, with "fog-like formations and bluish dots and lines of light. Violet light phenomena seemed to emanate from the walls."[97] His mind seemed once again to be unfurling. Reich admitted that when he closed his eyes the "surging and seething" continued, which would suggest he was having hallucinations, but he convinced himself the visions were real because they seemed to get larger and more intense when he held a magnifying glass to his eyes, and darkened when he put on the sunglasses that had been prescribed for his conjunctivitis.[98] He drew pictures of the rhythmic pulsation and spiraling flight paths of these "ghostly" apparitions, which illustrate his book on the discovery of the orgone.

One evening Reich spent five hours naked in this subterranean space; he started to see a blue vapor emanating from his body. "I'm radiating at the hands, palms, and fingertips, at the penis . . ." he wrote in his diary. "Madame Curie may have died of it. I must not go to pieces. But I'm radiating."[99] Erik Erikson claimed that when he visited Reich in Denmark in 1934, Reich told him that he'd seen a blue light being transmitted when he watched two people having intercourse.[100]

Reich's long periods of self-imposed subterranean isolation, where he sat locked in his iron cage, are testament to his increasing alienation; his diary is full of references to his loneliness. After several years together, Reich had separated from Elsa Lindenberg. When she was out late one night, supposedly rehearsing a routine with her pianist at the National Theater, Reich suspected her of having an affair, all the more painful because they'd just decided to have a child together. He turned up at the man's house unannounced and caused a scene (whether he was being paranoid or not is unclear: "She had taken her diaphragm along!" Reich noted in his journal).[101] He ridiculed Lindenberg's dancing, which he had previously so respected—she should be helping him with his more important work, he shouted—and he threatened to punch the composer in the face. He stormed out, knocking over some chairs and smashing a mirror. It didn't matter that Reich had had several affairs himself; he handled his jealousy by immediately sleeping with a prostitute, oblivious to his double standard ("Sex must be free and unencumbered," he wrote in his diary the next day). Lindenberg moved out after the fight.

Reich was waiting for an American visa that his former pupils in America had helped him secure, and also for the Norwegian alien's passport that he needed in order to leave Europe. The German embassy had issued him a passport in the name of Wilhelm Israel Reich—Israel wasn't his middle name—and stamped it "JEW."

When he begged Lindenberg to emigrate to America with him, she declined—"It was the hardest 'no' I ever had to say," she later said.[102] "I know what Elsa must have gone through in those days," Ilse Ollendorff wrote in her biography of her husband, "because 15 years later I went through the same experience. No matter how much love, devotion and understanding one might bring to the situation, there was a point when it became a question of life or death, a matter of retaining one's own integrity and individuality or submitting completely to Reich."[103]

"He was aware of his gifts and he knew that he had an outstanding contribution to make," Lindenberg remembered of her final days with Reich. But, she continued,

> he was also afraid for himself, afraid of where his developments might take him. At times he believed that he would achieve fame and recognition in his lifetime; in other moods he feared that it would go "kaput," that his life would end tragically in one way or another. Sometimes at night when he couldn't sleep he would speak to me about his fears, including the fear that he might go mad. He also spoke to me about his guilt over feeling responsible for his mother's death.[104]

# AMERICA

# Six

On a hot and humid day at the end of August 1939, the SS *Stavangerfjord* arrived in New York. Walter Briehl and Theodore Wolfe came to meet it, and waited for Wilhelm Reich to walk down the gangplank. Wolfe, a professor of psychiatry at Columbia University, had visited Reich in Norway for vegetotherapy, but Briehl had not seen Reich since he studied under him in Berlin in the early 1930s. Briehl noticed that Reich had put on weight over the intervening decade and, even though tanned from the nine-day crossing, looked weary and depressed. Reich's mood is reflected in his laconic diary entry of that day. In contrast to many émigrés' lyrical descriptions of the splendors of the skyscraper city, Reich simply wrote, "Uneventful arrival in New York. Children in the country. Gertrud [Gaasland] is well."[1]

In an attempt to lift Reich's spirits, Briehl took him to jazz clubs in Harlem, to see the neon lights in Times Square, and on a picnic to Jones Beach. Reich was impressed by New York's ethnic mix and apparent egalitarianism—"New York is a real city," he wrote in his diary after two days' exploration. He elaborated in a letter to Elsa Lindenberg: "New York is huge and totally different from Berlin, simpler and more impressive. People are quiet, not rushed, as I expected; they are friendly and courteous; in a word, they are not yet disappointed and corrupted."[2]

Reich's hope was that he would be granted a fresh start in the United States, and that his ideas about sex and politics would be embraced there. Briehl and Wolfe had personally put up the five thousand dollars needed to guarantee Reich's visa, and had arranged for him to teach a course called "Biological Aspects of Character Formation" at the New School for Social Research, which offered Reich a much longed-for academic affiliation. The affidavits they'd provided to the Immigration and Naturalization Service were laudatory to the point of hyperbole—they declared Reich the inventor of a therapy that would revolutionize the world and hailed him as a new Pasteur. Having been on the intellectual fringes in Europe, Reich was now a colleague of the scholarly elite: nearly two hundred European academics—including Hannah Arendt, Bronislaw Malinowski, Erich Fromm, and Leo Strauss—had sought refuge from Nazism at the New School, which was known as the "University in Exile."

Reich rented a large ivy-clad, Lutyens-style house with a ski jump of a roof in Forest Hills, Queens. It was a wealthy, leafy suburb half an hour from the center of the city that appealed to the nostalgia of many émigrés because it resembled certain suburbs of Vienna and Berlin. He put up a picture of Elsa Lindenberg on his study wall between photographs of his mother and Freud, and imagined, as he wrote to Elsa in a letter, that she might walk in at any moment.

Reich's house was only a short walk from Flushing Meadow Park, the 1,200-acre site of the 1939 World's Fair. Attended by 45 million people, the fair was dedicated to "The World of Tomorrow"; visitors could take a simulated rocket trip to London, be televised on one of the first-ever small screens, and watch a seven-foot golden robot called Elektro as it walked, told jokes, and smoked cigarettes. America was emerging from the Great Depression, and Roosevelt's anti-business policies, with its attacks on monopoly power and endorsement of strikes, was thought by many businessmen to be slowing recovery. The large corporations that contributed to the fair sought to represent themselves, rather than a paternalistic government, as the confident custodians of the future. One of the fair's attractions symbolized this hoped-for convergence of citizen and consumer: a monumental cash register the size of a three-story house.

There was no German pavilion in Flushing, but there was a Czechoslovak one—it stood unfinished as a reminder of the Nazi invasion of Czechoslovakia that March. A "Freedom Pavilion" that would highlight the plight of all those whom Hitler had exiled had been proposed but was never built. When he opened the fair, President Roosevelt delivered what the *Herald Tribune* called "a polite but pointed lecture to Chancellor Adolf Hitler on the advisability of peaceful co-operation among nations."[3] Like many of his European peers, Reich held President Roosevelt in extremely high regard (Thomas Mann enthusiastically described the president as "a match for the dictators of Europe").[4] Roosevelt was, according to the historian Anthony Heilbut, virtually canonized by refugees who generally regarded themselves as instinctive skeptics.

Roosevelt's domestic enemies on the right represented the New Deal as a breeding ground for radicals and Communists. Many on the left asked whether the New Deal was Roosevelt's solution to fascism or a sign of contamination by it. Nazi propaganda portrayed Roosevelt as an authoritarian leader who was following a trail Hitler had blazed. In November 1940, Reich wrote to a shocked A. S. Neill: "I feel myself completely confused and inclined to revise most of the things I learnt in Europe about what socialism should be. If you hear socialists and communists who have come over here claiming that Roosevelt is a dictator or fascist, then your stomach turns around. I have started to hate them." Reich thought Roosevelt had "done more in the field of social security than any communist in Russia would dream of getting."[5]

Since Hitler's takeover in 1933, America's most famous German émigré, Albert Einstein, had been living in Princeton, where an institute had been set up in his honor. He also gave a short talk at the World's Fair on its opening day. In a heavy German accent, Einstein spoke for five minutes about cosmic rays, subatomic particles that bombard the earth with energy. It was promised that at the end of Einstein's presentation ten rays from outer space would be harnessed by a device in the Hayden Planetarium, but when the great physicist switched on what should have been a dramatic light display, the electrics overloaded and the power failed.

The most popular attraction at the fair was Futurama, which had hour-long queues up the spiraling ramp to the tall, narrow cleft that served as an entrance. Inside, visitors stepped onto a moving platform and sat on pewlike seats before being taken on a gentle roller coaster ride over a utopian vision of 1960s America: "You somehow get an almost perfect illusion of flying," *The New Yorker* reported.[6] A loudspeaker built into the winged headrest of each seat boomed, "All eyes to the future!" as people were launched out over what was claimed to be the largest model ever built, a monumental landscape punctuated by glass domes, elevated walkways, revolving airports, and clusters of skyscrapers, all crisscrossed with seven-lane super-highways (Futurama was sponsored by General Motors). "Atomic energy," the ride's relentlessly optimistic narrator told the time travelers, "is being used cautiously."[7]

One can imagine Reich, a newcomer to America, looking down over Futurama's idealized United States, enraptured by the utopia depicted and daydreaming of the people who might inhabit it. (He visited the World's Fair at least three times.) Did he imagine it to be neurosis and disease-free, populated by the sexually liberated? What did he make of cosmic and atomic rays, which must have seemed to him no more likely to power the future than the orgone energy he'd discovered? As the ride ended, the train deposited visitors on a full-scale mock-up of an imagined metropolitan street intersection in two decades' time. Suddenly, it was the spring of 1960: the dawn of a decade that would be propelled by the aftershocks of Reich's ideas, in ways no one in 1939 could have guessed. As people stepped off the moving platform, they were handed a blue and white lapel pin that boasted I HAVE SEEN THE FUTURE.


On September 1, German tanks rolled into Poland and World War II began. "Because of the enormous distance," Reich wrote to Lindenberg, "the war in Europe appears to us like an unreal dream. I still feel that I am part of Europe, although I am already beginning to take root in American soil."[8] Needless to say, however, this transition wasn't without its difficulties, and Reich felt the emotional anxiety and strain experienced by many émigrés as he mourned the old world and sought yet another beginning. Reich's teaching at the New School wasn't to begin until the next semester, and in the meantime he suffered what he described as an "enormous depression."

Devastated by the political situation in Europe, Reich visited his children for the first time in four years. They had moved to New York with Annie and Arnold Rubenstein the previous year. Reich found Eva and Lore "reserved" and "uneasy" around him, "'well brought up,' restrained, and superficially cheerful"; their mother would not let them visit him, and he felt, he wrote, "spiritually and intellectually alone."[9]

Reich became increasingly reclusive in Forest Hills. His diary portrays his first few weeks there as a period of "gigantic metamorphosis"; it was a time of creative brooding similar to his weeks of isolation at the alpine sanatorium in Davos.[10] Reich's moods swung between feelings of "worry, doubt, hesitation . . . sleepless nights . . . worthlessness" and moments of elation in which he seemed absolutely sure of his genius and heroic destiny: "Oh yes, I will have many pupils," he wrote to Lindenberg. "I will be honored, loved; after years of hard work I will have rebuilt a group around me that will fight for what is naturally right."[11]

Reich's home was entirely given over to his science. The ground floor became a laboratory, cluttered with microscopes, electroscopes, and other scientific instruments; his office on the first floor doubled as the dining room and living room; and the spare room was used for therapy. The house had a large basement, a former playroom where Reich installed benches to seat thirty people, anticipating a new following. It was there that he reassembled his Faraday cage. The mesh box stood at center stage, the only prop in an empty subterranean theater.

Freud thought Americans to be tremendous prudes when he made his only visit to the land of the dollar barbarians, as he called it, in 1909; he wrote to Jung that they had "no time for libido" and in a letter to Jones he complained of America's virtuousness, lamenting "the strictness of American chastity."[12] However, by the time Reich arrived in Freud's "anti-paradise" exactly thirty years later, Alfred

Kinsey, a forty-four-year old professor of zoology at Indiana University, had already started collecting interviews for his monumental study of American sexuality, which would document in enormous and controversial detail a country with licentiousness seething below its prim façade.

In June 1938, Kinsey, an expert on gall wasps (he collected over a million specimens), began teaching what was quaintly referred to in the university curriculum as the "marriage course." Raised a strict Methodist, with a bullying puritanical father, Kinsey had once suffered the naïveté he now saw in his pupils. He told friends that his own lack of sex education had left him scarred and guilt-ridden, and he made it his mission to correct this in future generations. "In an uninhibited society"—Kinsey began the marriage class with a reference to the Trobriand Islanders—"a twelve-year-old would know most of the biology which I will have to give you in formal lectures."[13] Kinsey offered direct, graphically illustrated descriptions of sex; his course was nicknamed "the copulating class."

Kinsey married the first girl he ever dated, Clara McMillen, a chemistry student he met at a zoology department picnic soon after he arrived in Bloomington (he nicknamed her Mac; he was called Prok, short for Professor Kinsey). Both were virgins when they wed, and they would have four children together. Kinsey, his biographer James Jones has written, "thought that the best way to produce well-adjusted adults was to rear children who did not feel guilty about their sexuality."[14] Nudism, Kinsey wrote in a letter to a friend in 1934, enclosing two books on the nudist movement, has "been a healthy part of our children's education."[15] Future parents who took the marriage course were advised not to try to prevent their children's attempts at bodily exploration and were encouraged to include open talk about sexuality in front of their children "as part of the average dinner table conversation, as part of the average discussion of an average day."[16]

While researching material for the marriage course, Kinsey was surprised by the dearth of scientific literature available on sex—most of it, he said, was "morals masquerading under the name of science." He wanted to fill that void by collecting people's sexual histories, in order to build up a better portrait of the nation's sexual practices. In

*The Modernization of Sex*, the historian Paul Robinson describes Kinsey's interview technique as "his most brilliant creation, an authentic tour de force in which every scrap of sexual information available to memory was wrenched from the subject in less than two hours."[17] Kinsey asked 350 to 521 questions (it took him twenty minutes to get to the first explicitly sexual question), and by using a unique secret code he estimated that he was able to concentrate what would have taken twenty to twenty-five pages of narrative onto a one-page grid. It was, his colleague Paul Gebhard commented, an amazingly "compact, efficient (and, to a neophyte, diabolic) system."[18]

Kinsey quite deliberately made no moral evaluations of his subjects and guaranteed them complete confidentiality; he avoided euphemism, maintained eye contact, and rattled off his questions, employing subtle cross-checks to evaluate the reliability of his data. "We always assume that everyone has engaged in every type of activity," Kinsey wrote of his technique, which placed the burden of denial squarely on the subject. "Consequently we always begin by asking when they engaged in such activity."[19] The psychologist Frank Beach, who submitted to Kinsey's questioning, reported, "It wasn't 'Have you ever?,' it was 'When did you last make love to a pig?' You said 'Never!' OK—but he had you hooked if you were a pig lover" (Kinsey found that 17 percent of rural farmhands had engaged in bestiality).[20]

Kinsey, like Reich, wanted to change society, which he sought to do by presenting empirical proof that mores were out of sync with reality. The two men evidently never met, but they certainly corresponded: in 1943, only a couple of months after the English edition of *The Function of the Orgasm* was published, Kinsey wrote to Reich to request a copy (he also took out a subscription to Reich's newly founded *Journal of Sex Economy and Orgone Research*), including one of his own articles on homosexuality in scholarly exchange. As the copious marginalia in his copy of the book confirm, Kinsey shared Reich's celebration of the orgasm and his belief in the evils of sexual repression. In many ways they spoke the same language: Kinsey catalogued different kinds of orgasms with Reichian enthusiasm (he counted only experiences that led to orgasm in his statistical scheme), was against abstinence, maintained that masturbation was both healthy and necessary for alleviating nervous tension, and believed that there were "social values to be obtained by pre-marital experience in intercourse."[21] For Kinsey, as for Reich, sex held within it a utopian possibility, and he followed Reich in thinking that a Victorian morality present in twentieth-century America conspired to stifle it.

By the summer of 1939 Kinsey had grilled 350 people about their private practices, the majority of them university students. He began supplementing these repetitive "baby histories," as he dismissed them, by making trips to Chicago, some two hundred miles away, in search of people to interview. Kinsey brought the collecting mania that characterized his gall wasp research to his first field trips there: he took five to seven histories a day, many of them from members of the city's gay subculture—several of his interviewees, he wrote excitedly to a former graduate student, had enjoyed as many as two thousand to three thousand partners each. "[I've] been to Halloween parties, taverns, clubs, etc. which would have been unbelievable if realized by the rest of the world," he wrote.[22] By the end of 1940 he had collected 1,692 sex histories at a personal cost of $1,000, which was over a fifth of his salary.

The marriage class, though popular with students, disturbed many of Kinsey's colleagues. Thurman Rice, a member of the medical school who had previously been responsible for sex education, lobbied against the course and complained about the pornographic nature of the illustrations that accompanied Kinsey's lectures, confessing that one of the slides "was even stimulating to me."[23] In 1941 the Ministerial Association, a church organization, petitioned Herman Wells, the president of the university, to put a stop to the course. Wells forced Kinsey to choose between teaching it and collecting sexual histories. Three years after he began the marriage course, Kinsey decided to abandon two decades of work on gall wasps—to which he often dreamed of returning, but never did—and to give over his taxonomic expertise wholly to the field of sex research.

Thanks to a research grant that came through later that year from the Rockefeller Foundation, Kinsey was able to set up the Institute for Sex Research and hire young colleagues to help him amass many more sex histories. Kinsey and his new colleagues—the statistician Clyde Martin, the psychologist Wardell Pomeroy, and the anthropologist Paul Gebhard—set themselves the ambitious task of eliciting one hundred thousand sexual histories (the longest of which took seventeen hours to extract). Between 1938 and 1956 they managed only eighteen thousand—eight thousand were obtained by Kinsey himself.

Kinsey's team crisscrossed America with their boss like a team of traveling salesmen. Kinsey said that his researchers must have "the qualities of Fuller brush men"—in effect, their product was the sexual revolution. As they traveled they conducted interviews on planes, on trains, in cars, in library stacks, in diners, in bars, and in hotels, mapping the country in a new way. They recorded the nation's sex life in their secret code, the key to which took them six months to learn. It had never been written down; when they flew, they did so separately, so there would always be a survivor who knew the code. This code could even distinguish tonal inflection—YES, Yes, and Y-e-e-e-s. They communicated in a private language, for example: "My last history liked Z better than Cm, although Go in Cx madder him very er," Pomeroy said to Kinsey in a crowded elevator, which translated as "My last history liked intercourse with animals better than with his wife, but mouth-genital contact with an extramarital partner was very arousing."[24]

Gebhard compared the team to astronauts, pioneers who were sealed off from the world they studied: "We were kept so busy that, if you combined our home lives with the Institute, we didn't have much time left over for any other kind of socialization. For example, our interviewing trips would be two weeks long and we'd come home for two weeks, and during that period you'd have to teach. So it was a very confined life." (Someone joked that Mrs. Kinsey complained that she didn't see much of her husband anymore ever since he took up sex.) Vincent Nowlis, who did a brief stint of interviewing, described the endless car journeys and motel existence as like being in a submarine: "We were in a very isolated, self-contained world, sliding through dangerous waters on a difficult mission, desperate for time, moving in a self-contained world with a commander directing every movement, and the crew utterly dependent on him and on each other because the craft was so vulnerable. No one could afford to make a mistake."[25]

The Rockefeller Foundation would remain Kinsey's principal backer until 1954, when it ceased funding sex research, by which time Kinsey had been granted hundreds of thousands of dollars. Many critics have seen in the Rockefeller support of Kinsey's sex research an attempt by the ruling classes to manipulate human behavior by trying to find the means by which sex could be controlled. John D. Rockefeller, Jr., the neurasthenic son of the richest man in America, became interested in the study of sex when he was invited to head a 1910 New York City grand jury impaneled to investigate the city's prostitution rings. Rockefeller, whose only independent achievement to date had been to lead a Bible group in the Fifth Avenue Baptist Church, was inspired by his jury experience to throw himself into public service; he went on to use his huge fortune to support the campaign to wipe out this "social evil."

In 1909, the year of Freud's visit, panic about the "white slave trade" had swept across America. Sensationalist books on the subject such as *The Great War on White Slavery* and *The Cruel and Inhuman Treatment of White Slaves* were bestsellers, taking readers on titillating armchair tours of the nation's vice districts. Prostitution was a dominant issue in national politics; Theodore Roosevelt called for "the most relentless war on commercialized vice," by which he meant organized prostitution, and in 1910 Congress passed the Mann Act, which made it illegal to transport a woman across state lines for "immoral" purposes. The Immigration Act passed that same year gave police the power to arrest any foreign-born women found at dance halls and other places that were "frequented by prostitutes."[26]

Rockefeller joined forces with progessive reformers and in 1911 founded the Bureau of Social Hygiene, a charitable organization devoted to the "study, amelioration, and prevention of those social conditions, crimes, and diseases which adversely affect the well-being of society, with special reference to prostitution and the evils associated therewith." This allowed him to feel, as his father's biographer Ron Chernow put it, "politically liberal and modern while clinging to an old-fashioned aversion to gambling, prostitution, alcohol, and other vices traditionally shunned by Baptists."[27] The educational arm of his organization distributed millions of free pamphlets with titles such as *Social Hygiene vs. the Sexual Plagues* (1913). This last, which warned of the dangers of prostitution and venereal disease, was full of misinformation and judgment. It recommended that male infants be circumcised as a precaution against syphilis and warned that "excessive intercourse is silly, vulgar, brutal, and destructive."[28]

One of the bureau's first projects was to fund the Laboratory of Social Hygiene, an annex to a women's prison run by the pioneering sociologist Katharine Bement Davis, whom Rockefeller thought was the cleverest woman he'd ever met (Davis would go on to become the first woman to hold a cabinet post in the state of New York, and in 1915 was voted one of the three most famous women in America). Three-quarters of the inmates at Davis's overcrowded reformatory in Bedford Hills, New York, were prostitutes who had been arrested in New York and incarcerated for sex offenses, a prison population that had swelled as a result of the draconian measures made in an attempt to suppress the trade. The prison was designed to be a kind of university that would rehabilitate prostitutes, yet it made stringent proposals for those it deemed impossible to save.

Davis's laboratory conducted "a scientific study of the types of women psychologically and physiologically who enter upon the life of vice and crime."[29] The aim was to weed out the "moral imbeciles"—girls of "bad heredity" who simply could not "distinguish between right and wrong"—from those who might be reclaimed by society. Davis estimated that 20 percent of her charges exhibited "degenerate strains," with family histories of alcoholism, venereal disease, epilepsy, insanity, and tuberculosis. Davis's prisoners underwent three months of physical, mental, and sociological tests. They were kept in solitary confinement while they were subjected to Binet (intelligence) and Wassermann (syphilis) tests, humiliating medical examinations and an intrusive grilling about their sex lives. Fieldworkers would even visit their families to further determine their "social and moral condition."

The laboratory not only aimed to gain a more comprehensive knowledge of the social conditions that led women to prostitution but also promised to function as a kind of eugenics board. Davis didn't just think that the "feeble-minded" should be segregated from other prisoners because they might distract from the process of reform. She thought that they should be placed in permanent custodial care, at least during their childbearing years, to prevent them from bringing "into the world children who, if there is anything in heredity, have only to look forward to a life of hopeless misery."[30]

Rockefeller, like Davis, Kinsey, and many other reformers at the time, was a firm believer in eugenics. The family's interest in eugenics and sex research overlapped in the Rockefellers' concern with good breeding, reproducing their own class, and the campaign against prostitution and venereal disease. Rockefeller inherited his belief in eugenics from his father, who preached the survival of the fittest in business and rationalized his own meteoric rise as the result of superior biology. Rockefeller senior funded Charles B. Davenport's Eugenics Record Office, which opened in October 1910 in Cold Spring Harbor, Long Island (in 1920, benefiting from funds from another tycoon, the Eugenics Record Office became the Carnegie Institution Department of Genetics). Rockefeller senior paid the salaries of six researchers there to compile a huge number of family genealogies.

Davenport's team visited prisons and mental asylums, as well as the homes of the relatives of these inmates, in the hope of identifying the so-called submerged tenth, the 10 percent of the population that was thought to be dragging down the national gene pool. (Rockefeller senior attempted to redress this trend by having five children; his son had six.) The family trees Davenport collected were annotated with various social and physical characteristics written in a special code ("sx" stood for sexual pervert, "im" for immoral), much as Kinsey's later compilations of American sex life would be. By the time of his retirement in 1935, Davenport had completed eugenic assessments of thirty-five thousand names.

Davenport thought that if the feeble-minded were sexually segregated or sterilized, most "defectives" could be wiped out within fifteen to thirty years. "The most progressive revolution in history" he wrote, could be achieved if "human matings could be placed upon the same high plane as horse breeding."[31]

To Rockefeller junior, who supported the establishment of the

American Eugenics Society, Davis's proposed laboratory at the Bedford Hills reformatory gave eugenics an acceptable scientific gloss and, because each case would be judged by a panel of experts, a modicum of academic respectability (Rockefeller reassigned one of the eugenics workers whom his father sponsored at the Eugenics Record Office to Bedford Hills). He hoped that by bankrolling the laboratory for the state, he would prove its viability and that after five years the legislature would take it over and expand it.

Rockefeller junior's efforts and Davenport's work became part of a campaign to introduce sterilization laws, which came into effect in New York in 1912 and resulted in the compulsory sterilization of forty-five people, all inmates of mental asylums. The practice was declared unconstitutional six years later.

Over the next four decades of his life, John D. Rockefeller, Jr., would funnel almost six million dollars of his family foundation's money into sex research, including such large-scale projects as Margaret Sanger's Planned Parenthood. Sanger, also a believer in eugenics, would go on to become heavily involved in the research that led to the contraceptive pill. Indeed, according to the historian of sexology Vern Bullough, the Rockefellers were "about the sole supporters of sex research" in that period.[32] The Rockefellers were indispensable shapers of the field into which Reich brought his ideas about psychoanalysis and repression. Reich applied for Rockefeller grants in 1936 and 1941, but never received one—a rejection he took bitterly.

If the Rockefellers' hope was that by financing sex research they would help to police sexuality and control population growth, it backfired. The scientific data whose compilation they enabled eventually was used, by Kinsey and others, to support rather than stem sexual liberation, to explode rather than legislate morality. Kinsey started an avalanche of sexual confession that overwhelmed them, and the fifties began with a series of paranoid initiatives to contain sexuality.

Kinsey maintained that America's sex laws were antiquated, varied widely from state to state, were irregularly enforced, and didn't reflect the diversity of actual practices (in most states laws against homosexuality, adultery, and oral sex were on the books). Ninety percent of the nation's men and 80 percent of its women, Kinsey was fond of saying, could theoretically be sent to prison for what they'd done sexually. His subjects ranged from pedophiles to politicians, and sometimes they were both: "Kinsey never ceased to be amazed that people, especially in high places, would tell him the things that they did," wrote one of his assistants. "He came to believe, however, that people would tell him anything about themselves if the circumstances were right."[33] In a series of locked fireproof cabinets at the University of Indiana, Kinsey kept secret and carefully coded files that contained enough material, he boasted, "to blow up America."[34]

On September 22, three weeks into the war, Freud faced death in London with Socratic dignity. The wound on his jaw—or, as he put it, the "dear old cancer" with which he'd been sharing his body for the past sixteen years—now emitted such a fetid odor that his own dog wouldn't come near him. Virginia Woolf visited him at his Hampstead home and described him as "a screwed up shrunk very old man: with a monkey's light eyes, paralysed spasmodic movements, inarticulate: but alert . . . an old fire now flickering."[35] Freud, who had submitted to an unsuccessful round of X-ray treatments at a clinic in Harley Street, chose to extinguish those embers. He summoned his doctor, Max Schur, and asked him to administer an overdose of morphine, as they had previously agreed. Life, he said, was "only torture now." Schur carried out their agreement.

With Freud gone, the 20 members and 106 trainees of the New York Psychoanalytic Institute immediately began to argue over his legacy. Many of them were well-known to Reich: Annie Reich was now a senior figure at the institute, and two of Reich's former analysts, Sandor Rado and Paul Federn, were among its most vituperative combatants. The psychoanalytic mainstream turned to Anna Freud and Heinz Hartmann, whom Freud had invited to be his last analysand. In 1937 Hartmann had written an influential essay, "Ego Psychology and the Problem of Adaptation," which essentially turned the negative connotation of character armor on its head: he proposed that analysts try to strengthen their patients' egos so that they would be better able to control the drives of the id.

Hartmann, who became director of research at the New York Psychoanalytic Institute in 1941, believed the master's teachings could only be followed as a totality; the psychoanalytic dissenters who chose to take up only certain strands of Freud's thought were forced to found two splinter schools. Rado headed the Association for Psychoanalytic and Psychosomatic Medicine, affiliated with Columbia University; and Reich's old friend from Berlin, Karen Horney, founded the American Association for the Advancement of Psychoanalysis. Though influenced by character analysis, these self-described neo-Freudians felt that they had "made improvements on Reich's ideas," as one of their members, Clara Thompson, put it, by abandoning the libido theory.[36] They maintained that people were shaped by their desire for security and approval as much as they were by their sexual drives. Horney, for example, thought that neurotics were at war with themselves; she aimed to collect all the disassociated parts of their personalities in therapy and reintegrate them.

What all these schools shared was a desire to adapt their patients to the status quo rather than change it. Horney's position, as much as Hartmann's, implicitly assumed that the world was all right and that one only needed help in adjusting to it. This was not a revolutionary's view, and its conservatism is perhaps surprising, given that many of those who held it had narrowly escaped death in a world that was very evidently not all right at all. But the refugee analysts were all engaged in a hasty project of assimilation; they sought to adjust to, rather than change, their new environment, grateful for a second chance. As a result, psychoanalysis lost the radical edge it had had earlier in that decade in Europe.

Reich felt that he was the only truly radical analyst left—he was, he believed, drawing out the social consequences of the libido theory and using science to fight fascism. Reich recalled Freud's last words to him: that if Reich's theories of the orgasm and society were correct, Reich would have to carry the weight of psychoanalysis alone. Immune to the irony in Freud's farewell comment—the prediction and possible instruction that Reich would be forever out on a limb—Reich now arrogated to himself the role of intellectual heir. He noted in his diary, "Freud's legacy is a heavy burden!"[37]

But Reich carried what he saw as Freud's radicalism in a direction that few psychoanalysts could follow. A month after Freud's death, Reich sat in his Faraday cage and saw his hands glow blue yet again. He told Theodore Wolfe, he recorded in his diary, that he thought he was greater than Freud: "I have actually discovered life," Reich wrote. "It's truly incredible. I, a mere nonentity, a non-academician, a sexual scoundrel in the bourgeois sense, have made the discovery of the century."[38]

In October 1939 Reich met Ilse Ollendorff, a twenty-nine-year-old German divorcée and friend of Gertrud Gaasland's; Gaasland had left Willy Brandt and emigrated a few weeks before Reich. Reich described Ollendorff as "clever, pretty, and she has a body that reminds me of Elsa. Except that she is a brunette."[39] She was, in her own description, "very much impressed by him, even a little awed . . . He was a striking figure with his gray hair, ruddy complexion, and white coat. He showed me the laboratory, the house, and invited me to have a glass of wine."[40] Reich wrote in his journal that the meeting put an end to "six ghastly weeks of abstinence, interrupted only by emergency measures"—lack of sex had made him feel "lethargic and mean."[41]

Ollendorff moved in with Reich that Christmas Day. She was eight weeks pregnant, and Reich insisted that she have an abortion, as he feared a child would distract him from his research. She became Reich's (unpaid) secretary, laboratory assistant, and eventually third wife (Reich counted his seven-year relationship to Lindenberg, which he considered a "factual marriage," in the tally). Ollendorff was put in charge of the crates of cancerous mice that Reich now kept in his basement, where they were injected with SAPA-bions in the hope that these would dissolve their tumors. "Reich was a hard taskmaster," Ollendorff recalled of their isolated life together. "The records had to be kept meticulously as to every detail of treatment . . . At times I had the feeling that our whole life was ruled by the stopwatch."[42]

Reich devoted most of his time to trying to isolate the mysterious radiation given off by the SAPA-bions. He built a small wooden, metal-lined box with a magnifying glass in the front so that he could peek at the "blue moving vapors and bright, yellow-white streaks and dots of light" given off by the cultures inside.[43] He spent hours underground tracing the radiation's erratic paths. However, when he emptied, aired, and decontaminated his box, the phenomena were still visible, which confused him. They obviously did not emanate from the bions—were they the products of his imagination, as all the physicists he'd consulted in Oslo had implied?

In the summer of 1940, Reich and Ilse escaped the heat of New York and went on a monthlong camping trip to Mooselookmeguntic Lake in northern Maine, a remote region covered in pine and birch trees and gentle mountains that reminded Reich of Norway. "The war," he wrote to Eva Reich back in New York, "the emotional plague of mankind, and all the usual filth are so far away that it is almost impossible to believe that in two weeks' time we will be back in it again."[44] They rented a small, secluded log cabin that had no electricity and was situated right on the edge of the rocky shore of the lake (most of the holiday camps were restricted, clearly labeled: CHRISTIANS ONLY). Reich treated their stay as a kind of field trip; it was almost as if the similar landscape provoked flashbacks of the same strange visual phenomena he had observed in his basement during his final days in Europe.

When Reich looked at the night sky through a hollow tube, he saw "a vivid flickering" in the dark patches between the stars, occasionally punctuated by "flashes of fine rays of light."[45] A magnifying glass attached to the tube (which created a device he named an organoscope) made the comet-like forms appear larger, confirming to him that they were actually out there, in the cosmos. "Suddenly my box lost its mystery," Reich wrote of his resulting epiphany, which explained why he saw blue vapors, spirals, and dots in his orgone box even without the presence of SAPA-bions.[46] The "orgone energy" he'd discovered and concentrated in his Faraday cage, he now thought, was in fact omnipresent.

Reich seems to have spent the entire vacation staring through his tube at the pulsating fog that he saw in varying intensities wherever he looked. In *The Cancer Biopathy* (1948), he writes of nocturnal ramblings during which he examined sections of pavement, earth, lawn, shrubs, and flowers through his tube. It was like looking at the world through a kaleidoscope—everything he focused on seemed to disintegrate into firefly-like dots of light and mesmerizing, spinning waves. We live, Reich wrote in his journal, "at the bottom of an ocean of orgone energy. The air which we breathe is in reality orgone energy."[47]

When Reich returned to New York that September, after buying the cabin where he'd made his exciting discovery (he named it Orgonotic Lodge), he mounted a green light in his small box so that it might replicate the color of the night sky, and he drilled holes in the walls to "reproduce the flickering of the stars."[48] He also attached a bellows lens to it, so that it looked like a large old-fashioned camera. The lens was reversed, and when you looked through it into the box the magnified interior seemed to sparkle with blue light. He described this perforated version of the orgone accumulator as a sort of cosmos in a box. Reich planned to build one big enough for therapeutic purposes: "It is as if I were to let the patients sit in the middle of the aurora borealis," Reich wrote in his diary when he imagined the possible effects of this larger device.[49]

In December 1940, Reich built the first human-sized orgone energy accumulator, which was five feet high, and set it up in his Forest Hills basement. Reich acknowledged that the box, which improved on and replaced his Faraday cage, was an "unimpressive looking cabinet," but he asserted that it was "not at all the unremarkable box it seems to be . . . I sat in it twenty minutes naked to the waist. And it was very strong."[50] It was built of plywood and lined with sheet iron, and had a small window in the door to provide ventilation; you sat in it on a chair like a priest in a confessional. Reich thought that the organic material would absorb the orgone from the atmosphere and channel it into the metal interior. "How the energy penetrates the metal, we do not know," he admitted, and he also left unexplained why the orgone energy, if it could pierce metal, was reflected and concentrated in the interior of the machine, rather than disappearing through the other side.[51] The lining between the organic and inorganic layers was stuffed with rock wool, which was supposed to do something to prevent seepage. To increase the strength of the device he built up the layers, so that a series of up to twenty boxes were nested inside each other, like a Russian doll.

In the eighteenth century Franz Anton Mesmer discovered that the powers of his own animal magnetism were magnified if he stood with one foot in a pail of water with an iron rod in it. When he arrived in Paris from Vienna, where his reputation as an extraordinary healer had preceded him, Mesmer was besieged by more patients than he could hope to treat individually, as many as two hundred a day, so he invented the *baquet* to accommodate them en masse. The *baquet* was essentially a gigantic bucket, a huge Leyden jar supposedly charged by the animal magnetism or "vital fire" emanating from Mesmer's own person. Some *baquets* could seat twenty people, who would link fingers to complete an electrical circuit around the device, and Mesmer had four of these in his Paris treatment rooms at the Hôtel Bullion on rue Coq Héron. He would prowl around the expectant, highly charged circle with a magnetized wand, sending clients into fits of dramatic convulsions, hysterical laughter, and vomiting with his enthralling brown-eyed stare. Mesmer was speedily converting metropolitan hypochondria and ennui into "a steady stream of silver," and soon attracted the attention of King Louis XVI, who appointed a royal commission led by Benjamin Franklin to investigate Mesmer's technique.

Though you sat in it alone, Reich's orgone energy accumulator had certain parallels with the *baquet*. (For his most aristocratic patients, who included Marie Antoinette, Mesmer supplied miniature versions of his famous tubs so that they could take private baths in their own homes.) Reich was disillusioned by the ability of psychoanalysis to treat only one patient on the couch at a time and, after a radical attempt to take psychoanalysis to the "sickbed of society" by instituting a series of free and public clinics, he invented the orgone accumulator as a sort of psychoanalysis machine, with which he hoped more easily to achieve his messianic hopes for social change. Though Reich's psychoanalytically informed sexual theories were incredibly modern, even his supporters acknowledged that as a scientist he was a throwback to the eighteenth century. William Burroughs compared the orgone accumulator to a Leyden jar, and the legendary anarchist Paul Goodman, who was one of Reich's most enthusiastic American promoters, compared Reich to Alessandro Volta, who had created the first battery by wrapping metal rods in wet rags, "a device as primitive as Reich's box."[52]

Reich thought that when you sat in his box naked (as he advised), enveloped by orgone energy, a reaction was precipitated between its concentrated orgone system—three to five times as strong as in the open air—and the orgone in one's own body. He called this vibrant interaction "orgonotic lumination" and compared it to the fusion of energy systems in sexual contact, or when an infant is at the breast.[53] We were dealing, Reich asserted, with a "sexual energy," and—though he would later downplay this when his box became the object of controversy, preferring to emphasize its general health benefits—he claimed that you could feel "sexual excitation" when charged up by the machine.[54]

"It was put in the basement," Ilse Ollendorff recalled of being shut in the box, "and I remember the excitement when we all took turns sitting in it and, upon having our temperatures taken, saw Reich's prediction of a rise in temperature come true."[55] (It wasn't that the machine functioned as a sweatbox; the temperature rise was recorded even in an empty accumulator.) Reich also discovered that experimental subjects got a salty taste when they put their tongue an inch or so from the interior walls of the box and that they felt a prickling and warmth when they did the same with their palms; they experienced nausea and dizziness if they stayed in too long, for which Reich simply prescribed fresh air. This time limit varied; for repressed, "sluggish individuals" it sometimes took weeks for their bioenergetic fields to be charged up enough to feel these effects, whereas "lively" persons overdosed after only half an hour in the device.[56]

Reich made such extraordinary claims for his box that even this primitive contraption seemed as futuristic a device as those dreamed up at the World's Fair. He thought that in charging oneself with orgone energy one could increase one's resistance to disease and combat ailments from cancer to varicose veins and psoriasis. "It seems even more unbelievable," Reich wrote of these curative promises, "when one realizes that the accumulator contains no sophisticated components, wiring, buttons, or motors."[57] Reich applied for a patent for his orgone energy accumulator early the next year, but none was ever granted. A patent officer from Virginia wrote back to Reich, incredulously, "Do you think I want to go out on a limb and to make myself look ridiculous?"[58]

The month before Reich arrived in America, the Hungarian physicists Leo Szilard and Edward Teller had paid a visit to Albert Einstein at his summer retreat on Long Island. They presented him with a moral dilemma that would force Einstein to reconsider his long commitment to nonviolence: scientists in Berlin were stockpiling uranium and experimenting with nuclear chain reactions that would enable them to create superbombs. Einstein's colleagues urged him to write to President Roosevelt and encourage him to enter this deadly arms race.

Einstein agreed. His letter to the president warned that scientists at Einstein's own alma mater, the Kaiser Wilhelm Institute in Berlin, were experimenting with nuclear chain reactions, and that they now had a monopoly on uranium from the mines in Nazi-occupied Czechoslovakia. Unless America stockpiled enough uranium to compete, he advised, Germany would have an insurmountable advantage in the race to make "extremely powerful bombs."[59]

The letter initiated the Manhattan Project and launched the nuclear arms race. Later, Einstein would describe it as the "one great mistake in my life."[60] An article published in *Newsweek* in 1947, "Einstein, the Man Who Started It All," conferred on him the moral responsibility for, as Einstein himself put it, "opening that Pandora's box." After American bombs were dropped on Hiroshima and Nagasaki, sending mushroom clouds over ten miles into the air and incinerating over 210,000 people, the legendary pacifist told the magazine, "Had I known that the Germans would not succeed in developing the atom bomb, I would not have supported its construction."[61]

Though Reich thought of his creation—at least initially—as benign, his own box created its own storm of controversy. Reich contrasted his discovery of the healing "life rays" that he thought he could accumulate in his device with the guns capable of firing "death rays" that Nikola Tesla was working on in 1940 and which, as *The New York Times* reported, could supposedly melt a plane at a distance of two hundred fifty miles; Tesla thought that the military could use them to establish an invisible "Chinese Wall of Defense" around the United States.[62] Reich would later also oppose his beneficial orgone energy to the deadly atomic forces unleashed by Robert Oppenheimer and the Manhattan Project team's apocalyptic weapon.

Though they'd never met, Reich wrote to Einstein on December 30, 1940, asking if he could meet with him to discuss an "urgent scientific matter," namely his discovery of a hitherto unknown form of energy. Reich wrote:

> *Dear Professor Einstein,*
> *. . . Several years ago I discovered a specific, biologically effective energy which in many ways behaves differently from anything that is known about electromagnetic energy. The matter is too complicated and sounds too improbable to be explained clearly in a brief letter. I can only indicate that I have evidence that this energy, which I have called orgone, exists not only in living organisms but also in the soil and in the atmosphere; it is visible and can be concentrated and measured, and I am using it with some success in research on cancer therapy.*
> *This matter is becoming too much for me for practical and financial reasons, and broad cooperation is needed. There is some reason to believe that it might be of use in the fight against the fascist plague . . . I hesitate to follow the usual route of sending a report to the Academy of Physics, and you may find my caution strange, but it is based on extremely negative experiences.*[63]

Einstein, full of goodwill toward a fellow émigré and attracted to any idea that might help fight fascism, invited Reich to come to see him in Princeton two weeks later. Writing in 1971, Einstein's biographer Ronald Clark expressed surprise that his subject did not immediately see through what seemed so obviously a crank letter. But Reich had mentioned that he'd been the late Sigmund Freud's assistant at the Ambulatorium in Vienna for eight years; this would have recommended him to Einstein, who had met Freud in Berlin in 1926. On the occasion of Freud's seventy-fifth birthday Einstein had written to him saying that he reserved every Tuesday evening for reading Freud's essays. His interest was more literary than practical: Einstein preferred to "remain in the darkness of not-having-been-analyzed." The famous pair had conducted a public exchange of letters in 1932 in which Einstein asked Freud, "Why war?"

At 3:30 p.m. on January 13, 1941, Reich stood on the porch of Albert Einstein's home in eager anticipation of a meeting for which he had spent the last fortnight preparing. He was half an hour early. Reich thought that he'd discovered the "unified field theory," or theory of everything, that had so far eluded the famous scientist. (Reich had a legal document drawn up and notarized that laid claim to his unique orgonotic description of the universe.)

The two men spoke for almost five hours. It was, as Reich excitedly noted in his diary, "the first genuine and fruitful scientific discussion in ten years!"[64] Reich showed Einstein the telescopic tube, or organoscope, through which Einstein observed the same iridescence as Reich when they put out the lights in the room. "But I see the flickering all the time," Einstein reasoned when they turned the light back on and the effect continued. "Could it not be in my eyes?"[65] Reich assured him that when you looked at the rays through a magnifying glass they appeared bigger, so they had to be objective. Hesitantly, because he feared Einstein wouldn't believe him, Reich told him about his most astounding discovery—the unexpected rise in temperature he'd observed in the accumulator.

> To that he exclaimed: "That is impossible. Should it be true, it would be a great bomb!" (verbatim). He got rather excited and I too. We discussed it sharply and then he said that I should send him a small accumulator, and if the facts were true, he would support my discovery.[66]

It is notable, considering Einstein's preoccupation at the time with the atomic race and the specter of apocalypse, that he should have referred to Reich's alleged discovery of a free-energy machine as potentially a "bomb." Before departing, Reich asked the famously eccentric physicist if he could now understand why people considered him crazy. To this, Reich recalled in his account of the affair, Einstein uttered the ambiguous response: "I can believe that."[67]

Whatever he thought, Einstein decided to give Reich the benefit of the doubt, much as ten years earlier he'd granted Upton Sinclair's idea of "mental radio" (telepathy) a hearing. Reich had a small orgone accumulator built and took it to Princeton two weeks later. Reich and Einstein assembled the experimental box in Einstein's cellar without delay, placing it on a small table with a control thermometer hanging three or four feet above it in the air. Reich warned Einstein not to spend more than an hour in the room with the device, and to breathe some fresh air immediately after exposure to it.

"After some time he and I could both see that the temperature above the Accumulator was higher by about one degree than the temperature of the surrounding air," Reich wrote. "We were both very glad. He wanted to keep the Accumulator for about 2 or 3 weeks and then write to me. After about 10 days he wrote me a letter."[68]

Einstein wrote that he'd conducted several days' worth of experiments on the device, and together with an assistant he had found that there was a convection of heat from the ceiling to the tabletop. They took the accumulator apart and discovered that there was in any case a temperature difference between the areas above and under the table, thereby proving that the accumulator itself wasn't generating heat. What Reich observed, Einstein concluded, had a commonplace explanation: it was the result of air circulation and heat transfer within the room. "Through these experiments," Einstein wrote, "I regard the matter as completely solved."[69]

Reich had hoped Einstein would report his discovery to the Academy of Physics and invite him to join the exclusive Institute for Advanced Study at Princeton, where he thought he'd finally be among equals. He experimented frantically with his accumulator over the next fortnight to prove himself right, and wrote Einstein a twenty-six-page letter reasserting his claims and detailing data that summarized the spate of discoveries he'd made since 1934. Then he begged Einstein to help him in a striking formulation that implied the necessary rescue of his invention and his sanity: "I know that this is a great deal to accept all at once," Reich wrote. "It sounds 'mad,' and I cannot cope with it by myself."[70] Einstein did not reply.

Reich responded to this rejection, as he had to so many others, with a spurt of creativity and an avalanche of new discoveries. He took on his first cancer patient, whom he refers to in his journal only as Mrs. Pops. Mrs. Pops, who was estimated to have only six weeks to live, came to him in severe pain, as Reich later noted in *The Cancer Biopathy* (1948): "Her spine had been destroyed in two places, and several metastatic tumors (originating from her breast cancer) had been found in her pelvic bone."[71] Reich thought that Mrs. Pops had fallen victim to cancer as a result of her "sex-starvation," because she was a widow of twelve years whose husband had been impotent before he died.

Mrs. Pops came to Forest Hills every day for half-hour sessions in the box; it was Reich's hope that the accumulation of orgone energy would help to dissolve both her repressions and her tumors. According to his notes, her skin reddened when she sat in it, her blood pressure decreased, she sweated. Shortly afterward, Reich reported that Mrs. Pops seemed to be miraculously healed, "at least for the moment"; she could sleep without morphine and was no longer bedridden (he had also encouraged her to take on a lover in order to cement her cure).[72] Encouraged, Reich took on three other patients who were on the verge of death and went on to treat their cancers with orgone irradiation—effectively, he believed. He set up a dedicated clinic at his house in Forest Hills, the Orgone and Cancer Research Laboratories, to administer these cures.

Reich wrote to Einstein again, not once but regularly, reporting the results of his experiments. Einstein's secretary, Helen Dukas, consigned all of Reich's letters to the *"komische Mappe"* (the curiosity file), along with missives from flat-earthers and requests from organizations such as the New York Shoe Club, which asked Einstein to donate a right boot to their collection.

According to Ilse Ollendorff, Reich was baffled by Einstein's silence. He came to suspect that Einstein was covering up for his embarrassment at being proved wrong in his experiments with the accumulator. Reich wrote to a friend in 1944, "To this day I am convinced that [Einstein] is fully aware that I am right."[73] He suspected that "some of the pestilent rumors" being circulated by psychoanalysts about his sanity had reached Einstein, and that "obviously he wanted to be careful."[74]

Only when Reich threatened to publish their brief correspondence three years later did Einstein himself deign to reply to him. He wrote a curt note saying that he was unable to give the matter any more time and demanded that his name not be "misused for advertising purposes—especially in a matter that has not my confidence" (his secretary had by then returned Reich's accumulator and organoscope, the result of some pestering on Reich's part).[75]

Reich was so stung by his one-sided engagement with the physicist that he eventually published an account of it under the title *The Einstein Affair* (1953). By then Reich had become convinced that other forces were at work in his rejection. One of Einstein's early collaborators, Leopold Infeld, had left North America in 1950 and returned to Communist Poland, prompting speculation that America's nuclear secrets might be divulged. Reich cut out a newspaper article on the subject, and concluded that Infeld must have been the assistant who had tested the accumulator; he now suspected that a Communist conspiracy lay behind Einstein's rejection, which explained to him Einstein's "peculiar behavior after his initial enthusiasm." In fact, Infeld was not in Princeton in 1941. He had taken up a post as a professor at the University of Toronto two years earlier.

While he treated his cancer patients and waited for Einstein to reply, Reich wrote to Alvin Johnson, the head of the New School, with the news that he had "succeeded in rescuing several human beings from impending death" in his secret experiments with the orgone energy accumulator.[76] Hoping to contribute to the war effort, he also suggested teaching a new course, The Mass Psychology of Fascism. Johnson, who thought Reich's cancer cure claims sounded like quackery, thanked him for the "significant teaching" he'd done and politely dismissed him from his post; he advised Reich that his orgone work "belongs in a medical college or in your private laboratory, rather than in an institution like ours."[77]

In June 1941, a month after Reich's dismissal from the New School, the father of an eight-year-old girl who had cancer visited him to discuss possible treatment. The man then approached the American Medical Association (AMA) to inquire further about Reich's brand of therapy. They warned him that Reich was not a doctor and threatened to have him arrested for posing as one. (Reich had tried, and failed, to get his foreign medical license endorsed.)

Around the same time, he was evicted from his home on Kessel Street because his neighbors had complained to his landlord about his keeping experimental rodents there. He raised $14,000 from his supporters to buy a larger house nearby, just around the corner from the West Side Tennis Stadium. Among those who contributed to the loan was Walter Briehl, who was becoming increasingly frustrated with Reich and eventually fell out with him entirely. He had tried to persuade Reich to take the state medical exams, but Reich had refused: How could he be judged by people who he felt knew less than he did? Didn't his discoveries represent a paradigm shift in conventional science?

"At the first, I was a member of [Reich's] group," Briehl wrote in 1966 (in his entry on Reich in *Psychoanalytic Pioneers*),

> but it was obvious that personality changes had occurred and that he was not the Reich of old, of the psychoanalytic therapy seminars in Vienna. Finally, he began to act with increasing irritability and projected hostility to helpful advice offered in various categories (for example, whether to avoid conflict, how to effect adjustment, or suggestions pertaining to medical licensure); now with this state of affairs—offering no basis for personal or professional understanding—further association became impossible and our relationship terminated.[78]

It was not exactly the new start Reich had hoped for in America, and he became increasingly belligerent as a result. In July 1941 he composed a letter from his Maine retreat to his half-dozen supporters, asking them not to be too optimistic about his cancer cure; it was not that he himself doubted its efficacy, but he feared that the more hope they placed in it, the more virulent their reaction to any disappointments would be. Reich wrote that orgone therapy "definitely is able to destroy cancerous growth. This is proved by the fact that tumors in all parts of the body are disappearing or diminishing. No other remedy in the world can claim such a thing." But, Reich warned, "the neuroses and disastrous character habits are lurking behind the cancerous local tumor, at any moment ready to jump forth from the background and to smash our success in destroying the cancerous growth in many different ways."[79]

In *The Cancer Biopathy* (1948), Reich would list, rather defensively, a series of complications that had occasionally spoiled his fantastic cure: The accumulator could charge his patients sexually to a degree they couldn't tolerate, which might cause them to flee in fear from treatment. In one case orgone therapy reawakened a case of childhood claustrophobia, which made the beneficial use of the accumulator unbearable. Sometimes when the body tried to excrete the toxic waste left by the dissolving tumor it lodged elsewhere in the body, with disastrous consequences. Another patient didn't come to him early enough because he'd heard the rumor circulating that Reich was insane; in this instance "the babble of irresponsible colleagues cost a human life," Reich wrote sternly.[80]

In his letter, Reich advised his inner circle that they would have to stick together and steel themselves for "disastrous interferences and public disagreement" before the validity of their treatment would be widely accepted. Their work threatened the medical and radium industries, which would do anything they could to silence the competition orgone radiation represented (Reich made the analogy that Edison wouldn't have been able to rely on the producers of gas for help with his electric light). Anticipating defections, Reich told those disciples without the stomach for the fight to withdraw from the important work before the unpleasantness began.

"Having worked on the problem of biological energy since 22 years," Reich wrote in his still shaky English,

> and on the problem of cancer since about 14 years, I cannot go back and I cannot stop. I have to go on even if all the patients which we are taking into the experiment should die for 2, 3, or 4 years to come. I could not stop under any circumstances, because I have seen many times and quite clearly that the Orgone radiation exists, that it charges up the blood, that it destroys cancerous growth in any part of the body, that it strengthens the body and that it removes pain. That is for me personally, and I think it should also be for you, reason enough to bite yourself with your teeth and your fingers

deeply into the matter and to hold on to go through, even if it should take 10 or 20 years.[81]

In 1919 one of Freud's pupils, Viktor Tausk, committed suicide by hanging and shooting himself simultaneously. Tausk's suicide note was addressed to Freud. "I have no melancholy," it read. "My suicide is the healthiest, most decent deed of my unsuccessful life."[82] Tausk had been Freud's pupil but had been devastated when Freud refused to analyze him and sent him instead to see Helene Deutsch. When Tausk died, he'd just completed an essay, "On the Origin of the 'Influencing Machine' in Schizophrenia" (1919), which has since become a classic in the psychiatric literature. Reich met Freud in 1919, and it is often supposed that he took the seat Tausk's death had left empty in the psychoanalytic circle. In 1923 Reich gave a paper at a meeting of the Vienna Psychoanalytic Society on introspection in a schizophrenic patient, in which he confirmed many of Tausk's findings.

In his essay Tausk described the elaborate mechanical devices that paranoid schizophrenics invent in their imaginations in order to explain their mental disintegration. As the boundaries between the world and the schizophrenic's mind break down, Tausk wrote, the patient often feels persecuted by "machines of a mystical nature," which supposedly work by means of radio waves, telepathy, X-rays, invisible wires, or other mysterious forces. The machines are believed to be operated by enemies as instruments of torture and mind control, and the operators are thought to be able to implant and remove ideas and feelings and inflict pain from a distance. Patients typically invoke all the powers known to technology to explain these machines' obscure workings. Nevertheless, the machines always transcend attempts to give a coherent account of their function: "All the discoveries of mankind are regarded as inadequate to explain the marvelous powers of this machine."[83]

These "influencing machines" are described by their troubled inventors as complex structures constructed of "boxes, cranks, levers, wheels, buttons, wires, batteries and the like."[84] Sometimes these devices are thought to be their doubles, unconscious projections of their fragmented bodily experience and, more specifically, of their sexual organs. Tausk told the unhappy tale of Natalija A., a thirty-one-year-old former philosophy student, in order to shed light on the origins of this schizophrenic delusion. For the past six and a half years she had been haunted by her double, who took the form of the oustretched figure of a sargophagus; the torso, lined with velvet or silk, lifted off like the lid of a coffin to reveal the inner workings of the machine, which consisted of batteries supposed to represent the internal organs. She thought that the uncanny device which manipulated her worked by telepathy and was operated by a jealous suitor, one of her old college professors. When he struck the machine she felt pain; when he stroked the box's genitals, she felt aroused.

Tausk thought that all influencing machines were at some level the doubles of their inventor-victims, narcissistic projections conjured up by them. The machine, which always seemed to control the patient, was the embodiment of the schizophrenic's own sense of alienation from his or her body and a mad attempt to forestall that disintegration. In the course of his analysis of Natalija A., Tausk noticed how the machine ceased to resemble her. Her double became flat and indistinct in her descriptions of it, shedding its human attributes as it became purely mechanical. But Tausk maintained that all schizophrenics' machines were displaced representations of themselves, not merely indecipherable fictions. Tausk believed that all these confabulations, however mechanically complicated, were once the patients' doubles, which would inevitably become lost over time in the cogs and wheels of the influencing machine.

In the American edition of *The Function of the Orgasm* (1942), Reich praised Tausk's essay for its psychological insights: "It was not until I discovered bioelectric excitation in the vegetative currents that I correctly understood this matter," Reich wrote. "Tausk had been right: It is his own body that the schizophrenic patient experiences as the persecutor. I can add to this that he cannot cope with the vegetative currents which break through. He has to experience them as something alien, as belonging to the outer world and having an evil intent."[85]

The genius, like the schizophrenic, has a vivid sense of these terrifying forces, Reich suggested, but rather than fleeing from them into psychosis, the genius is able to harness them. Reich noted in his diary, in reference to himself, "'Genius' is knowledge of unarmoured life plus the courage which that knowledge produces."[86] Reich cited a pantheon of his heroes who had been characterized as "crazy": Ibsen, Nietzsche, Van Gogh, Galileo, and Beethoven. Of the fine line between sanity and madness, Reich wrote, "one could venture the assumption that the great creator in science or art is deeply engrossed in his inner creative forces; that he is and feels removed from petty, everyday noise in order to follow his creativeness more fully and ably. *Homo normalis* does not understand this remoteness and is apt to call him 'crazy.' He calls 'psychotic' what is foreign to him, what threatens his mediocrity."[87]

Reich declared his deep sympathy for mental patients: "The schizophrenic merely represents in grotesquely magnified condition what characterizes modern man in general. Modern man is estranged from his own nature, the biological core of his being, and he experiences it as something alien and hostile. He has to hate everyone who tries to restore his contact with it."[88] In vegetotherapy, Reich sought to make his patients feel this energy as a positive force coursing around their own bodies, dissolving the deadness, the repressions, to make libido fully accessible to them.

*The Function of the Orgasm* was written in part as a response to Reich's former colleagues' questions about his sanity. Soon after his arrival in New York, a rumor circulated that Reich had been institutionalized at the Utica State Mental Hospital. Though this was untrue (Reich suspected Fenichel, who was now in Los Angeles, of spreading the tale), it perhaps originated because of the superficial similarity between Reich's box and the "Utica Crib," a nineteenth-century restraining device that originated there and looked like a wooden cage.

In the fall of 1941 Reich took on a thirty-two-year-old schizophrenic woman for therapy and treated her for several weeks in the orgone energy accumulator. When Reich told her about the workings of the machine, she immediately understood it; she told him that he was the first person she'd met who could explain the powers surging within her in a way she understood. He tried to get her to accept these powers as currents in her own body, but she continued to project them as, in his account, "a foreign, strange force, which enlivened the things in the room."[89]

Though these outward forces seemed to Reich to be clear clinical symptoms of schizophrenia in his patient, he, too, had been sensing such forces ever since his bioelectric experiments, and he, too, now saw them as not only coursing around the body but as out there in the cosmos (since the nineteenth century, manic depression and schizophrenia have been seen as continuous, mania having many schizoid features). The shell of the orgone accumulator, which perhaps represented an attempt to contain these energies and to shield rather than merely to energize the patient, might be seen as a kind of coffin. Freud, discussing Tausk's patient Natalija A. with his Wednesday seminar group, had taken up the detail of the sarcophagus in her case, and noted that the ancient Egyptian mode of burial represented the comforting return to the mother's womb. In other words, the "influencing machine" into which Natalija A. withdrew embodied her paranoid attempt to rebuild a fragmented world. Had Reich, in retreating to a similarly comforting space, crossed the line between genius and schizophrenia that he himself had defined?

Tausk took the term "influencing machine" from a device invented in 1706 by Francis Hauksbee, a student of Isaac Newton's. Hauksbee's "influence machine" was a spinning glass globe that cracked like lightning when touched, transmitting an electrical spark and emitting a greenish neon-like light when rubbed—a mysterious luminosity that he called "the glow of life." These supernatural-looking effects were caused by the introduction of static electricity into a vacuum; it worked like the shimmering vacuum tube of the modern TV. (Its incarnation in the schizophrenic had similarly mesmerizing effects: "The influencing machine," Tausk wrote, "[often] makes the patient see pictures."[90]) Reich maintained that orgone energy glowed blue, and he designed his machine to collect this "life energy."

Reich's accumulator, which would go on to earn him worldwide fame and bring about his downfall, might be seen as a version of such a box with obscure powers from which can be inferred the autobiography of a sometimes brilliant and paranoid man—a device that also had an outward form of "influence" as a crucible for the sexual preoccupations of a generation and the aspirations of the radical left. In the ideological flux after the Second World War, Reich's ideas pointed the way to a new politics and were the subject of intense interest and debate. Reich identified barriers to political and sexual freedom and offered the users of the accumulator the means to override them. In the 1940s and '50s artists and intellectuals arrived at Reich's Orgone and Cancer Research Laboraties hoping to shed their repressions and enthusiastically built and shut themselves in his boxes, much as the fashionable and the curious flocked to Mesmer's rooms to see and experience the miraculous transformation promised by the *baquet*—a place that had to be reserved far in advance and cost roughly the same as desirable tickets to the opera. The novelist Stefan Zweig described this "collective frenzy" as "Mesmeromania." One might call the Reich craze Orgonomania.

At first Reich convinced thousands of people of the orgone accumulator's benevolent power. The removal of blockages from the sick body became a metaphor for the cleansing from the body politic of all barriers to freedom: a corrupt, artificial, and decadent society would be shaken up for the better. But he soon began to feel that the energy he had discovered could turn evil, and that its deadly impact was a threat to the world. He would invent ever more intricate devices to combat the spinning forces conjured by his own mind.

On December 7, 1941, the Japanese attack on Pearl Harbor killed 2,000 people and destroyed most of the U.S. Pacific Fleet. Germany was thought to have "induced" or "goaded" Japan to attack, and in the next few days the United States entered the war against not only Japan but the whole Axis coalition. On the evening of the Pearl Harbor attack, 770 Japanese were taken into custody on the orders of the FBI, and over the next few months almost 10,000 other Japanese, German, and Italian nationals were arrested. All the Japanese, German, and Italian nationals who lived in the United States found themselves classed as "enemy aliens." They were forced to carry identification cards, were forbidden to possess radios, cameras, or weapons, and were liable to be arrested, detained, and deported at any time.

Two years earlier, after the signing of the Hitler-Stalin Pact on

August 24, 1939 (when Reich was en route to America), the FBI hired one hundred fifty additional field officers and began assembling a list of potentially dangerous aliens to be arrested in a national emergency. Reich had renounced communism in Norway, well before many party members on the other side of the Atlantic who remained blind to Stalin's atrocities had done so, but nevertheless his name soon came up as a possible subversive. In July 1940, Theodore Wolfe's ex-wife, the psychiatrist Helen Flanders Dunbar, had been questioned as to whether Reich was a "fifth columnist." Unbeknownst to Reich, he had been under surveillance by the FBI as a suspected Communist since January 1941, the month he met Einstein (who was also being watched by the Bureau). His phone was tapped, his letters intercepted.

The American Communist Party, which had thrived during the Great Depression, hemorrhaged as a result of the Soviet alliance with Hitler because it had leaned so heavily on antifascist front groups for its support. Ironically, just as the threat represented by communism that preoccupied the United States for the next few decades was first being aired, the domestic party actually was in crisis. After Stalin's domestic crimes became well-known, and with the brutal suppression of the Soviet Union's satellite states, communism no longer looked so appealing. In the 1940 presidential election, which saw Roosevelt elected to a historic third term, only 46,000 voted for the leader of the American Communist Party, Earl Browder, half the number that had turned out for him four years earlier. As the historian Ted Morgan put it in *Reds: McCarthyism in Twentieth-Century America*, "From 1935 to 1939 the American Communist Party luxuriated in a popularity it would never regain."[91]

In 1940 Martin Dies, the cantankerous Democratic congressman from Texas who headed the House Un-American Activities Committee (HUAC), published *The Trojan Horse in America*. He maintained that fascists and especially Communists were eroding American life, just as they'd already done in Europe, and he blamed European immigrants for this decline. After witnessing a May Day parade in New York, he concluded that two thirds of the Communist Party membership were foreign-born. Dies, who strongly opposed the New Deal, which he sought to discredit by linking it with subversive groups, preceded Joseph McCarthy in alleging that 2,850 federal employees were Communist Party members. The Communists who had supposedly infiltrated the U.S. government included economist Maurice Parmelee, author of *Nudism in Modern Life: The New Gymnosophy* (1933), which advocated nudity in schools, homes, and the workplace. The well-illustrated book was brandished by Dies as evidence of Parmelee's supposed communism. For Dies, who saw Reds in and under every bed, Parmelee's "crackpot and immoral" ideas made him particularly suspect, and Dies managed to get the sexual utopian fired from his position at the Board of Economic Welfare.

The FBI was similarly suspicious of Reich's sex-political theories. It discovered that a Dr. Wilhelm Reich was on the medical advisory board of the American Communist Party and the editor of the board's health magazine, *Health and Hygiene*. An article in the Communist newspaper, the *Daily Worker*, dated November 7, 1941, noted that Reich taught political economy at the Workers' School. An American consul in Norway confirmed Reich's Communist past in Europe, reporting, "Dr. Reich had a considerable following in Austria, especially among the women doctors."[92] It was erroneously stated that Reich had been a party member in Norway until 1936, when he was expelled from the party for failing to adhere to the "party line."

On December 12, 1941, one day after Germany declared war on the United States, Reich was arrested at two-thirty in the morning. The two FBI agents who came to arrest and escort him to a detention center on Ellis Island wouldn't allow him to call a lawyer or even to go to the bathroom to get dressed without one of them being present. He reached Ellis Island at 4:20 a.m. and was fingerprinted, photographed, and incarcerated. Reich's FBI file read as follows:

INTERNAL SECURITY—ALIEN ENEMY CONTROL UNIT

| | |
|---|---|
| Age: | 44 yrs |
| Sex: | Male |
| Color: | White |
| Complexion: | Very ruddy |
| Eyes: | Brown |

| | |
|---|---|
| Hair: | Gray |
| Height: | 5'9½" |
| Weight: | 158 lbs |
| Build: | Stocky |
| Race: | Jewish |
| Nationality: | Austrian |
| Date and place of birth: | Dobzownica [*sic*], Austria, March 24, 1897 |
| Alien registration number: | 4505146 |

Reich slept on a spread-out newspaper in Ellis Island's crowded main hall, surrounded by members of the pro-Nazi German American Bund. In February 1939, 22,000 members of the Bund and their supporters had held a Nuremberg-style rally in Madison Square Garden at which their leader, Fritz Kuhn, criticized "Frank D. Rosenfeld's Jew Deal" (twice as many antifascists protested outside). Reich wrote in his appeal against his imprisonment that he feared that these other detainees might kill him if they learned about his long record of antifascist work.

As it had when he was under stress during the First World War and at the height of the Norwegian campaign, the psoriasis Reich had suffered from since adolescence again flared up, and the following night he was transferred to the hospital ward so that he could take regular baths to relieve his skin condition. Ollendorff was allowed to see him only two times a week; Annie Reich forbade her children from visiting their father. His lawyer, Lewis Goldinger, informed him that there was a 40 percent chance he'd have to sit out the war in an internment camp. Reich wrote, "I looked up every day from behind the bars to the Statue of Liberty in New York Harbor. Her light shone brightly into a dark night."[93]

Reich's house was searched; his basement laboratory intrigued the FBI agents, and in his thousand-volume library they turned up supposed evidence of his Communist and fascist sympathies: the FBI confiscated a biography of Lenin; a copy of Hitler's *Mein Kampf*; a book by Max Hodann, the German sex educator, on the Soviet Union; a Russian alphabet for children that Reich had brought back as a souvenir for his children when he visited Russia in 1929; and two books by Trotsky, the thinker who had led Reich to identify both Nazism and communism as variants of totalitarianism.

Special agents interviewed Alvin Johnson at the New School, who refused to discuss Reich's political beliefs. (Johnson's name is blacked out in the FBI file, but an FBI agent confirmed his identity to the Food and Drug Administration when it began investigating Reich in the late 1940s.) The year before, to counter charges of radicalism, Johnson had been forced to incorporate clauses in the New School's charter that barred any "communist or fellow traveler" from his institution's faculty and affirmed his staff's appreciation of America as a "citadel of liberalism."[94] Reich, who had become disillusioned with communism even before the Nazi-Soviet pact, would have happily signed such a document, but Johnson explained to the FBI that Reich's contract had not been renewed after his first year of teaching because Reich "is very egotistical and disregards the ideas of other scientists; and he claims to have a cure-all for cancer—all of which . . . smacked of 'quack' tactics on [Reich's] part."[95]

The FBI wasn't interested in Reich's purported cancer cure—rather, in determining his political sympathies. Reich had a hearing in a Brooklyn court on December 26, where he was grilled about his supposed Communist affiliations and as to whether his new house had been bought with money from Moscow. The U.S. attorney who oversaw the hearing determined that there was not enough evidence to substantiate charges and recommended in his report "that the alien be unconditionally discharged." ("The alien appears to be egotistical," he wrote in his summary of the proceedings, and made an anti-Semitic and xenophobic remark: "His personality definitely characterizes his race and country.")[96] Reich was released eleven days later—after he'd threatened to go on a hunger strike. He'd been detained for three and a half weeks.

Despite being free, Reich's name was still kept on what was referred to by the Enemy Alien Control Unit as the "key figures list." He was reclassified by Internal Security as Group B: "Individuals believed to be somewhat less dangerous but whose activities should be restricted." He was therefore still kept under surveillance. Reich got wind of these subsequent investigations after he discovered that two "policemen" had been making inquiries about him with his neighbors, which seemed to justify his sense of persecution. He was removed from the key figures list in July 1943, when the attorney general declared the danger classifications unconstitutional, by which time half of the ten thousand internees had been released.

Reich was sure that it was his ex-wife and Dr. Lawrence Kubie, then secretary of the New York Psychoanalytic Institute, who had informed on him to the FBI, representing him as an active Communist and potential spy; this allegation was based on something Lore Reich had said to him several months before his arrest: "Watch out, Willie," she warned him. "Annie has been discussing something negative about you with Dr. Kubie."[97] However, no doubt Lore was referring to the unpleasant rumors, mainly concerning Reich's mental health, that were circulating in the psychoanalytic community, of which he himself was all too aware.

It turned out that Reich had been the victim of an extraordinary mix-up. There was a William Robert Reich living in Newark, New Jersey, who operated a small bookstore that was used as a distribution center for Communist propaganda. William (Bill) Reich, born the same year as Wilhelm, was also state literature director of the Communist Party of New Jersey and taught political economy on Friday evenings at the Workers' School at 35 East Twelfth Street in Manhattan, only a few blocks from the New School at 66 West Twelfth Street.

In 1950, during the HUAC investigation titled "The American Aspects of [the] Assassination of Leon Trotsky," it was revealed that Bill Reich had worked as a Stalinist plant, recruited by agents of the Soviet secret police to infiltrate Trotsky's American supporters. In March 1936, when Trotsky was still in Norway, Bill Reich had written an article in the *Western Worker* under the headline "Johnson, Hallett, Reich Repudiate Trotsky"; he was recruited the following year by Louis Francis Budenz, managing editor of the *Daily Worker* and a colleague at the Workers' School. Budenz was head of the Buben group of spies, as it was known by Soviet intelligence, until he left the party in 1945 and became an FBI informant, a publisher of anti-Communist exposés, and a HUAC star witness.

It was Budenz who outed Bill Reich to HUAC as one of the most "prominent . . . concealed Stalinists acting as Trotskyites."[98] He also revealed that another of the Soviet secret police's plants among Trotsky's American supporters, Ruby Weil, introduced Ramón Mercader to Trotsky's secretary, Sylvia Ageloff. They began a whirlwind affair, which gained Mercader access to Trotsky's heavily fortified Mexico City compound, where he penetrated Trotsky's skull with an ice pick. What role Bill Reich played in the plotting that lead to Trotsky's assassination, if any, is unknown. In 1960 Reich found himself before HUAC and, presented with solid proof of his Communist affiliations, chose to take the Fifth Amendment on almost every question. (Even though members of the Communist Party were still being brought to trial in the sixties under the Smith Act, in 1963 the U.S. attorney declined prosecution in Bill Reich's case.)

Soon after Wilhelm Reich was released, William "Bill" Reich left the East Coast to take up a teaching post in San Diego, where the FBI began keeping tabs on him. On November 2, 1943, acknowledging the error in the classified files, J. Edgar Hoover declared Wilhelm Reich's case formally closed.

*Seven*

The sociologist and writer Paul Goodman was dismissed from his teaching post at the University of Chicago in 1940 for his open bisexuality and multiple affairs with students. He returned to his birthplace, New York City, where he soon became one of Greenwich Village's best-known bohemian personalities. He was an anarchist and self-proclaimed enfant terrible with, the literary critic Alfred Kazin wrote, "a deep apostolic sense of himself."[1] In his memoir, *New York Jew*, Kazin confessed to having envied the "scandalous" Goodman of the early 1940s:

> He was open about his pickups, his hopes and disasters, his love of boys; I was awed by his hungry searching and the unashamed naïve egomania with which he celebrated his desires. He seemed to press his self-declared difference as a writer and his boldness as a lover into everything he said and wrote. He was as assertive as Robespierre, Napoleon, Trotsky. Anything I picked up of his always seemed to me as roughly written as a leaflet.[2]

Goodman, who would become famous in 1960 for his bestselling study of adolescent delinquency, *Growing Up Absurd*, was a prolific writer who by the age of thirty-five already had a dozen books under his belt. He had published two volumes of his Empire City trilogy—which he described as "An Almanac of Alienation"—as well as books of literary criticism, community planning, and psychoanalysis, and he was working on *Parents' Day* (1947), a fictional account of his firing in 1944 from the progressive Manumit School in upstate New York. His sexual libertarianism and insistence on his right to pursue relationships with students had, once again, gotten him into trouble.

In the late summer of 1945, Goodman received a phone call from Wilhelm Reich, who asked him to come and visit him in Forest Hills. "I was pleased and puzzled," Goodman later wrote, "and fondly hoped that this remarkable man would put me to some activity."[3] He had just published an article about Reich in Dwight Macdonald's influential anarchist-pacifist magazine, *Politics*. "The Political Meaning of Some Recent Revisions of Freud," published in July 1945, a month before the atomic bomb was dropped, would introduce Reich to a new and deeply receptive audience: America's avant-garde.

In the ideological confusion of the postwar period, before the entrenched politics of the cold war took root, Reich's ideas swiftly became popular among the American intelligentsia. Goodman became one of Reich's most vocal torchbearers and Reich was upheld by a younger generation as the leader of a new sexual movement. His ideas reached larger audiences than he could ever have imagined in Europe. Elsworth Baker, one of Reich's most prominent American disciples, acknowledged, "Orgonomy in America first became popular in Greenwich Village among the Bohemians and beatniks, where it was hailed as a free sex philosophy and the accumulator as a device that would build up potency. It was perceived to a great extent as a place in which to masturbate."[4]

In his *Politics* essay, Goodman favorably contrasted Reich's ideas with those of the then-successful neo-Freudian analysts, Karen Horney and her former lover Erich Fromm, who had published a bestselling book, *Escape from Freedom* (1941), in which he had liberally borrowed from Reich in order to explain why people sought refuge from their own responsibilities in authority figures. (Fromm told Fenichel that he hadn't acknowledged his debt to Reich in the book because he was sick of Reich's megalomania, "pathological self-love and arrogance.")[5] Goodman maintained that neither analyst was as politically progressive as he thought he was.

Despite Horney and Fromm's superficial use of the rhetoric of freedom, Goodman wrote, all that their therapeutic innovations promised was the reintegration of sick and neurotic patients into the status quo. "What a fantastic proposal," Goodman wrote in mockery of this goal, "when a society creates emotional tensions, to reorientate not the society but the people!" Essentially the revisionists proposed "the continued and more efficient working, without nervous breakdowns, of the modern industrial system, war and peace."[6]

In contrast to the subtle conformism of the neo-Freudians, Goodman argued, Reich looked beyond the humble parameters of one-on-one treatment to propose a different world to set against the one that was currently consumed by war. Deeply disenchanted with communism, Reich now called for the "abolishment of politics" and referred to the sexual utopia of his imagination as a "work democracy." Where politicians and bureaucrats had once again led the world to the brink of apocalypse, Reich proposed a new self-organizing structure in which politics would take place at a grassroots level. Reich, who had turned away from communism, now had a new slogan with which he prefaced all his books: "Love, work and knowledge are the wellsprings of life. They should also govern it."

Goodman celebrated Reich as the author of the manifesto of a much-needed "psychology of the revolution." Reich promised, Goodman enthused, to restore a repressed populace "to sexual health and animal spirits" with apocalyptic orgasms, a condition of sexual bliss in which they would no longer be able to "tolerate the mechanical and routine jobs they have been working at, but turn (at whatever general inconvenience) to work that is spontaneous and directly meaningful."[7] Goodman was inspired by Reich's vision of what he interpreted as eroticized anarchy. "Unrepressed people," Goodman promised, "will provide for themselves a society that is peaceable and orderly enough."[8]

Goodman rang the doorbell of Reich's Forest Hills home with fantasies that Reich would thank him for his propagandist efforts or employ him on some intellectual collaboration. What Reich really wanted was to demand that Goodman stop linking his name with "anarchists or libertarians." Reich was, it seems, a reluctant figure-head, wary of nihilistic interpretations of his work.

When he read Goodman's essay, Reich noted in his diary that Goodman had carried out a "dangerous derailment" of his thinking. Goodman promoted Reich as the architect of the "psychology of the revolution" but then argued that after the big push, the "psychology of the post-revolution" should be essentially Freudian. Reich provided the directions, Goodman implied in a parenthesis, but his map of the future was "excessively simple and Rousseauian," and Freud was a better guide to its actual terrain. Reich, of course, thought that he had gone beyond Freud with his scheme of orgasmic liberation and he suspected Goodman of a loss of nerve in failing to fully imagine the future as he did. "Since there are millions of Goodmans," Reich wrote, "every revolutionary movement fails."

Goodman was stunned by Reich's reaction, and replied, "Really, Dr. Reich, what is it to you if we younger folk call you an anarchist or not?" A. S. Neill had often warned Reich against allowing himself to be held up as an anarchist mascot: when the Freedom Press wanted to publish Reich in Britain, Neill warned, "If they publish you then your public will be limited and the big public will be suspicious . . . Some anarchists are claiming you already, so be careful."[9] This advice, which proved prescient, was obviously on Reich's mind when he summoned Goodman because he explained that if Goodman persisted in portraying his sexual philosophy as anarchist, then A. S. Neill would find it hard to keep his middle-class pupils in Summerhill, an argument that failed to convince Goodman: "My guess was that the doctor was suffering from the understandable paranoia of the refugee from Hitler," he wrote later.[10]

An unsent letter by Reich to Goodman, written after that visit, does indeed record Reich's besieged thinking: "Restriction of this work to a definite political group by way of a label is only apt to impede its general influence on the social process," Reich lectured his admirer. "As I once tried to formulate it, I am neither left nor right, but forward." He added, by way of justification, "I am fighting a human disease, called emotional pestilence by me, which has ravaged human society for more than four thousand years . . . I have been standing 'on the firing line' for about twenty years."[11]

By 1946, Reich had self-published translations by Theodore Wolfe of three of his books—*The Function of the Orgasm* (1942), *Character Analysis*, and *The Sexual Revolution* (both 1945)—all of which had been extensively revised to include the story of his discovery of orgone energy and to reflect his new politics. (In the new editions Reich also substituted "progressive" for "Communist" and "social responsibility" for "class consciousness.") By 1947 the Orgone Institute Press was selling four to five hundred books a week, allowing Reich to boast that "'everyone' in New York is talking about my work" and that his writings were selling "like warm bread."[12] His work appealed to intellectuals and bohemians on both coasts. In his biography of Saul Bellow, James Atlas wrote, "Reich's *Function of the Orgasm* was as widely read in progressive circles as Trotsky's *Art and Revolution* had been a decade before."[13]

After the Hitler-Stalin pact and the Moscow trials, Reich's updated theory of sexual repression seemed to offer the disenchanted left a convincing explanation both for large numbers of people having submitted to fascism and for communism's failure to be a viable alternative to it. Reich presented guilty-feeling ex-Stalinists and Trotskyites with an alternative program of sexual freedom with which to combat those totalitarian threats. In creating a morality out of pleasure, Reich allowed postwar radicals—many of them GIs returning from a Europe perceived as sexually loose (fifty million condoms had been sent overseas with the military; eight per man a month)—to view their promiscuity as political activism. Reich made them feel part of the sexual elite, superior to the "frozen," gray, corporate consensus. He showed them how they might lead more authentic, unfettered lives against the grain of an increasingly affluent society.

The sociologist Philip Rieff noted in *The Triumph of the Therapeutic* (1961) that Reich flattered creative types, whom he described as closest to his "genital character." He offered bohemians and intellectuals who had lost faith in Marxism, but who didn't want to resign themselves to Freudian pessimism, a language of opposition: "The artists and writers who followed Reich," Rieff observed, "were, like him, defeated men of the left; for the defeated who, nevertheless, retained their pride of alienation, Reich's brave announcements of an end of politics turned failure itself into a kind of victory."[14] For

Reich, artists were revolutionaries by virtue of their chosen career: "All that . . . is genuinely revolutionary, all genuine art," Reich wrote in *The Mass Psychology of Fascism*, "stems from the natural biological nucleus"—and many followed him in believing that they were forging a new world with their anarchic orgasms.[15]

Dwight Macdonald, the editor of *Politics*, had warned of home-grown totalitarianism in his book *Fascism and the American Scene*, published the year before Reich emigrated to America, and he was struck by Reich's connection of sexual and social repression. In response he tried to be as sexually liberated as possible, embarking on an open marriage and numerous affairs for apparently ideological reasons. The nude cocktail parties and orgies in the dunes that Macdonald presided over at his Cape Cod retreat—attended by Goodman, Fritz Perls, Norman Mailer, and others—were, as he saw it, a form of politics. There was a responsibility in hedonism. As Michael Wreszin put it in his 1994 biography of Macdonald, "In the gloom of the cold war years, intellectuals whose historicism had been shaken faced the choice of either accommodating themselves to a prosperous anti-Communist society or taking a stand directly on what Mailer, citing Reich, called 'the rebellious imperatives of the self.'"[16]

In celebrating the anarchy of the orgasm, in trying to explode their sense of alienation with pleasure, the left were able to justify their retreat from traditional politics. Macdonald's antiestablishment set were, he later admitted, "ever hopeful, ever disillusioned."[17] After they lost faith in communism, Reich was their next enthusiasm. The orgone box's empty chamber reflected the political vacuum in which members of the radical left then found themselves.

"We were looking to break out," Mailer explained when I asked him why Reich was such an influence on his generation of postwar intellectuals. "We were living in an ideological box and a great many ideas appealed to us. Anything that would enable us to break out, to break loose, and find some better way to live. Naturally those ideas appealed only to people who lived in the Village, but we were a pretty free generation in the sense that we were ready to try pretty much anything—all kinds of sex, drugs, just about anything. Orgies were a big notion for us at the time: maybe that freedom was to be found in the orgy. There were very few orgies compared to how much talk there was about it, but still."[18]

Mailer was impressed with Reich the theorist but dismissed his clunky prose: in *The List* (1959) Mailer placed "Wilhelm Reich as a mind" under "Hip," whereas "Wilhelm Reich as a stylist" was under "Square."[19] "It gave a certain charm," Mailer said, "that he had such outrageous and hip things to say in that very formal, almost ugly, teutonic style." Goodman was no better a stylist. George Orwell, in his essay "Politics and the English Language" (1946), selected a passage from Goodman's article on Reich to illustrate bad, jargon-ridden, and convoluted writing. But Orwell, despite his criticism of Goodman's use of the medium, was evidently also fascinated by the message.

In *1984* (1949) Orwell made the Reichian link between sexual deprivation and totalitarianism, taking those ideas into the mainstream. In the novel, a spokesman for the oppressive New Order states, "The sex instinct will be eradicated . . . We shall abolish the orgasm." Julia, the free-spirited heroine of *1984*, explains why the authorities impose what they call antisexualism: "When you make love you're using up energy. And afterward you feel happy and don't give a damn for anything. They can't bear you to feel like that. They want you bursting with energy all the time. All this marching up and down and cheering is simply sex gone sour. If you're happy inside yourself, why should you get excited about Big Brother and Three Year Plans and all the rest of that bollocks?"[20]

Not all on the left were happy about Reich's revolutionary agenda. The young sociologists C. Wright Mills and Patricia Salter, colleagues at Columbia University's Bureau of Applied Social Research, accused Reich and Goodman of making a reactionary appeal to biology to legitimize their politics (hadn't the Nazis made similar claims?). Unlike Goodman and Reich, Mills and Salter hadn't yet relinquished faith in the radical labor movement. In their response to Goodman, published in the next issue of *Politics* as "The Barricade and the Bedroom," they mocked Reich's "gonad theory of revolution": was "orgastic potency" really "the key to freedom . . . or the lever of revolution"?[21]

Of course, Reich thought that it was, but he was uncomfortable with the way in which he had been taken up and distorted by America's avant-garde. He was campaigning for sexual freedom, he maintained, not sexual license. Paul Robinson wrote in *The Freudian Left* (1969), "Reich seemed to fear his would-be admirers even more than his critics. He was haunted by the thought that men with dirty minds would misuse his authority to unleash 'a free-for-all fucking epidemic.'"[22] For all his rhetoric of orgasms, Reich was surprisingly puritanical: he was against pornography and dirty jokes (which he thought would become obsolete after the sexual revolution), abhorred homosexuality, and preferred that sex not be detached from love.

The promiscuous Goodman disappointed him on this front, so much so that Reich sent him to be cured. He referred him to Alexander Lowen, who had just completed his own therapy with Reich. In his autobiography, Lowen recalled that Reich referred his first patient to him in 1945—an artist, whom he charged only two dollars. His next two patients must have included Goodman; both analysands "had more sense of themselves and were more substantial personalities," Lowen wrote. "They felt that they had been unjustly treated by Reich."[23] Lowen saw Goodman for about six months in his consulting room in a cheap downtown hotel. "They screamed their protests," Lowen wrote of his forceful attempts to dissolve his patients' character armor, "but my makeshift office was a room facing the streets. Their screaming brought the police."[24]

When I met him in 2004, and until his death in 2008 at the age of ninety-seven, Alexander Lowen still practiced a form of Reichian therapy and was one of only two people alive who were trained and treated by Reich (the other is Dr. Morton Herskowitz). Several people still made the pilgrimage to New Canaan, Connecticut, to have therapeutic sessions with him every week, and as a result, all the cabdrivers waiting at the train station knew where he lived. A ten-minute drive away, a large stone gateway marked THE CENTER FOR BIOENERGETIC ANALYSIS led to well-kept grounds and a large clapboard house. When I visited, two sun loungers were placed neatly next to each other on an immaculate lawn; an old Buick station wagon was parked in the driveway.

Lowen's secretary, Monica Souza, met me at the door and silently led me into a large living room, where the doctor was on the phone. The room had a seventies bohemian grandeur, with gold-colored sofas and a large pool table that had been turned into a display case for Lowen's many books, whose titles include *The Language of the Body* and *Love and Orgasm*. His phone call finished, Dr. Lowen stood up to shake my hand. "Shall we start work?" he asked. I followed him into his study, expecting to conduct my interview over his cluttered desk, but he continued on through his office into his cork-walled therapy room. (In Dušan Makavejev's 1971 cult film about Reich, *WR: Mysteries of the Organism*, Lowen is shown inducing what Reich called the "orgasm reflex" in a female patient in his treatment room: she throws herself around his couch in the throes of ecstasy). Souza was already there, putting a freshly laundered sheet onto the single bed that served as his analytic couch. There was a framed notice above it that said, simply, BREATHE.

Lowen asked me if I did any exercise, and I answered in the negative. "You have to do exercises every day!" he shouted in disbelief. "Get undressed and I'm gonna make you do it. You know how to do a somersault?"[25] I quickly explained that I'd come to ask him some questions about Reich, rather than for therapy. "I was in his classes," Lowen said. "Let me tell you about Reich—you put it down in your book: breathing is the essence of life. If you stop breathing, you know what they say about you? The moment you don't breathe, you die." He sat down, evidently satisfied with his truism, and told me to strip to my boxer shorts, determined to give me a practical demonstration of Reich's lesson.

Within minutes of our meeting, Alexander Lowen had me doing somersaults in my underpants on his analyst's couch. "Put your feet there, right at the edge of the bed, and put your head right next to your feet," Lowen instructed me. I flung myself off the bed. "Now watch yourself! You've got to look at the distances. You throw yourself like that in space and you're going to get killed. Go a little slower. Come on, do thirty-five to fifty of those. That's good. Can you hear your breathing? Well, that's what life's about and that's what therapy's about. That's the way—very good. You see, Reich thought that breathing gives your body life and if you do enough breathing your emotions become alive and suddenly you're crying and talking. BREATHE . . . otherwise you're half mechanical."

Lowen, a former law student who attended Reich's lectures at the New School, was, like Goodman, one of Reich's most politically engaged devotees. At the weekly seminars Reich held at his house in the early 1940s, Lowen urged Reich to pioneer a new program of community mental health and to lead a youth movement as he had done in Austria and Germany. Though these sex-pol clinics were never realized, Reich did initially plan a series of them along his European model, but he thought they could be established only with the backing of an official institution. To this end, Lowen approached Alvin Johnson at the New School to suggest the establishment of a Center for Social Research of Mental Hygiene, to be run by Reich. Johnson, who was perturbed by the path Reich had taken in his cancer research, turned Lowen down.

From 1942 to 1945 Lowen traveled to Reich's home in Forest Hills three times a week for therapy, for which he paid fifteen dollars a session. Reich was a large man, Lowen remembered, with soft brown eyes and strong, warm hands. In his first therapeutic session, Lowen lay in a pair of bathing trunks on Reich's bed, which also served as his couch. Reich simply told him to breathe and sat watching him silently in a nearby chair. After ten minutes Reich said, "Lowen, you're not breathing. Your chest isn't moving." He took his student's hand and held it to his own heaving chest. "His body was heavy," Lowen wrote of Reich in his autobiography, *Honoring the Body*, "puffed up, with a big chest."[26] Lowen, in imitation, started breathing more deeply. After several more minutes of silence, Reich suddenly instructed, "Lowen drop your head back and open your eyes wide."[27] Lowen spontaneously emitted a piercing and unexpected scream. "I hesitate to say that I screamed because I did not seem to do it," Lowen recalled. "The scream happened to me . . . I left the session with the feeling that I was not as all right as I thought."[28]

"My sessions with Reich centered around having me breathe, breathe, and breathe," Lowen told me. Reich applied forceful pressure with his hands to Lowen's tense muscles, especially the jaw muscles, the back of the neck, the lower back, and the abductor muscles of the thighs. "Some of it was very painful," he recalled of

Reich's pinching and punching. As Reich manipulated and dissolved Lowen's muscular blocks, supposedly allowing sexual energy to stream freely around the body, Lowen's unconscious hatred of his parents came flooding through the sluice gates of repression. On one occasion, as Lowen was instructed to lie on his front and pound the mattress with both fists, he imagined he saw his father's face in the crumpled sheet: "I suddenly knew I was hitting him for the spanking he had given me when I was a young boy." In another session he hallucinated his mother's angry-looking face on the ceiling; Lowen imagined himself at nine months, looking up at her from his baby carriage, and burst into tears. "Why are you so angry with me?" Lowen sobbed, using the words he didn't have then. "I am only crying because I want you."[29]

By the time I'd finished my prescribed number of somersaults the mattress had almost come off the bed; all the hyperventilating had made me giddy and nauseated. Without letting me pause for rest, Lowen had me bend backward over what looked like a padded sawhorse—he called it a "breathing stool" and considered it his major therapeutic innovation—and instructed me to reach back and lift an iron bell (I noticed that the ceiling was scuffed from people hitting the bed with a tennis racket to vent their anger). This "sexual exercise," as he described it, was designed to stretch and relax the pelvic muscles, allowing for "vibrations" in that region. "One, two, three, four, five—right, that's very good, now ten more."

Therapy with Lowen was more like having a personal trainer than an analyst. I was told to lie on the bed and kick my feet up and down, and then to assume a position that Charcot described as the "hysterical arc-de-cercle" when displayed by his patients at the Salpêtrière. "This is a basic exercise that Reich used," Lowen explained. "Now get your knees up, hold your feet, pull your ankles back, now lift your ass off the bed. Now arch more, move back on your feet—that's it, that's what Reich did. Arch, arch—that's it, now you've got the idea. Now put your knees together; breathe, breathe."

After almost an hour of such contortions my body began to give out with the effort. "There you go, you've got vibrations!" Lowen exclaimed as my legs began to shake and shudder. "There's a strong charge in your body now. Can you feel the breathing going through the whole length of your body? It's alive. That's it! You're doing very well—vibration IS LIFE!'

After two years of therapy with Reich, Lowen was able to summon up these rhythmic, convulsive movements—the orgasm reflex—at will. "Surrender to my body," Lowen wrote of this transition, "which also meant a surrender to Reich, became very easy."[30] The submission to the leader was both physical and mental. His orgasms became more potent, as Reich had promised: "What she felt, I didn't ask her, that's her business," Lowen told me of the first time he made love to his wife, "but I felt that there were power balls inside of me that flew out of me and into the stars. I could then imagine that there were stars that were out there that were really energetic forces."

After my session, Lowen took me down to his cellar to show me his orgone box. It was one of the older designs, without a window, and it was lined with fine mesh. Inside there was a supplemental orgone contrivance that looked something like a tea cozy and was used for putting over your breasts or head. "It had a very nice effect," he said unspecifically, having given up using the machine after five decades, "but it didn't have a great change on me."

In December 2001 Lowen's wife was diagnosed with ovarian cancer, which Reich had claimed his box could help cure. "When my wife was sick I got her to sit in there," Lowen said, looking into the coffin-like contraption. "But it didn't work. It wasn't strong enough."


One day in 1946, Fritz Perls walked into a café in Greenwich Village and overheard two men having a heated argument about politics. He went over and introduced himself; they turned out to be editors of the anarchist journal *Retort*. Perls wasn't volunteering to arbitrate the anarchists' heated discussion; he wondered whether they knew Paul Goodman. As it happens, the editors were friends with Goodman, and they offered to walk Perls over to his apartment.

Perls had recently arrived from South Africa, where he had spent the previous fourteen years, and which he now felt was becoming infected with the same fascistic spirit he'd fled when he left Europe. Perls had picked up a copy of Goodman's essay about Reich and the neo-Freudians when it was published the previous year, and had been encouraged to come to America by reading of his former colleagues' success. All the revisionists Goodman wrote about were people Perls had once known well, and, having written *Ego, Hunger and Aggression* (1942)—an attempt to build on Reich's Freudo-Marxism—Perls considered himself one of them (the book had the bold subtitle *A Revision of Freud's Theory and Method*). Indeed, Karen Horney, who had referred him to Reich in the early 1930s, sponsored his American visa, and Erich Fromm sent patients to him.

With his balding pate, jowly face, neat mustache, and pin-striped suit with spats and bow tie, Perls seemed untouched by his time in the subtropics. He looked the stereotype of a European émigré analyst, and must have cut a striking figure as he walked through Greenwich Village with his new acquaintances, on the way to meet his unlikely ally.

Goodman, who had not known of Perls's work, was thrilled to meet one of Reich's old-world allies, and grilled him about his sex-pol days. Once Perls had established himself (in a shabby cold-water flat on the Upper East Side, opposite the Jacob Ruppert Brewery), Goodman went on to introduce him to some of New York's most celebrated bohemians: avant-garde musicians and writers such as John Cage and James Agee; anarchists such as the Living Theatre founders Julian Beck and Judith Malina; and Dwight Macdonald, the most vocal of the New York intellectuals. Perls drew many of his patients from this circle. Within three weeks Perls had a flourishing practice, and his wife, Laura, and their two children were able to join him in the fall of 1947.

Reich was an important influence on the bohemian group's sexual game playing, open relationships, and devotion to exploring the limits of sexual pleasure. And Perls, who had been analyzed by the guru, easily fitted into this world of Reich's adherents. At fifty-three, he became a substitute master. As the permissive analyst, he offered the group some degree of license to live intense emotional lives, teaching them that it was good to unleash their feelings and to express their "authentic" selves, that personal transformation was akin to social transformation.

Influenced by the vogue for existentialism—in 1946 Jean-Paul Sartre and Albert Camus had made well-publicized trips to New

York—Perls thought that therapists should try to foster "unitary personalities who are willing to live dangerously and insecurely, but with sincerity and spontaneity"; integrated personalities, he said, "alone can guarantee the survival of mankind."[31] But, he added, pointing out the paradox Goodman had highlighted in his essay, "Can a really integrated personality function in a dissociated society?" Therapy as he imagined it would breed heroic misfits—the personal would be political.

Perls flirted with but did not join any of the dissident psychoanalytic groups in New York. In his autobiography he wrote that he had been invited to train future analysts but didn't, since that required him to have an American M.D. "I refused to accept the notion of adjusting to a society that was not worth adjusting to," Perls explained, in line with Goodman's view.[32] It was the so-called golden age of psychoanalysis, and Perls had ambitions to start his own school; he offered Goodman $500 to turn a fifty-page manuscript he'd written into readable English. It was the basis for *Gestalt Therapy* (1951).

Eventually he broke with Horney and Fromm. Though he cast the split as an ideological one, it has been suggested that there may have been another reason for the estrangement: Perls's shameless habit of fraternizing and sleeping with his analysands. One friend recalled that "he had a horrible reputation for sleeping with his patients," though she claimed that she "met many patients who slept with him and said it was one of the greatest experiences they ever had."[33]

"Fritz has a terrible reputation," Dwight Macdonald recalled. "Some 'mad power over women' in spite of the fact that he wasn't terribly attractive even then. Any woman would remember him. He had 'hand trouble.'"[34] Perls's colleague Elliot Shapiro put it, "He was quick to fondle. Right away, almost without introductions."[35]

Judith Malina, who later went into analysis with Goodman, described Perls in her diary at the time as "an imposing German who conducts himself like a 'Great Man.' He approached me, however, like a seducer. He admired my eyes and hands, but called my mouth 'all wrong.' He claimed that I despised people and should learn to spit at them."[36] Perls followed Reich in attacking people's character armor and was known for his devastating deflations. He was, Malina says, "a great star at this kind of 'public bitchiness.'" Most human encounters were sterile, either "mind-fucking or manipulation," Perls said in justification of what he called his "honest rudeness." At a party, Perls cornered Malina in an upstairs bedroom, caught hold of her, and whispered, "Tell me, Judith, do you have orgasms?"[37]

Shortly after Perls's arrival in New York, he met Reich for the first time in a decade. That encounter was as disastrous as Goodman's had been. "I really got a fright," Perls wrote of his onetime mentor. "[Reich] was blown up like an immense bullfrog, his facial eczema had become more intense."[38] They had last seen each other in 1936 at the Marienbad Psychoanalytic Congress, where Reich, unbeknownst to Perls, had been a toxic guest. Perls had found him remote and gloomy then; this time Reich was outraged that Perls was not current with the innovations he'd made in the interim. "His voice boomed at me pompously," Perls remembered, "asking incredulously: 'You have not heard of my discovery, the orgone?'"[39]

In a book of interviews about Perls, Alexander Lowen recounted the same event: "It was a short meeting; there was a kind of lack of communication, and I don't think Fritz ever saw Reich again. Fritz was put off by the fact that Reich wasn't interested in what Fritz was doing and I guess Reich, himself, was a little put off that Fritz had no awareness or interest in this whole big development that Reich was pursuing . . . [Fritz] was a little bitter about the whole experience with Reich."[40]

Perls was, however, intrigued enough by Reich's claim to have discovered a new energy that he decided investigate it. He visited a number of orgone box owners, one of whom was most likely the writer and critic Isaac Rosenfeld, a friend of his, whom the left-wing editor Irving Howe described as the literary scene's "golden boy" in the mid-1940s. Rosenfeld, who wore owlish glasses and combed his yellow-brown hair straight back, had read Reich's books hoping for a cure for his writer's block, which he felt might be a result of sexual inhibition. He spent much of the late forties working on dissolving these defenses. Rosenfeld and his wife were in therapy with Reich's student Dr. Richard Singer—"He goes to Queens for fucking lessons," a friend said dryly—and were enthusiastic users of the orgone box.[41]

Rosenfeld's tiny, messy fourth-floor walk-up on Barrow Street in Greenwich Village served as a sort of salon where Reich's ideas became the latest theoretical fashion, and as a disorderly showroom for the orgone accumulator in which Rosenfeld sat, as he later put it, "waiting for the moment when the Bourgeois Bubble of Sex shall at last be burst."[42] Alfred Kazin, who visited the apartment, described Rosenfeld's makeshift throne:

> Like so many of Isaac's attempts to apply his imaginative vision to life, this orgone box was compromised by his poverty and his many interests. It was too obviously a homemade, bargain-basement orgone box. It looked more like a cardboard closet or stage telephone booth than it did a scientific apparatus by which to recover the sexual energy one had lost to "culture." Isaac's orgone box stood up in the midst of an enormous confusion of bed clothes, review copies, manuscripts, children, and the many people who went in and out of the room as if it were the bathroom. Belligerently sitting inside his orgone box, daring philistines to laugh, Isaac nevertheless looked lost, as if he were waiting in his telephone booth for a call that was not coming through.[43]

According to Rosenfeld's friend and childhood rival, the novelist Saul Bellow, who had returned from a two-year stint in Paris to find Rosenfeld completely absorbed in Reichianism, Rosenfeld even grew tomatoes in his accumulator, claiming that the orgone rays yielded better fruit. He treated neighbors' sick pets in the box, and friends with headaches were encouraged to put on what Bellow described in a tribute to his friend as "a tin crown," a funnel on a bit of hose connected to a smaller box, which Reich referred to as a "shooter," that was supposed to focus the rays on colds, scratches, and cuts. Rosenfeld was so enthusiastic a devotee of Reich's theories that he turned his literature class at New York University into a seminar devoted to Reich. He was, Bellow said, "brilliantly persuasive."[44]

At Rosenfeld's urging, Bellow, who was also teaching at NYU, entered therapy with Dr. Chester Raphael, another member of Reich's circle, who goaded him in Reich's style about his stagnant, repressed body. In one of Bellow's unpublished manuscripts, a novel that was to have been based on Rosenfeld, there is a parody of a Reichian session in which the therapist taunts his patient, "You look to me like an overfed, jowly, snouty white pig. You have erectile potency, but you are not a potent man . . . I can tell by looking at you—the retracted pelvis, the stasis with accumulated fat, the shallowness of breathing. How can you have had real sexual experience?"[45] This script, with its allusions to animals, was close to the truth; Bellow once joked of his own therapy, "That wasn't sexology, that was zoology."[46] However, Bellow reported that he initially found the stimulation of his repressed rages therapeutic. In his novel *Henderson the Rain King* (1958) there is a passage that captures the dramatic catharsis sometimes achieved in Reichian therapy: "A sob came out of me," says Henderson. "It must have been laid down early in my life, for it was stupendous and rose from me like a great sea bubble from the Atlantic floor."[47]

Bellow, an ex-Trotskyite (he had traveled to Mexico to see his hero, only to find that Trotsky had been murdered the day before their appointment), also built an accumulator; like Rosenfeld's device it was homemade, built by a mutual friend from their Chicago days. Bellow would sit naked in the claustrophobic space for daily irradiations, reading under the glare of a bare bulb. He evidently believed in its efficacy: he told his biographer Ruth Miller that "he cured a couple of warts [with it] and improved his breathing." A New York orgonomist he'd met claimed to have cured a case of cervical cancer with the device, and to have got one "near remission," but Bellow's credulity had its medical limits—according to Miller, Bellow laughed at the uncomforting idea of a "near cure."[48]

Bellow would later claim to have been deluded in his belief in Reich's ideas and characterized his period on Raphael's couch as a "disaster"; in fact, in his later, more reactionary days, Bellow described the entire sexual revolution as "a thirty-year disaster." (Sexual liberation, Bellow said, "was terribly destructive to me; I took it as entitlement, the path to being a free man.")[49] He confided to his friend and fellow novelist Philip Roth that Reichian therapy was "really a horror," and he blamed his having submitted to it on Rosenfeld's influence. He only began therapy, he explained, so as not to lose his friend: "He insisted that I had to have this done, since he was doing it . . . Not anything I'm terribly proud of, but you could not keep your respect for yourself if you had not faced the ultimate rigors. And it was a link between Isaac and me. I felt that I could not let him go through this without going through it myself so that I would know what was happening to him."[50]

Chester Raphael remembered things differently when presented with this picture of a folie à deux: "That's a peculiar way to put it," he told Bellow's biographer James Atlas, remarking that Rosenfeld's name barely ever came up in sessions. "[Bellow] came because he had problems."[51] Bellow would later accuse Raphael of creating more problems than he cured by contributing to the breakup of his first marriage (he quit therapy in 1953 when his first marriage broke up). The "brutal candor" that Reichian therapy insisted on, in Bellow's estimation, had only made him "nastier." The Rosenfelds also split up at this time, finding marriage incompatible with their radical sex lives.

Rosenfeld died young from a heart attack in 1956. "At thirty-eight, [Rosenfeld] died in lonely sloth," Irving Howe wrote of the writer who had showed so much promise.[52] Alfred Kazin also characterized Rosenfeld as a worn-out failure, "as even the [Greenwich] Village desperados noticed" he had become. Rosenfeld, Kazin wrote, "sat in his orgone box looking for a message, for the Messiah, for the perfect freedom and happiness that would come to him as unprecedented sexual power—from the spheres." But he died, Kazin concluded, "a prisoner in his cell, the orgone box."[53]

Actually, before Rosenfeld died, he had ceased to use his accumulator, despite the assertions of Kazin and others that it was the box that finally suffocated him. As Steven Zipperstein noted in an essay on Rosenfeld published in *Partisan Review* in 2002, Rosenfeld did have the box with him in Chicago when he returned there toward the end of his life, but it was unused, dismantled and flat-packed in the corner of the room. The novel Rosenfeld was working on when he died was a dystopian tale that questioned the authoritarian nature of Reichian therapy: the action unfolded in a sex colony run by a scientist clearly based on Reich, who shows repressive intolerance to those who resist his call to pleasure.

Among Bellow's papers at the University of Chicago are eight hundred pages of his unpublished work on Reich and Rosenfeld, a study in failure. Bellow aborted it as too cruel a memorial, and wrote *Herzog* (1964) instead. (Moses Herzog parodies Reich's position when he muses that "to get laid is actually socially constructive and useful, an act of citizenship.") A small fragment of his Rosenfeld study was published as a short story, "Zetland: By a Character Witness." But these few pages take the reader only from Zetland's precocious Kant-reading childhood in Chicago to the moment he jettisoned the philosophy Ph.D. he was working on at Columbia, ready to head off to pursue a bohemian literary life in the Village. Even in this brief character sketch, however, Bellow includes clues of a life—and orgone box—to come: "Living in a kennel," Bellow writes of the bookish Zetland, "his thoughts embraced the universe."[54]

Bellow considered Rosenfeld to have been a victim of New York: "He came to take the town and he got took," Bellow told Philip Roth. "His considerable gifts as a writer never matured in New York. He became a follower of the onetime Freudian Wilhelm Reich. This would not have been possible in any other American city. It took Isaac years to cast off the Reichian influence. This ideological ordeal, one might say, followed him from Vienna to New York. He was ruined by this stuff," Bellow concluded.[55]

In 1945, Allen Ginsberg and Jack Kerouac were students at Columbia University and were lodging in Joan Vollmer's apartment on West 115th Street. Kerouac, a Catholic who had gotten in on a football scholarship, described Ginsberg as "this spindly Jewish kid with horn-rimmed glasses and tremendous ears sticking out . . . burning black eyes"; the two men had a brief, awkward affair.[56] Their friend William Burroughs was living nearby, on Riverside Drive, and after Kerouac and Ginsberg set him up with their landlady, he moved in, too. The gaunt and lanky Burroughs was more than a decade older than Ginsberg and Kerouac, and already seemed, Ginsberg recalled, to have the "ashen gray of an old-age cheek."[57] The younger pair admired him, Ginsberg wrote, like "ambassadors to a Chinese emperor." Kerouac hailed him as "the last of the Faustian men."[58] Burroughs returned the compliment by introducing the other members of the "libertine circle," as they dubbed themselves, to drugs, sailors, porn, bathhouses, and Wilhelm Reich.

After leaving Harvard in 1936, Burroughs had enrolled at the University of Vienna's medical school, Reich's alma mater, with vague plans of becoming a psychoanalyst, but his stay was dominated by the administration of arsenic shots for the syphilis he had contracted in America, which left him feeling nauseated and depressed. He left after a semester. Back in New York, Burroughs was analyzed by Paul Federn, who had been Reich's first therapist but whom Reich came to consider his nemesis. Burroughs was institutionalized in 1940 after he chopped off the tip of his finger in a Van Gogh–like gesture of unrequited love (Bellevue psychiatrists diagnosed him as a paranoid schizophrenic). Burroughs's parents gave him an allowance of two hundred dollars a month on the condition that he seek further help, and in 1946 Burroughs was undergoing narco-analysis with Dr. Lewis Wolberg, who used nitrous oxide and hypnosis to stimulate the unconscious.

Burroughs would return from his sessions with Wolberg to practice "wild analysis" on his friends, interpreting their dreams from the comfort of a wing chair. He also played a game that parodied the Reichian character analysis that he'd become interested in. The group would play an adaptation of charades to facilitate the exploration of the onion layers of their personality armor. Burroughs referred to these exercises in amateur dramatics as "routines." For example, underneath Burroughs's public persona as the distinguished heir of an important St. Louis family lurked a prissy, lesbian English governess ("My dear, you're just in time for tea. Don't say those dirty words in front of everybody!"). Scratch the governess surface and you reached Old Luke, a gun-toting, tobacco-chewing sharecropper from the Deep South ("Ever gut a catfish?"). The last stratum, at his very core, held a silent Chinaman, a contemplative, impassive character who sat meditating on the banks of the Yangtse. Ginsberg's hidden self was "the well-groomed Hungarian," and Kerouac liked to play the naïve American lost in the sophistications of Paris.[59]

Alfred Kinsey met Burroughs, Ginsberg, and Kerouac on one of their nocturnal trips to Times Square through their friend Herbert

Huncke, the male prostitute who coined the term "beat" and introduced Burroughs to recreational drugs. Kinsey paid Huncke for every interviewee he sent to his room at the Hotel Astor, and the beat trio were among them. (When Kinsey, who was fond of using slang in his interviews to put people at ease, asked Ginsberg directly, "Did you ever 'brown' anybody?" Ginsberg said that he had no idea what he meant. The house detectives at the Astor objected to the prostitutes, pimps, and drug addicts who were piling into the lobby from Times Square to catch the elevator up to Kinsey's room so as to earn the dollar he would give them for recounting their sexual histories. The manager wanted him out. "Nobody's going to undress in our hotel room," Kinsey assured him. "Yes," the manager replied insistently, "but you're undressing their minds.")[60]

After Burroughs left New York for Texas, sent home by a judge after he forged a prescription for morphine, Ginsberg wrote that his "wild analysis" with Burroughs, a bastardized version of Reichianism, had left him "with a number of my defenses broken, but centrally unchanged, with nothing to replace the lost armor."[61] Conflicted about his homosexuality (he was now having an affair with Neal Cassady, for whom sex was, according to Ginsberg, "a sort of joyful yoga"), Ginsberg wrote to Burroughs that he was thinking of going to see an analyst. "I think you would be better with the Reichians who sound a good deal more hip," Burroughs recommended in February 1947, certain that most other types of analysts were slaves to conformity, only content when they had turned their patients into "bank clerks . . . [all] scared and whipped down."[62] Reichianism appealed precisely because its practitioners, Burroughs thought, wouldn't dictate to you what to do.

Ginsberg wrote a letter to Reich the following month:

*My main psychic difficulty, as far as I know, is the usual oedipal entanglement. I have been a homosexual for as long as I remember, and have had a limited number of homosexual affairs, both temporary and protracted. They have been unsatisfactory to me, and I have always approached love affairs with a sort of self-contradictory, conscious masochism . . . I have had long periods of depression, guilt feelings—disguised mostly as a sort of Kafkian sordidness of sense of self—melancholy, and the whole gamut I suppose.*[63]

Reich, as Ilse Ollendorff noted, refused to treat homosexuals. He did, however, recommend three other orgonomists who might, and from among them Ginsberg chose Dr. Allan Cott, a member of Reich's inner circle who had a practice in Newark, New Jersey. Beginning in the winter of 1947, Ginsberg saw him for twice-weekly therapy and sessions in the accumulator. Ginsberg wrote of his vegetotherapy with Cott, "It was really remarkable, I felt this strange buzzing from disturbing the mouth area."[64]

Taking advantage of the proximity of Cott's office to his father's home, and still buzzing in the mouth, Ginsberg chose to come out during a posttherapeutic visit. "You mean you like to take men's penises in your mouth?" his father said unsympathetically.[65] But Cott thought homosexuality a perversion, as Reich did, and was working toward establishing heterosexual primacy rather than trying to persuade Ginsberg to come to terms with his queerness. "Frankly I won't trust that kind of straight genital Reichian," Burroughs wrote in disgust at this dogmatism. "Feller say, when a man gets too straight he's just a god damned prick."[66]

Cott terminated Ginsberg's therapy after three months because he continued to smoke pot against the doctor's advice. Ginsberg thought cannabis an integral part of his aesthetic education; Cott feared that it would lead to a psychotic episode. The summer he quit therapy, Ginsberg began experiencing auditory hallucinations. "It was like God had a human voice," Ginsberg wrote of his transcendental experience, in which he discovered his calling as a poet, "with all the infinite tenderness and mortal gravity of a living Creator speaking to his son."[67] Consumed by a desire to share his amazing experience, Ginsberg crawled out onto his fire escape and tapped on the next-door neighbor's windows, declaring to the two frightened girls inside, "I've seen God!"[68]

His father, still reeling from the discovery of his son's sexuality, feared that he was suffering from the paranoid schizophrenia that had caused his mother to be institutionalized in Pilgrim State, a mental hospital on Long Island. She also heard voices, feared her husband was trying to poison her, hallucinated Hitler's mustache in the sink, and thought spies were following her. When Ginsberg entered Reichian analysis, she was reportedly banging her head against the wall so ferociously that the doctors recommended a lobotomy.

Ginsberg phoned up Dr. Cott, his former therapist, and told him, "It happened, I had some kind of breakthrough or psychotic experience." Cott, who followed Reich in rejecting the talking cure, and who was obviously still angry at Ginsberg for chosing pot over therapy, said, "I'm afraid any discussion would have no value" and hung up on him.[69] Soon afterward, when Ginsberg was involved in a car chase in a stolen vehicle that ended in a dramatic crash, he was encouraged by a law professor at Columbia, where he was still a student, to plead insanity. Dr. Cott appeared in court to testify to his mental instability, and two months later Ginsberg was admitted to the Columbia Presbyterian Psychiatric Institute, where he stayed for eight months.

During Ginsberg's hospitalization, Burroughs wrote to Jack Kerouac to ask him to find out from Ginsberg what the "gadget made by Reichians" looked like. "I want especially to know its shape and if there is a window, and how one gets into it."[70] Kerouac doesn't seem to have been much help in providing a blueprint. Burroughs built his first accumulator in the spring of 1949 when he was living on a rented farm in Pharr, Texas, with Kells Elvins, a friend from his Harvard days. They were both enthusiastically reading Reich's *The Cancer Biopathy* and decided to build an accumulator in the orange grove Kells owned in the Rio Grande Valley. Built without recourse to any plans, the resulting device included some curious innovations. "Inside was an old icebox," Burroughs explained, "which you could get inside and pull on a contrivance so that another box of sheet steel descended over you, so that the effect was presumably heightened."[71] It took them a few days to construct the box. The result was eight feet high, much taller than the ones Reich manufactured: "It was a regular townhouse," Burroughs recalled.[72]

The pair took turns sitting in the accumulator and obtained, Burroughs wrote, "unmistakable results." Burroughs wondered what the Mexican farm laborers thought of this strange box that they entered "wrapped in old towels" and came out of feeling "much sexier and healthier," "with hard-ons." Burroughs and Kells also made one of Reich's smaller shooter boxes, with a funnel, which they used as a supplement to the big box. Their DIY was, Burroughs admitted, "a very sloppy job," but it still gave a powerful "sexual kick."[73]

"I have just been reading Wilhelm Reich's latest book *The Cancer Biopathy*," Burroughs wrote excitedly to Kerouac. "I tell you Jack, he is the only man in the analysis line who is on that beam. After reading the book I built an orgone accumulator and the gimmick really works. The man is not crazy, he's a fucking genius."[74] Kerouac described Burroughs enthusiastically promoting the box in *On the Road* (1955). According to Kerouac, Burroughs said, "Say, why don't you fellows try my orgone accumulator? Put some juice in your bones. I always rush up and take off ninety miles an hour for the nearest whorehouse, hor-hor-hor!"[75]

Burroughs used an orgone box on and off for the rest of his life. (There's picture of the rock star Kurt Cobain waving through the port-hole of Burroughs's last box, a scruffy, patched-up shed that he kept in the garden behind his house in Lawrence, Kansas.) In the 1970s he wrote an article for *Oui* magazine entitled "All the accumulators I have owned" in which he boasted, "Your intrepid reporter, at age thirty-seven, achieved spontaneous orgasm, no hands, in an orgone accumulator built in an orange grove in Pharr, Texas. It was the small, direct-application accumulator that did the trick."[76]


"What did you get out of it?" the anarchist Paul Mattick asked when Goodman told him he'd just had a session in an accumulator. "Nothing, nothing," said Goodman, as if it were more an existential than a therapeutic experience. "But that's it, that's what you get out of it."

Perls concluded that any positive claims for the orgone box were attributable to the placebo effect. "I invariably found a fallacy," he said of the orgone box users he met, "a suggestibility that could be directed in any way that I wanted."[77] Reich, Perls thought, had made a major contribution in giving Freud's notion of resistance a body, but he erred in trying to make a verifiable reality out of the libido. "Now resistances do exist, there is no doubt about it," Perls explained, "but libido was and is a hypothesized energy, invented by Freud himself to explain his model of man."[78] He thought Reich had hypnotized himself and his patients into the belief of the existence of the orgone as the physical and visible equivalent of libido.

Perls found that users of orgone boxes usually exhibited some paranoid symptoms. "Then I had another look at the armor theory," Perls went on, "and I realized that the idea of the armor itself was a paranoid form. It supposes an attack from, and defense against, the environment."[79] Perls criticized vegetotherapy for encouraging the formation of paranoid features by encouraging the patient to "externalize, disown, and project material that could be assimilated and become part of the self." Orgone energy, Perls concluded from his investigations into the orgone box, was "an invention of Reich's fantasy which by then had gone astray." The realization that the Reich he had met in New York was different from the one he had known in Europe, and that orgone mysticism was at the crackpot end of science, was tinged with melancholy. "The enfant terrible of the Vienna Institute turned out to be a genius," Perls wrote in his autobiography, "only to eclipse himself as a 'mad scientist.'"[80]

In his own elaboration of character analysis, which he called Gestalt therapy, Perls turned the idea of armor around: where Reich had come to see character armor as a defense against a hostile external world, Perls saw that same layer of self as a shield for one's own true drives—a straitjacket designed to safeguard against explosions of excitement from within. Thus, it wasn't a shell to be crushed but something integral, to be owned. (Laura Perls said they tried to convince Rosenfeld to give up his box, that he could increase his physical vitality and mental agility "entirely on his own, without external devices.")[81] He wanted his patients to be aware of their bodies, to feel the present vividly in the "here and now," to be "authentic," to act on their desires.

Perls got his patients to act out their feelings so that they could assimilate and take responsibility for them. He had originally wanted to be a theater director—he'd been a student of Max Reinhardt's when he was growing up in Berlin, and he'd become closely associated with the avant-garde Living Theatre troupe in New York. Julian Beck, a founder of the Living Theatre, explained to Perls's biographer, Martin Shepard, of Gestalt therapy, "[Perls] had something in mind that was halfway between the kind of performance we were doing [direct spectacle, aimed at challenging the moral complacency of the audience] and therapeutic sessions."[82]

"You are my client," Perls told one female patient. "I care for you like an artist, I bring something out that is hidden in you."[83] He described therapy as if it were a magic trick; the rabbit he claimed to pull out of the hat was a person shorn of the "neurosis of normalcy" and all the bourgeois niceties associated with it. This person, he hypothesized, was confident enough to be selfish, to act on rather than repress all her desires, whatever the social consequences. All the energy that others wasted on repression and concealment, Perls thought, should be available for creative self-expression. Another of Perls's patients recalled, "Fritz loved some types—open bastard-bitch—open defenses, that type. He didn't like anyone who would placate him or be too good to him or used good-girl or good-boy defenses—that drove him up the wall."[84]

Perls's views, and some of his methods, were much indebted to those pioneered by Reich in the thirties: Perls would habitually accuse his patients of being "phony" and was deliberately aggressive, much as Reich had been with him. Yet, his observations about the paranoid deviations in Reich's terminology and thinking were painfully perceptive, precisely because he had built on those very ideas.

In 1951, Perls, Paul Goodman, and a Columbia professor of psychology named Ralph Hefferline published *Gestalt Therapy: Excitement and Growth in the Human Personality*. Rewritten by Goodman, and bearing all the hallmarks of Goodman's exasperating style, the book blends Reich's ideas about energy blocks and flows with Sartre's café philosophy to create an American brand of existentialism turned therapy. The authors intended their self-help book to provide the reader with the tools for revolution: "In recommending [these experiments] to you," they warned of their mass-market therapy, "we commit an aggressive act aimed at your present status quo and whatever complacency it affords."[85] They promised immediate liberation, without the hard grind of political struggle; all you had to do was unleash your "authentic" self.

The "excitement" to which the subtitle of the book refers is a generalized libido, an élan vital that is seeking various outlets, not all of them sexual. Life, for Perls, was a series of "unfinished" or "undigested" situations, frustrations that were all waiting their turn for satisfactory closure. "After the available excitement has been fully transformed and experienced, then we have good closure, satisfaction, temporary peace and nirvana," Perls summarized his position. "[A mere] discharge will barely bring about the feeling of exhaustion and being spent."[86]

It sounded very like the Reichian orgasm. But for Perls, excitement was no longer exclusively genital, as it was for Reich, and this shift only served to open up numerous other slipways to pleasure. In Reich's view, the libido theory was an inviolable article of faith. In broadening its range to celebrate oral and anal pleasures, Perls heralded a polymorphously perverse and heretical vision—one that, ironically, would prove particularly amenable to exploitation under capitalism.

In 1952, Perls, his wife, Goodman, Isidore From, Elliott Shapiro, and two others founded the New York Institute for Gestalt Therapy, headquartered in the Perlses' apartment and with treatment rooms at 315 Central Park West. The seven founding members met on a weekly basis for group therapy. There was no bureaucratic hierarchy and everyone, including Perls, was subject to the honest criticism that was seen as the key to self-discovery. It was a very public form of character analysis: members of the group would draw one another's attention to every repression or hang-up, none of which was to be tolerated.

Elliott Shapiro, an ex-boxer and the head of a psychiatric school attached to Kings County Hospital in Brooklyn, brought a friend to one session; Shapiro's friend said he "had never witnessed the aggressive and profound battling that went on in those groups. Nobody, virtually nobody, was safe at any time."[87] Shapiro recalled, "We hammered at each other, and hammered, and hammered—every week. And it was the most vigorous hammering you can imagine . . . If you could live through these groups and take the corrections, the insults, the remarks . . ."[88] Not all the participants had sufficiently thick skins to take such brutal candor. The psychotherapist Jim Simkin left the group because he felt that everyone was "loading elephant shit on him," as did Ralph Hefferline, a coauthor of *Gestalt Therapy*.

To promote his new school, Perls traveled from city to city, introducing an audience of psychiatrists, social workers, and other interested parties to his "here and now" philosophy. He taught groups in Cleveland, Detroit, Toronto, and Miami how to be sensitive to their bodily needs and to follow their impulses, to be honest and unalienated. He'd be sharp and confrontational as he pushed his awareness techniques on the participants: What are you doing now? What are you experiencing? What are you feeling? Isadore From, who was part of the original New York group, remembers that these occasions were often very dramatic, with "a lot of shaking, trembling, anxiety"—effects that he thought were the result of the audiences' hyperventilating under the strain of Perls's relentless goading and questioning.[89]

The New York Institute of Gestalt Therapy also ran public seminars, including one by Goodman, "The Psychology of Sex" ("What you can't do, teach," he said with a laugh).[90] Following Reich, it was thought that neurosis could be treated by exposure to sexual pleasure. Goodman made this his area of expertise and people with sexual problems were often referred to him. One was a man who was worried about the quality of his orgasms after prostate surgery. Another thought he might be homosexual; the bisexual Goodman got his penis out and demanded that the patient touch it to help him make a diagnosis. In so doing he was no doubt influenced by Hitschmann, the Viennese analyst who had once asked Perls, then tormented by sexual inadequacy, to show him his penis.

In one of Goodman's group sessions, when someone complained of lack of sexual companionship, Goodman went around the circle and set up a week's worth of dates. "See, that wasn't so difficult," he reassured her. He was not beyond offering his own neurosis-busting services to patients of either sex, and once agreed to accompany a patient who invited him on an all-expenses-paid trip to Europe. He joked about setting up a College of Sex so as to put his vast experience to educational use. "I'm a sociopath," he warned a potential client. In a diary entry written in 1957, Goodman looked back on the previous decade and concluded that he'd made "a false cultus-religion (an obsession)" of sex: "The sexual act itself had just about the meaning of a ritual communion sacrifice."[91]

## Eight

I n late 1946, a journalist named Mildred Edie Brady visited
Reich in Forest Hills. Ollendorff opened the door and ushered
Brady upstairs. As Brady made her way up the staircase she observed the photographs of the Milky Way and other astrological formations that decorated the walls. They were hung almost as if to
give the impression that one was ascending to the heavens. Brady
entered Reich's second floor office to find a "heavy set, ruddy, brown
haired man of 50, wearing a long white coat and sitting at a huge
desk."[1] He looked up from his writing as if he were interrupting a
great thought, and sprang up from his desk to meet her.

An influential journalist already greatly respected in New York
and Washington for the diligent work she had done since 1930 on
politics and advertising, Brady, then forty, had become a pioneer in
the new consumer advocacy movement. She now lived in California
with her husband, Robert Brady, a professor of economics at Berkeley, with whom she had been instrumental in founding the Consumers Union in 1936. One of her colleagues at Berkeley described her as
"a highly articulate person with a well-developed sense of outrage."[2]

Brady was also something of a beguiling interviewer. A former
model with strawberry blond hair and striking green eyes, she was
by all accounts full of energy and charm. In her youth she had come

to New York from the Midwest with dreams of becoming an actress, and her thespian bent found an outlet in her undercover investigations into consumer issues.

Brady had first come across Reich when a friend of hers who had been diagnosed with cancer obtained an orgone box and begun to sit in it, hoping for a cure. When Brady, who considered this to be "crack-pot nonsense," made inquiries about Reich and his device, she was astonished to discover that many of the psychoanalysts she spoke to on the West Coast agreed with his theory of the orgasm and the psychic origins of cancer.

Brady told Reich that that she was bringing good and interesting news from friends on the West Coast. Though in retrospect this would seem to have been intentionally misleading, it was not entirely untrue; she had been to see many of his followers in California, and whatever her view of it, she was the first to relay to Reich in any detail his burgeoning influence there. Still, she had just had dinner with some of his analytic enemies, at a party hosted by Lawrence Kubie, the man whom Reich suspected of denouncing him to the FBI. The assembled guests had regaled her with stories of Reich's psychotic performance at the Lucerne congress in 1934, where he had set up camp on the lawn of the conference hotel. However, they defended his work prior to that.

"Reich's following is growing," Brady wrote to Dexter Masters, her Consumers Union colleague (he was a former lover).

> *If you talk to most of the analysts for any length of time, you generally find that they agree with Reich about everything except orgone. This embarrasses them. But actually I think Reich speaks the truth when he says that the only difference between him and his critics is that he dares to carry to its logical end the basic concept of Freud. And in that logic he reaches not only the psychoanalytic conclusions he does but the political implications as well—in a word, anarchism or nihilism.[3]*

Theodor Adorno famously wrote, in *Minima Moralia* (1951): "In psychoanalysis nothing is true except the exaggerations." From a different point of view, Brady essentially agreed with this sentiment.

Reich's excesses showed the true danger of psychoanalysis—the plague Freud had brought to America, in her view, was anarchy.

Brady believed that the vogue for psychoanalysis in the United States was akin to that for astrology in Rome in the first and second centuries. As Masters would later explain, "Her concern was less with Reich than it was with what she saw as a rather thin cultism growing out of a rather passionate nonsense . . . Mildred found the orthodoxy absurd and Reich a menace."[4]

Brady's article "The New Cult of Sex and Anarchy" appeared in the April 1947 issue of *Harper's Magazine*. It was the first time many Americans outside of a handful of radicals on both coasts had heard of Reich, and they came to know him as Brady cast him: the eccentric and misguided inventor of the orgone box, and the intellectual inspiration for a nascent youth movement in the San Francisco Bay area that was being led in Big Sur by the novelist Henry Miller (famous for his banned works of erotica, *Tropic of Cancer* and *Tropic of Capricorn*) and, to a lesser extent, in Berkeley by the anarchist poet Kenneth Rexroth (who presided over the anarchist forum, the Libertarian Circle). They were people Reich had never met and places he'd never been.

Miller had returned to America in 1940, after a sexually adventurous decade in Paris—the "Land of Fuck"—and immediately embarked on a three-year-long, 25,000-mile road trip across the country. His travelogue, *The Air-Conditioned Nightmare* (1945), was intensely critical of the United States, which he presented as spiritually bankrupt, full of conformity, prejudice, philistinism, and sexual repression. He acknowledged that the generation of émigrés with whom he'd returned to America saw it as a world of hope, as representative of the future, but Miller wrote, "To me it was a world I knew only too well, a world that made me infinitely sad." He found only glimmers of authenticity in the renegades and escapists he met on the road.[5] In 1944, at fifty-two, he settled with his third wife in Big Sur to escape a civilization he deemed to be sick, and to enjoy the hot sulfur springs and simple life. In keeping with Miller's outlaw infamy, they lived in a former convict's cabin on the edge of a cliff that plunged a thousand feet into the sea.

Miller, "the sage of Big Sur," was so destitute that he wrote an open letter to readers of *The New Republic* begging them to send him clothes ("love corduroys"), art supplies, and any sum of money in return for one of his watercolors. He used a child's cart to haul these gifts the mile and a half up the hill to his home, wearing nothing, he wrote in a memoir, "but a jock-strap."[6] His charity appeal was a "howling success." *Time* magazine called Miller a "free-loving, free-sponging American-from-Paris," but in Miller's mind, donors were sponsoring an idealistic venture: his attempt to fuse sex and mystical religion to discover a utopian alternative to the "villainous status quo."[7]

Miller's legend as a literary pornographer was enough to associate Big Sur with anarchy and sexual liberation. Battered contraband copies of his books, brought back from Europe by GIs, circulated in bohemian circles and assured his underground reputation (they would not be publicly available in the States until 1964). A martyr to censorship and a vocal pamphleteer against the war, Miller attracted his share of cultish acolytes, or "Millerites," who flocked to Big Sur hoping to emulate him. "They were all filled with a desire to escape the horrors of the present and willing to live like rats if only they might be left alone and in peace," Miller wrote of these postwar dropouts, both veterans and conscientious objectors, who were searching and struggling for a better way.[8] "The cyclotron not only smashed atoms," Miller wrote of the invention that had led to the atomic bomb, "it smashed our moral codes."[9]

Miller had inherited his shack from George Leite, a twenty-four-year-old poet who was nicknamed Blackie the Bandit because of his dark Portuguese good looks. Leite and his wife, Nancy, stayed on in Big Sur in a neighboring hut, where they absorbed Miller's philosophy. Miller would no doubt also have been affected by Leite's enthusiasm for Reich. Miller encouraged Leite to start *Circle*, an anarchist and pacifist literary magazine based in Berkeley that both he and Rexroth contributed to and that included laudatory articles about Reich. Outside Leite's office, like a sentry post, stood his homemade orgone box.

Mildred Brady's secretary, Lucille Marshall, told me that Brady was "entranced" by Leite because he had two live-in helpmates: his wife stayed home to raise their two children while his mistress helped him earn a living.[10] "We had a wild and crazy life," Nancy Leite bashfully explained when I asked her about this domestic arrangement. "In some ways it made life easier, in some ways it made life more difficult."[11] Jody Scott, Leite's mistress, arrived from Chicago in 1946 just in time to help Leite fold his struggling magazine; she had the job of returning manuscripts to Tennessee Williams, Anaïs Nin, and Lawrence Durrell. "I shared a house, his wife, and *Circle* magazine, and coauthored a book with George Leite," Scott remembered, "and he did indeed possess an orgone accumulator and used it daily, explaining to me that Wilhelm Reich was a genius who worked under Freud and that Reich had invented this marvelous device to step up an individual's vital powers, necessary because we've all been horribly crushed and injured by a suppressive society."[12]

Brady visited Leite and Miller, who, she wrote in her piece, were turning the coastal hills below San Francisco into "the cultural Mecca of the twentieth century."[13] Literary immigrants now flooded there, spilling out of San Francisco down Highway 1 and turning the Pacific coastline around Big Sur into what Brady describes as an unsightly shantytown version of Paris's Left Bank or 1920s Greenwich Village; she described these willing castaways as all "beards and sandaled feet . . . corduroys and dark shirts."

The anarchist-inclined literati were interested in poetry, philosophy, painting, but above all, she contended, sex. Reich was their guru—their "ultimate authority." According to Brady, *The Function of the Orgasm* (1942) was "the most widely read and frequently quoted" bible of the avant-garde group. "Even at the poetry-readings," Brady mocked, "you are likely to find someone carrying a volume of his turgid and pretentious prose."[14]

In a long, well-written, and well-researched piece, Brady skewered this fringe community for its avant-garde posturing. She ridiculed its members for their confident belief that they formed "a biological elite" of the "orgastically potent," beacons from a nonrepressed world amid a sea of "orgastic cripples." These conscientious objectors, dropouts from both war and life, had developed a

TOP: The second generation of psychoanalysts found themselves at the forefront of the avant-garde. (Top row) Wilhelm Reich, Otto Fenichel, Jenny Walder; (middle row) Grete Bibring-Lehner, Eduard Bibring; (bottom row) Edith Buxbaum, Claire Fenichel, and Annie Pink, 1927. (The Boston Psychoanalytic Society and Institute Archives)

CENTER: Members of the Vienna Psychoanalytic Ambulatorium, a radical attempt to make psychoanalysis free and accessible to the masses, 1922. Wilhelm Reich is seated at the center, next to the older Eduard Hitschmann; on Reich's left are Grete Bibring-Lehner, Richard Sterba, and Annie Pink. (The Freud Muscum Photo Library)

RIGHT: Anna and Sigmund Freud at the Gare de l'Est in Paris, June 1938, on their way to London, where Sigmund Freud lived in exile during the last year of his life. (The Freud Museum Photo Library)

TOP: Women dancing in a circle at Territory Adolf Koch, Koch's socialist body culture school on Lake Motzen just outside Berlin. Koch's "Alliance of People's Health" had 300,000 members in 1932. (Mel Gordon Collection)

BOTTOM LEFT: Annie Reich (née Pink), Wilhelm Reich's former patient and first wife, and the mother of two of his children, with Eduard Bibring at a fancy dress party, 1926. (The Boston Psychoanalytic Society and Institute Archives)

BOTTOM RIGHT: Mildred Edith Brady, a former model and the journalist who made Reich infamous in America as the leader of "the new cult of sex and anarchy," 1930s. (Joan Brady)

ABOVE: Annic, Wilhelm, and Eva Reich, with Edith and Richard Sterba (far right), in the late 1920s. Sterba described Reich as a "genital narcissist." (The Boston Psychoanalytic Society and Institute Archives)

BELOW: Erwin Stengel, Grete Bibring-Lehner, Rudolph Lowenstein, and Wilhelm Reich at the 1934 Lucerne Psychoanalytic Congress, during which Reich was expelled from the International Psychoanalytic Association. (The Boston Psychoanalytic Society and Institute Archives)

ABOVE. A Food and Drug Administration official holding the funnel of an "orgone shooter," used for directing orgone rays at localized wounds and infections, and modeling an orgone blanket and hat intended for bedbound patients, 1956. (Food and Drug Administration Archive)

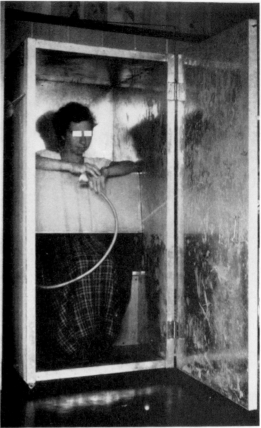

FIG. 7. AN ORGONE ENERGY ACCUMULATOR WITH CHESTBOARD AND SHOOTER IN USE

ABOVE: An image from Reich's booklet *The Orgone Energy Accumulator, Its Scientific and Medical Use* (Orgone Institute Press, 1951). Eva Reich is shown sitting in the orgone box, a device that Reich hoped might dissolve sexual repression and cancerous tumors. This image was used as evidence in the FDA's 1954 complaint for injunction.

LEFT: William S. Burroughs's orgone energy accumulator, stored in the garden of his home in Lawrence, Kansas. He claimed to have had a "spontaneous orgasm" in the box. (Lee Ranaldo)

ABOVE: Paul Goodman, writer and sexual libertarian, running a Gestalt group therapy session, c. 1960. (Sam Holmes)

LEFT: Harvey Matusow, the paid FBI informer who alleged that Communists were using sexual liberation to prey on youth. He later recanted and helped bring down McCarthy. Photos taken in December 1954. (The Harvey Matusow Archive, University of Sussex)

BELOW: Fritz Perls, Reich's patient in Berlin in the 1930s, at Esalen, where he became a guru to the counterculture and a central figure in the Summer of Love. Photo c. 1967. (Esalen Archives)

ABOVE: Ernest Dichter, the man who used sex to sell products by applying psychoanalysis to marketing, running a focus group, c. 1960. (Susan Schiff Faludi, Hagley Museum and Library)

BELOW: The Orgone Energy Observatory, the fieldstone house Reich built for himself in Rangeley, Maine, in 1948. He moved there from New York in 1950. Reich and Michael Silvert are visible in the photograph, at the left. (From *The Orgone Energy Accumulator, Its Scientific and Medical Use*, 1951)

AIR VIEW OF THE ORGONE ENERGY OBSERVATORY, ORGONON, RANGELEY, MAINE

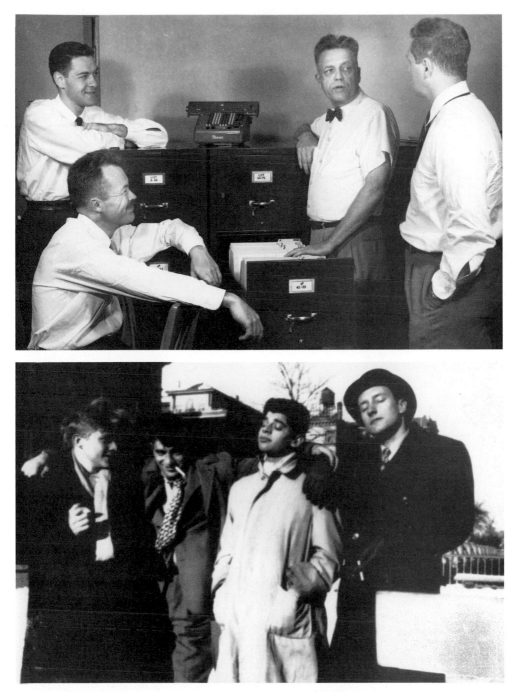

TOP: Clyde Martin, Paul Gebhard, Alfred Kinsey, and Wardell Pomeroy around the filing cabinets that contained the thousands of coded sexual histories they collected, c. 1948. (The Kinsey Institute)

BOTTOM: Hal Chase, Jack Kerouac, Allen Ginsberg, and William S. Burroughs in New York City, where they were living in Joan Vollmer's apartment on West 115th Street and becoming interested in the ideas of Wilhelm Reich. Photo dates from late 1944 or early 1945. (Allen Ginsberg Estate)

RIGHT: Aurora Karrer, with whom Reich had a tempestuous relationship during the last two years of his life, in 1957. (National Library of Medicine)

LEFT: Bill Moise, Wilhelm Reich, and Michael Silvert operating the "cloudbuster," 1955. Reich thought he could use the device to make it rain and shoot down UFOs. Reich posed for and distributed this image for publicity purposes. (Peter Reich)

belief system that rationalized their stubborn policy of nonpartici-
pation. Their anarchism and search for salvation through sex seemed
to echo 1920s bohemia, but she found them to be more snobbish
and reactionary than their forebears.

Brady disliked the new generation's largely misogynistic and less
progressive religion of ecstasy, for which she felt that Reich's ideas
were largely responsible:

> These builders of the new Paris in the nineteen-forties would pro-
> foundly shock their agnostic predecessors of the twenties with
> their sentimental mysticism; for bohemia today is profoundly re-
> ligious . . . A sojourn in the Greenwich Village of the twenties
> [wouldn't prepare] you for love as "the ecstasy of the cosmos" or for
> the "sexual sacrament" as the acme of worship. Back in the postwar
> of World War I, sexual emancipation was stoutly defended and
> practically furthered by the younger generation . . . but it never got
> mixed up with the deity. Sex in those days was a strictly worldly
> affair and nobody's business but our own. "The great oneness,"
> however, is an intimate participant in the sexual emotions of his
> worshippers. In fact, he reveals himself fully only in the self-effacing
> ecstasy of the sexual climax. This, they hold, is the moment of deep-
> est spiritual comprehension of "the other reality," the one moment
> when there is living communication between "the vital force" and
> the individual.[15]

The orgone box promised to channel these cosmic forces, which
is why Alfred Kazin later mocked Isaac Rosenfeld's homemade
contraption as a telephone box with a line to a higher power. But
Reich saw orgone energy as a scientific reality: the idea of "God"
was just a projection of man's awareness of the cosmic orgone ocean
that surrounded the earth. However, Brady was right to notice that
this distinction between science and mysticism was not always clear
in his writing, nor to his followers. In *The Triumph of the Therapeutic*,
Philip Rieff argued that the seeds of an ecstatic religiosity were always hidden in Reich's thought, "despite many clever, even bizarre,
rituals of avoidance."[16]

When Brady skeptically questioned one of Reich's followers

about the existence of orgone energy, he said, "Christ, Mrs. Brady, Reich's seen it—it's blue."[17]

"Mass orders for books are coming in from the West Coast," Reich noted in his journal in October 1945.[18] But he was an unwitting guru, far removed from the avant-garde who eagerly consumed his ideas on both coasts, and he lived a largely reclusive life, surrounding himself with a very few followers. Reich disappeared to Maine for increasingly long portions of the year, and conducted experiments with orgone energy in the Student Laboratory, a building he'd constructed on a newly acquired 200-acre estate four miles west of Dodge Pond, in the Rangeley Lakes region of western Maine. He thought of himself as a scientist, not a leader of a sex cult, and went to considerable effort to differentiate his political philosophy from anarchism.

Though Reich's ideas had national reach, the disciples in Reich's immediate "cult of no little influence," as Brady referred to his circle, were few in number. In 1945 Reich had only three trainees: Theodore Wolfe, Alexander Lowen, and an osteopath, William Thorburn. The following year Reich met Elsworth Baker, a senior doctor suffering from depression who worked at Marlboro State Hospital in New Jersey. Baker became Reich's most faithful adherent and would help him attract many more.

"He loomed large and powerful," Baker recalled in his memoir of his first encounter with Reich, "had a slow easy walk, snow white hair, and a florid face with piercing kindly eyes."[19] Reich X-rayed Baker's chest to see if his diaphram was free. He then asked him to take off his clothes, and began to prod Baker in the ribs and press down on his chest to get him to breathe more deeply. "It was downright frightening," Baker admitted. Reich ordered him to hit the couch and bite on a leather roll, and demanded that Baker try to hurt him by twisting the skin of his forearm with both hands. "He tried to make me angry," Baker wrote, "had me scream, and did succeed in making me sob as I had never before in my life."[20]

Reich diagnosed low energy—if he hadn't come to see him when he did, Reich said, Baker wouldn't have lived more than five years. He prescribed to Baker an orgone energy accumulator to redress his bioenergetic imbalance and demanded that he sign an affidavit acknowledging the device as experimental. When Baker said that wouldn't be necessary and that his word was enough, Reich said, "Do you think you're a king or something?" (It took six weeks of daily irradiations before Baker felt a warm tingling in the accumulator).[21] Reich said his fee was between twenty and thirty dollars and asked Baker how much he'd like to pay. After he settled on twenty-five dollars, Reich began teasing him about the money, and for a long time after, when Baker paid, Reich would pass the bills under his nose to smell.

Baker's wife, Marguerite, also began to see Reich for treatment. Reich, who always called people's wives by their maiden names, referred to her as Miss Maybury and, according to Baker, developed a small crush on her. On several occasions he tried to seduce her—unsuccessfully, according to her husband—and he painted two Chagall-like pictures of her. One of these, which used to hang in Baker's office, depicts a redheaded woman lying naked in a bed of poppies, her conical breasts massaged by spiraling and pulsating blue rays of orgone energy.

Two weeks into Baker's treatment Reich suggested that he start doing orgone therapy on his own patients. (He hadn't yet attained the orgasm reflex himself; it was three months and fifty-five sessions before he claimed to.) In his experiments with the new technique, Baker converted five of the physicians who worked under him to Reich, most notably Chester Raphael and Albert Duvall. The medical director at Marlboro State Hospital became perturbed by this cultish takeover—he thought that the hospital was becoming "a den of Reichian iniquity"—and he refused Baker's request to experiment with the orgone accumulator on the premises. (The director of social services, a social worker, and the hospital chaplain were all known to have orgone accumulators in their hospital quarters.) He had heard the false rumors that Reich had been institutionalized, that he was undergoing treatment for schizophrenia, and that vegetotherapy involved the masturbation of patients.

In May 1948, Baker was called before a medical tribunal and accused of quackery and the doctors under him at Marlboro State were all fired. Dr. Cotton, New Jersey's deputy commissioner for institutions and agencies, admitted that Baker might have helped some of his patients with orgone therapy, but he imputed this to Baker's own "enthusiasm and suggestion" rather than to the method itself—"You could help them with an electric belt," he claimed.[22] He asked Baker whether he masturbated patients and said that he'd heard that some of them screamed with pain and emerged from therapy sessions covered in bruises. "Yes, sometimes there are bruises," Baker admitted, "some people bruise very easily," but no one had ever complained, he added. Cotton dismissed Reich's methods as "a mixture of quackery, chiropractics and Christian Science."[23] Baker resigned soon after in order to devote the rest of his life to Reich's work.

"Of course we are exciting patients sexually," Reich told an audience of coworkers assembled in his Forest Hills home, in response to Cotton's charge, "but not with their dirty fantasy . . . And we don't manipulate the patient's genitals; but if we did, again, we wouldn't do it with their dirty fantasy."[24]

When the American Association for Medical Orgonomy was founded in 1947, at Reich's suggestion, a charter was drafted to safeguard the organization against "medical orgone quacks." The implication was that rather than being a distortion, Reich's science was itself subject to—and already the victim of—distortion. The charter stated that all members must go through "personal restructuring" (that is, vegetotherapy) before admission, and that they should accept the orgasm theory, orgone energy, and the sexual rights of children. In a parody of the government loyalty oaths, the bylaws asserted, furthermore, that members "must not be a member of a church or a subversive political party" or abuse "the sexuality of patients."[25]

A month after the *Harper's Magazine* piece appeared, Brady published another article, this time in *The New Republic*. "The Strange Case of Wilhelm Reich" also ridiculed Reich's theories, especially the orgone box and Reich's cancer cure claims. Under the title ran the line, "The man who blames both neuroses and cancer on unsatisfactory sexual activities has been repudiated by only one scientific journal."[26] It was a much more devastating and direct attack on Reich than Brady's *Harper's* essay. At the top of his own copy of Brady's *New Republic* piece Reich scrawled a message to posterity: "THE SMEAR."

Before Brady dismissed him in the national press as a fraud and a madman, accusations that he would never be able to shake off, his ideas had seemed to be getting traction. Just before Brady's visit, Reich had written to A. S. Neill: "I am looking calmly into the future and hopefully too. There is only one thing I fear. That is, some crooked frame-up, some abysmal *Gemeinheit* [dirty trick] which may still hit me in the back and destroy my work. But we are all alert and watchful."[27] He thought that Brady's article constituted just such a setup and later blamed Brady for his change of fortune in America. "Thus, without wanting it, we have been brought to the attention of a very broad public," Reich wrote to a colleague.[28] He complained in his journal: "They brought me into the public eye in America in a shabby way."[29]

"The Reichites," Brady wrote of the group that was crystallizing around Reich, "declare that orgastic impotence is the primary cause of cancer, all neuroses, all psychoses, impotence, frigidity, perversions, cardiovascular hypertension, hyperthyroidism, constipation, hemorrhoids, epilepsy, peptic ulcer, obesity, narcotic addiction, alcoholism and the common cold."[30]

Brady portrays Reich as a quack before mentioning incredulously that, even so, he was listed in *American Men of Science* ("First swallows!" Reich wrote when he heard of his inclusion), and his work was discussed in such high places as the *Journal of the American Medical Association* and the *American Journal of Psychiatry*. *Politics* and *The Nation* had also carried enthusiastic accounts of his sexual theories. Only one scientific journal had repudiated them: *Psychosomatic Medicine* characterized orgone theory as "a surrealistic creation" and dismissed *The Function of the Orgasm* as "nuttier than a fruitcake."[31]

Brady, apparently unaware of Reich and Fenichel's earlier collaboration, was astounded that Fenichel, one of the most prominent of the Californian exile analysts, "granted Reich considerable standing" in *The Psychoanalytic Theory of Neurosis* (1945), which she described as the "current bible of the American Psychoanalytic Association."[32] Reich, Brady wrote, had more patients than he could treat. In her article, Brady called for the American Psychiatric Association to regulate psychoanalysis, or for it to be under state control (as it was in Norway after the campaign against Reich there), so that a gullible public might be protected from threats such as that represented by Reich and the bogus aphrodisiacal box he sold. Brady portrays Reich's machine as entirely without worth, less a scientific implement than his own personal piggybank.

Brady's article was reprinted in the *Bulletin of the Menninger Clinic* (an editorial pointedly referred to Mr. rather than Dr. Reich), and in December 1947 was abridged in *Everybody's Digest*, which circulated in the millions, under the title "Is the World Sexually Sick?" (Brady had pointed out that Reich thought mankind "endemically neurotic and sexually sick.") Brady unleashed a tidal wave of other titles reporting on Reich's supposed sexual cure-all, which made him notorious beyond avant-garde circles. An article in *Collier's* in January 1948 contained the statement "The orgone and the accumulator can lick anything from cancer to the common cold, according to Reich."[33]

Reich issued a press release correcting some of Brady's statements, but no one printed it. In a long article in the *Journal of Orgonomy*, "Emotional Plague Versus Orgone Biophysics" (1948), Wolfe refuted the negative aspects of what he called (echoing the Norwegian press's hounding of Reich), "The 1947 Campaign." He insisted that the Orgone Institute Research Laboratories, the distributing organization for accumulators founded in 1945, was not a sexual racket but a nonprofit organization, with all profits plowed back into research. Reich made no claims to be able to cure cancer, Wolfe wrote (rather misleadingly, in light of previous statements by Reich), but attacked the underlying malaise from which tumors sprang; and some of the accumulators with which he did this were lent rather than rented to those who couldn't afford them.

Reich detected a Communist conspiracy behind Brady's attack. "It was typically communist, mudslinging propaganda under the guise of a factual, objective portrayal," he wrote. He dismissed Brady as "an intelligent but obviously sex hungry woman" and wrote in his diary, "It is obvious that Mrs. Brady believes that I am the only man who could help her to achieve an orgasm, which she so desperately needs. The tragedy is: she is not aware of her need."[34]

In September 1952, Reich wrote an angry, rambling, stream-of-consciousness note to himself recalling Brady's visit.

> Now I knew well why she said this when I recall her sitting there in front of me in the easy chair, with glowing eyes, glowing from genital frustration, with eyes as I have seen them many thousands of times in people of both sexes, of all ages and professions . . . who expected, I say, orgastic potency from me, expressing this yearning clearly in her eyes as she looks at me, and then smearing me up and down in public with that pornographic insinuation about the Or. accumulator which is supposed to provide orgastic potency. Thus she turned her normal, natural desire into mud, which she then throws in to my decent face.[35]

If Reich described Brady as a "Communist sniper," his suspicions seemed to be confirmed when his old friend, the psychologist Karl Frank, a card-carrying Communist in the 1920s and '30s, told him that he'd met the Bradys in California in 1936 and that they were definitely "fellow travelers."[36] Robert Brady was a known Communist, Frank told Reich, and "Mildred did not leave any doubt in her conversation that her Communist sympathies were stronger than her husband's."[37] Frank, who renamed himself Paul Hagen when he moved to the States, had done antifascist work for the OSS (Office of Strategic Services) in New York during the war and was himself under suspicion by the FBI of being a closet Communist (in Europe he had been a faithful party member and even served a prison sentence for kidnapping a political rival). "No other German exile was the subject of so many reports from American intelligence between 1941 and 1943" as Hagen, wrote Christof Mauch in his 2005 history of the OSS, *The Shadow War Against Hitler*.[38]

Joan Brady, Mildred's daughter, told me that although they were to the left, neither of her parents was ever a Communist or sexually repressed. They maintained a very open attitude to sex: her mother "lived a very adventurous sex life" (Joan Brady herself married Dexter Masters, the man with whom her mother had enjoyed an affair in the 1930s).[39] But it was not the first time the Bradys had been suspect. As early as 1939, the Consumers Union had been accused by HUAC of using its activities and publications to sabotage and destroy the capitalist system. Both Brady and her husband were singled out by Martin Dies as individuals who "don't believe in the American form of Government or the American economic system." Dies even read to the House of Representatives a passage from Robert Brady's *Spirit and Structure of German Fascism* (1937), in which Brady expresses his hope that America will turn its back on "fascist-inclined capitalism."

After much campaigning, the Consumers Union became the only organization to be taken off HUAC's list of subversive organizations in 1954, but though no connection to the Communist Party was ever proved, Mildred and Robert Brady were still under suspicion. That same year, Robert Oppenheimer, the "father of the A-bomb," who was recruited to the Consumers Union by the Bradys, was questioned by the FBI about his relationship with the couple. The Bradys were close friends with Alger Hiss and Haakon Chevalier, the man Oppenheimer claimed had tried to recruit him as a Soviet agent in 1942.

In 1949, Dwight Macdonald told Reich's student Myron Sharaf that Robert Brady "was definitely a Communist," a fact that was duly reported to Reich.[40] Macdonald, who renounced his own Trotskyism in 1942, also said that Fredric Wertham, Reich's other critic in the ranks of *The New Republic*, was a leading luminary of the American-Soviet Friendship League and a fellow traveler. Wertham may have had more pressing reasons for his negative review of Reich's work. He was a vocal crusader against children's comics ("the 10¢ plague"), which he considered a breeding ground for "unhealthy sexual attitudes" and juvenile delinquency, all of which Reich, too, seemed to encourage.[41]

Reich had been aware of *The New Republic*'s dislike of his politics for some time. In 1945 Paul Goodman, whom Macdonald had commissioned to write about Reich for *Politics*, had been commissioned to review translations of *The Sexual Revolution* and *The Mass Psychology of Fascism* for *The New Republic*. Goodman celebrated Reich's "enormous libertarian dynamism" and his call for the sexual freedom of children and adolescents. The editors rejected the review, writing back, "We cannot subject our readers to such opinions on your authority."[42] Goodman communicated this rejection to Reich, and instead published the article that November in *View*. *The New Republic* commissioned Wertham to write his scathing review instead, which labeled Reich's thinking "neo-fascist"; it came out six months before Brady's article.

Wertham thought that Reich's concept of "work democracy" was dangerously reactionary and called for "the intellectuals in our time . . . to combat the kind of psycho-fascism which Reich's book exemplifies."[43] Brady took up Wertham's baton in *Harper's*, making an uncharitable comparison between the new cult of sex and anarchy—with its deliberate assault on the state, church, and family— and the *Volk*-worshipping, proto-fascist circle that grew up around the German poet Stefan George in pre-Hitler Germany, "where a number of the Nazi leaders-to-be drank in the poet's songs of the divine power which manifests itself, 'not in the persons of the many . . . but only in the creative personality.'"[44] Brady argued that Miller and Rexroth's followers, steeped in Reich's thinking, shared George's elitist glorification of the instincts along with his sexual mysticism, and might therefore be construed as "neo-fascist."

In his diary Reich put the parenthesis "Wallace-Stalinist" after a reference to *The New Republic*.[45] Henry Wallace, who had been Roosevelt's vice president, became the editor of *The New Republic* in September 1946 after Truman sacked him as secretary of commerce for criticizing his foreign policy. Wallace used *The New Republic* as a vehicle to oppose Truman's cold war ideology and the escalating arms race that accompanied it, and he frequently defended the Soviet Union against what he considered to be Truman's overhysterical attacks. Brady's article might, indeed, be interpreted in this context; she wrote that Reich considered Russia "sex-reactionary" and "anti-sex," and seemed to defend the country's family values.

In the congressional elections at the end of 1946, the Republican Party picked up fifty-five seats and won a majority by linking communism with Truman's lingering New Dealism—it was the first time they'd controlled Congress since 1930. Though President Truman didn't think the "bugaboo of communism" was a significant threat, he had to take a convincing anti-Communist stand if he was going to win the presidential election two years later. In March 1947, hoping to silence his critics, he introduced the loyalty program, which required that 2.5 million federal employees be investigated by an expanded FBI to see if they had Communist sympathies (785 resigned; only 102 were fired).

In December 1947, when Wallace was contemplating running for president as head of the Progressive Party, *The New Republic*'s offices were "as crowded as Grand Central Station with Communist-controlled delegations falling over each other to entreat [Wallace], and tell him he had three million fans."[46] Truman argued that the Communists were trying to split the Democratic vote so as to get a Republican elected president, which would "lead to the confusion and strife on which Communism thrives."[47] He narrowly beat Dewey to serve a second term. Wallace had mistaken Communist support for popular appeal: the Progressive Party received no electoral votes and only 3 percent of the popular vote, mostly in New York; it represented, wrote Arthur Schlesinger, Jr., "the last hurrah of the era of the Popular Front of the 1930s."[48]

Laurence Duggan and Harry Dexter White, whom Wallace planned to appoint his secretary of state and secretary of the treasury, respectively, were revealed later to have been Soviet agents.[49] In 1952 Wallace published an article, "Why I Was Wrong," in which he explained that his too-trusting stance toward the Soviet Union and Stalin stemmed from inadequate information about Stalin's excesses and that he, too, now considered himself an anti-Communist.

*The New Republic*'s publisher when Brady's article came out was Michael Straight, a son of the New York banker Willard Straight and the heiress Dorothy Whitney, who were close friends of the Roosevelts. In 1948, when Wallace left to resume his political career, Straight became the magazine's editor. Straight had been recruited to the NKVD by Anthony Blunt in 1937 when he was an economics student at Cambridge. Under the code name Nigel, Straight passed secrets to the Soviets when he had a job at the State Department in 1938, and he recommended Alger Hiss as a possible recruit (Hiss is thought to have been an agent already), and he assisted in getting press credentials from *The New Republic* for someone he knew to be a Communist spy. "We were among the last of the utopians," he explained of these actions in his memoir, *After Long Silence.*[50]

Interestingly, the man who recruited Straight's contact, Anthony Blunt, and the other members of the notorious Cambridge Five (Kim Philby, Guy Burgess, John Cairncross, and Donald Maclean) was the stocky, charismatic Austrian psychologist Arnold Deutsch, known to them as "Otto."[51] He had been a collaborator of Wilhelm Reich's in the late twenties and early thirties, when he'd been an active member of Sex-Pol. At twenty-five, already engaged in undercover work for the Comintern, Deutsch ran Reich's Vienna publishing house, the Münster Verlag, which brought out two of Reich's booklets on sexual repression in 1929 and 1930 (Deutsch attracted the attention of the Viennese police's antipornography squad for his role in these publications). Reich was expelled from the Communist Party in 1933, by which time Deutsch was back in Moscow being trained as an NKVD agent, or "illegal." Reich was conveniently forgotten. Christopher Andrew, a historian of espionage, writes in *The Sword and the Shield* that Deutsch omitted all references to his youthful fad for Reich in his KGB-sponsored memoir, as did the Soviet intelligence agency in its official hagiography of Deutsch.[52]

Deutsch's enthusiasm for sexual liberation, a cornerstone of his politics, no doubt appealed to the Cambridge Five. Deutsch painted for them a picture of the Soviet Union as a land of equality and sexual tolerance, a vision that Reich had shared but that he disowned in *The Sexual Revolution.* Guy Burgess always insisted that Stalin's views on homosexuality were more liberal than "American propaganda" implied. Cairncross later wrote a history of polygamy, *After Polygamy Was Made a Sin: The Social History of Christian Polygamy* (1974), in which he boastfully quoted George Bernard Shaw: "Women will always prefer a 10 percent share of a first-rate man to sole ownership of a mediocre man."[53]

In 1947, the year the Brady piece came out, Donald Maclean was working as a double agent in the United States, where he was rumored to be passing atomic secrets to the Russians under the code name Homer (a pun on his bisexuality). But Straight had quit the "great game" by then; he refused to cooperate with Soviet intelligence after 1942, apparently disenchanted with the Soviet attack on Finland. Also in 1942 Deutsch drowned en route to New York, when his ship was sunk by a German torpedo.

Under Straight's editorship *The New Republic* supported Truman in 1948 rather than its former editor, Wallace. Straight eventually outed Blunt as a spy in 1963, by which time Philby, Burgess, and Maclean were already living in the Soviet Union. Philby had an affair with Maclean's wife there in the early sixties. A book he gave to Melinda Maclean at that time, Alex Comfort's *The Joy of Sex*, later turned up in a Sotheby's auction (Comfort, a British anarchist and poet, had been a regular contributor to George Leite's *Circle*). Philby's inscription neatly summarized Reich's philosophy: "An orgasm a day keeps the doctor away."[54]

Reich, who did not approve of marriage, lived with Ilse Ollendorff for five years before tying the knot. He wrote that he only agreed to do so because his lawyer, Arthur Garfield Hays, told him that the judge in the Naturalization Court would disapprove of their having a child out of wedlock and that this might affect their application for citizenship (Peter was a year old). "When I left the courthouse," Reich wrote in his journal the day they collected their marriage license, "I could have puked! My wife too!"[55]

The judge did question Reich about his having been found in 1941 with volumes by Lenin and Trotsky in his library: "And what has politics to do with biology?" he asked Reich.[56] Reich told the judge all his distinguished qualifications, mentioning that he was a member of the International Society of Plasmogeny. The stenographer made a Freudian slip and transcribed: "International Society of Polygamy." Reich and Ollendorff were subsequently granted citizenship in 1946, when Reich was forty-nine.

Ilse Ollendorff thought that a "Moscow-directed conspiracy" against Reich—which her husband, whom she describes as prone to paranoia, suspected—was a little far-fetched. Undoubtedly nothing so systematic was in process, but interestingly Kenneth Rexroth, the "Father of the Beats" who had been a member of the Communist Party, also saw in Brady's attack the hallmark of party influence. Referring to the *Harper's* article on Reich and his anarchist circle in his autobiography, Rexroth wrote: "It didn't take the Communist Party long to attack us."[57] At the time the Communist Party was in crisis. In 1946 Earl Browder, the leader of the American Communist Party, who wanted to take American communism in a more moderate and mainstream direction ("Communism is Americanism," he said), was accused of being a "social imperialist" and expelled from the party under orders from Moscow. His close associates were also purged for "petit bourgeois anarchism."

Rexroth thought that the Communist Party, weakened after the Second World War, was trying to make the anarchists look ridiculous by hitching their wagon to Reich's star in the public's imagination. In comparison with the Communists' withering group, the anarchists were thriving, largely because of their popular pacifist stance during the war. In *Autobiographical Novel*, so titled to avoid libel suits, Rexroth described a meeting in San Francisco held by his anarchist group, the Libertarian Circle. Devoted to the topic "Sex and Anarchy," the event became a legend that might have provided the title for Brady's article. "You couldn't get in the doors," Rexroth wrote. "People were standing on one another's shoulders, and we had to have two meetings, the overflow in the downstairs meeting hall."[58]

Before Brady's article appeared, Rexroth claimed, Henry Miller and many other supposed "Reichites" had never heard of Reich. "I have never met anybody in this circle who was a devotee of the dubious notions of the psychologist Wilhelm Reich," Rexroth wrote in response to Brady's claims. "In fact, few of them have ever read him, and those who have consider him a charlatan."[59] This is a highly doubtful claim in light of his enthusiastic promotion by anarchists such as George Leite, Paul Goodman, and Marie Louise Berneri. Reich was also on Rexroth's own reading list and was much discussed at the Libertarian Circle.

With the benefit of hindsight, Rexroth compared the orgone box to an earlier quack medical device, the Abrams box:

The whole Socialist movement after the First War, led by Frank Harris and Upton Sinclair, embraced the Abrams electronic diagnosis machine [the Abrams box could supposedly diagnose and treat diseased tissue with electrical vibrations]. Twenty years later, after the Second War, the reborn Anarchist movement committed suicide in the orgone boxes of Wilhelm Reich. Anyone who had taken a course in high school physics would have known that this stuff was arrant nonsense but the trouble was that these people had lost belief in high school physics along with their belief in capitalism or religion. It was all one fraud to them. Dr. Abrams had been San Francisco's leading diagnostician. He almost certainly was self-deluded. The same is true of Wilhelm Reich, who before he was persecuted first by Freud, then by the Nazis, then by the Stalinists, was one of the more valuable of the second generation of psycho-analysts. Both Abrams and Reich were taken up by criminal promoters who used their madness to defraud thousands of people and to make hundreds of American radicals ridiculous.[60]

Other anarchists also tried to distance themselves from Reich's controversial invention after Brady's attack. In 1949, when he outed Brady as a Communist to Sharaf, Dwight Macdonald was making daily trips to Reich's New York office for irradiations in the orgone box. According to Macdonald's Austrian friend and neighbor, the biologist and cancer specialist Theodore Hauschka, who was interviewed by the FDA in February 1953, Macdonald would sit in the box for "one-half hour each day in the nude with his tongue protruded in order to get the full effect of Orgone radiation."[61]

While meditating inside the accumulator, and unbeknownst to Reich, Macdonald was plotting his own denunciation of Reich's theories. He was researching an article he hoped to write for the radical magazine he edited, *Politics*, and in which he had previously allowed Goodman to so enthusiastically promote Reich. Provisionally titled "A Layman's Opinion of the Reichian Theory and Orgone Accumulator," it was to run alongside Hauschka's damning professional opinion of the box. *Politics* folded in 1950, so Macdonald never wrote his article, but according to Hauschka the only benefit Macdonald claimed to have derived from Reich's box was that he managed to finish reading *War and Peace* while sitting inside it.

Macdonald commissioned Hauschka to write his medical opinion of the accumulator. Hauschka never used the box, but on the basis of his study of Reich's books and the repetition of some of Reich's experiments outlined in them, he concluded that Reich's orgone theory was the "gibberish of a madman." In his own paper, which was also never published (but was cited in Clara Thompson's 1950 book on the neo-Freudians), Hauschka wrote that Reich's theories were "the ultimate in schizoid experience"; Reich substituted "a billion ameboid individualities for [his] disintegrating ego."[62]

"I did not know," Hauschka wrote, sarcastically quoting Reich, "that 'many cancer cells have a tail and move in the manner of fish.' Perhaps they are trying desperately to be spermatozoa, for cancer, according to Reich, is the direct consequence of sexual stasis and pleasure starvation." He refuted Reich's assumption with his own research on mice; according to Hauschka, 70 percent of the breeding females he studied died of breast tumors, whereas only 5 percent of the virgin mice developed cancer. He therefore concluded, "Sexual stasis does not cause malignancy but prevents it; but I should hesitate to let this finding tempt me into recommending nation-wide celibacy as a means of cancer-prevention."[63]

Hauschka thought Reich was sincere in his beliefs: "If Reich were a quack—and he most assuredly is not—he could never have dreamt up this nightmare of a book. What a tragic waste of enthusiasm and misdirected scientific curiosity! What a classic of systematized self-delusion, quite capable of deluding others as well!"[64]

However, if Brady hoped to ridicule the anarchists by linking them with Reich, this strategy backfired—despite the reservations of important spokesmen such as Rexroth and Macdonald, the negative publicity Reich received only attracted more people to his ideas. In 1949 the newspaper *PM* noted that *The Mass Psychology of Fascism* was the most frequently requested item in the New York Public Library. Henry Miller reported that a number of people came to Big Sur saying, "I came to join the cult of sex and anarchy."[65] Elsworth Baker wrote in his memoir, *My Eleven Years with Reich*, "The appearance of emotional plague articles only resulted in a further spread of interest . . . The telephone rang almost constantly."[66]

On the August 28, 1947, Charles Wood, a Food and Drug Administration inspector for Maine, made an unannounced visit to Orgonon, Reich's estate in Maine (named in honor of Reich's discovery of orgone energy there several years earlier). Wood drove up the half-mile-long driveway lined with blueberry bushes, past handwritten signs reading NO ADMITTANCE, NO TRESPASSING, and NO ADMISSION EXCEPT ON WRITTEN APPOINTMENT. Ilse Ollendorff came out of the Student Laboratory to greet the visitor and confirmed that Reich saw no one without prior arrangement. When Wood showed her his credentials she went back inside to confer with her husband, and Reich appeared.

"Dr. Reich," Wood's subsequent report in the FDA archive in Washington states, "is fifty years old, speaks with a German accent, and was dressed in blue dungarees and a work shirt at the time of the visit. His greeting was cordial." When Reich asked Wood how he'd heard about the box, he said a friend had sent him the Brady article; Reich complained about its "red-fascist" origin and called it "rotten" and "bitchy."[67]

Wood was visiting to determine whether the accumulator might be classed as a medical device and would therefore be under FDA jurisdiction; applications had to be filed with the FDA for all medical or therapeutic devices shipped in interstate commerce. The Consumers Union had played an active role in securing the passage of the Food, Drug, and Cosmetic Act, one of the last measures of Roosevelt's New Deal, in 1938. As one judge explained the act, "The purpose of the law is to protect the public, the vast multitude of which includes the ignorant, the unthinking, and the credulous who, when making a purchase, do not stop to analyze."[68] (Wood was already working on the Hoxsey cancer case, helping to gather evidence against Harry Hoxsey, who sold a dark brown herbal remedy that he claimed could cure cancer.)

Reich took Wood into the orgone room, an enormous accumulator lined with sheet iron, to show him the two accumulators kept inside. "It is a small cabinet affair, large enough to hold a small chair for the patient to sit in," Wood reported to Charles Wharton, chief of the eastern division of the FDA, evidently unimpressed. "Dr. Reich readily admitted that his 'Orgone Accumulator' was a device (in experimental stages) for the treatment of many diseases, including cancer."[69] The accumulator, Reich told him, was only ever used under a doctor's supervision, and volunteered the names of the five doctors who were working with him at that time. Patients paid a small rental fee. Having already gotten into trouble with the American Medical Association, Reich had scaled back his claims; he now asked patients to sign an affidavit in the presence of a notary that stated that they were participating in an experiment and that no cures were promised.

The Orgone Institute also sold as well as rented accumulators. One of the large devices retailed for $216, and a tabletop model, the shooter, cost $75. These were shipped by rail through Boston to New York City and on to New Jersey, Pennsylvania, Oregon, and California. Reich gave Wood some examples of the literature that was sent out with each box. An instruction sheet, "How to Use the Orgone Accumulator," addressed the "pioneers" who had volunteered to test Reich's new machine: "We do not promise any cures," users were told. "No mystical influence should be expected. No profit interest is behind the distribution of Orgone Accumulators. The chief aim is to define in the course of 2 to 4 years how many people who use the Akku regularly will still develop chronic colds, severe sinus trouble, pneumonia and diseases of the life system, (cancer, etc.)." Patients were instructed to sit in the box every day, preferably in the nude, until they'd "had enough" or felt there was "nothing happening any longer."[70]

A thirty-eight-year-old woman called Clista Templeton manufactured the boxes in Oquossoc, a small hamlet a few miles from Orgonon. Templeton told Wood, who visited her immediately after he met Reich, that she had been making accumulators since her father, Herman Templeton, died three years earlier. Herman Templeton had been a guide in the area and Reich had become friends with him on his first holiday in Maine (Reich had been staying in a cabin built by Templeton, which he then bought from him). Templeton started making rental accumulators for Reich on a one-off basis in 1942. By the end of the following year there were 20 accumulators in official use, most of them built by him, and he built the same number again in 1944. As Reich became better known after the war, demand shot up: in 1946, 56 new devices were constructed; the next year, when Brady's article came out, 65. By the time of Wood's visit, Templeton and his daughter had built 171 large accumulators and 85 smaller "shooters" between them. (Of course, many users, like Rosenfeld and Burroughs, simply built their own.)

When Templeton, sixty-nine, was diagnosed with advanced prostate cancer, Reich recommended he use an orgone accumulator. Templeton built his own box, becoming the first of Reich's patients to use one at home rather than in Reich's clinic in Forest Hills. Reich spent the summer of 1942 as Herman Templeton's informal physician, taking away urine samples to examine under the microscope and reappearing with reports of the residues of dead cancer cells that he had observed, proof that the tumors were being destroyed by sessions in the box. That summer, Clista Templeton told Wood, "Reich was much enthused over the possible development of the production of Accumulators on [a] big scale and that he indicated the need of all kinds of assistants, etc., to take care of the throngs of sufferers that were sure to crowd the gates of Orgonon."[71] Apparently he even made large road signs to direct people to Orgonon and put them up in the Rangeley Lakes region.

Templeton had been given six months to a year to live, but, as Reich reported in *The Cancer Biopathy* (1948), when he started using the accumulator his pains left him, he gained seven pounds, and his bedsores dried out. He lived for a further three years. Clista Templeton considered these statements to be "exaggerated or completely false."[72] According to Wood, Clista Templeton felt that her father had been exploited by Reich and planned to stop production in the near future. Her father, Clista said, had built himself an accumulator only after Reich's "consistent urging, and ... against his better judgment."[73] She thought that Reich's enthusiasm, and his hopes that Orgonon would become a new Lourdes, had given the family "false hopes." Though Templeton seemed to think the accumulator helped him in the fall and winter of 1942, Clista thought that these were probably the slow results of his earlier hospital treatment. Her father's health slumped early the next year and he died twenty-five months (not three years) after his cancer was diagnosed. Toward the end of his life, Clista said, her father "lost confidence in the Accumulator, and at one time told Dr. Reich that it was ineffective like all of the rest of the 'cure-alls.'"[74]

Before her father's death, his accumulator had been relegated to a shed, where lumber was piled on top of it, and it was now warped out of shape. It was about five and a half feet high and "a very crude affair," in Wood's description, "but probably as effective as any and a good exhibit of a worthless device." Wood thought it looked like a privy. "I told Clista that a slight alteration would make it a good back yard annex to a camp," he joked.[75]

After reading Wood's account of his visit to see Reich, Charles Wharton concluded that the orgone accumulator was "a fraud of the first magnitude being perpetrated by a very able individual fortified to a considerable degree by men of science."[76] Wharton, certain that Reich was cheating his customers with false medical claims, decided that the agency would pursue the investigation, and he instructed Wood to collect the names and addresses of every consignee, and of anyone who returned a box, so that the agency might identify potential "dissatisfied users" who might testify against Reich in court.

A month later Wood was back in Oquossoc on the first of several more covert investigations that he made before the year was out. In an effort to gauge the extent and modus operandi of Reich's business, Wood made trips to the local bank, to the postmaster, to the Railway Express office and the county registry. Wood also paid frequent visits to Clista Templeton's home; she was his key and most enthusiastic informant, and he kept his conspicuous government car hidden in her garage so that it wouldn't be seen by anyone connected with Orgonon.

Using Clista Templeton's records, Wood was able to collect a lengthy list of over one hundred consignees. It reads like a blacklist of names. Twenty of the devices had been shipped to doctors (Reich insisted that they use the device every day if they were to prescribe it to others), the others went to patients who paid ten dollars a month for a minimum period of three months for the privilege of "testing" it. According to Clista Templeton, the accumulators cost forty dollars to make, half for labor and half for materials. Wood estimated Reich's annual income from accumulators to be in the region of twenty thousand dollars. One Berkeley woman—perhaps Mildred Brady's friend—had returned her accumulator after three months. She might be a dissatisfied user, Wood wrote hopefully.

A week after his first visit, Wood visited Reich for a second time. Reich was examining a patient who was using the accumulator to treat his leg ulcers. "The Dr. was dressed in blue dungarees and heavy wool shirt. He looked anything but professional," Wood noted. "He is thick set with a ruddy complexion and at his time, as previously, his red face showed evidence of peeling skin with light colored skin around the left eye."[77] Wood adds that this skin condition was "probably caused by accumulator research activities," which seems an odd assertion if he was so sure the box was worthless.

Reich was warned that his accumulator was definitely classed as a device by the FDA and that therefore Wood would have to carry out a factory inspection. "Dr. Reich," apparently flustered by this news, "answered most questions by asking questions."[78]

Because it was the end of the summer and the Reichs were about to return to New York, much of the equipment in the Student Laboratory had been dismantled. Wood took down the serial numbers of all the remaining instruments. Two accumulators in the orgone room were marked with small labels reading ORGONE ENERGY ACCUMULATOR / MADE IN USA / ORGONON, RANGELEY, MAINE, and stamped with a production number and a wishbone-like symbol.

Wires ran from one of these boxes out into the laboratory to a Geiger-Müller counter. Reich explained that he was perfecting a "free energy machine, a motor powered by orgone energy," and told his patient that he hoped that it would be an even better device than the orgone accumulator for helping "suffering humanity."[79] (Saying that mankind was not ready for such a momentous discovery, Reich dropped the project in 1949 after one of his laboratory assistants allegedly absconded with the machine; he alerted the FBI that the student might be a Russian spy.)

After Reich's patient had left, Wood brought up Reich's conflict with Freud. Reich "completely exploded" and refused to answer any questions on the topic, declaring the dispute none of the FDA's business. "The newspaper campaign directed against him [in Norway] was another touchy subject he refused to discuss," Wood said. "His investigation by the FBI was not discussed as Reich was becoming very excited in relation to all of the troubles he confronted in his 'strife for the advancement of science.'"[80]

Reich complained to his lawyer Arthur Garfield Hays, who was general counsel to the American Civil Liberties Union:

> Our work is being confused with some pornographic . . . activities. It is too bad that inspectors in such a responsible position are not capable of distinguishing between science and pornography, and they never heard the name Sigmund Freud, and that they feel justified in asking hidden questions as, for instance, what kind of women we are employing or what we are doing with our women, etc. The implication is clearly that of indecent, smutty, pornographic behavior on our part. They should know with whom they are dealing. They seem to be disturbed by the insinuation in Miss Brady's article that the orgone accumulator gives the patient orgastic potency. I wished it did, but it does not. But to the average human mind, used to smutty sex activities going on everywhere, the word orgastic potency has a different meaning.[81]

There are certainly frequent indications in Wood's reports that he felt the FDA had stumbled across a vice ring or free-love cult in Rangeley. Wood said to one Orgone Institute employee when he interviewed her about the box, "Oh, since you're not married, you don't need one, do you?" Lois Wyvell at the Orgone Institute Press was asked if she handled "sex books."[82] Dr. Simeon Tropp, who as head of the Orgone Institute Research Laboratories in New York had taken over production of accumulators from Clista Templeton, was told by FDA inspectors that they were looking for a "sexy racket, mixed up with a strange box." Tropp's medical partner had agreed to cooperate with the FDA because he felt that Tropp "had come under the influence of Reich to such an extent that he appeared to be in a hypnotic state."[83]

Clista Templeton had a sketch made by Reich of a glass tube to be inserted into the vagina that she'd picked up by mistake from Reich's desk along with some other drawings, which seemed to hint at the accumulator's being some kind of masturbatory device. The glass tube was filled with steel wool and attached to the shooter hose for use with nasal and vaginal disturbances. According to the instructions, the tube was to be "inserted . . . gently and not for more than 2 minutes at a time, or until a slight burning sensation is felt."[84]

With Reich safely back in New York until the next summer, Wood, using Clista Templeton's list of people to whom accumulators had been sent, began interviewing Reich's patients in the Rangeley area. He discovered that there was a good deal of local enthusiasm for the box. A lady who worked at the Rangeley Tavern used one "in the nude [to] . . . overcome fatigue."[85] The police were called out one night to investigate a disturbance at the tavern and found a party in full swing. The chef had been locked in her orgone accumulator.

Reich hoped that one day every household might have an accumulator, which might be used to prevent cancer and other ailments, and to keep the nation charged up with bioenergy. In *The Cancer Biopathy* he imagined a whole city using it in a large-scale trial, so social workers could compare the incidences of cancer with those in similar places that didn't have the benefits of the box. "If it is possible to mobilize the populations of an entire planet for purposes of war, then it must be possible to mobilize a district of 10,000 inhabitants for the purposes of a crucial experiment," Reich wrote. "It must not be left undone."[86] But in the meantime, he used the Rangeley area as the testing ground for his theories.

Though you could rent or buy an accumulator, most of Reich's clients in this rural part of Maine were charity patients who got them on loan free of charge. "Like water and air, orgone energy can be obtained for nothing and is available in unending quantities," Reich wrote in 1948. "The purpose of collecting it in the accumulator (a process similar to filling a wash basin with water) is to supply it in concentrated form. It is important to provide a means of access to concentrated orgone energy for even the poorest people."[87] Some of his patients in Maine were so tearfully grateful for their orgone treatment, Reich wrote in *The Cancer Biopathy*, that he sometimes felt like "one of those mystical faith healers."[88]

Sylvester Brackett, a seventy-year-old who claimed the accumulator was a miracle cure for his arthritis, was described by Wood as Reich's "chief booster" in the Rangeley Lakes area. It was Brackett whom Reich had been examining when Wood last visited Orgonon. "Dr. Reich's treatment of Mr. Brackett," Wood reported, "consisted of having him repeat the miraculous benefits derived from the orgone accumulator several times for my benefit." (Wood warned his superiors that Brackett "was the real 'testimonial' type.")[89] Later, when Wood visited his home, Brackett told him that he had suffered crippling arthritis for over a decade; he used a small shooter on his joints, legs, and hands and sat in a large accumulator for about an hour a day, a habit he credited with his being able to walk again.

Both devices were set up in his living room, just outside his bedroom, but Brackett admitted that (against Reich's advice) he hadn't used either accumulator for the few months between his last meeting with Reich and Wood's visit, because he hadn't been suffering any excessive stiffness. But, Wood wrote, he stated that "he would under no circumstances be deprived of the use of the Accumulators and probably would resume treatments, if his condition became any worse."[90]

George Garland, Brackett's seventy-year-old brother-in-law, had used the accumulator to combat his asthma. He paid Reich five dollars a month and sat in it for fifteen to forty-five minutes each night, but he returned the box after about six months, feeling that it was not beneficial in his case. Another relation, Samson Brackett, who Wood thought looked like Rip van Winkle, had used an accumulator for leg sores for about a year, again free of charge, but returned it after deciding that it had "lost its power." A Mr. Beckworth, whose son married Brackett's daughter, sat in his accumulator to treat his asthma and arthritis. Also a charity patient, he claimed to have achieved good results with the device. He stored it in pieces in a corner of his bedroom, not having used it for several months, but said he planned to use it again in the spring.

Though several people had discontinued using or dismantled their accumulators, none would declare themselves dissatisfied with the device. No one would admit that they had been suckered. For example, Oscar Tubbs, sixty-one, lived on his own on a small farm and used the accumulator for "asthma, leg lameness, piles, ear and nose troubles" ("Aside from his belief in Orgone Accumulators," Wood wrote, "he appears to be intelligent"). Tubbs found sitting in it nude "rather harsh treatment in cold weather" and got Reich's permission to use it "lightly clad." He kept the shooter by his bed; Wood noticed dust in the larger accumulator and Tubbs admitted that he, too, was not using it, though he hung on to it in case of emergencies. He'd had a letter from Reich warning him of the FDA investigation and "was concerned over the possibility of being classed as a fraud victim and apparently put up a strong defense for three years' use of the boxes."[91]

Wood was aware that his findings would disappoint his Boston bosses. He had interviewed twelve of Reich's accumulator patients. "No dissatisfied users were located," Wood wrote to the FDA's central office on January 5, 1948.

> The users seem to be either satisfied with results or take the attitude that nothing was promised so they are not dissatisfied that no benefits were received . . . This entire Orgone Accumulator setup is a peculiar one and quite different from anything else I ever worked on. None of the Maine users have any literature put out by Reich or the Institute and most of them wouldn't understand it if they had it. The boxes are either loaned free of charge or rented at a low rate ($15 a month) to local people.[92]

A few months later Wood reported that it seemed as though the "orgone box business was petering out" in Reich's absence; it seemed almost as though most people planned to use their box only in the summer months when they could enjoy the free medical attention Reich extended to them.[93]

The following August, when Reich returned to Maine, Wood reported to Wharton that production of orgone accumulators had been resumed. Reich certainly made no secret about his inventory, which was painstakingly documented in Ollendorff's "Report on Orgone Energy Accumulators in the USA" (*Journal of Orgonomy*, 1950). At the time of writing, Ollendorff wrote, there were 322 accumulators in "official" use in the United States, which had earned the Wilhelm

Reich Foundation (established in 1949 by Reich's supporters) a total of $23,000—a much more modest sum than Wood had estimated.

Charles Wharton's war on Reich became an obsession for him. "He was crazy about that Reich case and didn't think of anything else during the whole time," Wood recalled. "He built it way up out of proportion."[94] Wharton was evidently sex-obsessed; according to Jerome Greenfield, author of *Wilhelm Reich vs. U.S.A.*, he kept a ceramic phallus in a drawer of his desk, which he used to take out to try to distract his secretary when she came in to take dictation. But this exhibitionistic streak masked an inner prudery. He suggested tipping off the post office to postal deliveries of *The Sexual Revolution*, thinking that they might have the grounds for an obscenity case, and he helpfully marked all the pages that spoke of adult and infantile masturbation for them. He kept an accumulator in the corner of his office. "This is a box," wrote Wharton, "in which a man is placed and thereby becomes permeated with orgone, which is a progenitor of orgasm . . . No kidding."[95]

Wood's own interest in the case was also somewhat personal. He was fifty-two and recently widowed. In December 1947, three months after his first visit to her workshop, he married Clista Templeton—which explains his excessive concern to paint her in a good light with his superiors in Boston. Several times in his reports, Wood refers to the importance of guarding the information she supplied to him so that Reich—who had quizzed her about Wood's initial visit—wouldn't find out that she was working to betray him. He repeatedly states her deep regret that she ever became involved with Reich and that she planned to discontinue working for him soon. Convinced by Wood that Orgonon was a criminal operation, Clista Templeton did hand in her notice, and the manufacture of accumulators was moved to New York. Nevertheless, by then it would have been difficult to argue that she was an independent witness in any potential case against Reich; Wood's quest had ended in love and compromise.

# Nine

Alfred Kinsey's *Sexual Behavior in the Human Male* was published in January 1948. It ran to 804 pages, with 162 tables and 173 graphs, and was published by a serious medical textbook house, W. B. Saunders. Nevertheless, as *Time* magazine commented, not since *Gone With the Wind* had there been such literary excitement: 200,000 copies were sold in two months. The media compared its appearance to the atomic bomb that had been dropped three years before, and anticipated its having as devastating a social effect. The head of the Salvation Army condemned the report as a "weapon for temptation," thinking it would legitimize sexual extremes.

Kinsey's Hollerith machine crunched a range of famously startling and revolutionary statistics from the mass of raw data he collected all around America. The press reveled in the book's salacious details, transforming "Dr. Sex," as Kinsey came to be known, into an instant celebrity: 92 percent of men masturbated; 85 percent had premarital coitus; 50 percent had extramarital coitus; and 69 percent had visited prostitutes. The most shocking facts at the time were those concerning the incidence of homosexuality: 37 percent of men had enjoyed a homosexual experience leading to orgasm ("more than one male in three," Kinsey emphasized), and 4 percent were exclusively homosexual.

Kinsey's book desentimentalized sex, looking at it outside of the rhetoric of love and the institution of marriage; he claimed to be dispassionately presenting his findings. "This is first of all a report on what people do," he wrote, "which raises no questions of what they should do."[1] But Kinsey was a lot more prescriptive than he liked to admit, and underneath his cool scientific detachment was a crusading humanitarianism that bubbled up between the lines of everything he wrote. The literary critic Lionel Trilling, for one, criticized the report for being "full of assumption and conclusion; it makes very positive statements on highly debatable matters and it editorializes very freely."[2]

Clara Kinsey later said that her husband's work represented "an unvoiced plea for tolerance." Kinsey hoped his data would encourage ridicule of the existing sex laws: "At least 85 percent of the younger male population," he wrote in an introduction, "could be convicted as sex offenders if law enforcement officials were as efficient as most people expect them to be" (as it stood, 3 percent of all prison inmates were sex offenders, and in some states, including California, the figure was as high as 10 percent).[3] In the face of the evidence of such wide sexual variation, Kinsey called for the dismantling of antiquated laws against homosexuality, prostitution, oral sex, sodomy, and bestiality. Nature, he argued, would always triumph over the moral restrictions men tried to impose on it.

Kinsey's book was, his biographer James Jones wrote, "an ode to Eros . . . a celebration of the 'human animal's' ability to find sexual outlets in a society obsessed with controlling and restricting sexual freedom."[4] Kinsey was dismissive of the Rockefellers' attempts at sex reform. "Millions of dollars have been spent by certain organizations" to curb prostitution, he said with reference to their antivice efforts, which had only resulted in a "transference of . . . premarital intercourse from prostitutes to girls who are not prostitutes."[5] The Rockefellers sought to legislate morality and control reproduction, but Kinsey thought that, with the exception of sexual violence, the only workable law in relation to sex was to have no laws at all.

"If society's only interest in controlling sex behavior were to protect persons," Kinsey wrote, "then the criminal codes concerned with assault and battery should provide adequate protection."[6] America's sex laws, he concluded, were not really about protecting people but about upholding custom, which is why, he thought, they were defended with so much emotion. (The sexual revolution that Kinsey inspired was also a legal revolution: in 1955 the American Law Institute drafted an influential Model Penal Code, which, drawing on Kinsey's study, rejected the concept of "deviant sexual behavior" and led to the reform of the sex laws.)

The Kinsey book came out in an election year, one in which Henry Wallace was running as the leader of a third party endorsed and sponsored by the Communists. The wartime alliance between East and West had crumbled that summer when the Soviet Union blockaded West Berlin. The blockade was bypassed with a massive 462-day airlift operation organized by the Western Allies, and the anticommunism that defined the next decade was just taking root. Truman's loyalty oath saw government workers scrutinized for their sexual practices, and "sex deviants" were sacked because they were thought to be potential targets of blackmail by Soviet agents.

J. Edgar Hoover, whose FBI had expanded so that it could carry out the loyalty screenings Truman had introduced, associated Kinsey and all sexual licentiousness with communism. According to Clara Kinsey, her husband voted Republican. "Revolutionary Russia hasn't got far," he wrote in his biology textbook, "for it tried to secure wealth and leisure without working for them, and the millions who have consequently starved to death in that country bear testimony to the truth of the scientific conviction that we can't get something for nothing."[7] But when Kinsey wanted to collect histories from senior members of the Communist Party in New York, he took the precaution of having his attorney get an assurance from the FBI director that there would be no attempt to secure the information obtained in these interviews, which cast him in Hoover's eyes as a sympathetic "fellow traveler."

The FBI—which was, in James Jones's memorable phrase, "possibly the only American institution more obsessed with sex than [Kinsey's] Institute for Sex Research"—assigned an agent to review Kinsey's book at J. Edgar Hoover's personal request. The agent declared the report to be "not as scientific as it is prejudicious" and thought it might "do incalculable harm in the hands of adolescents who read it as justification for their own sexual habits."[8] Hoover, who saw himself as a white knight upholding America's sense of decency, wrote an article for *Reader's Digest* warning of the possible impact of Kinsey's work: "It is important to the very future of our national life that we hold fast to our faith. Man's sense of decency declares what is normal and what is not. Whenever the American people, young or old, come to believe there is no such thing as right or wrong, normal or abnormal, those who would destroy civilization will applaud a major victory over our way of life."[9]

In 1949, the year after the publication of his report, Kinsey made a speech before the Marriage Counselors Association in New York City in which he was critical of the FBI's policies on sex crimes, especially their entrapment of homosexuals, and someone communicated to the bureau that Kinsey was "anti-FBI." Hoover launched an investigation into Kinsey—"What do we know of Kinsey's background?" he asked, initiating a large file on the scientist. They never found out that Kinsey, in creating his own sexual utopia, fostered a culture of wife swapping and bisexuality. He also filmed orgies within the inner circle of his senior staff and their spouses in the supposed interest of science. Hoover ordered that someone should "tackle Kinsey . . . and make him put up or shut up," which was exactly what Hoover requested be done when people were reported to have questioned his own sexuality.[10] A lifelong bachelor, he was widely thought to be in a long-term homosexual relationship with his deputy, Clyde Tolson. Truman Capote would nickname them Johnny and Clyde, which got him, he joked, "about 200 pages in an FBI file."[11]

Since 1925, the FBI had maintained an extensive "obscene publications file," to which Hoover denied access when Kinsey's researchers requested it in the late 1950s; and in 1951, as part of McCarthy's attempt to flush out Reds from under beds, the FBI would start collecting their own version of Kinsey's sexual histories. Hoover initiated a Sex Deviates Program that collected potentially embarrassing sexual details on a wide variety of people, with secret dossiers on presidents, a former first lady, members of the cabinet, and members of Congress. When it was destroyed in 1977 it contained 300,000 pages.[12] Hoover's sex files were used to opposite ends to Kinsey's: namely, to consolidate his power and to purge federal government of homosexuals and other "sex deviants," who were deemed security risks, a policy Hoover pursued with perhaps over-compensatory gusto.

A Gallup poll conducted at the time found that 78 percent thought the Kinsey study a good thing, but the 10 percent who dis-approved were a vocal minority. The psychoanalyst Lawrence Ku-bie, known for his uncompromising stance on homosexuality, wrote one of the most devastating critiques of the report (Kubie, Reich's nemesis, was Tennessee Williams's analyst and so disapproved of the writer's homosexuality that he apparently advised him to give up writing and practice abstinence). He criticized Kinsey for ignor-ing psychological factors in sexuality, and in trusting that his sub-jects' memories could evade the forces of repression, for justifying sexual perversions, and for his statistical technique.

Kinsey hadn't operated with a random sample because of the impossibility of forcing people to offer up their sexual histories; as a result, he was accused by Kubie of relying on volunteers who were less inhibited than the rest of the populace, which skewed his sta-tistics and presented the country as sexually dissolute. Kinsey sought to address this lack of random sampling by what he called the "100 percent sample," whereby he'd get all the members of a Rotary Club or college fraternity to give their histories.

It was this accusation that the Rockefeller Foundation took most seriously as they tried to extricate themselves from their relationship with Kinsey. President Harold Dodds of Princeton University, a trustee of the Rockefeller Foundation, compared the report to "small boys writing dirty words on fences," and the Rockefeller-funded American Social Hygiene Association criticized the report on reli-gious and moral grounds.[13] The foundation's board asked whether Kinsey's work fitted with their program to uphold "moral and spiri-tual values" and debated whether his funding should be continued.[14] Kinsey was arrogantly dismissive of all criticism, accusing his detrac-tors of falling short of scientific thinking and of being "sex shy."

Two months after the Kinsey book was published, Reich, whose *Function of the Orgasm* was quoted in it, wrote to A. S. Neill, "Here Kinsey's book, which has sold 600,000 copies [an exaggeration] and deals with the orgastic function in the human male, has helped quite a bit to break through the Chinese wall which had been erected [around discussions of sexuality] and is being kept up by psychoanalytic merchants and red fascist politicians in unison."[15] Reich perhaps had Kubie's criticisms in mind when he wrote about how psychoanalysts buttressed the wall of repression.

But Reich, like many others, criticized Kinsey for his cold scientific detachment in regard to sex. A frequent accusation against Kinsey, leveled by, among others, the psychiatrist Karl Menninger, was that Kinsey studied sexual behavior and not love, things that many—including Reich—thought to be inseparable. The anthropologist Margaret Mead, for example, regretted that Kinsey "atomized" sex, reducing it "to the category of a simple act of elimination," and criticized Kinsey for his residual puritanism: "Nowhere have I been able to find a single suggestion that sex is any fun," she said.[16]

For Kinsey, heterosexual coitus was only one of six possible sexual "outlets" (his word), along with masturbation, petting, nocturnal dreams, homosexual contacts, and bestiality—all of which were equally acceptable to him. Margaret Mead: "The book suggests no way of choosing between a man and a sheep."[17] Reich followed Freud in thinking that genital union was the only mature form of sexual behavior; orgastic potency, for him, was intimately bound up with heterosexual love, and every other avenue for pleasure was a perversion (unlike Kinsey, Reich thought homosexuality an aberration and, according to Ollendorff, never knowingly treated a gay man). Reich differentiated between the orgasm enjoyed when "making love," in which the opposite sex partner "is felt as 'somebody else,' if not as completely alien and foreign," and the more profound and rejuvenatingly potent orgasm enjoyed when you "fall in love," when you are totally "lost in the experience . . . ONE organism, as if united or melted into each other."[18]

"Now they want us to consider love," Kinsey once told his colleague Wardell Pomeroy with characteristic dryness. "If we started in on that, we'd never finish."[19]

In the summer of 1948, at the height of this debate about the nation's sex life, Reich organized the First International Orgonomic Convention, held in Maine and clearly modeled on the psychoanalytic congresses he had attended in the 1920s and 1930s. The FDA investigation seemed to have gone quiet, and Reich assumed—falsely, it turned out—that it had been abandoned. The "Chinese wall" of sexual repression seemed to be crumbling and the focus was on the role orgonomy might play in a liberated future. Reich had posters printed for the occasion with a slogan that reflected the optimistic spirit: IT CAN BE DONE.

There were thirty-five participants at the convention, including representatives from Norway, Israel, Argentina, and Britain. A. S. Neill came over from Summerhill; before traveling to Maine he gave a lecture to a packed auditorium at the New School for Social Research, where his frequent references to Reich were greeted with thunderous applause. "It was a wonderful, exciting time," remembered the vegetotherapist Morton Herskowitz. "There was a joie de vivre there. We felt like we were in the front ranks of people who were going to make a change."[20]

The orgonomists inspected the foundations for the substantial Orgone Energy Observatory, at the crest of a hill overlooking Dodge Pond, which they had all helped finance and which would be finished the following year; it was to house a laboratory, a study, and a telescope that would enable Reich to further pursue his biophysical investigations uninterrupted (at the time Reich was working on a series of "Basic Orgonomic Functional Equations" to explain the workings of his free energy machine).

The modernist structure, with two-foot-thick walls constructed of multicolored fieldstones, had an aggressive, stocky design that seemed almost an extension of Reich's personality. Reich had helped to design it, and had further ambitious but ultimately unrealized plans for Orgonon: an Orgone Research Hospital, an Orgone Research University, and an Orgone Energy Accumulator Factory. He had an architect create some designs and even had some woodland cleared to make way for them, still referred to as Hospital Field. One of his favorite hobbies was to pace out his property, putting red flags up to mark out where these buildings would be.

In recordings of Reich lecturing to his assembled orgonomists, he comes across as authoritarian, commanding, persistent—with a loud, thickly accented voice. "Is that right? Is that clear?" he said, giving them the time to catch up with his train of thought. When he asked a question, they groped like schoolchildren for the answer, and he encouraged them: "Yes, you're very close! . . . Give me a concrete example! Go ahead, jump!"[21] Because most of them had submitted to Reich physically in treatment, it was perhaps easier for them to submit to him intellectually. "Frankly, Reich, in 1948 I had the impression that hardly one of the assembled workers had the faintest idea of what you were talking about," Neill wrote to Reich after the summer conference, "myself included."[22]

Nevertheless, they were all mesmerized by him. Alexander Hamilton described Reich, who was explaining his free energy machine with the help of one of his mysterious diagrams, as "a big magician, doing parlor tricks surrounded by a maze of shiny, sparkling, glowing, ticking, turning gadgets in a tangle of insulated wires."[23]

"They were not 'unarmoured', 'orgastically potent', or anything else special," Myron Sharaf wrote in his biography of Reich's followers (he was one):

> Often they parroted Reich and were afraid to stand up to him. He in turn "used" them as much as they, in a different way, "used" him, to bask in his reflected glory, to have some sense of being part of great, expanding themes. People would work for him for nothing or for very little recompense. He claimed they were learning a lot, and so they were. He accepted, indeed asked for, considerable financial help from his followers. When people dropped out of his close circle, it hurt him but he went on relentlessly, replacing defectors with new adherents.[24]

Reich was always formal—even dictatorial—with his physicians, addressing them without fail as "Doctor." In the tolerant atmosphere of Scandinavia, everyone had referred to Reich as "Willie," but in America, Reich deliberately remained aloof, maintaining strict professional boundaries, and no one used his first name. "Since 1938," Reich told a seminar of orgonomists in 1949, "I have had no personal friendships . . . This is one of the greatest sacrifices I had to make for the work . . . Most of my enemies in the psychoanalytic movement developed out of friends; Fenichel, Annie Reich, Rado—

they were the ones who spread the rumors of my insanity, my alleged insanity."[25]

Dr. Morton Herskowitz—Reich's last trainee and the last of Reich's students still alive in 2010—occupies a substantial brick town house in Philadelphia. In the spacious waiting room there is a large portrait of Reich against an agitated dark red Van Gogh–like backdrop. He is shown wearing a lab coat over a scarlet shirt, whose color matches his ruddy cheeks, and he looks out of the frame from beneath an electrified mop of gray hair with sad, almond-shaped eyes. There is a long, specially constructed massage table in the middle of Herskowitz's treatment room; the table has a brown vinyl cover that's noticeably dented, presumably having been pummeled by five decades of patients. A photograph of Reich posing on the balcony of his house in Maine overlooks this therapeutic stage, and a few primitive sculptures decorate the wall.

I went to see Dr. Herskowitz, now in his nineties, to get a sense of what Reich's disciples saw in their guru—what it was like to be afflicted by "Reichitis," as one of them called it. Reich declared, "A person like me comes along once every thousand years." Clearly his followers felt honored to witness and be a part of his millenarian journey—and, because of the vogue for vegetotherapy, earn a decent living in the process. In *Listen, Little Man* (1948), Reich railed against a culture of mass conformity and settled a lifetime of scores, attributing every one of his setbacks to the gray, repressed bureaucratic "little man" who was envious of his great freedom (thereby confirming Fredric Wertham's view of him as contemptuous of the masses). The little man, Reich wrote, was "miserable and small, stinking, impotent, rigid, lifeless and empty."[26] Reich's followers similarly felt that they were members of a liberated elite that was forging a new way.

Herskowitz, who wears his hair combed back and has a distinguished aquiline look, reclined in his chair to answer my questions, folding his hands over his belly. There was a half-smoked cigar in an ashtray next to a pile of patient notes on his desk, and he spoke with a nasal voice that was punctuated by the occasional wheeze. "When Reich talked, we all had a kind of, maybe not quite fervor, but something approaching it," Herskowitz told me of being gripped by Reich's visionary message, "maybe something like what the first Christian disciples felt about what they were doing. This was going to revolutionize society."

Herskowitz was a young osteopath with Trotskyite sympathies when he met Reich in 1948. He was contemplating a career as a conventional psychoanalyst when a girlfriend's father asked him if he knew about Reich's work. "That guy? He's nuts," Herskowitz replied. "Everybody knows it."[27] However, he agreed to give Reich the benefit of the doubt and read *The Sexual Revolution*. Reich's books—which taught how to dissolve a starched, stiff world—were to Herskowitz "an intellectual and emotional banquet," and although he was a bit dismayed by Reich's concept of orgone energy, which sounded a little eccentric to him, he decided to seek Reich out for therapy.

When Reich came down the stairs to greet him he was wearing a lab coat. His large head and "leonine" hair, which Reich wore spiky and electrically wild, reminded Herskowitz of Einstein. "When you walked in did you see that painting?" Herskowitz asked me. "I painted it—it's my first impression of Reich. He was walking down the stairs, the first day I came to Forest Hills. He was like a tank, a battering ram, he was a force! You got the sense that he couldn't be subdued." Reich looked him straight in the eye as he introduced himself, with a gaze that somewhat undermined his confident entrance. Herskowitz described Reich as having hazel-colored eyes that were "clear, penetrating, and bespoke a deep sadness. There was no trace of self-pity, but of a deeply perceived *Weltschmerz* [world-weariness]."[28]

"What do you think of orgone energy?" Reich asked, to Herskowitz's horror. He responded awkwardly that the concept seemed very strange to him. "Of course it does," Reich answered sympathetically. "You've been trained in science and this is along a different path. If you stay in therapy long enough you'll do the lab work yourself and maybe you'll even change your mind." Reich agreed to take him on as a patient and asked him if he was willing to sign a document that would grant Reich permission to hospitalize him at any point he deemed necessary in the therapy. Herskowitz agreed, but was in fact never asked to sign such a form. It was Reich's way of testing his trust.

Herskowitz was instructed to bring his own bed linen when he traveled from Philadelphia to Forest Hills for his training sessions, which by then cost fifty dollars, twice what Baker had paid, and he kept his sheet in the cubbyhole allotted to him outside Reich's treatment room. He also bought an orgone box and used it at home. "Therapy was a unique and electrifying experience for me," Herskowitz said of Reich's hands-on technique. "I remember after each session I'd come out with a vigor like I'd never experienced. I knew something unique was happening." He wrote in his memoir of his time with Reich: "I left the therapeutic session and was walking towards the subway. I felt like I had never remembered feeling. I was flying."[29]

What did Reich do to achieve these powerful effects? "He'd show me how to breathe at the start of every session," Herskowitz said, "and he'd see if my chest was moving correctly and occasionally he'd give it a little push, that's all. He'd just work on a particular segment of armoring. It wasn't much but he'd always accomplish something. He'd do things—a poke or a look—and something would start to happen in my body; what we call 'streamings,' just an aliveness that I hadn't felt before."

Reich divided the body into several rings of armoring, and the first that needed to be attacked was the ocular segment. "He'd flash a light right in front of my eyes and ask me to follow it, and he did a lot of eye contact. We'd just look at each other softly, and he had wonderful eyes. And he could be very tender and you just felt almost like you were in the presence of a deer . . . Another time he asked me to look paranoid at him, so I was looking suspicious, and all the time my breathing was getting bigger, and he looked paranoid back at me. It got to a point where I said, 'Hey, I may really go crazy,' and I stopped. And that was just as well enough for him, I'd shown that I could be THAT paranoid." To dissolve the oral segment, the second barrier to orgastic potency, Reich would instruct Herskowitz to gag between visits and he showed him how to do this; he would also have him bite towels.

Reich could also be angry in sessions, "and that helped to loosen you up and to evoke the same thing in you. He'd say, 'Make an angry face and punch your cheek and get as angry as you can.' And he'd be looking at me angrily and egging me on. And it worked." Reich would imitate Herskowitz's stuttering responses to questions, which he interpreted as part of the defensive, censoring, superficial façade of polite sociality that he was trying to break through in therapy: "His imitations were wonderful," Herskowitz said. "He'd ask me a question and I'd say, 'It seems to me,' and he'd imitate my hesitation and 'er's,' and boy, that was annoying, he did it so well! . . .

"Reich . . . was a master of getting under one's skin," Herskowitz said. "Sometimes I would have loved to punch him in that mocking mouth." In one moment of negative transference, he did bring up the rumors then circulating that Reich was psychotic. Reich ran over to the fireplace and picked up a rifle that was propped up against it, pointed it at Herskowitz's head, and shouted, "I'm crazy! I'm crazy! I'm going to kill you!" Herskowitz burst out laughing—he says an image flashed through his mind of a possible *New Yorker* cartoon: "Psychiatrist uses rifle to solve all your problems." Reich began laughing, too, and replaced his weapon. Then he added as an afterthought, "Don't you ever do this to one of your patients." Reich was fond of such histrionic displays; when Theodore Wolfe's wife, Gladys Meyer, was in treatment with Reich, he once rushed at her holding a pair of antlers, forcing her to take refuge behind the couch.

It took two years of therapy before Herskowitz had any intimations of an orgasm reflex. "It just happens by itself, it happens at a certain point when you have enough excitation, and things start to tremble down here," he explained. "It just starts to move involuntarily." In Herskowitz's book *Emotional Armoring: An Introduction to Psychiatric Orgone Therapy*, he described the orgasm reflex as feeling "like a magnet is making your pelvis move, and you have nothing to do with it" (it sounds like a sexual version of the mystic's rapture).[30] "After you're pretty free of armoring," he told me, "it doesn't take much to get it started. If you just breathe [he inhales deeply] and let yourself remain open, you start to get excitations down in your pelvis and it just happens by itself."

———

Though Reich's followers identified with Christ's disciples, they didn't so much try to convert people as try to prevent children from becoming corrupted by the "emotional plague." As Reich wrote to Neill, full of disillusionment with the promises of conventional radicalism, "You can't make a crooked tree straight again. Therefore let's concentrate on the newborn ones, and let's divert human attention from evil politics towards the child."[31] Herskowitz explained: "We were going to raise the next generation of kids who were going to be totally different from everyone else, and have patients who were going to affect their kids. People would grow up confident, energetic, they'd be their own persons. They'd be a disciplined force for keeping on making things better."

The postwar baby boom was cause for concern in 1950: a "Mid-Century White House Conference on Children and Youth" had been scheduled for that December, and an interdisciplinary Fact Finding Committee had been appointed. Its members included Margaret Mead (author of *Coming of Age in Samoa* [1928], an account of a sexually permissive society in the South Seas), Dr. Spock (who had trained as a psychoanalyst under Reich's therapist Sandor Rado and whose famous manual on "permissive" child rearing had come out in 1946), and the psychologist Kenneth Clark (who came to the conference armed with a report on the effects of segregation on the attitudes of black children; it would go on to be central to the 1954 Supreme Court decision in *Brown v. Board of Education* that ended racial segregation in schools). The committee would offer advice on how best to foster "the development of a healthy personality in children."

Reich wanted to contribute to this national conversation about how a Freud-informed generation should bring up their children. In early 1950, Reich established an Orgonomic Infant Research Center (OIRC) in Forest Hills "to study healthy children and the prevention of armoring from birth onward."[32] About forty social workers, nurses, and physicians met in Reich's Forest Hills basement to discuss how infants and children should best be raised to save them from the sexual repressions that Reich thought would irreparably spoil them.

Reich planned eventually to build a children's home at Orgonon,

with a small hospital attached, where children's precious feral qualities might be more easily guarded from the emotional plague. This
was to cost $300,000—money he hoped to raise selling Christmas
trees grown on his estate and from accumulators manufactured in
the factory he planned to build there. Reich hoped at the Orgonomic
Infant Research Center to breed a new nonrepressed, armor-free
super-race.

In February 1950, Reich invited Neill to leave his "free" school
to become director of this new project. But Neill had no plans to
give up his own school to run what he considered a kind of experimental orphanage. He thought that "up until [age] 5 [children]
should be with their mothers." When Reich wrote that he was studying several newborns at OIRC, Neill responded, "Dammit, man,
you didn't do anything with Peter newborn, did you?"[33] He hated
the idea of children as test subjects. In fact, a chapter of Reich's
book *Children of the Future: On the Prevention of Sexual Pathology* (1952)
is devoted to an account of Reich's successfully curing a three-
week-old Peter of his "falling anxiety" by means of simulated drops
and muscle manipulation.[34]

Reich no doubt also had his own son's upbringing in mind when
he spoke to his followers about the importance of shielding children from a sick, neurotic world. Peter Reich, Neill's daughter, Zoë,
and Wolfe's daughter, Pussy, were seen as paragons of self-regulation:
supple, free, and sexually confident. But the utopia of their childhood seemed a precarious one. Neill recalled "one day when Peter
had been most difficult, anti-social, destructive, a real problem child.
Reich was baffled and so was I. Suddenly he burst out laughing.
'Here we have the greatest school master in the world and the greatest psychologist . . . and the two of us can't do a damn thing about
the kid.'" In 1950 Reich complained to Neill of his six-year-old,
"Lately Peter hates me, hits me with glee because I keep him going MY way and the world pulls him THEIR way."[35]

Reich treated his son with vegetotherapy to ensure that he maintained a relaxed belly. He also taught him to gag by swallowing warm
water before flicking his tonsils with the forefinger of his left hand
until he vomited it back up. Peter would lie on the couch and follow
his father's finger as he moved it around in front of him until he was

dizzy. In this hypnotized state, Reich would then poke his finger up under his chin so hard, Peter wrote in his memoir, *A Book of Dreams* (1973), that it was "as if it would come right out under my tongue, hurting, arrrgghhhh."[36] His descriptions of Reich's manipulation of his muscles in these therapy sessions are punctuated with cries of pain: "Ow! . . . No! No! No! It hurts." He begs Reich to stop as his father presses down on his stomach and chest: "Uuuuuuunnnnnnn oh Daddy it hurts. Please, Daddy, please uuuuunnnnnhhhh."[37]

Reich had his son kick, punch the pillow, and scream as he encouraged him to breathe deeply. "I didn't feel like it," Peter wrote of his vegetotherapy sessions. "I didn't want to do anything just get away from his hand. It hurt[.] I didn't want it there and grit[ted] my teeth and made a face. His hand was up at my throat and unlocking my jaw to let me scream with my face and my legs."[38] Years later Peter went to another orgone therapist looking for emotional help, but it was uncanny to be manipulated with his father's technique by someone else's hands. "I miss his hand on my chest," he wrote.[39]

Members of OIRC would report back on the similar problems they were having safeguarding their children's natural agility amid the distractions of New York, and they would discuss how to keep them healthy with vegetotherapy and regular sessions in the accumulator. In 1950 the four-and-a-half-year-old Paki Wright was paraded in front of an audience in Reich's Forest Hills basement. Wright, who wrote a novel about her Reichian upbringing, *The All Souls' Waiting Room* (2002), described herself to me as one of orgonomy's "key guinea pigs." Her mother, Miriam Sheppard, became an enthusiastic convert to Reich after reading *The Function of the Orgasm* in the late 1940s. "Reich was synonymous with God when I was growing up," Wright explained. "Every word he said, everything he did, was revered ridiculously and I don't remember any questioning. He was It. In terms of Guru worship, that's where I grew up."[40]

Like Peter Reich, Wright was raised according to Reich's principles, and she spent half an hour a day taking an orgone bath in the accumulator. "I think it was probably after school," she said. "It had a little reading lamp and I read my comic books." With its tiny window, the accumulator stood in the corner of their apartment like "a

mute, Cyclopean sentinel," she put it in her novel. She remembered sitting in it when the FDA came knocking on their door to
interview her mother about the device. She felt like Anne Frank
hiding in the attic from the Gestapo.

"I remember meeting [Reich] very vividly," Wright said. "I probably wasn't more than four, and he made such an impact. He was
very distinctive looking first of all and I remember he wore his white
lab coat." Her appearance was scheduled for the sixth meeting of
the Orgonomic Infant Research Center. Five other children, including Peter Reich, had already been presented at the previous five
meetings. Reich asked them to disrobe and examined them onstage,
illustrating to his audience how to work through any blockages he
detected in their supple naturalness. The subterranean audience
assembled in Reich's basement consisted of about thirty orgonomists, Reichian enthusiasts, nurses, social workers, and—bizarrely,
considering Reich's avowed atheism—a few priests. All, Reich
wrote, had been through "therapeutic restructuring," read the "orgonomic literature," and were joined in the "task of fighting the
emotional plague." However, it was on this occasion that Reich felt
the "emotional plague" erupt to destroy the center. "The structural
hatred against the living broke out in this meeting," he wrote, "and
only I was aware of it."

Reich wrote up Wright's case in *Children of the Future*. He described Wright's mother, Miriam Sheppard, as a "lively, intelligent,
and slightly belligerent, hardworking, self-supporting woman . . . a
bit high-strung."[41] She introduced her daughter and, in front of her,
spoke in frank detail about her own sex life, but the audience reaction was disapproving and, Reich wrote, she "became confused and
strained." Elsworth Baker was one of these critics: "She was apparently very promiscuous and enjoyed sex with any man who came
along," he wrote in his memoir. "She obviously enjoyed the lime-
light and went into all the minute details of her pregnancy, with
gestures, in a loud voice and using coarse language. It seemed a
rather crude and indelicate presentation, and it shattered any illusions about the beauty of this experience."[42]

Reich then asked the four-and-a-half-year-old Wright to undress
so that the audience could examine her free movement and lack of

muscular blocks. "The child, whom I had seen and examined the previous day, behaved very peculiarly," Reich wrote. "She clung to her mother; it was difficult to make contact with her. She refused to undress. I did not try to force the issue, feeling that the child should be free to choose her own way. The demonstration turned into a failure. I felt a definite coldness in the atmosphere, especially when the mother began to describe the genital habits of her child. There were very few questions from the audience. When the mother left, an icy stillness prevailed."[43] Reich felt that his followers were prudes, because they bristled at some of the inappropriateness of his philosophy of sexual liberation when it came to children. But even though psychoanalysts had long recognized that children were sexual beings, were children ready to have adult sexuality foisted upon them?

Wright recalled, "Reich was the one who, when he asked me to take my dress off and I refused, reassured me: 'Okay, fine.' He was very good about that, he was very respectful, and, ironically, I didn't get that from the other adults in my life." She wasn't the first child to have stage fright. Elsworth Baker's two-year-old son, Michael, who was in therapy with Felicia Saxe, also was frightened by the crowd, and didn't want his clothes removed. Dr. Baker persuaded him to strip to his underpants, but he objected to being examined and demanded his shirt be put back on: "Now you can't see my tummy."

This time, however, after their aborted viewing of the young Paki Wright, the disappointed audience began to criticize Reich, which embarrassed him—the guru felt their criticisms hitting him "with the force of machine-gun bullets."[44] Some in the audience thought that Wright might have been harmed by hearing her mother's description of her promiscuous sex life. Marguerite Baker called the presentation "pornographic." "It was perfectly clear to me that structural hatred against the public discussion of down-to-earth genitality had, for the first time, attacked the OIRC," Reich wrote. "The OIRC was doomed."[45]

In the early 1940s Reich had contemplated founding an American Sex-Pol Organization, but hadn't managed to find a home for it. The Orgonomic Infant Research Clinic embodied his first attempt at initiating a practical sociology in the United States, but it was a failure. "I realized that what drove people to me was my 'brilliance' and my 'radiant personality,'" Reich complained, "not the cause for which I bled in many ways. I wanted workers, fighters, knowers, searchers. What I got was a lot of mystical hangers-on who expected salvation from me. Orgastic potency, happiness in life, without doing anything to get and secure it. I should give it to them . . . Under such conditions it was imperative to decline to lead anything or try to do anything at all in the ocean of human filth."[46]

Reich moved permanently to Maine in the spring of 1950, imagining himself now as a thinker above the fray, as Freud had been on the Semmering. He gave over his house in Forest Hills to an Orgone Institute Diagnostic Clinic, which was run by Elsworth Baker, and OIRC, led by Albert Duvall, which continued without him. He would no longer face the criticisms of a wider public, and surrounded himself only with his most loyal followers. Nine of his devotees, six of whom were on the payroll, followed him to Maine, and doctors like Herskowitz made the fourteen-hour trip each way to continue therapy on the weekends. But Reich felt ambivalent about his "worshipful disciples," as he had once described himself in reference to Freud. In 1951 he wrote *The Murder of Christ* (1953), in which he put forward that Christ, the archetypal genital character in tune with cosmic forces, was killed by all the people who expected him to perform miracles; when these weren't delivered, they turned against him. He felt a similar burden of expectation—that he was being smothered by his disciples. "There are two ways of killing a great man," Reich wrote, "with a pistol or with a pedestal."[47]

Duvall was the head of OIRC and Michael Silvert, who had originally trained as a gynecologist, worked there as his assistant. Paki Wright's mother became a midwife for Silvert and ran a crèche in her Greenwich Village apartment, where it was hoped that children could be raised free of repressive societal mores. "She and Silvert performed home births for Reich's pregnant patients for several years, and were partners and lovers for a while," Wright told me. "And I was privy to this insane scene that was going on around me when I was growing up. It left me more or less . . . speechless."

Wright described Silvert as "very zealous": "Silvert was a tall man, he was six foot five [others told me he was closer to five feet eleven inches, but Paki remembered him through a child's eyes], with silvery hair, almost like a conch shell when I knew him, it was bald in the middle. He had a large nose, gray eyes, and long wavy lips, and a very intense energy, and no humor that I can remember, which to my mind is the worst thing about him. He just took everything so seriously." Even among orgonomists Silvert was seen as extremely dogmatic. Myron Sharaf described him as "fanatical, humorless"; Herskowitz didn't much like him, either, and told Reich that he thought Silvert an "orgonomic Communist," to which Reich replied, "Orgonomy can use its Communists."[48]

Silvert had been doing a stint as resident in psychiatry at the Menninger Clinic as part of his training at the Winter General Veterans Administration Hospital in Kansas when he came across orgonomy; before that he had been a flight surgeon for the air force serving in China. Dr. Boote, director of professional education at Winter, described him to the FDA as "a chronic complainer" who "showed progressively poorer adjustment to the work as the course continued."[49] His last hospital evaluation revealed his growing interest in the staged confrontations of character analysis: it was reported that he slapped patients to encourage them to fight him.

Wright described her Greenwich Village upbringing as "totally bohemian": "The circle around my mom consisted mostly of the parents of the children she took care of. Then there were Silvert and a few other therapists floating around the edges. My mother and Silvert bought a farmhouse in the country together as a little getaway—in South Valley, New York, which was a six-hour drive from Manhattan, and we used to go there together. The parents were a pretty cool group actually. They were very free love, they were very energetic, they were funny. There was a lot of sleeping around among the group—everyone was young, they were energetic, they were horny. I don't think it was any different from anything you'd see today, but it was maybe a little ahead of its time. This was in the early fifties, after all.

"When Mom felt I was getting 'plaguey,'" Paki Wright continued, "I would have to go to a session with Silvert, which was literally ironic, he was the last man in the world I'd want to see as a therapist or a doctor or a healer. But she didn't seem to get that. I'd lie down, always naked on the couch—it was extremely unpleasant for me to be around him in that position."

Wright told me how Silvert initiated her into sex when she was only five years old, almost as a therapeutic act. He apparently thought that her first sexual experience should be with someone orgastically potent like himself. The scene is made more disturbing by the fact that her mother was complicit in this; Wright remembers her "crying, pacing back and forth, looking distraught" as she prepared to send her daughter to her boyfriend. "She was madly in love with Silvert," Wright said, "and was very jealous of his interest in me. Ugh! It's just so horribly complicated."

"I found out many, many years later that Silvert did tell Reich what he was doing," Wright added, "or I guess it came out in his therapy with Reich, and Reich flipped out. It did redeem Reich in my mind a lot; I never thought he was responsible in a funny way. I never ascribed Silvert's behavior to Reich, it was an aberration." Elsworth Baker wrote in his memoir that Reich had forbidden Silvert from treating women patients for a year in 1950, and that he was later suspended from practicing orgonomy for a year—I suspect this was after learning of the incidents with Paki Wright.

However, Silvert's suspension could have been due to any other transgression. Baker once referred two of his female patients to Silvert for gynecological examinations, "both of whom refused to go back," Baker wrote. "He told them he liked vaginas, their looks, smell, touch, and taste and went into great detail concerning their sex lives. With each patient, he had examined her whole body and gave an orgonomic session before doing a pelvic."[50]

Reich did not suspend Silvert's boss, Duvall, when he heard similar allegations of sexual abuse raised about him. "Duvall, oh boy!" Herskowitz said when I asked him about ORIC. "He should not have been near children. I heard he sexually abused his kid patients. I first got to know about it because some guy who I'd treated as a kid wrote me a long letter when he was in his late adolescence, after he'd moved to California, about his relationship with Duvall before he'd seen me. And it was horrible.

"There was a community in southern New Jersey, which was like the Greenwich Village of southern New Jersey, where lots of people had been in therapy and had sent their kids into therapy with Duvall and Elsworth Baker, and I gradually heard stories about how all those kids hated to go to therapy, resented it, and much later I heard stories of sexual encounters between Duvall and some of those kids . . . Apparently the kids also regarded sessions with Baker as torture . . . There was a lot of craziness going on." I asked Herskowitz whether Duvall had been trained by Reich. "Yes, he was," Herskowitz replied. "That's one thing Myron Sharaf always held: that Reich should have done more talking with his patients than he did, because apparently he didn't know Duvall." One might say that Herskowitz didn't know his child patient, either, if his earlier abuse didn't come up in their therapy sessions.

Allan Cott, Allen Ginsberg's former therapist, who ran the American Association for Medical Orgonomy's Committee of Medical Ethics and Practice, went to Reich with the reports of some of the complaints about Duvall, but was told that Duvall had a great reputation with children. Reich felt that if sex couldn't express itself naturally, it came out in a distorted way, and he was keen to prevent this by encouraging the sexual spontaneity of children; but he did not seem to acknowledge the complications involved in this. In fact, Reich's idealistic program for a happy childhood sex life was cited by pedophile groups in the 1960s, such as the René Gunyon Society (its slogan was "Sex by age eight, or it's too late"). It is unclear what the evidence against Duvall was: Reich no doubt thought that his appointment of Duvall was appropriate and that it was the usual prudery and misunderstanding about the sensitive issue of childhood sexuality that had led to the allegations against him. Soon afterward he promoted Duvall to the board of the Wilhelm Reich Foundation. Cott resigned and would later collaborate with the FDA, whom he told that he no longer believed in orgone energy.

In his diary, written just after he arrived in America, Reich recorded that Annie Reich imposed time limits on his visits with his own children. "What's the matter—are you afraid I'll seduce her?" Reich asked when Lore was forbidden to stay overnight. "I wouldn't put it past you," Annie replied.[51] When I met Lore Reich in Pittsburgh she brought up this incident. "I had my own reasons not to touch the man," Lore said, and explained why she had so little interaction with her father in the States. "I think he was a sex abuser. I didn't trust him, I'm sorry. He was a very dangerous, difficult man and I think he was sexually unreliable, and I wouldn't be surprised if he molested my sister, though she would never admit that, I'm sure . . . I didn't want to spend the night at his place because I thought he would be sexually promiscuous with me, which I don't think is totally wrong—I don't know if he would have had intercourse, but he would have done something. He was really a sex abuser, excuse me for saying it—I don't have any evidence, but I think he was. At least a voyeuristic one, if nothing else. Anyway, I didn't want to stay the night at his house. He got very angry and he was sure that it was my mother who was preventing it, and it didn't occur to him that I may not have wanted to."

Someone once suggested to Lore Reich that her father's own precociously early sexual experiences had constituted abuse, and she'd never thought of them before in this light. "This guy thought that he had a precocious sexuality induced by adult seduction. And so, as is very common—I know this as a psychoanalyst—when you've been sex abused, you either become very frigid, or you become very obsessed with sex . . . and he went the oversexed way." She felt that he was "a victim and then a perpetrator": "There are all these pictures of my sister on the beach with Elsa [Lindenberg]; my sister, she already has breasts and she's running around nude . . . Those pictures on the beach, he's always fully clothed . . . I think he was more into watching other people's excitement, a voyeur."

Eva had advanced Alzheimer's when I attempted to contact her and I was unable to interview her (she died in 2008). However, the suspicions of abuse trace the chasm that divided their family. Lore Reich remained loyal to her mother, and was taught by her when she trained to be an analyst in New York. "We were the mecca, mecca school," Lore Reich reminisced, "or we thought we were, we were it, we were the most important, the most intellectual, most orthodox, most true." She seldom saw her father. "We had a number of stormy kickings out; once I remember he asked whether I thought he was crazy, and I said yes. Well, he wanted truthfulness! Then he kicked me out and I didn't see him for several years. So I'm the black sheep of the Reich family. Eva adores him, he's great, like God or something." Her sister went to Reich's lectures at the New School when she was fifteen years old; Reich wrote in November 1940 that, despite Annie Reich's attempts to pronounce him dangerous and mad, "Eva has turned over to me completely."[52] After she graduated from college, Eva Reich worked as Reich's assistant until he died.[53]

Myron Sharaf wrote that "Reich was sometimes criticized for being overly affectionate with Eva" when she was a young girl.[54] Reich's friend and onetime mistress Lia Laszky told Sharaf that she once left her four-year-old son, Tony, with the Reichs for a week or so while she went on holiday, and when she came to collect him she criticized Reich for cuddling his daughter too much, which would prevent healthy relationships with men forming later in life. He was furious. She reminded him that she was working for Sex-Pol as his expert on children, so her advice should be listened to, and he replied angrily that she wasn't the expert on raising his children. Reich's sister-in-law remembered disapprovingly that when Tony and Eva undressed to take a nap, Reich watched them through the keyhole, keen to see who made the first sexual advance (the pair just giggled and then fell asleep). Sharaf draws a parallel with Reich's spying on his mother and tutor as a small boy.

Reich's message about sexual liberation was undoubtedly a little overwhelming for the children at which it was aimed, and on whom he placed the burden of his utopian hopes. A childhood friend of Peter Heller's, Edith Kramer, who later became a therapist and whose mother attempted suicide at the bohemian playground of Grundslee, later commented, "The atmosphere in that bygone era," with its flaunting of sexual freedom, had perhaps "been too seductive for children."[55] Lore Reich may have no proof of her allegations against her father, but when she was growing up she certainly felt threatened by his constant emphasis on children's sexuality. Before they separated, Reich and Annie kept a diary on their children's sex education, informing them at about age four of the facts of life; sexuality, as one might expect, was a constant topic in their household. In *The Sexual Revolution* Reich argued that the only plausible reason one might give for not letting your children watch you have sex would be that it might interfere with your own pleasure, prompting speculation that he'd experimented with such a performance.

Reich was radically flawed in his judgment of Silvert and Duvall; it transpired that numerous other members of ORIC, whether Reich heard about it or not, did sexually abuse children. Susanna Steig, the niece of Reich's follower William Steig (a *New Yorker* cartoonist, who did the illustrations for Reich's *Listen, Little Man*), has published an online memoir, "My Childhood Experiences with Reichian Therapy," in which she claims to have been masturbated in vegetotherapy sessions with her Reichian therapist, "a gypsy-like woman dressed in shiny silks, with her breasts hanging out of her blouse." Steig wrote that she was also tortured by Elsworth Baker, who practiced a particularly rough vegetotherapeutic technique (he "pressed on my back so hard that I couldn't breathe," she remembered). She tells of another Reichian who repeatedly raped an eleven-year-old patient for months; apparently, the unnamed analyst was later put into a mental institution.[56]

On a holiday in Maine, when she was six or seven, Steig claims to have been encouraged by Sharaf and his wife, Grethe Hoff, to sleep with Peter Reich ("Peter knows everything about the act of mating since the age of three," Reich wrote in an unpublished paper called "The Silent Observer" [1952]. "He has had already his intimate genital experiences with girls of his own age group.")[57] On her return home Baker gripped Steig's leg in a session and said, "Is this where you feel it when you think of Peter?" That he knew of Hoff's sexual encouragement made Steig think that she "was part of an experiment."

"I have spent a lifetime dealing with the aftermath of my traumatic childhood, full of abuse and betrayal," Susanna Steig wrote. "I think the Reichians were megalomaniacs, true believers, and elitists. Not one of them had a bit of empathy or sympathy for children. Many of them were sadists. I really hope the truth of what happened to us becomes well known . . . This is a cautionary tale about true believers and the evil that they do."[58]

———

Two years after Reich's failed demonstration with Wright in the Forest Hills basement, Albert Duvall was investigated by the Department of Education for running Orgonomic Infant Research Center without the required New York medical license; he was licensed to practice only in New Jersey and Tennessee. The New York Medical Society had received a complaint accusing Duvall of running a "sexual racket involving children" at the clinic. The original complainant, a nurse from New Jersey, alleged that Duvall had done inestimable damage to her five-year-old son, who was mute, by teaching him how to "satisfy himself." Duvall had seen him for three months before his mother submitted to a few therapy sessions herself, in which she claimed Duvall made sexual advances to her. Duvall responded to the complaint by saying that she had "developed genital feelings she could not tolerate and had become plaguey."[59]

In March 1952 the Department of Education of New York City sent a special investigator, Helen Blau, to visit the clinic. She arrived for a therapy session with Duvall, "flashily dressed, heavily perfumed, and flirtatious," according to Baker, and "she complained of constant fatigue, dizziness, and loss of love for her husband."[60] He had her disrobe, lie on her back, and breathe deeply while he strategically pressed parts of her body. On another visit she was accompanied by her "husband," who asked to see the accumulator and to have its workings explained to him. The following week the "couple," accompanied by two other inspectors, returned to arrest Duvall on a "morals charge against children."

Reich agreed to close OIRC, and the case against Duvall was subsequently dropped. Duvall moved to California, where he set up a practice in Los Angeles. Judy Garland sent her daughter Lorna Luft to see him there.[61]

*Ten*

On September 23, 1949, President Truman announced the news that America's four-year monopoly on the atomic bomb had ended. The Soviets had exploded their first atomic weapon on August 29, 1949, two years before the CIA expected them to have this capability. In the wake of the new threat, fears about the dangers of radiation and spying entered the popular imagination. David Bradley, an army doctor from Wisconsin who had witnessed the atomic tests in the Bikini Atoll, published a bestselling book that warned of radiation's invisible and all-pervasive effects; it was ominously titled *No Place to Hide* (1949), a title that encapsulated the fear of the era. The cold war quickly escalated: the United States had 200 A-bombs in 1949 and 290 in 1950, and by 1952 it had stock-piled 841 devices. Truman also ordered the development of the considerably more powerful hydrogen bomb.

In 1949 Alger Hiss was indicted for perjury, suspected of lying in front of the House Un-American Activities Committee when he denied he was a Soviet spy—a young Richard Nixon, for one, didn't believe him. A senior official in the State Department who had attended the Yalta Conference and helped draw up the UN charter, Hiss had been accused of being a Communist and of passing sensitive information to the Russians by a former party member, Whittaker Chambers. This high-profile case was a year in the courts and became a focal point for the wildly escalating cold war climate of suspicion and distrust. That year anticommunism reached new heights when the Alien Registration Act of 1940, or Smith Act, was used to prosecute Communist leaders. They were classed as dangerous subversives intent on overthrowing the U.S. government, and the party was effectively bankrupted and outlawed, its remaining members forced to go underground.

Hiss was convicted in January 1950 and sentenced to five years in prison. Two weeks after he was sentenced, Klaus Fuchs, a physicist who worked at Los Alamos, confessed to stealing the atomic secrets that helped the Soviets develop the bomb, and that summer Julius and Ethel Rosenberg were arrested, accused of doing the same. The following month, sensing an inroad for the Republicans— who hadn't held the presidential reins since 1933—Senator Joseph McCarthy lent his name to an era when he burst onto the national stage with his dramatic but unfounded claim that there were 205 "known" Communists in the State Department. McCarthy later dropped this number to 57. Though lots of people lost their jobs, he never proved a single charge. McCarthy gave voice to the panic and uncertainty of a new political era. The CBS reporter Edward R. Murrow later said of McCarthy, "He didn't create the situation of fear; he merely exploited it, and rather successfully."[1]

In 1950, Margaret Chase Smith, a moderate Republican senator for Maine, criticized McCarthy's "totalitarian techniques." McCarthy, she said, was cynically trying to ride "the Republican Party to victory through the selfish exploitation of fear, bigotry, ignorance, and intolerance."[2] In this new atmosphere of fear, the members of Reich's circle, secreted away in Maine, were looked upon with suspicion by many local residents. They called them the "orgies" and portrayed the thickly accented Reich as a Dr. Caligari figure. When Tom Ross left his job at the local laundry to go and work for Reich as a caretaker, he said that everyone told him, "Gee, if you go and work for him, he'll have you in one of those boxes and you'll never see daylight again."[3] Reich's books were barred from the Rangeley Public Library because they advocated fostering children's sexual impulses; the FBI files are full of handwritten letters from people living nearby—their names blacked out—informing the bureau of the strange goings-on up at Orgonon.

Unsubstantiated rumors were circulating in Rangeley that Reich was building an atomic bomb on his estate, that the Reichians were a "Communist outfit," and that they used the box for "perverse sexual purposes." One local store owner said that there was "a lot of sexuality" going on at Orgonon. "They're interested in nudism and a lot of funny business."[4] Furthermore, it was alleged that Rolling Hill Farm, a summer camp run according to Neill's ideas and attended by Reich's son, Peter, was "a children's nudist camp connected with Reich's operations" and a "feeding center" for the pedophilic Reichians. One overimaginative correspondent even suggested that an amber light he'd seen shining at Orgonon one night—from the farm two miles away—was an illicit signal system.

In October 1949 the FBI dispatched an agent to investigate. The agent found no truth to any of the allegations—though he spotted an accumulator in the Rolling Hill Farm school's playroom. An FDA inspector who later visited the school was surprised to find the children fully clothed and the camp to be "a rather high-class place." In his report to the bureau the agent concluded, "Recent experience in Maine has indicated that the residents of rural areas in that state are particularly concerned about the current international situation and inclined to regard all persons residing in or passing through the area who are not lifelong residents with suspicion."[5]

In August 1950, at the close of a summer convention devoted to the topic "The Children of the Future," Reich asked Elsworth Baker, head of the American Association for Medical Orgonomy, to give a talk to the local townspeople he had invited up to an open day at Orgonon, in the hope that he might dispel some of the rumors that were circulating. "I am sure that, to many of you, Orgonon has an air of mystery and secrecy about it and that you have heard many rumors concerning it," Baker told the group that assembled in the Student Laboratory. "For example, the telescope that many of you saw in the room of the Orgone Energy Observatory today has been said to be a machine gun; Dr. Reich is said to have developed a miraculous cancer cure; and there has been a lot of questioning about the idea that a lot of sex is going on or a lot that concerns sex. The purpose of today's lecture is to try and clarify some of those questions."[6]

He evidently failed. In a letter sent to thirty Rangeley citizens that November and copied to the FBI, the "nine workers at Orgonon" sought to dispel the rumors that had been multiplied by Baker's talk:

> Now, after the upheaval around the lecture given by Dr. Elsworth F. Baker at Orgonon in the end of August has blown over, we may be permitted to tell you the following . . . We do not run a brothel as the Fowlers with their rumors imply; we have nothing to hide, we do not conduct sexual orgies and we are not "communists." Mr. Sharaf did not run after girls in town at night, and Peter Reich did not expose himself in school; he was forced to do so by a group of boys on the school grounds. We do not seduce small children and we do not commit sexual crimes on adolescent boys and girls. We do not "feed" patients to doctors; we do not sleep with another partner every night. We have no machine guns but only a telescope and scientific instruments in our observatory, and when there are lights in the windows at 3 or 4 in the morning, someone is sitting at his desk and taking readings or doing some writing or calculating.[7]

Peter Reich described his upbringing in Maine as "pretty hard. I was really ostracized quite a bit and it was a very difficult time." He was bullied at school in Rangeley, stripped, and pelted with stones. "I remember as a kid," Peter told me, "before *Playboy* and the porn magazines, there were these magazines called *Detective* and things like that. I remember very vividly one of these magazines, where the women would have little black things across their eyes—it made it illicit and kind of prurient; there was an illustration, hand drawn, not a photograph, of a whole row of orgone accumulators with men in them, looking out of the windows, and a girl in a negligée is dancing in front of them. And they're all beating off in these sex boxes. People really thought that if you got in this box you would have better orgasms and that was it. Imagine it, just think of it: here's a local barbershop and here's people reading a magazine about these guys four miles away, sitting in these boxes and jerking off. Jesus Christ! And this is the fifties, in a small rural town. Forget it—it's a no-brainer!"[8]

The Korean War, the first armed confrontation of the cold war, broke out in June 1950 and persisted for the next three years. With both superpowers possessing atomic weapons, and the race on to develop the H-bomb, there was wide-scale fear that the world was descending into global nuclear conflict: Armageddon. President Truman noted stoically in his diary: "It looks like World War III is here—I hope not—but we must meet whatever comes—and we will."[9]

Reich hoped that his orgone energy accumulator would play an important role in the war against what he now called "red fascism," treating wounds and burns and immunizing Americans against radiation sickness. He proposed sending a medical unit to Korea to treat wounded troops with the accumulator and raised money for Korean children orphaned by the war. In December of that year, his band of medical orgonomists planned defense units in and around New York City; each unit consisted of two doctors, a nurse, a social worker, and at least two assistants, all armed with orgone devices in case of atomic attack.

For the previous two years Reich had been trying to interest the Atomic Energy Commission (AEC) at Oak Ridge, Tennessee, in the orgone energy accumulator as a possible cure for radiation sickness. Reich also suggested that bomb shelters be built like huge orgone accumulators because he felt that the orgone energy field that built up inside might also deflect nuclear radiation. (One of these, built at the Hamilton School, was kitted out with copies of all Reich's books.)[10] The AEC decided then, as they reported to the FBI, that Reich's "scientific theories and experiments are mentally unsound and meaningless."[11]

Reich now wrote to Eleanor Roosevelt, who had a reputation as a champion of émigrés, to tell her about the benevolent role orgone energy might play in the war. She forwarded the letter and attached article to Robert Oppenheimer, the former head of the Manhattan Project at Los Alamos who was now director of the Institute for

Advanced Study at Princeton as well as a consultant to the AEC and a fierce opponent of the H-bomb. He wrote back, "I am afraid that the evidence of the paper [on orgone energy] makes me suspect that this undertaking is a hoax. I have been unable to find anything about it that is reassuring."[12]

In response to the global emergency, and keen to show doubters that he had something to contribute, Reich embarked on another frenzy of experiments. He wrote once again to the AEC to request some test samples of radioactive phosphorus-32, hoping to prove the efficacy of the orgone energy accumulator in neutralizing nuclear radiation. When the AEC, which had already branded Reich a time waster, failed to respond to his request, he ordered two one-milligram vials of pure radium from a private laboratory. He wanted to expose mice to these radium needles until they developed radiation sickness and then attempt to cure them in mouse-sized accumulators.

On January 5, 1951, Reich performed a preliminary test that he called, in keeping with his penchant for official-sounding acronyms, the Oranur (orgonomic antinuclear radiation) experiment. As the AEC conducted its atomic tests at Los Alamos, Reich felt as though he were doing parallel ones in Maine. He put one of the radium vials, still in its lead sheath, in an "orgone charger," a coffee can wrapped in layers of steel wool, and placed it in an accumulator constructed of twenty alternating layers of steel and fiberglass insulation to increase its power. The accumulator was in turn placed in the orgone room in the Student Laboratory. The orgone devices, stacked in this way like Chinese boxes, were supposed to act as a kind of atomic shelter in reverse, and Reich expected the radiation to be contained and neutralized.

However, it seemed to Reich that exactly the opposite happened: the radium was excited and aggravated and erupted with radioactive toxicity, spewing a dark and dangerous mushroom cloud over Orgonon. After five hours, according to his description, the atmosphere in the lab was still charged and oppressive, the walls seemed to be glowing, and the radioactivity levels were so high that his Geiger-Müller counter jammed.

The radium was removed and the lab was aired, but this didn't seem to clear it. Reich supposed that the orgone energy had been altered by the radioactivity into a dangerous pollutant that he called deadly orgone, or DOR: "angry, a killer itself, attempting to kill the irritating nuclear radiation."[13] Orgone energy, which until then had been exclusively a force for good, had somehow soured on him. "There is deadly orgone energy," Reich wrote after 1951. "It is in the atmosphere. You can demonstrate it on devices such as the Geiger counter. It's a swampy quality . . . Stagnant, deadly water which doesn't flow, doesn't metabolize."[14] The battle was no longer about how to accumulate the "life energy" but how to ward off its deathly aspect. In finding a place for Thanatos as well as Eros in his theory, Reich seemed to be finally embracing Freud's death instinct, against which he'd fought so strongly in the early 1930s.

According to Myron Sharaf, who was at Orgonon at the time, Reich was "tremendously excited" by the powerful reactions he was witnessing. "It was a terrible and at the same time exhilarating experience," Reich wrote to Neill, "as if I had touched the bottom of the universe. It is still rather confused, but never in my 30 years of research career have I experienced such an upheaval."[15]

Undeterred by the supposed dangers, Reich repeated the Oranur experiment for an hour a day over the next six days. On the last day, only a few minutes after placing the radium in the accumulator, he could see from 250 feet away that the atmosphere inside the laboratory was clouded: "It was moving visibly and shined blue to purple through the glass."[16] According to Baker, who arrived with Allan Cott and Chester Raphael a week after the original experiment, even at that distance Reich and others claimed that they "became nauseated and faint . . . They felt pressure in the forehead and were pale."[17]

After his attack of nausea, Reich withdrew to the observatory, where he had a stiff drink and fell asleep. When he woke up, Baker recalled, Reich said he felt "particularly clear and sharply aware of his environment."[18] In this heightened state, Reich took the three visiting physicians into the contaminated lab, where, influenced by Reich's descriptions of what had happened, they had the same sense of being poisoned. Baker felt a "heavy atmosphere with a peculiar, sickening, acrid odor" at fifty feet away, and when they entered the building they all "immediately felt nausea, weak, and pressure on the forehead and in the epigastrium."[19] They still felt giddy an hour later, Baker reported, even though they'd had lots of air and a large whiskey.

Reich had decided that alcohol, on which he was becoming increasingly dependent, might help alleviate what he called "Oranur sickness": he prescribed "alcoholic drinks, in moderation, at the right time, to the point of a warm gentle glow." All visitors were therefore "fortified with Whiskey," Baker said (Reich was, he added, generous with his supply). Everyone wore winter coats inside the observatory, as the windows were left open to ventilate the place of DOR. Reich also prescribed prolonged baths, cold-water compresses over the eyes, and "regular orgastic discharge in the natural embrace" to alleviate the symptoms of DOR contamination.[20]

Reich dispatched Baker, Raphael, and Cott to Washington, where they were instructed to report the dramatic results of the Oranur experiment to the Atomic Energy Commission. The physicians were disappointed when a representative of that agency gave them the brush-off. Baker wrote, "Though [the official] was schooled in diplomacy, I felt he was wracking his brain as to how he could politely get rid of these kooks."[21]

Sharaf recalled Reich repeatedly asking his coworkers who remained at Orgonon, "How do you feel now?" Every ailment was attributed to Oranur. The reactions described included a salty taste on the tongue, cramping and twitching of the muscles, hot and cold shivers, chronic fatigue, fainting spells, nausea, loss of appetite and balance, conjunctivitis, mottled skin, and a ringlike pressure around the forehead. The symptoms were so varied that Reich suspected that latent diseases—hidden fears and hatreds—had been brought to the surface as a result of exposure to Oranur, affecting each person in his or her Achilles' heel, each person's particular point of bioenergetic weakness.

Ilse Ollendorff and Peter Reich, then seven years old, were evacuated from Orgonon to nearby Rangeley at the end of March. According to Baker, Ilse developed an ovarian cyst that had to be operated on, and spent six weeks recuperating with the Bakers—her cyst turned out not to be cancerous. Reich claimed that Peter had developed a four-hour bout of scarlet fever that was catalyzed and then killed by the strange radiation emitted by the Oranur experiment. According to Baker, "Peter became seriously ill, with weakness in the legs, shooting pains, and a tendency towards immobilization even in breathing. He became pale, and developed cold perspiration and malaise."[22] Eva Reich, who had finished her medical studies and, to her mother's distress, had come to work with Reich, was also afflicted with Oranur sickness and left in the spring of 1951. She had been helping to disinfect the laboratory when she put her head into a metal cabinet and "immediately went into shock and seemed in severe distress. Her pulse became barely perceptible—46 beats per minute. She was pale and her lips were cyanotic . . . Her vision was impaired, and at times she could not speak."[23] Apparently her father revived her with cognac.

Reich claimed that, except for a two-week period after the experiment during which he felt "helpless and disturbed," he was the only one who did not suffer any severe malaise. Indeed, after this depressive period he felt "very vigorous" and enjoyed a surge of creativity. "I needed little sleep," he wrote, "worked much and without effort, better than usual, and I felt a peculiar pleasantness in moving my limbs."[24] Reich began painting large, expressive, gaudy Munch-like paintings, completing ten canvases in two weeks, many of which still hang at Orgonon. "If art is a disease," he wrote to Neill, "Oranur has brought out the artist in me . . . I am also playing and enjoying the organ, and have begun to write down melodies of which I am quite full."[25] He compared this episode to the creative flurry that led him to the discovery of SAPA-bions in 1939. Having been through this earlier episode, Reich claimed a certain invincibility to deadly orgone energy.

Peter Reich, despite his father's and Baker's reports of his health, maintains that he didn't feel anything during the Oranur experiment. He puts it all down to mass hysteria. His mother had to have a hysterectomy and Eva got ill, but, he said, Eva "was always a bit hysterical." Herskowitz told me that, after Oranur, Reich was "a little more off balance, edgier, a little bit more irritable . . . I was only there briefly one weekend during that period because Reich canceled sessions. Everyone was sick and complaining. I didn't have any big effects."

Lia Laszky, who had worked with Reich in the mobile clinics in

Vienna, was now practicing as a psychoanalyst in New York and made a trip up to Maine at this time to see her old friend. She had been convinced by Reich's cancer theories and impressed with the orgone accumulator when she was invited to try it in 1940; much to Reich's delight, she not only felt very hot but claimed to have seen blue flashes after fifteen minutes inside the box. But when Reich gave her a tour of the observatory in Maine, Laszky concluded that his descriptions of recent events there were totally paranoid and delusional. Reich was painting two or three paintings a day, and Laszky thought the results "totally schizophrenic." She pleaded with him: "Willie, in the name of our old friendship, get help for yourself!" "Who could I go to?" Reich replied. Laszky recommended her colleague Dr. Hyman Spotnitz, who believed in the reversibility of schizophrenia, an illness for which he hoped to pioneer a cure. Reich laughed and said that he treated himself. According to Laszky, "He became very hostile after that."[26]

Reich began traveling the area, taking readings to see the extent of the DOR field and sleeping in a tent or his car, never staying in the same place for more than two nights. He noticed that rocks around the area had begun to blacken, a physical index of the contamination, and he circled the black, sooty spots with red pencil to try to measure how these marks were spreading over the stone. Reich called this black substance "melanor," or "black OR." He'd stay periodically with his wife and son in Rangeley, and occasionally he'd return to his former home. "Reich went back to the observatory on several occasions," Ilse recalled, "suffered blackouts, and once fell asleep there for several hours and looked severely ill and almost in shock when he finally got out."[27] On one occasion he woke there shaking and with bleeding gums, his face a bright vermilion.

Reich's reaction to the Oranur experiment, Ollendorff wrote in her memoir, "came later than most." Despite his presumed resistance to DOR, Reich lay in bed in October 1951, struck down by a heart attack for six weeks, which he attributed to Oranur sickness. Reich had known he had heart trouble for some time, having suffered his first episode of rapid heartbeats at the end of 1949. During a therapy session with Herskowitz, Reich had handed the doctor a stethoscope and asked him to listen to his chest. "I told him I heard a murmur, a very significant murmur," Herskowitz said. "He just shook his head." The doctors who visited him after it happened recommended that he go to the hospital, but Reich insisted on treating himself solely with orgone therapy, lying in bed for a month with a shooter funnel over his chest. He also gave up smoking at this time. (He'd previously maintained that if you breathed deeply enough, tobacco would have no negative effects.) Ollendorff wrote to Baker, "He fluctuates very much between wanting to die, not wanting to die, and being afraid of dying."[28]

"When the outside world seemed threatening Reich's wrath turned against those closest to him," Ollendorff wrote in her book *Wilhelm Reich: A Personal Biography*. "I had suffered severely—both physically and emotionally—from the Oranur effect, and I was frightened. I was also disturbed by the insecurity of our living conditions. When Reich added to this his completely irrational accusations about my supposed infidelities, life became too difficult and our relationship started to deteriorate."[29]

After she succumbed to her own brand of Oranur sickness, Ollendorff had a hysterectomy performed by a surgeon who had been a patient of Reich's, and spent six weeks with Elsworth Baker and his family to recuperate. "I sit in the accu very regularly," she wrote to Reich, "so I really should be all right."[30] Baker gave her a course of vegetotherapy at Reich's request and he made frequent progress reports back to Reich, breaking the code of doctor-patient confidentiality out of blind discipleship.

Prone to bouts of pathological jealousy like his father, Reich accused Ollendorff of cheating on him with Wolfe, his first American disciple and translator, when he was incarcerated in Ellis Island. According to Baker, Reich was suspicious because the pair had been out celebrating the New Year while he was imprisoned. Ollendorff passed out drunk, and Wolfe carried her upstairs to bed—she awoke naked, unsure as to whether he had undressed her.

Baker tried to persuade Reich that the affair was a phantom, as Ollendorff and Wolfe had always maintained it was. Wolfe wrote to Reich protesting his innocence: "I hate to see a fine woman driven towards her death because a man will not rid himself of a groundless, foolish idea."[31] However, Baker reported that Ollendorff did confess a certain attraction to Wolfe. For Reich, these thought crimes were just as bad as a tangible infidelity, and he accused Baker, for all his efforts at appeasement, of also having slept with Ollendorff. Reich said that Wolfe, who had done so much to help him, was "out of contact" after the Oranur experiment and deliberately marginalized him.

Reich subsequently pressured Ollendorff for a divorce, because he thought it would improve their relationship, and Ollendorfff consented to this. The divorce was finalized on September 13, 1951. A sexual revolutionary who believed in his right to a healthy sex life, Reich signed on to the double standard: he had taken advantage of Ollendorff's recuperation at the Bakers' to begin an affair with thirty-eight-year-old Lois Wyvell, his devoted assistant, who ran the Orgone Institute Press in Rangeley. When Ollendorff returned after going through the humiliation of a divorce, she found out about his affair but stayed with him for three more unhappy years—a time she describes with understatement as one "of intense restlessness."[32] She lived with Peter, who was caught in the middle of his parents' volatile relationship, in a rented house in Rangeley and continuing to work at Orgonon as Reich's assistant. Reich would occasionally stay with them in Rangeley, but more often he traveled the area taking rock and wood samples, sleeping in his tent, in the car, or in motels, and spending the occasional troubled night in the observatory.

Peter Reich once pointed out to his father the house where the manager of Rangeley's local store lived, which started off another jealous wave of accusations. Reich filed in his archives a detailed report of his suspicion that Ollendorff was having an affair with this man. He tailed the manager like a private eye, and even though Ollendorff maintained that she had been at a parent-teacher meeting at that time, he imagined he'd seen her in the darkness of the manager's shop wearing nothing but white underwear. After confronting her, Reich stormed out in a jealous rage as Peter tried to hold him back. "You are either strong and the way I am," Reich told him, "then you will find your way to me; or, you are weak—then you will come to the dead world of your mother."[33]

Reich came back but his jealousy persisted and he used the

Stalinist techniques he despised to assuage it. Ollendorff wrote, "He demanded again and again that I write 'confessions' about my feelings of fear of the work, occasional feelings of fear and hate about him, and he took these 'confessions' and locked them away."[34] They were filed and preserved for posterity in the Archives of the Orgone Institute. Copies of several of these forced confessions and "protocols," transcripts of Reich's interrogations, survive. He also had others denounce her, and wrote his own statements detailing her infidelities. Reich wrote that Ollendorff "cheated Baker by not telling him anything over months" of therapy with him, and that "Baker stated to me once that he had never encountered such hiding as in her."[35] "I used my therapy with Baker mostly to complain about Reich," Reich made Ollendorff confess, "by making [Reich] bad instead of admitting my cheating."[36]

In Reich's assessment, as detailed in another "deposition" he wrote, Ollendorff "felt that she had failed in fulfilling her ideal of helping a great man, since she could not, with her structure, fulfill her own ideal, [and] she had to tear that ideal down in order to make herself appear innocent or decent. In other words, in order to cover up her own inadequacies, she had to tear down the one whom she was to serve."[37]

Lois Wyvell, with whom Reich was still sleeping, wrote a statement: "If unable to restrain herself, IO would probably try to make Reich seem paranoid, with herself as the innocent victim."[38] In November 1953 Reich filed the following "Examples of I.O.'s Defense Mechanisms": "In general, I.O. behaves like a person who is dreaming of flying high in the air while being safely on the ground. Awakening suddenly, she finds herself racing through space in full REALITY at 1000 miles per hour in a rocket ship. She starts screaming. She tried to tell the people in the ship that the pilot went crazy, and when this does not bring her down to safe earth, she attacks the hardworking pilot, tries to get hold of the steering device, to bring the ship down to earth. When this fails she collapses and shouts that the pilot has driven her crazy."[39]

Peter Reich took me to see his mother, who lived in a plush assisted-living residential community. Ollendorff had short-cropped hair, wore a hearing aid, and looked much younger than her ninety-five years (she died in 2008 at the age of ninety-nine). Despite her and Reich's differences, she still used an orgone blanket—two three-foot-high padded panels lashed together with leather laces, which were fraying at the edges. "Reich was an impressive person," she told me in a soft voice, "very stocky, and he had a very red face because he had a skin disease. He was an impressive person, very attractive and out of the ordinary, with a strong Austrian accent—much stronger than I had." (She was originally from Germany.)[40]

I asked Ollendorff whether she was ever worried about Reich's mental health. "I think it was okay," she replied softly. "He was drinking a lot and that was worrying me. He was always suspicious that I had an affair, with this one and the other one. Absolutely NOT true." In her book she wrote, "He often drank himself into an absolute stupor. At other times, drink would make him furiously angry, and at such times it was safer to be out of his way."[41] Ollendorff was unable to follow Reich's theoretical leaps, which Reich pressured her to do and greatly resented that she didn't. She concluded: "I think one has to recognize, as painful as the admission may be, that Reich's logic had carried him on and on, so far into space that at some point he began sometimes to lose contact with reality. He was able to pull himself back again and again, but the continued pressure forced him to seek escape into the outer regions, into a more benevolent world."[42]

In 1954, two years after their divorce, Ollendorff finally left Orgonon to work for the Hamilton School in Massachusetts, a free school, much like Summerhill, that was run by a couple who were former students of Reich's. (She applied for a job at Summerhill, but Neill advised against it, believing that she shouldn't be three thousand miles away from her son.) At Hamilton she found a refuge, as the couple had broken away from Reich's influence. Alexander Hamilton, having heard Ollendorff's complaints about her former husband—who had convinced her that she, rather than he, was going mad—wrote to Reich to say that he thought "everything that has come out of Orgonon since Oranur . . . rationalized defenses against untenable positions."[43]

———

As he tried to consolidate the latest events into his ever more elaborate theories, Reich's ideas took another leap forward into science fiction. Susan Sontag has pointed out that Reich's writing has "its own inimitable coherence" (earlier, she had called it "inimitable looniness"). "His description of orgone energy blocked," Sontag wrote in *Illness as Metaphor*, "and backing up as the crammed cells fight to the death, is already reminiscent of science fiction."[44] But not everyone could follow his new direction, and the Oranur phenomenon saw a dissipation and disintegration of the group.

Reich became increasingly dictatorial, aggressively seeking confirmation of his groping assumptions. "Reich probably was not too sure of his own theories and observations," Ollendorff concluded, "and therefore demanded from all of his assistants absolute identification with the work. Very few of us were able to do this." Among the few who could, she wrote, "there was an absolute belief in everything Reich said, whether it was against all logical appearances or not."[45] Anyone who expressed skepticism was felt by Reich to have strayed from his project: "His voice boomed, his skin reddened, he was all harshness," Sharaf wrote.[46] When Sharaf objected to these outbursts, Reich replied, as if to say that to repress his feelings would be worse, "What do you want me to get, cancer?"[47] He would accuse them, as he had Ollendorff, of being "armored," "caught in the trap," "hidden," or "poker-faced," or of "running" from him.

Reich wrote to his remaining Norwegian disciple, Ola Raknes, perhaps with memories of how his group had evaporated in Scandinavia before he came to America:

> The Oranur Experiment had the effect of bringing out the truth in everybody and resulted in the fact that the following persons have gone or have separated themselves: Myron Sharaf, Lois Wyvell, Allan Cott, Chester Raphael, Lee Wylie, Grethe Hoff, Albert Duvall, Theodore Wolfe and several others. This does not mean, with the exception of one or two, that they have become enemies. It only means that they are no longer close to the work.[48]

Reich made all his followers sign "confessions" of their feelings toward him and his work, which led some of them to compare him to Stalin. In one of these confidential memos, dated December 14, 1951, and duly filed and locked away in Reich's archive, Michael Silvert wrote that when he read Reich's *Cosmic Superimposition* (1951), in which he argues that the sexual embrace is mirrored in space as clusters of stars meet to spawn new galaxies, he had that "old familiar feeling" that Reich was "crazy, or schizophrenic":

> The homo normalis with his dead genital and cold pelvis within me felt that Reich could only be schizophrenic to be so different in his approach, so free, so open . . . to be so far ahead of classical general and stratophysical thinking. I, homo normalis, felt afraid, wondered whether Reich was not really leading me astray, up a dark, blind alley, from which I could not return. The other orgonomists, I feel, have similar reactions to the new book, though hidden. Dr. Gold, recently, said, "After reading it, I felt like jumping out of a window." His expression was one of wonderment and horror. At our literature seminar with Dr. Baker, the book was met with a cold silence, even more so than "The Oranur Project" [also published in 1951]. I think they all have their homo normalis within, who damns Reich as schizophrenic . . . My impression is that all orgonomists, in some degree, feel that Reich is schizophrenic.[49]

Another document in the archive, which is unsigned, calls this ambivalent reaction "Reichitis." The author, who claims to be talking for all Reich's colleagues but whose text reads as though he were taking dictation, wrote that Reich was "ten times better than even their best selves" and that "they loved him more deeply than they've ever loved," but this excessive admiration sometimes turned against itself and became destructive (this recapitulated the plot of *The Murder of Christ*): "We come to fear Reich and his capacities . . . 'we can't take it,' 'he is too much for us.' In order to deal with Reich, we have to be up to his devastating honesty, directness, efficiency, and sense of responsibility—and this becomes too difficult in the long run. It leaves no room for our own piddly pleasures and escapes—and it becomes more convenient to stay away and simply do nothing."[50]

Myron Sharaf left Orgonon at the beginning of 1952 "due to intolerance to Oranur."[51] He returned a year later, and Reich made him write a confession of his negative feelings, "Report on Impressions of Oranur and WR." "I was very annoyed and irritated when several assistants enthusiastically felt Oranur effects when I felt nothing," Sharaf recalled, "and I thought that they were prone to blame every pain and discomfort on Oranur." His report goes on:

> My "poker face" during this period which WR often commented on was undoubtedly due in part at least to my efforts to keep a "straight face" when discussing or participating in events I somewhere deep down felt were ludicrous. I did think to myself sometimes that WR, eager to find further confirmatory facts, was "imagining" that the rocks were blackening. The line between this and being crazy was admittedly thin, but it allowed me not to feel consciously dishonest when I answered "no" after WR once asked directly if the participants thought he were crazy.[52]

Later in the report Sharaf does admit—in the wary tone of someone whose schoolmaster is watching over him—to having thought Reich crazy at that time: "Yet actually I could not help but somewhere feel that he was childish and—though it is still with reluctance I use the word—'crazy' and 'grandiose.'"

There is a tape recording, titled simply "Alone," that Reich made after a meeting with the board of trustees of the Wilhelm Reich Foundation at Orgonon on April 3, 1952. Reich's speech is slow, full of poignant pauses, and his deep voice, full of elongated vowels and clipped consonants, has the elegant Germanic tones of a 1940s film star. He is on his own, as the title suggests, sitting in the large room of the Student Laboratory, talking into his recording device with angry restraint about the uselessness of his followers. Reich says in a steely tone to a biographer of a future time:

> I hope that someone will at some time in the future listen to this recording with great respect—respect for the courage that was necessary to sustain the research work in orgone energy—life energy—through the years. I shall not go into the great strain, into the details, the worries, the sleepless nights, the tears, the expenditure of money and effort . . . I would like only to mention the fact that there's nobody

around, there's not a single soul at Orgonon, or down in New York, who would fully and really, from the bottom of his existence, understand what I am doing . . . Every single one of them spites me . . . "Why did he have to start this Oranur experiment which gives us so much trouble?" They see only trouble. They don't see, or they don't want to realize, what it means for medicine, biology, and science in general, as well as to philosophy . . . to them it is mostly bother, an inducer of sickness, suffering. And at times I have the distinct feeling that they believe—but do not dare to admit their own thoughts—that I may have gone haywire.[53]

One morning in late April 1952, Alfred Stellato arrived for his appointment at the Orgone Institute Diagnostic Clinic, Reich's former residence in Forest Hills, Queens. Dr. Chester Raphael, who looked about thirty-two years old, according to Stellato, came out to greet him and ushered him into a small doctor's office. It looked less like an examination room, Stellato noted, than a "rather ill-supplied laboratory."[54] There was a microscope on a side table, a bottle of rubbing alcohol, and a supply of pipettes and quartz slides. Two pressure cookers for autoclaving blood samples—for a test Reich used to determine human vitality and susceptibility to cancer—sat on a gas range.

Alfred Stellato was not a genuine patient but an undercover agent for the Food and Drug Administration. Three years after Charles Wood's initial visit to Orgonon, the agency had stepped up its investigation as part of a new antiquackery campaign. Media interest in Reich had reached a new intensity following the publication of Martin Gardner's popular *Fads and Fallacies in the Name of Science* (1952), which included a debunking chapter on Reich in a rogues' gallery of quacks. The FDA was under a lot of pressure from the American Medical Association to do something about him.

Reich knew that the FDA continued to keep its eye on him: an accumulator user had written to him in the summer of 1951 saying that an official had visited his home, photographed his box, and taken a statement about how much he paid in rental and how he had first heard of Reich's device. Reich immediately wrote a letter of complaint to the FDA, asking them to contact him directly rather than harass his patients. Two weeks later Reich's institute sent a letter out to about five hundred users recommending that they refer the FDA to them if the agents called asking questions.

What Reich and his "firm," as the FDA insisted on calling it, didn't know was that, as well as continuing their search for dissatisfied users, FDA agents were soliciting the institute for products and literature, which they hoped to use in court as proof of a "promotional scheme" around the accumulator. Several agents corresponded with the institute, simulating a genuine and growing interest, in carefully worded letters (Reich would later call them "catch letters"). Their use of multiple addresses enabled them to buy items from Reich's catalogue without arousing suspicion. By the time of Stellato's visit the FDA had assembled an almost complete collection of orgonomic literature and orgone devices. Every envelope, packing crate, Railway Express receipt, and canceled check was carefully filed away in an FDA storage facility as possibly incriminating evidence. The organization's thoroughness is impressive: there is an endless inventory of exhibits in the FDA files; every shred of evidence was kept.

It was unusual for FDA agents to go undercover posing as patients; an FDA memo states, "Very few operations of this kind have been undertaken in the past."[55] Stellato was a particularly useful asset, since he had a slight heart murmur and a benign tumor on his tongue. The FDA persuaded his doctor to go along with their plan and pretend the tumor was potentially cancerous so as to try to entrap Reich by getting him to sanction the use of the accumulator as a cancer cure. Stellato duly wrote to the institute asking if his possibly malignant tumor might be treated with the accumulator he had acquired the previous year for $222.10. To Stellato's surprise, Reich himself wrote back.

Reich advised Stellato to keep using his accumulator so as to keep his bioenergetic levels beneficially high, but he was shrewd enough not to give any specific medical advice, and reserved judgment until he had seen a report by Stellato's own physician. Stellato sent his fake one in, and shortly afterward he got a letter from Dr. Simeon Tropp, who had given up his surgical practice in 1949 to work full-time for the Wilhelm Reich Foundation, suggesting that Stellato come to the Forest Hills clinic for a Reich Blood Test. Stellato made an appointment and traveled up to New York from Baltimore on the agreed-upon date.

According to Stellato, Raphael got "slightly excited" when he heard about the cancerous growth on his tongue. He pricked his patient's finger, sucked up a blood sample with a teat pipette, and examined it under a microscope, looking for spiky-looking T-bacilli (T for *Tod*, death) in the blood cells, which Reich thought were indicative of cancer. (One doctor the FDA consulted said of the Reich Blood Test, "It's a screwball thing": all the spiky T-bacilli represented was the natural crenellation of red blood cells.)[56] As he hunched over the instrument, Raphael advised Stellato to have the tumor removed as his doctor had advised and to continue using the orgone accumulator every day, just as he was doing, because it charged the body up so that it didn't become susceptible to disease.

"At one point," Stellato said, "he asked his receptionist if his explanation of how the accumulator works was comprehensible to her. She replied that it was the best discussion she heard on the subject in a long time. That remark seemed to please him." When Raphael asked him whether he had understood his explanation, Stellato sarcastically reported that he feigned a "very serious look" and replied, "Being a layman I couldn't understand everything he said but . . . I was doing my best to comprehend to the best of my ability."[57]

Raphael then quizzed him about his sex life. Did he go out with women? Why not? Was he homosexual? Did he masturbate? Did autoeroticism give him pleasure? (Stellato's colleagues at the FDA had decided that he should give the impression of being sexually repressed.) After about twenty minutes Raphael correctly diagnosed the blood sample as negative for cancer. He then asked his patient to undress for a physical examination and left the room while he did so. Stellato looked around and noticed *The Function of the Orgasm* on a shelf, but he was surprised to see no other medical books, nor any medical degrees on the wall. Raphael returned and asked him to remove his remaining garments. He lay naked on the couch, while Raphael sat in a chair to his left:

> As I lay on the cold couch, the doctor glanced at me from head to toe not saying a word . . . I noticed he would look at my penis and

stop, then his eyes would continue their journey to my neck and face. As he looked at my penis he asked me when I had been circumcised. I looked at him and replied that I had never been. This must have amazed him for he asked to closely examine the head of my sex. After he examined it front and back, he remarked that for an uncircumcised penis, the foreskin was extremely clear of the head and seemed very clean. I just nodded . . . His remarks and his manner of approach created some doubts in my mind as to his medical efficacy.[58]

Dr. Raphael diagnosed severe repression. Stellato was "full of pent-up emotions" and his musculature was knotted with "deep emotional strain," he noted. For a half hour the doctor expounded on the dangers of abstinence. Stellato wrote, "My belief is that he was merely building up a good case to ask me to pay a sizable fee." As Stellato got up to dress, Raphael noticed a stiff neck muscle and had him lie down again. "He tapped my neck, my shoulders and then my back manually," Stellato wrote in his report. "As he tapped the small of my back with his right hand his left hand rested on my right buttock for a second or two."[59] The fee for this visit was twenty-five dollars.

The first time the reality of the new investigation struck home to Reich was when a government car with three FDA employees arrived unannounced at Orgonon at the end of July 1952, three months after Stellato's visit to the Forest Hills clinic. Before the three FDA officials (an inspector, a doctor, and a physicist) entered Reich's property, they stopped to hide radioactivity-monitoring film badges in their jackets and pencil dosimeters in their shirt pockets. Reich's recent publication, *The Oranur Project*, had indicated that his premises were dangerously radioactive; the FDA wasn't sure whether to believe this or not, and these devices would warn of exposure to harmful levels of radiation.

They drove up to the pavilion marked "Student Laboratory," but no one answered when they knocked on the door. In fact, the place seemed deserted. There were DANGER signs everywhere (the laboratory had been quarantined after Oranur). The road to the observatory was also closed off. Suspended from the gate chain was a NO TRESPASSING sign. Another read, as it had when Wood first visited, ADMITTANCE BY WRITTEN APPOINTMENT ONLY. The inspectors ignored these warnings, dropped the chain, and drove in.

Reich had thought it now safe to move back into the building and Ilse Ollendorff came out to meet them—as always, she was Reich's last line of defense. She told them that Reich was far too busy with his research to see them. But when Inspector Kenyon said that the two doctors had come from Washington and would not be available indefinitely, Reich yelled from his office on the first floor, "I can come down, I can come down, Ilse." In a few moments, the FDA report states, "A large, robust man of plethoric appearance bounded down the steps."[60]

Reich demanded he see the FDA agents' credentials, and he took them into another room to examine them more closely. Reich suspected the men were really "pharmaceutic agents representing American industrial interests who were ready to sell out the country . . . via Moscow affiliations."[61] He got this idea from the conspiracy theorist Emmanuel M. Josephson's book *Rockefeller "Internationalist": The Man Who Misrules the World* (1952), which accused Nelson Rockefeller—who as undersecretary in the Department of Health was in charge of the FDA—of being in secret alliance with the Soviets. (In another mad stream-of-consciousness work, Josephson suggested that Stalin had murdered FDR at Yalta and that a look-alike had been reelected in 1944.) Three years earlier Reich had greeted Inspector Wood cordially and had willingly allowed an inspection—perhaps he was getting official approval at last!—but now, according to the inspector's later report, he was full of violently uncooperative rage. "After entering the front room, Reich became more violent in his speech and actions. He ordered the inspectors to sit down and then began a tirade concerning our investigation. This was accompanied by pacing and violent swinging of arms and pounding on a desk. He stated, in effect, that our investigation would create one of the greatest scandals in the country." Reich then "went into an explosive discourse to the effect that we were Red Fascists who had come to his place with the idea of controlling Orgone energy. He indicated that our visit was prompted by the pharmaceutical industry."[62]

After this paranoid tirade, Reich asked the doctors to tell him their qualifications; he was apparently taken aback when Dr. Heller said he was a specialist in nuclear physics. Reich showed him his Geiger-Müller counter, which was hooked up to an accumulator and was making audible clicks. Heller pretended to take a good look at it so as to expose his radiation testing equipment for as long as possible (no radiation was recorded that day), and Reich chastised him for not recognizing it immediately.

Reich yelled, arms flailing, that the earlier FDA campaign had cost him thousands of dollars, which could have been much better spent on developing his tremendous discoveries. He shouted that the accumulator wasn't a device, as he had indicated three years earlier (he now thought it could be more accurately described as an atomic pile, and thought it should be under the juristiction of the Atomic Energy Commission and not the FDA). He shouted that Wood had asked his patients whether they masturbated: "What right do you people have to come here and ask me whether my secretary has a lover or whether other goings-on of this character exist around here? What do you think we are up here, bums?" There was no answer, but Reich thought Dr. Brimmer's expression suggested that he thought just that and he charged at him with a threatening clenched fist, screaming in a high-pitched voice, "Take that smile off your face."[63]

Reich calmed down a little after smashing an ashtray in anger; he said that he wanted the confusions of the earlier inspection "cleaned up" before he would permit another. He gave them a copy of his pamphlet *The Orgone Energy Accumulator: Its Medical and Scientific Use* and ordered them to "study" all of the publications in its bibliography. After they'd done this, they'd have to attend an "Oranur course" to update themselves on more recent developments before he would grant them an inspection. "Get out!" he yelled when his unwanted guests protested these requirements. "We are not in Hitleria or Modjuland yet." ("Modju" was Reich's own neologism; it fuses "Mo"—taken from the Venetian patrician Giovanni Mocenigo, who denounced the philosopher Giordano Bruno to the Inquisition—with Stalin's real name, Djugashvili.)[64]

The three FDA men decided to cut their losses and instead inspect S. A. Collins & Sons, the Rangeley carpentry firm that manufactured accumulators for Reich. Reich had already phoned ahead and told Vernon Collins, the man who had built the observatory at Orgonon for him, not to allow the inspectors to touch any of the accumulators he had stored there. Collins complied with this request, but he did agree to be interviewed. Most of the accumulators Collins built for Reich, the inspectors learned, were built in the winter months, which was traditionally a slack period for the firm. The design was so simple that they followed not a blueprint but verbal instructions relayed by Reich. They built five accumulators at a time and had manufactured two to three hundred since production started a year and a half earlier. The boxes were marked with "CS" (Collins & Sons), and about 75 percent were shipped to New York and New Jersey; the company also made orgone blankets, "shooters," and "hats." A representative from the Orgone Institute, Collins said, came down to examine the boxes and other devices before they were crated.

In the FDA file in Washington, accompanying the inspectors' report are six pages of photographs of the Collins shop, a small timber shed with double doors, whose fitting motto, considering the merchandise, was "Everything to Build Everything." You can see the inspector's sleek black automobile parked out front. There are several pictures of the messy interior, which are framed and labeled as if they were of the scene of a crime. There is a picture of a six-foot stack of old accumulator panels, boards salvaged from returned machines. Another image shows a corner piled up with bundles of the steel wool, fiberglass, and galvanized wire mesh used to make the machines. Crated accumulators lean against a back wall, flat-packed and ready to be shipped.

After the FDA's unannounced call to Orgonon, Reich made official complaints to the FBI, asking them to verify the identities of the inspectors, and to the president, warning of the FDA's red fascist threat to the United States. He began his letter to President Truman as if they were old friends: "I have been bothered again by the Food and Drug Administration."[65]

## Eleven

Senator Joseph McCarthy, in an effort to garner headlines, spiced his anticommunism with hints of sexual scandal, straying from his main line of inquiry to accuse various government employees of being "sexual deviants" and therefore potential "security risks." Homosexuals were, it turned out, easier to identify than Communists. McCarthy soon broadened his antigay campaign to suggest that the loosening of sexual mores was a deliberate ruse by Communists to undermine the American family and way of life.

In February 1952, during two days of HUAC open hearings in Washington, the twenty-eight-year-old ex-Communist Harvey Matusow testified that Communists were cultivating and exploiting an atmosphere of sexual permissiveness to try to attract young members to the party. Matusow was, according to one observer, arrogant, grossly overweight, brash, and "talkative to the point of garrulousness."[1] He was also one of the FBI's most celebrated informers, employed by McCarthyite committees as a paid witness; in a second wave of Smith Act trials, he would go on to point the finger at Communists, most of whom had been his former friends in the party.

Matusow's mother was Russian-born and his father ran a cigar store in the Bronx where, Matusow claimed, Leon Trotsky had once bought ice cream from his grandfather. He joined the Communist

Party in 1946 as a young World War II veteran; he said he found the same "esprit de corps" there as he had in the army. Matusow was soon on the payroll, working in party bookstores, offices, and summer camps. In 1948 his junior party cell joined Youth for Wallace to support the former editor of *The New Republic* in his presidential bid; in photographs of Wallace's concession speech, Matusow is pictured standing alongside him. As if to confirm the extent of Communist infiltration, Matusow would boast that he had been a member of forty-five Communist front organizations.

The month after McCarthy made his famous allegation that the State Department was riddled with Communists, Matusow visited the New York office of the FBI and volunteered his services. He was angry because the party had recently demoted him, having accused him of "white chauvinism" when he took a job at a Harlem debt collection agency. A few days before the Korean War began, the FBI signed him up as an informer at seventy-five dollars a month. At the time the American Communist Party's leadership was on trial under the Smith Act. The party was revealed in court to be riddled with FBI infiltrators; thirteen ex-Communists—including Louis Budenz, who recruited William Reich, the man confused with Wilhelm by the FBI—testified that they had been taught that revolution was achievable only through violence. The party crumbled under the financial pressure of mounting a legal defense, and became so wary of spies that it stopped recruiting new members and instead purged thousands as a result of its own loyalty checks.

Matusow was expelled from the party in 1951, accused of being "an enemy agent"; he enlisted in the air force. He had a nervous breakdown during his second stint in the military, and was diagnosed as a manic-depressive "schizoid personality . . . manifested by nomadism, eccentricity, seclusiveness, [and] moderate stress of a break with the Communist Party."[2]

Matusow got over his period of depression by immersing himself more deeply in anticommunism. He was keen to join the ranks of Communists turned celebrity informants such as Matt Cvetic (author of *I Was a Communist for the FBI*), the "spy queen" Elizabeth Bentley, and the *Time* writer Whittaker Chambers, who had exposed Alger Hiss as a Communist. All three made a living from their former party affiliation and had been hailed in the press as national heroes.

Matusow realized, by his own admission, that he needed a "gimmick" if he was to make a career of the McCarthy hearings like these other professional and well-paid informers. He consciously decided to make his inside knowledge of the overlooked Communist youth movement his area of useful expertise. By making "something sinister out of much that was innocent," as he put it, Matusow persuaded America of a Communist plot to indoctrinate American youth.[3]

Before the Ohio Un-American Activities Commission, Matusow explained how the Communist Party had tried to infiltrate the Boy Scouts movement and stated that there were 3,500 Communists teaching in the New York City school system and that Communists taught toddlers politicized Mother Goose rhymes. A newspaper quoted one of these: "Jack Sprat could eat no fat, his wife could eat no lean. Because the Congress done them in and picked their pockets clean."[4] But he garnered the biggest headlines when he warned how Communists preyed on sexual weakness to recruit the young.

Matusow told HUAC that sexual immorality was rampant among the Communists of Greenwich Village and Camp Unity, a Communist youth camp in Wingdale, New York. Matusow recounted tales of the sexual permissiveness that was encouraged there: young campers made love openly in the grass by Lenin's Rock, a sculpted boulder of the Russian leader that made joking reference to Mount Rushmore. American youths were lured to the party, Matusow claimed, with promises of sexual promiscuity. The headline of the February 7, 1952, *New York Daily Mirror* proclaimed: "FBI Aide Says Reds Employ Sex as Snare." The editorial read: "The Matusow revelations about Communist use of intellectual and of sexual appeals to rope young people into the party's lower echelons pose a new light on the brutishly immoral and completely conscienceless strategies of the red traitors."[5] It was exactly the kind of connection between sexual immorality and radical politics that the FDA and other investigatory bodies saw in Reich's and Kinsey's work.

Matusow was catapulted into McCarthy's inner circle as a result of his testimony. He became assistant to the editor of *Counterattack*, a four-page weekly started by three former FBI men that published an ever-evolving blacklist and fed information from J. Edgar Hoover to McCarthy. He campaigned for his hero, Senator McCarthy, in the 1952 elections, delivering anti-Communist speeches in Wisconsin, Utah, Montana, Idaho, and Washington in which he detailed the "Communist plot against McCarthy."

Matusow was a "publicity addict," hooked, he later wrote, on the "narcotic of newsprint."[6] He named more than two hundred people as Communists and was a key witness in several high-profile cases. But he was so keen to incriminate Communists that he made false accusations and perjured himself in the process. He lied to help convict Clinton Jencks—whom he'd met in a left-leaning artists' colony near Taos presided over by the former Greenwich Village bohemian Mabel Dodge and D. H. Lawrence's widow, Frieda. Jencks led mineworkers in New Mexico in a strike depicted in the classic movie *Salt of the Earth* (1954), directed by the blacklisted director Herbert Biberman (Jencks played himself in the film), which was later banned as "Communist propaganda." Jencks stood accused of falsely signing an affidavit stating he was not a Communist, as was required of all union officials under the Taft-Hartley Act, and because of Matusow's false testimony he was sentenced to five years in prison.

In 1953 Matusow, riding high on his celebrity, married one of McCarthy's wealthy backers, the millionaire Arvilla Bentley, who had an oil portrait of McCarthy prominently displayed in her house. The couple had fallen in love when Matusow chaperoned her out of the country to the Bahamas Country Club so that she could dodge a subpoena that would have forced her to reveal that she'd given McCarthy's campaign more money than was allowed under the law. He was only twenty-six; "the Duchess," as he called her, was forty-three.

Matusow's marriage lasted only four months. In August 1953 he wrote to McCarthy from Reno, where they'd gotten divorced: "When I testified at the trial of the 16 Communist Leaders in New York, the defense said, 'You'd do anything for a buck.' I denied it, but he was right."[7] Matusow, a self-described "mess," went around telling everyone that he had lied under oath and wanted absolution. A Communist publisher, hoping to provide evidence that would necessitate a retrial of Jencks and others, persuaded him to write a book confessing to having been a false witness. Matusow himself was sentenced to five years for obstructing justice.

When Kinsey's second volume cataloguing American sexuality, *Sexual Behavior in the Human Female*, appeared in August 1953, it played right into the McCarthyite fears about sex and communism. (The Soviets had just tested their first H-bomb.) To those on the right, Kinsey seemed to be speeding up the deteriorating respectability of America by making controversial moral judgments that masqueraded as science. He reported, for example, that 50 percent of his interviewees had had sex before marriage, and went on to explain how he was in favor of premarital experimentation, arguing that those who enjoyed early sexual experiences adjusted more easily and happily to married sexual life.

Kinsey noted that there was "a marked correlation between experience in orgasm obtained from pre-marital coitus, and the capacity to reach orgasm after marriage."[8] Ten percent of women never did, for which Kinsey blamed the pernicious Judeo-Christian tradition of abstinence outside of wedlock. The orgasm remained his sole unit of measurement of sexual experience, and in the final chapter, "Anatomy and Physiology of Sexual Response and Orgasm," he provided a graphic description of climax, distilled from the many hours of secret footage he'd shot of the members of his inner circle having sex in his attic.

Conservatives furiously attacked Kinsey for eroding the sacred institution of the American family, on which so much of 1950s America's romanticized image of itself was based. Catholics and Protestants were in an uproar and there was a very public eruption of disapproval and disgust. One Baptist minister attacked Kinsey as a "deranged Nebuchadnezzar."[9] Louis Heller, the Democratic congressman for New York, tried to get the post office to ban the book (three years earlier the post office had confiscated some photographs that Kinsey had acquired for his collection, and it took several years of legal battles to win them back). Even the journal *Science* dismissed the book as propaganda for Kinsey's own subversive views.

Kinsey was not a sexual anarchist or Communist and he insisted that all his researchers be happily married (though this was largely for appearances' sake). Kinsey argued for sexual liberation ostensibly to safeguard the institution of the family rather than to subvert it. In America, Kinsey said, it took years to resolve the sexual repression that had been inculcated from childhood, and he thought that the delay in sexual activity until marriage was directly responsible for the high rate of divorce. "Judged by the departure from the physiologic normal and the damage wrought on the home and society," Kinsey argued, "the great distortions of sex are the cultural perversions of celibacy, delayed marriage, and asceticism."[10]

However, the Kinsey Reports reflected and fueled a new mood. The reports inspired Hugh Hefner to launch *Playboy*, which appeared, complete with Marilyn Monroe centerfold, in December of that year to mock America's puritan pretensions. (Within two years *Playboy* was selling 500,000 copies a month, at fifty cents a peek; by the end of the decade this figure had doubled.) One of Hefner's student papers, "Sex Behavior and the U.S. Law," was the basis for what would become the *Playboy* philosophy. "If Kinsey had done the research," Hefner reflected years later, "I was the pamphleteer, spreading the news of sexual liberation through a monthly magazine."[11]

The magazine *Washington Confidential* used Kinsey's national averages to calculate that 21 congressmen must be gay and 192 other politicians "bad behavior risks," which perhaps stirred Congressman B. Carroll Reece, Republican of Tennessee and later chairman of the Republican National Committee, to attack the Rockefeller Foundation for funding Kinsey's allegedly Communist-inspired efforts at "weakening American morality." The Reece Committee (the House Committee to Investigate Tax-Exempt and Other Comparable Organizations), established in 1952, was a sideshow to the McCarthy hearings. It aimed to prove that there was "a Moscow-directed, specific plot to penetrate the American foundations and to use their funds for communist propaganda and communist influence upon our society."[12]

The committee asked to see the Rockefeller Foundation's files. In right-wing circles it was commonly believed that the United States had recognized the Soviet Union in the early 1930s only under pressure from the Rockefeller Foundation, which wanted to help

Rockefeller's Standard Oil negotiate energy contracts with Russia's revolutionary leaders. The Rockefeller Foundation, and others like it, were seen as forming an "unofficial state department," and it was thought that they should be subject to the same scrutiny as government.[13] It was suspected that even if the trustees themselves were beyond reproach, the foundation staff was riddled with Communists. Reece dismissed the Kinsey Reports the foundation had funded as "a bunch of claptrap" and believed they were part of the Communists' "diabolical conspiracy" to undermine the American home.[14]

Even if he wasn't a Communist, Kinsey seemed to share the Communists' view of human nature and morality. Subversion, Reece said, "does not refer to outright revolution, but to a promotion of tendencies which lead, in their inevitable consequences, to the destruction of principles through perversion or alienation. Subversion, in modern society, is not a sudden, cataclysmic explosion, but a gradual undermining, a persistent chipping away at foundations upon which beliefs rest."[15] The Kinsey Reports did precisely that, negatively impacting on social mores, and Kinsey's case illustrated, for Reece, how "comparatively small donations may have big repercussions in the realm of ideas."[16]

In 1951, Kinsey had won another round of Rockefeller funding by a single vote. Now the foundation, keen to remain behind the scenes and not to have its dirty laundry aired in public, bowed to public prudery and cut off its support. Instead it awarded Union Theological Seminary $525,000, which was considerably more than its total support of Kinsey over thirteen years. (Henry Pitney Van Dusen, head of the seminary and Kinsey's fiercest critic, was a member of the Rockefeller board.) John Foster Dulles, a Rockefeller Foundation trustee (later Eisenhower's secretary of state), believed that the foundation should steer clear of the controversial subject of sex.

In 1953, Margaret Sanger, then sixty-eight, whose Planned Parenthood enjoyed the enthusiastic patronage of the Rockefellers, arranged for the seventy-six-year-old philanthropist Katharine McCormick, with whom she had become friends in the late 1920s, to meet the scientist Gregory Pincus, the man who would become known as "the father of the Pill." McCormick, who was the second woman to graduate from

MIT, with a degree in biology, had become interested in endocrinology when seeking a cure for her husband's schizophrenia. Stanley McCormick, the youngest son of the inventor of the mechanical reaper and the founder of International Harvester, had been institutionalized two years after they married (his older brother married John D. Rockefeller, Jr.'s sister, Edith, who was Carl Jung's chief enthusiast and patron). According to the Harvard gynecologist John Rock, who conducted the first human trials of the contraceptive pill, Katharine McCormick "was as rich as Croesus. She has a vast fortune . . . she couldn't even spend the interest on her interest." McCormick would put two million dollars of her inherited fortune into Pincus's research.[17] McCormick and Sanger, veterans of the first sexual revolution, would coordinate and fund the second.

As early as 1912 Margaret Sanger had envisioned a "magic pill" for contraception, so that sex might be freed from procreation. The founder and editor of *The Woman Rebel*, imprisoned in 1917 for distributing birth control devices, Sanger was described by Mabel Dodge as "an ardent propagandist for the joys of the flesh." She was married twice and had numerous lovers, enjoying, she said, "being ravaged by romances."[18] Sanger, a keen eugenicist, also saw birth control as an urgent imperative, predicting in 1950 that "the world and almost all our civilization for the next twenty-five years is going to depend upon a simple, cheap, safe contraceptive to be used in poverty-stricken slums and jungles, and among the most ignorant people."[19] It was because of their shared interest in eugenics that Sanger's Planned Parenthood organization enjoyed the enthusiastic patronage of the Rockefellers.

In 1952, in response to contemporary anxieties about the population explosion, John D. Rockefeller III started the Population Council, which was directed by Frederick Osborn, the leader of the American Eugenics Society. Populations were growing twice as fast in "developing" countries as in the United States and Europe, and this "population bomb," as one eugenicist called it, threatened to create breeding grounds for communism around the world.[20] John Rock, who conducted the first human trials of the contraceptive pill in 1954, wrote that "the greatest menace to world peace and decent standards of life today is not atomic energy but sexual energy."[21]

Overpopulation and communism were, in Rock's words, "more than synchronous." The technological breakthrough of the Pill offered a means to control this swarm, and it is interesting that Kinsey's avenue of research was closed down just as the Pill offered a means to achieve the goals to which the Rockefellers had hoped Kinsey would contribute.

When the Reece Committee submitted its final report in December 1954, the two Democrats on the committee appended a minority report denouncing the enterprise as a "complete waste of public money." They attributed its trumped-up charges to "the cloud of fear so evident in all phases of our national life in recent years." By then McCarthy's star was beginning to wane. The minority report diagnosed the era over which he'd reigned as characterized by "fear-sickness."[22]

Kinsey never got replacement funding, though after his death, in 1956, Hugh Hefner gave a grant to his institute in return for free access to its extensive collection of pornographic films. Like Reich, Kinsey publicly identified with scientists such as Copernicus and Galileo who had been persecuted for their discoveries. Kinsey embarked on a swan-song tour of Europe, visiting many places where Reich had left his mark. He interviewed Scandinavian transvestites and visited London brothels in his quest to collect impressions of European attitudes to sex. He found Scandinavia to be an enlightened sexual paradise, which had eluded Reich when he was there before the war.

In November 1953 an agent from the Immigration and Naturalization Service (INS) visited Reich at Orgonon to try to get information on two suspected Communists and to check Reich's own political beliefs. One of these men was the novelist Lion Feuchtwanger, the man who financed Bertolt Brecht's escape to America from Norway; Feuchtwanger was now living in Pacific Palisades, California. The INS thought Reich might have known him in Berlin.

In his report the INS agent noted the numerous paintings and sculptures of nudes that decorated the observatory, and the shotguns and rifles Reich kept propped up by the door, along with a supply of unboxed ammunition, "in position for instant use." Reich was a prolific writer, to which he now devoted much of his day, and he would take breaks on the deck for target practice. A pistol in a holster was slung over the back of the study chair that Reich sat in for the interview, which gave him—dressed in dungarees and a checked jacket, with a red bandana tied around his neck—the air of a revolutionary leader.

Reich's suspicious behavior led the agent to assume that their conversation was being recorded. He asked Reich how he felt about communism:

> SUBJECT stated he had not engaged in Communist activity "in over 20 years," that over six million Germans had been Communist [Party] members during his own membership, that he is opposed to Communism as Communism is against the three things that he considers most important in life, namely, "Love, Freedom and Babies," that he was in favor of the execution of the Rosenbergs but would not have wanted to be the executioner, that he hated persons who "hid behind the Fifth Amendment," and that his study of the face of Malenkov revealed Malenkov to be a psychopath. [Stalin had died that March, and Malenkov had become premier of the Soviet Union.][23]

The INS kept tabs on Reich from 1948 to 1956, initiating their investigation after A. H. Crombie, the author of various right-wing Christian antisex pamphlets and *Communism and the Moral Break-down in America* (1955), wrote to them questioning his political allegiance. (Reich had written a scathing critique of Crombie's attempts at sex education.) Reich was, of course, violently anti-Communist by this time; like Kinsey, he voted Republican. On November 4, 1952, Eisenhower had been elected president with 55 percent of the vote, bringing a Republican into the White House for the first time in two decades. Reich voted for him not because he was the conqueror of the Nazis, having led the invasion of Europe, but because he thought he had an "honest face." Eisenhower would be the last president to have been born, like Reich, in the nineteenth century. He had a ruddy complexion like Reich's and radiated an inner strength. Reich thought this indicated "the simplicity, the close-fulness and contactfulness of the genital character. I do not know him, really, personally; but that is what I feel about him, also his wife. Now that is a sexual revolution."[24] All of Reich's physicians were expected to follow him in voting Republican, which alienated some of them, as most were natural Democrats and would have preferred to support Adlai Stevenson. "None wished to buck Reich," Baker said (only he, Duvall, and Silvert were already conservatives).[25]

After Eisenhower was elected, several boys, led by a local druggist, went on a victory parade through Rangeley. Orgonon had been evacuated after the Oranur experiment and Ilse Ollendorff had rented a house in the center of the town. As the parade passed their windows, Reich heard the group shout, "Orgy, Orgy, Orgy, Commie, Commie, come out, you Commie!"[26] "I remember it vividly," recalled Peter Reich, who was eight at the time. "This mob came to our house and they were shouting down with the Commies, down with the orgies." Wilhelm Reich rushed out to confront them, and it was noticed that he held a gun behind his back as he harangued the group; this was subsequently reported to the FBI.

When the INS agent showed Reich photographs of the two "aliens" under suspicion of being Communists, Reich replied "almost instantly" that he didn't know either of them:

> SUBJECT then lost self-control. He paced the floor and pounded the table. His face reddened and his speech became at times incoherent. When asked if he had been offended in some way which caused his excitement, SUBJECT said he had been. SUBJECT then went on to say that in effect, he had been insulted in being asked to merely identify a suspected Communist, that I did not realize who he, SUBJECT, was, that I did not understand how minor was the importance of questioning him concerning individual Communists as he wanted it plainly understood that his personal knowledge of Communism extended beyond the "political field" of Communism and went deep into the heart of the philosophy of present day Communism—dictatorship as compared with Marxism.[27]

Reich had presumed that the agent hadn't come all this way to ask him to snitch on two individuals, but to ask for his psychological ideas on how the United States might, as he shouted to the agent, "understand and get to the root of the 'Communist disease.'"

Reich's lifelong obsession with the curative powers of the orgasm no doubt played a part in the FBI, INS, and FDA's dogged pursuit of him. In 1954 the American Medical Association, which had encouraged the FDA to bring Reich to court, had accused Kinsey of sparking a "wave of sexual hysteria" with the publication of his second volume.[28] If Kinsey's libertarianism was attracting attention, bringing Reich to trial held the potential to stem that tide; some popular magazines certainly fused the projects of the two men (see, for example, the December 1954 issue of *Uncensored* magazine).[29] Reich once again became the scapegoat for the new morality because, as the guru of the "new cult of sex and anarchy," he seemed to give a philosophical rationale to the data identified by Kinsey.

It is clear that the FDA did think of Reich's box as a sexual device, something that Reich was increasingly adamant it wasn't. Inspector Wood had always thought the accumulator business was the tip of the iceberg, a cover for some sort of vice ring: "I still think the accumulator is a smoke-screen proposition," he advised his boss.[30] When accumulator users were interviewed, the inspectors never failed to note a flirtatious demeanor or report a twinkling eye; sex was always seen to be bubbling under the surface of these encounters. Of course, many users who read about the accumulator in the magazines that ridiculed and popularized the machine did feel that the device would have libido-enhancing effects. One art student who was interviewed by the FDA—and who, it was noted with suspicion, at the time of the visit was reading *America and the Intellectuals* (1953), a transcript of a symposium organised by *The Partisan Review*—was especially embarrassed and nervous during questioning. Inspector Cassidy concluded his report: "I feel strongly that his interest in the accumulator pertained more to sex than to cancer."[31]

In 1953 the FDA, which had been unable to locate and tap into an anticipated reservoir of unhappy accumulator users, commissioned independent trials from several doctors and scientists. The accumulators that the FDA inspectors had bought from the Orgone Institute were photographed, initialed, and dated and then immediately sent to universities, laboratories, and hospitals around the country so that experts could test whether there was any energy emanating from them and, if so, whether it had any beneficial effect on health. Prestigious institutions such as the Mayo Clinic and MIT, where a physicist submitted a thesis-length rebuttal of Reich's theories, were awarded grants by the FDA to do this. The University of Chicago put together a three-man committee on mathematical biophysics who found the accumulator to be "a gigantic hoax with no scientific basis."[32] Dr. Nicolas Rashevsky, who led the group, said: "The material is beneath any refutation. Practically every paragraph exhibits complete ignorance of well-established facts of science. Other paragraphs contain wild speculations made without any scientific basis whatsoever. Sometimes wild claims are made . . . The argument of the claimant in such cases is usually that scientists must admit they do not know everything."[33]

Dr. Philip Thompson worked for the Maine General Hospital in 1953, when the FDA asked him to do tests on the accumulator. "They were selling them and saying that they had curative values," he told me over the phone from his home in Portland. "We proved that they didn't. We had two boxes down here, just as they were manufactured in Rangeley. My job was to test the orgone accumulator as a cure for arthritis—we observed six or seven patients for six months. We took it seriously, we followed Reich's directions."[34]

Another doctor at the hospital, Dr. Raymond Higgins, stuffed six glass vaginal tubes with steel wool and attached them with cable to a shooter box—as prescribed by the guidelines Clista Templeton had picked up by accident—and used them to do tests on twenty-two cases of trichomoniasis, the sexually transmitted disease known as "trich" caused by the protozoan *Trichomonas vaginalis*. Higgins described one case as an awkward "sore thumb" in the FDA's case against Reich, as the infection seemed to have cleared up immediately after treatment. His superior rationalized that the introduction of a cold glass tube might temporarily immobilize the parasite.[35]

Although Dr. Thompson claims to have taken Reich's procedures seriously when conducting his trial, most of the FDA tests weren't particularly thorough, as the time-pressed experts thought the whole exercise slightly ridiculous. Some test subjects were treated only a few times with orgone devices. (Furthermore, Reich's supporters later claimed the tests were invalidated by the close proximity of X-ray machines, which would have aggravated the orgone energy, turning it into therapeutically ineffective DOR.) Dr. Frank H. Krusen of the Mayo Clinic, who was testing for the accumulators' effects on the user's temperature, pulse, respiration, and blood pressure, appended the following covering note to his final report: "It was very difficult for me to bring myself to take the time to prepare this report because . . . this quackery is of such a fantastic nature that it seems hardly worthwhile to refute the ridiculous claims of its proponents."[36]

If the scientists thought the accumulator so absurd, why, one might ask, did the FDA consider it such a threat? "It wasn't a threat to the medical establishment," Thompson explained. "The threat was financial gain. They were making money claiming that they could cure cancer. It was a financial and legal thing. We were more interested in seeing people weren't buying a pig in a poke. I thought it was a complete hoax—and so it proved to be." Thompson thought the box was being marketed as some kind of aphrodisiac: "They claimed to be harnessing the sexual energy of the cosmos that they obviously lacked at home. But the box didn't seem to contain sexual energy or any other kind of energy. There are all sorts of hoaxes as far as sexual energy is concerned." He added, "There's a sucker born every minute."[37]

By the time the FDA was conducting its clinical trials of the orgone energy accumulator, Reich had ceased using one himself. In fact, A. S. Neill once admitted that he never actually saw Reich use an accumulator when he stayed at Orgonon, though he admitted that Reich might have been one of those "German five a.m." early risers who used the box first thing. "He did use it," Ilse Ollendorff told me. "Not in the last few years, but he did use it."[38]

When Bernard Grad, a biologist at McGill University in Montreal, visited Orgonon in April 1951, he found that everyone had developed an aversion to the accumulator after Oranur and all the contaminated devices at Orgonon had been removed from the Student Laboratory and placed two hundred yards away in the woods. When Simeon Tropp took Grad to see them, he felt giddy and faint when standing near them. "I seemed to lose contact for a moment," Grad said of their effect on him. He approached them again and "I almost keeled over." These effects were contagious, Grad believed; his own accumulator became contaminated, and he could bear sitting in it for only a few minutes: "I was irradiated and I felt a bit remote from people and things for a couple of weeks."[39]

Baker described Orgonon as under a cloud after Oranur, a "constant, heavy, dark mass." Perhaps this cloud reflected Reich's heightened emotional state.[40] After Oranur, Reich came to believe that atomic explosions and tests had disturbed the orgone energy envelope around the earth and that DOR (deadly orgone) now floated around the atmosphere like a huge flotilla of airborne cancers. Baker wrote of his own first sighting of one of these billowing horsemen of the apocalypse:

> It was an appalling sight, a dark cloud reaching clear to the ground. It was transparent but seemed like a mass of black specks. As it approached, the birds and insects became quiet, the leaves stopped their rustle and turned upside down. The sun could be seen, but it appeared that we were in shadow. Reich had us all crawl under pine trees which he said absorbed DOR and would protect us to some extent. We all developed headaches, a strong thirst, and a dusky skin. After half an hour, the cloud passed, and the world again became alive. The birds and insects became active, the leaves regained their luster, and the sun once more was bright. The shadow had gone. We soon recovered from our DOR effects.[41]

In response to the "DOR emergency," as Reich called it, the orgone box, his original "influencing machine," began to develop and sprout new features. Reich planned to transform the accumulator into a more complicated, mad, and intricate device with which he could do battle with the ominous DOR clouds he watched looming over the hills of Orgonon.

The first of these devices, a Duchamp-like construction, was built for him by Tom Ross, Reich's caretaker at Orgonon, who had also built accumulators for him. It had a wooden turret and rows of pipes that could be spun around with a revolving system made from several recycled bicycle wheels. Reich now thought that DOR was attracted to water, and his machine worked like a lightning rod to ground DOR as if it were electricity. Ross's prototype had a double row of five fifteen-foot-long aluminum pipes, which were connected by cables to water so as to draw off the DOR in the atmosphere and purify it. In 1940, when he had "discovered" orgone energy, Reich had directed his orgonoscope, a hollow tube, at Mooselookmeguntic Lake. He felt, like King Canute, that he was able to move the waves by pointing it.

The "cloudbuster," as it was dubbed, looked like an antiaircraft gun. Reich thought that when he pointed the battery of aluminum pipes at the sky, he was able to draw off the polluting DOR by moving his machine in a circular motion. After an hour or so of his massaging a black cloud in this way, it seemed, miraculously, to dissipate. Whereas Reich invented the accumulator to dissolve stagnant repressions in the body, this larger device was designed to get blocked orgone energy flowing in the atmosphere itself. Tom Ross once said that he was sure the cloudbuster worked, but that no one except Reich really knew how to work it.

The existence of DOR conveniently explained why the accumulator was not always effective: recent atomic energy explosions caused a dissipation of the orgone energy in the atmosphere, which made the accumulator less powerful and even reversed its effects, Reich theorized. Reich arranged for all accumulator users to be sent a new instruction sheet advising them to adapt their boxes by grounding the devices in water with cables so as to draw off dangerous DOR. Reich also had miniature models of the cloudbuster built that were the size of his shooter boxes. They looked like old-fashioned cameras with multiple lenses, but instead of a curtain at the back they had a cluster of hosepipes that were grounded in a bucket or sink. Reich taught his physicians how to use the cloudbuster in therapy to draw out the polluting DOR from the bodies of their patients as if it were some kind of psychoanalytic vacuum cleaner.

In May 1953, Baker, Duvall, and Raphael flew to Maine so that Reich could demonstrate his cloudbuster to them (Reich had had two more devices built in Portland) . "During the operation," Baker reported,

> the gravitational pull around the cloudbuster and for some distance away seemed to increase markedly, making it actually difficult to pick up one's feet from the ground. The atmosphere around the cloudbuster was highly charged, and, in a few minutes, our lips became blue and parched, our mouths dry. Soon our faces were blue, and we became dizzy and unsteady. We kept wet cloths on our faces. Smoke appeared to be gushing from the ends of the ten pipes. Reich said it looked like an anti-aircraft gun during firing. Whether the smoke-like material was being sucked into the pipes or being emitted from them I could not be sure.
>
> It was all very impressive and made us aware again of the tremendous forces at work, forces with which we had become familiar since the beginning of the Oranur experiment. We who have been through this experiment know how real and actually terrifying it all was and how frustrating to meet scoffers who belittle Reich's work and call him insane.[42]

Reich assumed the mythic status of rainmaker and felt that he could not only redirect storms but also summon them up. He offered to break the drought for a local blueberry farmer for the sum of one hundred dollars. According to Peter Reich, it rained.

On February 10, 1954, at the FDA's request, a twenty-seven-page complaint for injunction was filed against Wilhelm Reich, Ilse Ollendorff, and the Wilhelm Reich Foundation. Extensive tests, the report stated, had proved that orgone energy was nonexistent, and therefore the accumulators were "misbranded under the Food, Drug and Cosmetic Act because of false and misleading claims."[43] The FDA estimated that more than a thousand accumulators, shooter boxes, orgone energy blankets, and orgone energy funnels had been sold or rented, at costs of between $15 and $225. All Reich's publications, including the celebrated *Character Analysis* and *The Sexual Revolution*, were deemed part of a fraudulent "promotion of cures" to advertise accumulators, as the publications made frequent reference to this energy the FDA considered to be spurious.

Reich apparently went into shock for three days after a federal marshal delivered a copy of the complaint. He politely offered the marshal a drink, but Ollendorff claimed that she bore the brunt of his later anger: "Reich directed his whole fury against the outside world at me." He once hit her so hard he perforated an eardrum; she left Orgonon in August 1954.[44] The complaint was a devastating indictment of his life's work. To add insult to injury, it was signed by Peter Mills, Reich's lawyer in the late forties and early fifties, who had become U.S. attorney for the state of Maine in 1953.

Eventually Reich consulted a local lawyer, who suggested that he agree to stop selling orgone products, which he thought would then allow Reich to continue selling his literature. However, Reich refused to do this: "The moment we start to bargain . . . we would stamp the accumulator as fraud. It is not a fraud. Therefore we can not agree to any bargaining."[45]

Reich refused to cooperate with the courts, and instead of appearing for trial he sent a "Response," which stated: "It is not permissible, either morally, legally, or factually to force a natural scientist to expose his scientific results and methods of basic research in court." Reich hinted at the great power of the secrets he harbored. "Such disclosure," he wrote enigmatically, "would involve untold complications and possible national disaster."[46] It was interpreted as a "crank letter" and not treated as evidence.

There was no contest to the injunction because Reich, too proud to expose himself to ridicule in defending his discovery, failed to show up in court, so the FDA won its case by default. The judge decreed that all rented accumulators were to be recalled and destroyed and all paperback editions of Reich's literature was to be burned. Reich's more expensive hardbound books were not to be sold until the portions containing curative claims were deleted. Since Reich referred to orgone energy on almost every page of many of these volumes, this would have not only been costly but would have rendered the texts meaningless. The defendants, the judge ordered, were "perpetually enjoined and restrained from . . . making statements and representations pertaining to the existence of orgone energy."[47]

On March 19, 1954, FDA commissioner Charles Crawford sent letters to many official bodies—including the American Psychoanalytic Association, the American Psychiatric Association, and the American Medical Association—bragging over this easily won victory:

> Dr. Reich has long contended that only the hopelessly ignorant could disagree with his theories or doubt his miraculous cures with orgone energy accumulators. Repeated challenges were issued in literature, widely distributed by the Wilhelm Reich Foundation, daring medical physicists to test accumulators adequately. FDA accepted the challenge and has concluded that there is no such energy as orgone and that Orgone Energy Accumulator devices are worthless in the treatment of any disease or disease condition of man.
>
> Irreparable harm may result to persons who abandon or postpone rational medical treatment while pinning their faith on worthless devices such as these.[48]

In response, Reich fired off telegrams to the president, J. Edgar Hoover, and members of the press. "Established knowledge," he wrote, "must have no authority ever to decide what is NEW knowledge." Reich threatened to prove the existence of orgone energy by summoning up violent storms with his cloudbuster: "According to the Federal Food and Drug Administration, Orgone Energy does not exist. We are drawing east to west from Hancock, Maine, and Orgonon, Rangeley, Maine, to cause [a] storm to prove that orgone energy does exist . . . We are flooding the East as you are drying [in] the Southwest. You do not play with serious natural-scientific research."[49]

In March 1954, a seventy-ton hydrogen bomb was dropped on Bikini Atoll, unleashing the power of 1,200 atomic bombs when it vaporized the small island in the Pacific. The weapon, the Nobel Prize–winning physicist Arthur Crompton warned, threatened to draw the final curtain on humanity. One of the men who worked on the super, as the bomb was referred to, nicknamed it Campbell's—it promised to turn the planet to soup.

Reich was too caught up in his own private battles to take much notice, yet he might have registered the event. The slight to his ego that the FDA injunction represented caused him to retreat even further into a world of fantasy, which reflected in distorted ways the anxieties about the current political situation. Reich became convinced that creatures from outer space were attacking the earth, riding their spaceships, which were powered by orgone energy, on the "OR energy streams of the Universe." He thought that the exhaust, or "offal," from these machines was the black powdery substance he had seen around Orgonon, and which he referred to as melanor, or black-DOR, and that the spacemen were deliberately scattering it over the earth to render the planet dead and barren. Reich believed they were turning America into a wasteland, and he used his cloud-buster to combat them—in this fashion, he was dealing with the "planetary emergency" in his uniquely engaged way, re-creating his earthly struggles with the FDA on a cosmic scale. He wrote to Neill in August 1954, "I am far off in space as it were."[50]

Reich peppered the air force with letters detailing his weather control and UFO-busting discoveries. He was not the only person who believed in UFOs at that time: numerous sightings prompted a Pentagon press conference in 1952 and then an air force investigation, known as Project Blue Book. At the end of 1953 Reich read several books about flying saucers, including Donald Keyhoe's *The Flying Saucers Are Real* (1950). Keyhoe thought that the UFOs had been summoned by the atomic explosions; he reported that their "observation suddenly increased in 1947, following the series of bomb explosions in 1945."[51] After the explosion of the H-bomb there was an even bigger smoke signal to attract them.

UFOs seemed to account for all the loose ends of everything Reich had discovered; now anything that he could not explain was attributed to spacemen, even his German shepherd dog's mysteriously broken hind leg. It seemed that the visitors from outer space knew all the orgonomic secrets of the universe that he did, and therefore only he had the knowledge to match and outwit them.

Every new and curious phenomenon was incorporated into Reich's elastic orgonomic scheme of things. "Things were fitting well, even too neatly for my taste," he wrote in his posthumously published report on UFOs, *Contact with Space* (1957). "Therefore I hesitated to tell anything to anyone about them."[52]

Reich wanted to explain UFOs on an orgonomic basis, much as Carl Jung, who was also then much preoccupied with flying saucers, sought to explain them in terms of psychic projection. "At a time when the world is divided by an iron curtain," Jung wrote in 1958 after a decade of research into flying saucers, "we might expect all sorts of funny things, since when such a thing happens in an individual it means a complete dissociation, which is instantly compensated [for] by symbols of wholeness and unity."[53] Reich in his bipolar states suffered just such a split, and indeed his whole oceanic theory of orgone energy might be interpreted in that light. Some nights he would spot three or four Eas (energy alphas, as he called UFOs) hovering in the sky above Orgonon. They would leave the atmosphere heavy and black, but by mobilizing the cloudbuster Reich was able to clear the air and make the sky blue again.

As fact and fiction blurred, Reich's work took on the apocalyptic urgency of a science fiction film. Robert Wise's *The Day the Earth Stood Still* (1951) was a particularly important influence. The film tells the story of a humanoid extraterrestrial, Klaatu, who lands his spacecraft in Washington, bringing the message that something drastic needs to be done to stop impending nuclear catastrophe. In the film, the army, quick to violence in the face of the unknown, shoots and wounds the spaceman. The alien nevertheless manages to visit a famous scientist and to convince him, by completing a previously unsolved mathematical problem, to listen to his doom-laden message. After a feature-length manhunt, the military finally kills him, but Klaatu is resurrected in the spacecraft, which is powered by atomic energy, and delivers a final warning: he tells the scientists of the world, whom he has called together for an emergency briefing, that earth can either decide to abandon warfare and join other peaceful space-faring nations or it will be destroyed as a dangerous threat.

The film captured Reich's sense of alienation and he empathized with Klaatu, the gaunt but well-spoken alien peacemaker. "I had the distinct impression," he wrote, "that it was a bit of my story which was depicted there; even the actor's expression and looks reminded me and others of myself as I had appeared 15 to 20 years ago."[54] He felt that he was similarly hunted, and that no one—not even Einstein—heeded his warnings of a similarly dangerous threat, sexual repression, which only he had the knowledge and means to combat.

On December 14, 1954, Dr. Silvert traveled to Arizona from Orgonon in a chartered plane, bringing as his special cargo a one-milligram vial of "orur"—previously radioactive material from the Oranur experiment that had been buried in an iron safe for three years. The safe apparently acted like an accumulator; secreted there, the concentrated orgone energy supposedly worked to neutralize the nuclear radiation in just the way that Reich had anticipated it would when he set out on his fateful experiment. Reich used the orur to excite and bolster the cloudbuster, harnessing it to the device to increase its potency. The lead vial containing the radium was placed in a leather pouch and dangled, like testicles, from the base of the guns.

Silvert was delivering the orur to Arizona so that Reich could turn the cloudbuster into a powerful space gun with which to fight the aliens that he felt were attacking and destroying the earth. The orur was thought to be so potent that it was secured in an eight-inch-long tear-shape container and towed behind the aircraft on a 150-foot nylon line. When the plane landed the powerful load was reeled in, but because it was deemed so dangerous, it was never allowed closer than five feet to the plane, so was left to bounce and drag along the airstrip. Silvert, who took Paki Wright along for the ride, insisted that it be guarded at all times during the several refueling stops, and he monitored the pilots with a Geiger-Müller counter to see if they had been contaminated with radioactivity. When they got to Arizona he insisted they all take a Reich Blood Test.

Reich had established a base in a small rented house just outside Tucson, which he renamed Little Orgonon. His coworkers were now mainly family: Peter; Eva; his son-in-law, Bill Moise, an artist who had been an antiaircraft gunner during the war; and Robert McCullough, a biologist who worked at the University of New Hampshire when he first met Reich in 1953. Reich and Eva had driven the long distance down to Arizona in his brand-new white Chrysler convertible, and McCullough, Moise, and Peter drove down in Chevy trucks with two cloudbusters. They hoped to use the machines to attack UFOs and to clean up the DOR with which Reich thought these alien craft were deliberately polluting the desert. The operation was termed grandiosely OROP Desert (Orgone Energy Operation in the Desert), and the trucks that carried the cloudbusters had spinning wave logos emblazoned down the side to represent the cosmic waves Reich thought the spaceships rode on.

Peter Reich's memoir, *A Book of Dreams* (1973), tells the story of his eccentric upbringing as seen through a child's eyes. In Arizona he was a ten-year-old sergeant in Reich's "Corps of Cosmic Engineers," with red crayon stripes to prove it drawn on the pith helmet with which his father equipped all the operators of the cloudbuster. Peter would sit up at night alongside his father with a telescope and binoculars, on the lookout for UFOs, which were visible to them as "silvery disks" and "yellow pulsations." They saw one pulsating, speeding, red and green blob with such frequency that they christened it the Southern Belle.

Once a sighting had been made, they would rush to the cloudbuster to unplug the aluminum tubes and extend the pipes out like a telescope until they reached some fifteen feet. They would then chase the UFO across the night sky, cranking the wheels of the device to spin the turret around and to raise and lower the guns, until they managed to sap the flying saucer of energy. The UFOs began to blink erratically, to fade, sometimes to disappear completely, Peter later reported. Reich claimed to have shot down several UFOs in this manner. It was almost as if Reich and his group felt they were the last line of defense between America and the universe.

Reich first used the cloudbuster this way on May 12, 1954. Reich wrote in *Contact with Space* (1957):

Easy contact was made on that fateful day with what obviously turned out to be a heretofore unknown type of UFO. I had hesitated for weeks to turn my cloudbuster pipes toward a "star," as if I had known that some of the blinking lights hanging in the sky were not planets or fixed stars but SPACE machines. With the fading out of the two "stars," the cloudbuster had suddenly changed into a SPACEGUN . . . What had been left of the old world of human knowledge after the discovery of the OR energy (1936–40) tumbled beyond reprieve. Nothing could any longer be considered "impossible." I had directed [the] drawpipes, connected with the deep well toward an ordinary star, and the star had faded out four times.[55]

In Arizona they fought what Reich described as a heroic "full-scale interplanetary battle." (Reich had seen *War of the Worlds* earlier that year.)[56] This was so intense, Peter described in his memoir, that it required two cloudbusters, and he includes childhood sketches showing how they were mobilized. Reich acted like a military general, deploying them in strategic places, and the two gunners communicated with each other using whistles: one blast for north, three long blasts for west, three short ones for east, four for south, and two for "zenith," which meant guns straight up.

A huge black-purple mushroom cloud "looking like smoke from a huge fire" formed over Little Orgonon, which had an angry reddish glow. Reich's Geiger counter apparently went crazy, and the team "suffered from nausea, quivering, pain in the upper abdomen and discoloration of movements"; in one "battle" McCullough was apparently temporarily paralyzed on his right side.[57] It took an hour of furious work to clear the cloud, and when this had been done two B-52 bombers flew low over Little Orgonon, which Reich thought was an overflight intended to salute their good work.

I met Peter Reich for Sunday lunch at his home in Massachusetts, two hours outside of Boston. He works as assistant to the dean of the Harvard Medical School—an unlikely job for someone whose father devoted the last two decades of his life to battling the "pharmaceutical interest." Peter said, "I've spent sixteen years working for the enemy."

"What my kids don't understand," Peter told me as we sat in deck chairs in his garden, "was that people in Reich and my mother's generation really believed in a better world. It was probably going to look like a Socialist world. It wasn't going to be Communist, it wasn't going to be fascist. It was fair and honorable, and sexuality would be part of that better world. There was a vibrancy and a hope. But that better world didn't make it and people today don't know about that."

When I asked him to describe his father's obvious charisma, Peter Reich invoked movies. "When *Star Wars* came out and I saw the scene where Obi-Wan Kenobi tells Luke Skywalker about the Force, I really felt kind of ripped off. And that is the best description. He had that presence that Obi-Wan Kenobi projected and that same belief in that same force." To understand Reich, Peter told me, you had to understand how he modeled his life on the films he saw.

"He thought these movies were about him, and maybe they were, you see. It's hard to know where the circle starts. For example, *High Noon*, he was *really* into *High Noon*, and *Bad Day at Black Rock*. And this is why he wore a cowboy hat: he was Gary Cooper. And when the FDA came up to see him at Orgonon, he was just like Spencer Tracy. He'd say, 'Listen, mister'—he used that language. That was really part of his American persona, the movie person. He didn't make a distinction between that and real life.

"He could put his hands on you, and he was a healer, he really was. And I think he felt that he could heal the world, because these cloudbusters really seemed to work. So he really felt like he was in control of everything. And he didn't understand why other people didn't see that. He shared the moral certainty that Gary Cooper had in *High Noon* and Spencer Tracy had in *Bad Day at Black Rock*, and that Sir Thomas More had in *A Man for All Seasons*."[58]

I imagine Reich as the Burt Lancaster character in *The Rainmaker*, a naïve showman and energetic charlatan who charms a sexless old maid and then actually drums up a storm. The very idea of orgone energy might be seen as cinematic: in *The Blue Light* (*Das Blaue Licht* [1932]), a feral Leni Riefenstahl is the guardian of a high-altitude cavern that glows an ethereal blue during full moons and lures men to their deaths in the mountains.

I put it to Peter Reich that in every biography of Reich there seems to be a cutoff point, an eye-rolling threshold after which the biographer considers Reich to be mad. For the psychoanalysts it was Lucerne; for others it was one of his odd inventions, be it the orgone box, the cloudbuster, or the space gun. Even among his devotees, only a very few managed to follow him until the end. A. S. Neill, Reich's faithful friend since the 1930s, was exasperated when he received a copy of Reich's new journal, *CORE* (Cosmic Orgone Engineering), which described the "cloudbusting" experiments: "If I had never heard of Reich and had read *CORE* for the first time," he wrote to Reich in January 1955, "I would have concluded that the author was either meschugge [mad] or the greatest discoverer in centuries. Since I know you aren't meschugge I have to accept the alternative. I can't follow you . . . is there anyone who can?"[59]

Peter Reich replied: "Okay, I was on that operation when the blueberry growers paid Reich to make rain in '54, and it started to rain. I just couldn't believe it. Another time, this hurricane was heading right towards us and all of a sudden it veered off. You know, I participated in a lot of things that I think really happened. And I don't know what to make of them. I remember in Arizona, he'd bought his telescope and he was seeing these flying saucers, and I remember looking through the telescope and I didn't see the thin cigar shape with the little windows [this is how Reich described a UFO to him]. I remember thinking to myself, *Well, I don't know.* That's where I drew the line, I think, and that was as a ten-year-old boy. But I made it rain, I made the wind come up. I don't know, I just really don't know.

"He was a nineteenth-century scientist, he wasn't a twentieth-century scientist. He didn't practice science the way scientists do today. He was a nineteenth-century mind who came crashing into twentieth-century America. And boom! The FDA was hot to get a prosecution and he walked right into it. He was sending telegrams to the president of the United States, saying that he was stopping hurricanes and claiming that the FDA were Communists. He walked right into it, with his eyes wide open."

When *A Book of Dreams* came out in 1973, Peter Reich was criticized for not being able to state clearly whether he now believed in orgone energy or not, though it is precisely this irresolution that makes the book such a compelling read. In 1988, in a preface to a new edition of the book, Peter Reich wrote: "The forty-four-year-old husband and father is a private person to whom this all happened a long time ago. He waits, he watches. A critic once said that Wilhelm Reich had grabbed truth by more than its tail. How much more? Does anybody know? Does Orgone Energy exist? So, yes, the son is still hedging."[60] Almost twenty years later he is still equivocating; his is an ambivalent, complicated relationship to his father's ideas and inventions. "Perhaps it is the easy way out," Peter Reich speculated in his book. "Keeping one foot in the dream—but it is deeper than that. My childhood is the dream."[61]

"You know, he was like Obi-Wan Kenobi," he repeated. "He was all there, all the time. He would get drunk—he did have a bad drinking problem. And he beat my mother up. But it's funny, that doesn't detract in my mind. He would get drunk because he was so lonely. One by one [his friends] got to the eye-rolling point. They kept peeling off. At a certain point I just think he started spiraling and he knew that it couldn't go on anymore. [The Yugoslav filmmaker Dušan] Makavejev said that everybody has a blind spot when it comes to Reich, and I think that's true. But where does that blind spot begin?"

In 1956 Peter Reich spent the summer at Summerhill. When a military plane flew overhead he told Neill that it had been sent to protect him against his father's enemies. Neill told Peter that this was nonsense—the planes weren't his guardian angels but were passing overhead because there was a large U.S. atom bomb base several miles from Summerhill. When Reich heard of Neill's response, he told his inner circle that Neill was "unreliable" and was not to be trusted. "I was genuinely concerned about Peter and his fears of overhead planes," Neill protested to Reich when he heard he'd been blacklisted. "And his grown-upness which is not real, for he wants to be childish and play a lot of the time . . . He looks too anxious. I think he is trying to live a part . . . 'I am the only one who understands what Daddy is doing.' He may understand but his emotions are all mixed up. He isn't Peter Reich; he is Peter Reich plus Wilhelm Reich. And, dear old friend, call this emotional plague or what you will. To me it is just plain truth." After wishing Reich luck, Neill signed off, "Goodbye Reich, and God bless you."[62]

"And what if he did go mad?" Neill wrote in 1971. "Often [Reich] said that our asylums are full of people who aren't mad enough to live in our sick civilization . . . It is an odd world if Reich were mad and the politicians and the Pentagon and the color-haters are sane."[63]

Peter took me to a shed crammed full of bicycles, tools, and discarded car batteries. In the back of the shed, accessible via a path cleared through all the bric-a-brac, was an orgone energy accumulator. There was a blue chair inside it with a cushion on the seat. "This is like the first ones ever made," Peter said proudly, "like the one Eva is sitting in in the accumulator booklet, where she's pictured with a black band over her eyes. This is the real McCoy! Hop in." When I was shut inside the device he instructed me, "Breathe deeply, Chris, breathe deeply!"

On top of the box I noticed that someone had stowed an old multicolor hobbyhorse that looked as though it had been fashioned from driftwood. It struck me as an apt crown for Reich's machine—Freud had called Reich's orgasm theory his hobbyhorse.

I imagined how Peter must feel when he sits in his father's contraption, the device that caused his downfall. In his book, Peter wrote of all the emotions that bubbled back to the surface when he revisited Orgonon in the mid-sixties, the first time he'd been there since his father's funeral: "His father's world was still locked away inside of him; he was a kind of young soldier, guarding a mystery that nobody seemed to understand."[64] Perhaps, for Peter, sitting in the orgone accumulator was as close as he could get to such a vault. Perhaps it functioned as a sort of crypt. Sitting in there, surrounded by swirls of orgone energy, might be a bit like having his dad's comforting arms wrapped around him.

The FDA had a representative from its Los Angeles office visit Reich's property in Arizona at the end of 1954. They wanted to see whether he had transferred operations there and was still building accumulators in violation of the injunction. Reich, absorbed with the idea of a red fascist threat, refused to grant them permission to inspect the property. He suspected the FDA official was a spy, interested in finding out about the mysterious properties of the orur Silvert had brought down from Maine (Reich told the marshal that FDA agents were more like Russians than Americans). He wrote in *Contact with Space*, "The attack by the food and drug agents upon orgonomy was no more than an expresson of terror of the Cosmic Energy on the part of sick men. It, therefore, 'did not exist'; its discoverer was to this view either a 'quack' or a 'lunatic.'"[65]

Reich believed the injunction was unconstitutional—a mere "nuisance"—and wrote to Neill: "We have won the case against the FDA factually," sure that it would be overturned on appeal.[66] If it did stand, he thought, it would cut off only one strand of his research (albeit one that now brought in three thousand dollars a month) and free him to concentrate on his cloudbusting and "cosmic engineering" work.

No accumulators were being made in Arizona. But Reich, as the FDA was soon to find out, had not recalled any of the devices already on hire and was still collecting rental payments. Letters to users informing them that the device had been banned had been printed but were never sent. In his absence, Reich put Silvert in charge of affairs at Orgonon and the financial operations of the Wilhelm Reich Foundation, and Silvert continued to send bills to users of the boxes on Reich's behalf. These were now stamped on the bottom, "Make checks payable to ORUP DESERT and send to Orgone Institute Research Labs, Inc., 50 Grove Street, New York 14, N.Y." (This was Silvert's New York address.)

In early June 1955, after Reich got back from his desert trip, two FDA inspectors came to Rangeley to see whether Reich was complying with the terms set out in the decree. They traveled with a deputy marshal to protect them because Reich was known to carry firearms. The marshal went in to announce their arrival but Reich refused to see them, though he made a brief appearance on the observatory balcony to vent some spleen. The deputy marshal later told the U.S. attorney Peter Mills that he had been left with the impression from this brief encounter that "Reich was a madman." The FDA noted that Mills had "indicated that the court would not be too happy about having a madman in his court and we might have some difficulty in fostering contempt of court procedures against Reich."[67]

The next day the FDA officers sought out Tom Ross, who, despite having received a telegram from Reich instructing him not to cooperate with "FDA PHARMACEUTICAL MOSCOW AGENTS," agreed to be interviewed. He told them that the previous winter Silvert had picked up all of Reich's remaining banned literature and accumulator panels (enough, he thought, for one hundred boxes) and had driven them in a truck to New York. According to an affadavit Ross later gave, when he asked Silvert whether this action was legal, Silvert said that "consulting an attorney was like seeing a doctor—you ask his advice, and then you do what you think is best, whether or not it agrees with what he said." Whether Silvert acted with or without Reich's knowledge was later a subject of much debate. "I would say he didn't complain," Ross said when asked if Reich had been angry on hearing the news. "He said, 'I wonder if it was wise,' or something to that effect."[68] Reich certainly accepted the profits that Silvert passed on to him.

The FDA, with minimal detective work, soon came up with an inventory of everything that Silvert had tried to salvage: 4 bundles of wooden cabinets knocked down; 1 cabinet assembled; 361 loose panels; 338 cartons of books or literature. They also tracked down and visited a user who had written to Silvert asking where he should return his accumulator. Silvert instructed him to return it not to Rangeley, where it was supposed to be destroyed, but to Mr. Tom Mangravite at 25 West Third Street in Manhattan.

They began surveillance of Silvert's apartment in New York and Mangravite's loft. Inspectors were able to see piles of accumulator panels through Mangravite's windows and observed cars arriving and collecting accumulators. The FDA notes take on the air of a noir film: "While the premises were kept under surveillance, nocturnal activity in the traffic of orgone accumulators was observed. A resident of the neighborhood told an inspector that the windows are covered by blankets when there is activity in the building at night."[69] Inspector Irving Feldman tailed a Chevrolet that had been picking up panels, but lost the car when it raced through two red lights.

On July 13, at 5:15 p.m., Inspector F. P. Hamill, posing as a patient of Elsworth Baker, walked toward Mangravite's building. As he passed a colleague who was on surveillance in a nearby doorway, he switched on the "Midget Radio Transmitter" he carried in his pocket. He rang the doorbell, and when Hamill entered the dark hallway he could see a young man waiting for him at the top of a stairs. He estimated that Tom Mangravite was about twenty-six; he was approximately five feet ten inches, with black hair. Mangravite was a sculptor and an electromechanical designer for Bell Laboratories, where he worked on the invention of the first mechanical ten-digit telephone. He also did cabinetwork and carpentry on the side, which is where the accumulators came in. According to the straitlaced and besuited inspector, who insisted on describing Mangravite in his report as a "businessman," Mangravite "was attired in rather odd clothes, a white shirt and light brown pants. He seemed a little bit nervous."[70] They entered a basic carpentry workshop, where there was a "cache" of accumulator panels from Rangeley; Hamill estimated there were enough for sixty or seventy devices.

The undercover inspector told Mangravite that he'd bought an accumulator several years ago from the Wilhelm Reich Foundation but hadn't used it for some time. Recently he'd received a note from Dr. Silvert suggesting that he might want to improve his accumulator by adding some cables and he wanted to try these adaptations to treat some trouble he was having with sinusitis, a stiff neck, and a deaf left ear. Mangravite explained that the cables should be drilled through the walls of the box and placed in running water or, if that wasn't possible, simply a bucket, so that the accumulator could be "grounded" to draw off some of the deadly orgone energy (DOR) that might otherwise build up in the accumulator.

The FDA inspector had Mangravite mail him the cable he'd come to buy, so that Mangravite could be shown to have broken the law barring Reich from trading in orgone paraphernalia across state lines. Hamill said the cable wouldn't fit in his pocket, which Mangravite thought was odd, as he was wearing a bulky topcoat (to hide his recording device), even though it was June. The first time Mangravite knew that he'd been tricked was when the cable and its packaging appeared as evidence in the criminal trial in which he now found himself involved.

At 2:15 p.m. the next day different FDA officers arrived with an inspector from the New York City Department of Health to make an official inspection.

I met Tom Mangravite in his offices at New York University, where he teaches camerawork in the film program. A slight eighty-year-old man with sunken eyes, neatly parted white hair, and a gray mustache, Mangravite was wearing beige trousers and a white shirt— exactly the same wardrobe that the undercover FDA officer had described as strange: "I was a sculptor and a painter!" Mangravite replied incredulously when I pointed this out. "I was probably wearing khakis and a white shirt. That's my getup attire!

"These guys were completely square, I guess," he continued. "The FDA guy who came down to my studio on a Saturday morning—he was an odd man. He told me that Dr. Baker had sent him to see me. He was thin, he was gray, he was pinched. And it shocked me. I thought, *What the hell kind of a therapist is Baker if this guy's one of his patients*, because the man had nothing in his eyes. I still remember the feeling I had. He was just a complete drain. Apparently the FDA had rented a factory space and were watching my studio from across the street. What a waste of money. I also had a roof space, and they reported on the breast size of one of the young ladies I was sunbathing with . . . I think if there wasn't a sexual element to orgonomy, Reich would have been left alone. They figured that this group, with all the sexual freedom stuff, had to be a bad thing."[71]

Mangravite lived in Greenwich Village, moved in bohemian circles, and had read a few of Reich's books. When he suffered depression after separating from his first wife, a Reichian friend referred him to Silvert. Silvert's small treatment room-cum-studio in the neighborhood was furnished with a single bed that served as the couch. Mangravite had the impression that he lived as well as worked there. "You were nude, a lot of deep breathing, pounding on pillows, and screaming" is how Mangravite described the therapy that followed. "The aim was to attain a full orgasm, where your body's completely in it and everything goes with it."

Mangravite described the "big aura" and "the godlike qualities" that were projected onto Reich by his followers, and I asked him whether he thought the Reichians formed a sort of cult. "There was a real cliquish flavor to it," he acknowledged. "The apostles, the therapists, they were really bowing at his feet; he was very much the leader. They made the assumption that Reich was as healthy as he claimed he wanted other people to be, that he had accomplished it [orgastic potency], so it's a surprise when you read all these books, like his son's, saying that Reich never took a shower nude, that he always took a shower in his underpants. He had foibles. But obviously he was a genius, there's no question about that."

The physicians were a very formal lot who always referred to each other by their surnames, which Mangravite found very strange at first. But this formality was only a façade. "Everyone was very sexually active," Mangravite revealed. "There was a lot of free love involved. Casual encounters went all the way from, you know, 'Let's fuck,' to getting to know each other and having three or four relationships going at one time." Having read Ilse Ollendorff's memoir of her time with Reich, Mangravite concluded, "Reich was obviously screwing anyone he wanted, though he was married—she was very nice about it."

Mangravite characterized Silvert as a "very rigid" apostle: "He was trying to out-Reich Reich; any little thing Reich said, he'd jump on." Reich was "on his own little mountaintop up there" in Maine, and his version of Reich was seen through his therapist's eyes. "Every time [Reich] made a new discovery it became the law, as passed down through the therapists to the patients, and it all got digested and regurgitated in different ways. Everything was filtered and twisted by Silvert."

Silvert soon had Mangravite using an accumulator as an adjunct to therapy. Mangravite told me that he experienced a "sensation of warmth and pleasure" sitting in his device, and found that it quickly cleared up headaches and other small ailments. He was curious enough to repeat some of Reich's other experiments, and he kept a log of the temperature difference before and after he used the box. He custom-made forty or fifty devices, including some child-sized ones for the nursery run by Paki Wright's mother, over which he took particular care: "Some of the ladies wanted special colors and what not." Silvert sold Mangravite's carefully constructed creations for four hundred dollars, four times what he paid Mangravite to build them.

Mangravite also constructed a cloudbuster and he prided himself on his version's being more scientifically accurate than the more primitive devices Reich used. He added a "protractor-type thing," so that as you tilted it you could tell what angle it was pointed at and were therefore able to keep more accurate records. Mangravite and Silvert did weather work in New York: "We had a cloudbuster mounted on a truck near Canal Street," Mangravite recalled of the eight-wheeler and its strange load, "and we'd go out, myself and Silvert, at four or five in the morning, and in the evening, to work on the weather experiments. We'd go down to the piers on the Lower East Side, and to ground the thing we'd throw the cables into the river water." They did this every day for two years. Mangravite claims that they were able to clear up the DOR that accumulated over Manhattan's skyscrapers with the device.

A month after his return to Orgonon from his desert expedition, Reich was charged with contempt of the injunction. The FDA lawyers argued that he had violated the terms of the court order by failing to recall and destroy accumulators and literature, in refusing the FDA permission to inspect his property in Arizona and at Orgonon, and in shipping accumulator parts from Rangeley to New York, where they continued to be sold. Reich was asked to appear in court the following month "to show cause why legal proceedings shouldn't be initiated" against him.

On June 9, 1954, McCarthy lost the fearful grip he'd held over the country during the earlier fifties. In the Army-McCarthy hearings, in which McCarthy was accused of exploiting his position to get special privileges for one of his assistants, who had been drafted, the army's lawyer, Joe Welch, struck the killing blow. The hearings were televised, and the coup de grâce was watched by many in the twenty million households that had TV sets at the time. McCarthy was clearly drunk—he kept a bottle of boubon in his briefcase and started drinking in the morning—and his inebriated, red-faced, bullying ugliness was plain for all to see.

When Welch challenged McCarthy to give the attorney general a list of the one hundred thirty Communists who, he claimed, worked in military defense plants, the senator tried to undermine him by pointing out that someone from his Boston law office was a former member of the National Lawyers Guild, which he accused of being "the legal bulwark of the Communist Party," and therefore a Communist. Welch, in defense of a member of his law firm, uttered his now legendary putdown: "Until this moment, Senator, I think I never really gauged your cruelty or your recklessness." When McCarthy continued his character assassination of the young man, who was fresh out of Harvard Law School and was in fact the secretary of the Young Republicans League and not a Communist, Welch famously exclaimed, "'Have you no sense of decency, sir, at long last? At long last, have you left no sense of decency?"[72]

"In one black second," reported *The Wisconsin State Journal*, the normally supportive newspaper in the senator's home state, "McCarthy . . . wrecked it all. He blew his angry head of steam and cast out an ugly smear on a young man who had no connection with the case. It was worse than reckless. It was worse than cruel. It was reprehensible."[73] The fledgling lawyer McCarthy had attacked was Fred Fisher. Welch told McCarthy that he feared that Fisher would always "bear a scar" needlessly inflicted by him. That December, the Senate voted to censure McCarthy by a two-thirds majority. His credibility was finished.

The following year Fred Fisher served as Reich's lawyer, appearing at the hearing in Maine in the prelude to Reich's trial for contempt of the injunction. Even though Reich hated Communists, or "red fascists," as he commonly called them, Fischer's McCarthy-inflicted "scar" would have been less a black mark to him than a badge of honor. Reich thought that McCarthy was inspired by the same red fascism as the FDA—Stalin, Reich wrote, was "the father of both the Hitlers and McCarthys"—and he never supported him.[74]

A. S. Neill thought it unlikely that Senator McCarthy was a "red fascist" and wondered whether McCarthy could investigate the FDA, as he had so many other institutions, to reveal the Communist plot against Reich. "HE IS!" Reich scrawled in the margin of the letter, certain in his assessment.[75] Peter Reich once compared his father to the senator from Wisconsin: both saw Communists everywhere, and Reich often seemed to engage in McCarthyite tactics by demanding that his lovers and colleagues sign endless confessional protocols. Reich objected to the comparison. He told his son that McCarthy offered no solutions to the world's problems, whereas he had "made a discovery with which to fight evil."[76]

Fisher traveled from Boston up to Reich's hearing in Portland, Maine. He argued that criminal charges against his client should be dropped because the injunction exceeded the powers of the court that had issued it. There was no way, Fisher said, that Reich could carry out the recall of accumulators and literature the injunction demanded of him. He advised Reich to plead not guilty.

Reich then took center stage to address the judge directly. He spoke for half an hour, trying to summon up all his old powers of oratory. He objected that his accumulators and books were now so far out into the world that it was impossible for him to stop the spreading of his ideas. He also complained that the box on show as a courtroom exhibit was an old, badly maintained device that the FDA had deliberately chosen to make him look a charlatan (it had been delivered to the court on April Fool's Day). Reich maintained that neither the FDA nor the judiciary had any authority to decide whether orgone energy existed or not—it was purely a scientific matter.

Reich's paranoia and delusions of grandeur were evident in his discussions of space travel and UFOs and in his allusions to his high-powered friends in government and to the top secret nature of his research. An effort was being made, he said, to steal his equations, which explained the workings of the universe. Reich concluded his talk with a description of the fate of Giordano Bruno, the alchemist who had been burned at the stake by the Inquisition because of his heretical scientific ideas. Hundreds of years later a pope had apologized at his tomb. He implied that he was a similar martyr to free thought, as history would prove.

"He bellowed and raged and at times was cautioned by both defense attorneys," wrote Joseph Maguire, who was representing the government in the case. "He talked about how humble he is. In the next breath [he] indicated that he was one of the greatest scientists of the time."[77]

On the journey back to Boston, Fisher told Myron Sharaf that he'd never witnessed a day in court like it. He maintained, again, that the only way he could keep Reich out of prison, and his writing in print, would be if Reich disassociated himself from the accumulator business. Reich refused to do this as a matter of principle, because that would mean accepting the FDA's characterization of the box as a fraudulent device. Fisher later resigned from the case when Reich, bolstered by his court appearance, insisted on his right to cross-examine witnesses alongside his attorney. When the motion to dismiss his case was denied, Reich subsequently acted as the "counsel for the discoverer of life energy," proposing to represent himself in the trial that was tentatively scheduled for that December.

# Twelve

In the early 1950s the United States produced half the world's goods and possessed two thirds of its machinery; the resulting prosperity and automation increased standards of living and swelled the middle class.[1] Sociologists such as David Riesman and C. Wright Mills began to worry less about poverty than about the conformist, suburban nature of the American dream and the corrupting and alienating results of affluence. The "new little men," wrote Mills in *White Collar: The American Middle Classes* (1951), were "cheerful robots" and "political eunuchs," cogs in a bureaucratic machine that they were powerless to change. In *The Lonely Crowd* (1950), Riesman painted a similar portrait of an apathetic, status-obsessed, socially anxious citizenry dominated by the "marketing mentality."

Advertisers honed methods to exploit these anxieties and feed the fifties' orgy of consumption. The sexual revolution was accompanied and intertwined with a marketing revolution that reflected the postwar surge in standards of living in America. Since 1940 America's gross national product had soared more than 400 percent, and the average citizen had five times as many discretionary dollars to spend on luxuries as in the previous decade. By the late 1950s, to compete for this spending power, corporations blew nearly $12 billion on advertising (up from $2 billion in 1939) and three-fourths of the

largest advertising companies used "depth techniques": in a crowded
marketplace, businesses came to rely on methods inspired by psychoanalysis to make their products more seductive to the masses,
co-opting Reich's message of sexual liberation in order to sell things.
If ego psychologists thought of the id as something to be tamed,
and radical analysts wanted to set it free, advertisers sought to exploit
its repressed forces to ignite customers' desires and make them buy
things that they didn't really need or even know they wanted. Just
as Reich was being prosecuted for "false labeling," libidos were being freed not to liberate people, as he hoped, but further to enmesh
them in the capitalist system.

In the United States, psychoanalysis had long had a fluid relationship with business and commerce. Indeed, you might say that
psychoanalysis first came to America coupled with its commercial
usage. Freud's Vienna-born American nephew, the publicist Edward Bernays—whose mother was Freud's sister, and whose father
was Freud's wife's brother—founded the country's first public relations firm in 1919, and consciously used Freud's idea of a latent but
powerful sexuality as a form of subliminal seduction to manipulate
the masses. Freud spent time with Bernays during his 1909 tour of
America and became fond of him, but Ernest Jones dismissed him
as "an American 'sharper' and quite unscrupulous."[2] Bernays was instrumental in the publication of American editions of Freud's writings, and he was always on the lookout for different ways that
psychoanalysis might be popularized and exploited for profit—for
example, he tried, unsuccessfully, to get his uncle to write a column
for *Cosmopolitan* magazine. During his stay Freud had been exposed
to, and amused by, the aggressive marketing that Bernays was to make
his own specialty. He saw an advertisement outside an undertaker's
shop that read, "Why live, when you can be buried for $10?"[3]

Bernays visited Freud after the First World War and proved a
quick study. He returned determined to adapt his uncle's ideas about
sex to the realm of American commerce, setting up a public relations office and creating campaigns that were designed to appeal
directly to the unconscious desires of consumers. In 1929 he employed the analyst A. A. Brill to come up with a sales strategy for the
American Tobacco Company aimed at recruiting female smokers.

Bernays boasted in his autobiography that this "may have been the first instance of [psychoanalysis's] application to advertising."[4] Brill advised casting cigarettes as "torches of freedom" in the battle for women's liberation, and Bernays staged a march of debutante smokers down Fifth Avenue to impress this idea on the public mind. It was the first of many such campaigns of mass suggestion. With his office on Wall Street, Bernays successfully bridged the old and new worlds of psychoanalysis. In 1933 *Life* magazine joked that he had "probably made more money out of applied psychoanalysis than all Vienna ever saw."[5]

By the mid-1950s the corporate hero of applied psychoanalysis was Ernest Dichter, a man who, like Reich, had fled Europe to escape the Nazis. He went on to turn the commercialization of dreams into a fine science. Indeed, Dichter was described as "the Freud of Madison Avenue," "one of the great mass psychoanalysts of our era," and "Mr. Mass Motivations Himself." Through his psycho-detective work, Dichter promised the "mobilization and manipulation of human needs as they exist in the consumer," or, put bluntly, the "translation of sex into sales." Dichter, who came up with the Esso slogan "Put a Tiger in Your Tank," has been credited with inventing focus groups, overdraft facilities for checking accounts, and the idea of placing sweets near supermarket checkouts.[6] In a 1956 article, "Put the Libido Back into Advertising," Dichter wrote, "Libido is a basic life force, a pulsating, virulent, invisible power which is the very stuff of our inner lives."[7]

Dichter was born in Vienna in 1907 to a working-class family who lived in an apartment across the street from Freud. His carrot-red hair, he later said, made him predestined to be a psychologist because it always made him feel like an outsider, concerned with what people thought of him. A decade younger than Reich, whom he never met, he was shaped by his childhood in Vienna in very different ways. His father was a "spectacularly unsuccessful salesman," he wrote in his memoir, *Getting Motivated* (1979), a traveling haberdasher and peddler of textiles for whom Dichter grew up to have little respect. He was sometimes unable to provide for the family, and during the severe shortages of post–World War One Vienna the family ate bread made of flour and sawdust. Sometimes they starved, Dichter recalled, "with nothing to eat for three days in a row." But where Reich turned to socialism and then communism in response to these experiences, Dichter became an enthusiastic capitalist.

At fourteen, to help support the family, Dichter left school and went to work for his uncle Leopold, who owned the Dichter Department Store on Brunnengasse. Dichter worked there as a secretary and then a window dresser and was soon the family's principal bread-winner. His uncle became a substitute father figure, and while his two younger brothers became militant Communists, Dichter became an advocate of conspicuous consumption. He read American maga-zines and imported U.S. sales techniques, such as piped-in music and kinetic displays, and enjoyed his first, hurried sexual experiences with "a dark-haired, somewhat cross-eyed girl" in the company's storerooms: "behind rows of kitchen utensils and sundry chinaware, glasses, and, around Christmas time, behind dolls and electric trains, waiting to be given a place in the visible shelves at the front of the store."[8] Sex and commodities were inextricably intertwined, in Dichter's view.

Dichter, who went on to study psychology at the University of Vienna under Charlotte and Karl Bühler, was trained as an analyst by an American studying in Vienna who treated him in return for German classes. He came to New York the year before Reich did, with only a hundred dollars to his name, and found an apartment in the Bronx, then known as the Fourth Reich because it was so full of European immigrants. His first job was as a market researcher. Un-impressed with the discipline's bland empiricism, the thirty-one-year-old Dichter wrote to six corporate giants to try to interest them in a psychoanalytic approach to marketing. "I am a young psycholo-gist from Vienna," he wrote by way of introduction, "and I have some interesting new ideas which can help you be more successful, effective, sell more and communicate better with your potential cli-ents."[9] Four companies were intrigued enough to respond, and there followed a flurry of work that firmly established his reputation in America and made him the leading practitioner in the new field of "motivational research."

Dichter went to work for *Esquire* magazine, where he used psy-choanalytic methods to discover the perhaps obvious fact that subscribers were attracted to the publication because of the nude pictures (he told the company not to be embarrassed about this but to stress to potential advertisers that readers lingered longer on the page, and with wider eyes); he conducted a study for Procter & Gamble's Ivory Soap that laid bare that there was an erotic element to bathing, and that a bath was seen as a purification ritual whereby one washed one's troubles away. The resulting jingle was "Be Smart and Get a Fresh Start with Ivory Soap." He helped Chrysler market Plymouth cars, discovering that women most often made the decisions about which car a family bought and that, while convertibles sucked men into the salesroom, they were seldom sold—men associated them with the fantasy of having a mistress but settled for a wifely sedan.

Only eighteen months after arriving in the United States, Dichter's clever analyses of the sexual appeal of commodities earned him a write-up in *Time*, where he was described as "a small, neat, emphatic man who speaks almost perfect English."[10] Dichter claimed to be "the first to apply to advertising the really scientific psychology." Advertising agencies, Dichter liked to say, were "advanced laboratories in psychology." Consumers were docile and malleable, Dichter thought, and ads should try to bypass their rational minds and appeal to the softer ground of their unconscious: "Dr. Dichter scoffs at advertising that tries to reason with potential customers, to scare them or lecture them on their shortcomings," *Time* explained. "He believes in tapping hidden desires and urges." Chrysler was just about to launch its "Dichterized advertisements," which, the magazine concluded, would do just that. "Probable motif: the subconscious lure of the open road, the deep passion to master a machine."

In 1947 Dichter published *The Psychology of Everyday Living* (a play on Freud's *The Psychopathology of Everyday Life*), in which he introduced his ingenious psychoanalytic findings about soap, cars, appliances, and cigarettes to a wide public. The book was designed as an accessible self-help manual to help Americans "accept the morality of the good life."[11] Dichter thought that the country's traditional puritanical values were desperately out of sync with capitalist ideology. He wanted to encourage people to shed their guilty feelings about self-indulgent pleasures and find erotic satisfaction in the buying of things.

Dichter was, in his way, also an idealist. He embraced consumer culture wholeheartedly as a bulwark against fascism and the best weapon against communism. Like many European exiles, he felt that the totalitarian threat was simmering beneath the surface of American life. Dichter saw the motivational researcher as a psychoanalyst-at-large whose job was to safeguard democracy by assuaging the fears of an anxious society; he turned consumption into a kind of therapy. Whereas thinkers such as David Riesman and C. Wright Mills saw mass affluence as leading to an epidemic of alienation, Dichter interpreted it as the very thing that kept democracy and the economy on the march. "If we were to rely exclusively on the fulfillment of our immediate and necessary needs, our economy would literally collapse overnight," Dichter said.[12] Citizens bought into the American dream with their every purchase.

Like Reich, Perls, and other American interpreters of Freud, Dichter introduced a permissive version of psychoanalysis to America, one that identified sex with liberation. But Dichter was a Freudian ambassador to an entirely different sector of society—big business; he worked separately but to striking overall cultural effect. From a diametrically opposite position as that of Reich, Perls, et al., Dichter spoke the language of the counterculture: he called for hedonism, pleasure, and self-expression, which he thought would make people immune to dangerous totalitarian ideas. He promised to help members of an emerging generation that spurned convention and puritanism (but not materialism) discover their individuality and sense of inner satisfaction through owning objects.

As America entered the 1950s, the decade of commodity fetishism, Dichter offered consumers moral permission to embrace sex and consumption and forged a philosophy of corporate hedonism. "Hedonism," Dichter argued, "as defended by the old Greeks, has to be brought to the surface again. We have to learn to forget the guilt of original sin."[13] Dichter maintained that Americans had to shed their outmoded concept of morality if they were to discover their freedom in commodity culture without the destructive guilt that might lead to fascism or communism. "We are fighting a sham battle with rockets and hydrogen bombs," Dichter wrote, "while underneath the real struggle, the silent war, is for the possession of men's minds."[14]

Meanwhile, the philosopher Herbert Marcuse was framing the belief that the booming, automated, and advanced economy of 1950s
America might bring about an altogether different political structure. Capitalism, he wrote, had only resulted in "concentration
camps, mass exterminations, world wars, and atom bombs," and he
maintained that, perhaps for the first time, the great postindustrial
riches that were being enjoyed in America made the realization of a
leftist alternative a possibility.[15] In *Eros and Civilization* (1955), he
proposed an influential vision of a sexual utopia that was informed
by Reich's sex-pol vision.

Marcuse was perhaps the most radical member of the Frankfurt
School, a neo-Marxist interdisciplinary social theory associated with
the Institute of Social Research at the University of Frankfurt am
Main, relocated to Columbia University in 1934. The Frankfurt
School's other prominent members were Theodor Adorno, Max
Horkheimer, and Erich Fromm. In 1932 Reich, then at the height
of his Freudo-Marxism, had published an article in the first issue of
the Institute of Social Research's journal, and its members followed
his lead in grafting together psychoanalysis and Marxism, and acknowledged this debt. But during the Second World War, Adorno
and Horkheimer embraced Freud's theory of the death drive in order to help explain current events, which Reich had never done, and
emphasized Freud's political pessimism as a result—Erich Fromm,
for example, dismissed the revolutionary Freud as a myth.

In 1934, Marcuse emigrated to the United States. During the war
he worked for the Office of Strategic Services (OSS), a unit of the
American government's espionage and covert operations and the
forerunner of the CIA. There he developed the ideas Reich had outlined in *The Mass Psychology of Fascism* and applied them to government policy, identifying anti-Nazi groups within Germany and
working on ways in which the Americans could disseminate propaganda that would turn Hitler's people against him. ("Marcuse," argued the historian Paul Robinson, "was in substantial agreement
with Reich . . . Even in the 1930s Marcuse considered bodily repres-

sion, and in particular sexual repression, one of the most important attributes of the exploitative social order.")[16] When the OSS was disbanded in 1945, Marcuse moved to the State Department, where he compiled a 532-page report titled "The Potentials of World Communism." The historian H. Stuart Hughes, who claims to have received the equivalent of a second university education when he worked for the OSS under Marcuse, wrote, "It has seemed deliciously incongruous that at the end of the 1940s, with an official purge of real or suspected leftists in full swing, the State Department's leading authority on Central Europe should have been a revolutionary socialist who hated the Cold War and all its works."[17] Marcuse resigned in 1951, disenchanted with the virulent anticommunism of the McCarthy period, and returned to academia.

While teaching at Harvard University, Marcuse, then fifty-seven, published *Eros and Civilization* (1955), which took up where Reich left off in trying to fuse Freud and Marx—though, in a concession to the climate of more general political despair that permeated the mid-fifties, Marx isn't mentioned by name anywhere in the book. *Eros and Civilization* points the way to the possibility of a utopian society free from sexual repression. If *Civilization and Its Discontents*, which stated that sexual repression was an eternal and indispensable part of culture, was Freud's answer to the threat posed by Reich's youthful radicalism, Marcuse's book, whose title makes a glancing reference to Freud's, was an ingenious attempt to twist Freud's reactionary pessimism so that the revolutionary, liberationist Freud once again came to the fore.

Marcuse followed Paul Goodman in ripping into the neo-Freudians, including the Frankfurt School member Erich Fromm, whom he accused of practicing a therapy based on the claim that true happiness was available in this society, which promoted conformism (Fromm would retaliate by calling Marcuse a nihilist). Like Goodman, Marcuse singled out Reich as the most significant figure of the left-wing Freudians, and he paid tribute to him as an intellectual predecessor. But he chided Reich for ignoring Freud's idea of the death drive and the inevitability of repression. Marcuse also felt that Reich's dogmatic insistence on the orgasm as a panacea for all social malaise marred his significant insights with "a sweeping primitivism" that foreshadowed "the wild and fantastic hobbies of his later years."[18]

Marcuse thought that some degree of repression was necessary if a society was to function, something Reich never seemed to fully accept, but Marcuse felt that capitalism demanded excessive libido sacrifices by its subjects. He distinguished between "basic repression," required for any civilization, and "surplus repression" (alluding to Marx's notion of "surplus value"), which he felt was historically contingent and a tax often way above the necessary requirements of civilization. A capitalist sex economy, Marcuse argued, employed surplus repression to concentrate the libido in the genitals, so as to leave the rest of the body free for exploitation as an instrument of labor. Marcuse believed that Reich, in idealizing the "genital character," merely reinforced this "tyranny of the genital." Like Fritz Perls, Marcuse looked to the perversions—which Freud defined as "the persistence into adult life of id impulses that have escaped repression"—to short-circuit Freud's somber pessimism. "The perversions," Marcuse argued, "express rebellion against the subjugation of sexuality under the order of procreation, and against the institutions which guarantee this order."[19]

Marcuse proposed a resexualization of the whole body. A liberated body, he hoped, would be a nonaggressive but disruptive force for social change, leading to a utopia founded on the "polymorphous perversity" of the child, for whom Freud thought the entire body was capable of erotic sensation. (Norman O. Brown, Marcuse's colleague at OSS, proposed a similar vision in *Life Against Death* [1959].) In this new society, Marcuse envisaged work not as alienating but as in itself a form of sexual play.

Ironically, though he proposed a polymorphously perverse version of Reich's "work democracy," Marcuse was himself almost the opposite of a hedonist. "In terms of his sexual relationships, everything was very covert, very traditional," said his stepson Osha Neumann, "Insofar as [he had] a carnal, genital, sexual drive, it was concealed."[20] After his wife died of cancer, Marcuse began an affair with the wife of his best friend, Franz Neumann, who had worked with him at the OSS. When Franz Neumann died in a car crash in

1954, the two married and, despite his brief affair with a graduate student, remained happily so. Osha Neumann remembered Marcuse's telling him approvingly about how Thomas Mann used to wake up each morning, get dressed in a jacket and tie, and then write about characters consumed by passion, powers that Marcuse, too, seemed able to sublimate.

"I sometimes suspect that there's a barely repressed strain of Puritanism in Marcuse's make-up," wrote Paul Robinson, "a fastidiousness which allows him to treat sexuality with great abandon at the level of theory, but results in a squeamish 'That's not what I meant at all!' when confronted with the untidy reality of sex."[21] Indeed, almost a decade after *Eros and Civilization* was published, Marcuse realized that his optimistic belief in the radically oppositional nature of sexuality was deeply flawed and published a corrective vision, *One-Dimensional Man* (1964).

In the summer of 1955, as *Eros and Civilization* was being passed around on American college campuses, Reich was living alone at Orgonon, with the caretaker Tom Ross as his only company. Ilse Ollendorff had left him the previous summer, and had taken Peter to live at the Hamilton School in Massachusetts. In her absence Reich had a brief affair with Grethe Hoff, a former patient who worked as a social worker at the Orgonomic Infant Research Center in Queens. She left her husband, Myron Sharaf, with whom she had a one-year-old child, to be with Reich (resentment over this colors Sharaf's ambivalent biography of Reich). But she was soon disillusioned by Reich's "blatantly erroneous notions," such as his belief that air force planes were guarding him at Eisenhower's instruction, and when she expressed her doubt about these ideas she also found herself the subject of Reich's jealous rages. Hoff left him and moved back to Norway with her child. Reich wrote to her, begging her to return and signing off: "Goodbye, my sweet heart. You are running away from too much happiness."[22]

Reich was desperately alone, living off canned food and potatoes and onions dug from Ollendorff's now overgrown kitchen garden. He suffered a bout of depression—the underside of his mania—and was much preoccupied with death. ("It happens that, after a period of great productivity, an artist or a 'knower' breaks down psychotically," he had written in *Character Analysis*. "It is too much to carry.")[23] He began preparing a mausoleum for himself at Orgonon and asked Ross to begin digging a hole for his grave.

Reich had sold much of his laboratory equipment to pay his legal fees, and he used what money was left to build an extravagant dining room in the large, empty laboratory in the observatory. He told people that he was expecting an important dignitary, perhaps Eisenhower himself, and he redecorated the ground-floor room, buying new furniture, china, glass, and silverware for the anticipated event. Gladys Meyer, Theodore Wolfe's widow, was invited to dine with him there. "She told me that she will never forget the pathetic efforts Reich made to be the perfect host at dinner in that rather formal dining room," Ilse Ollendorff wrote of this evening.

> He had dressed up, while she arrived with her picnic basket for what she thought would be a very informal sort of dinner. The entire episode had something unreal about it, like a play. After dinner Reich played the organ and later in a conversation mentioned that he was rereading Rousseau and also the New Testament. She remembers sensing in Reich a need to be reassured that he was able to communicate, that he was not mad, that he was understood.[24]

That August, Aurora Karrer—the daughter of an eminent biophysicist, Dr. Enoch Karrer—attended a four-day conference at Orgonon devoted to the Reich medical DOR-buster. Karrer was thirty-three, the same age as Reich's eldest daughter, Eva, and worked as a medical researcher at the National Institutes of Health in Washington (which, it happened, encompassed the FDA), where she had done work on the effects of penicillin on the bloodstream. Her report on this subject had greatly impressed Reich when she sent it to him in the spring.

There are pictures of the dark-haired Aurora along with the other sixteen people who attended the 1955 conference. One of only two women present, she was photographed wearing a white smock, cupping a knee with her hands as she leaned forward to listen attentively to Reich as he demonstrated his latest therapeutic innovation. Reich is sitting in a chair by a camp bed, seemingly entwined in the DOR-buster's many lengths of grounding metal cable. He is wearing a red cravat, which, according to Sharaf, "highlighted his resemblance to a guerilla chief."[25]

Karrer all too happily stepped into the void left by Ollendorff and Grethe Hoff. Reich considered her his last wife. A photograph of Karrer is inscribed "To my beloved husband, Willie. Your loving and devoted wife, Aurora. April 27, 1957." It depicts her gazing off, with a strong, determined jaw, a pretty, pugnacious round face, a string of pearls, and carefully coiffed, curled hair.

"I only knew Aurora tangentially," Morton Herskowitz told me. "To me I always felt that she was like a . . . I don't know if she'd ever been Reich's patient, but she was like somebody possessed with a positive transference. Just the way she constantly adored him. I remember, I thought she reminds me of some of my patients whose positive transference is too strong."

In his lecture on the end phase of therapy, delivered in 1949, Reich told his physicians that he never accepted a patient if he felt that she was attracted to him. He also advised the assembled orgonomists, "Don't touch a patient, as long as they are a patient. If you feel attracted to them, don't accept them as a patient . . . You will try, of course, despite your own desire, to get her to someone else." Only if a patient had successfully reached orgastic potency and had "developed a healthy genital attachment" toward the therapist was it reasonable to break off therapy and begin an affair. You had to distinguish this "healthy desire," Reich warned, from the patient's narcissistic wish "to tear you down from your pedestal . . . and smash you to pulp."[26] (He no doubt had Annie Reich in mind.) Karrer had in fact been in analysis with Dr. Elsworth Baker, who "had found it impossible to continue to treat her" because of her strong transference toward him—and perhaps his own attraction to her—and he had broken off her analysis.[27] Baker referred Karrer to Dr. Raphael, who must have experienced similar problems, because he in turn referred her to Dr. Charles Oller.

The upcoming trial cast its shadow over the 1955 conference. "There were fewer smiles and jokes than there had been at past conferences," wrote Myron Sharaf, who attended despite having been deeply wounded by Reich's recent affair with his wife. "The mood was grim at times."[28] Reich wanted to DOR-bust everyone who attended the conference in front of the rest of the group, as if to symbolically purify them. He claimed that, using his DOR-busting device, he had cured himself of the laryngitis he had been afflicted with for several months, and even to have used it to elicit the orgasm reflex on Dr. Willie, one of his physicians. During one of these open sessions, Bill Moise burst into tears after the machine's numerous little guns had been pointed at his body, as if it were sucking out some inner grief.

When Baker refused to submit to the same treatment, not wanting to compromise himself in front of Karrer, a former patient, Reich lost his temper. "She knows more about orgone energy than you'll ever know," he told Baker harshly. He was evidently falling in love with Karrer. "He went on to tell me," Baker remembered, that "during her therapy with me, she had fallen in love with me, wanted me, and was ready, but I had not responded. He felt she was very healthy" and it was therefore permissible for him to initiate an affair with her.[29] Baker disagreed with Reich's diagnosis, though he didn't dare contradict him.

Baker was given a private DOR-busting session with Reich, which lasted twenty minutes. "It took a few minutes before I felt anything," he wrote, "and then I began to feel a strong, irresistible pulling on my lips, which was literally pulling out sobbing from the depths." After his third session, Baker wrote, "I felt better than I ever had in my life. I felt warm and kindly toward everyone. And I surprised myself by including Silvert, whom [sic] I thought was leading Reich to disaster."[30]

In November 1955, in the hiatus before his trial, Reich moved to Washington under the pseudonym Dr. Walter Roner (perhaps a reference to his mother's maiden name, Roninger) to be near Karrer, who lived in Bethesda, Maryland. They lived together in an apartment building called Alban Towers on Massachusetts Avenue, and he felt a comfort and reflected importance in being near the seat of government. He was deluded in thinking they were interested in his work, and he continued to write letters to President Eisenhower and other officials in which he assumed that they would protect him in his legal battle.

Reich's trial was delayed until April 30, 1956, when it got under way at the courthouse in Portland, presided over by Judge Sweeney. Reich assumed the court summons was fraudulent because the U.S. attorney hadn't personally signed his name, only had it typed in. Reich complained, "Only legally correctly signed and executed documents will be accepted by the Counsel for the Discovery of the Life Energy."[31] Ollendorff, who had also been subpoenaed (having now left Reich's orbit she was no longer named in the complaint), had sought the advice of a lawyer on this question and, having learned that the document was valid, showed up in court. Reich, Silvert, and Mangravite didn't, and they were arrested the following morning for contempt of court.

Mangravite was held in a federal jail for two days while he waited for a federal marshal to transport him in handcuffs to Maine. When they stopped for lunch en route he had to eat wearing his cuffs as if he were a dangerous felon. In Portland, Maine, he was put in the same jail cell as Reich, to whom he had spoken on the phone but had never met. "At the time I was a little bit in awe," Mangravite said of this awkward first meeting. "I was obviously in shock—I felt very isolated, it was a very unpleasant couple of days in prison. Reich was standing there, marching about his cell, still holding court, because it was a small holding cell and the doctors were there, too, sitting outside."

One of Reich's orgonomists put his house up as bail (set at $30,000), and Reich, his patient Silvert, and Silvert's patient Mangravite were released. Mangravite told me that while he was in Maine, Reich took the opportunity to give him six or seven therapy sessions in his study at Orgonon. The techniques Reich used sounded more like interrogation than therapy. Reich believed that Mangravite, as a "government witness"—as if he had a choice in the matter—was a traitor to orgonomy, and he was using his deep breathing techniques not to break down character armor but to extract a confession from the suspected double agent. Reich, increasingly paranoid, thought he was besieged with Communist spies.

"I was just in a chair," Mangravite recalled. "There were other people in the back of the room. He did much of the talking. At that point he had discovered this thing, the 'spy syndrome,' and he asked, 'Are you a spy?' He was putting me through this shit. A lot of the therapists used to make you tickle your throat until you vomited to get you loosened up—it was very unpleasant. He had me do that a lot, which I found annoying. . . . I thought, *Let's not pick on me because you're pissed that we're here on trial and everything's going against you.* I always had the feeling that he was performing for whoever was there. I don't know if he was frightened or not in the trial. He held the attitude that he was above all this and it's all going to disappear, because he was too important."

Reich was brought to the Portland courthouse in handcuffs; a picture of him holding up his cuffed wrists appeared in a local paper. Reich acted as his own defense attorney in the subsequent trial, dubbing himself a representative of the EPPO—the Emotional Plague Prevention Office. Many of the forty-odd devotees of Reich's cause who traveled up to Maine to offer their support on the first day of the trial thought that Reich's decision to represent himself was a mistake.

"He was the most unusual human being I'd ever had contact with," Herskowitz says, "but I always thought that I had more common sense than he did; I was aware of his political naïveté, I was aware at the beginning of the trial that if he persisted in this he was going to lose. I was aware he had misguided opinions. You know, he liked cowboy movies and he viewed politics as [being] like cowboy movies—Eisenhower was looking over him and would protect him. I assumed Eisenhower was hardly aware of him, if at all." (Ola Raknes, with whom Reich had once contemplated going into therapy, attributed Reich's Eisenhower delusion to "some sort of unsolved child-parent conflict.")[32]

Mangravite asked me, "Do you have any impression that he had a Christ complex and that he wanted to be persecuted? There are so many things, the more I think about it, the more stupid they were. It was almost like he didn't want to defend himself."

The three-day trial was well covered in the Portland papers, which reveled in Reich's eccentricities and the science fiction appeal of devices like orgone energy accumulators and DOR-busters, and the court was filled to capacity during each session. One local paper's headline read, as if it were a film to review, PLOT IS LOUSY, CAST IS GREAT, paying tribute to the trial's "colorful personalities." The article described how Reich scribbled notes on a yellow legal pad, shook and bobbed his head animatedly as he listened to witnesses, and frequently slid his fingers anxiously "through the somewhat thin white hair that draws a sharply defined border to the florid complexion." When his turn came to cross-examine, he was quick to jump from his seat to the stand, where "his examination was sometimes hampered by his accent."[33]

The government used several witnesses to outline in painstaking detail every single violation of the injunction. The first of these was Ilse Ollendorff, who hadn't seen Reich since they separated two years before. When quizzing her, Joseph Maguire, the government's lawyer, tried to paint a picture of Reich as the head of an underworld gang. He repeatedly referred to "the business," called Reich the "big boss," and used sinister-sounding terms like "drop in New York." Though Ollendorff admitted that rental payments had continued to be collected after the injunction, she took every opportunity to correct Maguire's misrepresentations: "She was a fine witness," Sharaf recalled in an article on the trial written two years later, "perhaps the clearest and most secure of any that took the stand during the trial."[34]

When it was Reich's term to question Ollendorff, he asked only what the money that he got from the sale of accumulators was used for. Ollendorff replied that it all went into research, such as Reich's desert operations. Reich said that that would be all, as if to counter Maguire's insinuations by simply showing the selfless nobility of his enterprise.

The next witness was Paul Berman, an accumulator user from New York, whom Sharaf described as "the epitome of a deeply sick neurotic."[35] He had been in treatment with Dr. John Pierakkos, who with Alexander Lowen later that year founded the Institute of Bioenergetics, a splinter group that developed Lowen's vegetother-apeutic gymnastics. Berman told Maguire that Pierakkos had sug-gested he begin using the box and that he had continued to pay rental payments after the injunction; no efforts had been made to recall his device. Reich asked him if the accumulator had helped him. Berman said it had, but his answer was ordered struck from the record. Judge Sweeney ruled that questions about the efficacy of the device should have been the subject of the earlier trial; this one was solely to determine the narrower question as to whether Reich had broken the injunction.

Maguire's questioning of his witnesses took two days. He sought to establish beyond doubt that Silvert had acted in concert with Reich in transporting accumulators in interstate commerce by show-ing how the accumulators had been sold or rented for Reich's finan-cial benefit. Reich complained of the "sleepy-making" quality of Maguire's examinations; on one occasion, when Maguire was going into minute detail about how Reich had spent Silvert's illegally got-ten gains, even the judge became impatient and interrupted him: "How far are you going in this thing—buying cigarettes, cigars and such things?"[36] Reich pointed out that he'd contributed $350,000 of his own earnings to orgone research, so it was ridiculous for Maguire to quibble over who might have paid a $21.50 bill.

On the third day of the trial it was Reich's turn to call up wit-nesses. He spent only an hour and a half questioning them, and his flamboyant amateurism, modeled on films such as *Mr. Smith Goes to Washington*, made a lively contrast to Maguire's dour professional-ism. The only physician to give evidence was Albert Duvall, who told the court that he wouldn't have asked his patients to return their accumulators even if Reich had asked him to. However, Reich didn't pursue the idea of the injunction being impossible to en-force. He instead sought to prove the absolute necessity of breaking the injunction in his examinations. Judge Sweeney was bemused by this tactic. "If you have admitted that you have disobeyed this injunction, then you are really wasting our time here," the judge told him. "I cannot listen to why you disobeyed it or why you had to. The fact is that if you admitted you disobeyed it your case is about over."[37] But Reich insisted he was not guilty and the judge, granting him a greater degree of laxity than he would have granted a lawyer, allowed him to proceed with his questioning.

Reich hinted at classified secrets he was unable to divulge, the threat of espionage, and the supporters he had in high places (the White House, the air force, the CIA). He told the court that FDA spies had to be kept out of Orgonon at all costs because they were intent on stealing his secret equations, and that his workers had been instructed to carry firearms to ensure that agents stayed out. When McCullough, who had been to Arizona with Reich, was asked by the judge if he was willing to shoot an FDA official, he answered that "under certain conditions" he would.[38] To assert the deadly seriousness of his work and to show how he was prepared to die protecting his secrets, Reich called Tom Ross to the stand and asked him to tell the court how he had instructed Ross to dig him a grave at Orgonon.

The only real embarrassment inflicted on the prosecution was when U.S. Attorney Mills was questioned by Reich about why he had crossed over from being Reich's lawyer to prosecuting the case against him. Mills claimed that he'd stopped working for Reich in 1952, before the FDA's complaint was issued, and that in any case he had only notarized a few documents for Reich. In fact, he had been present at meetings where the business of Reich's conflict with the FDA was discussed, as minutes show. Mills argued that he'd assigned Maguire as a special prosecutor on the case to settle any question of a conflict of interest. When Reich claimed they'd been friends, Mills claimed that their social interaction had consisted of only the occasional cup of coffee, to which the judge asked, "With milk and sugar in it?"[39] The judge pointed out that Mills could have removed himself completely from the case if he'd wished.

In a recess, Judge Sweeney suggested to Ollendorff that Reich have a psychiatric evaluation, as he thought an insanity claim was the only way he could avoid a guilty verdict. There were clear signs in his testimony that he had lost traction with reality. And indeed, in some intergalactic Oedipal struggle, Reich now supposed that his father might have been a visitor from outer space. In the posthumously published *Contact with Space*, Reich wrote:

> On March 20th, 1956 at 10 PM, a thought of a very remote possibility entered my mind which I fear will never leave me again: Am I a spaceman? Do I belong to a new race on earth, bred by men from outer space in embraces with earth women? Are my children offspring of the first interplanetary race? Has the melting pot of interplanetary society already been created on our planet, as the melting pot of all earth nations was established in the U.S.A. 190 years ago? Or, is this thought related to things to come in the future? I request my right and privilege to have such thoughts and to ask such questions without being threatened to be jailed by any administrative agency of society.[40]

However, Ollendorff never communicated the judge's recommendation to Reich:

> I very vigorously advised against a psychiatric examination. First, because it would have infuriated Reich and all his friends to a great extent, and second, because whatever Reich's delusions may have been in regard to the conspiracy or to the secret nature of his work, I felt that he was absolutely rational in the conduct of the trial so far as his basic premises were concerned, namely that scientific research should be free of political interference, that he had a duty to expose the biased and malevolent intentions of the FDA investigation which he felt to be against the public interest.[41]

The jury, which included an African-American for the first time in the history of that court, deliberated for only ten to fifteen minutes before announcing their verdict: guilty. In the notes on the case that he made at the time, Sharaf compared the scene to a passion play, and Reich to Christ: "Reflected in his face [was] a note of a bottomlessly deep hurt."[42] Reich stoically packed his papers into a briefcase. On the steps of the courthouse he declared that a "legal scandal" had been committed that day. His disciples, who had thought him invincible, felt "depressed and helpless" at the verdict. Some cried. "The sentence marked at least the end of one phase of an experiment," wrote Sharaf:

> The situation with the "followers" was a bad one . . . But to hang around in guilt-ridden circles wasn't much help either . . . All the mysticism was there—Reich will find a way out, he "knows" things we don't know, we don't understand it all. This was partially rational, but it was also deeply sick. At one point during the judge's summation, one person in the audience said: "It looks good, Reich is smiling," and he genuinely expected that the outcome would be different than it was . . . I think Reich himself contributed to this atmosphere because he was clinging staunchly to his own line.[43]

Sharaf heard Reich "speak sharply" to Mangravite on the steps outside of the court—"Look at him!" Reich told Silvert, indicating that Mangrivite looked emotionally sick, or "DOR-ish." (Reich later commented that Sharaf also looked "blackish" and asked him whether he was also a spy.) When Mangravite begged to be able to speak to Reich, he replied, "Yes, but the truth, please!" implying that Mangravite had lied when giving his evidence in court.[44]

I told Mangravite that during my research I'd discovered that, before their sentencing, Reich and Silvert had lodged a complaint of perjury against him. "What!" Mangravite exclaimed in disbelief. "I never heard about that. That's amazing!" It seems that Silvert was trying to save his own skin in Reich's eyes by buying into the paranoid fantasy that Mangravite, who had been dragged into all this by Silvert, was actually an FDA stooge. "Dr. Silvert has conceded that [Mangravite] may well have been unknowingly induced [to ship accumulators from Rangeley to New York] by subversive conspirators," Reich wrote in the brief for his later Supreme Judicial Court appeal, "in order to provide 'proof' of interstate shipment after the injunction was issued."[45]

"He knew me as a patient and as a friend," Mangravite said of Silvert's betrayal, "and he knew who I was and what I was, and we worked so closely together. I built all the accumulators, I stored all the books, he saw me practically every day and had known me as a therapist, and now he'd decided that I was some sort of evil left-wing spy?" Mangravite told me that Silvert began collecting denunciations about him from his friends and that he became an outcast from orgonomy, the science to which he'd devoted so much of his time, which left him feeling confused and resentful. "I assume that what was written about me was that I was 'plaguey.' Anybody that did anything wrong was plaguey—this was the emotional plague that was attacking Reich."

Two weeks later, Reich was sentenced to two years in prison and Silvert to one year and a day, and the Wilhelm Reich Foundation was fined $10,000. All remaining accumulators and Reich's paperback books that referred to orgone energy were to be destroyed under FDA supervision. "We have lost, technically only, to an incomprehensible procedure treadmill," Reich wrote in a speech that the judge read the court after he had passed sentence. "I and my fellow workers have, however, won our case in the true, historical sense. We may be destroyed physically tomorrow; we shall live in human memory as long as this planet is afloat in the endless Cosmic Energy Ocean as the 'Fathers' of the cosmic, technological age."[46]

On hearing of the several years of detective work that secured Reich's sentence, the writer Mildred Edie Brady, whose publications had initiated the investigation, wrote to John Cain of the FDA:

> *There is a kind of journalistic excitement in learning that an article you wrote years ago has been instrumental in bearing such fruit. The more I think about it, the more my fingers itch to do a book on the whole case . . . It would be a fine tale of really true adventure that ought to outsell any detective story . . . Let me give you the heartiest congratulations on a very tough job, very well done.*
>
> *Sincerely,*
> *Mildred E. Brady*[47]

Peter Reich was there on June 5, 1956, when the FDA agents Kenyon and Niss arrived at Orgonon to supervise the destruction of the accumulators banned by the injunction. As their dusty black car passed the twelve-year-old Peter, who was standing by the Student Laboratory, the deputy marshal escorting the agents flashed him his badge before they drove up the steep hill to the observatory. Peter phoned ahead to raise the alarm and ran as fast as he could after the government car. When he caught up with them, the two FDA inspectors were standing opposite Reich's desk. They were wearing narrow shiny ties, white shirts, and black suits and referred, Peter remembered, to Orgonon as "Orgy-non."

Reich, who was seated, was wearing a red-and-black-checked shirt and fidgeted with a pencil. They were discussing who would have to carry out the destruction: the inspectors were arguing that the defendants were supposed to do it under the supervision of the FDA. Reich refused to destroy his own work—to him, it was no less than an act of iconoclasm. "Mr. Ross," he eventually said to Tom Ross, not dropping his angry stare at the "red fascist" interlopers, "take Peter and go to the lab. Start dismantling the accumulators. Get some axes out."[48]

Tom Ross and Peter unscrewed the three accumulators in the Student Laboratory and built a pyre out of the fiberglass insulation on the grass at the bottom of the observatory's driveway. They then started wielding the axes, chopping gashes in the panels. When they had finished, Peter recalled, "the pile was crumpled and broken, and steel wool was hanging out of the panels all frothy and gray."[49]

"Well, gentlemen. Are you satisfied?" Reich asked the inspectors sarcastically. "We have gasoline! It would make a nice fire, no?" He asked them if they wanted to destroy the rest of his scientific equipment or burn his books. As they left, one of the officials, evidently embarrassed, said they were sorry that it had come to this. Reich replied, "Yes, you're sorry. Of course. Aren't we all. Good-bye, gentlemen. Someday you will understand."[50]

According to the FDA report written later that day, Silvert and Moise were also present at this meeting, along with two attorneys that Reich had hired. Although there were only a few accumulators left at Orgonon, Silvert admitted to having ten more devices in New York stored in a Thompson Street warehouse along with panels for twenty-five or thirty more. Reich had sold eighty-two other accumulators to the people who had rented them (earning $8,264.75), and his lawyers were arguing that he had no way of forcing the new owners to return them to Rangeley for destruction, as the injunction specified. "The defendants were quite civil and cautious," the report stated. "On a few occasions Dr. Reich became somewhat agitated and strode out of the room, only to return in a moment or two. Their attitude seemed to be that of martyrs. The Food and Drug Administration could take and destroy everything they had."[51]

According to this official account, there was an attempt to burn the accumulators, but they wouldn't ignite, so they had to be finished off with axes. Reich put an American flag atop the rubble and wreckage of the chopped-up accumulators as if he were commemorating the dead.

A few weeks later the inspectors returned to Orgonon to preside over a book burning. Reich took them down to the Student Laboratory and said, "There they are, burn them." As Inspector Niss was doing a count, Reich advised him to air himself occasionally, as the lab was contaminated, a warning that went unheeded. Reich had arranged for someone from Collins's workshop to carry out the job, which involved piling 251 volumes of Reich's writings on the bonfire. "During the burning," Niss wrote in his report, "Dr. Reich found himself just about to throw some of the literature on the fire. He stopped short and remarked, 'I promised myself that I would have nothing to do with the burning of this literature.'"[52] He told Niss that his books had also been burned by the Nazis, and that he couldn't believe that book burning could also happen in America.

In fact, in the early 1950s numerous "subversive" books were banned from schools and libraries, and thirty thousand books, by authors such as Jean-Paul Sartre and Langston Hughes, that were considered pro-Communist by McCarthy's henchmen were withdrawn from information centers in embassies and consulates abroad. Ironically, some of these same books had been burned in Germany. One senator pointed out that the term "book burning" was "symbolic of any effort to remove books from libraries," and quarantining books in basements and warehouses was just as bad as incinerating them. In June 1953, Eisenhower, who hated McCarthy—he thought him "a pimple in the path of progress"—made a speech condemning these actions: "Don't join the book burners," he told the graduating class at Dartmouth College. "Do not think you are going to conceal thoughts by concealing evidence that they ever existed. Don't be afraid to go in your library and read every book, as long as any document does not offend our own ideas of decency. That should be the only censorship."[53]

In late August the FDA destroyed the literature that was warehoused at the Orgone Institute Press in Greenwich Village. Silvert was there with Paki Wright's mother, Miriam Sheppard, and a few other hired helpers. Six tons of literature, valued at fifteen thousand dollars, was taken to the New York City Sanitation Department's Gansevoort Street incinerator. Included in the inventory were over twenty thousand journals as well as hardback volumes that should have been saved, according to the terms of the injunction (though not sold until references to orgone energy were struck out), including copies of *The Mass Psychology of Fascism* and *The Sexual Revolution*, both of which made only passing reference to orgone energy. The FDA looked on: "The truck dumped the material in the dumping area and the overhead crane picked it up and dumped it into the fire."[54]

The American Civil Liberties Union protested the book burnings in both a letter to the FDA and in a press release that was ignored by every major newspaper. Reich rejected the ACLU's offer of help, even though it was the only organization to come to his support. The ACLU had been formed to protect left-wingers during the Red Scare of 1920, and even though Communists had been barred from leadership positions since 1940, Reich maintained that it was a Communist front organization.

After his arrest and sentencing, Reich remained in Maine, sinking into an alcohol-numbed depression as he awaited the result of the decision of the Supreme Judicial Court. "I've never seen such bitterness and hatred as this man is capable of showing at times," Karrer wrote in her journal, "especially under the influence of liquor." Karrer, who spent most of that summer with him, was often the object of Reich's rage, as recorded in some of her diary entries and letters:

*August 14, 1956*
Willie violent and threatening. Said he felt the need to kill someone—might as well be me. He had been drinking heavily. Didn't remember his threats and violent flailing around the next day when sober.

Reich once told her that he thought murder under the influence of alcohol was pardonable, and she sometimes thought he might be capable of such an act.

### August 15, 1956

Willie violent and destructive—burned a whole file of something so "spies couldn't find his secrets." Finished off a bottle of cognac all by himself, didn't remember next day.

A month after the FDA burned his books, Reich was incinerating his own letters and files.

### October 6, 1956 [an unsent letter by Karrer to Reich]

*I do not plan to sit by calmly and be hit, slapped, or beaten by you under the influence of alcohol. I cannot and will not stand physical abuse. I'm sorry I simply do not know how to handle this phase of your personality, though I love you dearly. Now you know why I run; not from guilt of anything. How does one prevent such upheavals? I don't know. All I've ever wanted was for you to be happy.*[55]

After their quarrels, and fearful of his violent temper tantrums, Karrer would often disappear for a few days, but some masochistic streak in her would always see her return, and she would cover up for his drunken violence. They obviously had a complicated relationship, because the evening of this last incident, Karrer sent Reich a fifteen-dollar bouquet of flowers "to cheer him up." Karrer wrote that on two occasions Reich hit her, and on one occasion he rushed at her "with the look of a madman [and] with an ax." She also claims that he wounded his dog, Troll, with an iron bar—and that he later blamed this on extraterrestrials.

Karrer, as she recorded in her diary a week before the results of Reich's appeal were due, often felt trapped in their destructive relationship. She had given up her job at NIH to be with Reich:

I wanted to leave and go my own way last April, but then he was arrested here in Washington and I just couldn't desert at such a time, and similar upheavals have prevented me from freeing myself. He's

like a little child, [there's] something very pathetic and tragic about
him which makes it hard for me to just leave him when he is down . . .
I can assure you it's a nightmare to live with this man who is struggling so desperately to save himself. One can just see everyone desert as the ship sinks. He really has not a single real friend in the
world who really knows him. Yet the instant of his death he will be
hailed as the greatest man of our century.[56]

As his small fiefdom crumbled around him, Reich became increasingly paranoid. He would scrawl mad messages to those "red
fascists" who he thought were plotting to kill him, which he would
post around Orgonon. One in angry blue pencil that Karrer found
pinned to the lower cabin door read: "Want to make it kind of look
like suicide, don't you LM? By Proxy!!" "LM" stood for "Little Man,"
from the title of one of his books; it is a stern lecture to his "miserable
and small, impotent, rigid, lifeless and empty" critics. Another, found
inside the locked steel cabinet of the treatment room in the observatory, said, "You are not deeply ashamed of your rotten nature? You
cannot reach my realm." Another, left for those he feared were out to
kill him, stated: "I know you, public stinker, deep down, as a decent
fellow. Why don't you stop your stupidity. Go ahead through everything if you still can." Another one, propped up on a mantelpiece in
the observatory, read: "This room is wired for me and for you as an
equal citizen—sit down—have a good talk. Yours WR."

Suspecting that she was part of the "conspiracy" that was out to
destroy him, Reich used threats to make Karrer sign confessions—
as he had done with Ollendorff and other disciples. He went through
all her personal belongings, her purse and desk, impounding all the
written material therein. Karrer created an itemized list of these
confiscated things: "notes taken and collected from time to time on
the legal action and Wilhelm Reich's work, pictures given to me by
him and papers to hold for him, newspaper clippings of the trial, a
green diary and a sheet of equations." Reich, like Karrer, also obsessively kept notes. "Many times during times of rage he writes things
on a yellow legal pad which he locks in the bathroom," Karrer wrote.
"I really do not know what he has recorded. But I'm sure that the
most important thing to this man is how he goes down in history.

I've seen him defend himself at the expense of others, so I'm sure I'm no exception. If someone in the past has called him crazy, he's gone to great lengths to destroy that individual by his pen."

His legal pad was, in fact, as she later discovered, scrawled with paranoid signs: "These are the same equations I transmitted to CIA," Reich wrote on one sheet. "The Higs [hoodlums in government] did not get the real stuff . . . The true stuff is in my head. I planted many false equations."


At the National Library of Medicine in Washington, which is part of the National Institutes of Health, where Aurora Karrer had once worked, there is a series of boxes of Reich-related materials donated by her. Apparently Karrer planned to write a biography of Reich, which was to be called *The Genius: Personal Life and Loves of Wilhelm Reich*. One chapter was provisionally titled "Living with a Genius." She obsessively kept everything relating to Reich's life—letters, receipts, notes—which form a collage portrait of this time of strife.

The most developed bits of Karrer's text relate to the women who had preceded her in Reich's life: Annie Pink, Elsa Lindenberg, Ilse Ollendorff, and Grethe Hoff Sharaf. Perhaps she was jealous of them, perhaps she wanted to learn from their mistakes, perhaps Reich's unresolved past hung over their relationship, perhaps theory and practice crashed into each other in Reich's sex life. Karrer wrote in her notes that Reich obviously still loved Ilse Ollendorff— she reports that he broke down in sobs after one of Peter and Ilse's visits (Peter recalls that Reich showed him a gun at this time and, in tears, threatened to commit suicide with it rather than face prison). "I think that he has come to love me as much as any woman he has ever known, or more," Karrer reassured herself. "At times he's so sweet and kind and loving." Reich, she wrote, believed their life together was "the deepest and greatest love story of our time."

In the late 1970s, Aurora Karrer revisited the notes she had made toward the book that she had abandoned twenty years earlier. Over time, Karrer sought to defend Reich's legacy and assumed a position as the "grande dame of orgonomy," as Elsworth Baker's son, Courtney, described her, but she now poured out all her ambiva-

lence about Reich, scrawling over the collected pages and documents and underlining passages in red pen to create a catalogue of
bitter accusations.[57] Her red-penned notes dissect Reich and his
methods from a position outside of the Reich cult—she describes
Reichians as "submissive followers" in these later additions. Karrer asks rhetorically: "Is orgonomy a revolutionary force, a political
weapon, [or] a religious creed?"

With her angry marginalia Karrer creates, by default, a rough outline for a radically different book than the one she intended to write
in 1955. In this version Reich is no longer a "genius" but a conceited,
arrogant egotist, a fake, an abuser, a violent person who degraded
those around him, someone who trapped everyone in a therapeutic
web, a mentally unstable bully who made others feel as if it were
they—not he—who were mad. Karrer claims an Olympian perspective on Reich not only as his last wife but as his last analyst: "I completed his analysis! If I hadn't stayed with him he'd have shot
himself. As I look back on it that's what everyone was wishing he'd
do—Eva, Ilse, Baker, the orgonomists, etc."

Wilhelm Reich was, according to Karrer, "as ruthless and self-
serving as [the] cult-leader Jim Jones. He viewed himself as an
absolute ruler—and perfect in every respect." (Jim Jones was the
charismatic founder of the People's Temple, who attempted to set up
a utopian community in the jungles of Guyana—named Jonestown,
after himself—but ended up choreographing a mass suicide in
1977.) Her notes try to explain how Reich swept people up into his
world, how he brainwashed them, how he undermined them. As Karrer exorcised Reich's memory through Reich's memory, each one of
her bullet point notes reads like a sloughed skin:

- Wilhelm Reich thought of himself as more superior. He was the
  most sensitive and insecure man I ever met—to him the world had
  failed him.
- He always blamed all his ills on the world. To him everyone was
  always against him—he never said he was in any way at fault—only
  everyone else. Little wonder everyone deserted in droves.
- WR has the biggest ego I ever saw—a defense for deep feeling of
  inadequacy and insecurity and fears of lack of "manliness." If WR

couldn't help 4 wives and 3 children—[I] wonder how he expected to save the world? Saving people and children should start at home.

- No one could have an identity of their own around Wilhelm Reich. He forced them to become servants to him—to become subservient. He forbade them to keep "normal" contact with their families and friends and to have a normal life of their own.

- WR had massive delusions of grandeur. People believed him because their own lives were empty.

- Wilhelm Reich had the ability to impress people with his ideas—to win over all kinds of people by avoiding their vulnerabilities. He thrived on getting people to call him the greatest man alive, the saver of all mankind. Yet Wilhelm Reich destroyed every human being who came close to him. He could make them look bad if they seemed a threat to his own image of himself—the "king" of all mankind, as his daughter, Eva Reich Moise, put it.

- Wilhelm Reich first won people over by avoiding all their anxieties and weak points, then when he felt threatened by them—and he always did—he used their vulnerabilities to make them feel "insane" like they were so bad off they belonged in an insane asylum.

- In spring, 1956, WR believed himself a spaceman.

- Wilhelm Reich thrived on being the know it all, wise, advisor—never revealing his own weak points because to Wilhelm Reich he had none. He was perfect in his own mind's eye. Everyone around him was stabbing everyone else in the back in an attempt to justify following the great WR. Everyone close to Wilhelm Reich felt that he or she was the only one who understood him.

- What gets passed off as the effects of Oranur is really violent temper outbursts by WR. It's convenient to find something to blame a man's violence on—so everyone was brainwashed into calling it ORANUR.

- No one dared disagree with Wilhelm Reich. If they did they were part of the "conspiracy" to kill him or they were "sick." Some people succumbed to this and actually thought they were "sick" or were somehow being used by that "high up" conspiracy."

- Wilhelm Reich was impossible to be around when he drank. Under the influence of alcohol he got violent—often not remembering what he did. But he knew he'd beaten his dog Troll with an iron bar that led to the dog's death.

- All his wives needed protection from him . . . Everyone WR lived with and "loved" in the end WR destroyed. When Ilse ran, WR tried to make her out to be insane and have her locked up in a lunatic asylum. When Grethe ran back to her husband, Myron Sharaf, WR tried to get Grethe to have Myron Sharaf committed to an institution for the insane. But Grethe signed a statement saying she would take full responsibility for her husband. Elsa [Lindenberg] ran out of sheer fear and refused to come to America with him out of sheer fear of being alone with her husband.
- I'm the only one he didn't destroy. I never succumbed—Wilhelm Reich could never make me look bad to myself because I saw him as sick. He knew I saw him that way.

Back in Washington after his appeal had been rejected by the Supreme Judicial Court in Maine, and in the vain hope that the U.S. Supreme Court might take up his case, Reich grew distraught. On Valentine's Day 1957, he wrote to J. Edgar Hoover, "It is of crucial importance that I see you personally. Would you kindly let me know whether and when we will meet. Also where. Sincerely, Wilhelm Reich."[58] Two days after this imperious request, Reich wrote another letter to Hoover complaining of a prank caller who he thought was pretending to be Marilyn Monroe; he warned of "acute immediate danger." Later that day he wrote yet another letter detailing the conspiracy against him: "What the espionage is after," Reich reassured him, "is in my head only. They will never get it. I have sent out some false equations to keep them running in circles as these few psychopaths have kept the world running in circles so long." Reich informed Hoover of more imminent and apocalyptic threats and tried to whet his appetite with a few code words that he asked be kept on record: "'14:30'; 'Gaudeamus'; 'Moon'; 'Proto vegetation'; 'lo1 kr2.'"[59]

The day the Supreme Court turned down Reich's appeal, the FBI sent two agents to interview him in his Washington residence to collect the information that Reich had promised them the previous day. It is amazing that they took Reich's letters seriously enough to make the trip, considering their scattered content. Eva opened the door and welcomed them in. When the agents wouldn't sign their names in his appointment book, Reich phoned the bureau to check their credentials.

The FBI reported that when asked to give specific information on espionage or any other issue of national security, the "subject repeatedly dealt in generalities despite continued efforts to have him confine his train of thought in one direction . . . Subject went from one topic to another without making sense." When they tried to pin down why he had summoned them, Reich "would merely resort to general statements pertaining to cosmic energy, flying saucers, etc. When mentioning 'flying saucers' the subject was asked if his knowledge of these prompted his contacting the FBI, whereupon the subject replied in the affirmative but once again could not be specific."[60]

Reich made repeated references to Hoover's detailed knowledge of his work and produced three manila envelopes that were heavily sealed with wax and embossed with his initials. He wanted the agents to take one of these envelopes to the FBI director, which they wouldn't do unless he told them what they contained. Reich said the contents were too secret to divulge (one of them was perhaps the brown manila envelope containing his record of UFO sightings, which Reich had just rediscovered in Karrer's house—he had suspected her of stealing them). Before the agents could probe, Reich jumped to another subject.

It was the second time that month that Reich had been interviewed by FBI agents—a previous team, unimpressed with his hints of top secret work involving interplanetary travel, had stated that "Walter Roner" appeared to be "mentally unstable."[61] The pseudonymous Roner was soon connected to Wilhelm Reich, who had a large file at the bureau and had been sending them messages and materials for years on the conspiracy against him. "Since November, 1955, Reich and members of his staff have been bombarding FBI with complaints of perjury, fraud and other irregularities," a subsequent report stated. "He is described as a most unsavory character and is regarded in established scientific circles and by Government agencies as something of a 'quack.' As a matter of policy Reich's letters are unanswered by the bureau." After the FBI's second visit, since he had also failed "to furnish information which could be considered pertinent or comprehensible," the interviewing agents suggested that all further contact with Reich be avoided.

Two days before the FBI called, Reich wrote another missive to the president about the impending "planetary emergency," the last line of which read: "I am doing my best to keep in touch with an at times elusive and complicated reality."[62]

Reich and Silvert were taken to the federal penitentiary in Danbury, Connecticut, on March 22, 1957, for psychiatric evaluations. Reich was interviewed for an hour by a young consultant psychiatrist, Dr. Richard C. Hubbard, who had read and admired Reich's *Character Analysis* during his training. Reich told him about his more recent theoretical advancements and of the conspiracy against him. At one point a plane flew overhead, and Reich told Hubbard that the air force had sent it as a sign that they were protecting him ("There they are, watching me, encouraging me," Reich said). Hubbard thought this such an outlandish claim that he at first suspected Reich of trying to trick him into diagnosing him mentally unstable so as to escape serving his sentence. But he soon realized that Reich was quite sincere in his belief. Hubbard wrote in his report:

*Diagnosis*

Paranoia manifested by delusions of grandiosity and persecution and ideas of reference.

The patient feels that he has made outstanding discoveries. Gradually over a period of many years he has explained the failure of his ideas in becoming universally accepted by the elaboration of psychotic thinking. "The Rockefellows [*sic*] are against me." (Delusion of grandiosity.) "The airplanes flying over prison are sent by air force to encourage me." (Ideas of reference and grandiosity.)

The patient is relatively intact in the greater part of his personality though there is enough frank psychotic thinking to raise the question as to whether the diagnostic label might more appropriately be Schizophrenia Paranoid type. In general his emotional responses and behavior are consistent with his ideas. No hallucinations were elicited.

*Discussion*

In my opinion the patient is mentally ill both from a legal and a psychiatric viewpoint, hence should not stand convicted of a criminal charge.

*Treatment*

Observation in a mental hospital.[63]

Hubbard then interviewed Silvert; he diagnosed a case of folie à deux: "That is, by contact with Dr. Reich he has absorbed Dr. Reich's ideas including the delusional ones. During the interview he expressed some doubt concerning the truth of Dr. Reich's ideas ... but ended up with the statement that he believed them."[64] Hubbard advised that he be separated from the "primary psychosis."

Reich was duly moved to the federal penitentiary in Lewisburg, Pennsylvania, for further psychiatric evaluations, while Silvert remained in Danbury (where he made a nuisance of himself by protesting about the lack of conjugal rights). The chief probation officer of Maine had written a profile of Reich warning Lewisburg officials that Reich was "a man of great ego and vanity. He cannot submit to seeing his little kingdom destroyed. The only means he seems to find of perpetuating himself at this point is to present himself to his followers as a martyr."[65] Indeed, Reich wrote to his son from prison that he identified with "Socrates, Christ, Bruno, Galileo, Moses, Savonarola, Dostojewski [*sic*], Ghandi [*sic*], Nehru, Minscenti [*sic*], Nietzsche, Luther and many others who have fought the devil of ignorance, unlawful acts of Government, social evil."[66]

The two psychiatrists who interviewed him at Lewisburg also noticed that Reich got excited whenever planes went overhead, but though they noted the "nebulous concepts" Reich elaborated and his intricate system of "persecutory trends" (particularly concerning the Rockefeller Foundation), they concluded that Reich was legally sane:

The following represents the consensus of the Board of Examiners.

In our opinions:

During the interrogation, Reich gave no concrete evidence of being mentally incompetent. He is capable of adhering to the right and refraining from the wrong.

Although he expressed some bizarre ideation, his personality appears to be essentially intact.

In our opinion, it is felt that Reich could easily have a frank break with reality, and become psychotic, particularly if the stresses and environmental pressures become overwhelming.[67]

The opinions of the resident psychiatrists at Lewisburg took precedence over the opinion of Hubbard, who was only a visiting consultant, and Reich began his two-year sentence.

On the prison questionnaire he was required to fill in by his parole officer, Reich claimed that he was raised in an old-fashioned, "Bostonian" fashion. Asked to describe his family history, Reich chose not to disclose the pubertal drama of his mother's suicide. "She died from accidental food poisoning, I believe," he wrote. His father "died from grief > TB," and his brother, in this account, "from starvation due to War I" (in fact he hadn't died until 1926). Asked to describe how he got along with Karrer, Reich wrote, "Perfect." He planned to live with her on his release, "if she still wants me."[68] Reich had plans to emigrate to Switzerland with Karrer when he was released, as had so many other émigrés (Adorno, Horkheimer, Thomas Mann, Hermann Hesse, and Rilke all lived out their lives there): "well paid counseling earnings are quite certain," he wrote.

Reich's skin condition flared up once again in prison, as it had when he was incarcerated on Ellis Island; he soothed it by soaking in daily baths and by covering himself in Vaseline. In his report on the Oranur experiment, Reich had explained the high frequency of prison riots as the result of DOR being somehow concentrated in the barred cage of the prison cell. Eva and Bill Moise made occasional visits to the prison with a cloudbuster, with which they would try to clear the DOR over Lewisburg, hoping to make conditions there slightly more tolerable for Reich.

Silvert served his one-year sentence at Danbury. After his release from prison, and having lost his medical license, he worked as a bellhop captain in a Manhattan hotel. He committed suicide on May 29, 1958, by taking a dose of cyanide in Van Cortlandt Park in the Bronx.

The "great experiment," as the penitentiary in Lewisburg, the centerpiece of the Federal Bureau of Prisons, was known, was about a mile north of downtown Lewisburg. You had to drive along a meandering country road for about a mile, until, as one visitor in the 1950s described it, you reached "an abruptly impassable barrier, a massive concrete wall thirty feet high and more than one thousand feet long," like a "skyscraper on its side." There were redbrick watchtowers at each corner and inside were "factories, ball fields, lawns, and the huge main prison building, also built of brick."[69]

Alger Hiss had been imprisoned at Lewisburg from 1951 to 1954. "Three years in jail," Hiss said of his experience at Lewisburg, "is a good corrective to three years at Harvard."[70] Like Hiss, Reich was deemed important enough to have his own cell—everyone but the most prominent prisoners, and known homosexuals, slept in dormitories at Lewisburg. In the cell next door to Reich, sharing a view of the twenty-one-foot-high prison wall, was the thirty-year-old Harvey Matusow, the manic-depressive paid informer who had made the link between sexual permissiveness and communism before McCarthy's committees and contributed to the climate of fear that led to the witch hunts.

Matusow himself saw Reich as a victim of the conspiratorial culture he had helped fuel. As Matusow put it in an interview in 1995, "To me, Reich, although he was totally anti-communist, was the prime victim of McCarthyism. Because, if the silence that McCarthysim engendered had not existed at that time, the hue and cry about his persecution would have been much greater. But the intimidation of society in those times prevented any outbreak in defense of his rights."[71] Matusow, the paid informer, had testified against numerous Communists, including Elizabeth Gurley Flynn, a founding member of the ACLU, the only organization that rallied to Reich's defense (she was expelled when she joined the Communist Party).

In 1955, after his marriage to McCarthy's wealthy backer collapsed, Matusow admitted to having made up evidence against the union leader Clinton Jencks and published a confessional book, *False Witness* (1954), to explain why he had done so. For a brief moment Matusow was a household name—and a final embarrassment to the already discredited McCarthy—shedding an unfavorable light on the government system of shady paid informants (between 1952 and 1954 the Justice Department had eighty-three informants on its payroll).

Matusow's confession caused a sensation and he and his publishers were subpoenaed to appear before a federal grand jury, accused of having made the whole thing up. Matusow had begun a new career as "Cockyboo the clown," performing at children's parties, and appeared before the grand jury almost as a vaudeville star (as he told a government lawyer, to the amusement of the investigating committee, he was also developing a children's toy, which he called the "stringless yo-yo"). *The Washington Post* billed him as a "Congressional entertainer." He also had a nightclub act that satirized the army-McCarthy hearings by narrating the proceedings as if it were a baseball game. Matusow explained, "I was a clown on the nightclub floor in the evening and a government witness during the day."[72]

Conservatives claimed that Matusow's recantation was fake—if he was lying then, how did you know he wasn't lying now?—and the small radical press that published *False Witness* was portrayed as the control center of the latest Communist plot. Nevertheless, Matusow was sentenced to five years in prison for perjury, of which he served just under four years. But he felt that, in bringing down McCarthy and helping to end what he saw as McCarthy's reign of mass hysteria, he had finally become the hero he'd always wanted to be.

Matusow remembered the day in 1953 that he first heard of Reich, as it was also the day that Dylan Thomas died of alcoholism after a particularly long drinking bout. Matusow and some friends were mourning the death of the poet in his favorite haunt, the White Horse Tavern on Hudson Street in Lower Manhattan, when another regular burst in and announced excitedly that their cat had just delivered seven kittens in one of Reich's orgone accumulators. Four years later, Matusow found himself face-to-face with the machine's inventor when he was checking two books by Dylan Thomas out of the prison library (where Hiss had checked out the complete works of Lenin's widow). Reich, who had been assigned to work in the library, where he shuffled around stacking shelves, stamped the books with a two-week return date; Matusow asked him what it felt like to be surrounded by all this literature, knowing his own books would never be among them. "It's not the end of the world," Reich replied.[73]

Reich was optimistic that his friends in high government would swiftly work to free him. He was so confident of this, according to a "classification study" compiled by a prison social worker, that he was "merely living from day to day," not engaging with other prisoners and just waiting expectantly for his imminent release. " Reich had no friends in prison," Matusow remembered, describing how Reich used to spend sixteen hours a day alone in his cell:

> He kept to himself. Small talk in prison had him as a con man who got rich people to sit in strange boxes that allowed them to make love better. To others he was the flying saucer man who would stand in the exercise yard every day at lunchtime, looking directly into the sun. Just looking, and saying to the few cons who'd stand nearby, "They're coming, can't you see them, they're coming." Cons would smile, turn to one another, smile some more . . . Mad scientist in prison, just like in the movies.[74]

There was another reason for Reich's isolation: he told Karrer that he feared another inmate would murder him (William Remington, a former government official who had been one of the first victims of McCarthyism, had been beaten to death while incarcerated there in 1954). Reich applied to Eisenhower for a presidential pardon that May, and he was absolutely confident it would be granted by his fantasy friend. The document, "My Unlawful Imprisonment," was inscribed "To President Eisenhower Personally":

> I have "done wrong" in having disclosed to mankind the primordial, mass free Cosmic Energy that fills the Universe. This energy rules all living processes and the lawful behavior of celestial function; it determines our emotions, our First Sense of Orientation, judgment and balance. I have "done wrong" in having discovered and made politically accessible the basic force in nature that for millennia was called GOD in many tongues. God was made earthly,

reachable and understandable within man's heart and intellect, without in astrophysical manifestations.

The consequences of this discovery are truly dangerous to the emotional beliefs and intellectual constructions of man; to his total natural scientific outlook, to his accustomed social, planetary and emotional (= cosmic) existence. My technological achievements in the global atmosphere have already been adopted in special departments of the United States Air Force and were developed further... the US film "Earth vs Flying Saucers" depicts certain aspects of my contribution to the space problem technology, especially with regard to counter measures against Space Ships. I am certain that my implicit trust in my friends in the US Government will never be disappointed.[75]

The film Reich refers to, which had been released the previous year, depicts an antimagnetic gun that robs invading spaceships of their ability to defy gravity so that they crash like Icarus to the earth— once again, Reich felt he was living the movie; after all, hadn't he written in *Contact with Space* two years before that he had managed to extinguish UFO lights with his space gun?

In October 1957 the Russians launched Sputnik (which means "fellow traveler" in Russian). As the shiny twenty-three-inch ball orbited the earth, Matusow reflected on his anti-Communist-inspired crimes: "I was thinking every hour and a half, the consciousness of humanity is up there . . . Because we see ourselves for the first time. This little ball became this mirror going around the earth."[76] Reich was unimpressed by the Soviet achievement. He wrote to Peter that it was a "nice stunt like a ball thrown upon ocean waves and tossed about helplessly" but that it could never be an active navigation vessel like a spaceship run on orgone energy.[77]

On his release from prison in 1960 Matusow moved to England; he returned to America in the early seventies to live in a Massachusetts commune, and then in a Mormon community in Utah. He died in a car crash in 2002. In his unpublished memoir, *Cockyboo: The Stringless Yo-Yo*, the manuscript of which is held in the archives of Sussex University, there is a chapter called "The Day Reich Died." As well as being the "flying saucer guy," Matusow wrote, Reich was also known as the "Sex Box man." Matusow remembered that, in prison, rumors abounded about Reich and his machine: "There was a Sex Box story for every hour and every day." He described how the notorious Reich might be described to a new inmate:

> "Hey, man, see that mother with the red nose?"
> "Yeah, what about him?"
> "He's the Sex Box man!"
> "What the hell is the Sex Box man?"
> "Whatta you mean—you don't know? Everyone knows about the Sex Box man. It was in all the papers. He kinda made a big wooden sex coffin, and a guy and a chick would crawl into it. They'd have to make love for an hour before he'd let them out. It was a big porno raid. Everyone read about it."[78]

The fact that Reich had an angry skin condition but that the strikingly attractive Karrer, who was half his age, was a frequent visitor seemed to be living proof that the box worked, said Matusow. When Reich was seen in the refectory talking to the publisher Sam Roth, who was imprisoned in Lewisburg for the second time on pornography charges, more fuel was added to the rumors that were already circulating. When Roth's case reached the U.S. Supreme Court in 1957 it was ruled that, to be considered obscene, works had to be "utterly without redeeming social importance." Sexually explicit works by Henry Miller, D. H. Lawrence, and James Joyce could now be published and sold without censorship. Unfortunately, the "pornography" for which Roth was indicted, which included Victorian photographs of nude ten-year-old girls, was not thought to fall into this redeeming category.

On November 3, 1957, when Reich failed to appear for the 6:30 a.m. roll call, Matusow remembered, there was confusion as prison wardens checked to see that a convict hadn't escaped. The clanging sound of the steel doors echoed down the corridors as each cell in the block was searched. Reich was found at 7:04 a.m. Doctors estimated that he'd been dead for three to four hours. According to his prison file, "Reich [was] lying on his back, fully clothed except for shoes, on top of the bedclothes. The condition of the bedclothes indicated that the bed had been slept in, his eyes were closed . . . froth on his lips."[79] A postmortem showed "severe sortic stenosis and myocardial scarring," indicative of a massive heart attack.

Reich's death went almost unreported. Norman Mailer's *Village Voice*, the paper that would play a sizable role in turning Reich into an intellectual martyr of the counterculture, ran a short tribute. *Time* ran a brief obituary:

> Died. Wilhelm Reich, 60, once-famed psychoanalyst, associate, and follower of Sigmund Freud, founder of the Wilhelm Reich Foundation, lately better known for unorthodox sex and energy theories; of a heart attack in Lewisburg Federal Penitentiary, Pa., where he was serving a two-year term for distributing his invention, the "orgone energy accumulator" (in violation of the Food and Drug Act), a telephone-booth-size device which supposedly gathered energy from the atmosphere, could cure, while the patient sat inside, common colds, cancer and impotence.[80]

Reich, who had been much preoccupied by the idea of his death, had left detailed plans as to how he should be buried. Dr. Herskowitz arrived at Orgonon for the ceremony accompanied by a fellow orgonomist, Dr. Charles Oller, who had also joined Reich's circle in the late forties and who had been Karrer's last analyst. It was a cold and gray afternoon, just three days after Reich's death, and they brought with them a suitcase of clothes in which Reich was to be dressed for burial. They drove past an abandoned cloudbuster on the driveway, its guns pointed at the damp sky, creating a stark silhouette. A little farther up the hill was an even "greater shock," as Dr. Oller wrote in his account of the funeral: there were "three smashed accumulators scattered on the ground in haphazard fashion, burned and charred, the insides torn out and strewn on the grass."[81] Up at the observatory, workmen were building a makeshift mausoleum under the observatory porch; through the glass you could see Reich's open coffin on a large laboratory table covered with a Persian rug in the center of the long scientific hall.

One of Reich's paintings, *The Murder of Christ*, stood on an easel next to the coffin, and there were readings—as Reich had requested—from his book of the same name. Another of Reich's paintings hung near the entrance to the room. Dr. Oller was struck by the powerful image: "This one was of a darkly garbed woman, painted in grief, holding near her the bleeding head of a girl against a background that dissolved into flames. The inscription underneath carried the words, 'Twentieth Century.'"[82] It was as if Reich had failed to temper the flames that consumed that century, despite his most determined efforts.

About fifty people were in attendance. Ilse Ollendorff described it as a very theatrical occasion: "The atmosphere came very close to mass hysteria." Dr. Baker—who wrote a letter to all the readers of the latest Reichian journal, *Orgonomic Medicine*, stating that Reich had died "a victim of the emotional plague he had fought so valiantly"—gave a short eulogy:

> Friends, we are here to say farewell, a last farewell to Wilhelm Reich. Let us pause for a moment to appreciate the privilege, the incredible privilege of having known him. Once in a thousand years, nay once in two thousand, such a man comes upon this earth to change the destiny of the human race. As with all great men, distortion, falsehood, and persecution followed him. He met them all until organized conspiracy sent him to prison and there killed him. We have witnessed it all, The Murder of Christ.[83]

As the group listened to Reich's favorite recording, "Ave Maria" as sung by Marian Anderson, Reich's coffin was lowered into the vault Tom Ross had built. Peter Reich rushed upstairs to his father's study and lay on the floor crying, whispering "Come back, come back" into the purple carpet. When he got up he noticed that his tears had created a bloodred stain.

# *Thirteen*

In the year of Reich's death, Norman Mailer looked back over the decade and wrote: "These have been the years of conformity and depression. A stench of fear has come out of every pore in American life, and we suffer from a collective failure of nerve. The only courage, with rare exceptions, that we have been witness to, has been the isolated courage of isolated people."[1] Mailer held Reich to be one such hero, an "intellectual martyr" who "was on to something which will still change the course of human history."[2] Reich pointed the way to an orgastic future.

The debt to Reich was clear when Mailer, in his essay "The White Negro" (1957), described how the hipster "seeks love . . . love as the search for an orgasm more apocalyptic than the one which preceded it."[3] The hipster—stoked up with marijuana, existentialism, and Reich—was the prototype of the countercultural figure that emerged in the 1960s. Mailer's God, he wrote, was "energy, life, sex, force . . . the Reichian's orgone." Mailer dismissed psychoanalysts as "ball shrinkers"—the hipster didn't need to dissect his desires on the couch because the "orgasm is his therapy." Man, Mailer wrote, "knows at the seed of his being that good orgasm opens his possibilities and bad orgasm imprisons him."[4]

Just before he died, Mailer spoke to me about the direct influence Reich had on his thinking. "*The Function of the Orgasm* was like a Pandora's box to me," he said. "It opened a great deal because to speak personally, I'd been struck with an itch in my own orgasm. So much was good in it; so much was not good in it. And his notion that the orgasm in a certain sense was the essence of the character, which came out and was expressed in the orgasm, gave me much food for thought over the years. So there were many, many years when I felt that to a degree when your orgasm was improving, so were you improving with it . . . What was important to me was the force, and clarity, and power of [Reich's] early works, and the daring. And also the fact that I think in a basic sense that he was right."[5]

Irving Howe, the editor who published "The White Negro" in *Dissent*, dubbed Mailer the "thaumaturgist of orgasm." Mailer's essay initiated what Dan Wakefield, in his memoir of New York in the 1950s, called "the Great Orgasm Debate," which raged "not only in the pages of *Dissent* but in beds all over New York."[6] The orgasm became a battleground: Was the "apocalyptic orgasm" the key to revolution, as Reich and Mailer claimed, or a false aim that camouflaged the hipster's narcissistic and hedonistic selfishness? In a subsequent issue of *Dissent* the writer Ned Polsky argued that hipsters were "so narcissistic that inevitably their orgasms are premature and puny."[7]

Mailer admitted that the apocalyptic orgasm had always eluded him; after our interview he phoned me back to assert that "intellectuals never had good orgasms." Despite his belief that the orgasm was a mirror to the man, he never had vegetotherapy—although, he wrote in *The Village Voice* in February 1956, he had been analyzing himself. He added, "If I were ever to look for a therapist, I would be inclined to get me to a Reichian."[8] Mailer did build several variants of the orgone accumulator in his barn in Connecticut. One was carpet-lined so that he could scream his lungs out inside it as he combined Reich's regimen with Dr. Arthur Janov's primal scream therapy. Others were built like huge dinosaur eggs so that he could roll about inside them on the grass. "They were beautifully finished," remembered Mailer's friend the theater producer Lewis Allen, "and there was a big one that opened like an Easter egg. He climbed inside and closed the top."[9]

Mailer's enthusiastic promotion of Reich in *The Village Voice* and elsewhere introduced his ideas to a new generation of the counterculture. By October 1961 so many people were making the pilgrimage to Orgonon, now the Wilhelm Reich Museum, that the FDA sent an agent to make an "establishment inspection." The agent found Reich's laboratory much as he had left it, with photographs, scales, an oscilloscope, a Geiger counter, and a few glass slides scattered over the work surfaces—the record of an aborted scientific adventure. O. Spurgeon English, who had been analyzed by Reich in Vienna and Berlin but who never saw Reich in America, wrote of his own tour of Orgonon: "The whole place seems charged with an atmosphere of immense energy. The institution, while not large, represented the outward extension of a tremendous energetic man with his mind flooded with ideas; almost too many ideas for one person to put into action during one lifetime."[10] The director of the American Medical Association, who had suggested that the FDA make their visit, wrote, "The impression one receives is that this man, in the prime of a possible medical discovery, was clapped in prison."[11]

The FDA found that there were no accumulators being sold at that time, but in February 1963, six years after Reich's death (and, as Philip Larkin had it, "the year that sexual intercourse was invented"), an FDA official who had heard about the burgeoning interest in Reich's theories recommended further investigations. Executives at the Barnes and Noble bookstore were interviewed regarding their sale of Reich's books (which the FDA had banned Reich from distributing) and several Reichian therapists were investigated. All this renewed interest was attributed to Mailer. But no accumulators were being produced, and the FDA finally closed the case.

"Frankly, I always thought that the box was kind of crap," Mailer said, chuckling, when asked about the boxes he built, "and even people who had boxes always made jokes about them. It was a little bit like the embarrassment people used to feel during the atom bomb scare years of the early fifties, when once in a while someone who had a big house would confess that they had an atom bomb shelter down below in the cellar, and they were always very embarrassed by it, particularly after ten years had gone by and the bomb shelter down in the cellar was getting moldy. In that sense the orgone box was a fad." That Mailer should have chosen an atom bomb shelter as a point of comparison is perhaps not solely related to faddism: the orgone box was, similarly, a relic of the politics of the cold war.

In 1956, *Reader's Digest* conservatively estimated that 330,000 illegal abortions were performed in America, which resulted in the deaths of about 5,000 women. In 1957, the year of Reich's death, the FDA granted a license for the Pill to be used to treat menstrual disorders. In Massachusetts, where Gregory Pincus had developed the contraceptive pill, anyone supplying contraceptives faced up to five years in prison, and it was thought to be too controversial to market the Pill for that purpose. But doctors advised women that a "side effect" of the Pill was that it prevented ovulation, and 500,000 women knowingly took the Pill as contraception over the next two years. In 1960 the FDA allowed the Pill to be properly registered as a contraceptive, and by 1964 six million American and half a million British women were taking it. That year the Vatican publicly condemned the Pill, no doubt perturbed by how, as the journalist Malcolm Muggeridge put it, "the orgasm has replaced the Cross as the focus of longing and the image of fulfillment."[12] What started out as an exercise in population control had ended up freeing people to have orgasms without consequences.

By 1964, Reich's view that orgasms were the key to good health had become widely accepted. As President John F. Kennedy succinctly expressed it, "I get a migraine headache if I don't get a strange piece of ass every day."[13] Yet new social problems were presenting themselves in an environment increasingly characterized by sexual freedom. Some young women, *Time* reported in a 1964 cover story on Reich and "the Second Sexual Revolution," were seeing psychoanalysts not because they felt guilty about their sexual affairs but because, since everyone was telling them that sex was so good for them, they felt guilty about feeling guilty. Others, who worried that the sex they had wasn't as good as it should have been, also felt inadequate. Still more worried that they weren't getting any sex at all. "The great new sin today is no longer giving in to desire," *Time* concluded, "but not giving in to it fully or successfully enough."[14] *Time* cited Mailer, with his faith in the apocalyptic orgasm, as the leading representative of this inverted puritanism. Yet were the 1960s everything Reich would have wished for?

In response to the *Time* article, which stated that "it sometimes seems that all America is one big Orgone Box," five orgonomists—they signed themselves "The Ad Hoc Committee for the Study of the Emotional Plague"—published a tract criticizing the magazine for laying the current attitude of "sexual license and pornography" at Reich's door.[15] Reich was in favor of freedom, they asserted, not license; he was for love, not meaningless promiscuity. In their statement they distanced orthodox Reichianism, which stayed true to Reich's own undeniable streak of puritanism (he was against pornography, homosexuality, and dirty jokes), from what they considered to be the amateur distortions of the "truth peddlers," "crackpots," and "band-wagon riders" who had filled the vacuum left by Reich's death.

Elsworth Baker, who led the ad hoc committee, claimed that Reich, before his death, called him in and asked him to take responsibility for the continuation of orgonomy. He apparently advised him to sever all connections with the other disciples, apart from Duvall (whom he had exonerated of all accusations of sexual abuse) and Herskowitz. "They'll kill you," Reich warned. At that time, Baker was head of the Orgone Institute Diagnostic Clinic, responsible for assigning every patient who applied for psychiatric orgone therapy to an analyst. He also oversaw the organization's training program and the editorship of Reich's journal. He would go on to found the American College of Medical Orgonomists and invented a uniform for the members of the new organization. Many issues of *The Journal of Orgonomy* feature group photographs of them in their special blue and yellow robes, with which Baker hoped finally to achieve respectability and status.

Reich had renounced his sex-pol communism and become an enthusiastic Republican in the 1950s. Baker, a lifelong conservative, insisted on a similar political conversion from his left-wing patients. "Baker said that conservatives are healthier than liberals," recalled Orson Bean, the TV quiz-meister and comedian who had been on McCarthy's blacklist because of his communism before he entered therapy with Baker in the sixties, "because liberals are acting out a childish rebellion against their parents—so we all became more politically conservative to please Baker."[16] Baker cast the liberal character as a pathological type: "Only the most 'hideous distortions' of orgonomic truth," Baker wrote in *Man in the Trap* (1967), "could possibly equate [Reich's] work, thinking, and hopes for mankind with those of present-day liberals, leftists, and beatnik-bohemians who have in one way or another attempted to identify themselves with orgonomy."[17]

The year the *Time* article came out, 1964, was also the year that the twenty-two-year-old Jefferson Poland (who would later change his name by deed poll to Jefferson Fuck Poland) and Leo Koch, a friend of Allen Ginsberg's who had been fired from his job as professor of biology at the University of Illinois for encouraging sex among students, formed the Sexual Freedom League. They thought they were taking the name of Wilhelm Reich's Sex-Pol organization in Germany, but, Poland later admitted in a short history of the movement, they got Sex-Pol muddled up with the World League for Sexual Reform, founded by Magnus Hirschfeld.

According to Poland, the Sexual Freedom League's members were mainly denizens of the Lower East Side bohemia and Columbia University faculty and students, and included such counterculture stalwarts as Ginsberg, Fritz Perls's friends the avant-garde theater directors Julian Beck and Judith Malina, and Tuli Kupferberg, a member of the rock group the Fugs (which took its name from the euphemistic neologism Mailer was forced to use in *The Naked and the Dead*). Kupferberg would later star in the Makavejev film *WR: Mysteries of the Organism*. The league met at weekly gatherings in Greenwich Village to debate "sexual freedom"; they picketed the New York Public Library in order to make copies of Henry Miller's novels and the Kama Sutra, which were restricted to the eyes of scholars, more readily available; and they marched on a downtown women's jail chanting "Free the prostitutes." Paul Goodman and Albert Ellis, league members, taught a course for teenagers called "Freedom to Love."

The members of the Sexual Freedom League were just the sort whom Reich would have condemned for distorting his ideas in order to justify their promiscuous anarchism. Certainly, the league soon took an "orgiastic orientation," as Poland put it.[18] A large collection of magazine cuttings, flyers, press releases, memos, minutes of meetings, correspondence, and sex-related paraphernalia, now archived at the Bancroft Library at UC Berkeley and the Kinsey Institute, documents the Sexual Freedom League's quick transformation into an organization that sponsored orgies and sex parties rather than campaigning for the political ideals of sexual freedom.

Baker adopted Reich's hatred of those he called "freedom-peddlers," whom Baker felt would "bring the world to ultimate disaster in the name of 'peace,' 'freedom,' and 'justice.'"[19] Reich was all too aware, Baker wrote, of a fundamental contradiction between the longing for freedom and the biophysical incapacity to accept it. Patients would protect themselves against the wild streamings that emerged in therapy with a variety of reaction formations. Conversely, Reich believed that too much freedom all of a sudden in society would lead to uncontrollable excess, which people wouldn't be able to handle, and there would be sexual and political repression to counter it, as there had been after the Russian Revolution.

"Reich came to believe at the end that he had helped open a Pandora's box," Orson Bean recalled Baker telling him, "that might do more harm than good in at least the short term. Reich came to believe that human beings weren't ready for freedom yet, and that it had to be very gradually thrust upon them. If you went straight for the pelvic area in therapy, all hell would break loose."

Reich, who identified with Eisenhower, felt that his vision of sexual revolution had to be defended against the left as much as the right. In his book, Baker includes a table of sociopolitical types running the gamut from left to right, from Communist to fascist. On the extremes of that scale the Communist and fascist are most infected with the "emotional plague"; sex for them is purely physiological, and they don't believe in love. The modern liberal, who practices sex promiscuously, is also at the mercy of the demonic layer of secondary drives, against which his "political correctness" forms a weak defensive armor. The conservative, however, has free access to a core of human decency, "which allows for fuller self-expression and tolerance of aggression," and conservatives thus more closely approximate Reich's ideal of unarmored health; for the conservative "genital character," sex is an expression of love; but, Baker adds disapprovingly, many expect virginity to be maintained until marriage.[20]

The Reichians were an altogether different type of sexual conservative. Paul Goodman characterized them as "stupidly sectarian . . . narrow-minded and fanatical": "The Reichians are so high-minded and moral," he complained. "They always make me feel I don't know how to behave at all."[21] When patients approach health, Baker wrote, their attitude to society changes—one can't help thinking that they became more like Reich:

> Many social mores become incomprehensible; for example, living with a mate [a patient] does not love merely because the law says he is married, or an insistence on faithfulness out of duty. He has morals, true, but they are concerned with different values: sex is a desire only with one he loves, promiscuity is uninteresting, pornography is distasteful. He is not interested in perversion but feels tolerance toward it and intolerance toward the unbending attitude of society. He becomes self-regulating . . . His face becomes relaxed and expressive. His body loses its stiffness and appears more alive. He is able to give freely and react spontaneously to situations.[22]

Arguably the biggest "freedom peddler" of them all was Reich's former student Fritz Perls. In 1964 Perls visited the Esalen Institute, a cliffside community in Big Sur, California. Esalen, named after a local Indian tribe, had been founded in 1962 in a former health spa by two recent Stanford graduates, Michael Murphy and Dick Price, as an informal academy of the counterculture. Aldous Huxley had remarked that we use only 10 percent of our brains; at the alternative university of Esalen, residents would try to realize fully what Huxley called the "human potential." Perls compared Esalen to "the German Bauhaus, in which a number of dissident artists came together, and out of this Bauhaus came a re-catalyzation of art all over the world" (Perls had mingled with members of the original Bauhaus in Berlin).[23] He came to Esalen to deliver a seminar and ended up staying until the end of the decade.

Until then Perls had lived in relative obscurity, but he would become the charismatic figurehead of Esalen, its most famous celebrity, an important guru to the West Coast hippies, and, in 1967, a central figure in San Francisco's Summer of Love. Reich's idea of throwing off your repressions was Esalen's guiding philosophy, and Gestalt therapy, which unlike vegetotherapy could be done in groups, was seen as the most efficient technique for shedding such blocks. In California, Perls set himself up as Reich's heir—the latest guru of the new cult of sex and anarchy. He wrote in his autobiography with characteristic immodesty, "The target Esalen scored a bull's-eye with the arrow Fritz Perls."[24]

When he arrived at Esalen, Perls still retained a superficial veneer of respectability—he wore shirts and sport jackets. An early experimenter with LSD, he soon swapped these for brightly colored jumpsuits, walked barefoot, and grew his beard and hair long so that he resembled a dissolute Santa Claus. Laura Perls described her by then estranged husband as "half prophet, half bum." His neck was draped with strings of beads given to him by his many lovers, and he had a stone house built for himself on a cliff top, a round gun turret of a structure surrounded by eucalyptus trees, where he'd stage his group therapy sessions. It had a panoramic view over the Pacific Ocean and a balcony that looked directly down on Esalen's sulfur baths.

Perls, who turned seventy-one in 1964, used to drive a small car down to the bathtubs at five o'clock every day because his weak heart couldn't take the walk up and down the steep hill. Even so, he had a reputation as the pasha of the hot springs, where only the severely repressed would keep their clothes on, and he would successfully seduce women with such memorable lines as "You vant to suck my cock?"[25] His student Ilana Rubenfeld said that "women went up and wanted to have sex with Fritz all the time," and Perls boasted of these encounters in his rambling autobiography; he described himself as a polymorphous pervert.[26] "I like my reputation as being both a dirty old man and a guru," Perls wrote. "Unfortunately the first is on the wane and the second ascending."[27]

At Esalen people would come from Los Angeles and San Francisco to see Perls and his volunteers perform Gestalt therapy. He conducted his weekend "circus," as he called the public version of his act, in front of hundreds of onlookers. Perls once said that Freud had come up with the setup of his treatment room, where he sat behind his patients as they lay on the couch, because he was a mediocre hypnotist and hated eye contact. Perls's mise-en-scène was, by contrast, organized around his own exhibitionism. He was the director and was also at center stage; beside him was an empty chair, known as the "hot seat," a kind of therapeutic electric chair into which he'd invite volunteers who wished to work with him.

Perls would get his actors to move between the hot seat and another empty chair, playing out their conflicts, angers, and fears in an imaginary dialogue with themselves. This dramatized the perpetual battle between the "top dog," as he referred to the superego, versus the "underdog," or the rebellious id; of course, it was the underdog that Perls sought to release by making it aware of its shackles. He would sit there, chain-smoking, as he watched and dissected his victims' performances, getting them to repeat bits of dialogue that seemed inauthentic and commenting on how their bodies betrayed their various blocks. He was a master of improvisation and was often curt, rude, and scornful. Participants were encouraged, even expected, to be violently self-expressive ("Shit or get off the pot," Perls told them); they would often sob, scream, and verbally or physically attack him or other members of the group. After patients had finished working with Perls in the hot seat, it was customary for them to kiss him on the forehead, awarding him the honor accorded a traditional guru.

Perls was a master at stage-managing epiphanies. His brand of confrontational therapy became popular with an emerging counterculture already much impressed with Reich's thinking. It was, according to one of his students, "a theatrical and highly cathartic-orientated approach, arrogant, dramatic, simplistic, and promising quick change."[28] Goodman, who had by then become a star speaker at university campuses, visited Perls at Esalen and remarked that the bawdy, hippyish scene he presided over was "pathetic." He compared Perls's "hit and run" demonstration style to a one-night stand.

Perls sought to reintegrate people's fractured selves so that they could reclaim a sense of "wholeness" and "authenticity." He referred to his technique as akin to brainwashing, by which he meant not indoctrination but "washing the brain of all the mental muck we are carrying with us."[29] He didn't seem to realize that his ordering his patients to be more "genuine" and "authentic" might itself be a form of indoctrination. Perls's cultish and oft-repeated slogans were "Be here now," "Live in the present," "Re-own your projections," and "Be truly yourself." But if all one's repressions were exorcised, what was one left with?

Perls started his workshops by getting everyone to repeat the "Gestalt Prayer" after him:

I do my thing, and you do your thing.
I am not in this world to live up to your expectations
And you are not in this world to live up to mine.
You are you, and I am I,
And if by chance we find each other, it's beautiful.
If not, it can't be helped.[30]

He would end by chuckling "Amen."

In other words, Perls's basic philosophy was to be individualistic and self-interested (Perls's poem was prominently displayed at Sexual Freedom League parties, where it was known as the "Swinger's Credo").[31] For Perls, accusations of selfishness were just moralistic manipulations, an attempt by others to say, "Satisfy my-self, not your-self." Dick Price, one of the Esalen founders whom Perls had trained as a Gestalt therapist, took from the training this central lesson: "I think one of the really important things Fritz taught me is to be selfish, rather than continually driving myself 'unselfishly'— giving out and giving up."[32] The philosopher and student of Zen Alan Watts likewise recalled:

What I learned from Fritz was the courage to be me . . . There are times when the most loving thing you could do for other people is to be honestly selfish and say what you want. Because if you don't do that you will deceive them by making promises to do things which you are not going to come through with. So if you say, quite frankly, "Sorry. I can't be bothered with this. It's too much," they

are not deceived. And I think that's one of the most important things
Fritz had to say. To be honestly selfish is sometimes much kinder
than being formally loving.[33]

It was in Perls's philosophy of selfishness that sex, so large a part
of Esalen's brand of mystical psychoanalysis, and radical politics began slowly to become unstuck. By the end of the sixties, when Esalen was at the height of its notoriety, even Perls saw that there was
a problem. The Esalen Institute opened a branch in San Francisco,
which attracted 10,000 people in the first two months; hundreds of
hippies camped in the hills all around Esalen, and businessmen,
lawyers, and doctors flocked there on weekends hoping to recover
their dead feelings and get back in touch with their sensual and physical selves. Centers modeled on Esalen sprouted up all over America:
by the early 1970s there were more than a hundred such centers of
the "human potential movement" offering yoga, meditation, massage, nude therapy, encounter groups, and Gestalt therapy—all offering, as Perls put it, "instant joy."[34] Esalen, Perls lamented, was
threatened with being "drowned in a wave of faddism and fashion."
It was becoming a kind of rehabilitation center for lost souls—or, as
Perls put it, a "spiritual Coney Island"—and he distanced himself
from its tantric mysticism.[35]

Not only was Perls dismayed by how Esalen was becoming corporate and diluted by wishy-washy religious programs—"the discarded
soul was making a commercial reentry," Perls said, in acknowledgment of Esalen's sudden profitability—but he also dreaded the political situation in the United States. Perls thought he had a nose for
fascism; he'd left Germany just before Hitler's ascendancy, and escaped South Africa before the Nationalists came to power.[36] Now
that Nixon had been elected president and Reagan had been installed as the new governor of California, he felt that fascism was
imminent in America. In his rambling, stream-of-consciousness autobiography, published in December 1969, Perls wrote that he feared
that Nixon, like Hitler, would wage a war of "the fits" on "the unfits";
Negroes and hippies would be the new Jews. Michael Murphy, the
cofounder of Esalen, said that Perls was "semi-paranoid about the
political situation" in advising his friends to keep cash and passports

at hand so that they could make a speedy exit. The riots at the 1968 Democratic National Convention in Chicago had been the tipping point for Perls. "Ach, for me, this is the final decision," Perls told a friend. "We must leave America."[37]

In late 1969, Perls, then seventy-six, left Esalen and bought an old motel on Lake Cowichan on Vancouver Island, Canada, a location that would allow those who might be called up by the draft to avoid fighting in the Vietnam War. Many of his disciples, including Dick Price, then recovering from a psychotic breakdown, followed him there and helped create the Gestalt Institute of Canada (Price renamed the "hot seat" the "open seat" when he returned to Esalen, keen to make Gestalt therapy seem less confrontational). The motel consisted of two run-down rows of clapboard rooms, and could accommodate twenty-five to thirty people. Having pioneered group therapy, Perls now wanted to create a therapeutic community and a college that would correct some of the mistakes made at Esalen. The residents of his "Gestalt Kibbutz," as he described it, shared cooking and cleaning chores and participated in evening encounter sessions. Perls imagined Cowichan as a "leader-breeder" place where he'd train therapists who would then set up similarly utopian communities all around the world.

Perls's project at Cowichan was short-lived. In February 1970, having just returned from a visit to Europe, he was taken ill in Chicago with a high fever and was hospitalized. After an attempted biopsy, the heart that had long troubled him gave out. He died on March 14, 1970. When told by a nurse to lie down, he uttered his last words: "Nobody tells me what to do!"[38]


"I read the catalogs of the Esalen Institute," Herbert Marcuse said in a 1971 interview with *Psychology Today*. "To me this is sufficient to be horrified. This administration of happiness is nauseating to me. They teach people to touch each other and hold hands!"[39]

Marcuse was the theorist who did most to explain the machinations and paradoxes of sexual liberation. Whereas Reich offered the sexual revolution to the world in a box, Marcuse, after the initial optimism of *Eros and Civilization*, lifted the lid and saw the horrors contained within it. In *One-Dimensional Man*, published in 1964, Marcuse expressed cynicism about the revolutionary power of sex and the possibility of a sexual utopia in which technology could be used to free men and women, not to dominate them. "It makes no sense to talk about surplus repression when men and women enjoy more sexual liberty than ever before," he wrote. "But the truth is that this freedom and satisfaction are transforming the world to hell."[40]

Marcuse coined the new term "repressive desublimation" to analyze how societies manage to "extend liberty while intensifying domination"; radicalism was blunted because all liberated desire was swept into an existing capitalist system of production and consumption.[41] Advertisers, Marcuse argued, eagerly exploited for profit the new realm of unrepressed sexual feeling and used ideas from psychoanalysis to encourage consumers' apparently infinite desires and to foster what he called "false needs." Radical sexuality, for which he'd previously had grand hopes, was co-opted and contained: the libido was carefully, almost scientifically, managed and controlled.

Like Henry Miller, Marcuse held out hope for the "misfits," the conscientious objectors who might join with him in the "Great Refusal" of society's irrational values. In his foreword to the 1966 edition of *Eros and Civilization*, Marcuse confirmed his position as the antiwar movement's favorite philosopher by endorsing the radical slogan "Make love, not war!" The book transformed Marcuse into an icon of student revolutionaries; pupils at the University of Wisconsin even tried to set up a version of the erotic paradise that Marcuse had outlined. The historian Theodore Roszak wrote in 1968 that "the emergence of Herbert Marcuse as one of the major social theorists among the disaffiliated young of Western Europe and America must be taken as one of the defining features of the counterculture," and in 1970 *The New York Times* called Marcuse "the most important philosopher alive."[42] However, Marcuse's residual optimism sat uneasily with his comments on the place sexuality had in a one-dimensional, increasingly totalitarian world that could contain all apocalyptical orgasmic explosions.

The year Reich died, 1957, the sociologist Vance Packard published *The Hidden Persuaders*, a bestseller about the worrying symbiotic relationship between psychoanalysis and advertising that Marcuse cited as having contributed to his change of view. The book, an attack on Ernest Dichter's subliminal advertising methods, asked on its front cover, "What Makes Us Buy, Believe—and Even Vote—the Way We Do?" (In the 1956 election Adlai Stevenson had bemoaned the fact that candidates were now marketed like breakfast cereals.) Advertisers, Packard warned, employed "depth boys," as they were nicknamed, to try to puzzle out in indirect ways what really motivated people so that they could develop marketing strategies to best appeal to their selfish desires and whims. Dichter was, wrote Packard, "certainly the most famed of these depth probers."[43]

"Typically they see us as bundles of daydreams, misty hidden yearnings, guilt complexes, irrational emotional blockages," Packard complained of advertising's underhand manipulations. "We are image lovers given to impulsive and compulsive acts."[44] Their techniques were becoming increasingly "scientific," sophisticated, and insidious: researchers exposed test subjects to a battery of projective tests, psychoanalytic interviews, and free association games. They were subjected to hypnosis, lie detector tests, and eye-blink-rate analysis, all so that advertisers could best determine how to bait their hooks and "invade the privacy of our minds."[45] In one advertising company, Packard noticed, a copy of Reich's *Character Analysis* was consulted in the office library.

By the time Packard visited Dichter, Dichter had expanded his operations to a castle thirty miles north of Manhattan, in Peekskill, a twenty-six-room fieldstone mansion on a hill overlooking the Hudson River that could be approached only via a narrow, winding, mile-long private road. Inside there was a sixty-five-foot living room, a full-sized pipe organ, and an indoor pool. Dichter, dressed in a bow tie and horn-rimmed glasses, was described in the book as "jaunty . . . exuberant, balding."[46] Dichter called the focus groups he held in his Gothic mansion his "living laboratory." Children, Packard noted of the panel in progress when he was there, were watching televisions while resident psychologists, crouching behind special screens, secretly filmed and studied their every action so that they could inform advertisers how to subliminally manipulate them. One such session led to the invention of the Barbie Doll. "What they wanted was someone sexy-looking, someone that they wanted to grow up to be like," Dichter reported. "Long legs, big breasts, glamorous."[47] To Packard, Dichter's mansion was a sinister factory that manufactured and implanted self-destructive desires.

Ironically, Packard's bestselling attack (it sold over one million copies) made Dichter even more successful. It made him an instant celebrity and exposed his ideas to a large audience; he was invited onto TV and radio shows to explain and justify his Svengali-like techniques. A chapter in Dichter's autobiography is titled "Thank You, Vance Packard." Some clients even suspected that he'd commissioned *The Hidden Persuaders* for promotional purposes. Shortly after the book came out, Packard and Dichter confronted each other in a radio debate. Packard argued that, because of his commitment to "self-guidance and individuality," he had severe reservations about the way "advertisers are learning to play upon [our] subconscious needs without our awareness."[48] Packard thought that science was being used to menace and undermine democracy; he invoked "the chilling world of George Orwell and his Big Brother."[49]

Dichter, however, thought that motivational researchers were the invisible force that upheld democracy: salesmen peddled "a positive philosophy of life" and the people who bought what they sold declared their faith in the future and in the American dream. In *The Strategy of Desire* (1960), Dichter's book-length riposte to Packard, he described motivational researchers as "merchants of discontent" who created a world of psychological obsolescence and incessant demand for new things, and he believed that it was precisely in that endless quest and constant striving that people found political and psychological health:

> Our role, as scientific communicators, as persuaders, is one of liberating these desires, not in an attempt to manipulate but in an attempt to move our economic system forward and with it our happiness . . . The real definition of happiness is what I call constructive discontent. Getting there is all, not just half, the fun. Stress and insecurity and whatever its labels may be, are the most beneficial movers and springs of our life: Trying to reach a goal but having the goal recede is the real mystery of happiness.[50]

Citizens/consumers would never be sated, but would nevertheless enjoy, albeit not without anxiety, the demand feeding of their multitudinous desires. Dichter described himself as "a general on the battlefield of free enterprise." His was an elitist view: the masses were not ruled oppressively but rendered docile with things and images, like cattle led by golden rings through their noses, so that they wouldn't rise up and threaten democracy.

Advertisers, though serving the status quo, quickly allied themselves with the sexual revolution because it was good for business. They found a fertile field in the culture of self-improvement that Perls and others fostered. Perls educated his followers to throw off their inhibitions and gratify their every impulse. Advertisers were there to meet this demand for instant gratification and to help those in the counterculture express their individuality through things. Dichter wrote that the "psychological engineering" he practiced offered consumers the means to achieve "self-realization" through products without guilt. Products were sold as if they were the building blocks of one's sense of individuality and self-esteem: "Even a simple cake of soap may offer you unexpected satisfaction if you think of it not as a sober or boring necessity but rather as an opportunity for self-expression," Dichter advised.[51] As a result, the Yippies, the radical group who set out to disrupt the 1968 Democratic National Convention in Chicago—who intended, as their founder Jerry Rubin put it, to do "Gestalt theater on the streets," or "Gestalt therapy on the nation"—all too easily became the yuppies.[52]

The orgone energy accumulator offered a generation of seekers the opportunity to shed their repressions by climbing into a box, which turned out to serve as an apt symbol of their new imprisonment. In Roger Vadim's *Barbarella*, released in 1968, the evil scientist Durand-Durand, who seems to be partly based on Reich, uses a form of orgone accumulator as an instrument of torture when he attempts, unsuccessfully, to kill Barbarella with pleasure. And it is perhaps significant that in the Woody Allen movie *Sleeper* (1973), the Orgasmatron, a machine in which the Woody Allen character attempts to hide from the Secret Police, is a product of an authoritarian regime. These films might be seen to contain, hidden within their comedy, the sort of doubts raised by Marcuse about the efficacy of the sexual revolution. Sexual pleasure, they appear to argue, is not always revolutionary, but can be offered by the establishment as a panacea, thus becoming in itself a form of repression.

Aldous Huxley wrote in his 1946 preface to *Brave New World* (1932), a novel about a future dystopia in which sexual promiscuity becomes the law, "As political and economic freedom diminishes, sexual freedom tends compensatingly to increase. And the dictator . . . will do well to encourage that freedom . . . It will help to reconcile his subjects to the servitude which is their fate."[53] Sexual liberation, despite its apparent eventual successes, might be interpreted, as the philosopher Michel Foucault suggested with reference to Reich, as having ushered in "a more devious and discreet form of power."[54]

NOTES

BIBLIOGRAPHY

ACKNOWLEDGMENTS

INDEX

# NOTES

## INTRODUCTION

1. Nathan G. Hale, *Freud and the Americans: The Beginnings of Psychoanalysis in the United States, 1876–1917* (New York: Oxford University Press, 1971), 4.
2. Leslie Fishbein, *Rebels in Bohemia: The Radicals of the Masses, 1911–1917* (Chapel Hill: University of North Carolina, 1982), 88.
3. Samuel Tannenbaum, "Sexual Abstinence and Nervousness," in *Sexual Truths versus Sexual Lies, Misconceptions and Exaggerations*, ed. William J. Robinson (New York: Critic and Guide, 1919), 75–132.
4. The Oneida Community, a utopian commune that flourished in the mid-nineteenth century, was founded in 1848 by John Humphrey Noyes, whose bible was the Kama Sutra. Noyes instituted a form of polygamy that he dubbed "complex marriage." Members practiced what they called "male continence," whereby men were forbidden from ejaculating during sexual intercourse; this would, of course, have been anathema to Reich. (Despite this practice, forty children were born to the community of about two hundred and fifty people over twenty years.) In America Reich treated Humphrey Noyes, Jr., the children's therapist descended from the Oneida patriarch. See Taylor Stoehr, *Here Now Next: Paul Goodman and the Origins of Gestalt Therapy* (San Francisco: Jossey-Bass, 1994), 159.
5. On Reich's claim to have coined the term "sexual revolution," see Wilhelm Reich, *Reich Speaks of Freud*, ed. Mary Higgins and Chester M. Raphael (New York: Noonday, 1968), 44. There do seem to be earlier instances of the term's use, for example, in James Thurber and E. B. White's *Is Sex Necessary?: or, Why You Feel the Way You Do* (New York: Harper and Bros., 1929), which includes a chapter titled "The Sexual Revolution."

6. Wilhelm Reich, *Selected Writings: An Introduction to Orgonomy* (New York: Farrar, Straus and Giroux, 1973), 37.

7. Achieving "orgastic potency" was the end goal of orgone therapy: "Orgastic potency is the capacity to surrender to the flow of biological energy, free of any inhibitions; the capacity to discharge completely the dammed-up sexual excitation through involuntary, pleasurable convulsions of the body." See Wilhelm Reich, *The Function of the Orgasm* (New York: Farrar, Straus and Giroux, 1973), 102.

8. Richard Cook, *Alfred Kazin: A Biography* (New Haven: Yale University Press, 2007), 88.

9. James Baldwin, "The New Lost Generation," *Esquire*, July 1961, quoted in Steven J. Zipperstein, *Rosenfeld's Lives: Fame, Oblivion, and the Furies of Writing* (New Haven: Yale University Press, 2009), 117.

10. Reich, *Reich Speaks of Freud*, Freud to Annie Angel, 42.

11. Ilse Ollendorff, *Wilhelm Reich: A Personal Biography* (New York: St. Martin's Press, 1969), 36.

12. A. S. Neill, *Summerhill: A Radical Approach to Education* (London: Gollancz, 1962), 4.

13. Beverley R. Placzek, ed., *Record of a Friendship: The Correspondence Between Wilhelm Reich and A. S. Neill, 1936–1957* (London: Gollancz, 1982), 118.

14. Jonathan Croall, *Neill of Summerhill: The Permanent Rebel* (New York: Pantheon, 1983), 260.

15. Placzek, *Record of a Friendship*, Neill to Reich, 22.

16. Ray Monk, *Bertrand Russell, 1921–1970: The Ghost of Madness* (London: Jonathan Cape, 2000), 95.

17. Ibid., 95.

18. Placzek, *Record of a Friendship*, Neill to Reich, 322, 202.

19. Ibid., 256.

20. Zoë Redhead, author interview, February 2004.

21. Placzek, *Record of a Friendship*, Neill to Reich, 382.

22. Paul Roazen and Swerdloff Bluma, *Heresy: Sandor Rado and the Psychoanalytic Movement* (Northvale, N.J.: Jason Aronson, 1995), 84.

23. Louis Menand, "Road Warrior: Arthur Koestler and His Century," *The New Yorker*, December 21, 2009.

24. "Morals: The Second Sexual Revolution," *Time*, January 24, 1964, reprinted in *Sexual Revolution*, ed. Jeffrey Escoffier (New York: Thunder's Mouth, 2003).

25. Ibid.

26. Dagmar Herzog, *Sex After Fascism: Memory and Morality in Twentieth-Century Germany* (Princeton, N.J.: Princeton University Press, 2005).

27. Ibid., 159.

28. See Shulamith Firestone, *The Dialectic of Sex: The Case for Feminist Revolution* (New York: Morrow, 1970); Germaine Greer, *The Female Eunuch* (New York: McGraw-Hill, 1971); and Juliet Mitchell, *Psychoanalysis and Feminism: Freud, Reich, Laing and Women* (New York: Pantheon, 1974).

29. Eli Zaretsky, *Secrets of the Soul: A Social and Cultural History of Psychoanalysis* (New York: Knopf, 2004), 9.

## ONE

1. Wilhelm Reich, *Passion of Youth: An Autobiography, 1897–1922*, ed. Mary Higgins and Chester M. Raphael (New York: Farrar, Straus and Giroux, 1988), 80.
2. Wilhelm Reich, *The Function of the Orgasm* (New York: Orgone Institute Press, 1942), chapter 1.
3. Ibid.
4. Wilhelm Reich, *Reich Speaks of Freud*, ed. Mary Higgins and Chester M. Raphael (New York: Noonday, 1968), 39–40.
5. Martin Grotjahn, *My Favorite Patient: The Memoirs of a Psychoanalyst* (Frankfurt am Main: P. Lang, 1987), 32, 148.
6. Lore Reich Rubin, author interview, October 2004.
7. Ernest Jones, *The Life and Work of Sigmund Freud* (New York: Basic Books, 1957), 1:232.
8. Sigmund Freud and Carl G. Jung, *The Freud-Jung Letters: The Correspondence Between Sigmund Freud and C. G. Jung*, ed. William McGuire, trans. Ralph Manheim and R. F. C. Hull (London: Hogarth Press and Routledge and Kegan Paul, 1977), 300.
9. Sigmund Freud, *The Standard Edition of the Complete Psychological Works of Sigmund Freud*, ed. and trans. James Strachey (London: Hogarth, 1971), 2:271.
10. Ibid., 270.
11. Ibid., 19:49.
12. Brenda Maddox, *Freud's Wizard: The Enigma of Ernest Jones* (London: John Murray, 2006), 52.
13. Ernest Jones, *Free Associations: Memories of a Psychoanalyst* (New Brunswick, N.J.: Transaction, 1990), 159.
14. Ibid., 159.
15. Jones, *Life and Work of Sigmund Freud*, 3:412
16. Jones, *Free Associations*, 159.
17. Ibid., 160.
18. Jones, *Life and Work of Sigmund Freud*, 3:390.
19. Reich, *Reich Speaks of Freud*, 36.
20. Reich, *Passion of Youth*, 62
21. Ibid., 64.
22. Ibid., 65.
23. Ibid., 67.
24. Peter Gay, *Freud: A Life for Our Time* (New York: Norton, 1988), 377.
25. Maddox, *Freud's Wizard*, 146.
26. Sigmund Freud and Sándor Ferenczi, *The Correspondence of Sigmund Freud and*

*Sándor Ferenczi*, ed. Eva Brabant, Ernst Falzeder, and Patrizia Giampieri-Deutsch (Cambridge, Mass.: Harvard University Press/Belknap, 1996), 311.

27. Maddox, *Freud's Wizard*, 154.

28. Jones, *Life and Work of Sigmund Freud*, 3:17.

29. Untitled 46-page document. Aurora Karrer Reich Collection, National Library of Medicine, Washington, D.C.

30. H. J. Greenwal, "Soup Kitchens Feed Viennese Rotten Cabbage, Sawdust Flour, and Horse Meat Doled Out," *Poverty Bay Herald*, January 29, 1919.

31. Stefan Zweig, *The World of Yesterday: An Autobiography* (London: Hesperides, 2008), 14.

32. Ibid.

33. Stefan Zweig, *Mental Healers: Franz Anton Mesmer, Mary Baker Eddy, Sigmund Freud* (New York: Frederick Ungar, 1962), 267.

34. Brian R. Banks, *Muse and Messiah: The Life, Imagination, and Legacy of Bruno Schulz (1892–1942)* (Ashby-de-la-Zouch, U.K.: InkerMen, 2006), 138.

35. Helmut Gruber, *Red Vienna: Experiment in Working-class Culture, 1919–1934* (New York: Oxford University Press, 1991), 16.

36. Herman Sternberg, "On the History of the Jews in Czernowitz," in *Geschichte der Juden in der Bukowina* [History of the Jews in Bukovina], ed. Hugo Gold (Tel Aviv: Olamenu, 1962), 2:27–47.

37. "Abstract of Origin of WR," Aurora Karrer Reich Collection, National Library of Medicine.

38. Zweig, *World of Yesterday*, 223.

39. Martin Freud, *Glory Reflected: Sigmund Freud—Man and Father* (London: Angus and Robertson, 1957), 188.

40. Ibid.

41. Elizabeth Ann Danto, *Freud's Free Clinics: Psychoanalysis and Social Justice, 1918–1938* (New York: Columbia University Press, 2005), 26.

42. Reich, *Passion of Youth*, 74.

43. Ilse Ollendorff, *Wilhelm Reich: A Personal Biography* (New York: St. Martin's, 1969), 28.

44. Myron Sharaf, *Fury on Earth: A Biography of Wilhelm Reich* (London: Hutchinson, 1984), 51.

45. Reich, *Passion of Youth*, 76.

46. Ibid., 96.

47. Ibid., 87.

48. Ibid., 93.

49. Ibid., 129.

50. Sharaf, *Fury on Earth*, 60.

51. Reich, *Passion of Youth*, 105.

52. Ibid., 76.

53. John Updike, *Self-Consciousness: Memoirs* (New York: Knopf, 1989), 72.

54. Reich, *Passion of Youth*, 76.

55. Reich would later distance himself from "Weininger's misogyny, his attitude towards the Jews, and many other conspicuous peculiarities of his work." See Wilhelm Reich, *Early Writings* (New York: Farrar, Straus and Giroux, 1975), 8.

56. Chandak Sengoopta, *Otto Weininger: Sex, Science, and Self in Imperial Vienna* (Chicago: University of Chicago Press, 2000), 64.

57. Ibid., 221.

58. Ibid., 51.

59. Ibid., 139.

60. Reich, *Passion of Youth*, 63.

61. Ibid., 91.

62. Ibid., 9.

63. Ibid., 39.

64. Ibid., 95–96.

65. Ibid., 147.

66. Reich, *Function of the Orgasm*, 49.

67. Isidor Sadger, *Recollecting Freud*, ed. and with an introduction by Alan Dundes (Madison: University of Wisconsin Press, 2005), xxiv.

68. Ibid., xxxvii.

69. Paul Roazen, *Helene Deutsch: A Psychoanalyst's Life* (Garden City, N.Y.: Anchor/ Doubleday, 1985), 150.

70. Alison Fleig Frank, *Oil Empire: Visions of Prosperity in Austrian Galicia* (Cambridge, Mass.: Harvard University Press, 2005), 48.

71. Reich, *Passion of Youth*, 5.

72. Ibid, 26.

73. Ollendorff, *Wilhelm Reich*, 23.

74. Reich, *Passion of Youth*, 124.

75. Ibid., 29.

76. Ibid., 30.

77. Ibid., 31.

78. Ibid., 36.

79. Reich, *Early Writings*, 65.

80. Ibid., 68–69.

81. Ollendorff, *Wilhelm Reich*, 25.

82. Reich, *Passion of Youth*, 32.

83. Untitled 46-page document, Aurora Karrer Reich Collection, National Library of Medicine.

84. Reich, *Passion of Youth*, 90.

85. Ibid., 45.

86. Ibid., 42–43.

87. Ibid., 42.

88. Ibid., 46.

89. Ibid., 43.

90. Ibid., 46.

91. Ibid., 50.
92. Arie Schmelzer, "History of the Jews in the Bukowina (1914–1919)," in Gold, *Geschichte der Juden in der Bukowina*, 1:67–74.
93. The town was 40 percent Jewish before 1939. Only four hundred Jews remained in 1944; most of the others died in Belzec extermination camp. Schulz was shot dead in the streets by a Gestapo agent in 1942.
94. Reich, *Passion of Youth*, 56.
95. Eric Lohr, "The Russian Army and the Jews: Mass Deportation, Hostages, and Violence During World War I," *The Russian Review* 60, no. 3 (2001): 404–19.
96. Reich, *Passion of Youth*, 58.
97. Paul Roazen, *Freud and His Followers* (New York: Knopf, 1975), 504.
98. Reich, *Early Writings*, 5.
99. Allan Janik, *Wittgenstein's Vienna Revisited* (New Brunswick, N.J.: Transaction, 2001), 75.
100. Reich, *Early Writings*, 6.
101. Reich, *Function of the Orgasm*, 39.
102. Benjamin Harris and Adrian Brock, "Freudian Psychopolitics: The Rivalry of Wilhelm Reich and Otto Fenichel, 1930–1935," *Bulletin of the History of Medicine* 66, no. 4 (1992): 578–612.
103. Reich, *Passion of Youth*, 136
104. Ibid., 130.
105. Ibid., 115.
106. Ibid.
107. Freud and Jung, *Freud-Jung Letters*, 235.
108. Reich, *Passion of Youth*, 125.
109. Ibid., 124.
110. Bertha Maria Marenholtz-Bulow, *Reminiscences of Friedrich Froebel* (Boston: Lee and Shepard, 1892), 142.
111. Ibid., 125.
112. Ibid., 126.
113. Ibid., 125.
114. A statistic quoted in Wilhelm Reich, *The Sexual Revolution: Toward a Self-Regulating Character Structure* (New York: Farrar, Straus and Giroux, 1974), seems relevant here: "About 20,000 women per year died in Germany from abortions between 1920 and 1932, while 75,000 women per year became seriously ill from sepsis due to abortions" (30).
115. Reich, *Passion of Youth*, 141.
116. Lore Reich Rubin, author interview, October 2004.
117. Reich, *Passion of Youth*, 145.
118. Ibid., 153.
119. Ibid., 156.
120. Ibid.
121. Ibid.

122. Sharaf, *Fury on Earth*, 106.
123. Reich, *Passion of Youth*, 176.
124. Ibid., 176.
125. Ibid., 178.
126. Lia Laszky, interview by Kenneth Tynan, Tynan Archive, British Library, London.
127. Ibid.
128. Lou Andreas-Salomé, *The Freud Journal of Lou Andreas-Salomé* (New York: Basic Books, 1964), 41.
129. Ernst Federn, *Witnessing Psychoanalysis: From Vienna Back to Vienna via Buchenwald and the USA* (London: Karnac, 1990).
130. Ernst Federn, "The Relationship Between Sigmund Freud and Paul Federn: Some Unpublished Documents," *Revue internationale d'histoire de la psychanalyse* 2 (1989): 441–48.
131. Ollendorff, *Wilhelm Reich*, 25.


TWO

1. Eve Blau, *The Architecture of Red Vienna, 1919–1934* (Cambridge, Mass.: MIT Press, 1999), 27.
2. Stefan Zwieg, *The World of Yesterday: An Autobiography* (London: Hesperides, 2008), 223.
3. Helmut Gruber, *Red Vienna: Experiment in Working-Class Culture, 1919–1934* (New York: Oxford University Press, 1991), 61.
4. Ibid., 6.
5. Elizabeth Ann Danto, *Freud's Free Clinics: Psychoanalysis and Social Justice, 1918–1938* (New York: Columbia University Press, 2005), 17.
6. Ibid., 17.
7. Ibid., 3.
8. Ibid., 161.
9. Ibid., 130.
10. Paul Roazen, *Helene Deutsch: A Psychoanalyst's Life* (Garden City, N.Y.: Anchor/Doubleday, 1985), 253.
11. Helene Deutsch, *Confrontations with Myself: An Epilogue* (New York: Norton, 1973), 110.
12. Kurt R. Eissler, *Freud as an Expert Witness: The Discussion of War Neuroses Between Freud and Wagner-Jauregg* (New York: International Universities Press, 1986).
13. Reich, *The Function of the Orgasm* (New York: Orgone Institute Press, 1942), 41.
14. Ibid., 62.
15. Richard F. Sterba, *Reminiscences of a Viennese Psychoanalyst* (Detroit: Wayne State University Press, 1985), 41.
16. Reich, *Function of the Orgasm*, 74.

17. Danto, *Freud's Free Clinics*, 61.

18. Deutsch, *Confrontations with Myself*, 84.

19. Russell Jacoby, *The Repression of Psychoanalysis: Otto Fenichel and the Political Freudians* (Chicago: University of Chicago, 1986), 66.

20. Danto, *Freud's Free Clinics*, 4.

21. Reich, *Function of the Orgasm*, 47.

22. Ibid.

23. Wilhelm Reich, *Selected Writings: An Introduction to Orgonomy* (New York: Farrar, Straus and Giroux, 1973), 28.

24. In a 1922 essay, "Concerning Specific Forms of Masturbation," Reich claims to have cured a twenty-eight-year-old waiter of impotence by analyzing the unconventional method by which he attempted auto-affection; if this is the same patient, the claim of a cure was obviously premature. See Reich, *Early Writings* (New York: Farrar, Straus and Giroux, 1975), 125–32.

25. Wilhelm Reich, *Reich Speaks of Freud*, ed. Mary Higgins and Chester M. Raphael (New York: Noonday, 1968), 70.

26. Ibid., 67.

27. Reich, *Selected Writings*, 29.

28. Danto, *Freud's Free Clinics*, 92.

29. Sigmund Freud, "Lines of Advance in Psycho-Analytic Therapy" (1919), *Standard Edition*, 17:163.

30. Nathan G. Hale, *The Rise and Crisis of Psychoanalysis in the United States: Freud and the Americans, 1917–1985* (New York: Oxford University Press, 1995), 44.

31. Myron Sharaf, *Fury on Earth: A Biography of Wilhelm Reich* (London: Hutchinson, 1984), 68.

32. Hale, *Rise and Crisis of Psychoanalysis in the United States*, 45.

33. Reich, *Early Writings*, 159.

34. Ibid., 130.

35. Rachel Maines, *The Technology of Orgasm: "Hysteria," the Vibrator, and Women's Sexual Satisfaction* (Baltimore: Johns Hopkins University Press, 1998), 3.

36. Ibid., 35.

37. Jonathan Margolis, *O: The Intimate History of the Orgasm* (New York: Grove Press, 2004), 298.

38. Ibid., 298.

39. Reich, *Function of the Orgasm*, 95.

40. Ibid., 95.

41. Ibid.

42. Sigmund Freud, "Studies in Hysteria" (1895), *Standard Edition*, 2:137.

43. Ibid., 1:184

44. Sigmund Freud, "My Views on the Part Played by Sexuality in the Aetiology of Neuroses" (1906 [1905]), *Standard Edition*, 7: 274.

45. Deirdre Bair, *Jung: A Biography* (Boston: Little, Brown, 2003), 136.

46. Jacoby, *Repression of Psychoanalysis*, 42.

47. Brenda Maddox, *Freud's Wizard: The Enigma of Ernest Jones* (London: John Murray, 2006), 54.

48. Sigmund Freud, *Collected Papers*, 2:92.

49. Freud, "Inhibitions, Symptoms and Anxiety" (1926), *Standard Edition*, 20:92.

50. Reich, *Function of the Orgasm*, 85.

51. Ibid., 98.

52. Reich, *Reich Speaks of Freud*, 15.

53. Martin Shepard, *Fritz: An Intimate Portrait of Fritz Perls and Gestalt Therapy* (New York: Saturday Review Press, 1975), 38.

54. Hermann Nunberg and Ernst Federn, *Minutes of the Vienna Psychoanalytic Society: 1906–1908* (New York: International Universities Press, 1975), 42.

55. Reich, *Early Writings*, 202.

56. Reich, *Function of the Orgasm*, 96.

57. Wilhelm Reich, *Genitality in the Theory and Therapy of Neurosis*, ed. Mary Higgins and Chester M. Raphael (New York: Farrar, Straus and Giroux, 1980), 77.

58. Sándor Ferenczi, *Thalassa: A Theory of Genitality* (Albany: Psychoanalytic Quarterly, 1938), 38.

59. Reich, *Reich Speaks of Freud*, 24.

60. Reich, *Early Writings*, 209–10.

61. Ibid., 214.

62. Sterba, *Reminiscences of a Viennese Psychoanalyst*, 87.

63. Wilhelm Reich, *Character Analysis* (New York: Farrar, Straus and Giroux, 1972), 169.

64. Untitled 46-page document, Aurora Karrer Reich Collection, National Library of Medicine.

65. Wilhelm Reich, *People in Trouble*, volume 2 of *The Emotional Plague of Mankind*, trans. Philip Schmitz (New York: Farrar, Straus and Giroux, 1976), 107.

66. Roazen, *Helene Deutsch*, 219.

67. Reich, *Reich Speaks of Freud*, 149.

68. Wilhelm Reich, *Wilhelm Reich Biographical Material: History of the Discovery of the Life Energy, the Emotional Plague of Mankind*, volume 2 (Rangeley, Me.: Orgone Institute Press, 1953), 5.

69. Deutsch, *Confrontations with Myself*, 157–58.

70. Reich, *Early Writings*, 253.

71. Sharaf, *Fury on Earth*, 83.

72. Deutsch, *Confrontations with Myself*, 157.

73. Franz Alexander, Samuel Eisenstein, and Martin Grotjahn, eds., *Psychoanalytic Pioneers* (New Brunswick, N.J.: Transaction, 1995), 432.

74. Sterba, *Reminiscences of a Viennese Psychoanalyst*, 34.

75. Sharaf, *Fury on Earth*, 202. Richard Sterba, in "Character and Resistance," *Psychoanalytic Quarterly* 20 (1951): 72–76, wrote that Anna Freud's *The Ego and the Mechanisms of Defence*, "although it does away with much of Wilhelm Reich's *Character Analysis*, could hardly have been produced without the latter."

76. Eli Zaretsky, *Secrets of the Soul: A Social and Cultural History of Psychoanalysis* (New York: Knopf, 2004), 173.

77. Peter Gay, *Freud: A Life for Our Time* (New York: Norton, 1988), 472.

78. Ibid.

79. Reich, *Reich Speaks of Freud*, 66.

80. Reich, *Character Analysis*, 50.

81. Ibid., 45,

82. Ola Raknes, *Wilhelm Reich and Orgonomy* (Princeton, N.J.: American College of Orgonomy, 2004), 55.

83. O. Spurgeon English, "Some Recollections of a Psychoanalysis with Wilhelm Reich: September 1929–April 1932," *Journal of the American Academy of Psychoanalysis* 5, no. 2 (1977): 241.

84. Ibid.

85. Ibid.

86. Reich, *Reich Speaks of Freud*, 109.

87. Reich, *Character Analysis*, 148.

88. Sterba, *Reminiscences of a Viennese Psychoanalyst*, 87.

89. Richard Sterba, "Clinical and Therapeutic Aspects of Character Resistance," *Psychoanalytic Quarterly* 22 (1977): 1–20.

90. Sharaf, *Fury on Earth*, 100.

91. Reich, *Function of the Orgasm*, 166.

92. Freud to Andreas-Salomé, May 9, 1928, in Ernst Pfeiffer, ed., *Sigmund Freud and Lou Andreas-Salomé: Letters* (New York: Harcourt Brace Jovanovich, 1972), 174.

93. Ibid., 173.

94. Reich, *Reich Speaks of Freud*, 149.

95. Ibid., 151.

96. Ibid., 153–54.

97. Ibid., 59.

98. Ibid., 9.

99. Sharaf, *Fury on Earth*, 85.

100. Reich, *Reich Speaks of Freud*, 15.

101. Reich, *Genitality*, 8.

102. Reich, *Reich Speaks of Freud*, 40.

103. Reich, *Function of the Orgasm*, 75.

104. Reich, *Reich Speaks of Freud*, 34.

105. Reich, *People in Trouble*, 26.

106. Ibid., 33.

107. David S. Luft, *Eros and Inwardness in Vienna: Weininger, Musil, Doderer* (Chicago: University of Chicago, 2003), 151.

108. Reich, *People in Trouble*, 25.

109. Ibid., 33.

110. Ibid., 35.

111. Luft, *Eros and Inwardness in Vienna*, 4.

112. Jones, *Life and Work of Sigmund Freud*, 3:136

113. Martin Freud, *Glory Reflected: Sigmund Freud—Man and Father* (London: Angus and Robertson, 1957), 194

114. Zaretsky, *Secrets of the Soul*, 221.

115. Freud, *The Future of an Illusion* (1927), *Standard Edition*, 21:7.

116. Zaretsky, *Secrets of the Soul*, 219.

117. Edward L. Bernays, *Propaganda*, with an introduction by Mark Crispin Miller (Brooklyn: Ig, 2005), 38.

118. Ann Douglas, *Terrible Honesty: Mongrel Manhattan in the 1920s* (New York: Farrar, Straus and Giroux, 1995), 144.

119. Larry Tye, *The Father of Spin: Edward L. Bernays and the Birth of Public Relations* (New York: Crown, 1998), 111.

120. Elias Canetti, *The Conscience of Words*, trans. Joachim Neugroschel (New York: Farrar, Straus and Giroux, 1979), 205–6.

121. Zaretsky, *Secrets of the Soul*, 221.

122. Ibid., 221.

123. Ibid.

124. Reich, *People in Trouble*, 25.

125. Riccardo Steiner, *It Is a New Kind of Diaspora: Explorations in the Sociopolitical and Cultural Context of Psychoanalysis* (London: Karnac Books, 2000).

126. Ilse Ollendorff, *Wilhelm Reich: A Personal Biography*. New York: St. Martin's Press, 1969), 14.

127. W. R. Huggard and W. G. Lockett, *Davos as Health-Resort: A Handbook Containing Contributions by A. F. Bill, M.D.; A. Brecke [and Others] and Introduction by W. R. Huggard* (Davos: Davos Printing Company, 1907), 239.

128. Reich, *Genitality*, 10.

129. Helga Ferdmann, "Switzerland and Tuberculosis," in *Switzerland Unwrapped: Exposing the Myths*, ed. Mitya New (London: I. B. Tauris, 1997), 151.

130. Thomas Mann, *The Magic Mountain: A Novel*, trans. John E. Woods (New York: Vintage International, 1996), 125.

131. Ibid., 268.

132. Thomas Mann, "The Making of 'The Magic Mountain,'" *Atlantic Monthly*, January 1953, 42.

133. Albert Einstein, *The World as I See It* (San Diego: Book Tree, 2007), 35–36.

134. Reich, *People in Trouble*, 7.

135. Ibid., 7.

136. Ollendorff, *Wilhelm Reich*, 15.

137. Reich, *People in Trouble*, 204.

### THREE

1. Wilhelm Reich, *People in Trouble*, volume 2 of *The Emotional Plague of Mankind*, trans. Philip Schmitz (New York: Farrar, Straus and Giroux, 1976), 82.

2. Ibid., 87.

3. Ibid., 94.

4. Ibid., 92–93.

5. Ibid.

6. Myron Sharaf, *Fury on Earth: A Biography of Wilhelm Reich* (London: Hutchinson, 1984), 156.

7. Ibid.

8. Sigmund Freud, *The Question of Lay Analysis: An Introduction to Psychoanalysis* (New York: Norton, 1950), 124.

9. Wilhelm Reich, *Reich Speaks of Freud*, ed. Mary Higgins and Chester M. Raphael (New York: Noonday, 1968), 79.

10. Reich, *People in Trouble*, 74.

11. Ibid., 74.

12. Elizabeth Ann Danto, *Freud's Free Clinics: Psychoanalysis and Social Justice, 1918–1938* (New York: Columbia University Press, 2005), 197.

13. Reich, *People in Trouble*, 108.

14. Ibid.

15. Charlotte Wolff, *Magnus Hirschfeld: A Portrait of a Pioneer in Sexology* (London: Quartet, 1986), 251.

16. Reich, *People in Trouble*, 110.

17. Lia Laszky, interviewed by Kenneth Tynan, Tynan Archive, British Library, London.

18. Sharaf, *Fury on Earth*, 132.

19. Wilheim Reich, *Passion of Youth: An Autobiography, 1897–1951*. Ed. Mary Higgins and Chester M. Raphael (New York: Farrar, Straus and Giroux, 1988), 55.

20. Mikhail Stern and August Stern, *Sex in the USSR* (New York: Times Books, 1980), 24.

21. Anton Kaes, Martin Jay, and Edward Dimendberg, *The Weimar Republic Sourcebook* (Berkeley: University of California Press, 1995), 323.

22. Clara Zetkin, *Reminiscences of Lenin* (London: Modern Books, 1929), 49.

23. Wolff, *Magnus Hirschfeld*, 242.

24. Elisabeth Roudinesco, *Jacques Lacan & Co.: A History of Psychoanalysis in France, 1925–1985* (Chicago: University of Chicago Press, 1990), 40.

25. Richard F. Sterba, *Reminiscences of a Viennese Psychoanalyst* (Detroit: Wayne State University Press, 1985), 111.

26. Reich, *Reich Speaks of Freud*, 56,

27. Russell Jacoby, *Repression of Psychoanalysis: Otto Fenichel and the Political Freudians* (Chicago: University of Chicago, 1986), 80.

28. Freud, *Civilization and Its Discontents* (1930) *Standard Edition*, 21:76.

29. Reich, *Reich Speaks of Freud*, 44.

30. Freud, *Standard Edition*, 21:82.

31. Wilhelm Reich, *The Sexual Revolution; Toward a Self-Regulating Character Structure* (New York: Farrar, Straus and Giroux, 1974), 14.

32. Peter Heller, *A Child Analysis with Anna Freud* (Madison, Conn.: International Universities Press, 1990), 337.
33. Ibid., 340.
34. Ibid., 341.
35. Ibid., 337–38.
36. Ibid., 127.
37. Ibid., 340.
38. Reich, *Reich Speaks of Freud*, 51–52.
39. Ibid., 44, 53.
40. Reich to Dr. Baker, January 14, 1952, Wilhelm Reich Papers, Sigmund Freud Collection, Manuscript Division, Library of Congress, Washington, D.C.
41. Wolf von Eckardt and Sander L. Gilman, *Bertolt Brecht's Berlin: A Scrapbook of the Twenties* (Lincoln: University of Nebraska, 1993), 22.
42. Kaes, Jay, and Dimendberg, *Weimar Republic Sourcebook*, 720.
43. Gerald Hamilton, *Mr. Norris and I: An Autobiographical Sketch* (London: A. Wingate, 1956), 11.
44. Norman Page, *Auden and Isherwood: The Berlin Years* (Basingstoke, U.K.: Macmillan, 2000), 45.
45. David Clay Large, *Berlin* (New York: Basic Books, 2000), 229.
46. Reich, *People in Trouble*, 145.
47. Paul Roazen and Bluma Swerdloff, *Heresy: Sandor Rado and the Psychoanalytic Movement* (Northvale, N.J.: Jason Aronson, 1995), 83–84.
48. Wilhelm Reich, *The Mass Psychology of Fascism*, ed. Mary Higgins and Chester M. Raphael (New York: Farrar, Straus and Giroux, 1970), 13.
49. Large, *Berlin*, 238.
50. Anton Gill, *A Dance Between Flames: Berlin Between the Wars* (London: John Murray, 1994), 232.
51. Large, *Berlin*, 243.
52. Reich, *People in Trouble*, 143.
53. Ibid., 142.
54. R.H.S. Crossman, ed., *The God That Failed* (Freeport, N.Y.: Books for Libraries Press, 1972), 43.
55. Reich, *People in Trouble*, 136.
56. Edith Jacobson, oral history interview (1971), A. A. Brill Library, New York Psychoanalytic Institute.
57. Ola Raknes, *Wilhelm Reich and Orgonomy* (Princeton, N.J.: American College of Orgonomy, 2004), 53.
58. Reich, *Reich Speaks of Freud*, 179.
59. Jacoby, *Repression of Psychoanalysis*, 67.
60. Frederick S. Perls, *In and Out the Garbage Pail* (New York: Bantam, 1969), 49.
61. Ibid.
62. Frederick S. Perls, *Ego, Hunger, and Aggression: The Beginning of Gestalt Therapy* (New York: Random House, 1969), 248.

63. Ibid., 124.

64. Perls, *In and Out the Garbage Pail*, 202.

65. Perls, *Ego, Hunger, and Aggression*, 123.

66. Perls, *In and Out the Garbage Pail*, 53.

67. Jonathan Gathorne-Hardy, *Alfred C. Kinsey: Sex the Measure of All Things: A Life of Alfred C. Kinsey* (London: Pimlico, 1999), 153.

68. Sharaf, *Fury on Earth*, 162–3. Reich pointedly didn't refer to homosexuality in his program, as he, unlike Hirschfeld, considered it to be a perversion that would disappear after the revolution.

69. Reich, *People in Trouble*, 158.

70. Reich, *Reich Speaks of Freud*, 80.

71. Atina Grossmann, *Reforming Sex: The German Movement for Birth Control and Abortion Reform, 1920–1950* (New York: Oxford University Press, 1995), 125.

72. Ibid., 124.

73. Ibid., 122.

74. Adrian Brock and Benjamin Harris, "Otto Fenichel and the Left Opposition in Psychoanalysis," *Journal of the History of the Behavioral Sciences* 27 (1991): 157–65.

75. Reich, *The Sexual Revolution*, 127.

76. Ibid., 128.

77. Ibid.

78. Author interview, Lore Reich Rubin, October 2004.

79. Annie Reich, *Annie Reich: Psychoanalytic Contributions* (New York: International Universities, 1973), 88.

80. Reich, *Sexual Revolution*, 256.

81. Sharaf, *Fury on Earth*, 193.

82. Bronislaw Malinowski, *The Sexual Life of Savages in North Western Melanesia: An Ethnographic Account of Courtship, Marriage, and Family Life Among the Natives of the Trobriand Islands, British New Guinea* (Whitefish, Mont.: Kessinger Publishing, 2005), 64.

83. In Reich, *People in Trouble*, 121. Later published separately.

84. Grete Bibring, May 11, 1973, oral history interview records, Boston Psychoanalytical Society and Institute.

85. Joseph Wortis, *Fragments of an Analysis with Freud* (New York: Simon and Schuster, 1954), 106.

86. Reich, *People in Trouble*, 192.

87. Eli Zaretsky, *Secrets of the Soul: A Social and Cultural History of Psychoanalysis* (New York: Knopf, 2004), 230.

88. Sigmund Freud, *The Diary of Sigmund Freud, 1929–1939: A Record of the Final Decade*, ed. Michael Molnar (London: Hogarth Press, 1992), 13.

89. O. Spurgeon English, "Some Recollections of a Psychoanalysis with Wilhelm Reich: September 1929–April 1932," *Journal of the American Academy of Psychoanalysis* 5, no. 2 (1977): 239–53. English had been advised that if he fell under

Reich's influence he wouldn't be able to get a job at an American University. Helene Deutsch assured him that Reich's politics had nothing to do with his skill as an analyst, but it was a foretaste of prejudices to come.

90. Reich, *People in Trouble*, 190.
91. Riccardo Steiner, *It Is a New Kind of Diaspora: Explorations in the Sociopolitical and Cultural Context of Psychoanalysis* (London: Karnac, 2000), 128.
92. Ibid., 28.
93. Ibid., 128.
94. Paul Roazen, *Cultural Foundations of Political Psychology* (New Brunswick, N.J.: Transaction, 2003), 16.
95. Jacoby, *Repression of Psychoanalysis*, 3.
96. Jack Gaines, *Fritz Perls: Here and Now* (New York: Celestial Arts, 1979), 14.

## FOUR

1. Wilhelm Reich, *People in Trouble*, volume 2 of *The Emotional Plague of Mankind*, trans. Philip Schmitz (New York: Farrar, Straus and Giroux, 1976), 197.
2. Sigmund Freud, "On the History of the Psycho-Analytic Movement" (1914), *The Standard Edition of the Complete Psychological Works of Sigmund Freud*, ed. and trans. James Strachey (London: Hogarth Press, 1971), 14:34.
3. Ellen Siersted, *Wilhelm Reich in Denmark* (San Francisco: Reich Archive West, 1977), 2.
4. Reich, *People in Trouble*, 209.
5. Siersted, *Wilhelm Reich in Denmark*, 3.
6. Wilhelm Reich, *The Mass Psychology of Fascism*, ed. Mary Higgins and Chester M. Raphael (New York: Farrar, Straus and Giroux, 1970), 17.
7. Ibid., 30.
8. Reich, *People in Trouble*, 166.
9. Wolfgang Schivelbusch, *Three New Deals: Reflections on Roosevelt's America, Mussolini's Italy, and Hitler's Germany, 1933–1939* (New York: Picador, 2007), 63.
10. Dagmar Herzog, *Sex After Fascism: Memory and Morality in Twentieth-Century Germany* (Princeton, N.J.: Princeton University Press, 2005), 25.
11. Ibid., 26.
12. Ibid., 32.
13. Dagmar Herzog, ed., *Sexuality and German Fascism* (New York: Berghahn, 2005), 19.
14. Herbert Marcuse, *Technology, War, and Fascism*, ed. Douglas Kellner (London: Routledge, 1998), 90. Dagmar Herzog has argued that, on the surface at least, by the late 1930s the Nazis were thought by many to be sexual libertarians (Reich would no doubt have questioned the depth of their pleasure).
15. Reich, *People in Trouble*, 199.
16. Ibid., 200.
17. Ibid., 204.

18. Siersted, *Wilhelm Reich in Denmark*, 4.
19. Myron Sharaf, *Fury on Earth: A Biography of Wilhelm Reich* (London: Hutchinson, 1984), 185.
20. Reimer Jensen and Henning Paikin, "On Psychoanalysis in Denmark," *Scandinavian Psychoanalytic Review* 3 (1980): 106.
21. Siersted, *Wilhelm Reich in Denmark*, 3.
22. James Harvey Young, *The Medical Messiahs: A Social History of Health Quackery in Twentieth-Century America* (Princeton, N.J.: Princeton University Press, 1967), 194.
23. In 1935, after Magnus Hirschfeld's death, Leunbach, under Reich's influence, dissolved the World League for Sexual Reform after a dispute with the other surviving president. Leunbach and Reich believed that the league should join the revolutionary labor movement, but Norman Haire, in London, thought that sex reform should be independent of any party allegiance.
24. Siersted, *Wilhelm Reich in Denmark*, 4.
25. Ibid.
26. Ibid.
27. Riccardo Steiner, *It Is a New Kind of Diaspora: Explorations in the Sociopolitical and Cultural Context of Psychoanalysis* (London: Karnac Books, 2000), 154.
28. Reich, *People in Trouble*, 210.
29. Steiner, *It Is a New Kind of Diaspora*, 154.
30. Elizabeth Ann Danto, *Freud's Free Clinics: Psychoanalysis and Social Justice, 1918–1938* (New York: Columbia University Press, 2005), 270.
31. Reich, *People in Trouble*, 214–15.
32. Digne Meller-Marcovicz, director, *Wilhelm Reich: Viva Little Man* (2004). The footage of Lindenberg was shot in 1986.
33. Lilian Karina and Marion Kant, *Hitler's Dancers: German Modern Dance and the Third Reich*, trans. Jonathan Steinberg (New York: Berghahn, 2003), 54–55.
34. Karl Eric Toepfer, *Empire of Ecstasy: Nudity and Movement in German Body Culture, 1910–1935* (Berkeley: University of California Press, 1997), 152.
35. Sharaf, *Fury on Earth*, 195.
36. Ibid., 200.
37. Karina and Kant, *Hitler's Dancers*, 55.
38. Reich, *People in Trouble*, 216.
39. Ibid., 216.
40. Ibid., 222.
41. Ibid., 227.
42. Ibid., 242.
43. Danto, *Freud's Free Clinics*, 8.
44. Jacoby, *Repression of Psychoanalysis*, 88.
45. Benjamin Harris and Adrian Brock, "Otto Fenichel and the Left Opposition in Psychoanalysis," *Journal of the History of the Behavioral Sciences* 27 (1991): 599.

46. Lore Reich, "Wilhelm Reich and Anna Freud: His Expulsion from Psycho-analysis," *International Forum of Psychoanalysis* 12, nos. 2 and 3 (September 2003): 109–17.

47. Ernest Jones, *The Life and Work of Sigmund Freud* (New York: Basic Books, 1957), 3:193.

48. Peter Heller, *A Child Analysis with Anna Freud* (Madison, Conn.: International Universities Press, 1990), 340.

49. Elisabeth Young-Bruehl, *Anna Freud: A Biography* (New Haven: Yale University Press, 2008), 193.

50. Author interview with Lore Reich Rubin, October 2004.

51. Sharaf, *Fury on Earth*, 251.

52. Heller, *Child Analysis*, xxvii.

53. Ibid., xxv.

54. Ibid.

55. Sharaf, *Fury on Earth*, 200.

56. Sanford Gifford, Daniel Jacobs, and Vivien Goldman, eds., *Edward Bibring Photographs the Psychoanalysts of His Time, 1932–1938* (London: Taylor and Francis, 2005).

57. Steiner, *It Is a New Kind of Diaspora*, 177.

58. Reich, *People in Trouble*, 248.

59. Jacoby, *Repression of Psychoanalysis*, 84–85.

60. It was reported to Reich that Anna Freud said afterwards, "A great injustice has been done here," but this utterance so closely echoes Jones's record of Anna Freud's first-ever public utterance at a psychoanalytic congress (in 1927) that it seems likely that the two occasions were confused. Many years later, when Anna Freud was asked for her opinion on Reich, she simply said, "A genius or . . . ," confident that the listener would fill in the blank. See Sharaf, *Fury on Earth*, 202.

61. Siersted, *Reich in Denmark*, 8; Reich, *People in Trouble*, 245.

62. Sharaf, *Fury on Earth*, 187.

63. Ibid., 194.

64. Paul Roazen and Bluma Swerdloff, *Heresy: Sandor Rado and the Psychoanalytic Movement* (Northvale, N.J.: Jason Aronson, 1995), 84.

65. Ibid.

66. Wilhelm Reich, *Beyond Psychology: Letters and Journals, 1934–1939*, ed. Mary Higgins (New York: Farrar, Straus and Giroux, 1994), 3.

67. Wilhelm Reich, *Selected Writings: An Introduction to Orgonomy* (New York: Farrar, Straus and Giroux, 1973), 120.

68. Wilhelm Reich, *Character Analysis* (New York: Farrar, Straus and Giroux, 1972), 346.

69. Sharaf, *Fury on Earth*, 188.

70. Reich, *People in Trouble*, 250.

71. In January 1954, Reich sought revenge on all those who had accused him of

madness and immorality at Lucerne by compiling a long list of alleged psychoanalytic indiscretions (whether it is accurate or not is impossible to tell): "Ernest Jones slept with Alexander's wife during the Innsbruck Congress in 1927. Schjelderup slept with Bodil Tanberg, a patient of his. Zilboorg slept with Elizabeth Badgeley, also a patient. Feitelberg . . . fucked at Grundlsee like a rabbit, without love and with much joking." See statement dated 1954, Aurora Karrer Reich Collection, National Library of Medicine.
72. Edith Jacobson, oral history interview (1971), A. A. Brill Library, New York Psychoanalytic Institute.
73. Ibid.
74. Jacoby, *Repression of Psychoanalysis*, 82.

FIVE

1. Wilhelm Reich, *People in Trouble*, volume 2 of *The Emotional Plague of Mankind*, trans. Philip Schmitz (New York: Farrar, Straus and Giroux, 1976), 251.
2. Anthony Heilbut, *Exiled in Paradise: German Refugee Artists and Intellectuals in America from the 1930s to the Present* (Berkeley: University of California Press, 1997), 43.
3. Ibid., 440.
4. Ernest Jones, *The Life and Work of Sigmund Freud* (New York: Basic Books, 1957), 1:272.
5. Wilhelm Reich, *The Function of the Orgasm* (New York: Orgone Institute Press, 1942), 371.
6. Ibid., 274.
7. Ellen Siersted, *Wilhelm Reich in Denmark* (San Francisco: Reich Archive West, 1977), 14.
8. Reich, *People in Trouble*, 259.
9. Reich, *Function of the Orgasm*, 377.
10. Digne Meller-Marcovicz, director, *Wilhelm Reich: Viva Little Man* (2004).
11. Wilhelm Reich, *Beyond Psychology: Letters and Journals, 1934–1939*, ed. Mary Higgins (New York: Farrar, Straus and Giroux, 1994), 39–40.
12. Ibid., 56.
13. Ibid.
14. Ibid., 80.
15. Claire Fenichel, Otto Fenichel's wife, claims to have taught Lindenberg the principles of body work. See Claire Fenichel, oral history interview (May 1, 1984), Boston Psychoanalytic Society and Institute.
16. Reich, *Beyond Psychology*, 109.
17. See Robert Darnton, *Mesmerism and the End of the Enlightenment in France* (Cambridge, Mass.: Harvard University Press, 1968).
18. Reich, *Function of the Orgasm*, 271.
19. Siersted, *Wilhelm Reich in Denmark*, 7.

20. Randolf Alnæs, "The Development of Psychoanalysis in Norway: An Historical Overview," *Scandinavian Psychoanalytic Review* 3 (1980): 59.

21. A. S. Neill, *The New Summerhill*, ed. Albert Richard Lamb (London: Penguin Books, 1992), 282.

22. Ibid., 282.

23. A. S. Neill, *Neill! Neill! Orange Peel! An Autobiography* (New York: Hart, 1972), 190.

24. Ibid., 189–90.

25. A. S. Neill, *All the Best, Neill: Letters from Summerhill*, ed. Jonathan Croall (London: André Deutsch, 1983), 112.

26. A. E. Hamilton, "My Therapy with Wilhelm Reich," *Journal of Orgonomy* 13, no. 1 (Summer 1997), 11.

27. Neill, *An Autobiography*, 591–92.

28. Beverley R. Placzek, ed., *Record of a Friendship: The Correspondence Between Wilhelm Reich and A. S. Neill, 1936–1957* (London: Gollancz, 1982), 10–11.

29. A. S. Neill, *The Problem Teacher* (New York: International Universities Press, 1944), 35.

30. Reich, *People in Trouble*, 252.

31. Ibid.

32. Reich, *Beyond Psychology*, 7.

33. Ibid., 10.

34. Benjamin Harris and Adrian Brock, "Otto Fenichel and the Left Opposition in Psychoanalysis," *Journal of the History of the Behavioral Sciences* 27 (1991), 578.

35. Ibid., 605.

36. Ibid., 606.

37. Ibid.

38. Russell Jacoby, *The Repression of Psychoanalysis: Otto Fenichel and the Political Freudians* (Chicago: University of Chicago Press, 1986), 89.

39. David Boadella, *Wilhelm Reich: The Evolution of His Work* (London: Arkana, 1985), 361.

40. Ibid.

41. Henry Lowenfeld, oral history interview (October 8, 1984), Boston Psychoanalytic Society and Institute.

42. Ibid., 18–19.

43. Sigurd Hoel, *Sinners in Summertime*, trans. Elizabeth Sprigge and Claude Napier, afterword by Sverre Lyngstad (New York: Ig, 2002).

44. Alnæs, "Development of Psychoanalysis in Norway," 70.

45. After reading one of Reich's new publications, Fenichel told his colleagues in a 1937 *Rundbrief*, "Reich's themes are very exaggerated. Reich himself is monotonous or completely *meschugge* [mad]. Some of his theories are surely very interesting, even ingenious, but in the main, rational men must repudiate them." See Jacoby, *Repression of Psychoanalysis*, 90.

46. Reich, *People in Trouble*, 118–19.

47. Boris Nikolayevsky, "At the Dawn of the Comintern, the Narrative of 'Com-

rade Thomas,'" *Sozialistitshesky Vestnik* (Socialist Courier), April and October 1964, in Arnold Rubenstein's FBI file, FBI Headquarters, Washington, D.C.

48. Reich, *Beyond Psychology*, 69.

49. Ibid., 70.

50. Ibid., 46.

51. Jack Gaines, *Fritz Perls: Here and Now* (New York: Celestial Arts, 1979), 30.

52. Frederick S. Perls, *In and Out the Garbage Pail* (New York: Bantam, 1969), 49–50.

53. Leon Trotsky, *Writings of Leon Trotsky, 1936–37*, ed. Naomi Allen and George Breitman (New York: Pathfinder, 1978), 23.

54. Ibid., 36

55. Ibid., 22.

56. Leon Trotsky, *The Revolution Betrayed: What Is the Soviet Union and Where Is It Going?* with an introduction by David North (Detroit: Labor Publications, 1991), xxx.

57. Trotsky, *Writings of Leon Trotsky*, 39.

58. Isaac Deutscher, *The Prophet Outcast: Trotsky, 1929–1940* (New York: Verso, 2003), 239.

59. William J. Chase, *Enemies Within the Gates? The Comintern and the Stalinist Repression, 1934–1939* (New Haven: Yale University Press, 2001), 166.

60. Reich, *People in Trouble*, 205.

61. Trotsky, *Revolution Betrayed*, 131.

62. Wilhelm Reich, "The Bions: An Investigation into the Origins of Life," *Journal of Orgonomy* 10, no. 1 (1976): 24.

63. Reich, *Beyond Psychology*, 7.

64. Reich, *People in Trouble*, 261.

65. Ibid.

66. Aleksandr Ivanovich Oparin, *The Origin of Life* (New York: Dover, 2003), 32.

67. "They Will Kill Wilhelm Reich," February 4, 1949, Aurora Karrer Reich Collection, National Library of Medicine.

68. Reich, *Beyond Psychology*, 77.

69. David Boadella, *Wilhelm Reich: The Evolution of His Work* (London: Arkana, 1985), 358.

70. Placzek, *Record of a Friendship*, Neill to Reich, 30.

71. Siersted, *Wilhelm Reich in Denmark*, 13.

72. Reich, *Beyond Psychology*, 91.

73. Myron Sharaf, *Fury on Earth: A Biography of Wilhelm Reich* (London: Hutchinson, 1984), 230.

74. Ibid., 230.

75. Reich, *Beyond Psychology*, 147.

76. Reich, *People in Trouble*, 255.

77. Wilhelm Reich, "The Natural Organization of Protozoa from Orgone Energy Vesicles," in *International Journal of Sex-Economy and Orgone Research*, volume 1 (New York: Orgone Institute Press), 219.

78. Reich, *Beyond Psychology* 123.
79. Sharaf, *Fury on Earth*, 253.
80. Ibid., 253
81. Boadella, *Wilhelm Reich*, 360.
82. Reich, *Beyond Psychology*, 206.
83. Ibid., 197.
84. Ibid., 176.
85. Ibid., 120.
86. Ibid., 179.
87. Ibid., 76.
88. Ibid., 173.
89. Ilse Ollendorff, *Wilhelm Reich: A Personal Biography* (New York: St. Martin's Press, 1969). 37.
90. Robert N. Proctor, *The Nazi War on Cancer* (Princeton, N.J.: Princeton University Press, 2000).
91. Susan Sontag, *Illness as Metaphor* (New York: Farrar, Straus and Giroux, 1978), 86.
92. Wilhelm Reich, *Reich Speaks of Freud*, ed. Chester M. Raphael and Mary Higgins (New York: Noonday, 1968), 74–75.
93. Wilhelm Reich, *Selected Writings: A Introduction to Orgonomy* (New York: Farrar, Straus and Giroux, 1960), 204.
94. Reich, *Beyond Psychology*, 198–99, states, "In keeping with the orgasm theory, which equates the sexual and the vegetative, it must at the same time be the specific sexual energy, orgasm energy."
95. Reich, *Selected Writings*, 208.
96. Reich, *Beyond Psychology*, 206.
97. Reich, *Selected Writings*, 206.
98. Ibid., 206.
99. Reich, *Beyond Psychology*, 193.
100. Richard I. Evans, *Dialogue with Erik Erikson* (New York: Praeger, 1981), 85.
101. Reich, *Beyond Psychology*, 128.
102. Sharaf, *Fury on Earth*, 254.
103. Ollendorff, *Wilhelm Reich*, 45.
104. Sharaf, *Fury on Earth*, 196.

SIX

1. Wilhelm Reich, *Beyond Psychology: Letters and Journals, 1934–1939*, ed. Mary Higgins (New York: Farrar, Straus and Giroux, 1994), 231.
2. Ibid., 232.
3. David Hillel Gelernter, *1939: The Lost World of the Fair* (New York: Avon Books, 1996), 146.
4. Anthony Heilbut, *Exiled in Paradise: German Refugee Artists and Intellectuals in*

*America from the 1930s to the Present* (Berkeley: University of California Press, 1997), 196.

5. Wilhelm Reich, *American Odyssey: Letters and Journals*, ed. Mary B. Higgins (New York: Farrar, Straus and Giroux, 2004), 38

6. Gelernter, *1939*, 23.

7. Ibid., 24.

8. Reich, *Beyond Psychology*, 233.

9. Ibid., 238.

10. Reich, *American Odyssey*, 39.

11. Ibid., 62–63.

12. John Forrester, *The Seductions of Psychoanalysis: Freud, Lacan and Derrida* (Cambridge: Cambridge University Press, 1991), 45.

13. James H. Jones, *Alfred C. Kinsey: A Public-Private Life* (New York: Norton, 1997), 328.

14. Ibid., 258.

15. Jonathan Gathorne-Hardy, *Sex the Measure of All Things: A Life of Alfred C. Kinsey*. (Bloomington: Indiana University Press, 2004), 90.

16. Jones, *Alfred C. Kinsey*, 260.

17. Paul A. Robinson, *The Modernization of Sex: Havelock Ellis, Alfred Kinsey, William Masters, and Virginia Johnson* (New York: Harper and Row, 1976), 44.

18. Gathorne-Hardy, *Sex the Measure of All Things*, 175.

19. Alfred C. Kinsey, Wardell Baxter Pomeroy, and Clyde E. Martin, *Sexual Behavior in the Human Male* (Philadelphia: W. B. Saunders, 1948), 53.

20. Gathorne-Hardy, *Sex the Measure of All Things*, 210.

21. Kinsey, Pomeroy, and Martin, *Sexual Behavior in the Human Male*, 559.

22. Jones, *Alfred C. Kinsey*, 387.

23. Ibid., 410.

24. Wardell Baxter Pomeroy, *Dr. Kinsey and the Institute for Sex Research* (New York: Harper and Row, 1972).

25. Gathorne-Hardy, *Sex the Measure of All Things*, 299.

26. Marie Gottschalk, *The Prison and the Gallows: The Politics of Mass Incarceration in America* (New York: Cambridge University Press, 2006), 57.

27. Ron Chernow, *Titan: The Life of John D. Rockefeller, Sr.* (New York: Random House, 1998), 469.

28. Indiana State Board of Health, *Social Hygiene vs. the Sexual Plagues* (Indianapolis: 1910).

29. Ellen F. Fitzpatrick, *Endless Crusade: Women Social Scientists and Progressive Reform* (New York: Oxford University Press, 1990), 105.

30. Ibid., 100.

31. Daniel J. Kevles, *In the Name of Eugenics: Genetics and the Uses of Human Heredity* (Berkeley: University of California Press, 1986), 48.

32. Vern Bullough, "The Rockefellers and Sex Research," *Journal of Sex Research* 21, no. 2 (1985): 113–25.

33. Martin S. Weinberg, *Sex Research: Studies from the Kinsey Institute* (New York: Oxford University Press, 1988), 88.

34. Jones, *Alfred C. Kinsey*, 479

35. Eli Zaretsky, *Secrets of the Soul: A Social and Cultural History of Psychoanalysis* (New York: Knopf, 2004), 261.

36. Clara Thompson, *Psychoanalysis: Evolution and Development* (New Brunswick, N.J.: Transaction, 2002), 168.

37. Reich, *Beyond Psychology*, 240.

38. Ibid., 247.

39. Ibid., 246.

40. Ilse Ollendorff, *Wilhelm Reich: A Personal Biography* (New York: St. Martin's, 1969), 78.

41. Reich, *Beyond Psychology*, 246.

42. Ollendorff, *Wilhelm Reich*, 84.

43. Wilhelm Reich, *The Cancer Biopathy*, volume 2 of *The Discovery of Orgone* (New York: Farrar, Straus and Giroux, 1974), 91.

44. Reich, *American Odyssey*, 31.

45. Wilhelm Reich, *Selected Writings: An Introduction to Orgonomy* (New York: Farrar, Straus and Giroux, 1973), 214.

46. Reich, *Cancer Biopathy*, 94.

47. Reich, *American Odyssey*, 34.

48. Reich, *Selected Writings*, 226.

49. Reich, *American Odyssey*, 145.

50. Reich, *Cancer Biopathy*, 310; see also Reich, *American Odyssey*, 43.

51. Ibid., 116–17.

52. Paul Goodman, *Nature Heals: The Psychological Essays of Paul Goodman* (New York: Free Life Editions, 1977), 76.

53. Reich, *Cancer Biopathy*, 314.

54. Ibid., 317–18; Reich, *Selected Writings*, 249. After Mildred Brady's negative article about his device in *The New Republic*, Reich claimed that the machine didn't cause "sexual excitement" or provide "orgastic potency," though many users continued to sit in it because they thought it did. See Reich, *American Odyssey*, 433.

55. Ollendorff, *Wilhelm Reich*, 56.

56. Reich, *Cancer Biopathy*, 316.

57. Ibid., 310.

58. Beverley R. Placzek, ed., *Record of a Friendship: The Correspondence Between Wilhelm Reich and A. S. Neill, 1936–1957* (London: Gollancz, 1982), Reich to Neill, 107.

59. Ronald William Clark, *Einstein: The Life and Times* (New York: Avon Books, 1994), 676.

60. Ibid., 847.

61. Albrecht Fölsing, *Albert Einstein: A Biography* (New York: Penguin, 1998), 725.

62. Reich, *American Odyssey*, 100.

63. Ibid., 46–47.

64. Ibid., 55.

65. Ibid., 199.

66. Reich, *American Odyssey*, 199.

67. Ibid., 57.

68. Ibid., 199.

69. Einstein's letter of February 7, 1941, in Wilhelm Reich, *Biographical Material, History of the Discovery of the Life Energy, The Einstein Affair* (Rangeley, Me.: Orgone Institute Press, 1953), catalogue no. E-9.

70. Reich, *American Odyssey*, 74.

71. Ibid., 92.

72. Ibid., 85.

73. Ibid., 220.

74. Ibid., 211.

75. Ibid., 217.

76. Ibid., 96.

77. Ibid.

78. Franz Alexander, Samuel Eisenstein, and Martin Grotjahn, eds., *Psychoanalytic Pioneers* (New Brunswick, N.J.: Transaction, 1995), 436.

79. July 7, 1941, Aurora Karrer Reich Collection, National Library of Medicine, Washington, D.C.

80. Reich, *Cancer Biopathy*, 353.

81. July 7, 1941, Aurora Karrer Reich Collection, National Library of Medicine, Washington, D.C.

82. Paul Roazen, *Brother Animal: The Story of Freud and Tausk* (New York: Knopf, 1969), 127.

83. Victor Tausk, "On the Origin of the 'Influencing Machine in Schizophrenia,'" *Psychoanalytic Quarterly* 2 (1933): 519–56, reprinted in *Incorporations*, ed. Jonathan Crary and Sanford Kwinter (New York: Zone/MIT Press, 1992), 544.

84. Ibid.

85. Wilhelm Reich, *The Function of the Orgasm* (New York: Orgone Institute Press, 1942), 46.

86. Reich, *American Odyssey*, 363.

87. Wilhelm Reich, *Character Analysis* (New York: Farrar, Straus and Giroux, 1972), 430.

88. Reich, *Function of the Orgasm*, 46.

89. Reich, *Character Analysis*, 470.

90. Crary and Kwinter, *Incorporations*, 544.

91. Ted Morgan, *Reds: McCarthyism in Twentieth-Century America* (New York: Random House, 2003), 169.

92. Jerome Greenfield, "Wilhelm Reich: 'Alien Enemy,'" *Journal of Orgonomy* 16, no. 1 (1982): 93.

93. Reich, *American Odyssey*, 138.

94. Peter M. Rutkoff and William B. Scott, *New School: A History of the New School for Social Research* (New York: Free Press, 1986), 136. See also Claus-Dieter Krohn, *Intellectuals in Exile: Refugee Scholars and the New School for Social Research* (Amherst: University of Massachusetts Press, 1993).

95. December 24, 1941, Wilhelm Reich's FBI file, FBI Headquarters, Washington, D.C. The file, bloated with pamphlets Reich sent to the FBI, has 789 pages. Available at www.orgone.org/wr-vs-usa/fbi-files/wr-fbi-files.htm.

96. Greenfield, "Wilhelm Reich: 'Enemy Alien,'" 106.

97. Reich, *American Odyssey*, 128.

98. Louis F. Budenz, *Men Without Faces: The Communist Conspiracy in the U.S.A.* (New York: Harper and Bros., 1950), 247.

SEVEN

1. Alfred Kazin, *New York Jew* (New York: Syracuse University Press, 1996), 45.

2. Ibid., 45–46.

3. Paul Goodman, *Nature Heals: The Psychological Essays of Paul Goodman* (New York: Free Life Editions, 1977), 85.

4. Elsworth Baker, "Fourth Annual President's Address, July 6, 1972" (at the American College of Orgonomy), *Journal of Orgonomy*, Elsworth F. Baker Commemorative Issue, February 1986, 65–69.

5. Russell Jacoby, *Repression of Psychoanalysis: Otto Fenichel and the Political Freudians* (Chicago: University of Chicago, 1986), 109.

6. Goodman, *Nature Heals*, 54–55.

7. Ibid., 55.

8. Ibid., 55–56.

9. Taylor Stoehr, *Here Now Next: Paul Goodman and the Origins of Gestalt Therapy* (San Francisco: Jossey-Bass, 1994), 66.

10. Paul Goodman, *Nature Heals*, 85.

11. Wilhelm Reich, *American Odyssey: Letters and Journals*, ed. Mary B. Higgins (New York: Farrar, Straus and Giroux, 2004), 314.

12. Beverley R. Placzek, *Record of a Friendship: The Correspondence Between Wilhelm Reich and A. S. Neill, 1936–1957* (London: Gollancz, 1982), Reich to Neill, 178. Four of Reich's books had been translated and updated to include his latest discoveries, and four issues of the *International Journal of Orgonomy* had been published.

13. James Atlas, *Bellow: A Biography* (New York: Random House, 2000), 162.

14. Philip Rieff, *The Triumph of the Therapeutic: Uses of Faith After Freud* (Chicago: University of Chicago Press, 1987), 176.

15. Ibid., 176.

16. Michael Wreszin, *A Rebel in Defense of Tradition: The Life and Politics of Dwight Macdonald* (New York: Basic Books, 1994), 196.

17. Gregory D. Sumner, *Dwight Macdonald and the Politics Circle: The Challenge of Cosmopolitan Democracy* (Ithaca: Cornell University Press, 1996), 3.

18. Norman Mailer, author interview, June 2007.

19. Norman Mailer, *Advertisements for Myself* (Cambridge, Mass.: Harvard University Press, 1992), 424.

20. George Orwell, *1984: A Novel* (New York: Penguin/Signet Classics, 1977), 137.

21. C. Wright Mills and Patricia Salter, "The Barricade and the Bedroom," *Politics*, October 1945, 63–64.

22. Paul A. Robinson, *The Freudian Left: Wilhelm Reich, Geza Roheim, Herbert Marcuse* (New York: Harper and Row, 1969), 72

23. Alexander Lowen, *Honoring the Body: The Autobiography of Alexander Lowen, M.D.* (Alachua, Fla.: Bioenergetics, 2004), 44–45.

24. Ibid., 45.

25. Alexander Lowen, author interview, June 2004.

26. Lowen, *Honoring the Body*, 41.

27. Ibid., 38–39.

28. Alexander Lowen, *Bioenergetics* (New York: Coward, McCann & Geoghegan, 1975), 17–18.

29. Ibid., 21.

30. Ibid., 24.

31. Fritz Perls, "Planned Psychotherapy" (talk given in 1946 or 1947), *Gestalt Journal* 2, no. 2 (1989): 5–23.

32. Frederick S. Perls, *In and Out the Garbage Pail* (New York: Bantam, 1969), 266.

33. Jack Gaines, *Fritz Perls: Here and Now* (New York: Celestial Arts, 1979), 36.

34. Martin Shepard, *Fritz* (New York: Saturday Review Press, 1975), 57.

35. Ibid.

36. Judith Malina, *The Diaries of Judith Malina, 1947–1957* (New York: Grove Press, 1984).

37. Ibid.

38. Perls, *In and Out the Garbage Pail*, 50.

39. Ibid., 50.

40. Gaines, *Fritz Perls*, 35.

41. Atlas, *Bellow*, 163

42. Steven J. Zipperstein, *Rosenfeld's Lives: Fame, Oblivion, and the Furies of Writing* (New Haven: Yale University Press, 2009), 51.

43. Kazin, *New York Jew*, 51.

44. Isaac Rosenfeld, *Preserving the Hunger: An Isaac Rosenfeld Reader*, ed. Mark Shechner with a foreword by Saul Bellow (Detroit: Wayne State University Press, 1988), 16.

45. Atlas, *Bellow*, 163.

46. Ibid., 295.

47. Saul Bellow, *Henderson the Rain King* (London: Penguin, 1996), 298.

48. Ruth Miller, *Saul Bellow: A Biography of the Imagination* (New York: St. Martin's Press, 1991).

49. Atlas, *Bellow*, 385.

50. Philip Roth, "I Got a Scheme!" *The New Yorker*, April 25, 2005, 72.

51. Atlas, *Bellow*, 165.

52. Irving Howe, *A Margin of Hope: An Intellectual Autobiography* (San Diego: Harcourt, Brace, Jovanovich, 1984), 134.

53. Kazin, *New York Jew*, 51.

54. Saul Bellow, *Saul Bellow: Collected Stories*, ed. Janis Freedman Bellow and James Wood (New York: Viking, 2001), 241.

55. Roth, "I Got a Scheme!" 72.

56. David Halberstam, *The Fifties* (New York: Villard, 1993), 297.

57. Barry Miles, *Ginsberg: A Biography* (New York: Simon and Schuster, 1989), 41.

58. Steven Watson, *The Birth of the Beat Generation: Visionaries, Rebels, and Hipsters, 1944–1960* (New York: Pantheon, 1995), 28.

59. Miles, *Ginsberg*, 71.

60. Martin S. Weinberg, *Sex Research: Studies from the Kinsey Institute* (New York: Oxford University Press, 1988), 53.

61. Miles, *Ginsberg*, 89.

62. William S. Burroughs, *The Letters of William S. Burroughs: 1945–1959*, ed. Oliver C. G. Harris (New York: Penguin, 1994), 11.

63. Miles, *Ginsberg*, 95.

64. Ibid., 96.

65. Ibid.

66. Burroughs, *Letters*, 19.

67. Miles, *Ginsberg*, 99.

68. Ibid., 101.

69. Ibid., 102.

70. Burroughs, *Letters*, 53.

71. William S. Burroughs, *The Adding Machine: Selected Essays* (New York: Arcade, 1986), 164.

72. William Burroughs, "Orgone Accumulators I Have Owned," a draft of an article published in *Oui* as "My Life on Orgone Boxes" (October 1977), box 47, folder 459, William S. Burroughs Papers, Ohio State University, Columbus.

73. Ibid.

74. Burroughs, *Letters*, 51.

75. Jack Kerouac, *Road Novels, 1957–1960*, ed. Douglas Brinkley (New York: Library of America, 2007), 136.

76. Burroughs. "Orgone Accumulators I Have Owned."

77. Perls, *In and Out the Garbage Pail*, 51.

78. Ibid., 51.

79. Ibid., 50.

80. Ibid., 51.

81. *Rosenfeld's Lives:* (New Haven, Conn.: Yale University Press, 2009), 119.
82. Shepard, *Fritz*, 61.
83. Everett Shostrom, producer and director, *Three Approaches to Psychotherapy*, three-part film series, 1965.
84. Gaines, *Fritz Perls*, 37.
85. Frederick S. Perls, Ralph F. Hefferline, and Paul Goodman, *Gestalt Therapy: Excitement and Growth in the Human Personality* (New York: Delta Book, 1951), 144.
86. Ibid.,
87. J. Wysong, "An Oral History of Gestalt Therapy, Part 4: A Conversation with Elliott Shapiro," *Gestalt Journal* 8, no. 2 (Fall 1985): 15–26.
88. Ibid.
89. Edward Rosenfeld, "An Oral History of Gestalt Therapy, Part 2: Conversation with Isadore From," *Gestalt Journal* 1, no. 2 (Fall 1978): 7–27.
90. Taylor Stoehr, *Here Now Next: Paul Goodman and the Origins of Gestalt Therapy* (San Francisco: Jossey-Bass, 1994), 158.
91. Ibid., 240.

### EIGHT

1. Mildred E. Brady, "The Strange Case of Wilhelm Reich," *The New Republic*, May 26, 1947, 20.
2. Dexter Masters to Kenneth Tynan, quoted in Tynan's unfinished manuscript "A Study of Wilhelm Reich." Tynan Archive, British Library, London.
3. Ibid.
4. Ibid.
5. Henry Miller, *The Air-Conditioned Nightmare* (New York: New Directions, 1945), 23.
6. Henry Miller, *Big Sur and the Oranges of Hieronymus Bosch* (New York: New Directions, 1957), 12.
7. Kathryn Winslow, *Henry Miller: Full of Life* (Los Angeles: Jeremy Tarcher, 1986), 61–62.
8. Miller, *Big Sur*, 12.
9. Ibid., 168.
10. Lucille Marshall, author interview, December 2006.
11. Nancy Leite, author interview, December 2006.
12. Jody Scott, personal communication with author (e-mail), November 2006.
13. Mildred E. Brady, "The New Cult of Sex and Anarchy," *Harper's Magazine*, April 1947, 312.
14. Ibid., 314.
15. Ibid.
16. Philip Rieff, *The Triumph of the Therapeutic: Uses of Faith After Freud* (Chicago: University of Chicago, 1987), 141.

17. Lucille Marshall, author interview.

18. Wilhelm Reich, *American Odyssey: Letters and Journals*, ed. Mary B. Higgins (New York: Farrar, Straus and Giroux, 2004), 307.

19. Elsworth Baker, "My Eleven Years with Wilhelm Reich" (part 1), *Journal of Orgonomy* 10, no. 2 (1976): 178. Elsworth Baker's recollections, described as "a serialized book," were published in the *Journal of Orgonomy* in seventeen parts between 1976 and 1984.

20. Ibid., 178.

21. Ibid., 179.

22. Baker, "My Eleven Years with Reich" (part 2), *Journal of Orgonomy* 11, no. 1 (1977): 22.

23. Ibid., 22.

24. Myron Sharaf, "Further Remarks of Reich: 1948 and 1949," *Journal of Orgonomy* 6, no. 2 (1972): 238.

25. Baker, "My Eleven Years with Reich" (part 2): 158.

26. Brady, "Strange Case of Wilhelm Reich," 20.

27. Beverley R. Placzek, ed., Reich, *Record of a Friendship: The Correspondence Between Wilhelm Reich and A. S. Neill, 1936–1957* (London: Gollancz, 1982), 164.

28. Reich, *American Odyssey*, 412.

29. Ibid., 412.

30. Brady, "Strange Case of Wilhelm Reich," 22.

31. Ibid., 20.

32. Ibid., 22.

33. Myron Sharaf, *Fury on Earth: A Biography of Wilhelm Reich* (London: Hutchinson, 1984), 362.

34. Reich, *American Odyssey*, 392.

35. September 1952, Aurora Karrer Reich Collection, National Library of Medicine, Washington, D.C.

36. Reich, *American Odyssey*, 429.

37. Jerome Greenfield, *Wilhelm Reich vs. the U.S.A.* (New York: Norton, 1974), 77.

38. Christof Mauch, *The Shadow War Against Hitler: The Covert Operations of America's Wartime Secret Intelligence Service* (New York: Columbia University Press, 2003), 170.

39. Joan Brady, author interview, August 2006. Their parents' liberal attitude toward sex was confirmed by her sister, Judy Brady, in an author interview, November 2006.

40. Sharaf, *Fury on Earth*, 366.

41. Fredric Wertham, *Seduction of the Innocent* (Port Washington, N.Y.: Kennikat Press, 1972), 47.

42. Paul Goodman, *Nature Heals: The Psychological Essays of Paul Goodman* (New York: Free Life Editions, 1977), 82.

43. Fredric Wertham, "Calling All Couriers," review of *The Mass Psychology of Fascism* by Wilhelm Reich, *The New Republic* 115, no. 2 (December 2, 1946): 737.

44. Brady, "New Cult of Sex and Anarchy," 320.
45. Reich, *American Odyssey*, 392.
46. Ted Morgan, *Reds: McCarthyism in Twentieth-Century America* (New York: Random House, 2003), 309.
47. Ibid., 311.
48. Arthur Schlesinger, "Who Was Henry A. Wallace," *Los Angeles Times*, March 12, 2000.
49. See Robert Louis Benson and Michael Warner, eds., *VENONA: Soviet Espionage and the American Response, 1939–1957* (Washington, D.C.: National Security Agency/Central Intelligence Agency, 1996), and John Earl Haynes and Harvey Klehr, *Venona: Decoding Soviet Espionage in America* (Yale University Press, 2000). White's code names were "Lawyer," "Richard," and "Jurist"; Duggan was referred to as "Frank."
50. Michael Whitney Straight, *After Long Silence* (London: Collins, 1983), 93.
51. Miranda Carter, *Anthony Blunt: His Lives* (London: Macmillan, 2001), chapter 7.
52. Christopher M. Andrew and Vasili Mitrokhin, *The Sword and the Shield: The Mitrokhin Archive and the Secret History of the KGB* (New York: Basic, 1999), pp. 581–82.
53. Sarah J. Ormrod, *Cambridge Contributions* (Cambridge: Cambridge University Press, 1998), 213.
54. Ron Rosenbaum, "Kim Philby and the Age of Paranoia," *The New York Times*, July 10, 1994.
55. Reich, *American Odyssey*, 273.
56. Placzek, *Record of a Friendship*, Reich to Neill, 155.
57. Kenneth Rexroth, *An Autobiographical Novel*, ed. Linda Hamalian (New York: New Directions, 1991), 508.
58. Ibid., 510–11.
59. Kenneth Rexroth, *The Alternative Society: Essays from the Other World* (New York: Herder and Herder, 1970), 14
60. Rexroth, *Autobiographical Novel*, 119–120.
61. Interview with Theodore Hauschka, February 9, 1953. Food and Drug Administration (FDA) files, Wilhelm Reich, 1897–1957, National Library of Medicine, Washington, D.C.
62. Theodore Hauschka, "The Cancer Biopathy of Wilhelm Reich," FDA files, National Library of Medicine. Reich managed to obtain a copy of Hauschka's paper, referred to by Clara Thompson in *Psychoanalysis: Evolution and Development* (1950; rev. ed. New York: Transaction, 2002), which included a chapter on Reich that praised his early work but dismissed his orgone theories. He later threatened to sue both Thompson and Hauschka for libel.
63. Ibid.
64. Ibid.
65. Miller, *Big Sur*, 45.

66. Baker, "My Eleven Years with Reich" (part 4), *Journal of Orgonomy* 12, no. 1, 1978: 16.
67. Inspector's Report, September 8, 1947, FDA Archive. Two months after Brady's article appeared, the director of the medical advisory division of the Federal Trade Commission sent a copy to the FDA.
68. James Harvey Young, *The Medical Messiahs: A Social History of Health Quackery in Twentieth-Century America* (Princeton, N.J.: Princeton University Press, 1967), 191.
69. Inspector's Report, September 8, 1947.
70. "Instructions on how to use the Orgone Accumulator," FDA files, National Library of Medicine.
71. Inspector's Report, November 18, 1947, FDA files, National Library of Medicine.
72. Ibid.
73. Inspector's Report, November 26, 1947, FDA files, National Library of Medicine.
74. Inspector's Report, November 18, 1947, FDA files, National Library of Medicine.
75. Inspector's Report, January 5, 1948, FDA files, National Library of Medicine.
76. Greenfield, *Wilhelm Reich vs. the U.S.A.*, 66.
77. Inspector's Report, September 30, 1947, FDA files, National Library of Medicine.
78. Ibid.
79. Ibid.
80. Ibid.
81. Reich, *American Odyssey*, 412–13.
82. Greenfield, *Wilhelm Reich vs. the U.S.A.*, 84.
83. Ibid., 69.
84. Inspector's Report, Setember 30, 1947, FDA files, National Library of Medicine.
85. Ibid.
86. Wilhelm Reich, *The Cancer Biopathy*, volume 2 of *The Discovery of Orgone* (New York: Farrar, Straus and Giroux, 1974), 424.
87. Ibid., 415.
88. Ibid., 336.
89. Inspector's Report, September 8, 1947, FDA files, National Library of Medicine.
90. Inspector's Report, January 5, 1948, FDA files, National Library of Medicine.
91. Ibid.
92. Inspector's Report, January 5, 1948, FDA files, National Library of Medicine.
93. Inspector's Report, April 2, 1948, FDA files, National Library of Medicine.

94. Greenfield, *Wilhelm Reich vs. the U.S.A.*, 62.
95. Ibid., 62.

## NINE

1. Alfred C. Kinsey, Wardell Baxter Pomeroy, and Clyde E. Martin, *Sexual Behavior in the Human Male* (Philadelphia: W. B. Saunders, 1948), 7.
2. Lionel Trilling, "The Kinsey Report," *The Liberal Imagination* (New York: Doubleday, 1957), 218.
3. Kinsey, Pomeroy, and Martin, *Sexual Behavior in the Human Male*, 224.
4. James H. Jones, *Alfred C. Kinsey: A Public-Private Life* (New York: Norton, 1997), 516.
5. Kinsey, Pomeroy, and Martin, *Sexual Behavior in the Human Male*, 347.
6. Ibid., 4.
7. Jones, *Alfred C. Kinsey*, 195.
8. May 10, 1948, Kinsey's FBI file, FBI Headquarters, Washington, D.C., http://foia.fbi.gov/kinsey_alfred/kinsey_alfred_part03.pdf.
9. Jones, *Alfred C. Kinsey*, 632.
10. January 5, 1950, Kinsey's FBI file, http://foia.fbi.gov/kinsey_alfred/kinsey_alfred_part03.pdf. For Hoover's similar threat against Joseph Bryan III, who had called Hoover a "pansy in pants," see Athan G. Theoharis, *J. Edgar Hoover, Sex, and Crime: An Historical Antidote* (Chicago: Ivan R. Dee, 1995).
11. Richard Hack, *Puppetmaster: The Secret Life of J. Edgar Hoover* (Beverly Hills: New Millennium, 2004), 275.
12. Theoharis, *J. Edgar Hoover, Sex, and Crime*, 103–04.
13. Jones, *Alfred C. Kinsey*, 595.
14. Ibid., 596.
15. Beverley R. Placzek, *Record of a Friendship: The Correspondence Between Wilhelm Reich and A. S. Neill, 1936–1957* (London: Gollancz, 1982), 220. Kinsey cited Reich's *The Function of the Orgasm* to question Reich's notion of spontaneous ejaculation, which Kinsey thought impossible.
16. Jones, *Alfred C. Kinsey*, 579.
17. Ibid., 579.
18. Untitled 46-page document, Aurora Karrer Reich Collection, National Library of Medicine.
19. Wardell Baxter Pomeroy, *Dr. Kinsey and the Institute for Sex Research* (New York: Harper and Row, 1972), 195.
20. Morton Herskowitz, author interview, November 2004.
21. Wilhelm Reich, "Orgone Therapy: Critical Issues in the Therapeutic Process," tape recordings of lectures, summer 1949, Wilhelm Reich Museum, Rangeley, Me.
22. Placzek, *Record of a Friendship*, Neill to Reich, 238.

23. A. W. Hamilton, "Reactions to the First Orgonomic Conference," *Orgone Energy Bulletin* 1, no. 3 (1949): 117. The conference took place on October 1, 1948.

24. Myron Sharaf, *Fury on Earth: A Biography of Wilhelm Reich* (London: Hutchinson, 1984), 27.

25. Reich, "Orgone Therapy."

26. Wilhelm Reich, *Listen, Little Man!* (Rangeley, Me: Orgone Institute Press, 1948), 43.

27. Morton Herskowitz, "Recollections of Reich," *Journal of Orgonomy* 12, no. 2 (1978): 187.

28. Ibid., 188.

29. Morton Herskowitz, "Memories of Reich: Dr. Herskowitz Recalls His Experiences with Wilhelm Reich," available at www.orgonomicscience.org/history.html.

30. Morton Herskowitz, *Emotional Armoring: An Introduction to Psychiatric Orgone Therapy* (Hamburg, Germany: Lit, 2001), 85.

31. Placzek, *Record of Friendship*, Reich to Neill, 335.

32. Ibid., 271.

33. Ibid., Neill to Reich, 324.

34. Wilhelm Reich, "Falling Anxiety in a Three-Week-Old Infant," in *Children of the Future: On the Prevention of Sexual Pathology*, ed. Mary B. Higgins and Chester M. Raphael (New York: Farrar, Straus and Giroux, 1983).

35. Placzek, *Record of a Friendship*, Reich to Neill, 312.

36. Peter Reich, *A Book of Dreams* (New York: Harper and Row, 1973), 136.

37. Ibid., 137.

38. Ibid.

39. Ibid., 158.

40. Paki Wright, author interview, November 2005.

41. Wilhelm Reich, "Meeting the Emotional Plague," in Reich, *Children of the Future*, 78.

42. Elsworth Baker, "My Eleven Years with Reich" (part 1), *Journal of Orgonomy* 10, no. 2 (1976): 188.

43. Reich, "Meeting the Emotional Plague," 79.

44. Ibid., 81.

45. Ibid.

46. Ibid., 84.

47. Annotation to untitled 46-page document, Aurora Karrer Reich Collection, National Library of Medicine. See also Wilhelm Reich, *The Murder of Christ* (New York: Farrar, Straus and Giroux, 1966).

48. Sharaf, *Fury on Earth*, 420.

49. Interview with Dr. Boote, FDA files, National Library of Medicine.

50. Baker, "My Eleven Years with Reich" (part 5), *Journal of Orgonomy* 12, no. 2 (November 1978): 183.

51. Sharaf, *Fury on Earth*, 271.
52. Placzek, *Record of a Friendship*, 43.
53. Eva Reich, "I Was the Strange Doctor," *International Journal of Life Energy* 1, no. 1 (1979): 32–42.
54. Sharaf, *Fury on Earth*, 149.
55. Peter Heller, *A Child Analysis with Anna Freud* (Madison, Conn.: International Universities Press, 1990), 342.
56. Susanna Steig, "My Childhood Experiences with Reichian Therapy," pw1 .netcom.com/~rogermw2/Reich/others.html.
57. "The Silent Observer," February 1952, Wilhelm Reich Papers, Sigmund Freud Collection, Manuscript Division, Library of Congress, Washington, D.C. The "Silent Observer," or "SO," was the authorial voice used by Reich when he annotated or added to the documents preserved in his archive.
58. Steig, "My Childhood Experiences with Reichian Therapy."
59. Baker, "My Eleven Years with Reich" (part 6), *Journal of Orgonomy* 13, no. 1 (May 1979): 43.
60. Ibid., 40.
61. See Lorna Luft, *Me and My Shadows: A Family Memoir* (New York: Pocket Books, 1998), in which she describes her therapy visits to Dr. Duvall.

TEN

1. Ted Morgan, *Reds: McCarthyism in Twentieth-Century America* (New York: Random House, 2003), 477.
2. Fred J. Cook, *The Nightmare Decade: The Life and Times of Senator Joe McCarthy* (New York: Random House, 1971), 262.
3. Tom Ross, speaking in Digne Meller-Marcovicz, director, *Wilhelm Reich: Viva Little Man* (2004).
4. "Administrative Report," October 25, 1950, Reich's FBI file, FBI Headquarters, Washington, D.C. (For atomic bomb rumors, see "Office Memorandum," January 11, 1949.)
5. Reich's FBI file, October 13, 1950.
6. Elsworth Baker, "My Eleven Years with Reich" (part 4), *Journal of Orgonomy* 12, no. 1 (May 1978): 24.
7. Reich's letter "To 30 Rangeley citizens," dated November 13, 1950, Reich's FBI file.
8. Peter Reich, author interview, July 2005 and July 2007.
9. David Halberstam, *The Fifties* (New York: Villard, 1993), 69.
10. A. E. Hamilton, "My Therapy with Wilhelm Reich," *Journal of Orgonomy* 13, no. 1 (Summer 1977): 6.
11. Reich's FBI file, December 2, 1953.
12. Letter from Robert Oppenheimer to Eleanor Roosevelt, January 15, 1951. Somehow Reich came into possession of this letter, which he thought was part

of the conspiracy against him. Aurora Karrer Reich Collection, National Library of Medicine.

13. Myron Sharaf, *Fury on Earth: A Biography of Wilhelm Reich* (London: Hutchinson, 1984), 376.

14. Susan Sontag, *Illness as Metaphor* (New York: Farrar, Straus and Giroux, 1988), 67.

15. Beverley R. Placzek, *Record of a Friendship: The Correspondence Between Wilhelm Reich and A. S. Neill, 1936–1957* (London: Gollancz, 1982), Reich to Neill, 319.

16. Wilhelm Reich, *Selected Writings: An Introduction to Orgonomy* (New York: Farrar, Straus and Giroux, 1973), 370.

17. Elsworth Baker, "My Eleven Years with Reich" (part 5), *Journal of Orgonomy* 12, no. 2 (November 1978): 168.

18. Ibid.

19. Ibid.

20. Wilhelm Reich, *The Oranur Experiment: First Report, 1947–1951* (Rangeley, Me.: Wilhelm Reich Foundation, 1951).

21. Ibid., 169.

22. Ibid., 171.

23. Ibid., 172.

24. Reich, *Selected Writings*, 377.

25. Placzek, *Record of a Friendship*, Reich to Neill, 322.

26. Ken Tynan, interview with Lia Laszky, Tynan Archive, British Library, London.

27. Ilsa Ollendorff, *Wilhelm Reich: A Personal Biography* (New York: St. Martin's Press, 1969), 110–11.

28. Baker, "My Eleven Years with Reich" (part 5): 181.

29. Ollendorff, *Wilhelm Reich*, 108.

30. Ilse Ollendorff to Reich, Aurora Karrer Reich Collection, National Library of Medicine.

31. Sharaf, *Fury on Earth*, 389.

32. Ollendorff, *Wilhelm Reich*, 111.

33. Deposition by Wilhelm Reich Regarding Ilse Ollendorff, October 3, 1952, Aurora Karrer Reich Collection, National Library of Medicine.

34. Ollendorff, *Wilhelm Reich*, 113.

35. "Statement," November 1, 1952, Aurora Karrer Reich Collection, National Library of Medicine.

36. May 21, 1952, Aurora Karrer Reich Collection, National Library of Medicine.

37. "Deposition by Wilhelm Reich Regarding Ilse Ollendorff," October 3, 1952, Aurora Karrer Reich Collection, National Library of Medicine.

38. "Statement of Personal Impression," December 4, 1952, Aurora Karrer Reich Collection, National Library of Medicine.

39. "Examples of I.O.'s Defense Mechanisms," January 11, 1953, Aurora Karrer Reich Collection, National Library of Medicine.

40. Ilse Ollendorff, author interview, July 2005.
41. Ollendorff, *Wilhelm Reich*, 120.
42. Ibid., 128.
43. Sharaf, *Fury on Earth*, 441.
44. Sontag, *Illness as Metaphor*.
45. Ollendorff, *Wilhelm Reich*, 115.
46. Sharaf, *Fury on Earth*, 26.
47. Lois Wyvell, "Orgone and You," *Offshoots of Orgonomy* 3 (1981): 7.
48. Letter to Ola Raknes, January 24, 1953, Aurora Karrer Reich Collection, National Library of Medicine.
49. "Reaction to 'Cosmic Superimposition,'" December 14, 1951, Aurora Karrer Reich Collection, National Library of Medicine.
50. "Reichitis," 1951, Aurora Karrer Reich Collection, National Library of Medicine.
51. Report on impressions of Oranur and WR (Spring 1951), September 1953, Aurora Karrer Reich Collection, National Library of Medicine.
52. Ibid.
53. "Alone," recording made by Wilhelm Reich at Orgonon on April 3, 1952. Wilhelm Reich Museum, Rangeley, Me.
54. Inspector's report, April 30, 1952, FDA files, National Library of Medicine.
55. Memorandum of Interview, April 15, 1952, FDA files, National Library of Medicine.
56. Interview with Dr. Norcross (Lahey Clinic), February 5, 1954, FDA files, National Library of Medicine.
57. Inspector's report, April 30, 1952, FDA files, National Library of Medicine.
58. Ibid.
59. Ibid.
60. Inspector's report, July 29, 1952, FDA files, National Library of Medicine.
61. Elsworth Baker, "My Eleven Years with Wilhelm Reich," *Journal of Orgonomy* 17, no. 1 (1983), 53.
62. Inspector's report, July 29, 1952, FDA files, National Library of Medicine.
63. Ibid.
64. Ibid.
65. WR letter to Truman, August 13, 1952, Tynan Archive, British Library, London.

ELEVEN

1. Harvey Matusow, *False Witness* (New York: Cameron and Kahn, 1955), 55.
2. Ted Morgan, *Reds: McCarthyism in Twentieth-Century America* (New York: Random House, 2003), 530.
3. Matusow, *False Witness*, 102.
4. Ibid., 77.
5. Ibid., 74.
6. Ibid., 71.

7. Morgan, *Reds*, 535.

8. Alfred C. Kinsey, *Sexual Behavior in the Human Female* (Philadelphia: W. B. Saunders, 1953), 328.

9. Jonathan Gathorne-Hardy, *Sex the Measure of All Things: A Life of Alfred C. Kinsey* (London: Pimlico, 1999), 395.

10. James H. Jones, *Alfred C. Kinsey: A Public-Private Life* (New York: Norton, 1997), 307.

11. James R. Petersen, *The Century of Sex: Playboy's History of the Sexual Revolution, 1900–1999* (New York: Grove, 1999).

12. René Albert Wormser, *Foundations: Their Power and Influence* (New York: Devin-Adair Company, 1958), 47.

13. "Funds and Foundations—Information Concerning Central Research Matter," May 19, 1959, Kinsey's FBI file.

14. Special House Committee to Investigate Tax-Exempt Foundations, *Tax-Exempt Foundations* (Washington, D.C.: U.S. Government Printing Office, 1954), 124.

15. Wormser, *Foundations*, 84.

16. Ibid., 32.

17. David Halberstam, *The Fifties* (New York: Villard, 1993), 287.

18. Lara Marks, *Sexual Chemistry: A History of the Contraceptive Pill* (New Haven: Yale University Press, 2000).

19. Ibid.

20. *The Population Bomb* (New York, 1954) was the title of a pamphlet by Hugh Moore that was mailed to one thousand business and political leaders, including Rockefeller (Moore would eventually print half a million copies of his anti-Communist tract).

21. Ibid.

22. Jones, *Alfred C. Kinsey*, 736.

23. See Jerome Greenfield, "Reich and the INS: A Specific Plague Reaction," *Journal of Orgonomy* 17, no. 2 (1983): 205–66. Greenfield's papers, including INS material, are at the Taminent Library and Robert F. Wagner Labor Archives, New York University.

24. Myron Sharaf, *Fury on Earth: A Biography of Wilhelm Reich* (London: Hutchinson, 1984), 413.

25. Elsworth Baker, "My Eleven Years with Reich" (part 8), *Journal of Orgonomy* 14, no. 1 (May 1980), 33.

26. Ibid.

27. Greenfield, "Reich and the INS."

28. David Allyn, *Make Love, Not War: The Sexual Revolution, an Unfettered History* (New York: Routledge, 2001), 17.

29. "The Sex Theory They Tried to Suppress!" *Uncensored*, December 1954.

30. Inspector's report, June 1951, FDA files, National Library of Medicine.

31. Interview with Mr. John Nash, December 2, 1953, FDA files, National Library of Medicine.

32. Interview with Dr. Nicolas Rashevsky, May 12, 1952, FDA files, National Library of Medicine.

33. Ibid.

34. Philip Thompson, author interview, July 2005.

35. Interview with Dr. Higgins (Maine General Hospital), February 1, 1954, FDA Archive. Reich claimed that the FDA's tests were inadequate. A supporter, Richard Blasbland, wrote to him to say that there was X-ray equipment in one of the laboratories conducting the tests, which aggravated the orgone energy, turning it into therapeutically ineffective deadly orgone (DOR) instead. See "The Pharmaceutical Industry and Medical Practice: A Discussion, Wilhelm Reich and Students," recording made at Orgonon, Rangeley, Me. August 24, 1953. Wilhelm Reich Museum, Rangeley, Me.

36. Jerome Greenfield, *Wilhelm Reich vs. the U.S.A.* (New York: Norton, 1974), 126.

37. Philip Thompson, author interview, July 2005.

38. Ilse Ollendorff, author interview, July 2005.

39. Baker, "My Eleven Years with Wilhelm Reich" (part 5), *Journal of Orgonomy* 12, no. 2 (1978): 172.

40. Ibid., 174.

41. Baker, "My Eleven Years with Wilhelm Reich" (part 6), *Journal of Orgonomy* 13, no. 1 (May 1979): 54. Reich describes DOR clouds in similar terms; see Reich, *Selected Writings: An Introduction to Orgonomy* (New York: Farrar, Straus and Giroux, 1960), 43–44.

42. Baker, "My Eleven Years with Wilhelm Reich" (part 9), *Journal of Orgonomy* 14, no. 2 (1980): 158.

43. Greenfield, *Wilhelm Reich vs. the U.S.A.*, 133.

44. Sharaf, *Fury on Earth*, 404.

45. "Notes Taken During Discussion WR and Mr. Richardson," February 25, 1954, Aurora Karrer Reich Collection, National Library of Medicine.

46. Greenfield, *Wilhelm Reich vs. the U.S.A.*, 302.

47. Ibid., 150

48. Press release, March 19, 1954, FDA files, National Library of Medicine.

49. Ibid., 154.

50. Beverley R. Placzek, *Record of a Friendship: The Correspondence Between Wilhelm Reich and A. S. Neill, 1936–1957* (London: Gollancz, 1982), Reich to Neill, 379.

51. Donald E. Keyhoe, *The Flying Saucers Are Real* (New York: Fawcett Publications, 1950), 179.

52. Wilhelm Reich, *Contact with Space: Oranur Second Report, 1951–1956; Orop Desert Ea, 1954–1955* (New York: Core Pilot, 1957), 71.

53. Carl Jung, *Flying Saucers: A Modern Myth of Things Seen in the Skies* (New York: Harcourt, Brace, 1959).

54. Reich, *Contact with Space*, 2.

55. Ibid., 4.

56. Ibid., 199.
57. Ibid., 180.
58. Peter Reich, author interview, July 2005.
59. Placzek, *Record of a Friendship*, Neill to Reich, 385.
60. Peter Reich, *A Book of Dreams* rev. ed., (New York: Harper and Row, 1988), preface.
61. Ibid.
62. Placzek, *Record of a Friendship*, Neill to Reich, 417–18.
63. Orson Bean, *Me and the Orgone* (New York: St. Martin's Press, 1971), xiii.
64. Reich, *Book of Dreams*, 112.
65. Reich, *Contact with Space*, 8.
66. Placzek, *Record of a Friendship*, Reich to Neill, 378.
67. Greenfield, *Wilhelm Reich vs. the U.S.A.*, 180.
68. Affidavit by Thomas Ross, June 18, 1955, FDA files, National Library of Medicine.
69. Inspector's report, July 13, 1955, FDA files, National Library of Medicine.
70. Ibid.
71. Thomas Mangravite, author interview, April 2006.
72. Morgan, *Reds*, 495–96.
73. Ibid., 497.
74. Anthony Heilbut, *Exiled in Paradise: German Refugee Artists and Intellectuals in America from the 1930s to the Present* (Berkeley: University of California Press, 1997), 443.
75. Placzek, *Record of a Friendship*, Neill to Reich, 396.
76. Sharaf, *Fury on Earth*, 476.
77. Greenfield, *Wilhelm Reich vs. the U.S.A.*, 184.

### TWELVE

1. Daniel Horowitz, *The Anxieties of Affluence: Critiques of American Consumer Culture, 1939–1979* (Amherst: University of Massachusetts, 2004), 50.
2. Sigmund Freud and Ernest Jones, *The Complete Correspondence of Sigmund Freud and Ernest Jones, 1908–1939*, ed. R. Andrew Paskauskas (Cambridge, Mass.: Harvard University Press/Belknap, 1993), 383.
3. Sigmund Freud to Marie Bonaparte, August 13, 1937, *Letters of Sigmund Freud, 1873–1939* (London: Hogarth Press, 1961), 436–37.
4. Edward L. Bernays, *Biography of an Idea: Memoirs of Public Relations Counsel Edward L. Bernays* (New York: Simon and Schuster, 1965), 395.
5. Ibid., 779.
6. Franz Kreuzer, *A Tiger in the Tank: Ernest Dichter, an Austrian Advertising Guru* (Riverside, Calif.: Ariadne, 2007).
7. Ernest Dichter, "Put the Libido Back into Advertising," *Motivations* 2 (July 1957): 13–14.

8. Ernest Dichter, *Getting Motivated: The Secret Behind Individual Motivations by the Man Who Was Not Afraid to Ask Why* (New York: Pergamon, 1979), 147–48.

9. Ibid.

10. "Science: Psychoanalysis in Advertising," *Time*, March 25, 1940.

11. Ernest Dichter, *The Strategy of Desire* (New Brunswick, N.J.: Transaction, 2002), xxi.

12. Ibid., 169.

13. Ibid., 263.

14. Ibid., 20.

15. Herbert Marcuse, *Eros and Civilization: A Philosophical Inquiry into Freud* (London: Routledge, 1998), 4.

16. Paul A. Robinson, *The Freudian Left: Wilhelm Reich, Geza Roheim, Herbert Marcuse* (New York: Harper and Row, 1969), 147.

17. H. Stuart Hughes, *The Sea Change: The Migration of Social Thought, 1930–1965.* (New York: McGraw-Hill, 1977), 175.

18. Marcuse, *Eros and Civilization*, 239.

19. Ibid., 49.

20. David Allyn, *Make Love, Not War: The Sexual Revolution, an Unfettered History* (New York: Routledge, 2001), 203.

21. Robinson, *Freudian Left*, 239.

22. Letter to Grethe Hoff, April 20, 1955, Aurora Karrer Reich Collection, National Library of Medicine. According to Myron Sharaf, "running" was one of Reich's favorite words—"one 'ran' from the depths, from strong feelings, from truth." See Myron Sharaf, *Fury on Earth: A Biography of Wilhelm Reich* (London: Hutchinson, 1984), 31.

23. Wilhelm Reich, *Character Analysis* (New York: Farrar, Straus and Giroux, 1972), 448.

24. Ilse Ollendorff, *Wilhelm Reich: A Personal Biography* (New York: St. Martin's Press, 1969), 163.

25. Sharaf, *Fury on Earth*, 441.

26. Wilhelm Reich, "Orgone Therapy: Critical Issues in the Therapeutic Process," tape recordings of lectures, summer 1949, Wilhelm Reich Museum, Rangeley, Me.

27. Elsworth Baker, "My Eleven Years with Reich" (part 14), *Journal of Orgonomy* 17, no. 1 (1983): 43.

28. Sharaf, *Fury on Earth*, 440–41.

29. Baker, "My Eleven Years with Reich" (part 14), 44.

30. Ibid., 45.

31. Jerome Greenfield, *Wilhelm Reich vs. the U.S.A.* (New York: Norton, 1974), 202.

32. Sharaf, *Fury on Earth*, 462.

33. Franklin Wright, "Plot Is Lousy, Cast Is Great," *Portland Evening Express*, May 5, 1956.

34. Greenfield, *Wilhelm Reich vs. the U.S.A.*, 205.

35. Sharaf, *Fury on Earth*, 448.

36. Greenfield, *Wilhelm Reich vs. the U.S.A.*, 209–10.

37. Ibid., 210.

38. Myron Sharaf, "The Trial of Wilhelm Reich," in *Wilhelm Reich Memorial Volume*, ed. Paul Ritter (Nottingham, U.K.: Ritter Press, 1958), 69.

39. Ollendorff, *Wilhelm Reich*, 178.

40. Wilhelm Reich, *Contact with Space: Oranur Second Report, 1951–1956; Orop Desert Ea, 1954–1955* (New York: Core Pilot, 1957), 1.

41. Ollendorff, *Wilhelm Reich*, 179–80.

42. Myron Sharaf, "The Sentencing of WR, Silvert, and the WRF," May 27, 1956, Aurora Karrer Reich Collection, National Library of Medicine.

43. Ibid.

44. Ibid.

45. Greenfield, *Wilhelm Reich vs. the U.S.A.*, 224–25.

46. Ibid., 226.

47. Letter from Mildred Brady to John Cain, May 1956, FDA files, National Library of Medicine.

48. Peter Reich, *A Book of Dreams* (New York: Harper and Row, 1973), 53.

49. Ibid., 57.

50. Inspector's report, June 7, 1956, FDA files, National Library of Medicine.

51. Ibid.

52. Ibid.

53. Dwight D. Eisenhower, address at Dartmouth College, June 14, 1953, "The President Speaks," *Library Journal* 78 (July 1953): 1206.

54. Inspector's report, August 23, 1956, FDA files, National Library of Medicine.

55. 1956 diary, Wilhelm Reich Papers, Aurora Karrer Reich Collection, National Library of Medicine.

56. Ibid.

57. Courtney Baker, author interview, March 2005.

58. Reich to Hoover, February 14, 1957, Wilhelm Reich's FBI file.

59. Reich to Hoover, February 16, 1957, Wilhelm Reich's FBI file.

60. February 25, 1957, Wilhelm Reich's FBI file.

61. February 18, 1957, Wilhelm Reich's FBI file.

62. Reich to Eisenhower, February 23, 1957, Aurora Karrer Reich Collection, National Library of Medicine.

63. Greenfield, *Wilhelm Reich vs. the U.S.A.*, 262–63.

64. Ibid.

65. Sharaf, *Fury on Earth*, 471.

66. Ollendorff, *Wilhelm Reich*, 195.

67. Greenfield, *Wilhelm Reich vs. the U.S.A.*, 264.

68. Wilhelm Reich's Prison File, Steamshovel Press no. 6, St. Louis, Mo.

69. Tony Hiss, *The View from Alger's Window: A Son's Memoir* (New York: Knopf, 1999), 31.

70. Ibid., 65.
71. "Tail-Gunner Joe Meets Cockyboo the Clown," *Flatland Magazine*, November 12, 1995, 36–40.
72. Robert M. Lichtman and Ronald D. Cohen, *Deadly Farce: Harvey Matusow and the Informer System in the McCarthy Era* (Urbana: University of Illinois, 2004), 96.
73. Harvey Matusow, "The Death of Wilhelm Reich," chapter 14 of his unpublished autobiography, "The Stringless Yo Yo," Harvey Matusow Archive, University of Sussex (U.K.) Library Special Collections.
74. Ibid.
75. "My Unlawful Imprisonment," Wilhelm Reich's prison file.
76. Cohen and Lichtman, *Deadly Farce*, 153.
77. Ollendorff, *Wilhelm Reich*, 196.
78. Matusow, "Stringless Yo Yo."
79. Wilhelm Reich's prison file.
80. *Time*, November 18, 1957.
81. Charles Oller, "At Reich's Funeral," November 6, 1957, Aurora Karrer Reich Collection, National Library of Medicine.
82. Ibid.
83. Baker, "My Eleven Years with Reich" (part 17), *Journal of Orgonomy* 18, no. 2 (1984): 169.

## THIRTEEN

1. Norman Mailer, *Advertisements for Myself* (Cambridge, Mass.: Harvard University Press, 1992), 328–29.
2. Norman Mailer to Kenneth Tynan, 1972, Tynan Archive, British Library, London.
3. Mailer, *Advertisements for Myself*, 347.
4. Ibid., 347.
5. Norman Mailer, author interview, June 2007.
6. Dan Wakefield, *New York in the Fifties* (Boston: Houghton Mifflin/Seymour Lawrence, 1992), 241.
7. Ibid., 221.
8. Roger Kimball, *The Long March: How the Cultural Revolution of the 1960s Changed America* (San Francisco: Encounter, 2000), 155.
9. Hilary Mills, *Mailer: A Biography* (New York: McGraw-Hill, 1984), 190.
10. O. Spurgeon English, "Some Recollections of a Psychoanalysis with Wilhelm Reich: September 1929–April 1932," *Journal of the American Academy of Psychoanalysis* 5, no. 2 (1977): 252.
11. Jerome Greenfield, *Wilhelm Reich vs. the U.S.A.* (New York: Norton, 1974), 274.
12. Malcolm Muggeridge, *Tread Softly for You Tread on My Jokes* (London: Collins, 1966), 46.

13. Ted Morgan, *Reds: McCarthyism in Twentieth-Century America* (New York: Random House, 2003), 561.
14. "Morals: Second Sexual Revolution," *Time*, January 24, 1964.
15. Elsworth Baker, "Orgonomy: The Years after Reich," *Journal of Orgonomy* 20, no. 1 (1986): 17.
16. Orson Bean, author interview, December 2005.
17. Elsworth F. Baker and Charles Konia, *Man in the Trap* (Princeton, N.J.: American College of Orgonomy, 2000), xvi.
18. Jefferson Poland and Sam Sloan, *Sex Marchers* (Los Angeles: Elysium, 1968). By 1976, Poland was offering child care for those attending the league's Saturday night orgies. "This project," it was claimed in a newsletter, "is intended as a small step towards helping children be free." When I tried to track Poland down for an interview I discovered that he'd served five years in jail in the 1980s for sexually abusing one of the children in his charge. He'd tried to castrate himself in prison and on his release was prescribed regular injections of female hormones to depress his libido. See www.meganslaw.ca.gov and Nikki Craft, "Jefferson Clitlick Freedom Poland: Convicted Naturist Pedophile" (www.nostatusquo.com/ACLU/NudistHallofShame/Clitlick.html).
19. Baker and Konia, *Man in the Trap*, xvii.
20. Ibid., 14–16.
21. Paul Goodman, *Nature Heals: The Psychological Essays of Paul Goodman* (New York: Free Life Editions, 1977), 85.
22. Ibid., xxiii.
23. Frederick S. Perls, *Gestalt Therapy Verbatim* (Lafayette, Calif.: Real People, 1969), 214.
24. Frederick S. Perls, *In and Out the Garbage Pail* (New York: Bantam Books, 1969), 145.
25. Martin Shepard, *Fritz* (New York: Saturday Review Press, 1975), 159.
26. Jack Gaines, *Fritz Perls: Here and Now* (New York: Celestial Arts, 1979), 216–17.
27. Perls, *In and Out the Garbage Pail*, 99.
28. Petruska Clarkson and Jennifer Mackewn, *Fritz Perls* (London: Sage, 1993), 135.
29. Perls, *In and Out the Garbage Pail*, 35.
30. Shepard, *Fritz*, 3.
31. Dan Greenburg, "My First Orgy," in *The Twentieth Anniversary Playboy Reader*, ed. Hugh M. Hefner (Chicago: Playboy, 1974), 610.
32. Gaines, *Fritz Perls*, 148.
33. Martin Shepard, *Fritz: An Intimate Portrait of Fritz Perls and Gestalt Therapy* (New York: Saturday Review Press, 1975), xv.
34. Leo E. Litwak, "A Trip to Esalen Institute—Joy Is the Prize," *The New York Times Magazine*, December 31, 1967.
35. Ibid., 161.
36. Perls, *In and Out the Garbage Pail*, 102.

37. Gaines, *Fritz Perls*, 337.

38. Shepard, *Fritz*, 192.

39. Sam Keen and John Raser, "A Conversation with Herbert Marcuse: Revolutionary Eroticism, the Tactics of Terror, the Young, Psychotherapy, the Environment, Technology, Reich," *Psychology Today*, February 1971.

40. Herbert Marcuse and Douglas Kellner, *Towards a Critical Theory of Society* (New York: Routledge, 2001), 98.

41. Herbert Marcuse, *One-Dimensional Man: Studies in the Ideology of Advanced Industrial Society* (London: Routledge, 2002), 76.

42. David Allyn, *Make Love, Not War: The Sexual Revolution, an Unfettered History* (New York: Routledge, 2001), 196–97.

43. Vance Packard, *The Hidden Persuaders* (New York: David McKay, 1957), 31.

44. Ibid., 7.

45. Ibid., 266.

46. Ibid., 31.

47. Betty Friedan would criticize Dichter for stereotyping women in "The Sexual Sell," a chapter of *The Feminine Mystique* (New York: Norton, 1963).

48. Daniel Horowitz, "The Birth of a Salesman: Ernest Dichter and the Objects of Desire," unpublished paper, Hagley Library and Archive, Wilmington, Delaware, 37 (www.hagley.org/library/collections/historicalref/articles/HOROWITZ_DICHTER.pdf). See also Daniel Horowitz, "The Émigré as Celebrant of American Consumer Culture: George Katona and Ernest Dichter," in *Getting and Spending: European and American Consumer Societies in the Twentieth Century*, ed. Susan Strasser, Charles McGovern, and Matthias Judt (Cambridge: Cambridge University Press, 1998), 149–66.

49. Packard, *The Hidden Persuaders*, 5

50. Ernest Dichter, *The Strategy of Desire* (New York: Doubleday, 1960), 258.

51. Horowitz, "Birth of a Salesman," 28.

52. Rubin took a "smorgasbord course in New Consciousness" and had Reichian therapy, which he said broke down his inhibitions, but he described its philosophy as "disturbingly conservative." See Jerry Rubin, *Growing Up at Thirty-seven* (New York: M. Evans, 1976), 20, 50.

53. Aldous Huxley, *Brave New World* (New York: Harper and Bros., 1946).

54. Foucault questions the naïve optimism of what he calls Reich's "repressive hypothesis." See Michel Foucault, *The History of Sexuality, Volume 1: An Introduction* (New York: Vintage, 1980), 11.

# BIBLIOGRAPHY

## BOOKS

Alexander, Franz, Samuel Eisenstein, and Martin Grotjahn, eds. *Psychoanalytic Pioneers*. New Brunswick, N.J.: Transaction, 1995.

Allyn, David. *Make Love, Not War: The Sexual Revolution, an Unfettered History*. New York: Routledge, 2001.

Anderson, Walt. *The Upstart Spring: Esalen and the Human Potential Movement; The First Twenty Years*. Lincoln, Neb.: IUniverse, 2004.

Andreas-Salomé, Lou. *The Freud Journal of Lou Andreas-Salomé*. New York: Basic Books, 1964.

Andrew, Christopher M. *The Sword and the Shield: The Mitrokhin Archive and the Secret History of the KGB*. New York: Basic Books, 1999.

Appignanesi, Lisa, and John Forrester. *Freud's Women*. New York: Basic Books, 1992.

Appleton, Matthew. *A Free Range Childhood: Self Regulation at Summerhill School*. Brandon, Vt.: Foundation for Educational Renewal, 2000.

———. *Wilhelm Reich, A. S. Neill and Orgonomy*. Suffolk, U.K.: Friends of Summerhill Trust, 1990.

Atlas, James. *Bellow: A Biography*. New York: Random House, 2000.

Bair, Deirdre. *Jung: A Biography*. Boston: Little, Brown, 2003.

Baker, Elsworth F., and Charles Konia. *Man in the Trap*. Princeton, N.J.: American College of Orgonomy, 2000.

Banks, Brian R. *Muse and Messiah: The Life, Imagination and Legacy of Bruno Schulz (1892–1942)*. Ashby-de-la-Zouch, U.K.: InkerMen Press, 2006.

Bean, Orson. *Me and the Orgone*. New York: St. Martin's Press, 1971.

Bellow, Saul. *Henderson the Rain King*. Harmondsworth, U.K.: Penguin Books, 1996.

————. *Saul Bellow: Collected Stories*. Ed. Janis Freedman Bellow and James Wood. New York: Viking Press, 2001.

Bernays, Edward L. *Propaganda*. Ed. Mark Crispin Miller. Brooklyn: Ig, 2005.

Birken, Lawrence. *Consuming Desire: Sexual Science and the Emergence of a Culture of Abundance, 1871–1914*. Ithaca, N.Y.: Cornell University Press, 1988.

Blau, Eve. *The Architecture of Red Vienna, 1919–1934*. Cambridge, Mass.: MIT Press, 1999.

Boadella, David. *Wilhelm Reich: The Evolution of His Work*. London: Arkana, 1985.

Brady, Joan. *The Unmaking of a Dancer: An Unconventional Life*. New York: Harper and Row, 1982.

Brown, Norman O. *Life Against Death: The Psychoanalytical Meaning of History*. New York: Vintage, 1959.

Budenz, Louis F. *Men Without Faces: The Communist Conspiracy in the U.S.A.* New York: Harper, 1950.

Bullough, Vern L. *Science in the Bedroom: A History of Sex Research*. New York: Basic Books, 1994.

Burlingham, Michael John. *The Last Tiffany: A Biography of Dorothy Tiffany Burlingham*. New York: Atheneum, 1989.

Burroughs, William S. *The Adding Machine: Selected Essays*. New York: Arcade, 1986.

————. *The Letters of William S. Burroughs: 1945–1959*. Ed. Oliver C. G. Harris. New York: Penguin, 1994.

Canetti, Elias. *The Conscience of Words*. Trans. Joachim Neugroschel. New York: Farrar, Straus and Giroux, 1979.

————. *Crowds and Power*. Trans. Carol Stewart. New York: Farrar, Straus and Giroux, 1984.

————. *The Torch in My Ear*. New York: Farrar, Straus and Giroux, 1982.

Carsten, F. L. *The First Austrian Republic, 1918–1938: A Study Based on British and Austrian Documents*. Aldershot, Hants, U.K.: Gower, 1986.

————. *The Rise of Fascism*. Berkeley: University of California Press, 1967.

Carter, Miranda. *Anthony Blunt: His Lives*. London: Macmillan, 2001.

Cattier, Michel. *The Life and Work of Wilhelm Reich*. New York: Horizon, 1971.

Chase, William J. *Enemies Within the Gates? The Comintern and the Stalinist Repression, 1934–1939*. New Haven: Yale University Press, 2001.

Chernow, Ron. *Titan: The Life of John D. Rockefeller, Sr.* New York: Random House, 1998.

Clark, Ronald W. *Einstein: The Life and Times*. New York: Avon, 1994.

Clarkson, Petruska, and Jennifer Mackewn. *Fritz Perls*. London: Sage, 1993.

Cook, Fred J. *The Nightmare Decade: The Life and Times of Senator Joe McCarthy*. New York: Random House, 1971.

Cooper, Arnold M., Otto F. Kernberg, and Ethel Spector Person. *Psychoanalysis: Toward the Second Century*. New Haven, Conn.: Yale University Press, 1989.

Corrington, Robert S. *Wilhelm Reich: Psychoanalyst and Radical Naturalist*. New York: Farrar, Straus and Giroux, 2003.

Crabtree, Adam. *From Mesmer to Freud: Magnetic Sleep and the Roots of Psychological Healing*. New Haven, Conn.: Yale University Press, 1993.

Crary, Jonathan, and Sanford Kwinter, eds. *Incorporations*. New York: Zone/MIT Press, 1992.

Crossman, R.H.S. *The God That Failed*. New York: Columbia University Press, 2001.

Danto, Elizabeth Ann. *Freud's Free Clinics: Psychoanalysis and Social Justice, 1918–1938*. New York: Columbia University Press, 2005.

Darnton, Robert. *Mesmerism and the End of the Enlightenment in France*. Cambridge, Mass.: Harvard University Press, 1968.

Deutsch, Helene. *Confrontations with Myself: An Epilogue*. New York: Norton, 1973.

Deutscher, Isaac. *The Prophet Outcast: Trotsky, 1929–1940*. New York: Verso, 2003.

Dichter, Ernest. *Getting Motivated: The Secret Behind Individual Motivations by the Man Who Was Not Afraid to Ask Why*. New York: Pergamon, 1979.

———. *The Psychology of Everyday Living*. New York: Barnes and Noble, 1947.

———. *The Strategy of Desire*. New Brunswick, N.J.: Transaction, 2002.

Dickstein, Morris. *Gates of Eden: American Culture in the Sixties*. Cambridge, Mass.: Harvard University Press, 1997.

Didi-Huberman, Georges. *Invention of Hysteria: Charcot and the Photographic Iconography of the Salpêtrière*. Cambridge, Mass.: MIT Press, 2003.

Djerassi, Carl. *This Man's Pill: Reflections on the 50th Birthday of the Pill*. Oxford: Oxford University Press, 2001.

Douglas, Ann. *Terrible Honesty: Mongrel Manhattan in the 1920s*. New York: Farrar, Straus and Giroux, 1995.

Eckardt, Wolf von, and Sander L. Gilman. *Bertolt Brecht's Berlin: A Scrapbook of the Twenties*. Lincoln: University of Nebraska Press, 1993.

Einstein, Albert. *The World as I See It*. San Diego: Book Tree, 2007.

Eissler, Kurt. R. *Freud as an Expert Witness: The Discussion of War Neuroses Between Freud and Wagner-Jauregg*. New York: International Universities Press, 1986.

Ellis, Edward. *A Chronological History of the Rangeley Lakes Region*. Rangeley, Me.: Rangeley Lakes Region Historical Society, 1983.

Escoffier, Jeffrey. *Sexual Revolution*. New York: Thunder's Mouth, 2003.

Evans, Richard I., and Erik H. Erikson. *Dialogue with Erik Erikson*. New York: Praeger, 1981.

Ewen, Stuart. *PR! A Social History of Spin*. New York: Basic Books, 1996.

Federn, Ernst. *Witnessing Psychoanalysis: From Vienna Back to Vienna via Buchenwald and the USA*. London: Karnac, 1990.

Fenichel, Otto. *119 Rundbriefe (1934–1945)*. Ed. Johannes Reichmayr. Frankfurt am Main: Stroemfeld, 1998.

———. *The Psychoanalytic Theory of Neurosis*. New York: W. W. Norton, 1945.

Ferenczi, Sándor. *Thalassa: A Theory of Genitality*. Albany, N.Y.: Psychoanalytic Quarterly, 1938.

Firestone, Shulamith. *The Dialectic of Sex: The Case for Feminist Revolution*. New York: Morrow, 1970.

Fishbein, Leslie. *Rebels in Bohemia: The Radicals of the Masses, 1911–1917*. Chapel Hill: University of North Carolina Press, 1982.

Fitzpatrick, Ellen F. *Endless Crusade: Women Social Scientists and Progressive Reform*. New York: Oxford University Press, 1990.

Fölsing, Albrecht. *Albert Einstein: A Biography*. New York: Penguin Books, 1998.

Forrester, John. *Dispatches from the Freud Wars: Psychoanalysis and Its Passions*. Cambridge, Mass.: Harvard University Press, 1997.

Foucault, Michel. *The History of Sexuality*, Volume 1: *An Introduction*. New York: Vintage, 1980.

Frank, Alison Fleig. *Oil Empire: Visions of Prosperity in Austrian Galicia*. Cambridge, Mass.: Harvard University Press, 2005.

Freud, Martin. *Glory Reflected: Sigmund Freud—Man and Father*. London: Angus and Robertson, 1957.

Freud, Sigmund. *Collected Papers: Authorized Translation Under the Supervision of Joan Riviere*. Ed. Joan Riviere. New York: Basic Books, 1959.

———. *The Diary of Sigmund Freud: 1929–1939: A Record of the Final Decade*. Ed. Michael Molnar. London: Hogarth Press, 1992.

———. *The Question of Lay Analysis: An Introduction to Psychoanalysis*. New York: Norton, 1950.

———. *The Standard Edition of the Complete Psychological Works of Sigmund Freud*. Ed. and trans. James Strachey. London: Hogarth Press, 1971.

Freud, Sigmund, and Lou Andreas-Salomé. *Sigmund Freud and Lou Andreas-Salomé: Letters*. Ed. Ernst Pfeiffer. New York: Harcourt Brace Jovanovich, 1972.

Freud, Sigmund, and Sándor Ferenczi. *The Correspondence of Sigmund Freud and Sándor Ferenczi*. Ed. Ernst Falzeder. Cambridge, Mass.: Harvard University Press/ Belknap, 1996.

Freud, Sigmund, and C. G. Jung. *The Freud-Jung Letters: The Correspondence Between Sigmund Freud and C. G. Jung*. Ed. William McGuire. Trans. Ralph Manheim and R.F.C. Hull. London: Hogarth and Routledge and Kegan Paul, 1977.

Friedan, Betty. *The Feminine Mystique*. New York: W. W. Norton, 1963.

Fromm, Erich. *Sigmund Freud's Mission: An Analysis of His Personality and Influence*. New York: Harper, 1959.

Gaines, Jack. *Fritz Perls: Here and Now*. New York: Celestial Arts, 1979.

Gardner, Martin. *Fads and Fallacies: In the Name of Science*. New York: Dover, 1957.

Gardner, Sheldon, and Gwendolyn Stevens. *Red Vienna and the Golden Age of Psychology: 1918–1938*. New York: Praeger, 1992.

Gathorne-Hardy, Jonathan. *Sex the Measure of All Things: A Life of Alfred C. Kinsey*. London: Pimlico, 1999.

Gay, Peter. *Freud: A Life for Our Time*. New York: Norton, 1988.

———. *Freud, Jews, and Other Germans: Masters and Victims in Modernist Culture*. New York: Oxford University Press, 1978.

———. *Weimar Culture: The Outsider as Insider*. New York: Harper and Row, 1970.

Gelernter, David Hillel. *1939: The Lost World of the Fair*. New York: HarperPerennial, 1996.

Gellner, Ernest. *The Psychoanalytic Movement: The Cunning of Unreason*. London: Fontana, 1993.

Gifford, Sanford, Daniel Jacobs, and Vivien Goldman. *Edward Bibring Photographs: The Psychoanalysts of His Time, 1932–1938*. Giessen, Germany: Psychosozial-Verlag, 2005.

Gill, Anton. *A Dance Between Flames: Berlin Between the Wars*. London: John Murray, 1994.

Gold, Hugo. *Geschichte der Juden in der Bukowina* [History of the Jews in the Bukovina], Volume 2. Tel Aviv: Olamenu, 1958.

Goodman, Paul. *Nature Heals: The Psychological Essays of Paul Goodman*. New York: Free Life, 1977.

Grant, Linda. *Sexing the Millennium: A Political History of the Sexual Revolution*. London: HarperCollins, 1993.

Greenfield, Jerome. *Wilhelm Reich vs. the U.S.A.* New York: Norton, 1974.

Greer, Germaine. *The Female Eunuch*. New York: McGraw-Hill, 1971.

Grossmann, Atina. *Reforming Sex: The German Movement for Birth Control and Abortion Reform, 1920–1950*. New York: Oxford University Press, 1995.

Grotjahn, Martin. *My Favorite Patient: The Memoirs of a Psychoanalyst*. Frankfurt am Main: P. Lang, 1987.

Gruber, Helmut. *Red Vienna: Experiment in Working-class Culture, 1919–1934*. New York: Oxford University Press, 1991.

Grunberger, Béla, and Janine Chasseguet-Smirgel. *Freud or Reich? Psychoanalysis and Illusion*. New Haven, Conn.: Yale University Press, 1986.

Hack, Richard. *Puppetmaster: The Secret Life of J. Edgar Hoover*. Beverly Hills: New Millennium, 2004.

Halberstam, David. *The Fifties*. New York: Villard, 1993.

Hale, Nathan G. *Freud and the Americans: The Beginnings of Psychoanalysis in the United States, 1876–1917*. New York: Oxford University Press, 1971.

———. *The Rise and Crisis of Psychoanalysis in the United States: Freud and the Americans, 1917–1985*. New York: Oxford University Press, 1995.

Hamilton, Gerald. *Mr. Norris and I: An Autobiographical Sketch*. London: A. Wingate, 1956.

Hefner, Hugh M. *The Twentieth Anniversary Playboy Reader*. Chicago: Playboy, 1974.

Heilbut, Anthony. *Exiled in Paradise: German Refugee Artists and Intellectuals in America from the 1930s to the Present*. Berkeley: University of California Press, 1997.

Heller, Peter. *A Child Analysis with Anna Freud*. Madison, Conn.: International Universities Press, 1990.

Herskowitz, Morton. *Emotional Armoring: An Introduction to Psychiatric Orgone Therapy*. Hamburg, Germany: Lit, 2001.

Herzog, Dagmar. *Sex After Fascism: Memory and Morality in Twentieth-Century Germany*. Princeton, N.J.: Princeton University Press, 2005.

———, ed. *Sexuality and German Fascism*. New York: Berghahn, 2005.

Hiss, Tony. *The View from Alger's Window: A Son's Memoir*. New York: Knopf, 1999.

Hoel, Sigurd. *Sinners in Summertime*. Trans. Elizabeth Sprigge and Claude Napier. Brooklyn: Ig, 2002.

Horowitz, Daniel. *The Anxieties of Affluence: Critiques of American Consumer Culture, 1939–1979*. Amherst: University of Massachusetts Press, 2004.

Howe, Irving. *A Margin of Hope: An Intellectual Autobiography*. San Diego: Harcourt Brace Jovanovich, 1984.

Huggard, W. R., and W. G. Lockett. *Davos as Health-Resort: A Handbook Containing Contributions by A. F. Bill, M.D., A. Brecke and Others and an Introduction by W. R. Huggard*. Davos, Switzerland: Davos Printing Company, 1907.

Hughes, H. Stuart. *The Sea Change: The Migration of Social Thought, 1930–1965*. New York: Harper and Row, 1975.

Hulbert, Ann. *Raising America: Experts, Parents, and a Century of Advice About Children*. New York: Knopf, 2003.

Huxley, Aldous. *Brave New World*. New York: Harper and Bros., 1946.

Jacoby, Russell. *The Repression of Psychoanalysis: Otto Fenichel and the Political Freudians*. Chicago: University of Chicago Press, 1986.

———. *Social Amnesia: A Critique of Conformist Psychology from Adler to Laing*. Hassocks, U.K.: Harvester, 1977.

Janik, Allan. *Wittgenstein's Vienna Revisited*. New Brunswick, N.J.: Transaction, 2001.

Jay, Martin. *The Dialectical Imagination: A History of the Frankfurt School and the Institute of Social Research, 1923–1950*. Berkeley: University of California Press, 1996.

Jones, E. Michael. *Libido Dominandi: Sexual Liberation and Political Control*. South Bend, Ind.: St. Augustine's Press, 2000.

Jones, Ernest. *Free Associations: Memories of a Psychoanalyst*. New Brunswick, N.J.: Transaction, 1990.

———. *The Life and Work of Sigmund Freud*. 3 volumes. New York: Basic Books, 1957.

Jones, James H. *Alfred C. Kinsey: A Public-Private Life*. New York: Norton, 1997.

Jung, C. G. *Memories, Dreams, Reflections*. New York: Pantheon Books, 1963.

Kaes, Anton, Martin Jay, and Edward Dimendberg. *The Weimar Republic Sourcebook*. Berkeley: University of California Press, 1995.

Karina, Lilian, and Marion Kant. *Hitler's Dancers: German Modern Dance and the Third Reich*. New York: Berghahn, 2003.

Kazin, Alfred. *New York Jew*. New York: Syracuse University Press, 1996.

Kerouac, Jack. *Road Novels, 1957–1960*. Ed. Douglas Brinkley. New York: Library of America, 2007.

Kevles, Daniel J. *In the Name of Eugenics: Genetics and the Uses of Human Heredity*. Berkeley: University of California Press, 1986.

Kimball, Roger. *The Long March: How the Cultural Revolution of the 1960s Changed America*. San Francisco: Encounter, 2000.

Kinsey, Alfred C., Wardell Baxter Pomeroy, and Clyde E. Martin. *Sexual Behavior in the Human Male*. Philadelphia: W. B. Saunders, 1948.

Kreuzer, Franz, Gerd Prechtl, and Christoph Steiner. *A Tiger in the Tank: Ernest Dichter, an Austrian Advertising Guru*. Riverside, Calif.: Ariadne, 2007.

Kripal, Jeffrey John. *Esalen: America and the Religion of No Religion*. Chicago: University of Chicago Press, 2007.

Krohn, Claus-Dieter. *Intellectuals in Exile: Refugee Scholars and the New School for Social Research*. Amherst: University of Massachusetts Press, 1993.

Large, David Clay. *Berlin*. New York: Basic Books, 2000.

Lasch, Christopher. *The Culture of Narcissism: American Life in an Age of Diminishing Expectations*. New York: Norton, 1978.

Lichtman, Robert M., and Ronald D. Cohen. *Deadly Farce: Harvey Matusow and the Informer System in the McCarthy Era*. Urbana: University of Illinois Press, 2004.

Lindemann, Albert S. *A History of European Socialism*. New Haven: Yale University Press, 1983.

Lowen, Alexander. *Bioenergetics*. New York: Penguin Books, 1976.

———. *Honoring the Body: The Autobiography of Alexander Lowen, M.D.* Alachua, Fla.: Bioenergetics, 2004.

———. *Love and Orgasm*. New York: Macmillan, 1965.

Luft, David S. *Eros and Inwardness in Vienna: Weininger, Musil, Doderer*. Chicago: University of Chicago Press, 2003.

Maddox, Brenda. *Freud's Wizard: The Enigma of Ernest Jones*. London: John Murray, 2006.

Mailer, Norman. *Advertisements for Myself*. Cambridge, Mass.: Harvard University Press, 1992.

Maines, Rachel. *The Technology of Orgasm: "Hysteria," the Vibrator, and Women's Sexual Satisfaction*. Baltimore, Md.: Johns Hopkins University Press, 1998.

Makari, George. *Revolution in Mind: The Creation of Psychoanalysis*. New York: HarperCollins, 2008.

Malina, Judith. *The Diaries of Judith Malina, 1947–1957*. New York: Grove Press, 1984.

Malinowski, Bronislaw. *The Sexual Life of Savages in North-Western Melanesia: An Ethnographic Account of Courtship, Marriage, and Family Life Among the Natives of the Trobriand Islands, British New Guinea*. Whitefish, Mont.: Kessinger, 2005.

Mann, Thomas. *The Magic Mountain: A Novel*. Trans. John E. Woods. New York: Vintage International, 1996.

Mann, W. E. *Orgone, Reich and Eros: Wilhelm Reich's Theory of Life Energy*. New York: Simon and Schuster, 1973.

Mann, W. Edward, and Edward Hoffman. *The Man Who Dreamed of Tomorrow: A Conceptual Biography of Wilhelm Reich*. Los Angeles,: Jeremy Tarcher, 1980.

Marcuse, Herbert. *An Essay on Liberation*. Boston: Beacon Press, 1969.

————. *One-Dimensional Man: Studies in the Ideology of Advanced Industrial Society.* London: Routledge, 2002.

————. *Technology, War, and Fascism.* Ed. Douglas Kellner. London: Routledge, 1998.

Marcuse, Herbert, and Douglas Kellner. *Towards a Critical Theory of Society.* New York: Routledge, 2001.

Margolis, Jonathan. *O: The Intimate History of the Orgasm.* New York: Grove Press, 2004.

Marks, Lara. *Sexual Chemistry: A History of the Contraceptive Pill.* New Haven, Conn.: Yale University Press, 2001

Martin, Jim. *Wilhelm Reich and the Cold War.* Fort Bragg, Calif.: Flatland Books, 2000.

Masson, J. Moussaieff. *The Assault on Truth: Freud's Suppression of the Seduction Theory.* New York: Farrar, Straus and Giroux, 1984.

Mauch, Christof. *The Shadow War Against Hitler: The Covert Operations of America's Wartime Secret Intelligence Service.* New York: Columbia University Press, 2003.

McMillan, Priscilla Johnson. *The Ruin of J. Robert Oppenheimer and the Birth of the Modern Arms Race.* New York: Viking Press, 2005.

Miles, Barry. *Ginsberg: A Biography.* New York: Simon and Schuster, 1989.

Miller, Henry. *The Air-Conditioned Nightmare.* New York: New Directions, 1945.

————. *Big Sur and the Oranges of Hieronymus Bosch.* New York: New Directions, 1957.

————. *The World of Sex.* New York: Grove, 1965.

Miller, Martin A. *Freud and the Bolsheviks: Psychoanalysis in Imperial Russia and the Soviet Union.* New Haven, Conn.: Yale University Press, 1998.

Miller, Ruth. *Saul Bellow: A Biography of the Imagination.* New York: St. Martin's Press, 1991.

Mitchell, Juliet. *Psychoanalysis and Feminism: Freud, Reich, Laing and Women.* New York: Pantheon, 1974.

Morgan, Ted. *Reds: McCarthyism in Twentieth-Century America.* New York: Random House, 2003.

Muggeridge, Malcolm. *Tread Softly for You Tread on My Jokes.* London: Collins, 1966.

Neill, A. S. *All the Best, Neill: Letters from Summerhill.* Ed. Jonathan Croall. London: André Deutsch, 1983.

————. *Neill! Neill! Orange Peel! An Autobiography.* New York: Hart, 1972.

————. *The New Summerhill.* Ed. Albert Richard Lamb. London: Penguin Books, 1992.

————. *The Problem Teacher.* New York: International Universities Press, 1944.

New, Mitya. *Switzerland Unwrapped: Exposing the Myths.* London: I. B. Tauris, 1997.

Nunberg, Hermann, and Ernst Federn. *Minutes of the Vienna Psychoanalytic Society.* New York: International Universities Press, 1975.

Odier, Daniel, and William S. Burroughs. *The Job: Interviews with William S. Burroughs.* New York: Grove Press, 1970.

Ollendorff, Ilse. *Wilhelm Reich: A Personal Biography*. New York: St. Martin's Press, 1969.

Ormrod, Sarah J. *Cambridge Contributions*. Cambridge: Cambridge University Press, 1998.

Orwell, George. *1984: A Novel*. New York: Penguin/Signet Classics, 1977.

Packard, Vance. *The Hidden Persuaders*. New York: David McKay, 1957.

Page, Norman. *Auden and Isherwood: The Berlin Years*. Basingstoke, U.K.: Macmillan, 2000.

Peña, Carolyn. *The Body Electric: How Strange Machines Built the Modern American*. New York: New York University Press, 2003.

Perls, Frederick S. *Ego, Hunger, and Aggression: The Beginning of Gestalt Therapy*. New York: Random House, 1969.

———. *Gestalt Therapy Verbatim*. Lafayette, Calif.: Real People, 1969.

———. *In and Out the Garbage Pail*. New York: Bantam Books, 1969.

Petersen, James R. *The Century of Sex: Playboy's History of the Sexual Revolution, 1900–1999*. New York: Grove Press, 1999.

Placzek, Beverley R., ed. *Record of a Friendship: The Correspondence Between Wilhelm Reich and A. S. Neill, 1936–1957*. London: Gollancz, 1982.

Poland, Jefferson, and Sam Sloan. *Sex Marchers*. Los Angeles: Elysium, 1968.

Pomeroy, Wardell Baxter. *Dr. Kinsey and the Institute for Sex Research*. New York: Harper and Row, 1972.

Prochnik, George. *Putnam Camp: Sigmund Freud, James Jackson Putnam, and the Purpose of American Psychology*. New York: Other Press, 2006.

Proctor, Robert N. *The Nazi War on Cancer*. Princeton, N.J.: Princeton University Press, 2000.

Quinn, Susan. *Marie Curie: A Life*. New York: Simon and Schuster, 1995.

———. *A Mind of Her Own: The Life of Karen Horney*. New York: Summit, 1987.

Rabinbach, Anson. *The Austrian Socialist Experiment: Social Democracy and Austromarxism, 1918–1934*. Boulder: Westview, 1985.

———. *The Human Motor: Energy, Fatigue, and the Origins of Modernity*. New York: Basic Books, 1990.

Raknes, Ola. *Wilhelm Reich and Orgonomy*. Princeton, N.J.: American College of Orgonomy, 2004.

Reich, Annie. *Annie Reich: Psychoanalytic Contributions*. New York: International Universities Press, 1973.

Reich, Peter. *A Book of Dreams*, rev. ed. New York: Harper and Row, 1988.

Reich, Wilhelm. *American Odyssey: Letters and Journals, 1940–1947*. Ed. Mary Higgins. New York: Farrar, Straus and Giroux, 1999.

———. *Beyond Psychology: Letters and Journals, 1934–1939*. Ed. Mary Higgins. New York: Farrar, Straus and Giroux, 1994.

———. *The Bioelectrical Investigation of Sexuality and Anxiety*. Ed. Mary Higgins and Chester M. Raphael. New York: Farrar, Straus and Giroux, 1982.

————. *Biographical Material, History of the Discovery of the Life Energy, The Einstein Affair*. Rangeley, Me.: Orgone Institute, 1953.

————. *Character Analysis*. New York: Farrar, Straus and Giroux, 1972.

————. *Children of the Future: On the Prevention of Sexual Pathology*. Ed. Mary Higgins and Chester M. Raphael. New York: Farrar, Straus and Giroux, 1983.

————. *The Cancer Biopathy*. New York: Farrar, Straus and Giroux, 1973.

————. *Contact with Space: Oranur Second Report, 1951–1956; Orop Desert Ea, 1954–1955*. New York: Core Pilot, 1957.

————. *Cosmic Superimposition* and *Man's Orgonotic Roots in Nature*. Rangeley, Me.: Orgone University Press, 1951.

————. *Early Writings*. New York: Farrar, Straus and Giroux, 1975.

————. *Ether, God, and Devil: Cosmic Superimposition*. New York: Farrar, Straus and Giroux, 1973.

————. *The Function of the Orgasm: Sex-Economic Problems of Biological Energy*. New York: Farrar, Straus and Giroux, 1973.

————. *Genitality in the Theory and Therapy of Neurosis*. Ed. Mary Higgins and Chester M. Raphael. New York: Farrar, Straus and Giroux, 1980.

————. *The Invasion of Compulsory Sex-Morality*. New York: Farrar, Straus and Giroux, 1971.

————. *Listen, Little Man!* Ed. Theodore P. Wolfe. New York: Noonday, 1971.

————. *The Mass Psychology of Fascism*. Ed. Mary Higgins and Chester M. Raphael. New York: Farrar, Straus and Giroux, 1970.

————. *The Murder of Christ*. New York: Noonday, 1977.

————. *The Oramur Experiment: First Report, 1947–1951*. Rangeley, Me. Wilhelm Reich Foundation, 1951.

————. *The Orgone Energy Accumulator: Its Scientific and Medical Use*. Wilhelm Reich Foundation, 1951.

————. *Passion of Youth: An Autobiography, 1897–1922*. Ed. Mary Higgins and Chester M. Raphael. New York: Farrar, Straus and Giroux, 1988.

————. *People in Trouble*, Volume 2: *The Emotional Plague of Mankind*. New York: Farrar, Straus and Giroux, 1976.

————. *Reich Speaks of Freud*. Ed. Chester M. Raphael and Mary Higgins. New York: Noonday, 1968.

————. *Selected Writings: An Introduction to Orgonomy*. New York: Farrar, Straus and Giroux, 1960.

————. *Sex-Pol: Essays, 1929–1934*. Ed. by L. Baxandall, introduction by B. Ollman, trans. A. Bostock. New York: Vintage, 1972.

————. *The Sexual Revolution: Toward a Self-Regulating Character Structure*. New York: Farrar, Straus and Giroux, 1974.

————. *Wilhelm Reich Biographical Material: History of the Discovery of the Life Energy, the Emotional Plague of Mankind*, volume 2, documentary volume. Rangeley, Me.: Orgone Institute, 1953.

Rexroth, Kenneth. *The Alternative Society: Essays from the Other World*. New York: Herder and Herder, 1970.

———. *An Autobiographical Novel*. Ed. Linda Hamalian. New York: New Directions, 1991.

Rickett, Frances. *Tread Softly*. New York: Simon and Schuster, 1964.

Rieff, Philip. *The Triumph of the Therapeutic: Uses of Faith After Freud*. Chicago: University of Chicago Press, 1987.

Ritter, Paul, ed. *Wilhelm Reich Memorial Volume*. Nottingham, U.K.: Ritter Press, 1958.

Roazen, Paul. *Brother Animal: The Story of Freud and Tausk*. New York: Knopf, 1969.

———. *Cultural Foundations of Political Psychology*. New Brunswick, N.J.: Transaction, 2003.

———. *Freud and His Followers*. New York: Knopf, 1975.

———. *Freud: Political and Social Thought*. New York: Knopf, 1968.

———. *Helene Deutsch: A Psychoanalyst's Life*. Garden City, N.Y.: Anchor/Doubleday, 1985.

———. *Meeting Freud's Family*. Amherst: University of Massachusetts Press, 1993.

Roazen, Paul, and Bluma Swerdloff. *Heresy: Sandor Rado and the Psychoanalytic Movement*. Northvale, N.J.: Jason Aronson, 1995.

Robinson, Paul A. *The Freudian Left: Wilhelm Reich, Geza Roheim, Herbert Marcuse*. New York: Harper and Row, 1969.

———. *The Modernization of Sex: Havelock Ellis, Alfred Kinsey, William Masters, and Virginia Johnson*. New York: Harper and Row, 1976.

Robinson, William J. *Sexual Truths Versus Sexual Lies, Misconceptions and Exaggerations*. New York: Critic and Guide, 1919.

Rosenfeld, Isaac. *Preserving the Hunger: An Isaac Rosenfeld Reader*. Ed. Mark Shechner. Detroit: Wayne State University Press, 1988.

Roudinesco, Elisabeth. *Jacques Lacan & Co.: A History of Psychoanalysis in France, 1925–1985*. Chicago: University of Chicago Press, 1990.

Rubin, Jerry. *Growing Up at Thirty-seven*. New York: M. Evans, 1976.

Sadger, J. *Recollecting Freud*. Ed. Alan Dundes. Madison: University of Wisconsin Press, 2005.

Saunders, Frances Stonor. *The Cultural Cold War: The CIA and the World of Arts and Letters*. New York: New Press, 2001.

Schivelbusch, Wolfgang. *Three New Deals: Reflections on Roosevelt's America, Mussolini's Italy, and Hitler's Germany, 1933–1939*. New York: Picador, 2007.

Sengoopta, Chandak. *Otto Weininger: Sex, Science, and Self in Imperial Vienna*. Chicago: University of Chicago Press, 2000.

Sharaf, Myron. *Fury on Earth: A Biography of Wilhelm Reich*. London: Hutchinson, 1984.

Shepard, Martin. *Fritz: An Intimate Portrait of Fritz Perls and Gestalt Therapy*. New York: Saturday Review Press, 1975.

Stern, Mikhail, and August Stern. *Sex in the USSR*. New York: Times Books, 1980.

Siersted, Ellen. *Wilhelm Reich in Denmark*. Reich Archive West: San Francisco, 1977.

Sontag, Susan. *Illness as Metaphor*. New York: Farrar, Straus and Giroux, 1978.

Steiner, Riccardo. *It Is a New Kind of Diaspora: Explorations in the Sociopolitical and Cultural Context of Psychoanalysis*. London: Karnac, 2000.

Stephan, Alexander. *"Communazis": FBI Surveillance of German Emigré Writers*. Trans. Jan van Heurck. New Haven, Conn.: Yale University Press, 2000.

Sterba, Richard F. *Reminiscences of a Viennese Psychoanalyst*. Detroit: Wayne State University Press, 1985.

Stoehr, Taylor. *Here Now Next: Paul Goodman and the Origins of Gestalt Therapy*. San Francisco: Jossey-Bass, 1994.

Straight, Michael Whitney. *After Long Silence*. London: Collins, 1983.

Strasser, Susan, Charles McGovern, and Matthias Judt. *Getting and Spending: European and American Consumer Societies in the Twentieth Century*. Cambridge: Cambridge University Press, 1998.

Sumner, Gregory D. *Dwight Macdonald and the Politics Circle: The Challenge of Cosmopolitan Democracy*. Ithaca, N.Y.: Cornell University Press, 1996.

Theoharis, Athan G. *J. Edgar Hoover, Sex, and Crime: An Historical Antidote*. Chicago: Ivan R. Dee, 1995.

Thompson, Clara. *Psychoanalysis: Evolution and Development*. New Brunswick, N.J.: Transaction, 2002.

Toepfer, Karl Eric. *Empire of Ecstasy: Nudity and Movement in German Body Culture, 1910–1935*. Berkeley: University of California Press, 1997.

Trilling, Lionel. *The Liberal Imagination*. New York: New York Review Books, 2008.

Trotsky, Leon. *The Revolution Betrayed: What Is the Soviet Union and Where Is It Going?* Introduction by David North. Detroit: Labor Publications, 1991.

———. *Writings of Leon Trotsky*. Ed. Naomi Allen. New York: Pathfinder Press, 1973.

Tye, Larry. *The Father of Spin: Edward L. Bernays and the Birth of Public Relations*. New York: Crown, 1998.

Ulam, Adam Bruno. *Stalin: The Man and His Era*. New York: Viking Press, 1973.

Updike, John. *Self-Consciousness: Memoirs*. New York: Knopf, 1989.

Wakefield, Dan. *New York in the Fifties*. Boston: Houghton Mifflin/Seymour Lawrence, 1992.

Watson, Steven. *The Birth of the Beat Generation: Visionaries, Rebels, and Hipsters, 1944–1960*. New York: Pantheon, 1995.

Weinberg, Martin S. *Sex Research: Studies from the Kinsey Institute*. New York: Oxford University Press, 1988.

Weitz, Eric D. *Weimar Germany: Promise and Tragedy*. Princeton, N.J.: Princeton University Press, 2007.

Wertham, Fredric. *Seduction of the Innocent*. Port Washington, N.Y.: Kennikat Press, 1972.

Wilson, Colin. *Wilhelm Reich*. London: Olympic Marketing, 1974.

Winslow, Kathryn. *Henry Miller: Full of Life*. Los Angeles: Jeremy Tarcher, 1986.

Wolff, Charlotte. *Magnus Hirschfeld: A Portrait of a Pioneer in Sexology*. London: Quartet, 1986.

Wormser, René Albert. *Foundations: Their Power and Influence*. New York: Devin-Adair, 1958.

Wortis, Joseph. *Fragments of an Analysis with Freud*. New York: Simon and Schuster, 1954.

Wreszin, Michael. *A Rebel in Defense of Tradition: The Life and Politics of Dwight Macdonald*. New York: Basic Books, 1994.

Young, James Harvey. *The Medical Messiahs: A Social History of Health Quackery in Twentieth-Century America*. Princeton, N.J.: Princeton University Press, 1967.

Young-Bruehl, Elisabeth. *Anna Freud: A Biography*. New Haven, Conn.: Yale University Press, 2008.

Zaretsky, Eli. *Secrets of the Soul: A Social and Cultural History of Psychoanalysis*. New York: Knopf, 2004.

Zipperstein, Steven J. *Rosenfeld's Lives: Fame, Oblivion, and the Furies of Writing*. New Haven: Yale University Press, 2009.

Zweig, Stefan. *Mental Healers: Franz Anton Mesmer, Mary Baker Eddy, Sigmund Freud*. Trans. Eden Paul and Cedar Paul. London: Cassell, 1933.

———. *The World of Yesterday: An Autobiography*. Reprint. London: Hesperides, 2008.

## ARTICLES

Alnæs, Randolf. "The Development of Psychoanalysis in Norway: An Historical Overview." *Scandinavian Psychoanalytic Review* 3 (1980).

Baker, Elsworth F. "My Eleven Years with Wilhelm Reich." Serialized book in seventeen parts. *The Journal of Orgonomy*, 1976–1984.

———. "Wilhelm Reich." *The Journal of Orgonomy* 1 (1–2), 1967.

Blasband, David. "In Memoriam: Albert Ing Duvall." *The Journal of Orgonomy* 14, no. 1 (1980).

Brady, Mildred, "The New Cult of Sex and Anarchy." *Harper's Magazine*, April 1947.

———. "The Strange Case of Wilhelm Reich." *The New Republic* 116 (May 26, 1947).

Brock, Adrian, and Benjamin Harris. "Freudian Psychopolitics: The Rivalry of Wilhelm Reich and Otto Fenichel, 1930–1935." *Bulletin of the History of Medicine* 66, no. 4 (1992).

———. "Otto Fenichel and the Left Opposition in Psychoanalysis." *Journal of the History of the Behavioral Sciences* 27 (1991).

Bullough, Vern L. "Katherine Bement Davis, Sex Research, and the Rockefeller Foundation." *Bulletin of the History of Medicine* 62, no. 1 (1988).

———. "The Rockefellers and Sex Research." *Journal of Sex Research* 21, no. 2 (1985).

Danto, Elizabeth Ann. "The Ambulatorium: Freud's Free Clinic in Vienna." *International Journal of Psycho-Analysis* 79 (1998).

———. "A New Sort of 'Salvation Army': Historical Perspectives on the Confluence of Psychoanalysis and Social Work." *Clinical Social Work Journal* 37, no. 1 (2009).

———. "Sex, Class and Social Work: Wilhelm Reich's Free Clinics and the Activist History of Psychoanalysis." *Psychoanalytic Social Work* 7, no. 1 (2000).

Dichter, Ernest. "Put the Libido Back into Advertising." *Motivation* 2 (July 1957).

Federn, Ernst. "The Relationship Between Sigmund Freud and Paul Federn: Some Unpublished Documents." *Revue internationale d'histoire de la psychoanalyse* 2 (1989).

Gifford, Sanford. "'Repression' or Sea Change—Fenichel's *Rundbriefe* and the 'Political Analysts' of the 1930s." *International Journal of Psycho-Analysis* 66 (1985).

Greenfield Jerome. "Examination of Wilhelm Reich by the Immigration and Naturalization Service." *Journal of Orgonomy* 16, no. 2 (1982).

———. "Reich and the INS: A Specific Plague Reaction." *Journal of Orgonomy* 17, no. 2 (1983).

———. "Wilhelm Reich: Enemy Alien." *Journal of Orgonomy* 16, no. 1 (1982).

———. "Wilhelm Reich in Prison." *International Journal of Life Energy* 2, no. 1 (Winter 1979–80).

Hale, Nathan G. "From Berggasse XIX to Central Park West: The Americanization of Psychoanalysis, 1919–1940." *Journal of the History of the Behavioral Sciences* 14 (1978).

Hamilton, A. E. "My Therapy with Wilhelm Reich." 2 parts. *Journal of Orgonomy* 1997.

———. "Reactions to the First Orgonomic Conference, October 2, 1948." *Orgone Energy Bulletin* 1, no. 3 (1949).

Herskowitz, Morton. "Memories of Reich: Dr. Herskowitz Recalls His Experiences with Wilhelm Reich." The Institute of Orgonomic Science. www.orgonomicscience.org/history.html.

———. "Recollections of Reich." *The Journal of Orgonomy* 12, no. 2 (1978).

Hitschmann, Edward. "A Ten Years' Report of the Vienna Psycho-Analytical Clinic." *International Journal of Psycho-Analysis* 13 (1972).

Horowitz, Daniel. "The Birth of a Salesman: Ernest Dichter and the Objects of Desire" (unpublished paper). Hagley Library Web site.

Jensen, Reimer, and Henning Paikin. "On Psychoanalysis in Demark." *Scandanavian Psychoanalytic Review* 3 (1980).

Keen, Sam, and John Raser. "A Conversation with Herbert Marcuse: Revolutionary Eroticism, the Tactics of Terror, the Young, Psychotherapy, the Environment, Technology, Reich." *Psychology Today* 4, no. 2 (February 1971).

Levine, Norman. "Wilhelm Reich: Culture as Power." *History of European Ideas* 5, no. 3 (1984).

Lohr, Eric. "The Russian Army and the Jews: Mass Deportation, Hostages, and Violence During World War I." *The Russian Review* 60, no. 3 (2001).

Matusow, Harvey. "Tail-gunner Joe Meets Cockyboo the Clown." *Flatland Magazine* 12 (1995).

Mills, C. Wright, and Patricia Salter. "The Barricade and the Bedroom." *Politics* 2 (October 1945).

Pietikainen, Petteri. "Utopianism in Psychology: The Case of Wilhelm Reich." *Journal of the History of the Behavioral Sciences* 38, no. 2 (2002).

Rabinbach, Anson. "The Politicization of Wilhelm Reich: An Introduction to 'The Sexual Misery of the Working Masses and the Difficulties of Sexual Reform.'" *New German Critique* 1 (1973).

Reich, Lore. "Wilhelm Reich and Anna Freud: His Expulsion from Psychoanalysis." *International Forum of Psychoanalysis* 12, nos. 2 and 3 (September 2003).

Rosenbaum, Ron. "Kim Philby and the Age of Paranoia." *The New York Times*, July 10, 1994.

Rosenfeld, Edward. "A Conversation with Isadore From." *The Gestalt Journal* 1, no. 2 (Fall 1978).

Schlesinger, Arthur. "Who Was Henry A. Wallace?" *Los Angeles Times*, March 12, 2000.

Sharaf, Myron. "Further Remarks on Reich." 14 parts. *Journal of Orgonomy*, 1970–1977.

———. "Some Remarks on Reich." 4 parts. *Journal of Orgonomy*, 1968–1970.

———. "Thoughts About Reich: Reich's Sense of His Historic Mission." 7 parts. *Journal of Orgonomy*, 1977–1979.

Steiner, Riccardo. "It Is a New Kind of Diaspora . . ." *International Review of Psycho-Analysis* 16 (1989).

Sterba, Richard F. "Character and Resistance" (1948). *Psychoanalytic Quarterly* 20 (1951).

Wyvell, Lois. "An Appreciation of Reich." *The Journal of Orgonomy* 7, no. 2 (1973).

———. "Orgone and You." A serialized book. *Offshoots of Orgonomy*, 1980–1986.

Zipperstein, Steven. "Isaac Rosenfeld's Dybbuk and Rethinking Literary Biography." *Partisan Review* 99, no. 1 (Winter 2002).

# ACKNOWLEDGMENTS

In 2004, Wilhelm Reich's last lover, Aurora Karrer (he referred to her as his wife and she considered herself one, but they never legally married), donated several densely packed boxes of papers to the National Library of Medicine (NLM) in Washington, D.C. I was there, examining the Food and Drug Administration's copious files on the orgone energy accumulator case, when John Rees, then assistant curator of the Archives and Modern Manuscripts Program, brought this uncatalogued and previously unexamined material to my attention. The discovery of these 12,500 pages of documents, not elsewhere available, contributed greatly to my understanding of aspects of Reich's private life.

Reich decreed that after his death, his papers should be sealed for fifty years. But before the papers were sealed, Aurora Karrer microfilmed all Reich's published works so that they would be more readily available to researchers (seven reels of microfilm were deposited in the Firestone Library at Princeton University). She also copied extensively from his personal papers, to which she had access as his "wife," for a biography she was planning but never wrote. It is this material—which relates more to Reich's private life than his experiments—along with her own notes on Reich's final days, that she donated to the NLM. "If everything in the archive is destroyed," she wrote to Reich's daughter Eva, "history will be preserved."

The sealed archives of the Orgone Institute were eventually deposited at the Countway Library of Medicine at Harvard University, and when they were unsealed in 2008, I applied for access. The gatekeepers are three of Reich's second generation of devotees, none of whom personally knew Reich. They declined to give me permission, because they objected to the "tone" of an article I had written for the *London Review of Books* that questioned some of Reich's later ideas. They also objected to the title of this book. It seems that the price of admission to the collection is that you must abandon any critical or thoughtful attempt to understand Reich's puzzling and controversial career. The gatekeeper committee acknowledged that they might be accused of "impeding genuine scholarship," and it is unfortunate that Harvard has agreed to house these archives under such censorial terms. Given these circumstances, Aurora Karrer's papers at the NLM provided an invaluable corrective.

Reich's surviving family, when they realized I was nonpartisan, were extraordinarily open and helpful to me. I am particularly grateful to Peter Reich, who was a gracious host, inviting me to stay at his home to discuss his father's life and thought, and who has become a friend. His mother, Ilse Ollendorff, since deceased but at the time fiercely independent at the age of ninety-six, also shared her memories with me, as did Reich's daughter Lore Reich Rubin, who, as a former psychoanalyst herself, was able to elucidate Reich's contribution to that field and suggest a diagnosis of his later mental state. Her sister Eva Reich was too ill to see me and had lost her memory, but Eva's daughter, Renate Moise, trusted me with a pile of videotapes and transcripts and rare books that helped explain her mother and grandfather's complicated relationship.

I'm also indebted to Reich's students Morton Herskowitz and the late Alexander Lowen, who helped me understand the utopian fervor felt by Reich's first American disciples. Roxana Tynan granted me permission to see her father's papers at the British Library; Kenneth Tynan had planned a biography of Reich in the early 1970s and I found myself following in his footsteps as I researched this book, meeting many of the same people he had met thirty years earlier. Tynan had three vegetotherapy sessions with Elsworth Baker while researching his aborted work. Baker's son, Courtney, who is also a Reichian therapist and who knew Reich as a child, agreed to repeat the experiment on me, offering me three trial sessions for which he charged me no fee. This painful experience allowed me to comprehend something of what Reich's own patients went through. Elsworth Baker's former patients Orson Bean and Arthur Geller also shared with me their dramatic experiences of Reichian therapy and explained how submitting to it was once the vogue.

Others who generously shared their memories include Steven and Renate Perls, Peter Marcuse, Paki Wright, Zoë Redhead, and Ann Call (née Kinsey); Mildred Edith Brady's children, Joan and Judy Brady, and her former secretary Lucille Marshall; Kinsey sex researcher Paul Gebhardt; psychiatrist Robert Spitzer; Living Theatre founder Judith Malina; Clista Templeton, Tom Mangravite, and Tiny Collins, who all built orgone boxes for Reich; the trustee of the Wilhelm Reich Infant Trust, Mary Boyd Higgins; Henry Miller's friends Nancy Leite and Jodie Scott; FDA doctor Philip Thompson; and Norman Mailer.

Many people have helped me at one stage or another, and to degrees they might not know. They include James Atlas, John Lahr, Jennifer Bass, Margaret Salinger, Val Miller, Adam Curtis, Robert Glazer, Zoë Heller, Giselle Sharaf, Tuli Kupferberg, Steven Zipperstein, James Graverholz, John Bennett, Paul Roazen, Ernst Falzedar, George Prochnik, Ruben Gallo, John Forrester, Matthew von Unwerth, David Silver, Kevin Hinchey, David Allyn, Beverly Lindholm, Richard Turner, Tony Wood, Mark Cousins, Colin MacCabe, Douglas Kellner, Rebecca Fishwick, James M. Carpenter, Jennifer Hill Karrer, Cecile Banke, Catherine Johnson-Roehr, and Karen Maine.

I'm grateful to the librarians at the various archives my research took me to: the FBI archive, the Columbia University Libraries, the Kinsey Institute Library, the British Library, the Harvard University libraries, the New York Public Library, the New York Psychoanalytic Society and Institute, the Boston Psychoanalytic Society and Institute, the Princeton University Library, the Ohio State University Libraries, the National Library of Medicine, the Library of Congress (where the papers Reich deposited to the Sigmund Freud archive were opened in 2004), the New York University Libraries, the Freud Museum, the Rockefeller Archive Center, the Wellcome Library, the American Museum of Natural History, and the Rangeley Historical Society.

My colleagues at *Cabinet* magazine, Sina Najafi and Jeffrey Kastner, allowed me to rehearse ideas in that publication under their watchful editorial eye, as did Paul Laity and Mary-Kay Wilmers at the *London Review of Books*. Claire Barliant, Inigo Thomas, and Michael Wood generously read various stages of the manuscript and offered invaluable suggestions.

I'm grateful to Hal Foster and Rosalind Krauss for sponsoring me as a visiting scholar at Columbia University, where I began this book. An early draft won a Royal Society of Literature Jerwood Award, which allowed me to spend time traveling in America, conducting interviews and doing research; a residency at the MacDowell Colony offered me the splendid isolation in which to finish it. Christine Burgin and William Wegman, Mary and Alan Turner, Elena and Michael Wood, and Niki and Alf Coles have also offered me writerly sanctuary.

Thank you to my agent Natasha Fairweather, who helped initiate this book and made it possible, and to my editors on both sides of the Atlantic—Philip Gwyn Jones, Nicholas Pearson, Robin Harvie, and Paul Elie—who, with exemplary patience and intelligence, encouraged me to broaden its scope.

And above all I'd like to thank Gaby Wood, to whom this book is dedicated and without whom it would never have been written.

# INDEX

abortions, 55–56, 153, 220, 432, 454*n114*; sex reform and, 129, 130, 132; in Soviet Union, 115, 116, 118, 189
Abraham, Karl, 65–66, 72, 73, 85, 88, 90, 129, 170
Abrams box, 289–90
"Ad Hoc Committee for the Study of the Emotional Plague,"433
Adler, Alfred, 18, 22, 113, 139
Adler, Victor, 31
Adorno, Theodor, 273–74, 394, 421
*Aftenposten* (newspaper), 193–94
*After Long Silence* (Straight), 287
*After Polygamy Was Made a Sin* (Cairncross), 287
Agee, James, 256
Ageloff, Sylvia, 243
Agrarian League, 100
*Air-Conditioned Nightmare, The* (Miller), 274
air force, U.S., 320, 352, 370, 397, 405, 419, 425
Alexander, Franz, 95, 466*n71*
Alien Registration Act (1940), 328
Allen, Lewis, 430
Allen, Woody, 6, 445
*All Souls' Waiting Room, The* (Wright), 316
Alnaes, Rudolf, 195
Ambulatorium (Vienna), 70, 73, 74, 85, 95, 96, 113, 114, 165, 226; establishment of, 64, 66–69; Hitschmann as director of, 66, 79; technical seminar at, 72, 88, 89

American Association for the Advancement of Psychoanalysis, 219
American Association of Medical Orgonomists, 280, 329; Committee of Medical Ethics and Practice, 322
American Civil Liberties Union (ACLU), 297, 411, 422
American College of Medical Orgonomists, 433
American Eugenics Society, 217, 358
*American Journal of Psychiatry*, 281
American Law Institute, 303
American Medical Association (AMA), 230, 293, 344, 362, 369, 431; *Journal of*, 281
*American Men of Science*, 281
American Psychiatric Association, 281–82, 369
American Psychoanalytic Association, 369
American Social Hygiene Association, 306
American-Soviet Friendship League, 284
American Tobacco Company, 389–90
anal stage, 73, 83, 270
anarchist(s), 4, 6, 53, 189, 267, 278, 434; Brady's attacks on Reich and, 273, 276–77, 289–91; British, 288; in California, 274–77, 289; Goodman as, 223, 244, 245, 247; Perls and, 255, 256
Anderson, Marian, 428
Andreas-Salomé, Lou, 60, 94

Andrew, Christopher, 287
Angel, Anny, 113
animal magnetism, 20, 177, 223
"Anna O." case, 20, 54
*Anschluss*, 5, 25
anticommunism, 242, 249, 286, 328,
    351–54, 360, 395, 422, 425, 485*n20*
antifascists, 152, 238, 240, 283
Anti-Nazi League, 128
anti-Semitism, 21, 29, 48, 52, 154, 241
*Arbeiderbladet* (newspaper), 195
*Arbeiterblad* (newspaper), 150, 151
*Arbeiter-Zeitung* (newspaper), 97, 98, 113
Arendt, Hannah, 206
Aristotle, 191
Army-McCarthy hearings, 384–85
*Art and Revolution* (Trotsky), 248
Association for Psychoanalytic and
    Psychosomatic Medicine, 219
*Atlantic Monthly, The*, 107
Atlas, James, 248, 261
atomic bomb, 200, 225, 245, 275, 284, 302,
    327–29, 377, 394, 431; *see also* hydrogen
    bomb
Atomic Energy Commission (AEC), 331,
    332, 334, 349
Auden, W. H., 123, 124
Auschwitz concentration camp, 144
Austrian Psychoanalytic Association, 149
Austrian Revolution, 24–25
*Autobiographical Novel* (Rexroth), 289

Bachofen, Johann Jakob, 103
*Bad Day at Black Rock* (film), 375
Badgeley, Elizabeth, 466*n71*
Baker, Courtney, 414
Baker, Elsworth, 86, 245, 291, 321, 326,
    381, 382, 414, 435–36; on "Ad Hoc
    Committee for the Study of the
    Emotional Plague," 433; children
    treated by, 322, 325; cloudbuster
    demonstrated to, 367; conservative
    politics of, 361, 433–34; DOR (deadly
    orgone) described by, 365; Karrer in
    analysis with, 399, 400; literature
    seminars of, 342; at Marlboro State
    Hospital, 278–80; Ollendorff treated by,
    337, 339; on Oranur experiment, 333–35;
    at Orgonomic Infant Research Center
    meetings, 317, 318; Rangeley
    townspeople addressed by, 329–30; at
    Reich's funeral, 428; and Reich's

pathological jealousy, 337–38; training
    sessions of, 312
Baker, Marguerite, 279, 318, 334
Baker, Michael, 318
Baldwin, James, 7
Baptists, 214, 355
*Barbarella* (film), 445–46
Barnes and Noble, 431
"Barricade and the Bedroom, The"
    (Wright and Salter), 250
Bauer, Otto, 31, 64, 69, 98, 100, 109
Beach, Frank, 211
Bean, Orson, 433–35
"Beating Fantasies and Daydreams"
    (Freud), 45
Beck, Julian, 256, 268–69, 434
Bedford Hills (New York) women's
    reformatory, 215–17
Beethoven, Ludwig van, 36, 235
Bellevue Hospital (New York City), 263
Bell Laboratories, 381
Bellow, Saul, 248, 259–62
Belzec extermination camp, 454*n93*
Benjamin, Harry, 198
Bentley, Arvilla, 354
Bentley, Elizabeth, 352–53
Bergler, Edmund, 113
Berlin Opera, 158
Berlin Poliklinic, 65–66, 68, 69, 143
Berlin Psychoanalytic Institute, 126, 139
Berlin Psychoanalytic Society, 129, 165
Berman, Paul, 403–404
Bernays, Edward, 101–102, 389–90
Berneri, Marie Louise, 289
Bernfeld, Siegfried, 122, 139
Bettelheim, Bruno, 52, 53
*Beyond the Pleasure Principle* (Freud), 78
Biberman, Herbert, 354
Bibring, Eduard, 34, 165
Bibring, Grete (née Lehner), 33–34,
    138, 165
Binet intelligence tests, 215
*Bioelectric Investigation of Sexuality and
    Anxiety, The* (Reich), 174
Biological Institute (Copenhagen), 192
*Bion Experiments, The* (Reich), 193
bions, 191–93, 196; SAPA, 199–200,
    220–21, 335
birth control pill, 12, 356–59, 432
Black Hand, 48
Blasbland, Richard, 485*n35*
Bloch, Iwan, 33
*Blue Angel, The* (film), 115

*Blue Light, The* (film), 375
Blunt, Anthony, 286–88
Boehm, Felix, 143
Bohr, Niels, 145, 200
Bolshevism, 4–5, 30, 63, 139, 147, 166
Bolshevo Commune (Moscow), 118
*Book of Dreams, A* (Reich), 316, 373, 376–77
*Book of the It, The* (Groddeck), 107
Boote, Dr., 320
Bornstein, Berta, 59, 122, 161–63, 183–84
Bornstein, Steff, 122
Bourneville, Desiré Magloire, 75–76
Brackett, Samson, 299
Brackett, Sylvester, 298–99
Bradley, David, 327
Brady, Joan, 283–84
Brady, Mildred Edie, 272–74, 276–78, 280–87, 289–92, 294, 296, 408, 471*n54*
Brady, Robert, 272, 283, 284
Brandt, Willy, 174–75, 220
Braun, Heinrich, 31
*Brave New World* (Huxley), 446
Brecht, Bertolt, 145, 150, 172, 196, 359
Breuer, Josef, 20, 21, 54
Briehl, Walter, 89, 114, 205, 206, 231
Brill, A. A., 143, 389–90
Brimmer, Dr., 349
Browder, Earl, 238, 289
Brown, Norman O., 396
*Brown v. Board of Education* (1954), 314
Brownian motion, 192–93
Brownshirts, 125, 141
Bruno, Giordano, 349, 386
Bryan, Joseph, III, 480*n10*
Budenz, Louis Francis, 242, 352
Bühler, Charlotte and Karl, 391
Bullitt, William, 26
Burgess, Guy, 287, 288
Burlingame, Dorothy, 162–63
Burlingame, Mabbie, 164
Burlingame, Robert, 162–63
Burroughs, William, 6, 223, 262–67, 294
Butyrka prison (Moscow), 118
Buxbaum, Edith, 58, 59

Cage, John, 256
Cain, John, 408
Cairncross, John, 287
California, University of, Berkeley, 435
*Call for Sexual Tolerance, A* (Ujhely), 123
Cambridge University, 8, 286
Camus, Albert, 256

cancer, 196–200, 253, 280–82, 290–94, 329, 341, 344, 362; of Freud, 84, 90, 101, 144, 198, 218; Nazism and, 196–97; orgone accumulator treatment for, 5, 200, 224, 226, 229–32, 241, 255, 260, 273, 280, 282, 294–95, 298, 336, 345–46, 364, 427; SAPA-bions and, 199–200, 220
*Cancer Biopathy, The* (Reich), 221, 229, 232, 266, 267, 294, 298
Cancer Hospital (Oslo), 200
Canetti, Elias, 102
Capote, Truman, 305
Carlsberg Foundation, 192
Carnegie Institution Department of Genetics, 216
"Case of Pubertal Breaching of the Incest Taboo, A" (Reich), 43–44
Cassady, Neal, 264
Cassidy (FDA Inspector), 362
castration anxiety, 58, 71, 147
Catholic Church, 114, 115, 137, 139, 262, 355
Central Intelligence Agency (CIA), 327, 384, 405, 414
Centre Universitaire Méditerranéen, 192
*Chalk Triangle, The* (Reich), 138
Chambers, Whittaker, 327, 352–53
character analysis, 35, 127, 172, 178, 219, 263, 268, 270, 320
*Character Analysis* (Reich), 90–91, 139, 150, 164, 248, 368, 398, 419, 443, 457*n76*
character armor, 9, 91, 93, 128, 137, 218, 251, 257, 268, 402
Charcot, Jean-Martin, 19–20, 76, 254
Chernow, Ron, 214
Chevalier, Haakon, 284
Chicago, University of, 244, 262, 363
*Children of the Future* (Reich), 315, 317
Christianity, 36
Christian Social Party, Austrian, 29, 30, 36, 63–64, 67, 97, 98, 100, 142; Militia of, *see* Heimwehr
Chrobak, Rudolf, 76
Chrysler Corporation, 382
*Circle* (magazine), 275, 276, 288
*Civilization and Its Discontents* (Freud), 120–21, 395
"Civilized Sexual Morality and Modern Nervousness" (Freud), 77
Clark, Kenneth, 314
Clark, Ronald, 226
Clark University, 3

cloudbusters, 11, 366–67, 369–76, 384, 421, 427
Cobain, Kurt, 267
"Coitus and the Sexes" (Reich), 58
cold war, 8, 245, 249, 285, 327, 328, 331, 395, 432
Collier's magazine, 282
Collins, Vernon, 350, 410
Columbia Broadcasting System (CBS), 328
Columbia Presbyterian Psychiatric Institute (New York), 266
Columbia University, 126, 205, 219, 262, 266, 269, 394, 434; Bureau of Applied Social Research, 250
Comfort, Alex, 288
Coming of Age in Samoa (Mead), 314
Committee of Revolutionary Social Democrats, 112
Communism and the Moral Breakdown in America (Crombie), 360
Communist International (Comintern), 150, 184, 188, 189, 287
Communist Manifesto, The (Marx and Engels), 113
Communists, 189, 355, 357, 375, 376, 410, 435; in Austria, 30, 53, 98, 100, 101, 108–12, 121, 391; in Denmark, 145, 150–52, 188; in Germany, 12, 117, 124–25, 129, 131, 132, 135–38, 140, 147, 148, 156–58, 184, 287, 360; in Hungary, 29; in Poland, 230; psychoanalysts' antagonism toward, 146, 155, 166, 170; Reich's break with, 248, 282–83, 290, 360–62, 433; Reich's paranoid delusions about, 376, 385–86, 402; in United States, 161, 207, 238–43, 284, 288–89, 304, 320, 327–30, 359–60, 411, 422, 423; see also anticommunism
"Compulsory Marriage and Enduring Sexual Relationship" (Reich), 133
"Concerning Specific Forms of Masturbation" (Reich), 456n24
Congress, U.S., 214, 285, 305, 353
Connery, Sean, 6
Conscience of Words, The (Canetti), 102
Constitution, U.S., Fifth Amendment, 243, 360
Consumers Union, 272, 273, 284, 292
Contact with Space (Reich), 371, 373–74, 379, 406, 425
contraception, 133; see also birth control pill
"Contributions to the Psychology of Jealousy" (Fenichel), 181

Cooper, Gary, 375
Copenhagen, University of, Institute of Theoretical Physics, 145, 200
Copernicus, Nicolaus, 359
CORE (journal), 376
Cosmic Superimposition (Reich), 342
Cosmopolitan magazine, 389
Cossacks, 50
Cott, Allan, 265, 266, 322, 333, 334, 341
Cotton, Dr., 279–80
Counterattack (weekly), 353–54
Crawford, Charles, 369
Crombie, A. H., 360
Crompton, Arthur, 369–70
Crowds and Power (Canetti), 102
Curie, Eva, 199
Curie, Marie, 199, 201
Curie, Pierre, 199
Cvetic, Matt, 352–53

Dachau concentration camp, 140
Daily Worker (newspaper), 239, 242
Danbury Federal Penitentiary, 419, 421
Danish-Norwegian Psychoanalytic Society, 153, 180
Danto, Elizabeth, 70, 80, 143
Dartmouth College, 410–11
Davenport, Charles B., 216
Davis, Katharine Bement, 215–17
Day the Earth Stood Still, The (film), 371–72
deadly orgone (DOR), 333–36, 364–66, 370, 373, 381, 384, 407, 485n35, 486n41; device for busting, 398–400, 403; in prisons, 421
death instinct, 93, 138, 333
defenses, 20, 90, 258, 264, 269, 340
Dell, Floyd, 4
Democratic Party, U.S., 238, 286, 355, 359, 361; 1968 National Convention, 441, 445
Demons, The (Doderer), 101
Detective magazine, 330
Deutsch, Arnold, 137, 287, 288
Deutsch, Felix, 61, 66, 84
Deutsch, Helene, 37, 39, 61, 66, 67, 69–70, 85, 88, 89, 114, 233, 463n89
Deutscher, Isaac, 188
Deutsches Volkstheater (Vienna), 51
Development of Psychoanalysis, The (Ferenczi and Rank), 89
Dewey, Thomas E., 286
Dialectics of Nature (Engels), 191
Dichter, Ernest, 390–93, 443–45

Dichter, Leopold, 391
Dies, Martin, 238–39, 284
Dietrich, Marlene, 115
Dikemark Sykehus (Oslo), 174, 175
*Dissent* (journal), 430
*Dr. Zhivago* (film), 99
Dodds, Harold, 306
Doderer, Heimito von, 101
Dodge, Mabel, 4, 354, 358
Dollfuss, Engelbert, 142
Doolittle, Hilda, 17
DOR, *see* deadly orgone
"Dora" case, 31
Dorno, Carl, 104
dreams: commercialization of, 390;
  interpretation, 18, 52, 70, 96, 196, 263
Dukas, Helen, 229
Dulles, John Foster, 357
Dunbar, Helen Flanders, 238
Durrell, Lawrence, 276
Duvall, Albert, 279, 319, 321–22, 325, 326,
  341, 361, 367, 404


*Earth vs. Flying Saucers* (film), 425
Eastman, Max, 4, 196
Economic Welfare, Board of, 239
*Ecstasy* (film), 157
Edison, Thomas Alva, 232
*Ego, Hunger and Aggression* (Perls), 127, 256
"Ego and the Id, The" (Freud), 71
*Ego and the Mechanisms of Defense, The*
  (Freud), 163–64, 457n76
ego psychology, 91
"Ego Psychology and the Problem of
  Adaptation" (Hartmann), 218
Einstein, Albert, 5–6, 107, 207, 225–30,
  238, 311, 372
*Einstein Affair, The* (Reich), 230
Eisenhower, Dwight D., 357, 360–61,
  369, 397, 398, 401, 402, 410–11, 419,
  424–25, 435
Eissler, Kurt, 96, 131–32, 198
Eitingon, Max, 22, 65, 66, 69, 139, 143
"Elisabeth von R." case, 76
Ellis, Albert, 434
Elvins, Kells, 266, 267
*Emotional Armoring* (Herskowitz), 313
"emotional plague," 221, 291, 314, 315,
  317, 378, 408, 428, 435
"Emotional Plague Prevention Office
  (EPPO)," 402
*Empire of Ecstasy* (Toepfer), 157

Enemy Alien Control Unit, 241
Engels, Friedrich, 103, 105, 191
English, O. Spurgeon, 92, 114, 140, 431,
  462n89
Enlightenment, 191
Erikson, Erik, 146, 201
*Eros and Civilization* (Marcuse), 394, 395,
  397, 441, 442
Esalen Institute, 436–41
*Escape from Freedom* (Fromm), 149, 245
"Esoterik" (Fenichel), 53
*Esquire* magazine, 391–92
Esso, 390
eugenics, 115, 153, 215–16, 358
Eugenics Record Office, 216
*Everybody's Digest*, 282
existentialism, 256–57
Experimental Home for Children
  (Moscow), 118–19


*Fads and Fallacies in the Name of Science*
  (Gardner), 344
*False Witness* (Matusow), 422, 423
Faraday cage, 200, 209, 220–22
fascism, 4–6, 8, 109, 166, 219, 226, 248, 284,
  375, 435; in Austria, 29, 100–101, 109;
  cancer and, 196–98; consumer culture as
  bulwark against, 393; in Denmark, 158;
  in Germany, 142 (*see also* Hitler, Adolf;
  Nazis); in Italy, 111; neo-, 285; in
  Norway, 186–90, 193; opponents of, *see*
  antifascists; red, 291, 307, 331, 348, 350,
  379, 385, 409, 413; Roosevelt accused of,
  207; in South Africa, 255, 440
*Fascism and the American Scene*
  (Macdonald), 249
Federal Bureau of Investigation (FBI),
  238–43, 283, 296–97, 353, 361, 362;
  Atomic Energy Commission report on
  Reich to, 331; books confiscated by, 189;
  Bradys investigated by, 284; Enemy
  Alien Control Unit of, 241; informants
  of, 242, 273, 351–52; Kinsey investigated
  by, 304–305; Rangeley rumors and
  allegations investigated by, 328–29;
  Reich file of, 6, 239, 241, 472n95;
  Rubenstein file of, 184; search of
  Reich's house by, 240–41; "secret
  information" offered by Reich to,
  417–19; Sex Deviates Program, 305–306;
  Truman's loyalty program carried out
  by, 286

Federal Bureau of Prisons, 422
Federn, Ernst, 60–61
Federn, Paul, 19, 22, 60–61, 66, 68, 84–85, 87–89, 95, 167, 218, 263
Feist, Herta, 157
Feitelberg, Sergei, 466n71
Feldman, Irving, 380
feminism, 55, 76, 116
Fenichel, Claire, 466n15
Fenichel, Otto, 57, 66, 88, 139, 144, 171, 173, 181–83, 245, 309, 466n15; adolescence of, 52–53; at Annie Pink and Reich's wedding, 59; "children's seminar" for young analysts of, 70, 122, 126; and Reich's expulsion from IPA, 156, 165, 166, 180–81; Rundbriefe (newsletters) circulated by, 159–61, 166, 170, 181, 182, 467n45; sexology seminars of, 18, 55; in United States, 235, 281
Ferenczi, Sándor, 22, 26, 54, 71, 72, 80, 89–91, 95, 114, 142, 170
Fest, Joachim, 148
Feuchtwanger, Lion, 359
Firestone, Shulamith, 14
Fischer, Albert, 192–93
Fisher, Ernest, 98
Fisher, Fred, 385–87
Five Lectures on Psychoanalysis (Freud), 3
Fliess, Wilhelm, 76–77
Flying Saucers Are Real, The (Kehoe), 370
Flynn, Elizabeth Gurley, 422
Food, Drug, and Cosmetic Act (1938), 282, 367, 427
Food and Drug Administration (FDA), 12, 241, 308, 329, 353, 375, 376, 398, 431; birth control pill licensed by, 432; contempt charges against Reich brought by, 384–87, 405, 407; former Reichian as collaborator with, 322; injunction against Reich obtained by, 367–70, 378–79, 384; investigation of orgone accumulator by, 6, 290, 292–301, 317, 344–50, 362–64, 379–82, 485n35; Leunbach's uterine paste banned by, 153; at Reich's Arizona property, 378–79; seizure and destruction of accumulators and books by, 408–12
Forbidden Love (manifesto), 132
Forel, Auguste, 33
Foucault, Michel, 446, 492n54
Frank, Karl, 54–55, 121–22, 144, 184, 283
Frankfurt, University of, 13, 394
Frankfurt School, 394, 395
Franklin, Benjamin, 223

Franz Ferdinand, Archduke of Austria-Hungary, 48
free association, 21, 70, 71, 443
Free Associations (Jones), 22
Freedom Press, 247
French Academy of Sciences, 20
Freud, Anna, 19, 108, 142–44, 155, 156, 161–65, 185, 218, 457n76; Annie Reich analyzed by, 103, 134, 161, 163; child analysands of, 121–22, 162–64; fictionalization of self-analysis of, 45; and Reich's expulsion from IPA, 155, 156, 165–66, 181, 465n60; Reich's technical seminar attended by, 89
Freud, Ernst, 65
Freud, Martin, 25, 29, 20, 101
Freud, Sigmund, 25, 57, 96–97, 127, 152, 206, 247, 276, 297, 307, 319, 390, 427; active therapy criticized by, 90; American analysands of, 63; Anna's relationship with, 45, 134; apartment block named after, 63; Bernays and, 101–102, 389; birthday celebrations of, 83–84, 185; break with Reich, 103, 104, 138–39, 142, 146, 151, 154, 155, 159, 161, 165–66, 170, 172, 219, 290, 296; Burlingame analyzed by, 162; burning of books of, 141; cancer of, 84, 85, 90, 101, 198; creation of psychoanalysis by, 19–22; death of, 218–20; death instinct theory of, 138, 333, 394; developmental theory of, 72–73; Dichter and, 390, 392–93; Einstein and, 226–27; and Federn's antagonism toward Reich, 84–85, 87–89, 95; free clinics launched by, 65–69, 72, 112; Hirschfeld admired by, 129; id concept of, 107; at International Congresses of Psychoanalysis, 64–65, 71; Jones's biography of, 61, 161, 173; last meeting of Reich and, 122–23; libido theory of, 73, 77, 78, 96, 173, 174, 209, 267–68; in London, 164, 199; Nazi attacks on, 141–44; opposition of Marxist psychoanalysts to, 126; orgasm theory rejected by, 94, 120–22, 378; politics of, 31; in post–World War I Vienna, 26–28, 32; referral of patients to Reich by, 18, 38–39, 71; Reich becomes disciple of, 17–19, 22, 36, 50–52, 59, 60, 157; Reich considered heir apparent to, 8–9; on repression, 5, 76–78, 113, 136, 396; on resistance, 91, 93, 267; at Salpêtrière

Hospital, 19, 75–76; on Soviet Union, 119–20; Tausk and, 233, 236; therapeutic technique of, 71–72, 95–96, 176, 438; on transference, 54; in United States, 3–4, 214, 274; at University of Vienna, 19, 22, 24; on Weininger, 37; works of, *see titles of specific works*
Freud, Sophie, 27
Freudianism, 6, 83, 93, 119, 161, 173, 247, 262, 393; Lenin's denunciation of, 117; Marxism and, 5, 106, 115, 130, 131, 155, 248, 256, 395; orthodox, 26, 137, 195; *see also* neo-Freudians
*Freudian Left, The* (Robinson), 251
Friedjung, Josef K., 60
Froebel, Friedrich, 55
From, Isidore, 270, 271
Fromm, Erich, 70, 126, 149, 160, 206, 245–46, 256, 257, 394, 395
Fuchs, Klaus, 328
Fugs, the, 434
*Function of the Orgasm, The* (Reich), 5, 11, 51–52, 82, 235, 276, 281, 316, 346; American editions of, 211, 234, 248; Freud's response to, 94, 120; Mailer influenced by, 429–30; publication of, 84, 105–106, 125–26; quoted in Kinsey Report, 306, 480*n15*
*Future of an Illusion, The* (Freud), 101

Gaasland, Gertrud, 174, 205, 220
Galileo, 195–96, 235, 359
Gallup polls, 306
Gardner, Martin, 344
Garland, George, 299
Garland, Judy, 326
Gebhard, Paul, 211, 213
General Motors, 208
George, Stefan, 285
German American Bund, 240
German Association for Proletarian Sexual Politics, *see* Sex-Pol
German Institute for Psychological Research and Psychotherapy, 143
German Medical Society for Psychotherapy, 149
German People's Theater (Vienna), 51
German Psychoanalytic Society, 139, 142, 143, 149, 159
German Soviet Friendship Society, 129
Gerö, George, 160, 167
Gestalt therapy, 257, 268–71, 437–41, 445

*Gestalt Therapy* (Perls, Goodman and Hefferline), 257, 269, 270
Gestapo, 140, 144, 193, 317, 454*n93*
*Getting Motivated* (Dichter), 390
Ginsberg, Allen, 6, 262–66, 322, 434
Glover, Edward, 90
*God That Failed, The* (Koestler), 125–26
Goebbels, Joseph, 102, 124
Goethe, Johann Wolfgang von, 44–45, 99
Goethe Institute (Boston), 161
Gold, Dr., 342
Goldinger, Lewis, 240
Goldman, Emma, 4
*Goodbye to Berlin* (Isherwood), 123–24
Goodman, Paul, 223, 244–45, 249, 253, 284–85, 289, 436; Marcuse compared with, 395; orgone accumulator use of, 6, 267; Perls and, 255–57, 269–71, 438; *Politics* essay on Reich by, 245–47, 250, 255, 284; in Sexual Freedom League, 434; treatment by Lowen of, 251
Göring, Hermann, 140, 143
Göring, Matthias, 149
Grad, Bernard, 364–65
Graf, Cäcilie, 61
Great Depression, 116, 145, 206, 238
Greenfield, Jerome, 301
Greer, Germaine, 14
Groddeck, Georg, 107
Gross, Otto, 77
Grossman, Atina, 132
Grosz, George, 125
Grotjahn, Martin, 19, 93
*Group Psychology* (Freud), 102
*Growing Up Absurd* (Goodman), 244
Gruber, Helmut, 64
Gyömröi, Edith, 160, 171, 173

H.D., 17
Habsburg monarchy, 24
Hagen, Paul, *see* Frank, Karl
Haire, Norman, 464*n23*
Hale, Nathan G., 73
Hamill, F. P., 380–81
Hamilton, Alexander, 309, 340
Hamilton School (Massachusetts), 307, 331, 340, 397
Harnick, Eugen, 127
Harnick, Jenö, 146
*Harper's Magazine*, 6, 274, 280, 285, 289
Harris, Frank, 289
Hartmann, Heinz, 167, 218

Harvard University, 263, 266, 358, 395, 422; Law School, 385; Medical School, 374
Hauksbee, Francis, 236
Hauschka, Theodore, 290–91, 478n62
Hayden Planetarium (New York), 207
Hays, Arthur Garfield, 288, 297
Health, U.S. Department of, 348
Health and Hygiene (magazine), 239
Hefferline, Ralph, 269, 270
Hefner, Hugh, 356, 359
Heifetz, Ottilie Reich, 32
Heilbut, Anthony, 207
Heimwehr, 100, 109–11, 142; shock troops (Frontkämpfer) of, 110
Helldorf, Wolf Heinrich von, 125
Heller, Louis, 355
Heller, Peter, 121–22, 162, 164, 324, 349
Henderson the Rain King (Bellow), 260
Herskowitz, Morton, 251, 308, 310–14, 319–22, 335–37, 399, 402, 427, 433
Herzog (Bellow), 262
Herzog, Dagmar, 13–14, 148, 463n14
Hesse, Hermann, 421
Hidden Persuaders, The (Packard), 442–44
Higgins, Raymond, 363
High Noon (film), 375
Himmler, Heinrich, 140
Hindenburg, Paul von, 139–40
Hippocrates, 75
Hiroshima, atomic bombing of, 225
Hirschfeld, Magnus, 5, 118, 129–30, 141, 434, 462n68, 464n23
Hiss, Alger, 284, 286–87, 327, 352, 422, 423
Hitler, Adolf, 12, 130, 143, 147–48, 150, 189, 207, 240, 247, 266; cancer obsession of, 197–98; Lore Reich's comparison of Reich and, 169–70; pact with Stalin, 237–38, 241, 248; propaganda of anti-Nazi groups against, 394; rise to power of, 100, 124, 139–41, 168; as struggling artist in Vienna, 29; Weininger applauded by, 36
Hitler Youth, 52
Hitschmann, Eduard, 22, 35, 66, 69, 70, 72, 79, 80, 127, 271
Hodann, Max, 129, 240
Hoel, Sigurd, 182–83, 194, 195
Hoff, Grethe, 325, 341, 397, 399, 414, 417
Hoffmann, Ferdinand, 149
Hoffmann, Wilhelm, 175
Holocaust, 6, 152
homosexuality, 18, 129, 130, 211, 271, 346, 422; of Ginsberg, 264–65; Kinsey on, 217, 302, 303, 305–307; McCarthy's campaign against, 351; Nazi persecution against, 149; Reich's abhorrence of, 251, 265, 307, 433, 462n68; in Soviet Union, 116, 118, 287
Honoring the Body (Lowen), 253
Hoover, J. Edgar, 243, 304–306, 354, 369, 417, 418, 480n10
Horkheimer, Max, 394, 421
Horney, Karen, 70, 126, 127, 219, 245–46, 256, 257
House of Representatives, U.S.; Committee to Investigate Tax-Exempt and Other Comparable Organizations, 356, 359; Un-American Activities Committee (HUAC), 238–39, 242–43, 284, 327, 351, 353
Howe, Irving, 258, 261, 430
Hoxsey, Harry, 292
Hubbard, Richard C., 419–21
Hughes, H. Stuart, 395
Hughes, Langston, 410
Huncke, Herbert, 263–64
Huxley, Aldous, 436, 446
hydrogen bomb, 331–32, 355, 369–70, 393
hypnosis, 19–21, 54, 76, 263, 443
hysteria, 19–20, 75–76, 78, 362; mass, 335, 423, 428

Ibsen, Henrik, 19, 50–52, 187, 235
id, 71, 93, 107, 134, 218, 389, 306, 438
Ideal of Marriage (Van de Velde), 82
Illinois, University of, 434
Illness as Metaphor (Sontag), 197–98, 341
Immigration Act (1910), 214
Immigration and Naturalization Service (INS), U.S., 206, 359–62
impotence, 80, 81, 129, 281, 427, 456n24; psychonalytic treatment of, 38–39, 74, 79
Impulsive Character, The (Reich), 73, 85, 174
incest taboo, 47, 96, 136
Indiana University, 210–12, 218
Infeld, Leopold, 230
influencing machine, 233–34, 236
Inhibitions, Symptoms and Anxiety (Freud), 78
In and Out of the Garbage Pail (Perls), 128
Inquisition, 196, 349, 386
Institute of Bioenergetics, 404
Institute of Sex-Economic Bioresearch, 172, 182

Institute for Sex Research, 212–13, 304
Institute for Sexual Science, 129, 141, 435
Inter-Allied Commission on Relief of
  German Austria, 27
International Bureau of Revolutionary
  Youth Organizations, 174
International Congresses of
  Psychoanalysis, 307–308; Berlin (1922),
  71; Budapest (1918), 64; Innsbruck
  (1927), 466n71; Lucerne (1934), 164–70,
  180, 185, 376, 465n71; Marienbad
  (1936), 185–86, 258; Salzburg (1908,
  1924), 21, 80
Internationale Arbeiter-Hilfe (Workers
  International Relief), 100
International Harvester, 358
International Herald Tribune, 26–27
International Journal of Orgonomy, 473n12
International Journal of Psychoanalysis, 138
International Orgonomic Convention
  (Rangeley, Maine, 1948), 307–308
International Psychoanalytical Association
  (IPA), 8, 19, 139, 143–44, 154–56, 159,
  161, 165–69, 180, 185
International Society of Plasmogeny, 288
Interpretation of Dreams, The (Freud), 18
Introductory Lectures on Psychoanalysis
  (Freud), 78
Invasion of Compulsory Sex-Morality, The
  (Reich), 137
Isherwood, Christopher, 123–24, 129
Is Sex Necessary? (Thurber and White),
  449n5
I Was a Communist for the FBI (Cvetic), 352


Jacobsen, Jo, 146
Jacobson, Edith, 70, 126–27, 144,
  160, 170
James, William, 3
Jahrbuch für sexualle Zwischenstufen
  (journal), 130
Janov, Arthur, 430
Jazz Age, 13
Jeder Achte (film), 197
Jekels, Ludwig, 70
Jencks, Clinton, 354, 422
Jerubbaal (youth journal), 53
Jessen, Friedrich, 106
Jews, 28–29, 32, 49, 53, 54, 162, 194, 262,
  440, 452n55; Nazi persecution of, 5, 102,
  124, 125, 130, 140–45, 147–49, 158, 201,
  454n93; Russian pogroms against, 48;

scapegoating of, 28, 30, 36; in
  Wandervögel youth movement, 52; see
  also anti-Semitism
Johnson, Alvin, 230, 241, 253
Jokl, Robert, 85
Jones, Ernest, 77, 101, 103, 136, 142–43,
  161, 181, 389, 465n60; affairs of, 54,
  466n71; autobiography of, 22, 39;
  biography of Freud by, 61, 161, 173;
  character theory of Abraham and, 72, 73,
  90; clinic established by, 66; first
  meeting of Freud and, 21–22; in
  post–World War I Vienna, 26; refugees
  from Nazis aided by, 144, 154–55, 186;
  and Reich's expulsion from IPA, 154–56,
  165–67, 180
Jones, James, 210, 303, 304
Jones, Jim, 415
Josephson, Emmanuel M., 348
Journal of Orgonomy, 282, 300, 433
Journal of Political Psychology and Sex
  Economy, 160
Journal of Sex Economy and Orgone
  Research, 211
Joyce, James, 426
Joy of Sex, The (Comfort), 288
Judeo-Christian tradition, 355
Julius, Deso, 53–54
Jung, Carl Gustav, 4, 36, 54, 61, 77, 209,
  358; anti-Semitism of, 21; flying saucer
  research of, 371; Freud's break with, 22,
  89, 139, 170
Justice Department, U.S., 423
Justice Ministry, Danish, 152, 153


Kafka, Franz, 25
Kahn, Lore, 54–58, 108, 122
Kaiser Wilhelm Institute (Berlin), 175, 225
Kama Sutra, 434, 449n4
Kant, Immanuel, 33
Kapital, Das (Marx), 103
Karl-Marx-Hof (Vienna), 63, 142
Karrer, Aurora, 398–400, 411–15, 418, 421,
  424, 426, 427
Kaufman, M. Ralph, 114
Kazin, Alfred, 6–7, 244, 259, 261, 277
Kennedy, John F., 432
Kenyon (FDA Inspector), 348, 408–409
Kerouac, Jack, 6, 262–63, 266, 267
Keyhoe, Donald, 370
KGB, 287
Kings County Hospital (Brooklyn), 270

Kinsey, Alfred, 4, 209–14, 216–18, 263–64, 353, 355–57, 359, 360, 362, 480*n15*
Kinsey, Clara (née McMillen), 210, 303, 304
Klein, Melanie, 155
Klimt, Gustav, 27
Knobel, Otto, 188
Koch, Leo, 434
Koestler, Arthur, 12, 125–26
Kokoschka, Oskar, 27
Kolisch, Rudolf, 33
Kollontai, Alexandra, 116–18
Korean War, 331, 352
Kramer, Edith, 324
Kraus, Karl, 36
Kreyberg, Lejv, 193
Krusen, Frank H., 364
Kubie, Lawrence, 242, 273, 306, 307
Kuhn, Fritz, 240
Kun, Béla, 29
Kupferberg, Tuli, 434

Laban, Rudolf von, 157
Labor Party, Norwegian, 186, 187, 193, 195
Lamarr, Hedy, 157
Lancaster, Burt, 375
*Lancet, The* (journal), 192
Lange, Helene, 157
*Language of the Body, The* (Lowen), 252
Larkin, Philip, 431
Laszky, Lia, 34–35, 38, 55, 59–60, 66, 114–16, 133, 324, 335–36
Laszky, Tony, 324
Lawrence, D. H., 354, 426
Lawrence, Frieda, 354
Law to Restore the Professional Civil Service (Germany, 1933), 141
League of Nations, 63
Le Bon, Gustav, 101, 102
Leite, George, 275–76, 288, 289
Leite, Nancy, 275, 276
Lenin, V. I., 105, 117–18, 124, 138, 184, 189, 288, 423
Leunbach, J. H., 152–53, 158, 193, 464*n23*
Lewisburg Federal Penitentiary, 12, 420–27
Leyden jars, 223
Leydig cells, 198
Libertarian Circle, 274, 289
"Libidinal Conflicts and Delusions in Ibsen's *Peer Gynt*" (Reich), 19, 50–51
libido theory, 13, 58, 93, 362, 396; advertising and, 390, 442; genitality in, 80–81, 128, 396; of Freud, 73, 77, 78, 96, 173, 174, 209, 267–68; neo-Freudian rejection of, 219; Perls on, 267–70; Reich's experiments on quantification of, 173–74, 190; sex-economy and, 166, 172; social consequences of, 219; in vegetotherapy, 235
Lie, Trygve, 187
Lieberman, Herman, 70
*Life Against Death* (Brown), 396
*Life* magazine, 390
*Life of Galileo* (Brecht), 196
Lindenberg, Elsa, 157–58, 172, 174–75, 205, 206, 208, 209, 220, 466*n15*; abortion undergone by, 56; breakup of Reich and, 201–202; dancing of, 157, 176, 201; Karrer on, 414, 417; at Lucerne congress, 164, 167
*List, The* (Mailer), 250
*Listen, Little Man* (Reich), 310, 325
Living Theatre, 256, 268
Loewenstein, Rudolph, 165
*Lonely Crowd, The* (Riesman), 388
Loos, Adolf, 65
Los Alamos National Laboratory, 328, 331, 332
Louis XVI, King of France, 223
*Love and Orgasm* (Lowen), 252
Lowen, Alexander, 251–55, 258, 276, 404
Löwenbach, H., 175
Lowenfeld, Henry, 160–61, 182
Lubbe, Marinus van der, 140
Lueger, Karl, 29
Luft, David S., 99
Luft, Lorna, 326

Macdonald, Dwight, 245, 249, 256, 257, 284, 290, 291
Maclean, Donald, 287, 288
Maclean, Melinda, 288
*Magic Mountain, The* (Mann), 106–107
Maguire, Joseph, 386–87, 403, 405
Mahler, Gustav, 39
Mailer, Norman, 6, 249–50, 427, 429–32, 434
Maine General Hospital, 363
Maines, Rachel, 75, 76
Makavejev, Dušan, 252, 377, 434
Malenkov, Georgy, 360
Malina, Judith, 256–58, 434
Malinowski, Bronislaw, 131, 136–37, 155, 159, 185, 206
*Man for All Seasons, A* (film), 375

Mangravite, Tom, 380–84, 401–403, 407–408
Manhattan Project, 225, 226, 331
manic depression, 162, 163, 169, 236, 352, 422
Mann, Thomas, 106–107, 141, 207, 397, 421
Mann Act (1910), 214
Manumit School, 245
*Man in the Trap* (Baker), 434
Marcuse, Herbert, 14, 149–50, 394–97, 441–43, 446
Marie Antoinette, Queen of France, 223
Marlboro State Hospital (New Jersey), 278, 279
Marriage Counselors Association, 305
Martin, Claude, 212
Marx, Karl, 4, 102–103, 105, 113, 395, 396
Marxism, 128, 139, 155, 166, 248, 256, 361, 394; of Fenichel, 126, 156, 159–60; Freudianism and, 5, 9, 106, 115, 130, 131, 155, 248, 256, 395; neo-, 394; sexual freedom and, 137, 138; of Social Democrats, 31
masochism, 45, 86, 87, 115, 129, 138, 166, 264, 412
Massachusetts Institute of Technology (MIT), 358, 363
*Masses, The* (journal), 4
*Mass Psychology of Fascism, The* (Reich), 13, 147, 150–52, 166, 179, 188, 189, 249, 284, 291, 394, 411
Masters, Dexter, 273, 274, 283–84
masturbation, 4, 18, 74, 129, 279–80, 346, 349, 456*n*; in childhood and adolescence, 47, 86, 119, 135, 149, 194, 301; Freud on, 76; Kinsey on, 211, 302, 307; in orgone accumulator, 245, 298; in Reich's laboratory experiments, 175, 178; Sadger and, 39, 59; in therapy, 178, 195; in vegetotherapy, 279, 325
Mattick, Paul, 267
Matusow, Harvey, 351–55, 422–26
Mauch, Christof, 283
Mayo Clinic, 363, 364
McCarthy, Joseph, 12, 239, 305, 356, 359, 385–86, 395, 424, 433; allegations of Communists in State Department by, 328, 352; book banning and, 410; hearings discredited, 384–85; homosexuals denounced as security risks by, 351; Matusow and, 353–54, 422–23
McCormick, Edith (née Rockefeller), 358
McCormick, Katharine, 357–58

McCormick, Stanley, 358
McCullough, Robert, 372–74, 405
McGill University, 364
Mead, Margaret, 307, 314
*Mein Kampf* (Hitler), 143, 147, 197, 240
Menand, Louis, 12
Meng, Heinrich, 84, 95
Menninger, Karl, 307
Menninger Clinic, 320; *Bulletin* of, 282
*Mental Healers* (Zweig), 176
Mercader, Ramón, 243
Mesmer, Franz Anton, 20, 176–77, 222–23
Methodists, 210
Meyer, Gladys, 313, 398
Mid-Century White House Conference on Children and Youth (1950), 314
Miller, Henry, 5, 274–76, 285, 289, 426, 434
Miller, Ruth, 260
Mills, C. Wright, 250, 388, 393
Mills, Peter, 368, 379–80, 405
*Minima Moralia* (Adorno), 273
Ministerial Association, 212
*Mr. Smith Goes to Washington* (film), 404
Mitchell, Juliet, 14
Mocenigo, Giovanni, 349
*Modernization of Sex, The* (Robinson), 211
Moise, Bill, 372–73, 400, 409, 421
Moise, Eva (née Reich), 158, 221, 323–24, 378, 398, 415–17; adolescence of, 163, 183–85, 209; birth of, 83; childhood of, 115, 134–36, 138, 140–41, 161, 164, 240; as Reich's assistant, 324, 335, 372–73
Moll, Albert, 33
Monroe, Marilyn, 356, 417
Montessori schools, 115
Moore, Hugh, 485*n20*
More, Thomas, 375
Morgan, Ted, 238
Mormons, 425
Muggeridge, Malcolm, 432
Müller-Braunschweig, Carl, 143, 165
Municipal Opera House (Berlin), 157, 158
Münster Verlag, 287
*Murder of Christ, The* (Reich), 319, 342, 427–28
Murphy, Michael, 436, 440
Murray, John, 114
Murrow, Edward R., 328
*My Eleven Years with Reich* (Baker), 291

Naevestad, Marie, 183
Nagasaki, atomic bombing of, 225

*Naked and the Dead, The* (Mailer), 434
Nasjonal Samling (National Union) Party, 186
"Natalija A." (case), 234, 236
*Nation, The* (magazine), 186, 281
National Institutes of Health (NIH), 398, 412, 414
National Lawyers Guild, 385
National Library of Medicine, 83, 414
Naturalization Court, U.S., 288
Nazis, 132, 139–50, 159, 174, 186, 250, 285, 290, 390; Austrian, 101; books burned by, 152, 410; Czechoslovakia invaded by, 207, 225; Eisenhower and defeat of, 360; eugenics of, 115; former Communists as, 156–57; German American Bund support for, 240; nationalistic appeals to youth of, 137; opposition within Germany to, 394; persecution of Jews by, 5, 102, 124, 125, 130, 140–45, 147–49, 158, 201, 454*n93*; public health campaign of, 197; refugees in New York from, 206; rise to power of, 139–40; sexual libertinism of, 148–50, 463*n14*; Soviet pact with, 237–38, 241, 248; Trotsky accused of plotting with, 187
Neill, A. S., 8–12, 192, 207, 281, 306, 314, 370, 379; anarchists and, 247; influence in U.S. of educational ideas of, 340, 329; on McCarthy, 385; Oranur effects described to, 333, 335; orgone accumulator of, 10–11; at Orgonon, 308, 309, 364; Peter Reich and, 9, 12, 315, 377; Reich's break with, 11–12, 377–78; Reich's treatment of, 8–9, 178–80
neo-Freudians, 219, 245–46, 255, 291, 395
neo-Marixsm, 394
Neumann, Franz, 396
Neumann, Osha, 396–97
New Beginning movement, 144
New Deal, 207, 238, 285, 292
New Hampshire, University of, 372
"New Lost Generation, The" (Baldwin), 7
*New Republic, The*, 275, 280–81, 284–88, 352, 471*n54*
New School for Social Research, 206, 209, 230, 241, 242, 253, 308, 324
*Newsweek*, 225
Newton, Isaac, 236
New York City; Department of Education, 326; Department of Health, 382; Department of Sanitation, 411

*New York Daily Mirror*, 353
*New Yorker, The*, 208, 313, 325
*New York Herald Tribune*, 207
New York Institute for Gestalt Therapy, 270–71
*New York Jew* (Kazin), 244
New York Medical Society, 326
New York Psychoanalytic Institute, 133, 218–19, 242
New York Psychoanalytic Society, 143
New York Public Library, 291, 434
New York Shoe Club, 229
*New York Times*, 110, 225, 442
New York University, 259, 382
Nietzsche, Friedrich, 60, 235
Nikolayevsky, Boris, 184
Nin, Anaïs, 276
*1984* (Orwell), 250
Niss (FDA Inspector), 408–10
Nissen, Ingjald, 195
Nixon, Richard M., 327, 440
NKVD, 286, 287
Nobel Prize, 67, 102, 107, 196, 199, 369
*No Place to Hide* (Bradley), 327
Nowlis, Vincent, 213
Noyes, Humphrey, Jr., 449*n4*
Noyes, John Humphrey, 449*n4*
nuclear weapons, 225, 230, 331, 371; *see also* atomic bomb; hydrogen bomb
*Nudism in Modern Life* (Parmelee), 239
Nunberg, Hermann, 22, 58, 72

"Observations on the Psychological Effect of Imprisonment on Female Political Prisoners" (Jacobson), 144
October Revolution, 116, 187, 189
Oedipus complex, 46, 54, 73, 120, 122, 135, 136, 264, 405
Office of Strategic Services (OSS), 283, 394–96
Ohio Un-American Activities Commission, 353
Ollendorff, Ilse, 220–21, 229, 240, 272, 341, 413; author's interview with, 339–40, 364; biography of Reich by, 41, 45, 61, 104, 202, 336, 383; breakup of marriage of, 340, 397–99; during FDA investigation, 292, 348; injunction served against Reich and, 367, 368; Karrer on, 414, 415, 417; marriage of Reich and, 169, 288; after Oranur experiment, 334, 336–37, 361; orgone

accumulator use of, 224, 340; Peter on, 374–75, 377; at Reich's funeral, 428; on Reich's homophobia, 265, 307; Reich's jealousy of, 337–39; at Reich's trial, 401, 403, 405–406; report on orgone accumulators by, 300–301; on vegetotherapy, 9

Oller, Charles, 399, 427, 428

*One-Dimensional Man* (Marcuse), 442

*On Education* (Russell), 10

Oneida Community, 4, 499*n4*

"On Genitality" (Reich), 74

"On the Origin of the 'Influencing Machine' in Schizophrenia" (Tausk), 233

*On the Road* (Kerouac), 267

Oparin, Aleksandr, 191

Oppenheimer, Robert, 226, 284, 331, 482*n12*

oral stage, 73, 83

Oranur experiment, 332–38, 340–44, 347, 361, 365, 367, 372, 421

*Oranur Project, The* (Reich), 347

orgasm reflex, 9, 178, 252, 255, 279, 313, 400

orgastic potency, 80–83, 250, 283, 312, 319, 383, 399, 450*n7*; heterosexuality and, 307; orgone accumulator and, 5, 297, 471*n54*; laboratory experiments on, 174–75; vegetotherapy for, 178

orgone accumulator, 5–14, 249, 221–25, 236–37, 267, 274–77, 376, 423, 430, 433; Abrams box compared with, 289–90; anarchist opponents of, 290–91; Baker's use of, 279; for cancer treatment, 5, 200, 224, 226, 229–32, 241, 255, 260, 273, 280, 282, 293–95, 298, 336, 345–46, 364, 427; children in, 316–17; deadly orgone (DOR) and, 365; Einstein and, 228; FDA investigation of, 6, 292–301, 317, 344–50, 362–64, 379–82; films satirizing, 445; Mailer on, 430–32; media-perpetrated rumors about, 330–31; Perls and, 258, 268; Peter in, 378; Rosenfeld's use of, 258–59, 261, 262

Orgone and Cancer Research Laboratories, 229

*Orgone Energy Accumulator, The* (Reich), 349

Orgone Energy Observatory (Rangeley, Maine), 308, 329

Orgone Energy Operation in the Desert (OROP), 373

Orgone Institute, 293, 297, 350, 363; Archives of, 339; Diagnostic Clinic, 319,

344, 433; Press, 248, 297, 338, 411; Research Laboratories, 282, 297, 379

Orgonomic Infant Research Center (OIRC), 314–19, 325, 326, 397

*Orgonomic Medicine* (journal), 428

*Origin of Life, The* (Oparin), 191

*Origins of the Family, Private Property and the State* (Marx and Engels), 103

Orwell, George, 250, 444

Osborn, Frederick, 358

Oslo, University of, 172, 178–79, 193

*Oui* magazine, 267

Øverland, Arnulf, 182

Packard, Vance, 442–44

Palace of Justice (Vienna), 97–98, 102

Pan-Germans, 30, 100

Pappenheim, Bertha (Anna O.), 20, 54

paranoia, 57, 77, 184, 268, 312, 440; and cancer as metaphor, 198; in initiatives against sexuality, 271; of Reich, 11, 12, 84, 85, 108, 133, 167, 170, 181, 182, 201, 236, 247, 269, 288, 336, 339, 349, 386, 402, 407, 413–14, 419; *see also* schizophrenia, paranoid

*Parents' Day* (Goodman), 245

Parmelee, Maurice, 239

*Partisan Review, The* (magazine), 261, 362

*Passion of Youth* (Reich), 33, 36, 38, 40, 41, 44, 46, 55

Pasteur, Louis, 191, 193, 206

*Peer Gynt* (Ibsen), 19, 50–52, 86, 108

*People in Trouble* (Reich), 99, 131, 141, 180, 190

People's Temple, 415

Perls, Fritz, 79, 127–29, 146, 249, 393, 396, 434, 445; at Esalen Institute, 436–41; Gestalt therapy developed by, 268–71; and Goodman's New York bohemian circle, 255–58; and orgone accumulator, 258, 267–68; in South Africa, 144, 185–86, 255

Perls, Grete, 144

Perls, Laura, 144, 186, 256, 268, 270, 437

*Petroushka* (ballet), 158

Philby, Kim, 287, 288

Philipson, Tage, 153, 158

*Picture Post*, 11

Pierakkos, John, 404

Pilgrim State Mental Hospital (New York), 265–66

Pincus, Gregory, 357–58, 432

Pink, Alfred, 59
Pink, Annie, *see* Reich, Annie
Pink, Fritz, 57
*Plan* (journal), 151, 152
Planned Parenthood, 217, 358
*Playboy* magazine, 330, 356
*PM* (newspaper), 291
Poland, Jefferson, 434, 435, 490*n18*
"Political Meaning of Some Recent
  Revisions of Freud, The" (Goodman),
  245
*Politics* (magazine), 245, 249, 250, 281,
  284, 290
"Politics and the English Language"
  (Orwell), 250
Polsky, Ned, 430
Pomeroy, Wardell, 212, 213, 307
*Population Bomb, The* (Moore), 485*n20*
Population Council, 358
pornography, 13, 41, 75, 118, 151–52, 194,
  251, 287, 436; Kinsey and, 212, 359;
  literary, 275; Reich accused of, 194, 297,
  318, 433; Sam Roth imprisoned for, 426
*Pravda*, 115
Price, Dick, 436, 439, 441
primal scream therapy, 430
Princeton University, 306; Institute for
  Advanced Study, 228, 331–32
Procter & Gamble, 392
Progressive Party, 286
Project Blue Book, 370
*Propaganda* (Bernays), 102
"Prophylaxis of Neuroses, The" (Reich), 120
Protestantism, 187, 355
"Psychic Contact and Vegetative
  Streamings" (Reich), 168–69
*Psychoanalytic Education in Soviet Russia*
  (Schmidt), 119
Psychoanalytic Institute (Moscow), 118–19
*Psychoanalytic Pioneers* (Briehl), 231
*Psychoanalytic Theory of Neurosis, The*
  (Fenichel), 281
*Psychology of Everyday Living, The*
  (Dichter), 392
*Psychology Today*, 441
*Psychopathology of Everyday Life, The*
  (Freud), 3, 18, 392
*Psychosomatic Medicine* (journal), 281
Puritanism, 4, 397

*Question of Lay Analysis, The* (Freud), 112
Quisling, Vidkun, 186, 187

Rabinbach, Anson, 28, 112
Radek, Karl, 124
Rado, Sandor, 11, 122, 124, 133, 134,
  167–68, 170, 218, 219, 309, 314
*Rainmaker, The* (film), 375
Raknes, Ola, 12, 91–92, 126, 180–82, 198,
  341, 402
Rank, Otto, 22, 72, 89–90, 95, 139
Raphael, Chester, 259–60, 279, 333, 334,
  341, 344, 346–47, 367, 399
Rashevsky, Nicolas, 363
*Reader's Digest*, 305, 432
Readhead, Zoë, 9, 11, 12, 315
Reagan, Roland, 440
Red Cross, 110
*Red Flag, The* (Communist newspaper),
  53, 111
Red Front, 125
Red Scare (1920), 411
*Reds: McCarthyism in Twentieth-Century
  America* (Morgan), 238
Reece, B. Carroll, 356–57
*Reforming Sex* (Grossman), 132
Reich, Annie (née Pink; first wife) 57–59,
  113, 122, 137–38, 144, 163, 181, 190, 399;
  on Ambulatorium staff, 70; analyzed by
  Anna Freud, 103, 134, 163; birth of
  children of, 83, 108; breakup of marriage
  of, 133–35, 140–41, 157–58, 161, 164,
  167; custody battle of Reich and, 162,
  183–85, 322–23; and Eva's reconciliation
  with Reich, 324, 335; Karrer on, 414;
  marriage of Reich and, 59; in New York,
  209, 218, 240, 242, 323; and Reich's
  mental deterioration, 103, 108, 167–68,
  170, 183, 309–10; *Rundbriefe* of, 160, 182;
  in Soviet Union, 116, 118; in Vienna
  demonstration against Christian Social
  government, 98, 99
Reich, Arnold (uncle), 32, 42, 47
Reich, Cäcilie (née Roninger; mother),
  40–47, 57, 132, 202, 206, 324, 421
Reich, Eva (daughter), *see* Moise, Eva (née
  Reich)
Reich, Leon (father), 40–48, 87, 104, 421
Reich, Lore (daughter), 134–35, 160–63,
  169–70, 176, 322–24; birth of, 108;
  childhood of, 134–36, 138, 140–41, 161,
  164, 167, 183–85, 209, 240, 323, 324
Reich, Ottilie (née Heifetz; sister-in-law),
  87, 136
Reich, Peter (son), 329–31, 339, 361, 367,
  374–78, 386, 414; in Arizona, 372–74;

and breakup of parents' marriage, 338, 397; childhood sexual experiences of, 325; and father's death, 428; FDA destruction of accumulators witnessed by, 408–409; infancy of, 288; letters from prison to, 420, 425; after Oranur experiment, 334–35; at Orgonomic Infant Research Center meetings, 317; at Summerhill, 9, 12, 377; vegetotherapy on, 315–16

Reich, Robert (brother), 31, 41, 43, 46, 48, 87–88, 104, 421

Reich, Sigrid (niece), 87

Reich, Wilhelm: affairs of, 115, 134, 157–58, 201, 338, 339, 397–400; at Ambulatorium, 66, 69–70, 72–74, 79, 80, 85, 89, 95, 96; analysis of, 39, 41, 44, 60, 61, 84, 133, 218; antagonism of psychoanalytic establishment toward, 84–85, 87–89, 94–97, 138–39, 154–56, 161–64, 180–81; anti-Communist conspiracy theories of, 282–85, 291, 307, 350, 361–62, 379, 385–86, 409, 411, 413; Arizona expedition of, 372–74, 384; birth of, 39–40, 288; birth of children of, 83, 108; bohemians and intellectuals influenced by, 6, 7, 245–51, 255–67, 274–78, 288–91, 429–31; Brady's articles attacking, 272–74, 280–87, 289–92, 408; breakup of marriages of, 133–35, 140–41, 157–58, 161, 164, 167, 340, 397–99, 416; burning of books of, 152, 410–12; cancer theory of, 196–200, 231–33, 341; character analysis technique of, 35, 90–94, 172, 178, 219, 263; childhood and adolescence of, 28, 40–48; child-rearing principles of, 136, 137, 314–22, 324–26, 328; Communist Party membership of, 12, 108–12, 124–25, 137–38, 150–52, 172; custody battle over children of, 162, 183–85, 322–23; daughters' relationships with, 164, 185, 209, 322–24, 335, 372–73; death of, 11, 12, 426–27, 442; disciples and, 307–310, 314, 319, 341–43, 382–84, 399–400; DOR emergency of, 365–66; Einstein and, 5–6, 226–30; Eisenhower and, 360–61; emigration to United States of, 4, 5, 201–202, 205–209, 225; experiments conducted by, 172–76, 190–92, 199–201, 209, 220–22 (*see also* Oranur experiment); expulsion from IPA of, 8, 161, 164–70, 172, 185–86; FBI and, 6, 189, 239–42, 328–31, 362, 417–19; FDA investigation of, 6, 292–301, 344–50, 362–64; free clinics established by, 112–15; Freud as mentor of, 17–19, 22, 36, 50–52, 59, 60, 157; funeral of, 427–29; homophobia of, 251, 265, 307, 433, 462*n68*; imprisonment of, 12, 419–24; injunction against, 367–70, 378–82, 384; INS investigation of, 359–62; Jewish background of, 28, 29, 32–33; Kinsey and, 211–12, 306–307; last meeting of Freud and, 122–23; legacy of, 432–36; Marcuse and, 394–97, 441–42, 446; marriage of Annie Pink and, 59; marriage of Ollendorff and, 220, 288; Marxism of, 4, 9; in medical school, 17, 24, 26, 31–35, 52–53; mental deterioration of, 103, 108, 167–70, 182, 183, 202, 309–10; and Nazi rise to power, 139–43, 147–49; Neil and, 8–12, 178–80, 377–78; neuropsychiatric postgraduate studies of, 67–68; orgasm theory of, 74–75, 77–85, 88, 90, 93–94, 107, 120–21, 128, 270, 362, 432; orgone energy discovery of, 8, 171, 199, 201, 208, 220–22, 258 (*see also* orgone accumulator); paranoid delusions of, 11–12, 288, 370–71, 400–401, 412–19, 424–25; pathological jealousy of, 201, 337–40; Peter's reminiscences of, 374–78; prosecution of, 386–87, 389, 400–408, 411, 412, 417; psychoanalytic practice of, 8, 38–39, 54–58, 69–72, 85–87; Scandinavian exile of, 8, 144–59, 164, 171–75, 178–83, 185, 187, 190–96, 309, 359; schizophrenic patients of, 234–36; second generation of analysts influenced by, 126–29; sexual revolution advocated by, 4–5, 12–14, 122, 124–26, 129–33, 136–38; in Soviet Union, 116–20; therapeutic innovations of, 176–78, 269 (*see also* vegetotherapy); therapists trained in America by, 251–55, 278–80, 310–13; Trotsky and, 187–89; tuberculosis rest cure of, 104–108; in Vienna demonstration against Christian Social government, 98–103; works of, *see titles of specific books and articles*; during World War I, 23, 24, 32, 48–50, 53; youthful sexual relationships of, 34–38, 54–58

Reich, William Robert, 242–43, 352

Reich Blood Test, 344–45, 372

*Reichspost* (newspaper), 98
Reichstag fire, 140, 150
Reik, Theodor, 22
Reinhardt, Max, 268
Remington, William, 424
René Gunyon Society, 322
repression, 4–5, 10, 101, 119, 120, 180, 217, 237, 306–307, 446, anxiety and, 78; authoritarian, 114, 147, 149; breaking down physical manifestations of, 168, 173, 177, 235, 254, 347; cancer and, 229; Marcuse on, 396, 442; orgone accumulator used to dissolve, 366, 445; Perls on, 269, 270, 437, 439; political, 189, 435; sexual, *see* sexual repression; social, 69–70, 249
Republican Party, U.S., 285, 286, 304, 328, 356, 360–61, 433
Republikanischer Schutzbund (Republican Defense League), 98, 100, 109–12, 142
resistance, 10, 71, 91–93, 128; oral, 186; physical manifestations of, 91, 168, 267; unconscious, 70
*Retort* (journal), 255
*Reunion, The* (Reich), 47
*Revolution Betrayed, The* (Trotsky), 189
Rexroth, Kenneth, 274, 275, 285, 288–91
Rice, Thurman, 212
Riefenstahl, Leni, 375
Rieff, Philip, 248, 277
Riesman, David, 388, 393
Rilke, Rainer Maria, 60, 421
Riviere, Joan, 155
Roazen, Paul, 88
Robinson, Paul, 211, 251, 394–95, 397
Rock, John, 358
Rockefeller, John D., Jr., 214–17, 358, 485n20
Rockefeller, John D., Sr., 216, 217
Rockefeller, John D., III, 358
Rockefeller, Nelson, 348
*Rockefeller "Internationalist"* (Josephson), 348
Rockefeller Foundation, 145, 192, 193, 212, 214, 217, 303, 306, 356–58, 420
Roheim, Geza, 136
Roosevelt, Eleanor, 286, 331, 482n12
Roosevelt, Franklin D., 206, 207, 225, 286, 292, 348
Roosevelt, Theodore, 214
Rosenberg, Julius and Ethel, 328, 360
Rosenfeld, Isaac, 258–62, 268, 276, 294

Ross, Helen, 72
Ross, Tom, 328, 366, 380, 397, 398, 405, 409, 428
Roszak, Theodore, 442
Roth, Philip, 260, 262
Roth, Sam, 426
Rubenfeld, Ilana, 437
Rubenstein, Arnold, 144, 184, 209
Ruben-Wolf, Martha, 138
Rubin, Jerry, 445, 492n54
Russell, Bertrand, 10
Russell, Kate, 10
Russian Revolution, 30, 435; *see also* October Revolution

S. A. Collins & Sons, 350
Sachs, Hanns, 22, 25
Sachs, Wulf, 144
Sachter, Dr., 42
Sadger, Isidor, 19, 22, 39, 41, 44, 50, 59–61, 76, 84
sadism, 40, 73, 77, 86, 94, 106, 115, 129, 136, 138, 164, 325
Salinger, J. D., 6
Salpêtrière Hospital (Paris), 19, 75–76, 254
*Salt of the Earth* (film), 354
Salter, Patricia, 250
Salvation Army, 302
Sanger, Margaret, 217, 357, 358
"sand packet (SAPA) bions," 199–200, 220–21, 335
Sartre, Jean-Paul, 256, 269, 410
Schiele, Egon, 27
Schilder, Paul, 24, 57, 67, 88
schizophrenia, 11, 37, 108, 169, 233–36, 279, 358; eugenics and, 115; hysteria and, 152; paranoid, 12, 223, 233, 263, 265, 419; psychoanalytic treatment of, 68, 87; Reich diagnosed with, 11, 167, 336, 342
Schjelderup, Harald, 172, 180, 466n71
Schlamm, Willy, 53
Schlesinger, Arthur, Jr., 286
Schmidt, Alik, 119
Schmidt, Vera, 118–20, 135
Schnitzler, Arthur, 78
Schober, Johann, 98
Schoenberg, Arnold, 33
Schopenhauer, Arthur, 33
Schultz, Johannes, 149
Schulz, Bruno, 40, 48, 454n93

Schur, Max, 218
*Science* (journal), 355
Scott, Jody, 276
Seipel, Ignaz, 63, 100, 111, 112
Senate, U.S., 385
Settlement House (Vienna), 60
*Sex and Character* (Weininger), 36, 50
*Sex and Repression in Savage Society*
    (Malinowski), 137
sex-economy, 166
*Sex—Love—Marriage* (Schultz), 149
sexology, 18, 33, 35, 52, 55, 58, 128–30, 152,
    217, 260
Sex-Pol, 130–32, 138, 140, 153, 287, 324,
    433, 434
Sexpol Verlag, 150, 174
sexual abuse, 21, 321–25, 433, 490*n18*
*Sexual Behavior in the Human Female*
    (Kinsey), 355–57
*Sexual Behavior in the Human Male*
    (Kinsey), 302–307
Sexual Freedom League, 434–35, 439,
    490*n18*
*Sexual Lives of Savages in Northwestern
    Melanesia, The* (Malinowski), 137, 185
"Sexual Maturity, Abstinence, Marital
    Morality" (Reich), 122
sexual repression, 14, 45, 70, 86, 108, 114,
    137, 287, 308, 372; child-raising without,
    314; as cornerstone of class submission,
    111, 113; fascism and, 148, 149, 248;
    inroads by youth movement against, 53;
    as intrinsic to civilizing process, 113,
    136, 395; Kinsey on, 211, 356; Mann's
    literary exploration of, 106–107;
    Marcuse on, 395; in Miller's view of
    America, 274; neuroses caused by,
    77–78, 106, 130; orgone accumulator as
    cure for, 13; overthrow of, 4; societal
    norms responsible for, 96; Stalinist,
    189, 248
*Sexual Revolution, The* (Reich), 6, 122, 248,
    284, 287, 301, 311, 324–25, 368, 411
*Sexual Struggle of Youth, The* (Reich), 137,
    140, 150, 189
*Shadow War Against Hitler, The* (Mauch), 283
Shakespeare, William, 4
Shapiro, Elliot, 257, 270
Sharaf, Myron, 322, 325, 330, 341, 387,
    399–400, 417, 488*n22*; biography of
    Reich by, 34, 56, 84, 187, 309, 397;
    Macdonald denounces Brady as

Communist to, 284, 290; on Oranur
    experiments, 333, 342–43; and Reich's
    daughters, 163, 324; on Reich's trial,
    403–404, 406–407; on Silvert, 320
Shaw, George Bernard, 287
shell shock, 65, 80
Shepard, Martin, 268
Sheppard, Miriam (Paki Wright's mother),
    316, 317, 319–21, 383, 411
Siersted, Ellen, 146, 152–54, 164, 167, 173,
    178, 192
Sigmund Freud Archives, 96, 169
Silberer, Ernst, 22
Silberer, Herbert, 170
"Silent Observer, The" (Reich), 325
Silvert, Michael, 319–20, 342, 372, 379–81,
    400, 404, 409, 411; arrest of, 401;
    conservative politics of, 361;
    imprisonment of, 419–21; Mangravite
    and, 382–84, 407–408; sexual abuse of
    child patients by, 320–21, 325
Simkin, Jim, 270
Simmel, Ernst, 65
Sinclair, Upton, 228, 289
Singer, Richard, 258
*Sleeper* (film), 6, 445–46
Smith, Margaret Chase, 328
Smith Act (1940), 243, 328, 351, 352
Social Affairs Ministry, Danish, 195
Social Democrats; Austrian, 30–31, 63–64,
    66, 97–101, 103, 109–13, 142; Danish,
    145, 150; German, 124, 125, 140, 187
Social Hygiene, Bureau of, 214–15
*Social Hygiene vs. the Sexual Plagues*
    (pamphlet), 215
Socialists, 52, 60, 101, 187, 289, 375
Socialist Society for Sex Counseling and
    Sex Research, 113
Society of Heart Specialists, Viennese,
    68, 72
Society of Physicians, Viennese, 67
Sontag, Susan, 197–98, 341
Sorbonne, 13
*Sorrows of Young Werther, The* (Goethe),
    44–45
Souza, Monica, 252
Spengler, Alexander, 103
*Spirit and Structure of German Fascism*
    (Brady), 284
Spock, Benjamin, 314
Spotnitz, Hyman, 336
Sputnik 1, 425

Stalin, Joseph, 12, 124, 184, 238, 286, 342, 349, 385; death of, 360; enmity toward Trotsky of, 187, 190, 242; five-year plans of, 116; Hitler's pact with, 237–38, 241, 248; Kollontai's sex reforms reversed by, 118; psychoanalysis denounced by, 119; views on homosexuality of, 287; at Yalta, 348

Stalin, Vasily, 119
Stalinism, 285, 290, 339
Standard Oil, 357
Stanford University, 436
*Star Wars* (film), 375
State Department, U.S., 286, 327, 328, 352, 395
Staub, Hermann, 128
Steig, Susanna, 325
Steig, William, 325
Steinhof State Lunatic Asylum (Vienna), 68
Stekel, Wilhelm, 18, 22, 54, 113, 139, 179–80
Stellato, Alfred, 344–47
Stengel, Erwin, 165
Sterba, Richard, 69, 82, 89, 94, 113, 162, 164
Stern, Victor, 111
Sternberg, Josef von, 115
Stevenson, Adlai, 361, 443
Strachey, James, 155
Straight, Michael, 286–88
Straight, William, 286
*Strategy of Desire, The* (Dichter), 444
Strauss, Leo, 206
*Street of Crocodiles, The* (Schulz), 40
Strømme, Johannes Irgens, 178, 195
Student Laboratory (Rangeley, Maine), 278, 292, 296, 329, 332, 343, 347, 365, 408–410
student uprisings of 1968, 13–14
*Studies on Hysteria* (Freud and Breuer), 20, 76
Summerhill, 8–12, 178, 247, 308, 340, 377
*Summerhill: A Radical Approach to Childhood* (Neill), 12
Summer of Love (1967), 437
Supreme Court, U.S., 314, 417, 426
Supreme Judicial Court, 407, 411, 417
Sussex University, 425
Swales, Peter, 21
Swarowski, Hans, 38, 55, 59, 115
Sweeney, George C., 401, 404–406

*Sword and the Shield, The* (Andrew), 287
syphilis, 67, 147, 169, 197, 215, 263
Szilard, Leo, 225

Taft-Hartley Act (1947), 354
Tanberg, Bodil, 466n71
Tandler, Julius, 31, 64, 114
Tannenbaum, Samuel A., 4
Tausk, Victor, 170, 230–31, 236
*Technology of Orgasm, The* (Maines), 75
Teil, Roger du, 192
Teller, Edward, 225
Templeton, Clista, 293–95, 297–98, 301, 363
Templeton, Herman, 293–95
Tesla, Nikola, 225
*Thalasa* (Ferenczi), 80
"Therapeutic Significance of Genital Libido, The" (Reich), 81
Thomas, Dylan, 423
Thompson, Clara, 219, 291, 478n62
Thompson, Philip, 363
Thorburn, William, 278
*Thousand and One Nights, A*, 61
Thurber, James, 449n5
Tiffany, Charles, 162
*Time* magazine, 13, 275, 302, 352, 392, 432–34
Tjøtta, Thorstein, 193
Toepfer, Karl, 157
Tolson, Clyde, 305
Toronto, University of, 230
*Tractacus logico-philosophicus* (Wittgenstein), 36
Tracy, Spencer, 375
transference, 54, 70, 77, 90, 126, 183; negative, 95, 313; positive, 87, 93, 399; in Reich's relationship with Annie, 57–58, 141
Trilling, Lionel, 303
*Triumph of the Therapeutic, The* (Rieff), 248, 276
*Trojan Horse in America, The* (Dies), 238
*Tropic of Cancer* (Miller), 274
*Tropic of Capricorn* (Miller), 274
Tropp, Simeon, 297, 345, 365
Trotsky, Leon, 186–90, 241–43, 248, 260, 288, 351
Trotsky, Zina, 188–89
Trotskyism, 186, 188, 242, 248, 260, 284, 311

Truman, Harry S., 285–86, 288, 304, 327, 331, 350
Tubbs, Oscar, 299–300
tuberculosis, 65, 87, 103–104, 215, 421
Tynan, Kenneth, 115

UFOs, 11, 370–71, 373–74, 376, 386, 418, 425
Ujhely, Grete, 123
*Uncensored* (magazine), 362
unconscious, 17–19, 73, 90, 93, 101, 147, 233, 263; and consumer behavior, 389, 392; in hysteria, 20–21; in impulsive characters, 86; resistance and, 70, 71; Weininger on, 51
*Unconscious, The* (Freud), 18
Union Theological Seminary, 357
United Nations, 327
Unity Committee for Proletarian Sex Reform, 132
University Hospital (Vienna), 34
Updike, John, 35
Utica (New York) State Mental Hospital, 235

Vadim, Roger, 445
Van Dusen, Henry Pitney, 357
Van Gogh, Vincent, 235, 263
Van de Velde, Theodoor H., 82
vegetotherapy, 9, 182–83, 205, 235, 279–80, 337, 430, 437; children subjected to, 315–16; Ginsberg and, 265; Neill and, 12, 178–79; Perls's critique of, 268; technique of, 178, 191
Verlag für Sexualpolitik, 150, 174
Versailles Treaty, 124
*Vicissitudes of Instincts, The* (Freud), 18
Victorianism, 13, 212
Vienna, University of, 17, 19, 22, 24–26, 57, 59, 102, 263, 391; Clinic for Psychiatry and Nervous Diseases, 67
Vienna Anatomical Institute, 29
Vienna City Council, 84
Vienna Psychoanalytic Society, 39, 79, 85, 88, 94–96, 233; Ambulatorium and, 67, 96; Federn's leadership role in, 60, 61, 84; Reich accepted into, 19, 50; Training Institute of, 88–89, 268; women in, 37
Vietnam War, 441
*View* magazine, 285

*Village Voice, The*, 427, 430
*Völkischer Beobachter* (newspaper), 140
Vollmer, Joan, 262
Volta, Alessandro, 223
*Vossische Zeitung*, 125

W. B. Saunders Company, 302
Waal, Nic, 160, 180–82, 192, 195
Wagner, Otto, 63
Wagner-Jauregg, Julius, 24, 34, 67–68, 88
Wakefield, Dan, 430
Wallace, Henry, 285, 286, 288, 303, 352
Wall Street crash (1929), 116
Wandervögel youth movement, 52, 57
*Warte, Die* (journal), 132
*War of the Worlds* (film), 374
*Washington Confidential* (magazine), 356
*Washington Post*, 423
Wassermann syphilis tests, 215
Watts, Alan, 439–40
Wednesday Society, 60
Weil, Ruby, 243
Weininger, Otto, 36–37, 50–51, 55, 452n55
Weir-Mitchell, Silas, 76
Welch, Joseph, 384–85
Wells, Herman, 212
Wertham, Fredric, 284, 285, 310
*Western Worker* (periodical), 242
Wharton, Charles, 292, 295, 301
*When Your Child Asks Questions* (Reich), 137
White, E. B., 449n5
*White Collar* (Mills), 388
"White Negro, The" (Mailer), 429, 430
Whitney, Dorothy, 286
*Wilhelm Reich: A Personal Biography* (Ollendorff), 337
Wilhelm Reich Foundation, 300–301, 322, 343, 345, 367, 369, 379, 381, 408, 427
Wilhelm Reich Museum (Rangeley, Maine), 431
*Wilhelm Reich vs. USA* (Greenfield), 301
Williams, Tennessee, 276, 306
Wilson, Woodrow, 26
Winter General Veterans Administration Hospital (Kansas), 320
Wisconsin, University of, 442
*Wisconsin State Journal, The*, 385
Wise, Robert, 371
Wittgenstein, Ludwig, 36
Wolberg, Lewis, 263

Wolfe, Pussy, 315
Wolfe, Theodore, 205, 206, 220, 238, 248,
  278, 282, 313, 337–38, 341, 398
Wolff, Charlotte, 115, 118
*Woman Rebel, The* (magazine), 358
Wood, Charles, 292–301, 344, 348,
  349, 362
Woolf, Virginia, 218
Workers' Opposition, 118
Workers' School (New York), 239, 242
Workers' University, 128
World League for Sexual Reform, 130,
  131, 434, 464*n23*
*World of Yesterday, The* (Zweig), 27–28
World Radiation Center (Davos), 104
World's Fair (New York, 1939),
  206–208, 224
World War I, 17, 23, 27, 48–50, 53, 57,
  64–66, 83, 88, 240, 421
World War II, 184, 208, 218, 230, 237, 352,
  372, 394
Wortis, Joseph, 138

*WR: Mysteries of the Organism* (film),
  252, 434
Wreszin, Michael, 249
Wright, Paki, 316–19, 326, 372, 383, 411
Wylie, Lee, 341
Wyvell, Lois, 297, 338, 339, 341

Yalta Conference, 327, 348
Yeats, W. B., 198
Yippies, 445
Young Republicans League, 385

Zaretsky, Eli, 14
Zen, 439
Zetkin, Clara, 117
"Zetland: By a Character Witness"
  (Bellow), 262
Zilboorg, Gregory, 466*n71*
Zipperstein, Steven, 261
Zweig, Stefan, 27–29, 62, 176